THE OFFICIAL

PRICE GUIDE TO

COLLECTOR CARS

EIGHTH EDITION

ROBERT H. BALDERSON

HOUSE OF COLLECTIBLES

NEW YORK

Important Notice: All of the information, including valuations, in this book has been compiled from the most reliable sources, and every effort has been made to eliminate errors and questionable data. Nevertheless, the possibility of error, in a work of such immense scope, always exists. The publisher will not be held responsible for losses that may occur in the purchase, sale, or other transaction of items because of information contained herein. Readers who feel they have discovered errors are invited to *write* and inform us, so they may be corrected in subsequent editions. Those seeking further information on the topics in this book are advised to refer to the complete line of *Official Price Guides* published by the House of Collectibles.

Copyright © 1996 by Robert H. Balderson

All rights reserved under International and Pan-American Copyright Conventions.

This is a registered trademark of Random House, Inc.

Published by House of Collectibles
201 East 50th Street
New York, NY 10022

Distributed by Ballantine Books, a division of Random House, Inc., New York, and simultaneously in Canada by Random House of Canada, Limited, Toronto.

http://www.randomhouse.com

Manufactured in the United States of America

ISSN: 8756-1654

ISBN: 0-676-60024-7

Cover design by Michelle Gengaro

Cover photos by FPG International

Eighth Edition: August 1996

10 9 8 7 6 5 4 3 2 1

THE OFFICIAL®
PRICE GUIDE TO
COLLECTOR CARS

To Janelle, in her
first year of driving

CONTENTS

Preface ix
Acknowledgments xi
Note to Readers xiii
Market Review 1
The Birth and Growth of the Hobby 2
The History of Cars 3
Cars: Collector, Antique, or Classic? 8
    Collector Car 8
    Antique Car 9
    Classic Car 10
List of Registered Classic Cars, 1925–1948 10
Advice on Buying and Selling 13
    Evaluating Condition 13
    Buying for Investment 16
    Buying at Auction 16
    Selling the Collector Car 18
        Selling to a Dealer 19
        Selling to a Private Party 19
    Further Tips 19
Weatherizing 20
Safety Tips 20
Theft Prevention 21
Wheels for the Masses 21
Automobilia 24
    Advertising Brochures 25
    Books 25
    Engine Parts 25
    Hood Ornaments 25
    Hubcaps 25
    License Plates 25
    Magazine Ads 26
    Photographs 26
    Posters 26
    Repair Manuals 26
Production Figures, 1897–1985 (Model Year and Calendar Year) 26
Scope of the Book 58

How to Use This Book	58
Price Index (A–Z)	59
Introduction to Trucks	461
Introduction to Motorcycles	475
Collector Car Clubs	483
Collector Car Museums	503
Suggested Readings	513
Reference Periodicals	519
Glossary	521

PREFACE TO THE EIGHTH EDITION

To a nation of immigrants and wanderers, the advent of the automobile must have seemed a divine blessing. The car became our instrument of individual freedom—although humans could not soar with the eagles, they could "go somewhere." Farm families were now connected to society, people could drive off in search of a better life, young people were able to escape parental oversight and quickly recognized the back seat as a place to enjoy their blossoming passions. Today, for many people, solitude is only known inside their car.

For a child, a car trip is when they first see themselves in relation to the world, instead of the other way around. The sights along an endless run of highway conjure up personal revelations. This sense of getting somewhere, that they have actually been somewhere, lasts a lifetime.

For those who desire to possess them, the collector cars listed in this book are more than inanimate objects, they are a manifestation of an attitude and spirit. A bus, train, or plane will do for a tourist; a traveler requires his own motor car. The traveler is openly romantic about the exploration, adventure, and experience of "going," rather than of merely being taken from place to place. Satisfaction of this independent spirit is the impetus to go, and makes "getting there" half the fun.

For the dreamer, rambler, drifter, and writer the collector car represents a period before we became generic, when there were thriving towns with main streets, inviting motor courts to welcome the weary traveler at sundown, home cooking at roadside cafes where the only thing fast was the service, fun drive-in movies, amusing billboards, grateful hitchhikers, the lore of the road, people who cared, and summers that just seemed to last longer. We look back at flat tires, overheated radiators, no air conditioning, tourist traps, treacherous curves, narrow lanes, speed traps, and detour signs with an acceptance that can only indicate a hundred-year love affair with the damned things.

The automobile has influenced our history, literature, music, and art. It has made us a nation of dreamers. Jack Kerouac may have expressed the sentiment best in his 1955 book *On the Road* with the passage, "a fast car, a coast to reach, and a woman at the end of the road."

The ownership of a collector car makes it seem possible to live more than once, so enjoy!

ACKNOWLEDGMENTS

EIGHTH EDITION

I would like to express my profound appreciation to the associates and friends who so graciously gave their time and valued assistance. Without them this work would have been difficult; with them, it was a pleasure. My heartfelt gratitude goes to the following: Stephen Sterns, formerly Senior Editor at House of Collectibles, for his kindness, patience, and guidance; Patricia Voorhees and her staff at Fulton Court Secretarial Service for their devoted efforts to the seemingly never-ending rewrites, and for their lending an ever-ready ear; Stan Lukowicz for freely sharing his wealth of knowledge; Frank Just for his wise advice and unstinting help with reference material; George Giumarra, Del Denny, and Tom Sheehan for their valuable support, encouragement, and counsel; Jackie Frady (Executive Director), Sandy Saunders (Support Services Manager), and Don Geyer of the Harrah Foundation, National Automobile Museum, for graciously opening the museum for study and photographs, as well as for the use of their invaluable archives; Michael Forte for his assistance with Porsche; Mike McHugh for his assistance with exotic cars; Albert Mroz for his assistance with trucks; Steve Fields for the suggested readings; Nick Todd for help with data processing; Ben Davis of the Hayes Antique Truck Museum; Peter Hischier for answering endless questions; Jerry Britt, Director of Marketing, duPont Registry, and Katie Robbins, Executive Administrator, Classic Car Club of America, for their continuing support; and Mary, Pete, and Dave for keeping my operation running.

PREVIOUS EDITIONS

The House of Collectibles would like to extend sincere gratitude to the following: Rob Burchill of White Post Restorations; Gar Rosenthal of Philadelphia, Pennsylvania; Stanley Roe of Motor Vehicle Information Services; Bill Siuru for his article of interest, as well as Henry Austin Clark; Edwin K. Niles of Van Nuys, California; Cadillac Convertible owners of Thistle, New York; Paul Marchetti of Silver Spring, Maryland; and Von Reece Auctioneers of Austin, Texas.

Our thanks also go to the following for the Motorcycles section of this book: William T.G. Litant, President of the BSA Owners' Club of New England, Lincoln, Massachusetts; and Ted Faber, California Ariel Owners' Club, Seal Beach, California.

NOTE TO READERS

The Official Price Guide to Collector Cars is continually updated and revised with new factual material. Readers' comments and suggestions are respectfully solicited. The author is interested in previously unpublished information, articles, and photographs for future editions. Anyone interested in having their collection or institution featured in a subsequent edition is also encouraged to contact the author. All material may be submitted to: Robert H. Balderson, P.O. Box 254886, Sacramento, CA 95865.

MARKET REVIEW

In the mid-1990s the economic environment, encompassing the collector car market, is complex and unsteady. Before making my forecast for the market, it is appropriate to share with the reader the economic assumptions that form its basis.

Starting in the 1870s, developed countries became "industrialized." America transformed from agrarian to industrial, increasing workers' standard of living and creating a true "middle class" in our economy. Wage earners worked in specialized jobs being paid with money. They exchanged the money for consumer goods. After World War II, many workers' earnings increased to a point in excess of their living expenses; spending on leisure activities thus ensued. These people and their children, utilizing this buying power, produced the collecting boom that continued through the 1980s.

Today, in the 1990s, the American economy is again going through a transition, moving toward an "information" economy, and is being complicated by environmental concerns, the national debt, and the fact that a major block of the population ("baby boomers"), now beyond the age of peak consumption, is saving for retirement. The prosperous middle class that, by their spending patterns, create demand in specific markets, is impaired and shrinking. Until this precarious situation in the middle class reaches an equilibrium, any forecast for the market it supports will be based on uncertain data.

The market for collector cars is also studied in economic terms. The money spent on collectibles, including cars, is discretionary income, that is, the amount left over after paying for necessities. All forms of consumption and investment are in competition for these funds. The decision maker (buyer) will put the money in the place providing him/her the most satisfaction, at any point in time. This "place" could be anywhere from under the mattress to a sophisticated land deal. These financial decisions are all a balance of risk and return, and how much risk is acceptable relates directly to the level of confidence one has in the economy. Generally, the more quickly the item can be converted to cash, referred to as "liquidity," the lower the risk.

The market for collectibles is attempting to readjust after the inflation of the 1970s and overheated prices of the 1980s. With inflation down, the bulk of investment money going to the stock market and other forms of savings, and a glut of collector cars no longer being held as the status symbol of choice for the wealthy, the price of collector cars should have uniformly descended. In a free market, when supply exceeds demand, prices come down until supply and demand are equalized. With the massive volume and organization of the stock market, this reconciliation takes place ostensibly automatically. The stagnation in the collectibles market is explained in the economic axiom: "prices are strictly on the up side." No one wants to incur a loss. Refusing to sell until the amount invested can be recovered may be illogical, but enough collectors are doing it, whether out of ignorance or ego, to disrupt the market adjustment. Although we have all heard of the extreme example of individual cars of models that have plunged in price, these do not represent the aggregate of the market.

When an economic market cannot adjust into a state of equilibrium as is the case with many collectibles, including cars, it stagnates and acts as an inefficient and erratic manner. Currently, market events are more prevalent and attendance is up, but the number of purchases and the total dollars realized from sales are down. An increase in sales at a few events or a media star making major purchases may cause what is referred to as a "spike," but overall the market is flat.

As an additional complication, what was once "buyer's remorse" after the sale has become "buyer's paranoia" beforehand. Remember, no one needs to buy a collectible. It is not clear if buyers are holding back because of a lack of confidence in their assessment of the economy, or they do not have the personal conviction to evaluate and value the individual item, knowing the "greater fool theory" is suspended. At any rate, what we have is a market in unrest, reluctant sellers, and paralysis of analysis on the part of the buyers.

The constant exception to the above, in all areas of collecting, relates to any merchandise deemed to be the "best." If the car is first in production, extremely rare, in pristine condition, or generally held in esteem, a buyer is always ready, willing, and able to buy. Another area of cars in growing demand are those that are practical, reasonable, and fun. These cars express the owner's individuality, and include all convertibles and other styles that are sporty, interesting, or unique. Lastly, cars selling between enthusiasts, as within a car club, are solid, and motorcycles are experiencing a resurgence in demand.

In summary, the collector car market reflects its dependence on our national economy. The national economy is in transition from being industrial to becoming informational. This dynamism is going to cause economic instability in the foreseeable future. Now, more than ever, knowledge is power. A potential collector must methodically determine his economic position, calculate how much can be spent, and extensively research his area of interest and method of buying and selling.

The future of the collector car market for the enthusiast, the proud one-car owner, and the collector of a few cars is bright. It is again possible to buy a car "for what it is worth." This was made possible by the speculators' exit from the market. For you, the small-time car collector, the economic cycle has again reached your position—take advantage of it!

THE BIRTH AND GROWTH OF THE HOBBY

Car collecting is only about forty years old, and auctions, shows, and specialized publications are younger than that. Though still young, car collecting is a solid hobby and may be one of the most influential hobbies of the future.

Those who collected cars in the early days of motoring, such as Henry Ford, were usually involved in car production. While there were many auto enthusiasts during the Brass Era, they didn't view their cars as potential museum pieces.

Later the collector car hobby centered around the Brass Era. Cars from the '20s and '30s were on the market in the '30s and '40s, and people bought them because they were lower priced than current models from the same manufacturers.

The pace quickened in the '50s. Though finding parts was a challenge and there were no shows to exhibit finished products, more people turned to cars for a hobby. By the late '50s, car collecting had increased greatly, though prices for collector cars were still low.

The nostalgia boom of the '60s produced an increased interest in the Brass Era and later Classic Car Era. Bought by collectors and celebrities, collector cars were being driven more and more. This led to a heightened collecting market.

Such activity during the '60s helped in the location and restoration of many cars that otherwise would be lost. It also helped to establish restoration specialists.

Car shows and high prices sprouted in the '70s and continued through the mid-1980s. Restoration put more top Classics on the market, though demand was higher than supply. Record prices were set all over the country at car auctions. By the mid-'80s, the "hobby" had evolved into high stakes speculation. Many collectors who had loved the vehicles were priced out or pulled out in disgust. Greed had taken over, and greedy people are always vulnerable to shylocks. Investors were buying without knowledge. Unscrupulous dealers and auctions began "sheering the sheep."

By market manipulation and "fools buying," the car prices, in many instances, had exceeded their value by 100% or more. Today, after a period of readjustment, cars bought in the mid-1980s are now selling for half their purchase price. The speculators are gone; for the most part prices equal value, and informed collectors and investors are again making rational purchase decisions.

You could join them in this fascinating and rewarding hobby.

THE HISTORY OF CARS

How do you construct a self-propelled vehicle? Although not fully solved until the 19th century, mankind has pondered this question for thousands of years. Researchers believe that the Chinese had an advanced knowledge of steam power as far back as 3,000 years ago. Da Vinci, certainly one of the greatest minds of all time, theorized several self-propelled vehicles, including a primitive form of the helicopter. His insights helped develop several advancements in transportation, including the spoked wheel, which was much more efficient than the slab wheel.

In 1698, Thomas Severy, an Englishman, developed an atmospheric steam engine. It was not the first, but it is notable as being the first dependable as well as financially successful steam engine. His engine was used primarily as a water pump in Britain's copper mines.

The military was also responsible for much research into this area. A French army engineer, Nicholas Cugnot, is credited with building the first steam-powered vehicle. It was designed to carry large artillery pieces. It did so at a very low speed and often not very dependably, but it was an incredible achievement for the time.

In 1776, Jeremiah Wilkinson discovered how to handle material in a metalworking machine so that each part was interchangeable. In 1792 the first toll roads opened in Pennsylvania and Connecticut, and in 1886 Germany produced the first internal combustion–powered motor vehicle.

Charles E. Duryea developed America's first workable gasoline engine vehicle with a four-wheel design in 1893. James Ward Packard finished the design for his first car, and by 1894 Ransom E. Olds had sold a steam car overseas and built his first gasoline-powered vehicle. The following year yielded J. Frank Duryea's "Duryea Machine," featuring a water-cooled four-stroke engine, three forward speeds, and a reverse. It weighed 700 pounds and went 18 m.p.h. It was considered an advanced, dependable car. In 1897, the Duryea Motor Wagon Company was established and thirteen cars were produced before business stopped.

Henry Ford operated his first car in 1896—a twin-cylinder, 4 h.p. quadricycle. The first independent automobile dealership and the first franchised dealership began in 1898.

1900–1910

The 20th century began with James Gordon Bennett sponsoring his first international cup races. The race was won by a French entrant. It was a competition of endurance as well as speed. The course was 341 miles long, which was a considerable strain on the automobiles of the day. There were at least four major showings of automobiles in the United States and the typical American vehicle either had high buggy wheels for the country or light bike wheels for city use. European vehicles were more advanced. They had custom-crafted bodies, sported steering wheels, and no longer had a "motorized carriage" look.

The Olds Motor Works plant was destroyed by fire in 1901 and only one vehicle, the experimental curved dash, survived. Prior to this disaster, the heads of the Olds company couldn't agree on what kind of car to build. Several of them wanted to build smaller cars for local trips, others wanted bigger, more versatile (but also more expensive) cars. Since they only had one auto left after the fire, their problem was solved. They went with the curved dash model.

Because most of their facilities were in ruin, they had to sub-contract the manufacturer of many parts of their cars. They were located in Detroit, and since they offered business opportunities to a wide variety of industries, many new companies sprang up or relocated to the Detroit area. This, then, was the beginning of the Detroit-based, American automobile industry.

A new Olds car was assembled and driven over 800 miles in about seven days. This test drive encouraged orders for more than 1,000 vehicles.

Thomas B. Jeffery, producer of the Rambler Bicycle, produced Rambler cars in Kenosha, Wisconsin. Henry B. Joy took over Packard and moved the business to Detroit. In 1903, the Ford Motor Company was formed. All Fords were made at Dodge machine shops. The first Model A weighed more than 1,200 pounds and cost about $850. Ford produced the Model T in 1908—15 million were built before the model was discontinued nineteen years later. Organized in 1903, the Buick Car Company sold sixteen vehicles their first year then sold thirty-seven vehicles the following year. The first American coast-to-coast road trip was made in 1903. It took over a month. It's important to note, however, that in addition to low speeds and low dependability, the motorists had to deal with a scarcity of good road conditions. Most of the country still had dirt roads. A Frenchman broke the 100 m.p.h. barrier in 1904 by going 103 m.p.h.

Between the years 1905 and 1909, Cadillac's one-cylinder and four-cylinder engines began to outsell both Olds and Ford. U.S. cars were following European styles with the engine forward, followed by the transmission, and then the drive. In 1906, the Rolls-Royce Silver Ghost was introduced and sold for close to $5,000. Howard Marmon introduced America's first air-cooled V-8 engine.

Other developments included the formation of the American Automobile Association, the Society of Automobile Engineers, and the Association of Licensed Automobile Manufacturers who brought suits against Ford and others for infringing on the Selden patent. Perhaps the most famous antique car of all time was introduced in 1908. The Model T (or Tin Lizzy) became America's most popular car. It was easy to fix, ran well, was dependable, and, at about 30 m.p.h. cruising speed, got you to where you were going in good time.

By the end of the decade, the top American car makers included Buick, Ford, Maxwell-Briscoe, and REO.

1910–1919

In 1910, General Motors Company owned twenty car and accessory makers in America. Overall vehicle production was more than 180,000, including 6,000 trucks and buses. Almost half a million cars were registered in the United States. In 1911,

Billy Durant formed the Chevrolet Motor Company and Walter Chrysler became the plant manager for Buick. California offered the first school bus system. Ford's first moving assembly line was developed in 1912. Both the Duesenberg Motor Company and the Stutz Motor Company began production that year also.

An important legal milestone was passed in 1911 when the United States Appellate Court ruled that Ford and other motor companies had not infringed upon the Selden patent. The court went on to say that the Selden patent covered only two-cycle engines, not the four-cycle models then being used by Ford. This safeguarded auto production from any threat of a monopoly.

Cadillac's innovation of a dependable starter did away with the unwieldy crank start. This development also put down the electric automobile whose one advantage over the gas powered cars was that it had been easier to start. The story goes that Byron Carter, an auto pioneer himself, was killed by a faulty crank. Henry Leland, the head of Cadillac, decided that enough was enough and started his drive to develop a safe, dependable ignition system.

It was discovered in 1915 that Chevrolet was gaining large masses of General Motors stock. Dodge was doing well with "dependability" as its trademark, and Packard introduced a V-12 engine that featured aluminum pistons. Nash took over the Thomas B. Jeffery Company and it became Nash Motors Company.

World War I produced shortages of necessary vehicle building materials. Oregon imposed the first gasoline tax, and all states qualified for assistance under the Federal Highway Act. Headlamps were also introduced at this point, making night driving possible.

1920–1929

During this period, many relatively unknown car makers emerged, and quickly disappeared, while larger firms continued to grow.

Walter P. Chrysler left Buick to head Willys Overland, and Charles Kettering became the head of General Motors research laboratories. During this decade more new cars had enclosed bodies, ethyl gasoline was available to buy, quick drying spray finishes were put to use, Buick offered four-wheeled brakes, and Dodge produced the first all-steel closed body.

Every state began a gas tax, and house trailers made their way to the market. European automobiles were expensive, handcrafted, and in greater variety than American cars, but American production outstripped the Europeans by far. The American auto industry had by now become the largest industry in the nation. One very important step was taken by the government. They began to develop the U.S. highway system. More and more money was being channeled into roads which obviously helped to increase auto sales.

Production figures retreated slowly in the early and mid-1920s but they bounced back as 1930 approached. A record 5,337,097 automobiles were produced in 1929. It wasn't until 1949 that this record would be broken. The approaching depression would hit the auto industry hard, but only stunned, it would quickly bounce back.

1930–1939

The auto industry chugged along during the Depression, though the 1932 vehicle production of more than one million was the lowest number in seventeen years. The automobile had become a part of American life. Many families, hard hit by the economic depression, travelled across the country in search of better conditions. Whether they found them or not, the search was usually conducted in a car or truck. Trains, which had formerly been the standard mode of American travel, would never again challenge the automobile in popularity. Even if they were poor, the American family looked upon the car as a virtual necessity.

In 1934 Nash sold its one-millionth model. "Airflow" models were introduced by DeSoto and Chrysler, but these streamlined production cars did not attract many buyers. The first Lincoln Zephyr with a twelve-cylinder engine was introduced in 1935. During the same year, Chevrolet produced an all-steel station wagon.

An important step was taken in 1937 when General Motors and Chrysler both recognized the United Auto Workers union as the official representative of their workers. The car companies, directly or indirectly through contractors, employed hundreds of thousands of workers. The U.A.W. resolved to work for better conditions and wages for the workers.

The Fiat 500A Coupe was the most famous car in Europe, while in the United States Stutz went bankrupt and Hupp declined. By 1938, due to economic stress, car makers pushed their lower-priced merchandise.

In 1938, many Americans saw World War II approaching. Many also thought that with wartime production it wouldn't be easy to get a new car. They were right. So many people bought their new cars in the late 1930s, production went up by 800,000 cars in 1938 alone. Statistics show that by this time there was an average of just under one car per family in the United States. But the car industry wouldn't be the same in the 1940s. The war changed just about everything.

1940-1949

With German troops in France, Belgium, and the Netherlands, William S. Knudsen resigned as president of General Motors to head the Council on National Defense. General Motors produced its twenty-fifth-millionth car; Olds produced the first reliable automatic transmission; and car size became more massive. By 1941, Chrysler was mass-producing army tanks, and soon other companies became involved. In 1942 auto tires became rationed items, production of civilian passenger cars and trucks was stopped, speed limits were posted, and gasoline stamp rationing was imposed. Only 139 passenger cars came off the production line in 1943, but more than 13 billion dollars worth of wartime items had been produced. By 1944, gas rationing was down to two gallons each week. Strict speed limits were also imposed to conserve fuel.

"Rosie the riveter" became a popular figure as more women joined the work force than ever before. With so many men lost to the war effort, women had to take up the slack in manufacturing and the automobile companies were no exception. Their factories turned out everything from PT boat engines to tanks. There is no doubt that the tremendous manufacturing capability of the United States played a major role in defeating the axis powers, more than any other factor. The car companies were instrumental in that effort.

By 1945, automobile companies became concerned with how to convert the auto industry back to peacetime production. Two new corporations were announced: Kaiser-Frazer Corporation, which immediately launched into series production, and Tucker corporation, which had an advanced design.

Passenger car production was increased by almost 1,300,000 by 1947 and assembly plants began to pop up everywhere. Packard produced its one-millionth car. The first tail fins on Cadillacs were on the market in 1948. They also sported 160 h.p. and a V-8 high-compression engine. Olds also had a high-compression V-8. Fewer than fifty Tuckers were on the road.

In Europe the noted car was the Citroen 2CV with a 375-cc flat twin engine. Production couldn't keep up with the sales. The soldiers were all back from Europe. The G.I. Bill was helping to educate them. The country was more affluent than it had ever been before. The baby boom was on and people were moving to the suburbs. Everyone had a car—they expected it. There was an incredible optimism in the air. The 1950s were going to be even better. The car, now nearly as integral to the

American family as the home, was moving into the 1950s more popular than ever before.

1950–1959

More than eight million civilian vehicles were produced in 1950, along with heavy contracts for military supplies for the Korean War. Chrysler celebrated its silver anniversary and Mack its golden. Looking for public opinion about small cars, Kaiser-Frazer introduced the Henry J., a compact four-seater, and Nash-Kelvinator introduced the NXI, a small two-seat personal car. Ford introduced automatic transmission and Buick produced nonglare tinted glass.

Car styles changed some in the 1950s. Tail fins became popular, along with double-curvature windshields. Grilles became wider, windows became larger, and air conditioning and automatic transmission became more frequently available. Dodge offered its first V-8 engine in 1953. Chevrolet began work on the Corvette, a plastic-laminated fiberglass-body sports car. Experimental cars were shown at auto shows, including Hudson Italia, DeSoto Adventurer, Packard Balboa, and Buick Wildcat.

A sad aspect of driving started to impress itself on the American public. Automobile deaths rose to nearly 40,000 in the mid-1950s. Seat belts were still optional equipment and would be for a long time. Speeding regulations were strictly enforced, but the public's fascination with the automobile and the new high-performance models combined to make irresponsible driving a very deadly thing. There's a well-known story that in the early 1910s there were only two cars in the state of Kansas and they had an accident. In those days, with the low speeds, an accident was not much of a problem. But times had changed. The standard family car of the 1950s could reach 100 m.p.h. Handled unwisely, this made cars very dangerous.

Kaiser-Frazer bought Willys Overland to form Kaiser Motors Corporation. Ford and Buick celebrated their fiftieth anniversaries.

Hardtops became popular, along with wraparound windshields and safety padding on instrument panels.

Although it was constantly being improved, the automobile was becoming more and more short-lived. It's difficult to say whether this was because of failing workmanship or because with increased prosperity, the public could buy a new automobile more often. In any case, the average life of a car was just over five years.

The Thunderbird was introduced in 1954 as Ford's answer to the Corvette. The 1955 Buicks and Oldsmobiles featured four-door hardtops. Other new features included seat belts and safety door latches. The Edsel, produced by Ford, was introduced in 1957. Not popular, it was the wrong car at the wrong time. Buick offered aluminum brake drums with cooling fins and a dual-headlight system. American Motors dropped the Nash and Hudson in 1958, and the Continental was introduced by Lincoln. More compact cars were introduced.

1960–1969

Close to eight million vehicles were produced in 1960 and it marked the last year for the DeSoto. Much work was done on radiator coolant to prevent freezing in the winter and boil-overs in the summer. New cars were introduced to combat foreign imports. Factory-installed seat belts were offered in 1961 by American Motors. Sporty cars such as the Mustang and Barracuda were introduced in 1964. Belted radial designs for U.S. tires were developed in 1965 and many experimental and show cars were seen.

The Department of Transportation was formed in 1966 to insure safety standards. There was a renewed interest in electric cars as a result of worries about air pollution. Safety items became more important and emission control systems and seat belts were required by 1968.

1970–1979

Our car mentality, like the rest of the American experience, spilled the period of the 1960s over into the early 1970s. This decade transition brought with it an end of innocence in this country. The Vietnam War dissension, Watergate, and the energy crisis, with its 55 m.p.h. speed limit, stole the fun.

The "Muscle Cars" of the 1960s dwindled in production and the subcompact arrived. The engine's breath was choked away by emission controls and it became illegal to alter the components. No more "hot rod" physics in the quest for power. Lights, buzzers, and later voices began advising you of what you were doing wrong. Sports cars were replaced by grand touring (GT) types and the bureaucrats came within the thickness of canvas of killing the convertible. For the first half of the century the automobile was the source and symbol of individual freedom; now it was being reduced to simply another form of transportation. The time of romance, adventure, and a feeling of personal involvement was lost.

Not to worry, however—auto manufacturers may never produce the raw power of a 409, 427, or 426 Hemi again, but armed with the information in this book you can still own one!

CARS: COLLECTOR, ANTIQUE, OR CLASSIC?

Since it seemed very unfitting to refer to a 1926 Rolls or a 1932 Duesenberg as a "used car" or "secondhand car," collectors have evolved a variety of more appropriate terminology. In Britain the term "veteran car" is all-encompassing. Americans prefer terms such as collector car, antique car, and Classic car. There's just one problem: they tend to get misused and interchanged to mean the same thing by persons who aren't really informed on the subject. There is actually a distinct set of guidelines to determine whether a car falls into the category of collector, antique, or Classic . . . or possibly into more than one of them.

COLLECTOR CAR

The most encompassing term is *collector car.* A collector car is any car in which an adequate demand exists to create a market beyond mere transportation. Cars with collector appeal, as when one goes out of production, may be termed potential future collectibles, but not a collector car. Buying at this point is speculative. If you re-sell in the open market, you will only receive utility value. If a person bought early Mustangs, for example, they would have won; on the other hand, except for very unique models, Studebakers would have been a loss. Generally, sporty, high-end models that were popular when in production are good bets for the future. The ones with the most original amenities will become the most valuable. As with all collectibles and antiques, the key is "expensive when new." Exotic cars, with their limited production and high initial price, are the only vehicles that may be "instant" collectibles.

Eight or ten or twelve years after discontinuance, collectors are apt to start taking an interest in collector cars. By that time, the total in existence has dropped somewhat; it may be down to one-third the quantity manufactured or less, depending on circumstances. Gradually, it becomes something more than just a used car. Designing has changed considerably in the meantime. So have construction and interior detailing. Now that the car can be seen in retrospect, it takes on a different kind of character than it had originally, when you were hearing ads for it on radio and TV. All the hype is gone. The sticker price and the rebates and the idea of being "right in style" are forgotten. So you notice the workmanship more than you did originally, and you begin to think in terms of *what this car means today.* It wasn't built for the

1990s. Its manufacturer and its original owner were not concerned in the least about whether it would survive to the present time. But since it *has* survived, what does it have to offer the buyer of today? If all it has to offer is a low price, it can't be termed a collector car, regardless of its age. The mere fact that a car will provide transportation does not elevate it into the collector category. What about the body design? Does it typify the mood, the taste of its era? Is there a little hunk of the American Dream wrapped up in it? Does the styling represent some bold forward step of its day—which possibly turned a lot of auto industry heads and led to further, bolder steps? The tail fins on '50s Caddies are long gone now, to the point where we might forget their original significance and impact. Caddy fins were supposed to make the cars look like rockets. It was an era when rockets were in the news and car manufacturers tried numerous ways to achieve tie-ins. (Remember the Rocket V-8 engine?) The concept, of course, was that your car was more than just a car. It was a powerful, magical machine in which all sorts of wonderful things happened. Most makers tried to imitate the Caddy fins in one way or another.

Whenever a car has something interesting or appealing to recommend it, even if it isn't superior in performance, it has the potential to become a collector car. Sooner or later its market value will rise, as collector car enthusiasts begin seeking it out. It may never become really valuable. Obviously it won't get into the class of early Pierce-Arrows or Bugattis, because they have a lot more going for them: super styling, a high scarcity factor, and loads of accumulated glamor from years and years of being driven by celebrities. But not every collector can afford one of those. And, even if they could, there wouldn't be enough to go around. Growth of the hobby, and its spread into various economic classes, are partly responsible for so many cars of the '60s gaining collector ranking. And that's the beautiful part . . . you don't need to be rich to own a collector car. The listings in this book will reveal many makes and models which you can acquire for less than the sticker price on showroom cars.

A term that is often used interchangeably with collector car is "classic" car (lower case "c"). A more accurate usage of the term is with a capital "C", referring to cars designated by the Classic Car Club of America and discussed later in this section.

ANTIQUE CAR

This classification includes makes and models from the earliest years of commercial auto manufacturing up to about 1925. Those from the 1890s to about 1907 or 1908 are normally referred to as "vintage" cars, while models from 1908 to 1925 are called "Brass Era." These distinctions are drawn because of changes in design that occurred in or about the years indicated.

The earliest antique cars (up to 1907–08) are museum pieces in the true sense of the term, and it was actually these vintage cars that got the hobby started; originally, collectors were more interested in them than in Classics. There's a high rarity factor, as they were not only manufactured in limited numbers but destroyed in very large numbers. If the historical side of motoring intrigues you, they may be for you. They're available but, of course, quite expensive—and you won't be able to take one on the freeway. For local driving on city roads, though, they're entirely serviceable if restored to top running condition. Since the usual state of condition is rather low, fully restored specimens command large premiums.

The somewhat later Brass Era antiques are from the era of brass components and trim, usually featuring brass mounted headlamps and brass radiators (1907–08 to about 1925). In the early teens, all American auto makers were producing "brassy" cars. Following World War I, which ended in 1918, some continued using brass while others made changes and tried to take new directions. By 1925 nickel components had taken the place of brass throughout the industry and body designs had drastically changed.

Antique autos of the Brass Era are available, both in restored and unrestored condition. Prices are sometimes very temptingly low on unrestored specimens, but restoring a "brassy" is quite expensive. It usually runs higher than restoring a car of later vintage, especially if you try to get all original replacement parts. You can generally save some money by getting a Brass Era car that was fully restored five to ten years ago when restoration costs were much lower. This is almost certain to be cheaper than buying a newly restored specimen, or restoring one yourself. Of course, you'll want to make sure that the car was well cared for in the meantime and is not in need of further labor.

CLASSIC CAR

The Classic Car Club of America defines a Classic as a "fine" or "distinctive" automobile, American or foreign built, produced between 1925 and 1948. Generally, a Classic was high-priced when new and was built in limited quantities. Other factors, including engine displacement, custom coachwork, and luxury accessories such as power brakes, power clutch, and "one-shot" or automatic lubrication systems, help determine whether a car should be considered a Classic.

By 1925 the last vestiges of Brass Era manufacturing had disappeared from the auto industry. Putting the cutoff date at 1948 makes sense, too, as another epochal period began with the postwar auto boom. While antique (pre-1925) cars are significant and often very valuable, they fall far short of the Classics in performance. The Classic cars can be driven if restored to top working order. Of course, the earlier ones won't attain super high speeds and you might miss the power steering, if you learned to drive in the age of power steering. However, the oft-repeated warnings that you need enormous muscle power to maneuver a Classic really aren't true. Driving them just takes getting used to.

Not every car made from 1925 to 1948 is regarded as a Classic. The lower-priced American makes are excluded from this ranking in most instances. For example, no Buicks qualify, except those with custom bodies. In the case of makes with glamorous reputations—Bugatti, Duesenberg, Cord, Pierce—Arrow, and others—all models are deemed Classics. The relatively low output plays a role, along with the esteem in which these makes are held.

Of course, values vary a great deal. The designation into which a car falls does not automatically determine its cash value. A Classic is not always worth more than a non-Classic. This is why it's imperative to know the values before you buy or sell.

LIST OF REGISTERED CLASSIC CARS, 1925–1948

Note: The editor wishes to thank the Classic Car Club of America for their permission to reproduce this list for our readers. For questions or membership information write to the club at 1645 Des Plaines River Road, Suite 7, Des Plaines, Illinois 60018.

A.C.—All
ADLER—Please Apply.
ALFA ROMEO—All
ALVIS—Speed 20, Speed 25, and 4.3 litre
AMILCAR—Please Apply.
ARMSTRONG SIDDELEY—Please Apply.
ASTON-MARTIN—All 1927 through 1939
AUBURN—All 8- and 12-cylinder
AUSTRO-DAIMLER—All
BALLOT—Please Apply.
BENTLEY—All

BENZ—Please Apply.
BLACKHAWK—All
B.M.W.—327, 328, 327/318 and 335
BREWSTER—All Heart Front Fords
BROUGH SUPERIOR—Please Apply.
BUCCIALI—TAV 8, TAV 30, TAV 12 and Double Huit
BUGATTI—All except type 52
BUICK—1931–1942 90 Series
CADILLAC—All 1925 through 1935
    All 12's and 16's
    1936–1948—All 63, 65, 67, 70, 72, 75, 80, 85, 90 Series
    1938-1947—60 Special
    1940–1947—All 62 Series
CHENARD-WALCKER—Please Apply.
CHRYSLER—1926 through 1930 Imperial 80, 1929 Imperial L, 1931 through 1937
    Imperial Series CG, CH, CL, and CW.
    Newports and Thunderbolts
    1934 CX
    1935 C-3
    1936 C-11
    1937 through 1948 Custom Imperial, Crown Imperial Series C-15, C-20, C-24, C-27,
      C-33, C-37, C-40
CORD—All
CUNNINGHAM—Series V6, V7, V8, V9
DAGMAR—6-80
DAIMLER—All 8- and 12-cylinder
DARRACQ—8-cylinder and 4-litre 6-cylinder
DELAGE—Model D-8
DELAHAYE—Series 135, 145, 165
DELAUNAY BELLEVILLE—6-cylinder
DOBLE—All
DORRIS—All
DUESENBERG—All
DUPONT—All
EXCELSIOR—Please Apply.
FARMAN—Please Apply.
FIAT—Please Apply.
FN—Please Apply.
FRANKLIN—All models except 1933–34 Olympic
FRAZER NASH—Please Apply.
GRAHAM—1930–1931 Series 137
GRAHAM-PAIGE—1929–1930 Series 837
HISPANO-SUIZA—All French models
    Spanish models T56, T56BIS, T64
HORCH—All
HOTCHKISS—Please Apply.
HUDSON—1929 Series L
HUMBER—Please Apply.
INVICTA—All
ISOTTA FRASCHINI—All
ITALA—All
JAGUAR—1946–48 2½ litre, 3½ litre (Mark IV)
JENSEN—Please Apply.

JORDAN—Speedway Series Z
JULIAN—All
KISSEL—1925–26, 1927 8-75, 1928 8-90, and 8-90 White Eagle, 1929–31 8-126
LAGONDA—All models except 1933–40 Rapier
LANCHESTER—Please Apply.
LANCIA—Please Apply.
LASALLE—1927 through 1933
LINCOLN—All L, KA, KB, and K, 1941 168 H, and 1942 268 H
LINCOLN CONTINENTAL—All
LOCOMOBILE—All models 48 and 90, 1927–29 Model 8-80, 1929 8-88
MARMON—All 16-cylinder, 1925–26 74, 1927 75, 1928 E75, 1930 Big 8, 1931 88 and Big 8
MASERATI—Please Apply.
MAYBACH—All
MCFARLAN—TV6 and 8
MERCEDES—All
MERCEDES-BENZ—All 230 and up, K., S., S.S., S.S.K., S.S.K.L., Grosser and Mannheim
MERCER—All
M.G.—1935–39 SA, 1938–39 WA
MINERVA—All except 4-cylinder
N.A.G.—Please Apply.
NASH—1931 Series 8-90, 1932 Series 9-90, Advanced 8, and Ambassador 8, 1933–34 Ambassador 8
PACKARD—All sixes and eights 1925 through 1934
All 12-cylinder models
1935 Models 1200 through 1205, and 1208
1936 Models 1400 through 1405, 1407, and 1408
1937 Models 1500 through 1502 and 1506 through 1508
1938 Models 1603 through 1605, 1607 and 1608
1939 Models 1703, 1705, 1707, and 1708
1940 Models 1803, 1804, 1805, 1806, 1807, and 1808
1941 Models 1903, 1904, 1905, 1906, 1907, and 1908
1942 Models 2023, 2003, 2004, 2005, 2055, 2006, 2007, and 2008
1946–47 Models 2103, 2106, and 2126
All Darrin-bodied
PEERLESS—1925 Series 67, 1926–28 Series 69, 1930–31 Custom 8, 1932 Deluxe Custom 8
PEUGEOT—Please Apply.
PIERCE-ARROW—All
RAILTON—Please Apply.
RAYMOND MAYS—Please Apply.
RENAULT—45 h.p.
REO—1931–34, 8-35, 8-52, Royale Custom N1, 1934 N1, N2
REVERE—All
RILEY—Please Apply.
ROAMER—1925 8-88, 6-54e, 4-75, and 4-85e, 1926 4-75e, 4-85e, and 8-88, 1927–29, 8-88, 1929 and 1930 8-120
ROCHET SCHNEIDER—Please Apply.
ROHR—Please Apply.
ROLLS-ROYCE—All
RUXTON—All
SQUIRE—All

S.S. AND SS JAGUAR—1932 through 1940 S.S. 1, S.S. 90, SS Jaguar and SS Jaguar 100

STEARNS KNIGHT—All

STEVENS DURYEA—All

STEYR—Please Apply.

STUDEBAKER—1929–33 President except Model 82

STUTZ—All

SUNBEAM—8-cylinder and 3-litre twin cam

TALBOT—105C and 110C

TALBOT LAGO—150C

TATRA—Please Apply.

TRIUMPH—Dolomite 8 and Gloria 6

VAUXHALL—25-70 and 30-98

VOISIN—All

WILLS-SAINTE CLAIRE—All

WILLYS-KNIGHT—Series 66, 66A, 66B-Custom bodied only—Please Apply.

ADVICE ON BUYING AND SELLING

EVALUATING CONDITION

When you buy a collector car, its price will, or should, depend to a large extent on its condition. You already know that condition counts in the value of a used car. Collector cars are used cars and many of the same considerations apply—along with some extra ones that we'll get into in a minute. Even though collector cars are collectors' items, the value is much less when their state of preservation leaves a lot to be desired. The basic difference is that most collector cars are worth restoring, as a complete professional restoration greatly increases their value, while the average used car is not worth fully restoring. Fully restoring a car means to get it back into the original condition, inside and out, including upholstery and everything, as near as possible to the shape in which it left the factory. Depending on the car and the type of work that needs to be done, full restoration can be many times more costly than simply getting the car to run.

Usually when you shop for a collector car you will need to rely mostly on your own ability to evaluate its condition and the amount of work that would be required for a full restoration. This may not be the case if you buy from a dealer who specializes in collector cars, but then, of course, you'll be paying the full market price without any hope of getting a "buy." If you know something about restoration and can evaluate condition, you're certain to do better. There are many bad buys on collector cars, offered by people who want to unload them on an unsuspecting buyer. But there are also some real bargains to be had, even sometimes on ordinary used car lots.

We can't go into this subject as comprehensively, in the available space, as it deserves. The following should, however, prove a helpful "crash course."

The first point to consider is the purpose for which you're buying a collector car. If it's merely for transportation, you can treat the purchase as a used car and not think in terms of a full restoration. Quite a few collector cars from the 60s and early 70s can be had inexpensively in unrestored condition and are certainly suitable for transportation when they're in running shape—except that the m.p.g. will not be as high as for recent used cars in most cases.

If you want the car for transportation plus an investment, it will require a full restoration. If you intend to show the car at an antique auto show, it must have a full restoration with special attention to the bodywork, paint, and interior. At some shows it is not a requirement that cars be in running condition. In order to attract the showing of Vintage and Brass Era models, these shows will accept nonrunning cars. Even when running condition is demanded, it is usually necessary only to drive the car across the show floor or lot, not get it revving up to freeway speed or driving for a long period of time. But don't let this fool you. Most of the labor and expense that goes into a restoration will have to be done anyway, if you're going to show the car. There is no way to skimp on this. The only way to save money is to buy a car that doesn't need to have every part replaced. If a collector car is running when you buy it, and you intend to show it rather than use it for transportation, you may be able to bypass work on the engine and concentrate on the bodywork, trim, upholstery, and other details.

As you will note in the listings in this book, the difference in value between unrestored and restored condition varies from make to make and often from model to model. This is an extremely important consideration. Usually the more recent and more common collector cars are not worth a big premium when fully restored because (a) collector demand is not as strong for them, and (b) fully restored specimens are not that hard to find. When you buy such a car with the intention of restoring it, you're apt to end up putting more cash into the car than it's really worth. Say a certain car is worth $1,500 in good and $2,800 in excellent condition. It may appear that you're getting a "buy" if you find it selling for $1,250 in good condition (running, but far from fully restored). However, after paying for the restoration you will have to put more than $2,800 in the car—yet you will only raise its market value to $2,800. You cannot raise its value any higher than the optimum no matter how good the restoration job is. This is why it just doesn't pay to restore unless you're starting with a car whose market value can be hiked up considerably. The simple fact of the matter is that a full restoration by a professional restorer will cost about the same, regardless of the value of the car. If you're going to spend $8,000 or $10,000 on a restoration project, you'll want to start with a car whose value can be raised more than $8,000 or $10,000. There are numerous such collector cars on the market, and you can save money by buying them unrestored and having the work done afterward. Generally speaking, the more valuable the car is (when fully restored), the better candidate it is for restoration. Even if you have to spend $10,000 to restore a car which is worth $60,000 when fully restored, that car is an awfully good buy in unrestored condition for $20,000.

This is precisely what the collector car dealers do. They look for models that can be bought inexpensively because of their condition, then hand them over to a restorer who usually works under contract for them. When a dealer buys a car that's already fully restored, he knows he has very little leeway in which to work because there's nothing he can do to increase the value.

If the engine needs rebuilding this is a major undertaking which you probably will not be able to accomplish yourself. Quite possibly a large number of the original parts can be salvaged if a professional does the job. You can evaluate the condition of the engine and other working parts by checking for rust and other signs of neglect. Many collector cars have spent years in drydock without being driven, and rust and corrosion have set in. A professional restorer has the tools to buff off rust and rework parts that can be salvaged. Usually the bodywork will need sandblasting and repainting. Any car with serious dents or corroded bodywork requires major surgery from the restorer and this adds to the bill. Bodywork can always be repaired but everything done in a restoration increases the cost and may tip the scales between a profitable and unprofitable restoration. You will also have to consider the availability of replacement parts when parts are so corroded or otherwise deteriorated that they cannot be reworked. This does not necessarily relate to the age of the car or whether it was manufactured in the United States or abroad. Some replacement parts are simply more difficult to get than others because they were not kept in the manufacturer's line for more than few years. Cadillac V-16's from the early 1930s are an example of a model for which replacement parts are very, very hard to find.

When you do hand over a car for restoration, be sympathetic—at least a little—to the problems faced by the restorer. It may seem as though he's charging exorbitantly, but he has to cover the cost of labor plus the replacement parts. If hard-to-get components are involved, these are not likely to be on his shelves. The restoration people have good contacts in the trade and nearly always can find the right parts to do the job. It's a matter of time and money.

On the whole, most Classic cars of the 1930s require more expensive bodywork when being restored than cars from any other era. This is because the styling of that time, especially in the more exotic makes and models, included a great deal of intricate shaping and detailed chrome trim. Unless it's restored perfectly, the car is not in "show" condition. Real artistic skill is necessary to rework the bodies of many Classics and it isn't a task that can be hurried. Show judges examine these cars from all angles and they're very adept at recognizing when something is not quite right. Since you will be increasing the market value considerably by restoring the bodywork, there should be no hesitancy to do this.

Special attention must be given in evaluating the condition of any unusual features that the car may have. If there's wood paneling on the body, you'll want to see whether all the slats are original or if some have been replaced over the years. Quite often replacements are discovered, and when this is the case it's usually necessary to replace them all in restoration, since an exact match is very difficult to make. However, if the slats are all original but are merely in deteriorated condition, a restorer can almost always refurbish them by sanding and lacquering. Deep scratches or gouges are filled in, just as on old furniture, and when this work is complete it's very hard to distinguish from mint condition original state. If you prefer, you can instruct your restorer to merely prime the wood after sanding it down. In this way it will take a high polish and look more "woody" than with a lacquering job. Of course, the polish has to be redone periodically.

As far as the interior goes, the goal in restoration is to achieve a look and quality compatible with the original, even if the original is not really faithfully duplicated. There is some margin for exercising personal taste here, since interiors varied a great deal more than exteriors. Many Classic cars had custom interiors and you can examine quite a few specimens before finding two alike. Dealers in those days "pushed" custom interiors and many classes of customers—especially those in show business and high society—wanted the unusual. If you restore a Cord and put in leopard-skin upholstery, you aren't setting a precedent, and you might be going a step further toward copping a show award. When you plan an upholstery restoration, think in terms of the personality of the car and the era in which it was manufactured. Obviously, vinyl upholstery is a no-no on a Classic; if you're going for the leather look it has to be real leather, despite the high cost. Fur should also be genuine. But before going to extremes, consider how much you'll be driving the car and whether bizarre upholstery will be comfortable for you. Also, if you're going to drive the car, the durability of different types of upholstery has to be considered too. You'll get a lot more wear out of leather and it's sure to prove cheaper in the long run. Keep it well oiled at all times, whether the car is being driven or not. If you live in a cold climate with low humidity, oiling will need to be done more frequently. Leather dries out quickly and when it's dry it cracks.

Repainting is a standard step in restoration. You're at liberty to paint the car any color you like, and some collectors let their imaginations run wild. It's true enough that a shocking pink 1927 Rolls draws plenty of attention anywhere it goes, but, again, think of what you want to accomplish with your car. If your basic intent is to travel around to antique auto shows and exhibit it, you're likely to get a much more positive reaction from show judges when the color is authentic-looking (a color the car would have had originally, or at least not too far from it). If you want to go in for eye-catching color, pick a car with sporty lines.

BUYING FOR INVESTMENT

Collector cars have, for some time, drawn attention from investment-minded buyers. Many individuals who bought collector cars in the 1970s to mid-1980s realized substantial profits, but others suffered losses. Successful investing calls for being informed about cars, understanding the market, and careful planning.

To be a successful investment, a collector car must return more buying power to its owner than was put into it. Buying power is governed by the rate of national inflation, which has been averaging from 5% to 10% per year. This means that all money decreases in buying power at that rate, regardless of whether it is held as cash or in the form of objects. To reverse the decrease, money must be used to purchase things which rise in value faster than the rate of inflation, and which yield a "buying power profit" after all costs of selling are deducted. Many investors, not just in cars but all forms of financial investment, think they've profited while in fact they have suffered a loss. With a collector car investment, you must consider all the initial costs as only your first step. This includes the purchase of the car as well as repair work and incidental expenses. If you can sell the car quickly, a profit of 10% might be satisfactory. However, as time passes and inflation erodes the buying power of money, you will need a larger return. An important factor is the cost involved in selling. You will incur some expenses in the sale. These could be minimal if you sell to a private party. But if you sell to a dealer, a large percentage of the car's value will be deducted at the time of sale. A collector car will not generally be a profitable investment if it fails to double in retail value within five years from the time of purchase. If it doubles in five years it will be marginally profitable. A really worthwhile profit would usually not be possible unless it doubles in value within three to four years. This is assuming that the rate of national inflation remains in the 5–15% range. If it rises significantly, even a doubling in value within three to four years, it would not return a profit.

BUYING AT AUCTION

Auction buying has been the traditional and most popular method for acquiring collector cars. One reason is that many sellers prefer having their cars bid upon in competition instead of selling them to a dealer.

Cars passing through a major auction are much more thoroughly scrutinized than those offered by a a retail dealer. Any shortcomings will be noticed, and competition will not develop for any questionable car. The very fact that other bidders find the car appealing is a sign of assurance that you do not have when buying from a retail dealer. Even if you fail to obtain the car you want, the fun of attending the sale and being involved in the bidding pays its own reward. You will have a first-hand taste of what auctions are all about, and possibly on the next try or at some point in the future your efforts will prove successful.

At an auction, the auctioneer usually has more demand for cars than he can supply. Using this book as your guide, you need only compare the prices against auction sale realizations to discover that some auctioned cars are bargains. On the other hand, there are many instances of collector cars fetching more at auction than the "book" value—even two or three times as much. When this happens, a beginner is likely to be confused. Why should at $20,000 car sell for $60,000? The explanation is that there are no standard retail prices on collector cars. A rough idea of current values can be given in terms of recent sales realizations. This shows how much a car has been selling for, but it is not necessarily an indication of its real worth or potential.

Today's realization will go toward influencing the book values of tomorrow. This is why we repeatedly advise you to use this volume as a *guide* or yardstick to prices, and not to regard the prices as fixed or firm. A very high price for a car obtained at auction is always more impressive than if a dealer were to charge a comparable sum. The dealer might be accused of starting high and overpricing his stock with the intention of accepting counteroffers. This is obviously not the case at auction. Whatever price is realized by a car at auction is a true price in cold hard cash. Somebody is paying that price, not just naming it. It may seem unrealistically high or low, but it is an authentic price achieved in open competition. Note that the buyer must verify the auction company's reputation. If it is not a "clean operation," the price may *not* be authentic nor the competition open. Be informed, and read and converse with other collectors; knowledge is your most valuable asset.

There is the chance that you could find a collector car at an ordinary auction of secondhand cars. Once in a while a collector car will pass through a noncollector sale and the price is apt to be below book value. Most of these secondhand auto auctions are attended by dealers who look for cars that can be profitably resold to the general public. They are not looking for collector material because they do not deal in it, though they may be well aware of its value and collectibility. On the other hand, the condition of any collector car found in a noncollector auction may be disappointing. The car may be in need of major repair or restoration work. The mere fact that the car is being sold at a noncollector sale is cause for some suspicion; it would be going to a collector car auction if it had the potential to realize a really strong price. You will certainly want to conduct a thorough inspection before making any bids, or, if you are not personally equipped to do this, entrust the task to some knowledgeable mechanic.

At an auction, the auctioneer has the option of buying cars outright from their owners or of selling them on commission (also known as consignment); in the latter case he makes no personal investment and acts merely as an agent for the owner. It is generally to an owner's advantage to sell by commission rather than attempting to find an auctioneer who will buy his car(s) outright.

At every auction there is a pre-sale exhibition. The autos are arranged on a lot, each marked with its lot number (corresponding to the auctioneer's sale list or catalog). Prospective bidders are encouraged to attend the pre-sale exhibition. Any car on which you intend to bid should be closely examined. You should determine the extent of restoration needed, if any. Check under the hood and look at the interior. While it may not be possible to make quite so detailed an inspection as you would like, you will at least be able to spot any major repair jobs that need to be done, and this should enable you to calculate the amount of your bid. It is wise to settle on a bid limit before the auction. If you go into a sale with merely a vague notion of how much to spend on a car, you may end up overbidding. Figure out how much the car is worth to you in its current condition. Quite possibly it may be worth somewhat more or less to you than the book value. In other words, you might want the car if it sells at a real bargain price, but not at the full retail value. On the other hand, if you have long sought this particular model you may feel justified in bidding more than the book value. A bargain is a bargain only if you think it's a bargain. A high price is too high only if you feel guilty about paying that much. Your own personal satisfaction is the determining factor. This is what makes the market—the fact that certain people want certain cars very badly and are willing to give almost anything for them.

Generally, inspections are not permitted once the sale has begun. Do not count on making a last-minute inspection. Do your inspecting as early as possible. There is usually a last-minute inspection rush which results in bidders crowding around the vehicles. Under these circumstances a proper examination is difficult. The earlier the better, always.

At most auctions you will be required to register before the sale in order to make bids. There may be a small registration fee, but in return for this you receive a reserved seat in the bidders' gallery or possibly two seats for one registration fee (if you have a nonbidding person with you). This arrangement varies from one auction to the next. You will be assigned a bidder's number, which is entered in the auctioneer's bid book under your name, and you will probably be given a paddle bearing this number. This is done for the auctioneer's convenience in identifying bidders during the sale. You bid by simply raising this paddle or placard.

The cars will be sold in the order listed in the catalog or auction list. Generally, each car is driven out past the bidders and its lot number is announced by the auctioneer. It remains in view of the bidders while the bidding on that lot is in progress, then is removed. The bidding may start with an absentee bid if the auctioneer has one for that lot. There are generally no absentee bids at a collector auction, as the bidders want to make a personal inspection and be on hand to take the car away if they buy it. If there are no absentee bids, the auctioneer will usually ask that the bidding be opened at a specified sum. In the event nobody bids at that sum, he may then ask for a lower amount. The sum asked to open the bidding could be above or below the reserve price. The sale then progresses in the usual fashion of an auction. Bids are received very quickly on most lots, without the auctioneer ever having to ask for raises. As soon as a bid is made, another bidder instantly waves or raises his paddle. There may be a number of bidders raising their paddles simultaneously, in which case the auctioneer must decide whose bid it is.

After you've made a winning bid, you may be asked to sign an acknowledgment form. The auctioneer's assistant will bring this to your chair right before bidding begins on the next car. However, you will not be asked to pay for the car until the entire sale is completed. The reason for having buyers sign these acknowledgment forms is to prevent people from claiming, after the auction, that they did not buy anything. The acknowledgment form will have the lot number on it of the car you bought, as well as the amount of the winning bid.

You will be required to pay in full for all cars you purchased when the sale is concluded. Auctioneers do not accept personal checks unless accompanied by a letter of credit from the bidder's bank (and, even then, some do not). The methods of payment at an auction are cash or bank draft. Some auctioneers accept credit cards but the majority do not. Since it is unwise to carry a large sum in cash, the best procedure is to obtain bank drafts or cashiers' checks. You must have the amount filled in at the bank. Since you will not know precisely the amount you're spending, have the draft made out for a sum which is certain to be sufficient. The difference will be refunded to you by the auctioneer, either in cash or check.

SELLING THE COLLECTOR CAR

If you are holding a collector car purchased as an investment, the timing of your sale is important. There are trends in the collector car market that affect current values. Trends occur in all collector fields but they are more prevalent with cars because *current taste* is a strong factor with many buyers. The trend may really have nothing to do with the car itself. If so, you could wait it out. If you sell at the top of a trendy market, you will always make a greater profit than if you wait until demand has slackened.

Trends can come and go. You never can be in a position of knowing for sure—either about the right investment car to buy or sell. But to bring your chances of making an error down to their minimum, we advise you to read and study this book and keep abreast of the market. This involves subscriptions to collector car magazines, attendance at shows, and checking the results of auction sales. You should be able to notice trends developing as early as possible and be in a better position to make buying and selling decisions. You must also take care to include all costs in the investment, not just the initial purchase price of the car.

Selling to a Dealer

Usually the quickest way to sell a collector car is to a dealer. This is the route to follow in an emergency, when the speed of sale is more important than the amount received. If you have a running car in clean condition, most dealers will buy it from you—if you're willing to take the sum they offer.

Do not expect to get the full retail value from a dealer. Retail value is exactly that: the prices at which dealers sell to the public. Figured into the retail value are all their operating expenses plus their margin of profit.

Selling to a Private Party

Selling to a private party offers you the best chance of getting the price you want for your car. It allows you to set the price and terms, and it eliminates the uncertainty of an auction and the substantial discount incurred when selling to a dealer.

The main drawback in selling to a private party is the length of time it may take. Running advertisements can be costly, especially if it takes a long time to find a buyer.

In planning your ad, you will not want to use much space. A good collector car classified ad gives the make, model, condition, and price, along with any information that might qualify as a major selling point.

It is generally best to give a price in the ad. In many newspapers you may advertise a car or other merchandise without giving the price. This is to your benefit, as it prevents you from being swamped with calls by people. Nearly everybody who buys a collector car from a private owner (or even from a dealer) will try to work down the price. You could plan ahead for this by setting the price slightly higher than you're prepared to accept. However, you should not state a price of higher than 10% above the sum you would really like to get.

Your phone number should be included in your ad. Running the address is not advisable, as people may come by when you are not at home and there is the danger of theft. Also, you will draw many "lookers" by publishing your address.

The manner in which the car is displayed could be a determining factor. If the car is housed in a garage, be sure that the lighting is good and strong. Have the garage reasonably neat, without tools lying near the car. Make sure the car's interior is not littered.

If the car remains unsold after your initial advertising period, you may lower the price or spread out your ads into more publications—possibly the daily newspapers of surrounding towns.

FURTHER TIPS

When shopping for a collectible vehicle, many things should be checked. Always look for rust, especially in the following areas:

- Rear edges of front fenders
- Rocker panels
- Rear wheel arches
- Beneath the rear bumper
- Around parking and headlights
- Hood, doors, and trunk lid unless aluminum

Watch for torn, badly worn, or split cloth, leather, and carpet in the interior of the car. If just dirty, cloth or carpeting should clean easily.

Wood trim should be checked for cracking or splitting. Trim can be refinished, but you should decide if the possible repairs are worth it to you.

Look under the hood. Usually a car that runs is worth more than one that doesn't. Also keep in mind that a six-cylinder engine usually is easier to work on than a V-8 engine. Be sure to test the brakes before driving the vehicle. Finally, remember that a vehicle with a good body, but in need of mechanical work, is usually less expensive to repair than a car in the opposite condition.

WEATHERIZING

Most collectors who live in areas with harsh winters store their collectible vehicles for the season. If storing the vehicle in a building with a concrete floor, place an old carpet on top of the floor. A concrete floor needs covering because it will probably sweat. The moisture will travel through the car resulting in rust, mold, and mildew. Prepare the concrete floor with a layer of plastic and then a layer of old carpet. Ask a carpet dealer to save some of the old carpets he removes when installing new ones.

To prepare the vehicle for storage:

- Change oil, filter, and lubricate the chassis, then drive the car for ten to fifteen miles to make sure the mechanical parts are coated with oil.
- Wash and wax the exterior.
- Clean the interior and remove the rubber mats.
- Place mouse poison in the trunk and on the floor inside the vehicle.
- Fill the gas tank to prevent moisture which builds in an empty tank.
- Either remove the battery and store it in a cool, dry place, or charge the battery two or three times during the winter.
- Change and flush the antifreeze if it has not been done in the last two years.
- Coat mechanical parts and body with a lubricating fluid. Rustproof your vehicle if it has not been done. You can do it yourself with a kit, or contact a commercial rustproofing service.
- Only genuine wood parts should be cleaned and waxed.
- Any genuine leather pieces should be cleaned.
- Increase the tire pressure to about fifteen pounds above the normal pressure.
- Do not set the parking brake because moisture in the cables could rust it. Set an automatic transmission in park and a straight shift in reverse.
- Beware of car covers which do not allow moisture to escape. Actually, old sheets, blankets, etc. work well.

SAFETY TIPS

When working on a vehicle, whether a Classic or the family car, put safety ahead of everything else. It only takes one careless mistake for disaster to occur. Following are some do's and don'ts for car hobbyists.

- Do Not smoke in the workshop. Ashes could ignite any flammable liquid or material.
- Do Not throw old rags, especially those covered with a flammable liquid, in a waste can where they can ignite from spontaneous combustion.
- Do Not get under a car supported only by cement blocks or a small jack; instead use a heavy-duty floor jack.
- Do Not start a vehicle in a closed area. This is especially important for people with respiratory problems. The fumes can overcome a healthy person in five minutes. A person with breathing difficulties will be affected in half the time.
- Do wear safety goggles. Eyes are a precious commodity too often taken for granted.
- Do keep a fire extinguisher in your workshop. Although an obvious requirement for any work place, it is often forgotten.

- Do weld in a clear, open space. Welding sparks can easily ignite flammable items.

Although these suggestions are basic and well known to the public, many accidents occur because these rules were not heeded. A casual approach to safety is a dangerous one.

THEFT PREVENTION

Collectible vehicles should be safely secured so they won't invite theft. There are several possible methods used that may deter thieves.

Though you may not have an alarm system, place a manufacturer's sticker, which reads "protected by John Doe's alarm system," in a visible spot on your vehicle. This alone should deter thieves. A phony alarm switch put in an obvious place is another deterrent.

Of course, some thieves will try to steal in spite of such precautions. You may want to consider alarm systems. One popular alarm is connected to the doors, trunk, and hood. If any of these is opened the alarm, which could be a siren or car horn, will sound.

Other preventive measures include:

- A toggle switch on the battery that controls its circuit
- A "chapman" lock that grounds the ignition and prevents the hood from being opened
- A fuel lock that stops the fuel flow to the carburetor; the car will start and can be driven, but it will run only a short distance

While any of these devices should help to frustrate a thief, some are better than others. Check with an alarm company to determine the best option for your vehicle.

WHEELS FOR THE MASSES

EXCERPTED FROM *PEOPLE'S CARS*, BY BILL SIURU

There are many cars that are considered great because of their engineering, technical ingenuity, or styling. A few cars have achieved greatness because they provided basic automotive transportation to great masses of people and at very affordable prices, both in terms of initial investment and in daily operation. While there have been many attempts at minimum cost cars, only a handful can be considered great in terms of offering motoring to huge segments of the population.

These "people's cars" often represented the first automobile for a great many people around the world. Some have actually been termed "people's cars" while others have acquired this title by inference. Besides being extremely economical and produced in vast quantities for many years, most incorporated some very innovative engineering, even though they represented basic transportation. Indeed, in many cases the designs, optimized for lightweight and economical transportation, resulted in very unique approaches rather than just the scaling down of larger contemporary cars.

FORD MODEL T, 1908–1927

Only one American vehicle can really be called a people's car. This was Henry Ford's Model T. Produced for 18 years, more than 16 million were made, records that would only recently be repeated by another people's car, the Volkswagen Beetle. Not only did the Tin Lizzie put the United States on wheels, but it was also produced in Great Britain, Germany, and France, and exported to just about everywhere else. For example, in 1919 over forty percent of the cars registered in England were Fords. Prices for new Model Ts got as low as $260, and for this small amount you got pretty reliable transportation, especially considering the infancy of the automobile. The Tin Lizzie was a pretty basic piece of machinery with its two-wheel mechanical brakes, planetary transmission, 20 horsepower engine, top speed of slightly over 40 m.p.h., and lack of creature comforts even for its day. However, it did offer reliable transportation at a price just about every American could afford. We could go on with the Model T story, but most of it would be repetitious to just about every old car enthusiast.

The Model T—The world's first "people's car."

VOLKSWAGEN BEETLE, 1938–PRESENT

Again, the Volkswagen story is a well known one and will not be repeated here. Suffice it to say it was Adolf Hitler's dream to provide a car for all Germans through the Kraft durch Freude (Strength Through Joy) organization. Hundreds of thousands of Germans saved their marks in the program hoping for the day they could take delivery of a "Volksauto." However, World War II intervened and none were delivered. While designed by Ferdinand Porsche in the 1930s and unveiled to the public in 1938, very few VWs were actually built until 1945 and those that were went to the military. The VW would go on to become the world's most popular car, with versions still being produced in third-world countries.

By people's car standards, the Volkswagen was not a tiny car. Weighing in at 1,700 pounds, it was easily able to accommodate four people. What really made it so popular, especially under harsh American driving conditions, was its reliability and relatively good performance. It might be noted that the durability and reliability came as much from the quality craftsmanship that went into building the car as the basic design itself. The air-cooled engine, originally displacing 1131 cc and producing 30 horsepower and upgraded through the years, was quite capable of pushing the car to 70 m.p.h. and still gave m.p.g.s in the 25 range. The car was simple to repair and maintain, important attributes in a people's car.

BMC MINI, 1960–PRESENT

The BMC Mini was quite a revolutionary car and set the future trend for subcompact cars around the world. First of all, it used a transverse-mounted four-cylinder engine driving the front wheels. The 848 cc engine (later boosted to 998 cc) was coupled to a four-speed transmission that after 1968 was fully synchronized. While only 120 inches long, the car could accommodate four passengers, a tribute to very efficient packaging. The design came from Alex Issigonis. Another innovative feature was the rubber-sprung, fully independent suspension system.

The Mini came in many versions, the Morris and Austin badged engineered twins, as well as upgraded models such as the Wolseley Hornet and Riley Elf, which included such features as distinctive grilles and even trunks. For the enthusiast, of course, there was the Mini-Cooper, with engines ranging up to 1275 cc and 76 horsepower. These "roller-skate" hot rods had such other items as beefed-up drivetrains to handle the added power, disc brakes in front, and slightly better instrumentation. Even on tiny 10-inch wheels the cars are famous for their handling.

The Volkswagen Beetle—*The world's most popular "people's car."*

Of all the world's cars, it is interesting to look at these models that provided, and in fact are still providing, transportation for millions of people around the world. It is also amazing to see how long these cars were popular with the motoring public, whose tastes change quite rapidly. Indeed, some are still being bought today, many decades after they were first introduced, a real tribute to their design and engineering.

The BMC Mini—*Sets the standard for today's subcompacts.*

AUTOMOBILIA

Collecting anything which pertains to the history of the auto industry has become an extremely popular hobby around the world. Many clubs and societies have been established for car memorabilia collectors, and a number of special magazines and books are also available. Specialist dealers are also active. They buy and sell auto items and auto-related collectibles.

There are many choices for the auto memorabilia hobbyist. He can specialize in a single manufacturer or even in a single model of car, and even restrict himself to a given production year. An alternative to this is general collecting, or centering one's attentions on a particular component. For example, the collector may choose to be a historian and collect printed memorabilia from the early days of auto making.

Following is a list of items that could be included in auto memorabilia collections:

- Any manufactured item with an auto's name or illustration
- Ashtrays
- Autographs of auto personalities (Henry Ford, etc.)
- Auto mechanic tools
- Auto repair manuals
- Avon cars
- Banks
- Bills of sale
- Books
- Bulb horns (brass)
- Calendars and prints
- Cigarette and trade cards
- Clocks
- Club badges
- Door handles
- Driving instruction books
- Gasoline cans
- Gas pump globes
- Headlamps
- Horns
- Household items in the shape of autos
- Hubcaps
- License plates
- Miscellaneous brass and chrome trim
- News clippings
- Oil gauges
- Old drivers' licenses
- Original oil paintings and drawings
- Photographs
- Posters
- Radiator ornaments
- Roadside emergency kits
- Roadsigns (all materials)
- Steering wheels
- Tin and cast-lead toy models
- Tire pumps
- Trophies
- Valve caps
- Windshield wipers

As with other collectors' items, the selling prices depend upon supply and demand. Some articles are in rather short supply but do not sell high because of a limited buyer demand. On the other hand, there are some relatively easily obtainable auto antiques—such as hood ornaments—whose prices continually escalate due to collector competition. With the hobby becoming much more sophisticated and specialized, items of little artistic or historical significance tend to rise less rapidly in price, while, for example, motoring guides of the early 1900s are drawing intense competition. Some rare-book dealers have put out lavish catalogs devoted wholly to the car and feature repair manuals, road books, motoring atlases, etc., at sums that would have seemed remarkable ten years ago.

ADVERTISING BROCHURES
Not every manufacturer issued brochures every year. Values hinge on age, manufacturer, size of brochure, and presence of color illustrations.

BOOKS
After the widespread sale of autos began, publishers started producing guide books. These motoring guides included where to find roads, gas stations, and interesting sights. Since the books deal primarily with the road and sightseeing, they aren't prime collecting material.

Technical car books and general repair manuals are avidly sought; so are works about inventions and the development of automobiles.

ENGINE PARTS
Engine parts from the Brass Era tend to be collector favorites, especially for the mechanical-minded hobbyist. Parts from the Brass Era show the greatest change of design compared to parts of today. They are also handsome.

HOOD ORNAMENTS
Hundreds of types of hood ornaments have been cataloged by specialists who have found that the fanciest varieties date between 1925 and 1935. Most hobbyists collect ornaments by subject; some by manufacturer.

The collectibility of hood ornaments has long been recognized; in fact, they have been collected as long as they have been made.

HUBCAPS
The wide variety and abundance of hubcaps make them a good choice for the collector. Many styles and designs have been used on hubcaps, and they usually carry the name or symbol of the manufacturer.

Hubcaps of the Brass Era are the most stately. They were usually made of cast brass. The 1920s brought a more flashy style to hubcaps, and some even carried slogans on them.

LICENSE PLATES
The first auto collectible to attract widespread interest, license plates can be collected in a variety of ways. Collectors may try to get one from each state or concentrate on older plates. Older plates show the changes in size, design, and color over the years. Pre-1910 plates reflect a variety of types as well as material (leather, for example).

Because of the types used, most plates are not in mint condition. Some quickly deteriorated.

License plates from celebrity cars are very popular.

MAGAZINE ADS

Collecting magazine ads is a good option for the budget-minded collector. There is so much material available that most collectors specialize either by manufacturer or publication. Most interest is in full-page and double-page color ads. Ads from front or back covers are also desirable because they are on heavier paper.

By buying and clipping old magazines yourself, you will accumulate more ads for a lower cost than by buying them individually. The mid to late autumn issues usually have the most and the best ads for cars.

PHOTOGRAPHS

Most photograph collectors are interested in snapshot or portrait photos from the 1890s and early 1900s. Many photos were taken then since both the car and the portable box camera were novelties.

These photos represent one of a few ways to document the Brass Era, and current value is based on the type of car, size, quality, and preservation of the photo. Photos of cars being worked on are more valuable than simple portraits of family members.

POSTERS

Billboard posters featuring a car or advertising cars or car races are also collected. No effort has been made to save these posters and not many survived over the years. Mint condition, therefore, is not expected, especially for posters that date to the Brass Era.

Values depend on age, type of car, size of poster, rarity of poster, artist, and physical condition.

Posters are also bought by collectors of artists, so the value of a poster of an average car could be high if done by a popular artist.

REPAIR MANUALS

Valued according to age, maker, and physical condition, repair manuals have usually received heavy handling and are not in mint condition.

Repair manuals for cars recognized as Classics sell for the most money. However, a double market exists: manuals are sought by collectors as well as by car restorers.

Collectibles of this type can be found just about anywhere, but you have to know what you are looking for and what price you are willing to pay. Competition is becoming fierce in this highly popular collector field.

PRODUCTION FIGURES, 1897–1985 (MODEL YEAR AND CALENDAR YEAR)

The following statistics on year-by-year American auto production are the most accurate available, though they may not be 100% correct. Figures for 1897 to 1945 show *Model Year* production. Beginning in 1946, when post-war production began, auto manufacturers began to record *Calendar Year* output. Thus, when using these figures, it is important to keep in mind that those up to and including 1945 are for model year, and those from 1946 onward are for calendar year.

Since the following information was compiled partially as the result of original research by the publishers, it is fully protected by copyright and may not be reproduced without permission.

Production figures reflect increasing auto production over the years. In 1900, total recorded production was a mere nine vehicles. It jumped the next year to 399, even though no new manufacturers were added (Oldsmobile and Packard were the only makers). Then, in 1902, production passed 3,000. Enormous leaps occurred until

World War I, which put a damper on the industry. However, in the 1920s, production once again zoomed upward, despite competition from many foreign makers.

Until 1901, the horseless carriage was truly a novelty. It took a while to "catch on." Production in 1899 was no greater than in 1898. Even in 1901, Olds was the only maker mass-producing cars.

Obviously, quantities manufactured are not necessarily a reliable indicator of quantities still in existence. In general, models that sold originally in the lower price range suffered a slightly higher loss ratio over the years. They tended to be subjected to heavier wear, abuse, and neglect, while high-priced models were usually given better care by their owners. This does not mean that these cars are more valuable from a collector's viewpoint. We strongly advise you not to attempt judging values from the production figures, but to refer instead to the price listings in this book.

HOW TO USE THESE FIGURES

Figures from 1897 to 1945 are for makes and are arranged by volume, the highest-output make listed first, the second-highest next, and so on.

Beginning with the 1946 figures, total outputs for each manufacturer (including all makes) are given. This information is stated *before* the figures for each individual make and is indicated by the word *"all"* in parentheses. For example, "General Motors (*all*)" means *every passenger car made by General Motors that year*. The individual makes for each manufacturer are arranged with the *highest output first*, and with figures for models (when available) given *before the total output for that make.*

MODEL YEAR FIGURES, 1897–1945

1897
Oldsmobile 4

1898
Oldsmobile 6

1899
Oldsmobile 5
Packard 1

1900
Oldsmobile 6
Packard 3

1901
Oldsmobile 394
Packard 5

1902
Oldsmobile 2,531
Cadillac 640
Packard 22

1903
Oldsmobile 3,910
Cadillac 1,720
Ford 1,708
Packard 34
Buick 6

1904
Oldsmobile 5,598
Cadillac 2,418
Ford 1,695
Packard 281
Studebaker 260
Buick 37

1905
Oldsmobile 6,437
Cadillac 3,712
Ford 1,599
Buick 750
Packard 443
Studebaker 340

1906
Ford 8,802
Cadillac 3,319
Oldsmobile 1,663
Buick 1,428
Packard 928
Studebaker 410

1907
Ford 14,814
Buick 4,461

Cadillac 2,409
Packard 1,215
Oldsmobile 1,104
Studebaker 563

1908
Ford 10,116
Buick 8,940
Studebaker 8,137
Cadillac 1,967
Packard 1,607
Oldsmobile 1,251

1909
Ford 17,857
Buick 14,109
Cadillac 7,903
Studebaker 7,843
Packard 3,083
Oldsmobile 1,575

1910
Ford 30,794
Buick 28,416
Studebaker 16,421
Cadillac 8,008
Hudson 4,640
Oakland 4,028
Packard 2,242

1911
Ford 71,021
Studebaker 26,480
Buick 14,401
Cadillac 10,018
Hudson 6,391
Oakland 3,429
Packard 2,812
Oldsmobile 1,250

1912
Ford 161,409
Studebaker 28,611
Buick 21,804
Hudson 13,995
Oakland 5,421
Chevrolet 3,106
Packard 2,238
Oldsmobile 1,075

1913
Ford 211,469
Studebaker 41,642
Buick 24,901
Cadillac 15,018
Oakland 7,840
Hudson 7,391
Chevrolet 4,861
Packard 2,835
Oldsmobile 1,175

1914
Ford 331,862
Buick 31,641
Studebaker 29,830
Cadillac 10,002
Hudson 9,648
Chevrolet 7,841
Oakland 7,100
Packard 3,018
Oldsmobile 1,400

1915
Ford 477,762
Studebaker 54,730
Buick 41,756
Dodge 39,147
Cadillac 17,141
Oakland 12,461
Hudson 11,961
Chevrolet 8,609
Oldsmobile 6,842
Packard 5,600

1916
Ford 756,436
Buick 119,811
Dodge 68,471
Cadillac 18,004
Chevrolet 51,402
Studebaker 35,388
Hudson 28,491
Oakland 26,736
Cadillac 18,004
Oldsmobile 10,911
Packard 5,600

1917
Ford 600,726
Buick 118,438

Chevrolet 109,416
Dodge 88,471
Studebaker 39,748
Hudson 32,464
Oakland 32,116
Oldsmobile 22,613
Cadillac 19,006
Nash 11,811
Packard 7,696

1918
Ford 417,862
Buick 128,632
Chevrolet 72,491
Dodge 57,331
Oakland 26,219
Oldsmobile 19,169
Studebaker 18,419
Cadillac 14,285
Hudson 11,910
Nash 9,080
Packard 3,196

1919
Ford 838,481
Buick 165,997
Chevrolet 131,891
Dodge 104,791
Oakland 43,220
Oldsmobile 39,042
Hudson 38,491
Studebaker 35,051
Nash 26,414
Cadillac 20,678
Packard 3,196

1920
Dodge 148,621
Buick 123,000
Chevrolet 118,416
Hudson 48,216
Studebaker 47,981
Nash 35,606
Oldsmobile 34,504
Oakland 33,356
Cadillac 19,628
Packard 9,126

1921
Ford 956,841
Dodge 77,496

Studebaker 69,863
Buick 67,537
Chevrolet 57,439
Hudson 26,501
Nash 19,761
Oldsmobile 19,157
Cadillac 15,250
Oakland 10,444
Packard 9,126

1922
Ford 1,216,543
Chevrolet 211,916
Dodge 161,912
Buick 117,191
Studebaker 107,378
Hudson 64,380
Nash 38,919
Cadillac 26,296
Oldsmobile 21,499
Oakland 18,486
Packard 9,127

1923
Ford 1,775,093
Chevrolet 396,411
Buick 172,876
Dodge 171,421
Studebaker 89,418
Hudson 86,904
Nash 54,687
Oldsmobile 39,926
Oakland 25,576
Cadillac 24,707
Packard 13,652

1924
Ford 1,801,492
Chevrolet 248,309
Dodge 207,687
Buick 171,561
Studebaker 159,782
Hudson 136,840
Chrysler 69,161
Nash 53,481
Oldsmobile 44,542
Oakland 37,080
Cadillac 18,827
Packard 16,653

1925

Ford 1,591,630
Chevrolet 461,092
Hudson 261,400
DeSoto 197,831
Buick 186,483
Chrysler 128,417
Nash 98,764
Studebaker 80,365
Oldsmobile 37,786
Packard 30,477
Oakland 29,425
Cadillac 21,673

1926

Ford 1,289,653
Chevrolet 584,293
Dodge 249,869
Buick 238,543
Hudson 238,461
Studebaker 158,463
Chrysler 150,101
Nash 137,601
Pontiac 132,276
Oakland 58,827
Oldsmobile 53,783
Packard 37,734

1927

Chevrolet 1,678,540
Ford 434,918
Hudson 276,491
Buick 250,116
Pontiac 182,277
Chrysler 179,140
Dodge 146,001
Nash 127,164
Studebaker 123,474
Oldsmobile 69,282
Oakland 44,658
Packard 40,875
Cadillac 36,396
LaSalle 10,767

1928

Chevrolet 746,394
Ford 659,841
Hudson 291,840
Buick 235,009

Pontiac 224,784
Chrysler 151,306
Nash 139,004
Studebaker 105,968
Oldsmobile 78,879
Oakland 60,121
Packard 53,690
Plymouth 51,860
Cadillac 40,000
LaSalle 16,038

1929

Ford 1,511,312
Chrysler 884,680
Chevrolet 846,743
Hudson 346,876
Buick 201,182
Pontiac 200,503
Dodge 121,457
Nash 117,411
Oldsmobile 99,857
Plymouth 92,184
DeSoto 62,191
Studebaker 57,790
Oakland 50,693
Packard 45,788
LaSalle 22,961
Cadillac 18,004

1930

Ford 1,124,735
Chevrolet 640,980
Buick 138,155
Hudson 116,407
Pontiac 82,888
Plymouth 76,950
Studebaker 76,781
Nash 54,698
Oldsmobile 52,133
Chrysler 43,594
Packard 25,982
Oakland 21,943
Cadillac 15,492
LaSalle 14,986

1931

Chevrolet 847,979
Ford 537,918
Plymouth 106,896

Buick 97,661
Pontiac 84,708
Hudson 55,201
Dodge 52,690
Chrysler 51,145
Oldsmobile 47,277
Studebaker 44,218
Nash 38,467
Cadillac 15,197
Oakland 13,408
Packard 13,262
LaSalle 10,095
Lincoln 3,311

1932
Chevrolet 313,395
Ford 234,678
Plymouth 123,910
Buick 55,499
Hudson 51,046
Studebaker 47,950
Pontiac 45,340
Dodge 27,229
Chrysler 25,699
Oldsmobile 19,169
Nash 17,413
Cadillac 8,688
Packard 5,538
Lincoln 3,388
LaSalle 3,386

1933
Chevrolet 486,280
Ford 330,261
Plymouth 298,557
Dodge 106,107
Pontiac 90,198
Hudson 46,894
Buick 45,365
Studebaker 45,074
Oldsmobile 36,648
Chrysler 32,192
DeSoto 22,736
Nash 14,805
Packard 14,340
LaSalle 3,482
Cadillac 3,173

1934
Ford 573,807
Chevrolet 551,371
Plymouth 321,171
Dodge 95,001
Hudson 87,401
Pontiac 78,859
Oldsmobile 78,574
Buick 66,177
Studebaker 51,773
Chrysler 36,491
Nash 27,013
DeSoto 13,940
LaSalle 7,195
Packard 5,960
Cadillac 5,819
Lincoln 2,149

1935
Ford 938,465
Chevrolet 548,212
Plymouth 450,884
Oldsmobile 180,374
Pontiac 169,468
Dodge 158,999
Buick 109,961
Hudson 97,016
Packard 65,402
Nash 47,754
Chrysler 41,553
Studebaker 36,504
DeSoto 27,581
Cadillac 13,636
LaSalle 8,651
Lincoln 2,381

1936
Chevrolet 921,461
Ford 811,551
Plymouth 520,025
Dodge 265,005
Buick 251,059
Oldsmobile 191,357
Pontiac 176,270
Hudson 121,400
Packard 91,810
Studebaker 63,664
Chrysler 59,248
DeSoto 53,710

Nash	52,814
Lincoln	16,453
LaSalle	13,004
Cadillac	12,880

1937

Ford	837,419
Chevrolet	815,420
Plymouth	551,994
Buick	295,915
Dodge	295,047
Pontiac	236,189
Oldsmobile	206,830
Hudson	116,200
Chrysler	106,300
Packard	89,157
Nash	85,843
Studebaker	82,627
DeSoto	82,561
LaSalle	32,000
Lincoln	30,974
Cadillac	14,152

1938

Chevrolet	465,156
Ford	391,006
Plymouth	279,388
Buick	159,726
Dodge	114,529
Pontiac	97,139
Oldsmobile	88,045
Hudson	56,480
Chrysler	53,832
Packard	51,062
Studebaker	45,220
DeSoto	39,203
Lincoln	19,527
LaSalle	15,575
Cadillac	9,375

1939

Chevrolet	586,632
Ford	547,664
Plymouth	417,529
Buick	201,141
Dodge	179,300
Pontiac	154,340
Oldsmobile	137,227
Studebaker	92,200

Hudson	82,291
Mercury	74,107
Chrysler	72,309
Packard	72,213
Nash	65,451
DeSoto	55,699
LaSalle	24,130
Lincoln	15,406
Cadillac	13,581

1940

Chevrolet	767,744
Ford	594,155
Plymouth	499,155
Buick	278,784
Pontiac	247,001
Oldsmobile	197,154
Dodge	195,505
Studebaker	120,543
Chrysler	92,448
Packard	85,437
Mercury	81,059
Hudson	74,219
DeSoto	67,790
Nash	62,119
Cadillac	43,046
Lincoln	21,948

1941

Chevrolet	1,020,029
Ford	576,773
Plymouth	429,811
Buick	352,780
Pontiac	330,061
Dodge	236,999
Oldsmobile	235,852
Chrysler	161,704
Studebaker	92,289
DeSoto	89,580
Nash	83,211
Hudson	79,654
Mercury	76,481
Packard	66,428
Cadillac	66,130
Lincoln	21,994

1942

Studebaker	85,339
Chevrolet	58,087

Nash	53,817
Ford	47,488
Chrysler	46,586
Plymouth	29,480
Dodge	18,522
Buick	18,091
Oldsmobile	16,303
Pontiac	13,555
Packard	6,776
Lincoln	6,567
Hudson	5,291
DeSoto	4,471
Mercury	3,821
Cadillac	3,511

1943
——

1944
——

1945

Ford	33,921
Chevrolet	11,407
Nash	6,340
Pontiac	5,421
Hudson	4,614
Oldsmobile	3,102
Packard	2,652
Mercury	2,649
Studebaker	2,637
Buick	2,460
Cadillac	1,609
DeSoto	948
Plymouth	749
Lincoln	487
Chrysler	468
Dodge	376

CALENDAR YEAR FIGURES, 1946–1985

1946

GENERAL MOTORS *(all)*	827,845
Chevrolet	397,109
Buick	156,080
Pontiac	131,538
Oldsmobile	114,674
Cadillac	28,444
CHRYSLER *(all)*	539,592
Plymouth	241,656
Dodge	158,926
Chrysler/Imperial	76,642
DeSoto	62,368
FORD *(all)*	457,368
Ford	372,917
Mercury	70,955
Lincoln/Continental	13,496
AMERICAN MOTORS *(all)*	193,409
Nash	98,769
Hudson	94,640
STUDEBAKER *(all)*	119,668
Studebaker	77,566
Packard	42,102
KAISER *(all)*	11,753

1947

GENERAL MOTORS *(all)*	1,437,727
Chevrolet	695,992
Buick	267,830
Pontiac	223,015
Oldsmobile	191,454
Cadillac	59,436
CHRYSLER *(all)*	776,783
Plymouth	347,946
Dodge	237,735
Chrysler/Imperial	108,870
DeSoto	82,232
FORD *(all)*	755,552
Ford	601,665
Mercury	124,612
Lincoln/Continental	29,275
AMERICAN MOTORS *(all)*	217,058
Nash	113,315
Hudson	103,743
STUDEBAKER *(all)*	179,118
Studebaker	123,641
Packard	55,477
KAISER *(all)*	144,506

1948
GENERAL MOTORS (all) . . 1,565,926
    Chevrolet 775,990
    Buick 275,503
    Pontiac 253,469
    Cadillac 66,209

CHRYSLER (all) 835,154
    Plymouth 381,139
    Dodge 240,547
    Chrysler/Imperial 120,099
    DeSoto 93,369

FORD (all) 747,467
    Ford 549,077
    Mercury 154,702
    Lincoln/Continental 43,688

STUDEBAKER (all) 263,651
    Studebaker 164,754
    Packard 98,897

AMERICAN MOTORS (all) . . 262,740
    Hudson 144,119
    Nash 118,621

KAISER (all) 181,809

WILLYS (all) 9,968

CHECKER (all) 4,458

1949
GENERAL MOTORS (all) . . 2,206,827
    Chevrolet 1,109,958
    Buick 398,482
    Pontiac 333,957
    Oldsmobile 282,885
    Cadillac 81,545

CHRYSLER (all) 1,114,941
    Plymouth 569,260
    Dodge 298,053
    Chrysler/Imperial 140,454
    DeSoto 107,174

FORD (all) 1,077,641
    Ford 841,170
    Mercury 203,339
    Lincoln/Continental 33,132

STUDEBAKER (all) 332,995
    Studebaker 228,402
    Packard 104,593

AMERICAN MOTORS (all) . . 285,054
    Nash 142,592
    Hudson 142,462

KAISER (all) 60,405

WILLYS (all) 3,938

CHECKER (all) 1,465

1950
GENERAL MOTORS (all) . . 3,048,357
    Chevrolet 1,520,583
    Buick 552,827
    Pontiac 467,655
    Oldsmobile 396,757
    Cadillac 110,535

FORD (all) 1,556,688
    Ford 1,187,122
    Mercury 334,081
    Lincoln/Continental 35,485

CHRYSLER (all) 1,193,456
    Plymouth 567,381
    Dodge 331,220
    Chrysler/Imperial 167,425
    DeSoto 127,430

STUDEBAKER (all) 340,237
    Studebaker 268,099
    Packard 72,138

AMERICAN MOTORS (all) . . 331,798
    Nash 167,869
    Hudson 142,255
    Rambler 21,674

KAISER (all) 118,554

HENRY J (all) 30,947

WILLYS (all) 5,846

CHECKER (all) 2,715

1951
GENERAL MOTORS (all) . . 2,255,497
    Chevrolet 1,118,101
    Buick 404,695
    Pontiac 343,795
    Oldsmobile 285,634
    Cadillac 103,272

CHRYSLER (all) 1,228,645
    Plymouth 607,691

Dodge. 336,656
Chrysler/Imperial 163,541
DeSoto 120,757

FORD *(all)* 1,165,010
Ford 900,770
Mercury 238,854
Lincoln/Continental. 25,386

STUDEBAKER *(all)*. 298,075
Studebaker. 222,000
Packard. 76,075

AMERICAN MOTORS *(all)* . . 254,473
Nash. 101,438
Hudson. 93,333
Rambler 59,702

HENRY J *(all)*. 58,228

KAISER *(all)*. 41,308

CHECKER *(all)*. 3,085

WILLYS *(all)*. 2,097

1952
GENERAL MOTORS *(all)* . . 1,801,450
Chevrolet 877,950
Buick 321,048
Pontiac 277,156
Oldsmobile. 228,452
Cadillac. 96,844

FORD *(all)* 1,004,784
Ford 777,531
Mercury 195,261
Lincoln/Continental. 31,992

CHRYSLER *(all)*. 952,660
Plymouth 466,289
Dodge. 268,094
Chrysler/Imperial 120,692
DeSoto 97,585

AMERICAN MOTORS *(all)* . . 228,440
Nash. 99,086
Hudson. 76,354
Rambler 53,000

STUDEBAKER *(all)*. 224,508
Studebaker. 161,520
Packard. 62,988

KAISER *(all)*. 44,570

WILLYS *(all)*. 35,954

HENRY J *(all)*. 30,543

CHECKER *(all)* 694

1953
GENERAL MOTORS *(all)* . . 2,799,615
Chevrolet. 1,477,299
Buick 485,353
Pontiac 414,011
Oldsmobile. 319,414
Cadillac. 103,538

FORD *(all)* 1,546,518
Ford. 1,184,187
Mercury 320,369
Lincoln/Continental. 41,962

CHRYSLER *(all)* 1,246,577
Plymouth 654,414
Dodge. 301,827
Chrysler/Imperial 160,377
DeSoto 129,959

STUDEBAKER *(all)*. 267,215
Studebaker. 186,844
Packard. 80,371

AMERICAN MOTORS *(all)* . . 212,427
Nash. 93,504
Hudson. 77,098
Rambler 41,825

WILLYS *(all)*. 35,146

KAISER *(all)*. 14,313

HENRY J *(all)*. 7,459

CHECKER *(all)*. 2,974

1954
GENERAL MOTORS *(all)* . . 2,874,271
Chevrolet. 1,414,365
Buick 531,463
Oldsmobile. 433,810
Pontiac 370,887
Cadillac. 123,746

FORD *(all)* 1,687,224
Ford. 1,394,762
Mercury 256,729
Lincoln/Continental. 35,733

CHRYSLER *(all)* 720,051
  Plymouth 396,702
  Dodge. 151,761
  Chrysler/Imperial 101,744
  DeSoto 69,844

STUDEBAKER *(all)* 112,967
  Studebaker 85,660
  Packard. 27,307

AMERICAN MOTORS *(all)* . . . 95,182
  Rambler 37,779
  Nash. 29,371
  Hudson. 28,032

WILLYS *(all)* 9,339

KAISER *(all)* 5,756

CHECKER *(all)* 2,627

1955
GENERAL MOTORS *(all)* . . 3,989,987
  Chevrolet. 1,830,038
  Buick 781,296
  Oldsmobile. 634,459
  Pontiac 581,860
  Cadillac. 581,334

FORD *(all)* 2,240,661
  Ford. 1,764,524
  Mercury 434,911
  Lincoln/Continental. 41,226

CHRYSLER *(all)* 1,370,736
  Plymouth 746,361
  Dodge. 316,584
  Chrysler/Imperial 176,038
  DeSoto 131,753

STUDEBAKER *(all)* 181,397
  Studebaker 112,723
  Packard. 68,674

AMERICAN MOTORS *(all)* . . 161,790
  Rambler 83,852
  Nash. 51,315
  Hudson. 26,623

WILLYS *(all)* 4,778

KAISER *(all)* 1,021

CHECKER *(all)* 7

1956
GENERAL MOTORS *(all)* . . 3,062,426
  Chevrolet. 1,621,018
  Buick 535,364
  Oldsmobile. 432,903
  Pontiac 332,268
  Cadillac. 140,873

FORD *(all)* 1,669,165
  Ford. 1,373,542
  Mercury 246,628
  Lincoln/Continental. 48,995

CHRYSLER *(all)* 870,623
  Plymouth 452,918
  Dodge. 205,820
  Chrysler/Imperial 107,490
  DeSoto 104,395

AMERICAN MOTORS *(all)* . . 104,185
  Rambler 79,162
  Nash. 17,841
  Hudson. 7,182

STUDEBAKER *(all)* 96,387
  Studebaker 82,955
  Packard. 13,432

CHECKER *(all)* 3,970

1957
GENERAL MOTORS *(all)* . . 2,816,445
  Chevrolet. 1,522,549
  Buick 407,271
  Oldsmobile. 390,091
  Pontiac 343,298
  Cadillac. 153,236

FORD *(all)* 1,889,705
  Ford. 1,522,408
  Mercury 274,820
  Edsel 54,607
  Lincoln 37,870

CHRYSLER *(all)* 1,223,035
  Plymouth 655,006
  Dodge. 293,616
  Chrysler 118,718
  DeSoto 117,750
  Imperial 37,945

AMERICAN MOTORS *(all)* . . 114,084
  Rambler 109,178

Nash 3,561
Hudson 1,345

STUDEBAKER *(all)* 72,889
Studebaker 67,394
Packard 5,495

CHECKER *(all)* 3,871

1958
GENERAL MOTORS *(all)* . . 2,169,186
Chevrolet 1,255,943
Oldsmobile 310,795
Buick 257,124
Pontiac 219,823
Cadillac 125,501

FORD *(all)* 1,219,422
Ford 1,038,560
Mercury 128,428
Edsel 26,563
Lincoln 25,871

CHRYSLER *(all)* 581,300
Plymouth 366,758
Dodge 114,665
Chrysler 49,504
DeSoto 36,700
Imperial 13,673

AMERICAN MOTORS *(all)* . . 217,332

STUDEBAKER *(all)* 56,920
Studebaker 55,175
Packard 1,745

CHECKER *(all)* 3,267

1959
GENERAL MOTORS *(all)* . . 2,555,247
Chevrolet 1,349,562
Corvair 79,418
CHEVROLET TOTAL 1,428,980

Pontiac 388,856
Oldsmobile 366,305
Buick 232,579
Cadillac 138,527

FORD *(all)* 1,745,409
Ford 1,427,835
Ford Falcon 100,757
FORD TOTAL 1,528,592

Mercury 156,756
Lincoln 30,375
Edsel 29,677

CHRYSLER *(all)* 737,799
Plymouth 393,213
Valiant 19,991
PLYMOUTH TOTAL 413,204

Dodge 192,798
Chrysler 69,411
DeSoto 42,423
Imperial 20,963

AMERICAN MOTORS *(all)* . . 401,446

STUDEBAKER *(all)* 153,823

CHECKER *(all)* 5,768

1959
GENERAL MOTORS *(all)* . . 3,193,181
Chevrolet 1,614,342
Corvair 259,276
CHEVROLET TOTAL 1,873,618

Pontiac 418,154
Tempest 32,052
PONTIAC TOTAL 450,206

Oldsmobile 362,681
Olds F-85 39,931
OLDSMOBILE TOTAL 402,612

Buick 271,071
Special 36,733
BUICK TOTAL 307,804

Cadillac 158,941

FORD *(all)* 1,892,005
Ford 1,004,305
Ford Falcon 507,199
FORD TOTAL 1,511,504

Mercury 161,787
Comet 198,031
MERCURY TOTAL 359,818

Lincoln 20,683

CHRYSLER *(all)* 1,019,295
Plymouth 252,453
Valiant 231, 516
PLYMOUTH TOTAL 483,969

Dodge. 362,808	Dodge. 166,158
Lancer 48,858	Lancer 54,621
DODGE TOTAL 411,666	DODGE TOTAL 220,779
Chrysler 87,420	Chrysler 104,747
DeSoto 19,411	Imperial 12,699
Imperial 16,829	

AMERICAN MOTORS (all) . . 485,745

STUDEBAKER (all). 105,902

CHECKER (all) 6,980

AMERICAN MOTORS (all) . . 372,485

STUDEBAKER (all). 78,664

CHECKER (all) 5,683

1961

GENERAL MOTORS (all) . . 1,726,577
- Chevrolet. 1,201,811
- Corvair 316,679
- Chevy II 86,330
- CHEVROLET TOTAL 1,604,820

- Pontiac 244,391
- Tempest. 115,945
- PONTIAC TOTAL 360,336

- Oldsmobile. 253,944
- Olds F-85 67,894
- OLDSMOBILE TOTAL 321,838

- Buick 191,392
- Special 99,893
- BUICK TOTAL 291,285

- Cadillac. 148,298

FORD (all) 1,689,940
- Galaxie 710,392
- Falcon. 486,081
- Thunderbird 88,207
- Fairlane. 60,444
- FORD TOTAL 1,345,124

- Mercury Comet 185,844
- Monterey 109,755
- Meteor 16,037
- MERCURY TOTAL. 311,636

- Lincoln 33,180

CHRYSLER (all). 648,670
- Plymouth 188,170
- Valiant. 122,275
- PLYMOUTH TOTAL 310,445

1962

GENERAL MOTORS (all) . . 3,741,538
- Chevrolet. 1,495,476
- Chevy II 369,246
- Corvair 296,687
- CHEVROLET TOTAL 2,161,409

- Pontiac 401,674
- Tempest. 145,676
- PONTIAC TOTAL 547,350

- Oldsmobile. 356,058
- Olds F-85 102,301
- OLDSMOBILE TOTAL 458,359

- Buick 256,766
- Special 159,126
- BUICK TOTAL 415,892

- Cadillac. 158,528

FORD (all) 1,935,203
- Galaxie 722,642
- Fairlane. 386,192
- Falcon. 381,558
- Thunderbird 75,536
- FORD TOTAL 1,565,928

- Mercury Comet 144,886
- Monterey 109,347
- Meteor 81,213
- MERCURY TOTAL. 335,446

- Lincoln 33,829

CHRYSLER (all). 716,809
- Plymouth 177,651
- Valiant. 153,248
- PLYMOUTH TOTAL 331,079

Dodge. 251,722
Chrysler 111,958
Imperial 18,051

AMERICAN MOTORS (all) . . 454,784

STUDEBAKER (all). 86,974

CHECKER (all) 8,029

AMERICAN MOTORS (all) . . 480,365
Classic 321,916
American 129,655
Ambassador 28,794

STUDEBAKER (all). 67,918

CHECKER (all) 7,231

1963
GENERAL MOTORS (all) . . 4,077,272
Chevrolet. 1,625,931
Chevy II 312,097
Corvair 251,513
Corvette 113,774
CHEVROLET TOTAL 2,303,315

Pontiac. 481,652
Tempest. 143,616
PONTIAC TOTAL 625,268

Oldsmobile. 371,033
Olds F-85 133,522
OLDSMOBILE TOTAL 504,555

Buick 327,173
Special 152,226
Cadillac. 164,735

FORD (all) 1,963,869
Ford 911,496
Falcon. 341,871
Fairlane. 318,018
Thunderbird 66,681
FORD TOTAL 1,638,066

Mercury 118,815
Mercury Comet 150,694
Meteor 22,577
MERCURY TOTAL. 292,086

Lincoln 33,717

CHRYSLER (all) 1,047,722
Plymouth 274,735
Valiant. 221,677
PLYMOUTH TOTAL. 496,412

Dodge. 246,425
Dart 174,876
DODGE TOTAL 421,301

Chrysler 111,958
Imperial 18,051

1964
GENERAL MOTORS (all) . . 3,956,637
Chevrolet. 1,420,304
Chevelle 320,941
Corvair 195,780
Chevy II 157,799
Corvette 19,894
CHEVROLET TOTAL 2,114,718

Pontiac 443,306
Tempest. 250,328
PONTIAC TOTAL 693,634

Oldsmobile. 335,637
Olds F-85 175,294
OLDSMOBILE TOTAL 510,931

Buick 257,438
Special 188,980
Riviera 36,313
BUICK TOTAL 482,731

Cadillac. 154,623

FORD (all) 2,145,943
Ford 881,061
Mustang. 303,408
Falcon. 279,109
Fairlane. 233,718
Thunderbird 90,239
FORD TOTAL 1,787,535

Comet 195,227
Mercury 125,431
MERCURY TOTAL. 320,658

Lincoln 37,750

CHRYSLER (all) 1,242,162
Fury 266,683
Belvedere. 63,757
Barracuda. 50,110
PLYMOUTH TOTAL. 571,339

Polara 215,896
Dart 208,646
Coronet 80,552
DODGE TOTAL 505,094

Chrysler 145,338
Imperial 20,391

AMERICAN MOTORS (all) . . 393,863
Classic 201,506
American 151,969
Ambassador 40,388

CHECKER (all) 6,310

STUDEBAKER (all) 577

1965
GENERAL MOTORS (all) . . 4,949,395
Chevrolet 1,821,266
Chevelle 370,188
Corvair 204,007
Chevy II/Nova 164,348
Corvette 27,700
CHEVROLET TOTAL 2,587,509

Pontiac 534,633
Tempest/LeMans 326,019
PONTIAC TOTAL 860,652

Buick 368,973
Special/Skylark/Century 243,441
Riviera 41,424
BUICK TOTAL 653,838

Oldsmobile 400,664
Olds F-85/Cutlass 233,154
Toronado 16,983
OLDSMOBILE TOTAL 650,801

Cadillac 196,595

FORD (all) 2,565,776
Ford 1,048,388
Mustang 580,187
Fairlane/Torino 251,647
Falcon/Club Wagon 208,970
Thunderbird 75,710
FORD TOTAL 2,164,902

Mercury 193,069
Comet 162,335
MERCURY TOTAL 355,404

Lincoln 45,470

CHRYSLER (all) 1,467,553
Fury/Gran Fury 305,425
Belvedere/Satellite/Fury 179,823
Valiant 139,436
Barracuda 54,855
PLYMOUTH TOTAL 679,539

Coronet/Charger 240,199
Dart 173,199
Dodge 134,133
DODGE TOTAL 547,531

Chrysler 224,061
Imperial 16,422

AMERICAN MOTORS (all) . . 346,367
Classic/Rebel/Matador 173,374
Rambler/Hornet 100,217
Ambassador 72,776

CHECKER (all) 6,136

1966
GENERAL MOTORS (all) . . 4,448,668
Chevrolet 1,431,022
Chevelle 423,317
Chevy II/Nova 155,726
Camaro 94,426
Corvair 73,362
Corvette 24,939
CHEVROLET TOTAL 2,202,792

Pontiac 481,591
Tempest/LeMans 384,794
PONTIAC TOTAL 866,385

Oldsmobile 318,667
Olds F-85/Cutlass 237,982
Toronado 37,420
OLDSMOBILE TOTAL 594,069

Buick 315,639
Special/Skylark/Century 216,709
Riviera 48,073
BUICK TOTAL 580,421

Cadillac 198,797
El Dorado 6,204
CADILLAC TOTAL 205,001

FORD *(all)* 2,425,422	
Ford 948,462	
Mustang. 580,767	
Fairlane/Torino 304,659	
Falcon/Club Wagon 131,793	
Thunderbird 72,734	
FORD TOTAL 2,038,415	

Mercury 153,680
Comet 133,165
Cougar 48,013
MERCURY TOTAL. 334,858

Lincoln 52,169

CHRYSLER *(all)* 1,445,616
Fury/Gran Fury 289,676
Belvedere/Satellite/Fury 174,295
Valiant. 134,683
Barracuda 41,796
PLYMOUTH TOTAL. 640,450

Coronet/Charger. 278,531
Dart 146,361
Dodge. 107,134
DODGE TOTAL 532,026

Chrysler 255,487
Imperial 17,653

AMERICAN MOTORS *(all)* . . 279,225
Classic/Rebel/Matador 122,036
Rambler/Hornet 85,107
Ambassador 68,084
Marlin. 3,998

CHECKER *(all)*. 5,761

1967
GENERAL MOTORS *(all)* . . 4,117,860
Chevrolet. 1,150,264
Chevelle 375,831
Camaro. 216,210
Chevy II/Nova. 135,884
Corvette 23,775
Corvair 18,701
CHEVROLET TOTAL 1,920,665

Pontiac. 445,956
Tempest/LeMans. 288,924
Firebird 122,291
PONTIAC TOTAL 857,171

Buick 336,366
Special/Skylark/Century 194,355
Riviera 43,145
BUICK TOTAL 573,866

Oldsmobile. 277,910
Olds F-85/Cutlass. 256,643
Toronado 18,444
OLDSMOBILE TOTAL 552,997

Cadillac. 192,339
El Dorado 20,822
CADILLAC TOTAL. 213,161

FORD *(all)* 1,696,224
Ford 699,356
Mustang. 394,482
Fairlane/Torino 190,383
Thunderbird 59,640
Falcon/Club Wagon 33,527
FORD TOTAL 1,377,388

Cougar 131,743
Mercury 96,309
Comet 56,451
MERCURY TOTAL. 284,503

Lincoln 34,133

AMERICAN MOTORS *(all)* . . 229,057
Classic/Rebel/Matador 88,532
Rambler/Hornet 63,291
Ambassador 50,391
Javelin/AMX 26,595
Marlin 248

CHECKER *(all)*. 5,822

1968
GENERAL MOTORS *(all)* . . 4,592,114
Chevrolet. 1,217,255
Chevelle 432,302
Camaro. 229,344
Chevy II/Nova. 225,265
Corvette 32,473
Corvair 11,490
CHEVROLET TOTAL 2,148,129

Pontiac. 484,849
Tempest/LeMans. 352,878
Firebird 105,526
PONTIAC TOTAL 943,253

Buick 384,575
Special/Skylark/Century 216,594
Riviera 50,880
BUICK TOTAL 652,049

Oldsmobile 331,586
Olds F-85/Cutlass 276,269
Toronado 29,924
OLDSMOBILE TOTAL 637,779

Cadillac 187,765
El Dorado 23,139
CADILLAC TOTAL 210,904

FORD (all) 2,396,924
Ford 961,839
Fairlane/Torino 467,069
Mustang 345,194
Thunderbird 76,789
Falcon/Club Wagon 60,545
FORD TOTAL 1,911,436

Montego 149,391
Mercury 142,048
Cougar 129,813
MERCURY TOTAL 421,252

Lincoln 45,774
Mark III/IV 18,462
LINCOLN TOTAL 64,236

CHRYSLER (all) 1,585,591
Fury/Gran Fury 279,762
Belvedere/Satellite/Fury 250,550
Valiant 114,816
Barracuda 38,550
PLYMOUTH TOTAL 683,678

Coronet/Charger 315,685
Dart 199,780
Dodge 105,671
DODGE TOTAL 621,136

Chrysler 263,226
Imperial 17,551

AMERICAN MOTORS (all) . . 268,514
Rambler/Hornet 89,369
Ambassador 65,770
Javelin/AMX 58,051
Classic/Rebel/Matador 55,324

CHECKER (all) 5,477

1969
GENERAL MOTORS (all) . . 4,420,442
Chevrolet 1,069,544
Chevelle 400,460
Chevy II/Nova 298,738
Camaro 159,202
Monte Carlo 41,342
Corvette 26,920
Corvair 3,103
CHEVROLET TOTAL 1,999,309

Pontiac 453,241
Tempest/LeMans 269,300
Firebird 49,563
PONTIAC TOTAL 772,104

Buick 434,382
Special/Skylark/Century 226,061
Riviera 53,389
BUICK TOTAL 713,832

Oldsmobile 373,020
Olds F-85/Cutlass 265,987
Toronado 29,392
OLDSMOBILE TOTAL 668,399

Cadillac 239,584
El Dorado 27,214
CADILLAC TOTAL 266,798

FORD (all) 2,163,109
Ford 876,320
Fairlane/Torino 334,282
Mustang 275,391
Maverick 130,041
Falcon/Club Wagon 77,265
Thunderbird 50,143
FORD TOTAL 1,743,442

Mercury 142,509
Montego 121,597
Cougar 90,338
MERCURY TOTAL 354,444

Lincoln 43,290
Mark III/IV 21,933
LINCOLN TOTAL 65,223

CHRYSLER (all) 1,392,526
  Fury/Gran Fury 259,054
  Belvedere/Satellite/Fury 221,994
  Valiant. 120,514
  Barracuda 49,562
  PLYMOUTH TOTAL 651,124

  Coronet/Charger. 241,196
  Dart 144,046
  Dodge. 57,902
  Challenger 53,041
  DODGE TOTAL 496,185

  Chrysler 226,590
  Imperial 18,627

AMERICAN MOTORS (all) . . 242,898
  Rambler/Hornet 87,817
  Ambassador. 64,023
  Classic/Rebel/Matador 45,733
  Javelin/AMX. 45,325

CHECKER (all). 5,417

1970
GENERAL MOTORS (all) . . 2,979,248
  Chevrolet 550,596
  Chevelle 354,839
  Chevy II/Nova. 254,245
  Camaro. 143,675
  Monte Carlo 130,659
  Vega. 48,005
  Corvette 22,595
  CHEVROLET TOTAL 1,504,614

  Buick 287,904
  Special/Skylark/Century 153,334
  Riviera 18,693
  BUICK TOTAL 459,931

  Olds F-85/Cutlass. 246,567
  Oldsmobile. 179,936
  Toronado 13,129
  OLDSMOBILE TOTAL 439,632

  Pontiac. 182,000
  Tempest/LeMans. 144,755
  Firebird. 58,757
  Grand Prix. 36,700
  PONTIAC TOTAL 422,212

  Cadillac. 137,365
  El Dorado 15,494
  CADILLAC TOTAL 152,859

FORD (all) 2,017,152
  Ford 812,617
  Fairlane/Torino 327,288
  Maverick. 187,087
  Mustang. 165,414
  Pinto. 88,928
  Thunderbird 40,512
  Falcon/Club Wagon 26,072
  FORD TOTAL 1,647,918

  Mercury 124,540
  Montego. 82,908
  Cougar 71,035
  Comet 31,980
  MERCURY TOTAL. 310,463

  Lincoln 34,503
  Mark III/IV. 24,268
  LINCOLN TOTAL 58,771

CHRYSLER (all) 1,273,455
  Valiant. 279,615
  Fury/Gran Fury 266,116
  Belvedere/Satellite/Fury 123,033
  Barracuda 30,267
  PLYMOUTH TOTAL. 699,031

  Coronet/Charger. 154,314
  Dodge. 104,402
  Dart 104,358
  Challenger 42,625
  DODGE TOTAL 405,699

  Chrysler 158,614
  Imperial 10,111

AMERICAN MOTORS (all) . . 276,127
  Rambler/Hornet 79,670
  Ambassador. 56,990
  Classic/Rebel/Matador 56,711
  Gremlin. 49,539
  Javelin/AMX. 33,200

CHECKER (all). 4,146

1971
GENERAL MOTORS (all) . . 4,853,015
  Chevrolet 942,067
  Vega. 393,030

Chevelle 375,009
Chevy II/Nova 298,933
Camaro 148,379
Monte Carlo 136,515
Corvette 26,844
CHEVROLET TOTAL 2,320,777

Oldsmobile 390,173
Olds F-85/Cutlass 338,674
Toronado 46,352
OLDSMOBILE TOTAL 775,199

Buick 463,785
Special/Skylark/Century 242,612
Riviera 45,464
BUICK TOTAL 751,861

Pontiac 300,587
Tempest/LeMans 195,721
Grand Prix 89,512
Ventura 76,708
Firebird 66,087
PONTIAC TOTAL 728,615

Cadillac 236,499
El Dorado 40,064
CADILLAC TOTAL 276,563

FORD (all) 2,176,335
Ford 812,923
Fairlane/Torino 321,487
Pinto 299,867
Mustang 130,488
Maverick 127,414
Thunderbird 46,277
Falcon/Club Wagon 22,656
FORD TOTAL 1,761,112

Mercury 134,756
Comet 78,494
Montego 76,786
Cougar 53,156
MERCURY TOTAL 343,192

Lincoln 37,801
Mark III/IV 34,230
LINCOLN TOTAL 72,031

CHRYSLER (all) 1,313,306
Fury/Gran Fury 291,357
Valiant 236,386

Belvedere/Satellite/Fury 91,836
Barracuda 17,013
PLYMOUTH TOTAL 636,592

Coronet/Charger 159,951
Dart 152,925
Dodge 132,054
Challenger 28,901
DODGE TOTAL 473,831

Chrysler 188,360
Imperial 14,523

AMERICAN MOTORS (all) . . 235,669
Rambler/Hornet 67,875
Gremlin 54,615
Classic/Rebel/Matador 46,489
Ambassador 42,187
Javelin/AMX 24,503

CHECKER (all) 5,328

1972
GENERAL MOTORS (all) . . 4,775,344
Chevrolet 955,237
Vega 368,743
Chevy II/Nova 367,733
Chevelle 358,568
Monte Carlo 186,171
Camaro 35,943
Corvette 27,376
CHEVROLET TOTAL 2,299,771

Oldsmobile 389,089
Olds F-85/Cutlass 341,130
Toronado 51,267
Omega 25,708
OLDSMOBILE TOTAL 807,194

Pontiac 304,545
Tempest/LeMans 198,411
Grand Prix 98,587
Ventura 85,200
Firebird 15,828
PONTIAC TOTAL 702,571

Buick 425,813
Special/Skylark/Century 226,534
Riviera 36,210
BUICK TOTAL 688,557

Cadillac................. 233,456	Vega.................. 359,882
El Dorado 43,795	Chevelle.............. 314,755
CADILLAC TOTAL............ 277,251	Monte Carlo............ 246,533
	Camaro................ 117,828
FORD (all)............. 2,400,871	Corvette................ 32,616
Ford 812,718	CHEVROLET TOTAL......... 2,334,113
Fairlane/Torino 365,532	
Pinto.................. 322,338	Olds F-85/Cutlass........ 422,477
Maverick............... 165,934	Oldsmobile............. 383,623
Mustang............... 118,972	Toronado 56,468
Thunderbird 58,582	OLDSMOBILE TOTAL......... 918,119
Falcon/Club Wagon 23,934	
FORD TOTAL 1,868,010	Pontiac................ 345,214
	Tempest/LeMans......... 205,135
Mercury 150,671	Grand Prix............. 168,803
Montego............... 140,477	Ventura................ 89,150
Comet 83,101	Firebird................ 58,296
Cougar 53,594	PONTIAC TOTAL 866,598
MERCURY TOTAL............ 427,843	
	Buick 425,207
Mark III/IV................ 55,561	Special/Skylark/Century 311,879
Lincoln 49,457	Apollo................. 59,128
Lincoln total 105,018	Riviera 29,992
	BUICK TOTAL 826,206
CHRYSLER (all).......... 1,367,354	
Fury/Gran Fury 268,724	Cadillac................ 252,767
Valiant................ 250,583	El Dorado 54,931
Belvedere/Satellite/Fury..... 75,089	CADILLAC TOTAL............ 307,698
Barracuda................ 19,090	
PLYMOUTH TOTAL........... 613,486	**FORD** (all)............. 2,495,863
	Ford 752,468
Dart 182,122	Pinto.................. 366,748
Coronet/Charger.......... 178,261	Fairlane/Torino 298,545
Dodge................. 145,441	Mustang............... 193,129
Challenger 27,770	Maverick............... 184,810
DODGE TOTAL 533,594	Thunderbird 90,414
	Falcon/Club Wagon 23,105
Chrysler 204,881	FORD TOTAL 1,909,219
Imperial 15,393	
	Montego............... 146,565
AMERICAN MOTORS (all) .. 279,132	Mercury 132,896
Rambler/Hornet 83,213	Comet 103,275
Gremlin................ 69,773	Cougar 70,514
Classic/Rebel/Matador 52,343	MERCURY TOTAL............ 453,250
Ambassador............. 44,698	
Javelin/AMX............. 29,105	Mark III/IV................ 76,137
	Lincoln 57,257
CHECKER (all)............. 5,504	LINCOLN TOTAL 133,394
1973	**CHRYSLER** (all).......... 1,556,377
GENERAL MOTORS (all) .. 5,252,734	Valiant................ 335,816
Chevrolet 866,826	
Chevy II/Nova........... 395,673	

Fury/Gran Fury 245,058
Belvedere/Satellite/Fury 140,745
Barracuda 21,338
PLYMOUTH TOTAL 742,957

Dart 239,598
Coronet/Charger. 188,584
Dodge. 134,470
Challenger 30,211
DODGE TOTAL 592,863

Chrysler 205,601
Imperial 14,956

AMERICAN MOTORS (all) . . 355,855
Rambler/Hornet 114,839
Gremlin. 93,597
Classic/Rebel/Matador 72,476
Ambassador 43,676
Javelin/AMX 31,267

CHECKER (all) 6,333

1974
GENERAL MOTORS (all) . . 3,585,513
Chevrolet 472,292
Chevy II/Nova 386,947
Vega 327,707
Chevelle 292,719
Monte Carlo 232,410
Camaro. 157,909
Corvette 33,869
Monza 8
CHEVROLET TOTAL 1,903,861

Olds F-85/Cutlass 312,004
Oldsmobile. 166,424
Omega 50,751
Toronado 19,479
OLDSMOBILE TOTAL 548,658

Pontiac 122,037
Tempest/LeMans 144,786
Firebird 78,919
Grand Prix. 78,793
Ventura. 78,701
Astre. 28,847
PONTIAC TOTAL 502,083

Buick 172,562
Special/Skylark/Century 158,438

Apollo 52,126
Riviera 17,136
BUICK TOTAL 400,262

Cadillac. 192,729
El Dorado 37,920
CADILLAC TOTAL 230,649

CHRYSLER (all) 1,176,662
Valiant. 370,316
Belvedere/Satellite/Fury 137,636
Fury/Gran Fury 90,715
Barracuda 3,939
PLYMOUTH TOTAL 602,606

Dart 268,323
Coronet/Charger. 126,432
Dodge. 63,175
Challenger 6,063
DODGE TOTAL 463,993

Chrysler 96,630
Imperial 13,433

AMERICAN MOTORS (all) . . 352,088
Rambler/Hornet 127,680
Gremlin. 113,776
Classic/Rebel/Matador 83,618
Javelin/AMX 15,953
Ambassador 11,061

CHECKER (all) 4,996

1975
GENERAL MOTORS (all) . . 3,679,126
Chevrolet 318,400
Citation/Nova 296,413
Monte Carlo 266,578
Malibu/Chevelle 246,759
Vega 193,245
Monza 82,954
Chevette. 80,394
Corvette 45,948
CHEVROLET TOTAL. 1,687,091

Cutlass 363,814
Oldsmobile. 226,845
Omega 37,261
Toronado 22,535
Starfire 3,887
Buick 227,732

Century/Regal	212,948
Skylark/Apollo	74,443
Riviera	16,759
Skyhawk	3,938
BUICK TOTAL	535,820

Grand Prix	112,896
Pontiac	104,073
Firebird	94,198
LeMans	88,364
Phoenix/Ventura	60,405
Astre	55,805
Sunbird	7,728
PONTIAC TOTAL	523,469

Cadillac	193,444
El Dorado	48,134
Seville	36,826
CADILLAC TOTAL	278,404

FORD (all)	1,808,038
Granada	336,864
Ford	191,405
Mustang	187,554
Pinto	163,510
Torino	153,510
Maverick	105,418
Elite	90,738
Thunderbird	37,776
Club Wagon	34,639
FORD TOTAL	1,301,414

Monarch	108,103
Mercury	79,507
Bobcat	60,706
Cougar	57,215
Lincoln	55,499
Montego	52,751
Comet	46,822
Mark IV/V/VI	46,021
Lincoln–Mercury total	506,624

CHRYSLER (all)	902,902
Valiant	204,462
Fury	122,703
Gran Fury	71,670
Volare	33,416
Voyager	11,299
PLYMOUTH TOTAL	443,550

Dart	161,615
Coronet	72,417
Dodge	53,463
Sportsman	41,858
Aspen	25,129
DODGE TOTAL	354,482

Chrysler	102,940
Imperial	1,930

AMERICAN MOTORS (all)	323,704
Pacer	145,528
Hornet	69,533
Matador	57,172
Spirit/AMX/Gremlin	51,471

CHECKER (all)	3,181

1976

GENERAL MOTORS (all)	4,891,982
Citation/Nova	391,309
Chevrolet	370,934
Monte Carlo	364,233
Malibu/Chevelle	319,812
Camaro	201,653
Chevette	154,381
Vega	136,284
Corvette	47,431
Monza	21,064
Acadian	5,311
CHEVROLET TOTAL	2,012,412

Cutlass	560,055
Oldsmobile	304,071
Omega	67,127
Toronado	24,781
Starfire	8,391
OLDSMOBILE TOTAL	964,425

Century/Regal	345,201
Buick	309,099
Skylark/Apollo	128,599
Riviera	22,940
Skyhawk	11,830
BUICK TOTAL	817,669

Grand Prix	271,276
Pontiac	151,695
Firebird	125,018
LeMans	89,713
Phoenix/Ventura	86,750

Astre. 43,103
Sunbird. 17,076
PONTIAC TOTAL 784,631

Cadillac. 233,575
El Dorado 39,995
Seville. 39,275
CADILLAC TOTAL. 312,845

FORD (all) 2,053,799
Granada 415,390
Ford 248,550
Mustang. 183,369
Torino. 136,989
Pinto. 108,140
Thunderbird 106,949
Elite 105,989
Maverick. 92,378
LTD II 61,318
Club Wagon 34,982
FORD TOTAL 1,494,054

Monarch. 133,734
Cougar 105,811
Mercury 91,509
Lincoln 64,584
Mark IV/V/VI 60,296
Bobcat 39,063
Montego. 33,238
Comet 31,510
LINCOLN–MERCURY TOTAL 559,745

CHRYSLER (all) 1,333,402
Volare. 435,625
Fury 114,265
Gran Fury 57,466
Valiant. 35,696
Voyager 14,968
PLYMOUTH TOTAL. 658,020

Aspen. 342,509
Coronet 77,656
Sportsman 50,946
Dodge. 49,845
Dart 26,960
DODGE TOTAL 547,916

AMERICAN MOTORS (all) . . 213,918
Pacer 74,030
Hornet 63,722

Spirit/AMX/(Gremlin) 39,419
Matador 36,747

CHECKER (all). 4,792

1977
GENERAL MOTORS (all) . . 5,259,657
Chevrolet 590,113
Citation/Nova 363,181
Monte Carlo 356,065
Malibu/Chevelle 271,939
Camaro. 229,637
Chevette. 192,431
Corvette 46,357
Vega 40,361
Monza 38,773
Acadian. 4,546
CHEVROLET TOTAL 2,133,403

Cutlass 580,866
Oldsmobile 403,373
Omega 55,844
Toronado 33,057
Starfire 6,701
OLDSMOBILE TOTAL 1,079,841

Grand Prix. 268,990
Pontiac 221,870
Firebird 169,856
Phoenix/Ventura 87,565
LeMans 72,058
Sunbird. 35,599
Astre. 20,019
PONTIAC TOTAL 875,957

Buick 384,835
Century/Regal. 284,167
Skylark/Apollo. 102,272
Riviera 23,573
Skyhawk. 6,355
BUICK TOTAL 801,202

Cadillac. 267,581
El Dorado 52,483
Seville. 49,190
CADILLAC TOTAL. 369,254

FORD (all) 2,555,867
Thunderbird 365,986
Granada 357,076

Ford 275,868
LTD II 232,839
Mustang 170,315
Pinto 152,195
Fairmont 111,713
Maverick 48,792
Club Wagon 46,589
FORD TOTAL 1,761,373

Mercury 170,478
Cougar 164,437
Monarch 119,601
Lincoln 105,979
Mark IV/V/VI 84,593
XR-7 47,536
Bobcat 40,835
Zephyr 27,931
Versailles 20,867
Comet 12,237
LINCOLN–MERCURY TOTAL 794,494

CHRYSLER (all) 1,236,359
Aspen 259,540
Monaco 77,164
Diplomat 76,195
Sportsman 47,706
Royal Monaco 30,739
Omni 5,888
DODGE TOTAL 497,232

Volare 327,429
Fury 114,603
Gran Fury 30,822
Voyager 12,927
Horizon 6,282
PLYMOUTH TOTAL 492,063

Chrysler 130,128
LeBaron 116,936

AMERICAN MOTORS (all) . . 156,994
Pacer 40,034
Hornet 35,937
Concord 31,598
Spirit/AMX/(Gremlin) 29,006
Matador 20,419

CHECKER (all) 4,777

1978
GENERAL MOTORS (all) . . 5,284,499
Chevrolet 524,094
Malibu/Chevelle 373,454
Monte Carlo 325,890
Citation/Nova 309,941
Chevette 301,614
Camaro 281,735
Monza 166,951
Corvette 48,972
Acadian 13,585
CHEVROLET TOTAL 2,346,155

Cutlass 416,458
Oldsmobile 400,714
Omega 47,279
Toronado 28,251
Starfire 17,547
OLDSMOBILE TOTAL 910,249

Grand Prix 206,605
Firebird 195,378
Pontiac 184,327
LeMans 124,035
Sunbird 88,714
Phoenix/Ventura 67,951
PONTIAC TOTAL 867,010

Century/Regal 352,212
Buick 300,677
Skylark/Apolo 107,276
Riviera 25,179
Skyhawk 24,980
BUICK TOTAL 810,324

Cadillac 244,355
Seville 59,794
El Dorado 46,612
CADILLAC TOTAL 350,761

FORD (all) 2,557,197
Thunderbird 326,873
Fairmont 286,046
Ford 278,949
Granada 246,407
Mustang 240,162
Pinto 185,091
LTD II 134,608
Club Wagon 45,309
FORD TOTAL 1,743,445

XR-7 179,648
Mercury 152,149
Lincoln 98,119
Monarch. 89,974
Zephyr 88,254
Mark IV/V/VI 75,845
Cougar 38,460
Capri. 37,143
Versailles 15,559
LINCOLN-MERCURY TOTAL 813,752

CHRYSLER (all) 1,126,168
Volare 221,761
Horizon. 162,011
Fury 49,176
Voyager 10,673
Caravelle. 4,493
PLYMOUTH TOTAL. 448,114

Aspen. 162,651
Omni 126,225
Diplomat. 75,755
Aries. 33,220
Monaco 28,246
St. Regis. 15,453
DODGE TOTAL 441,550

LeBaron 150,908
Chrysler 85,596

AMERICAN MOTORS (all) . . 164,352
Concord 106,697
Spirit/AMX/(Gremlin) 37,466
Pacer 15,386
Matador 4,803

CHECKER (all). 4,225

1979
GENERAL MOTORS (all) . . 5,091,908
Chevrolet 447,343
Chevette. 413,648
Citation/Nova 343,821
Malibu/Chevelle 322,764
Camaro. 257,872
Monte Carlo 227,043
Monza 157,979
Corvette 48,568
Acadian. 17,133
CHEVROLET TOTAL. 2,236,171

Cutlass 509,726
Oldsmobile. 365,327
Omega 58,032
Toronado 53,552
Starfire 21,609
OLDSMOBILE TOTAL 1,008,246

Century/Regal. 330,560
Buick 252,220
Skylark/Apollo. 121,625
Riviera 58,029
Skyhawk. 24,715
BUICK TOTAL 787,149

Firebird 194,033
Pontiac 144,486
Sunbird. 105,988
Grand Prix. 93,158
LeMans 88,652
Phoenix/Ventura 88,184
PONTIAC TOTAL 714,511

Cadillac. 230,958
El Dorado 66,565
Seville. 48,308
CADILLAC TOTAL. 345,831

FORD (all) 2,043,014
Mustang. 365,357
Thunderbird 264,451
Fairmont 213,761
Pinto. 172,619
Ford 167,170
Granada 139,402
Club Wagon 36,177
LTD II 22,667
FORD TOTAL 1,381,604

XR-7 133,479
Capri. 107,094
Mercury 100,937
Lincoln 71,783
Mark IV/V/VI 68,313
Zephyr 62,837
Monarch. 59,810
Bobcat 43,374
Versailles 11,864
Cougar 1,919
LINCOLN–MERCURY TOTAL 661,410

CHRYSLER (all)	936,146
Omni	148,125
Aspen	132,610
Diplomat	50,610
St. Regis	25,846
Sportsman	23,124
DODGE TOTAL	380,315
Volare	183,486
Horizon	169,981
Caravelle	9,213
Voyager	6,312
Gran Fury	5,412
PLYMOUTH TOTAL	374,404
LeBaron	103,678
Chrysler	77,749
AMERICAN MOTORS (all)	184,636
Concord	88,580
Spirit/AMX/(Gremlin)	64,363
Eagle	25,964
Pacer	5,729
CHECKER (all)	4,766

1980
GENERAL MOTORS (all)	4,064,556
Citation/Nova	459,388
Chevette	454,068
Malibu/Chevelle	231,594
Monza	150,544
Chevrolet	134,909
Monte Carlo	125,474
Camaro	118,211
Corvette	44,190
Acadian	18,958
CHEVROLET TOTAL	1,737,336
Century/Regal	370,880
Skylark/Apollo	218,502
Buick	149,668
Riviera	44,525
BUICK TOTAL	783,575
Cutlass	395,784
Oldsmobile	233,845
Omega	115,673
Toronado	37,923
OLDSMOBILE TOTAL	783,225

Cadillac	115,424
El Dorado	54,267
Seville	34,300
CADILLAC TOTAL	203,991
Sunbird	149,239
Phoenix	136,210
Firebird	79,568
Grand Prix	76,030
Bonneville/LeMans	64,870
Pontiac	50,512
PONTIAC TOTAL	556,429
FORD (all)	1,306,948
Mustang	232,507
Fairmont	198,219
Thunderbird	117,856
Granada	113,281
Escort	108,450
Ford	91,135
Pinto	68,179
FORD TOTAL	929,627
Capri	68,070
Zephyr	66,657
Mercury	55,524
XR-7	42,927
Monarch	41,264
Lynx	37,641
Mark IV/V/VI	28,146
Lincoln	22,781
Bobcat	12,445
Versailles	1,866
LINCOLN–MERCURY TOTAL	377,321
CHRYSLER (all)	638,974
Horizon	145,036
Reliant	75,822
Volare	51,735
Gran Fury	14,472
Caravelle	6,277
PLYMOUTH TOTAL	293,342
Omni	121,703
Aries	60,666
Aspen	36,881
Diplomat	30,733
St. Regis	13,186
DODGE TOTAL	263,169

LeBaron 62,592
Chrysler 19,871

AMERICAN MOTORS (all) .. 164,725
Concord 68,344
Spirit/AMX/(Gremlin) 54,223
Eagle 42,223

CHECKER (all) 3,197

1981
GENERAL MOTORS (all) .. 3,904,083
Chevette 376,951
Citation 300,652
Celebrity/Malibu 213,628
Chevrolet 147,337
Monte Carlo 139,899
Cavalier 139,837
Camaro 99,059
Corvette 27,990
CHEVROLET TOTAL 1,445,353

Century/Regal 370,676
Skylark 239,175
Buick 171,834
Riviera 58,275
BUICK TOTAL 839,960

Supreme/Ciera 385,674
Oldsmobile 276,452
Omega 132,268
Toronado 43,929
OLDSMOBILE TOTAL 838,333

Grand Prix 97,051
Phoenix 96,597
2,000 91,465
1,000 88,871
Bonneville/A6000 88,293
Firebird 48,961
Pontiac 10,064
PONTIAC TOTAL 521,302

Cadillac 155,622
El Dorado 57,861
Seville 23,344
Cimarron 22,308
CADILLAC TOTAL 259,135

FORD (all) 1,320,197
Escort 353,167

Fairmont 176,246
Grenada 103,702
Thunderbird 64,328
Mustang 53,719
Ford 40,886
FORD TOTAL 892,043

Lynx 117,991
Marquis 65,720
Zephyr 51,868
Capri 50,336
Cougar 49,831
Cougar XR7 28,223
Lincoln 26,651
Mark 25,640
Continental 11,895
LINCOLN–MERCURY TOTAL 428,154

CHRYSLER (all) 748,774
Reliant 216,901
Horizon 139,014
Gran Fury 7,448
Caravelle 2,139
PLYMOUTH TOTAL 365,502

Aries 170,139
Omni 125,650
Dodge 13,817
Diplomat 12,644
St. Regis 3,682
DODGE TOTAL 325,932

LeBaron 52,478
Chrysler 4,862

VOLKSWAGEN (all) 167,755

AMERICAN MOTORS (all) .. 109,319
Concord 49,480
Spirit 35,143
Eagle 24,696

CHECKER (all) 3,010

1982
GENERAL MOTORS (all) .. 3,173,144
Camaro 214,107
Chevette 208,417
Celebrity/Malibu 169,872
Citation 159,069
Cavalier 96,124

Monte Carlo	81,181
Chevrolet	42,648
Corvette	22,838
CHEVROLET TOTAL	994,256
Supreme/Ciera	328,086
Oldsmobile	284,440
Omega	71,392
Firenza	40,636
Toronado	35,077
OLDSMOBILE TOTAL	759,631
Century/Regal	320,766
Buick	183,325
Skylark	137,810
Skyhawk	65,555
Riviera	43,882
BUICK TOTAL	751,338
Firebird	127,861
Bonneville/A6000	97,814
Grand Prix	63,509
Phoenix	45,469
1,000	44,830
2,000	41,834
PONTIAC TOTAL	421,317
Cadillac	156,618
El Dorado	56,638
Seville	22,716
Cimarron	10,630
CADILLAC TOTAL	246,602

FORD (all) . . . 1,104,054

Escort	270,299
Fairmont	128,519
Mustang	127,371
Granada	74,051
LTD 83	57,983
Thunderbird	29,326
Ford	2,034
EXP	1,062
FORD TOTAL	690,645
Grand Marquis	88,404
Lynx	82,475
Lincoln	47,609
Zephyr	40,406
Cougar	35,953
Capri	32,704

Mark	29,959
Marquis 83	24,858
Continental	20,052
Cougar 83 XR7	10,580
LN 7	409
LINCOLN–MERCURY TOTAL	413,409

CHRYSLER (all) . . . 600,502

Reliant	162,097
Horizon	77,572
Caravelle	1,556
PLYMOUTH TOTAL	241,225
Aries	129,213
Omni	72,456
Dodge	43,164
DODGE TOTAL	244,833
LeBaron	95,361
E Class	19,083

AMERICAN MOTORS (all) . . 109,412

Renault Alliance	57,613
Eagle	21,674
Concord	17,143
Spirit	12,982

VOLKSWAGEN (all) . . . 84,246

CHECKER (all) . . . 2,000

1983
GENERAL MOTORS (all) . . 3,975,111

Cavalier	308,440
Celebrity	244,471
Chevette	201,841
Camaro	193,116
Monte Carlo	124,926
Chevrolet	91,228
Citation	86,878
Corvette	28,174
CHEVROLET TOTAL	1,279,074
Ciera	527,388
Oldsmobile	365,542
Omega	59,967
Firenza	54,799
Toronado	43,135
OLDSMOBILE TOTAL	1,050,831

Regal	411,256
Buick	249,838
Skylark	112,843
Skyhawk	79,169
Riviera	52,503
BUICK TOTAL	905,609
2000	116,975
Firebird	100,228
LeMans/6000	55,560
1000	48,178
Grand Prix	41,797
Fiero	29,630
Phoenix	25,060
Pontiac	12,457
PONTIAC TOTAL	429,885
Cadillac	180,555
El Dorado	73,026
Seville	34,873
Cimarron	21,258
CADILLAC TOTAL	309,712

FORD (all) 1,547,680

Escort	290,045
Thunderbird	186,566
LTD	179,192
Mustang	124,225
Tempo	106,977
Ford	93,768
Fairmont	23,728
EXP	4,298
FORD TOTAL	1,008,799
Cougar XR7	126,395
Grand Marquis	90,805
Marquis	77,147
Lynx	73,413
Lincoln	58,872
Mark	34,143
Topaz	31,005
Capri	24,697
Continental	13,513
Zephyr	8,601
LN7	290
LINCOLN-MERCURY TOTAL	538,881

CHRYSLER (all) 904,286

Reliant	186,496

Horizon	117,744
Caravelle	5,329
Grand Fury	1,255
PLYMOUTH TOTAL	310,824
Aries	144,042
Omni	126,443
Dodge 600	49,181
Daytona	19,428
Dodge 400	18,478
Diplomat	1,241
DODGE TOTAL	358,813
LeBaron	86,261
E Class	73,597
New Yorker (E)	31,402
Laser	23,656
Fifth Avenue	19,733
CHRYSLER TOTAL	234,649

AMERICAN MOTORS (all) . . 200,385

Renault Alliance	153,878
Renault Encore	42,436
Eagle	4,068

VOLKSWAGEN (all) 84,246

HONDA (all) 55,335

1983
GENERAL MOTORS (all) . . 3,975,291

Cavalier	308,461
Celebrity	244,480
Chevette	201,841
Camaro	193,118
Monte Carlo	124,926
Chevrolet	91,228
Citation	86,878
Corvette	28,174
CHEVROLET TOTAL	1,279,106
Ciera	527,391
Oldsmobile	365,554
Omega	59,966
Firenza	54,800
Toronado	43,135
OLDSMOBILE TOTAL	1,050,846
Regal	411,255
Buick	249,838
Skylark	112,843

Skyhawk. 79,166
Riviera 52,503
BUICK TOTAL 905,608

2000 117,013
Firebird 100,225
Bonneville. 55,560
1000 48,178
Grand Prix. 41,797
Fiero 29,630
Phoenix 25,080
Pontiac 12,457
PONTIAC TOTAL 429,920

Cadillac. 180,654
El Dorado 73,026
Seville. 34,873
Cimarron. 21,258
CADILLAC TOTAL. 309,811

FORD (all) 1,547,680
Escort. 290,045
Thunderbird 186,566
LTD. 179,192
Mustang. 124,225
Tempo 106,977
Ford 93,766
Fairmont. 23,728
EXP. 4,298
FORD TOTAL 1,008,799

Cougar 126,395
Grand Marquis 90,805
Marquis 77,147
Lynx 73,413
Lincoln 58,872
Mark. 34,143
Topaz 31,005
Capri. 24,697
Continental. 13,513
Zephyr 8,601
LN7 290
LINCOLN–MERCURY TOTAL 538,881

CHRYSLER (all). 904,286
Reliant 186,496
Horizon. 117,744
Caravelle. 5,329
Grand Fury 1,255
PLYMOUTH TOTAL. 310,824

Aries. 144,042
Omni 126,443
Dodge 600 49,181
Daytona 19,428
Dodge 400 18,478
Diplomat. 1,241
DODGE TOTAL 358,813

LeBaron 86,261
E Class 73,597
New Yorker (E). 31,402
Laser 23,656
Fifth Avenue. 19,733
CHRYSLER TOTAL 234,649

AMERICAN MOTORS (all) . . 200,385
Renault Alliance 153,878
Renault Encore. 42,436
Eagle 4,068

VOLKSWAGEN (all). 98,207

HONDA (all). 55,335

1984
GENERAL MOTORS (all) . . 4,344,737
Cavalier. 400,254
Celebrity. 280,653
Camaro. 230,082
Chevette. 174,044
Chevrolet 134,072
Citation. 104,045
Monte Carlo 97,922
Corvette 35,661
CHEVROLET TOTAL 1,456,733

Oldsmobile 88 282,378
Ciera. 251,506
Supreme. 147,458
Oldsmobile 98 109,321
Firenza 67,986
Toronado 44,396
Calais 33,195
Omega 29,288
OLDSMOBILE TOTAL 1,065,528

Century. 227,973
Le Sabre 178,500
Regal 174,120
Skyhawk. 127,327

Skylark	110,649
Electra	87,819
Riviera	53,093
Somerset	28,352
BUICK TOTAL	987,833

2000	136,582
Fiero	114,002
Firebird	108,396
Pontiac	48,356
1000	25,063
Grand Am	24,667
Acadian	14,729
Phoenix	14,195
Bonneville	10,612
Grand Prix	9,391
6000	106
PONTIAC TOTAL	506,099

Cadillac	199,542
Eldorado	75,957
Seville	38,683
Cimarron	14,362
CADILLAC TOTAL	328,544

FORD (all)	1,775,257
Escort	341,901
LTD	225,913
Tempo	165,320
Thunderbird	146,203
Mustang	140,338
Ford	83,081
EXP	42,388
FORD TOTAL	1,145,144

Marquis	121,051
Cougar	116,517
Lincoln	106,998
Grand Marquis	89,312
Lynx	69,709
Topaz	46,566
Continental	36,105
Mark	25,601
Capri	18,254
LINCOLN–MERCURY TOTAL	630,113

CHRYSLER (all)	1,247,785
Reliant	172,416
Horizon	159,247

Caravelle	25,349
Grand Fury	21,263
PLYMOUTH TOTAL	378,275

Omni	146,350
Aries	142,487
Dodge 600	74,710
Daytona	52,986
Diplomat	41,100
Lancer	8,218
DODGE TOTAL	465,851

LeBaron	126,999
Fifth Avenue	116,802
Laser	70,075
New Yorker	65,057
E Class	24,726
CHRYSLER TOTAL	403,659

AMERICAN MOTORS (all) . .	192,196
Renault Alliance	110,170
Renault Encore	82,026

HONDA (all)	138,572

VOLKSWAGEN (all)	74,785

1985

GENERAL MOTORS (all) . .	4,887,079
Cavalier	492,004
Chevrolet	289,821
Celebrity	264,097
Camaro	214,429
Chevette	152,769
Monte Carlo	138,532
Nova	64,601
Corvette	46,304
Citation	28,697
CHEVROLET TOTAL	1,691,254

Ciera	356,798
Supreme	235,496
Delta 88	192,400
Calais	149,829
Oldsmobile 98	143,277
Firenza	62,152
Toronada	29,030
OLDSMOBILE TOTAL	1,168,982

Century	299,104
Electra	138,682

Regal	137,018
Somerset/Skylark	125,593
LeSabre	106,612
Skyhawk	105,617
Riviera	47,882
Skylark X	40,953
BUICK TOTAL	1,001,461

Grand Am	143,259
Sunbird/2000	142,947
Firebird	114,290
Fiero	109,569
Parisienne	90,989
6000	58,952
1000	24,895
Acadian	17,716
PONTIAC TOTAL	702,617

Cadillac	214,083
Eldorado	53,301
Seville	28,678
Cimarron	26,703
CADILLAC TOTAL	322,765

FORD (all)	1,636,150
Escort	344,548
Tempo	188,124
Mustang	187,776
LTD	184,431
Thunderbird	170,513
Taurus	12,250
Ford	7,122
EXP	3,863
FORD TOTAL	1,098,627

Cougar	129,788
Lincoln	119,787
Marquis	84,862
Lynx	75,098
Topaz	54,060

Continental	25,259
Capri	20,095
Mark	18,031
Sable	5,810
Grand Marquis	4,733
LINCOLN–MERCURY TOTAL	537,523

CHRYSLER (all)	1,266,068
Reliant	162,690
Horizon	142,611
Caravelle (E)	44,785
Gran Fury	15,179
Caravelle (M)	2,446
Caravelle (K)	1,776
PLYMOUTH TOTAL	369,487

Fifth Avenue	106,116
LeBaron	96,339
LeBaron GTS	95,187
New Yorker (E)	64,342
Laser	52,209
CHRYSLER TOTAL	414,193

Omni	136,823
Aries	135,186
Lancer	65,097
Daytona	47,746
Dodge 600 (E)	38,171
Diplomat	30,701
Dodge 600 (K)	28,664
DODGE TOTAL	482,388

AMERICAN MOTORS (all)	109,919
Renault Alliance	73,422
Renault Encore	36,497
HONDA (all)	145,337
VOLKSWAGEN (all)	96,458
NISSAN (all)	43,810

SCOPE OF THE BOOK

As you, the collector, know, and as evidenced by the information in preceding sections, a work covering "collector cars" is a monumental task. Parameters must be set, and for this book "used cars" have been excluded. Cars that are simply used can be old or of recent manufacture. Thousands of makes and models have come and gone in the last hundred years. If significant collector interest was not aroused to create a market for the old marque, it will not be listed. The other segment of the used car market, extending back fifteen years from the current model year, is termed "recently manufactured" and is covered by industry publications (Blue Book, etc.); they are, therefore, omitted here. If you are not able to locate the car you are researching, ask yourself if it may be categorized as simply a "used car." For omissions you do feel exist, please write with your input to improve future editions.

Note: This book represents an analysis of prices for which collectible cars have actually been selling for during the preceding period. Although every reasonable effort has been made to compile an accurate and reliable guide, car prices vary significantly depending on such factors as the locality of the sale and changing economic conditions. Accordingly, no representation can be made that cars listed may be bought or sold at the prices indicated, nor shall the author be responsible for any error made in compiling and recording the prices.

HOW TO USE THIS BOOK

Listings in this book are arranged alphabetically by manufacturer, with country of origin and period of production. Within the listing for each manufacturer, models are listed chronologically, along with model number or name, engine type, and body style.

Three price columns, based on condition, are listed—fair (F), good (G), and excellent (E).

- **FAIR:** A car that runs and is drivable. It is in need of mechanical and/or cosmetic repair and may be in the process of restoration. Conditions below this level are "poor/restorable" and "parts car."
- **GOOD:** A clean road-worthy vehicle, mechanically sound and attractive in both body and interior. When inspected, the car will show wear. This is an entry-level show car.
- **EXCELLENT:** This vehicle is in original or restored top condition. These cars are prize winners. They are NOT 100 point, "Concours d'Elegance," objects of industrial art; such cars would be termed "perfect" and only valued on an individual basis.

In the Trucks and Motorcycles sections of this book, we have used a two-column format to indicate price range. For these sections, the lower price refers to a specimen in good condition, and the higher price refers to a specimen in excellent condition.

The prices in this book are averages based on sales throughout the country and should be used strictly as a guide.

PRICE INDEX

(A - Z)

YEAR	MODEL	ENGINE	BODY	F	G	E

A

ABADAL *(Spain, 1912; 1913; 1930)*

YEAR	MODEL	ENGINE	BODY	F	G	E
1912		4 cyl.	Touring	4,500	6,500	12,000
1930	Standard	6 cyl.	Sedan	1,500	2,500	4,500

ABARTH *(Italy, 1950–71)*

YEAR	MODEL	ENGINE	BODY	F	G	E
1950	Tipo 207/A		Spyder	3,500	6,000	10,000
1951		600cc (Fiat)	Sport	3,500	6,500	10,000
1952			Sport	3,500	6,000	9,500
1957		2.2 Litre	Coupe	2,500	5,500	8,500

ABBOTT-DETROIT *(United States, 1909–18)*

YEAR	MODEL	ENGINE	BODY	F	G	E
1909		4 cyl.	Touring	4,500	9,500	25,000
1911		6 cyl.	Touring	4,500	9,500	25,000
1913		8 cyl.	Touring	6,000	14,000	27,500
1918		8 cyl.	Touring	3,500	10,000	15,000

A.B.C. *(United States, 1906–10)*

YEAR	MODEL	ENGINE	BODY	F	G	E
1906	High-wheel	2 cyl.	Runabout	3,500	8,500	12,500
1910	High-wheel	2 cyl.	Runabout	4,000	7,000	13,000

ABINGDON *(Great Britain, 1902–03)*

YEAR	MODEL	ENGINE	BODY	F	G	E
1902	Meredith	2 cyl.	Tonneau	3,500	6,500	12,500
1903	Abington	1 cyl.	Voiturette	3,000	5,500	10,000
1922	Dorman	4 cyl.	Dickey	3,500	6,000	9,500

A.C. *(Great Britain, 1908–66)*

YEAR	MODEL	ENGINE	BODY	F	G	E
1910	Sociable	1 cyl.	2 Passenger	3,000	5,000	12,500
1913		4 cyl.	Light	3,000	5,500	13,000
1927		2 Litre	2 Passenger	2,500	4,500	10,000
1936		80 hp	Sport Roadster	12,000	20,000	35,000
1937	1680	60 hp	Touring	6,000	12,000	25,000
1938		70 hp	Cabriolet	6,000	12,000	20,000
1947		74 hp	Sedan	4,500	9,000	15,000
1957		6 cyl.	Coupe	7,000	12,000	25,000
1958		85 hp	Roadster	6,000	15,000	40,000

YEAR	MODEL	ENGINE	BODY	F	G	E
A.C.	*(Great Britain, 1908–66) (continued)*					
1965	Cobra 289	V 8 cyl. (Ford)	Roadster	35,000	75,000	100,000

AC – 1963 " Cobra 289" Courtesy of A Motors, Grand Junction, Colorado

1966	Cobra 427	V 8 cyl. (Ford)	Roadster	50,000	90,000	150,000
ACCLES-TURRELL	*(Great Britain, 1900–02)*					
1900	10/15	2 cyl.	2 Passenger	3,000	5,500	12,500
1903	8	2 cyl.	2 Passenger	3,000	5,500	12,500
ACE	*(United States, 1920–22)*					
1920		4 cyl.	Touring	4,000	8,000	17,000
1921		6 cyl.	Touring	4,500	9,000	18,000
ACHILLES	*(Great Britain, 1903–08)*					
1903		1 cyl. (DeDion)	Coupe	3,500	6,000	15,000
1904		2 cyl. (DeDion)	Coupe	3,000	5,500	14,000
1905		2 cyl. (DeDion)	Coupe	3,000	5,500	14,000
1906		2 cyl. (DeDion)	Coupe	3,000	5,500	14,000
1907		2 cyl. (DeDion)	Coupe	3,000	5,500	14,000
1908		2 cyl. (DeDion)	Coupe	3,000	5,500	14,000
ACME II	*(United States, 1908–09)*					
1908	High-wheel		Buggy	3,500	7,500	15,000
ADAMS	*(Great Britain, 1903–06)*					
1903		2 cyl.	Touring	3,500	7,500	10,000
1905		2 cyl.	Touring	3,500	7,500	10,000
1906		2 cyl.	Touring	3,500	7,500	10,000

YEAR	MODEL	ENGINE	BODY	F	G	E
ADAMS or ADAMS-HEWITT until 1907 *(Great Britain, 1905–14)*						
1905		1 cyl.	Touring	3,000	7,000	12,000
1914	35/40	V 8 cyl.	Touring	3,500	8,000	17,000
ADAMS-FAREWELL *(United States, 1904–13)*						
1904		3 cyl. (Radial)	Brougham	5,500	12,000	20,000
1906	40/45	5 cyl.	Touring	4,000	13,000	22,500
1907	40/45	5 cyl.	Touring	5,000	14,000	25,000
1908	40/45	5 cyl.	Touring	5,000	14,000	25,000
1909	40/45	5 cyl.	Touring	6,000	15,000	27,500
1910	40/45	5 cyl.	Touring	6,000	15,000	27,500
1911	40/45	5 cyl.	Touring	6,000	15,000	27,500
1912	40/45	5 cyl.	Touring	6,000	15,000	27,500
1913	40/45	5 cyl.	Touring	6,000	15,000	27,500
ADELPHIA *(United States, 1920)*						
1920	Export	4 cyl.	Touring	2,200	5,000	10,000
ADER *(France, 1900–07)*						
1900		V 2 cyl.	Limousine	4,000	8,000	16,000
1902		V 2 cyl.	Limousine	4,000	8,500	17,000
1903		V 4 cyl.	Limousine	5,000	8,800	18,000
1905		20 hp	Limousine	5,500	9,500	19,000
ADLER *(Germany, 1900–39)*						
1900		1 cyl. (DeDion)	Voiturette	4,000	9,000	18,000
1905		V 2 cyl.	Voiturette	3,500	9,000	18,500
1913	Tandem		2 Passenger	3,700	10,500	19,000
1913	19/45	4 cyl.	Touring	3,900	8,500	20,000
1913	30/70	4 cyl.	Roadster	4,500	12,500	20,000
1925	6/25	6 cyl.	Touring	5,000	15,000	22,500
1930		8 cyl.	Sport Roadster	10,500	18,000	45,000
1934		8 cyl.	Landau	6,500	16,500	45,000
1936		8 cyl.	Sport Touring	7,500	16,000	35,000
1936		8 cyl.	Phaeton	9,500	20,000	35,000
1937		8 cyl.	Roadster	9,500	20,000	48,000
A.E.C.; ANGER *(United States, 1913–14)*						
1913	Open	6 cyl. (T-head)	Touring		RARE	
1914	Open	6 cyl. (L-head)	Touring		RARE	
AERO I *(Czechoslovakia, 1929–47)*						
1929	Type 500	1 cyl. (2 Stroke)		2,000	3,500	10,000
1929	Type 20	2 cyl.		2,500	4,000	10,000
1932	Type 30	2 cyl.	2 Passenger	2,500	4,000	10,000

YEAR	MODEL	ENGINE	BODY	F	G	E

AERO I *(Czechoslovakia, 1929–47) (continued)*

| 1937 | Type 30 | 4 cyl. | Drop Head Coupe | 2,500 | 5,000 | 15,000 |
| 1947 | Type 30 | 4 cyl. | Drop Head Coupe | 2,000 | 4,000 | 12,500 |

AERO III *(United States, 1921–24)*

| 1921 | | 2 cyl. | Roadster | | RARE | |

AEROCAR *(United States, 1906–08)*

1906	A	4 cyl.	Touring	3,500	9,500	20,000
1907	F	4 cyl.	Touring	3,500	9,500	20,000
1908	F	4 cyl.	Touring	4,500	10,000	22,000

AGA *(Germany, 1919–28)*

1921	6/20	1420cc	Roadster	3,500	5,000	12,500
1924	6/30	1½ Litre	Sport	3,000	4,500	10,000
1924	Targa Florio		Roadster	4,000	9,500	18,000
1926	10/45	6 cyl.	Roadster	7,500	10,000	25,000

AILLOUD *(France, 1897–1904)*

1897		Air-cooled	Roadster	3,500	6,000	12,500
1900		2 cyl.	Roadster	5,000	7,500	15,000
1904		4 cyl.	Roadster	5,500	9,500	17,500

AJAX *(United States, 1914–15)*

| 1914 | | 6 cyl. | Touring | 6,000 | 12,500 | 30,000 |
| 1915 | | 6 cyl. | Touring | 6,000 | 12,500 | 30,000 |

AJAX NASH *(United States, 1925–26)*

1925		6 cyl. 3 Litre	Sedan	2,000	2,000	4,500
1925		6 cyl.	Touring	3,000	4,000	9,000
1926		6 cyl.	Roadster	3,500	5,000	12,000

ALBA *(France, 1913–28)*

1913		4 cyl.	Runabout	2,700	5,000	12,000
1921		4 cyl.	Coupe	3,500	4,500	10,000
1926	SP		Sport	4,500	6,500	15,000

ALBANY *(United States, 1907–08)*

| 1907 | 6/7 | 1 cyl. (Air-cooled) | Surrey | 2,000 | 4,000 | 10,000 |
| 1908 | 18/20 | 2 cyl. (Air-cooled) | Runabout | 1,500 | 3,500 | 9,000 |

ALBANY *(Great Britain, 1971–72)*

| 1971 | RP | | Runabout | 2,000 | 3,000 | 10,000 |

ALBION *(Great Britain, 1900–13)*

1900	BG	2 cyl.	Runabout	3,000	4,000	10,000
1904	16	16 rt.-twin	Runabout	5,000	6,500	15,000
1906	24/30	4 cyl. (Chain-drive)	Touring	4,500	6,500	15,000
1913	15	4 cyl.	Touring	4,500	6,500	15,000

YEAR	MODEL	ENGINE	BODY	F	G	E
ALCO *(United States, 1905–13)*						
1905	24	4 cyl. (Chain-drive)	Touring	6,000	10,000	25,000
1905	60	6 cyl.	Touring	6,500	14,000	35,000
1910	5 Ps.	6 cyl.	Touring	6,000	15,000	45,000
1911		4 cyl.	Roadster	9,000	19,500	48,000
1913	5 Ps.		Touring	8,500	17,000	45,000
ALCYON *(France, 1906–28)*						
1906		4 cyl.	Voiturette	1,400	3,800	11,000
1907		1 cyl.	Voiturette	1,200	3,400	10,000
1909			Voiturette	1,200	3,400	10,000
1911			Coupe	1,800	3,400	10,000
1912		6 cyl.	Racing	4,000	9,500	35,000
ALES *(Japan, 1921)*						
1921		4 cyl.	Touring	2,000	3,500	9,000
1921		4 cyl. (Air-cooled)	Touring	2,100	3,600	10,000
ALFA-ROMEO *(Italy, 1910 to date)*						
1910		4 cyl. 4.1 Litre	Sport	10,000	17,500	30,000
1911		4 cyl. 2.4 Litre	Touring	7,500	10,000	25,000
1912			Touring	7,500	10,000	25,000
1913	40/60	6.1 Litre	Sport	12,500	20,000	50,000
1914	GP	4 cyl. 4.5 Litre	Sport	8,500	12,000	32,000
1922	RL	6 cyl. 3 Litre	Touring	10,000	18,000	48,000
1923	RM	4 cyl. 2 Litre	Sport	9,000	16,000	45,000
1923	P1	6 cyl.	Sport Roadster	8,500	12,500	30,000
1924	P2	8 cyl. (Supercharged)	Sport		RARE	
1925	RLSSS	3 Litre	Drop Head Coupe	5,000	7,500	17,500
1926	RLT	3 Litre	Touring	3,600	8,500	20,000
1926	GS 1750	6 cyl. 1500cc	Sport	9,500	12,500	27,500
1931		8 cyl.	Sport			
1931		(Supercharged)	2 Passenger		RARE	
1932	BP3 GP 1750	2.65 Litre	Roadster	7,500	10,000	22,500
1933	Bogato	2.6 Litre	Roadster	9,500	12,000	25,000
1933	8 C 2300	2.6 Litre	Touring	7,500	10,000	22,500
1934	1750	6 cyl. 2.9 Litre	Roadster	9,500	12,500	27,500
1935	P3	3.8 Litre	Touring	10,000	15,000	40,000
1936	GP	8 cyl.	Roadster	15,000	20,000	50,000
1937	8 C	8 cyl. 2.9 Litre	Cabriolet	7,500	12,000	35,000
1939	GP 2500	V 12 cyl.	Roadster	18,000	25,000	75,000
1947	6 C-2500	2 ½ Litre	Sport Convertible	6,600	13,000	24,000
1949	Super Sport	4 cyl.	Convertible	8,800	22,000	38,000

YEAR	MODEL	ENGINE	BODY	F	G	E
ALFA-ROMEO	*(Italy, 1910 to date) (continued)*					
1950	2500		Cabriolet	2,600	5,200	10,200
1950	1900	4 cyl.	Sedan	2,400	4,800	8,800
1951	"159"	6 cyl.	Sport	2,600	5,200	10,600
1953		3 Litre	Sport	3,300	6,600	10,400
1955	1900	4 cyl.	Coupe	3,000	5,000	9,000
1955		4 cyl.	Coupe	2,200	3,000	4,400

Alfa Romeo – 1955 "Coupe"

YEAR	MODEL	ENGINE	BODY	F	G	E
1957		3 Litre	Coupe	1,600	3,300	6,600
1959		3 Litre	Coupe	1,600	3,300	6,600
1960	Spider	4 cyl.	Roadster	5,000	10,000	15,000
1960	Spider					
	Veloce	4 cyl.	Roadster	7,500	12,500	17,500
1960	2000 Spider	4 cyl.	Roadster	10,000	15,000	20,000
1961	Spider	4 cyl.	Roadster	5,000	10,000	15,000
1961	Spider					
	Veloce	4 cyl.	Roadster	7,500	12,500	17,500
1961	2000 Spider	4 cyl.	Roadster	10,000	15,000	20,000
1962	Spider	4 cyl.	Roadster	5,000	10,000	15,000
1962	Spider					
	Veloce	4 cyl.	Roadster	7,500	12,500	17,500
1962	2000 Spider	4 cyl.	Roadster	10,000	15,000	20,000
1963	Spider	4 cyl.	Roadster	5,000	10,000	15,000
1963	2600 Spider	6 cyl.	Roadster	6,000	12,500	17,500
1964	Spider	4 cyl.	Roadster	5,000	10,000	15,000
1964	2600 Spider	6 cyl.	Roadster	6,000	12,500	17,500

YEAR	MODEL	ENGINE	BODY	F	G	E
ALFA-ROMEO *(Italy, 1910 to date) (continued)*						
1965	Spider	4 cyl.	Roadster	4,000	10,000	15,000
1965	Spider					
	Veloce	4 cyl.	Roadster	5,000	11,000	12,500
1965	2600 Spider	6 cyl.	Roadster	6,000	12,500	17,500
1966	Spider	4 cyl.	Roadster	4,000	10,000	15,000
1966	Spider					
	Veloce	4 cyl.	Roadster	5,000	11,000	12,500
1966	2600 Spider	6 cyl.	Roadster	6,000	12,500	17,500
1967	1600 Spider	4 cyl.	Roadster	3,000	7,500	10,000
1967	1750 Spider					
	Veloce	4 cyl.	Roadster	4,000	8,000	12,000
1967	2600 Spider	6 cyl.	Roadster	6,000	12,500	17,500
1968	1600 Spider	4 cyl.	Roadster	3,000	7,500	10,000
1968	1750 Spider					
	Veloce	4 cyl.	Roadster	4,000	8,000	12,000
1969	1600 Spider	4 cyl.	Roadster	3,000	7,500	10,000
1969	1750 Spider					
	Veloce	4 cyl.	Roadster	4,000	8,000	12,000
1970	1750 Spider					
	Veloce	4 cyl.	Roadster	4,000	8,000	12,000
1971	2000 Spider	4 cyl.	Roadster	3,000	6,000	7,500
1972	2000 Spider	4 cyl.	Roadster	3,000	6,000	7,500
1973	2000 Spider	4 cyl.	Roadster	3,000	6,000	7,500
1974	2000 Spider	4 cyl.	Roadster	3,000	6,000	7,500
1975	Spider					
	Veloce	4 cyl.	Roadster	2,500	5,000	6,500
1976	Spider					
	Veloce	4 cyl.	Roadster	2,500	5,000	6,500
1977	Spider					
	Veloce	4 cyl.	Roadster	2,500	5,000	6,500
1978	Spider					
	Veloce	4 cyl.	Roadster	2,500	5,000	6,500
1979	Spider					
	Veloce	4 cyl.	Roadster	2,500	5,000	6,500
ALFI *(Germany, 1927–28)*						
1927	3-Wheel	(D.K.W.)	Coupe	4,500	6,000	15,000
1928			Sport	7,500	10,000	25,000
ALLARD *(Great Britain, 1937–60)*						
1937		V 12 cyl.	Sport			
			Roadster	35,000	50,000	125,000
1946	M	V 8 cyl.	Convertible	20,000	30,000	70,000
1950	J.2	V 8 cyl.	Roadster	15,000	20,000	50,000

YEAR	MODEL	ENGINE	BODY	F	G	E
ALLARD *(Great Britain, 1937–60) (continued)*						
1951	K2	V 8 cyl.	Roadster	17,000	22,000	55,000
1952	JX2	V 8 cyl.	Roadster	25,000	35,000	85,000
1953	JR	V 8 cyl.	Roadster	30,000	40,000	95,000
1955	Palm Beach	4 cyl.	Roadster	10,000	15,000	40,000
1959	Palm Beach	6 cyl.	Roadster	15,000	20,000	50,000
ALLDAYS *(Great Britain, 1898–1918)*						
1898	Traveller	1 cyl. (DeDion)	Runabout	5,000	6,500	15,000
1903		1 cyl.	Runabout	5,000	6,500	15,000
1905	10/12	V 2 cyl.	Runabout	5,000	6,500	15,000
1906		4 cyl.	Touring	5,000	7,500	17,500
1911		6 cyl.	Touring	7,500	10,000	22,500
1912	30/35	6 cyl.	Limousine	7,500	10,000	22,500
1913	990	V 2 cyl.		6,000	8,000	15,000
ALLRIGHT *(Germany, 1908–11)*						
1908		2 cyl.	Vioturette	5,000	7,500	17,500
1911		4 cyl.	Touring	4,500	6,000	15,000
ALPHI *(France, 1929–31)*						
1929		6 cyl.	Sport Roadster	4,500	6,500	15,000
1929		6 cyl. 1.5 Litre	Racing	7,500	7,500	17,500
1931		6 cyl. 2.6 Litre	Touring	4,500	7,000	16,000
1931		8 cyl. 5 Litre	Touring	15,000	20,000	50,000
ALPINE *(France, 1955–71)*						
1955	Mille Miles	4 cyl.	Sport Coupe	4,500	6,000	12,500
1957	Dauphine	845cc	Coupe	4,000	5,500	12,000
1961	2 + 2		Gran Turismo Coupe	4,500	6,000	12,500
1961	Aerodynamic		Berlinette	5,000	6,500	15,000
1966	Berlinette	996cc	Coupe	3,000	4,000	9,500
1967	F3	V 8 cyl.	Sport	3,500	4,500	10,000
1971	A310 2 + 2	1605cc	Touring Coupe	3,000	4,000	8,500
ALTA *(Great Britain, 1931–54)*						
1931			Roadster	7,500	10,000	25,000
1945	G.P.	2 Litre	Coupe	5,000	7,000	15,000
1953		2 Litre	Sedan	5,000	7,000	15,000
ALVA *(France, 1913–23)*						
1913		4 cyl.	Touring	4,000	6,500	15,000
1916		4 cyl.	Touring	5,000	7,500	17,500

YEAR	MODEL	ENGINE	BODY	F	G	E
ALVIS	*(Great Britain, 1920–67)*					
1920	10/30	4 cyl. 1460cc	2 Passenger	7,500	9,500	20,000
1921	10/30	4 cyl.	4 Passenger	8,000	10,000	22,500
1922		4 cyl.	Super Sport	9,000	12,000	25,000
1923	12/50	1598cc	Touring	10,000	13,000	30,000
1928		6 cyl.	Sport Coupe	9,000	12,000	25,000
1929	Silver Eagle	6 cyl.	Sedan	9,000	12,000	25,000
1932	Speed Twenty	6 cyl.	Touring	15,000	20,000	55,000
1933	Firefly	4 cyl.	Touring	7,000	9,000	20,000
1935	Speed Twenty-five	3571cc	Saloon Sedan	10,000	15,000	35,000
1938	Silver Crest	2762cc	Saloon Sedan	7,200	12,000	26,000

Alvis – 1938 "Speed 25 Saloon Sedan"

YEAR	MODEL	ENGINE	BODY	F	G	E
1946	TA-14	4 cyl. 1892cc	Saloon Sedan	3,300	6,600	14,000
1951	TA-21	6 cyl.	Sport Roadster	7,500	10,000	25,000
1954	TB-21	6 cyl.	Saloon Sedan	7,500	10,000	25,000
1955	TA-21/100	6 cyl.	Saloon Sedan	10,000	12,500	30,000
1959	TD-21	6 cyl.	Saloon Sedan	6,500	8,500	20,000
1960	TD-21	V 8 cyl.	Convertible	10,000	12,500	30,000
AMCO	*(United States, 1919–20)*					
1919	Right-hand Drive	4 cyl.	Touring	3,500	9,000	20,000
1919	Left-hand Drive	4 cyl.	Touring	3,700	9,500	22,000
AMEDEE BOLLEE	*(France, 1885–1922)*					
1885		Steam	Runabout	10,000	15,000	35,000
1896		2 cyl.	Vis-a-vis	9,000	12,000	32,500
1898		2 cyl.	Racing	8,000	10,000	25,000
1899		4 cyl.	Racing	10,000	15,000	40,000

YEAR	MODEL	ENGINE	BODY	F	G	E
AMEDEE BOLLEE *(France, 1885–1922) (continued)*						
1912	30	4 cyl.	Touring	9,500	14,000	35,000
1914		4 cyl.	Touring	9,500	14,000	35,000
AMERICA *(Spain, 1917–22)*						
1917	Type A	Valveless		3,500	4,500	10,000
1918	Type B	4 cyl.	Runabout			
			Light	4,500	7,000	15,000
1919	Type C	4 cyl.	Sport	3,500	6,000	12,500
AMERICAN AUSTIN; BANTAM *(United States, 1930–41)*						
1930	Seven	4 cyl.	Coupe	4,000	6,000	12,500
1933	2-75	4 cyl.	Roadster	5,500	7,500	15,000
1940	65	4 cyl.	Convertible	5,500	7,500	15,000
1940	65	4 cyl.	Roadster	5,500	7,500	15,000
AMERICAN ELECTRIC *(United States, 1899–1902)*						
1899		Electric	Dos-a-dos	3,000	4,000	9,000
1902	4 S	Electric	Dos-a-dos	3,000	4,000	9,000
AMERICAN MERCEDES *(United States, 1904–07)*						
1904		4 cyl.	Touring	12,500	25,000	60,000
1907		4 cyl.	Demi-Limo	12,000	24,000	50,000
AMERICAN SIMPLEX *(United States, 1906–10)*						
1906	A	4 cyl.	Touring	6,000	8,000	20,000
1910	35	4 cyl.	Roadster	10,000	15,000	35,000
1910	35	4 cyl.	Limousine	8,000	12,000	30,000
1910	35	4 cyl.	Touring	9,500	13,000	32,500
AMERICAN STEAMER *(United States, 1922–24)*						
1922		2 cyl.	Touring	7,000	10,000	22,500
1923		2 cyl.	Roadster	8,000	12,000	25,000
1924		2 cyl.	Coupe	3,500	5,000	12,000
1924		2 cyl.	Sedan	3,500	5,000	12,000
AMERICAN UNDERSLUNG *(United States, 1906–14)*						
1907		4 cyl. (T-head)	Roadster	20,000	30,000	60,000
1909		4 cyl. (T-head)	Roadster	30,000	40,000	100,000
1913	666	6 cyl.	Touring	45,000	65,000	135,000
AMILCAR *(France, 1921–39)*						
1921		4 cyl.	Sport			
			Voiturette	10,000	12,500	30,000
1924	Grand SP	1074cc	Coupe	12,500	15,000	32,000
1925	CGS	4 cyl.	Touring	15,000	17,000	35,000
1927	C6 Course	6 cyl.	Sport			
			Roadster	15,000	20,000	45,000
1930	C8	8 cyl.	Touring	17,500	22,500	50,000

YEAR	MODEL	ENGINE	BODY	F	G	E
AMILCAR *(France, 1921–39) (continued)*						
1936	Pegase		Drop Head Coupe	6,000	8,000	17,000
1939	Compound	4 cyl. 1185cc	Sedan	4,000	7,000	15,000
1939		4 cyl.	Sport Sedan	3,500	5,000	12,000
AMPHICAR *(Germany, 1961–68)*						
1961	Amphibian	4 cyl.	Cabriolet	3,000	6,000	12,000
1963	Amphibian	4 cyl.	Convertible	3,000	6,000	12,000
1967	Amphibian	4 cyl.	Convertible	3,500	6,500	14,000
AMX *(United States, 1968–70)*						
1968		V 8 cyl. (390 cid)	2 Passenger Coupe	3,000	4,000	8,500
1969		V 8 cyl. (390 cid)	2 Passenger Coupe	3,000	4,000	8,500

Amx – 1969 "Passsenger Coupe" courtesy of AC Motors, Grand Junction, Colorado

YEAR	MODEL	ENGINE	BODY	F	G	E
1970		V 8 cyl. (401 cid)	2 Passenger Coupe	4,500	5,500	12,000
ANDERSON *(United States, 1907–10)*						
1907	A	2 cyl.	Buggy	3,000	7,000	16,000
1910	E	2 cyl.	Buggy	4,000	8,000	16,000
ANGUS-SANDERSON *(Great Britain, 1919–27)*						
1919		4 cyl.	Roadster	4,000	5,500	10,000
1923		4 cyl.	Roadster	3,000	5,000	9,500
1927		4 cyl.	Touring	4,500	6,000	15,000
ANSALDO *(Italy, 1919–36)*						
1919	4 A	4 cyl.	Touring	2,500	3,500	8,500
1923	6 A	6 cyl.	Touring	3,500	4,500	9,500
1923	4 C	6 cyl.	Touring	3,500	4,500	9,500
1931		8 cyl.	Sedan	3,000	4,000	9,000

YEAR	MODEL	ENGINE	BODY	F	G	E
ANTOINE *(Brazil, 1900–02)*						
1900	4	1 cyl.	Voiturette	2,000	3,000	6,500
1902	4	1 cyl.	Tonneau	2,500	3,500	8,000
A.P.A.L. *(Brazil, 1964–69)*						
1964	2 S	4 cyl. (VW)	Gran Turismo			
			Coupe	1,600	3,200	6,500
APOLLO *(Germany, 1910–26)*						
1910	B 4/12	960cc	Roadster	2,500	6,000	12,000
1924	4/20	960cc	Sport	2,800	8,000	16,000
APOLLO *(United States, 1962–64)*						
1962		V 8 cyl. (Buick)	Gran Turismo			
			Coupe	3,000	6,000	12,000
APPERSON *(United States, 1902–26)*						
1902	A	4 cyl.	Touring	6,000	8,000	18,000
1913	Jack Rabbit	4 cyl.	Touring	9,000	12,000	30,000
1920	1920	V 8 cyl.	Touring	8,000	10,000	28,000
1923	8-23S	V 8 cyl.	Touring	8,000	10,000	25,000
1925	Straight					
	Away	8 cyl.	Phaeton	10,000	12,000	28,000
AQUILA ITALIANA *(Italy, 1906–17)*						
1906	30/45	6 cyl.	Runabout	3,000	4,000	9,500
1913		6 cyl.	Coupe	2,000	3,000	7,000
ARABIAN *(United States, 1915–17)*						
1917		4 cyl.	Roadster	2,500	3,200	7,500
ARBENZ *(United States, 1911–18)*						
1911	C	4 cyl.	Touring	7,000	9,000	18,000
ARDEN *(Great Britain, 1912–16)*						
1913		2 cyl.	2 Passenger	1,200	4,000	10,000
1914	Alph	4 cyl.	4 Passenger	1,400	6,000	16,000
ARDENT *(France, 1900–01)*						
1900	4 Ps.	V 2 cyl.	Vis-a-vis	2,500	6,000	12,000
ARGONAUT *(United States, 1959–63)*						
1959	State	12 cyl.	Limousine	2,500	7,000	17,500
ARGYLL *(Great Britain, 1899–1932)*						
1899		2 cyl.	Runabout	1,200	2,500	7,750
1905	16/20	4 cyl.	Touring	1,400	3,000	9,000
1911	15	6 cyl.	Touring	2,000	6,900	14,000
ARIEL *(Great Britain, 1898–1915; 1922–25)*						
1906		4 cyl.	Touring	1,600	3,000	11,000
1924		4 cyl.	Touring	1,200	2,400	7,500

YEAR	MODEL	ENGINE	BODY	F	G	E
ARIES *(France, 1903–38)*						
1905	30	4 cyl.	Touring	6,000	8,000	18,000
1908		6 cyl.	Touring	7,000	9,000	19,000
1922	CC2	6 cyl.	Sport	8,000	10,000	20,000
1929	CC4S	6 cyl.	Sport	8,000	10,000	20,000
1934	9 CV	4 cyl.	Sedan	5,000	7,000	14,000
ARISTA *(France, 1912–15)*						
1912		1 cyl.	Coupe	1,800	5,000	9,000
ARISTA *(France, 1956–63)*						
1956	Passy		Roadster	1,200	4,000	6,000
1956	Passy	848cc	Coupe	1,000	3,000	4,000
ARMSTRONG SIDDELEY *(Great Britain, 1919–60)*						
1919		4 cyl.	Coupe	5,000	7,000	15,000
1930	12	4 cyl.	Coupe	6,000	8,000	16,000
1935	30	4 cyl.	Sedanca de Ville	9,000	12,000	24,000
1939			Limousine	10,000	15,000	30,000
1952	Hurricane	6 cyl.	Drop Head Coupe	5,000	7,000	15,000
1955	Sapphire 236	6 cyl.	Limousine	4,000	6,000	12,500
1956	Sapphire 346	6 cyl.	Limousine	4,000	6,000	12,500
1960	Star Sapphire	4 Litre	Sedan	6,000	8,000	16,000
ARNOLT *(United States, 1953–64)*						
1955	GT	1917cc (Bristol)	Coupe	5,000	12,000	26,000
ARROLL-JOHNSTON; ARROLL-ASTER *(Great Britain, 1897–1931)*						
1897		2 cyl.	Dogcart	3,500	7,000	16,000
1914		3 cyl.	Dogcart	3,000	6,000	15,000
1922		4 cyl.	Sport	3,000	6,000	16,000
1927	17/50	6 cyl.	Sport	3,500	6,500	17,000
1930	23/70	8 cyl.	Sedan	3,500	7,000	15,000
A.S.A. *(Italy, 1962–67)*						
1962		4 cyl.	Gran Turismo Coupe	2,000	4,000	10,000
1967	Rorrbar	6 cyl.	Gran Turismo Spyder	2,000	4,000	10,000
ASCOT *(Great Britain, 1928–30)*						
1928			Sedan	2,500	6,500	13,000
1930	18/50	6 cyl.	Sedan	3,000	7,000	15,000
ASHLEY *(Great Britain, 1958–61)*						
1958			Coupe	1,000	2,000	7,000
1961	Sportiva	100 E	Coupe	1,000	2,000	7,000

YEAR	MODEL	ENGINE	BODY	F	G	E
ASHLEY (Great Britain, 1958–61) (continued)						
1961	GT 4 S	100 E	Sedan	1,200	2,400	7,800
ASTAHL (Germany, 1907)						
1907		1 cyl.	Open	2,000	4,500	9,500
1907		4 cyl.	Open	3,500	5,500	11,500
ASTER (Great Britain, 1922–30)						
1922	18/50	2618cc	Sedan	2,500	4,800	10,500
ASTON (United States, 1908–09)						
1908		25 hp	Custom		RARE	
1909		40 hp	Custom		RARE	
ASTON MARTIN (Great Britain, 1922 to date)						
1922	Lionel					
	Martin	1½ Litre	Sport	17,000	20,000	40,000
1931	International	1½ Litre	Sedan	18,000	22,000	45,000
1932	LeMans	1½ Litre	Touring	20,000	25,000	55,000
1932	LeMans	1½ Litre	Roadster	25,000	30,000	65,000
1934	Aston Martin					
	Mark II	4 cyl.	Roadster	15,000	18,000	40,000
1935	Ulster	4 cyl.	Roadster	25,000	35,000	60,000
1936		2 Litre	Roadster	8,000	13,000	29,000
1936		2 Litre	Sport			
			Touring	7,000	12,000	29,000
1937		2 Litre	Touring	6,000	11,000	25,000
1938		2 Litre	Roadster	7,000	11,000	26,000
1939		2 Litre	Sport			
			Roadster	7,000	12,000	24,000
1949	DB1	4 cyl.	Coupe	8,000	10,000	20,000
1950	DB2	6 cyl.	Coupe	9,000	11,000	23,000
1953	DB 2/4					
	LeMans	2.9 Litre	Convertible	3,000	15,000	30,000
1953	DB 2/4	2.9 Litre	Coupe	8,000	10,000	20,000
1956	DB 2/4					
	MK III	2.5 Litre	Coupe	4,000	6,000	12,000
1957	DB 2/4					
	MK III	2.9 Litre	Convertible	20,000	25,000	50,000
1959	DB4	3.7 Litre	Convertible	20,000	35,000	75,000
1959	Mark III	2.9 Litre	Coupe	7,000	9,000	18,000
1959	DB 2/4					
	Mark III	2 cyl. 3 Litre	Coupe	2,000	6,000	20,000
1959	DB 2/4	6 cyl.	Convertible	25,000	75,000	125,000
1959	DB 2/4	6 cyl.	Coupe	12,500	40,000	65,000
1960	DB4 (1)	6 cyl.	Coupe	11,000	35,000	60,000
1961	DB4 (2)	6 cyl.	Coupe	15,000	40,000	75,000

YEAR	MODEL	ENGINE	BODY	F	G	E
ASTON MARTIN *(Great Britain, 1922 to date)* *(continued)*						
1961	DB4 (3)	6 cyl.	Coupe	15,000	40,000	75,000
1961	DB4 (4)	6 cyl.	Convertible	25,000	75,000	125,000
1961	DB4 (4)	6 cyl.	Coupe	15,000	40,000	75,000
1962	DB4 (4)	6 cyl.	Convertible	25,000	75,000	125,000
1962	DB4 (4)	6 cyl.	Coupe	20,000	35,000	50,000
1962	DB4 (5)	6 cyl.	Convertible	25,000	75,000	125,000
1962	DB4 (5)	6 cyl.	Coupe	20,000	35,000	50,000
1963	DB4 (4)	6 cyl.	Convertible	25,000	75,000	125,000
1963	DB4 (4)	6 cyl.	Coupe	25,000	40,000	55,000
1963	DB4 (5)	6 cyl.	Convertible	27,500	85,000	130,000
1963	DB4 (5)	6 cyl.	Coupe	25,000	40,000	55,000
1964	DB5	6 cyl.	Convertible	27,500	85,000	130,000
1964	DB5	6 cyl.	Coupe	25,000	40,000	55,000
1965	DB5	6 cyl.	Convertible	27,500	85,000	130,000
1965	DB5	6 cyl.	Coupe	25,000	40,000	55,000
1966	DB6	6 cyl.	Coupe	15,000	40,000	75,000
1966	Volante	6 cyl.	Convertible	25,000	75,000	125,000
1967	DB6	6 cyl.	Coupe	15,000	40,000	75,000
1967	Volante	6 cyl.	Convertible	25,000	75,000	125,000
1968	DB6	6 cyl.	Coupe	15,000	40,000	75,000
1968	DB5	6 cyl.	Coupe	10,000	25,000	50,000
1969	DB5 MK II	6 cyl.	Coupe	12,500	35,000	70,000
1969	DB5 MK II Volante	6 cyl.	Convertible	25,000	75,000	125,000
1970	DB5 MK II	6 cyl.	Coupe	12,500	35,000	70,000
1970	DB5 MK II Volante	6 cyl.	Convertible	25,000	75,000	125,000
1970	DB5 V8	V-8	Coupe	10,000	30,000	65,000
1971	DB5	6 cyl.	Coupe	10,000	25,000	50,000
1971	DB5 V8	V-8	Coupe	10,000	30,000	65,000
1972	AM V8 (2)	V-8	Coupe	12,500	35,000	70,000
1972	DB5 V8	V-8	Coupe	10,000	30,000	65,000
1972	DB5	6 cyl.	Coupe	10,000	25,000	50,000
1973	AM V8 (3)	V-8	Coupe	10,000	20,000	40,000
1974	AM V8 (3)	V-8	Coupe	10,000	20,000	40,000
1975	AM V8 (3)	V-8	Coupe	10,000	20,000	40,000
1976	AM V8 (3)	V-8	Coupe	10,000	20,000	40,000
1977	AM V8 (3)	V-8	Coupe	10,000	20,000	40,000
1978	AM V8 (3)	V-8	Coupe	10,000	20,000	40,000
1979	Vantage	V-8	Coupe	10,000	25,000	50,000
1979	Volante	V-8	Convertible	15,000	40,000	75,000
1979	Lagonda	V-8	Sedan	10,000	25,000	60,000

YEAR	MODEL	ENGINE	BODY	F	G	E
ASTRA *(Romania, 1922–24)*						
1922	45/60	4 cyl.	Roadster		RARE	
ATLANTA *(Great Britain, 1937–39)*						
1937		4 cyl. 1.5 Litre	Sport	5,000	7,000	12,000
1938		V 12 cyl.	Sedan	7,000	9,000	18,000
1938	2 Dr.	V 12 cyl.	Drop Head Coupe	8,000	10,000	22,000
ATLAS *(United States, 1907–13)*						
1911	O	4 cyl.	Touring	7,000	10,000	20,000
1912	Knight 12	4 cyl.	7 Passenger Touring	10,000	12,000	24,000
ATOMETTE *(Great Britain, 1922)*						
1922		(Villiers)		2,000	3,500	7,000
A.T.S. *(Italy, 1962–64)*						
1962		V 8 cyl. 2.5 Litre	Gran Turismo Coupe	2,500	4,800	9,800
AUBURN *(United States, 1900–36)*						
1904	A	2 cyl.	Touring	7,400	11,200	25,200
1905	B	2 cyl.	Touring	7,200	11,200	25,200
1906	C	2 cyl.	Touring	7,200	11,200	25,200
1907	D	4 cyl.	Touring	7,200	11,200	25,200
1908	G	2 cyl.	Touring	7,200	12,000	24,200
1908	H	2 cyl.	Touring	7,200	12,000	24,200
1908	K	2 cyl.	Runabout	7,500	11,500	25,500
1909	G	2 cyl.	Touring	7,200	12,000	24,200
1909	H	2 cyl.	Touring	7,400	12,400	25,400
1909	K	2 cyl.	Runabout	7,500	13,000	24,750
1909	B	4 cyl.	Touring	7,200	12,000	24,200
1909	C	4 cyl.	Touring	7,800	13,200	25,500
1909	D	4 cyl.	Runabout	8,200	14,000	28,000
1910	G	2 cyl.	Touring	7,000	12,000	24,000
1910	H	2 cyl.	Touring	7,500	13,000	24,750
1910	K	2 cyl.	Runabout	7,750	13,200	25,500
1910	B	4 cyl.	Touring	7,750	13,200	25,500
1910	C	4 cyl.	Touring	7,500	13,000	24,750
1910	D	4 cyl.	Runabout	7,800	13,200	25,500
1910	X	4 cyl.	Touring	7,800	13,200	25,500
1910	R	4 cyl.	Touring	8,000	13,700	27,500
1910	S	4 cyl.	Runabout	8,000	13,700	27,500
1911	G	2 cyl.	Touring	7,000	12,000	24,000
1911	K	2 cyl.	Runabout	7,500	13,250	24,750
1911	L	4 cyl.	Touring	7,500	13,000	24,750
1911	F	4 cyl.	Touring	7,500	13,000	24,750

YEAR	MODEL	ENGINE	BODY	F	G	E
AUBURN *(United States, 1900–36) (continued)*						
1911	N	4 cyl.	Touring	7,700	12,750	25,500
1911	Y	4 cyl.	Touring	7,500	13,000	24,750
1911	T	4 cyl.	Touring	7,500	13,000	24,750
1911	M	4 cyl.	Roadster	8,000	13,700	27,500
1912	30L	4 cyl.	Touring	7,000	12,250	24,000
1912	30L	4 cyl.	Roadster	7,500	13,000	24,750
1912	40H	4 cyl.	Touring	7,500	13,000	24,750
1912	40M	4 cyl.	Roadster	7,250	12,500	26,000
1912	40N	4 cyl.	Touring	7,750	13,000	26,500
1912	6-50	6 cyl.	Touring	8,000	13,700	27,500
1913	33L	4 cyl.	Touring	7,000	12,000	24,000
1913	33M	4 cyl.	Roadster	7,500	13,000	26,000
1913	40A	4 cyl.	Roadster	7,750	13,500	26,500
1913	40L	4 cyl.	Touring	7,250	12,250	25,500
1913	45	6 cyl.	Touring	7,750	13,500	26,000
1913	45B	6 cyl.	Town Sedan	7,250	12,500	25,250
1913	45B	6 cyl.	Coupe	7,000	12,000	24,000
1913	45B	6 cyl.	Roadster	7,750	13,250	26,250
1913	50	6 cyl.	Touring	8,000	13,700	27,500
1914	4-40	4 cyl.	Touring	7,750	13,250	25,500
1914	4-40	4 cyl.	Coupe	7,000	12,000	24,000
1914	4-40	4 cyl.	Roadster	7,750	13,200	25,500
1914	4-41	4 cyl.	Touring	8,000	13,700	27,500
1914	6-45	6 cyl. (Testor)	Touring	8,000	13,700	27,500
1914	6-45	6 cyl.	Roadster	8,250	14,250	28,500
1914	6-46	6 cyl.	Touring	8,500	14,500	28,500
1915	4-43	4 cyl.	Touring	7,750	13,100	26,500
1915	4-43	4 cyl.	Roadster	8,000	13,700	27,250
1915	4-36	4 cyl.	Touring	7,750	13,100	26,500
1915	4-36	4 cyl.	Roadster	8,000	13,700	27,500
1915	6-40	6 cyl.	Touring	7,500	13,000	25,500
1915	6-40	6 cyl.	Roadster	8,000	13,700	27,750
1915	6-40	6 cyl.	Coupe	7,500	12,000	24,500
1915	6-47	6 cyl.	Touring	7,800	13,200	26,750
1915	6-47	6 cyl.	Roadster	8,000	13,700	27,250
1916	4-36	6 cyl.	Touring	8,100	13,500	26,000
1916	4-38	4 cyl.	Touring	7,500	13,000	24,750
1916	4-38	4 cyl.	Roadster	7,800	13,200	25,500
1916	6-38	4 cyl.	Touring	7,800	13,200	25,500
1916	6-38	4 cyl.	Roadster	7,800	13,200	25,500
1916	6-40	6 cyl.	Touring	8,250	14,250	28,500
1916	6-40	6 cyl.	Roadster	8,250	14,250	28,500
1917	4-36	4 cyl.	Touring	7,800	13,200	25,500

YEAR	MODEL	ENGINE	BODY	F	G	E
AUBURN *(United States, 1900–36) (continued)*						
1917	4-36	4 cyl.	Roadster	8,250	14,250	28,500
1917	6-39	6 cyl.	Touring	8,250	14,250	28,500
1917	6-39	6 cyl.	Roadster	8,250	14,250	28,500
1917	6-44	6 cyl.	Touring	8,500	14,500	28,500
1917	6-44	6 cyl.	Roadster	8,500	14,500	28,500
1918	6-39	6 cyl.	Sport Touring	8,250	14,250	28,500
1918	6-39	6 cyl.	Touring	8,250	14,250	28,500
1918	6-39	6 cyl.	Roadster	8,250	14,250	28,500
1918	6-44	6 cyl.	Sport Touring	8,500	14,500	28,500
1918	6-44	6 cyl.	Touring	8,250	14,250	28,500
1918	6-44	6 cyl.	Roadster	8,250	14,250	28,500
1918	6-44	6 cyl.	Sedan	6,000	10,000	16,500
1919	6-39	6 cyl.	Touring	8,500	14,500	28,500
1919	6-39	6 cyl.	Roadster	8,500	14,500	28,500
1919	6-39	6 cyl.	Coupe	6,000	10,000	16,500
1919	6-39	6 cyl.	Sedan	6,000	10,000	16,500
1920	6-39	6 cyl.	Sport Touring	8,500	14,500	28,500
1920	6-39	6 cyl.	Touring	8,500	14,500	28,500
1920	6-39	6 cyl.	Roadster	8,500	14,500	28,500
1920	6-39	6 cyl.	Coupe	6,000	10,000	16,500
1920	6-39	6 cyl.	Sedan	6,000	10,000	16,500
1921	6-39	6 cyl.	Sport Touring	9,000	16,000	32,500
1921	6-39	6 cyl.	Touring	8,500	14,500	28,500
1921	6-39	6 cyl.	Roadster	9,000	16,000	32,500
1921	6-39	6 cyl.	Coupe	6,000	10,000	16,500
1921	6-39	6 cyl.	Sedan	6,000	10,000	16,500
1921	6-39	6 cyl.	Cabriolet	9,000	16,000	32,500
1922	6-51	6 cyl.	Sport Touring	9,000	16,000	32,500
1922	6-51	6 cyl.	Touring	8,500	14,500	28,500
1922	6-51	6 cyl.	Roadster	9,000	16,000	32,500
1922	6-51	6 cyl.	Coupe	6,000	10,000	16,500
1922	6-51	6 cyl.	Sedan	6,000	10,000	16,500
1923	6-43	6 cyl.	Touring	9,000	16,000	32,500
1923	6-43	6 cyl.	Sedan	6,000	10,000	16,500
1923	6-51	6 cyl.	Sport Touring	10,000	17,000	34,500
1923	6-51	6 cyl.	Touring	9,250	16,500	33,500
1923	6-51	6 cyl.	Sedan	6,000	10,000	16,500

YEAR	MODEL	ENGINE	BODY	F	G	E
AUBURN *(United States, 1900–36) (continued)*						
1923	6-51	6 cyl.	Brougham	6,000	10,000	16,500
1923	6-51	6 cyl.	Phaeton	10,000	17,000	34,500
1923	6-63	6 cyl.	Sport			
			Touring	10,000	17,000	34,500
1923	6-63	6 cyl.	Touring	9,250	16,500	33,500
1923	6-63	6 cyl.	Sedan	6,000	10,000	16,500
1923	6-63	6 cyl.	Brougham	6,000	10,000	16,500
1924	6-43	6 cyl.	Sport			
			Touring	10,000	17,000	34,500
1924	6-43	6 cyl.	Touring	9,000	16,000	32,500
1924	6-43	6 cyl.	Coupe	6,000	10,000	16,500
1924	6-43	6 cyl.	Sedan	6,000	10,000	16,500
1924	6-43	6 cyl.	2 Door	5,500	9,000	15,500
1924	6-63	6 cyl.	Sport			
			Touring	10,000	17,000	34,500
1924	6-63	6 cyl.	Touring	9,250	16,500	33,500
1924	6-63	6 cyl.	Sedan	6,000	10,000	16,500
1924	6-63	6 cyl.	Brougham	6,000	10,000	16,500
1925	6-43	6 cyl.	Coupe	6,000	10,000	16,500
1925	6-43	6 cyl.	Phaeton	10,000	17,000	34,500
1925	6-43	6 cyl.	Sport			
			Phaeton	11,000	18,000	35,500
1925	6-43	6 cyl.	2 Door Sedan	5,500	9,000	15,500
1925	6-43	6 cyl.	4 Door Sedan	6,000	10,000	16,500
1925	6-66	6 cyl.	Touring	10,000	17,000	34,500
1925	6-66	6 cyl.	Roadster	10,000	17,000	34,500
1925	6-66	6 cyl.	Brougham	5,500	9,000	15,500
1925	6-66	6 cyl.	2 Door	5,500	9,000	15,500
1926	4-44	4 cyl.	Touring	10,000	17,000	34,500
1926	4-44	4 cyl.	Roadster	10,000	17,000	34,500
1926	4-44	4 cyl.	Coupe	5,500	9,000	15,500
1926	4-44	4 cyl.	4 Door	5,500	9,000	15,500
1926	6-66	6 cyl.	Touring	11,000	18,000	35,500
1926	6-66	6 cyl.	Roadster	11,500	18,500	36,500
1926	6-66	6 cyl.	Coupe	6,000	10,000	17,000
1926	6-66	6 cyl.	Brougham	5,500	9,000	15,500
1926	6-66	6 cyl.	4 Door	5,500	9,000	15,500
1926	8-88	8 cyl.	Touring	11,500	18,500	36,500
1926	8-88	8 cyl.	Roadster	12,000	19,000	38,000
1926	8-88	8 cyl.	Brougham	6,200	10,400	17,600
1927	6-66	6 cyl.	Touring	12,000	19,000	38,000
1927	6-66	6 cyl.	Roadster	12,400	19,600	39,500
1927	6-66	6 cyl.	Sedan	6,000	10,000	16,500

YEAR	MODEL	ENGINE	BODY	F	G	E
AUBURN	*(United States, 1900–36) (continued)*					
1927	6-66	6 cyl.	Brougham	5,500	9,000	15,500
1927	6-66	6 cyl.	Cabriolet	11,000	18,000	35,000
1927	8-88	8 cyl.	Touring	12,000	19,000	38,000
1927	8-88	8 cyl.	Roadster	12,400	19,600	39,500
1927	8-88	8 cyl.	Coupe	6,000	10,000	16,500
1927	8-88	8 cyl.	Sedan	5,500	9,000	15,500
1928	6-66	6 cyl.	Roadster	12,000	19,000	38,000
1928	6-66	6 cyl.	5 Passenger Sedan	5,500	9,000	15,500
1928	6-66	6 cyl.	5 Passenger Sport Sedan	6,000	10,000	16,500
1928	6-66	6 cyl.	Cabriolet	11,000	18,000	35,500
1928	8-88	8 cyl.	Touring	12,700	20,000	41,000
1928	8-88	8 cyl.	Roadster	13,000	21,000	42,500
1928	8-88	8 cyl.	Sedan	6,000	10,000	16,500
1928	8-88	8 cyl.	Cabriolet	12,400	19,600	39,500
1928	76	6 cyl.	Roadster	12,400	19,600	39,500
1928	76	6 cyl.	5 Passenger Sedan	6,000	10,000	16,500
1928	76	6 cyl.	5 Passenger Sport Sedan	6,400	10,700	18,000
1928	76	6 cyl.	Cabriolet	12,000	19,000	38,000
1928	88	8 cyl.	Roadster	13,000	21,000	42,500
1928	88	8 cyl.	Sedan	6,000	10,000	16,500
1928	88	8 cyl.	Sport Sedan	6,400	10,700	18,000
1928	88	8 cyl.	Cabriolet	12,700	20,000	41,000
1928	115	8 cyl.	Roadster	13,500	22,500	45,000
1928	115	8 cyl.	Sedan	6,700	11,200	19,000
1929	6-80	6 cyl.	5 Passenger Sedan	7,000	11,000	19,500
1929	6-80	6 cyl.	5 Passenger Sport Sedan	6,400	10,700	18,000
1929	6-80	6 cyl.	Cabriolet	13,500	22,500	45,000
1929	6-80	6 cyl.	Victoria	6,200	10,400	17,600
1929	6-90	8 cyl.	Touring	13,000	21,000	42,500
1929	6-90	8 cyl.	Sedan	6,000	10,000	16,500
1929	6-90	8 cyl.	Phaeton	15,000	30,000	50,000
1929	6-90	8 cyl.	Victoria	11,000	18,000	35,500
1929	6-90	8 cyl.	Boattail Speedster	25,000	50,000	80,000
1929	76	6 cyl.	Touring	13,000	21,000	42,500
1929	76	6 cyl.	Roadster	13,500	22,500	45,000
1929	76	6 cyl.	Sedan	6,000	10,000	16,500

YEAR	MODEL	ENGINE	BODY	F	G	E
AUBURN	*(United States, 1900–36) (continued)*					
1929	76	6 cyl.	Cabriolet	12,700	20,000	41,000
1929	88	8 cyl.	Touring	13,000	21,000	42,500
1929	88	8 cyl.	Roadster	13,500	22,500	45,000
1929	88	8 cyl.	Sedan	6,200	10,400	17,600
1929	88	8 cyl.	Cabriolet	13,000	21,000	42,500
1929	115	8 cyl.	Roadster	15,000	30,000	50,000
1929	115	8 cyl.	Cabriolet	14,500	28,000	47,500
1929	115	8 cyl.	Victoria	10,500	17,800	35,200
1929	120	8 cyl.	5 or 7 Passenger Sedan	6,000	10,000	16,500
1929	120	8 cyl.	Cabriolet	14,500	28,000	47,500
1930	6-85	6 cyl.	Sedan	6,000	10,000	16,500

Auburn – 1930 "Roadster"

1930	6-85	6 cyl.	Cabriolet	14,000	27,000	46,500
1930	8-95	8 cyl.	Sedan	6,400	10,700	18,000
1930	8-95	8 cyl.	Cabriolet	14,000	27,000	46,500
1930	8-95	8 cyl.	Phaeton	15,000	30,000	50,000
1930	125	8 cyl.	Sedan	6,400	10,700	18,000
1930	125	8 cyl.	Cabriolet	15,000	30,000	50,000
1931	8-98	8 cyl.	5 or 7 Passenger Sedan	6,400	10,700	18,000

YEAR	MODEL	ENGINE	BODY	F	G	E
AUBURN *(United States, 1900–36) (continued)*						
1931	8-98	8 cyl.	Coupe	6,400	10,700	18,000
1931	8-98	8 cyl.	Cabriolet	13,500	22,500	45,000
1931	8-98	8 cyl.	Phaeton	17,500	35,000	55,000
1931	8-98 (custom)	8 cyl.	Coupe	7,500	13,000	24,750
1931	8-98 (custom)	8 cyl.	Cabriolet	14,000	27,000	46,500
1932	8-100	8 cyl.	5 or 7 Passenger Sedan	6,400	10,700	18,000
1932	8-100	8 cyl.	Coupe	7,500	13,000	24,750
1932	8-100	8 cyl.	Cabriolet	13,500	22,500	45,000
1932	8-100	8 cyl.	Brougham	6,000	10,000	16,500
1932	8-100A	8 cyl.	5 or 7 Passenger Sedan	7,250	12,500	26,000
1932	8-100A	8 cyl.	Coupe	7,500	13,000	24,750
1932	8-100A	8 cyl.	Cabriolet	14,000	27,000	46,500
1932	8-100A	8 cyl.	Phaeton	13,000	21,000	42,500
1932	12-160	12 cyl.	Sedan	7,500	13,000	24,750
1932	12-160	12 cyl.	Coupe	10,000	17,000	34,500
1932	12-160	12 cyl.	Cabriolet	15,000	30,000	50,000
1932	12-160	12 cyl.	Brougham	7,500	13,000	24,750
1932	12-160A	12 cyl.	Sedan	7,500	13,000	24,750

Auburn – 1932 "V-12 Sedan"

1932	12-160A	12 cyl.	Coupe	10,500	17,800	35,200
1932	12-160A	12 cyl.	Cabriolet	15,000	30,000	50,000
1932	12-160A	12 cyl.	Brougham	7,500	13,000	24,750
1932	12-160A	12 cyl.	Phaeton	17,500	35,000	55,000

YEAR	MODEL	ENGINE	BODY	F	G	E
AUBURN *(United States, 1900–36) (continued)*						
1933	8-101	8 cyl.	5 or 7 Passenger Sedan	7,500	13,000	24,750
1933	8-101	8 cyl.	Coupe	7,500	13,000	24,750
1933	8-101	8 cyl.	Cabriolet	17,500	35,000	55,000
1933	8-101	8 cyl.	Brougham	6,000	10,000	16,500
1933	8-101A	8 cyl.	5 or 7 Passenger Sedan	7,000	12,000	24,000
1933	8-101A	8 cyl.	Coupe	7,500	13,000	24,750
1933	8-101A	8 cyl.	Cabriolet	17,500	35,000	55,000
1933	8-101A	8 cyl.	Phaeton	17,500	35,000	55,000
1933	8-105	8 cyl.	Sedan	6,200	10,400	17,600
1933	8-105	8 cyl.	Phaeton	17,500	35,000	55,000
1933	12-161	12 cyl.	Sedan	8,000	13,700	27,250
1933	12-161	12 cyl.	Coupe	8,000	13,700	27,500
1933	12-161	12 cyl.	Cabriolet	17,500	35,000	55,000
1933	12-161	12 cyl.	Brougham	6,400	10,700	18,000
1933	12-161A	12 cyl.	Sedan	7,500	13,000	24,750
1933	12-161A	12 cyl.	Coupe	8,000	13,700	27,250
1933	12-161A	12 cyl.	Brougham	7,200	12,000	24,200
1933	12-161A	12 cyl.	Phaeton	20,000	42,000	70,000
1933	12-165	12 cyl.	Sedan	7,800	13,200	25,500
1933	12-165	12 cyl.	Cabriolet	17,500	35,000	55,000
1933	12-165	12 cyl.	Brougham	7,500	13,000	24,750
1933	12-165	12 cyl.	Phaeton	18,000	37,500	60,000
1934	652X	6 cyl.	Sedan	5,500	9,000	15,500
1934	652X	6 cyl.	Cabriolet	14,500	28,000	47,500
1934	652X	6 cyl.	Brougham	5,500	9,000	15,500
1934	652X	6 cyl.	Phaeton	17,500	30,000	55,000
1934	850X	8 cyl.	Sedan	6,200	10,400	17,600
1934	850X	8 cyl.	Cabriolet	17,500	35,000	55,000
1934	850X	8 cyl.	Brougham	6,200	10,400	17,600
1934	850X	8 cyl.	Phaeton	18,000	37,500	60,000
1934	1250	12 cyl.	Sedan	6,200	10,400	17,600
1934	1250	12 cyl.	Cabriolet	15,000	30,000	50,000
1934	1250	12 cyl.	Brougham	6,200	10,400	17,600
1934	1250	12 cyl.	Phaeton	19,000	40,000	64,000
1935	653	6 cyl.	Sedan	6,000	10,000	16,500
1935	653	6 cyl.	Coupe	5,500	9,000	15,500
1935	653	6 cyl.	Cabriolet	14,500	28,000	47,500
1935	653	6 cyl.	Brougham	5,500	9,000	15,500
1935	653	6 cyl.	Phaeton	17,500	35,000	55,000

YEAR	MODEL	ENGINE	BODY	F	G	E
AUBURN *(United States, 1900–36) (continued)*						
1935	851	8 cyl.	Sedan	6,200	10,400	17,600
1935	851	8 cyl.	Coupe	6,000	10,000	16,500
1935	851	8 cyl.	Cabriolet	15,000	30,000	50,000
1935	851	8 cyl.	Brougham	6,000	10,000	16,500
1935	851	8 cyl.	Phaeton	18,000	37,000	60,000
1936	654	6 cyl.	Sedan	6,200	10,400	17,600
1936	654	6 cyl.	Coupe	6,000	10,000	16,500
1936	654	6 cyl.	Cabriolet	22,000	43,500 ·	76,000

Auburn – 1936 "Cabriolet" Courtesy of White Post Restorations, White Post, Virginia

1936	654	6 cyl.	Brougham	6,000	10,000	16,500
1936	654	6 cyl.	Phaeton	20,000	42,000	70,000
1936	852	8 cyl.	Sedan	7,500	13,000	24,750
1936	852	8 cyl.	Coupe	7,000	12,000	24,000
1936	852	8 cyl.	Cabriolet	22,000	43,500	76,000
1936	852	8 cyl.	Brougham	7,000	12,000	24,000

YEAR	MODEL	ENGINE	BODY	F	G	E

AUBURN *(United States, 1900–36) (continued)*

YEAR	MODEL	ENGINE	BODY	F	G	E
1936	852	8 cyl.	Phaeton	20,000	42,000	70,000

Auburn – 1936 "Boattail Speedster"

AUBURN *(United States, 1967–80)*

YEAR	MODEL	ENGINE	BODY	F	G	E
1967	866 GP	V 8 cyl. (Ford)	Speedster	14,000	19,000	28,000
1968	866 GP	V 8 cyl. (Ford)	Speedster	14,000	19,000	28,000
1969	866 GP	V 8 cyl. (Ford)	Speedster	14,000	19,000	28,000
1970	866 GP	V 8 cyl. (Ford)	Speedster	14,000	19,000	28,000
1970	866 GP	V 8 cyl. (Pontiac)	Speedster	14,000	19,000	28,000
1971	866 GP	V 8 cyl. (Lincoln)	Speedster	15,000	20,000	29,000
1971	866 GP	V 8 cyl. (Pontiac)	Speedster	14,500	19,500	28,500
1972	866 GP	V 8 cyl. (Lincoln)	Speedster	15,000	20,000	29,500
1972		V 8 cyl. (Pontiac)	Speedster	14,000	18,000	30,000
1980		V 8 cyl. (Ford)	Speedster	16,000	24,000	36,000

AUDI *(Germany, 1910–39)*

YEAR	MODEL	ENGINE	BODY	F	G	E
1910	B	2612cc	Sport			
			Touring	4,500	9,000	16,000
1912	C		Sport			
			Touring	4,750	9,500	16,500
1914	D		Coupe	3,000	8,000	11,000
1916	E		Coupe	3,000	8,000	11,500
1924	M	6 cyl.	Cabriolet	4,000	10,000	18,000
1928	R	8 cyl.	Cabriolet	6,000	13,000	20,000
1937	Zwickau	8 cyl.	Drop Head			
			Coupe	5,000	8,000	15,500
1939	Dresden	6 cyl.	Sedan	4,000	7,000	13,000

AUSTIN *(United States, 1903–21)*

YEAR	MODEL	ENGINE	BODY	F	G	E
1903	XXV	2 cyl.	Touring	3,500	8,000	16,000

YEAR	MODEL	ENGINE	BODY	F	G	E
AUSTIN *(United States, 1903–21) (continued)*						
1915	66	6 cyl.	4 Passenger Touring	6,500	14,000	32,000
AUSTIN *(Great Britain, 1906–71)*						
1906	25/30	4 cyl.	Limousine	17,000	20,000	40,000
1910	Ten	4 cyl.	Touring	10,000	15,000	30,000
1919	Twenty	4 cyl.	Limousine	10,000	11,000	20,000
1922	Twelve	4 cyl. 1661cc	Touring	6,000	8,000	15,000
1924	Seven	747cc	Limousine	4,000	6,000	12,000
1929	20/6	6 cyl. (Supercharged)	Sport	7,000	10,000	22,000
1929	Seven Fabric		Saloon Sedan	4,000	5,000	7,000
1933	Ten	1.1 Litre	Saloon Sedan	4,000	5,000	7,000
1938	Cambridge Ten	900cc	Saloon Sedan	3,000	4,000	8,000
1945	Sixteen	4 cyl. 2.2 Litre	Sedan	2,500	3,000	5,000
1947	Sheerline	4 cyl. 4 Litre	Sedan	1,000	1,000	2,000
1948	Devon	4 cyl.	Sedan	1,000	1,000	2,000
1949	A 90	4 cyl.	Convertible	6,000	7,000	14,000
1954	A 40	4 cyl. 1.5 Litre	Coupe	2,000	2,000	3,000
1955	A 50	1.5 Litre	Convertible	2,000	2,000	3,000
1958	Princess	6 cyl.	Limousine	1,000	1,500	2,000
AUSTIN *(Australia, 1959)*						
1959	A 95	6 cyl.	Sedan	2,000	4,000	10,000
1959	Mini 850	4 cyl.	Sedan	1,700	4,000	8,000
AUSTIN-AMERICAN;BANTAM *(United States, 1931–1940)*						
1931	Austin	4 cyl.	Coupe	3,000	4,000	8,000
1931	Austin	4 cyl.	Roadster	4,000	6,000	12,000
1932	Austin	4 cyl.	Roadster	4,000	6,000	12,000
1933	Austin	4 cyl.	Roadster	4,000	6,000	12,000
1934	Austin	4 cyl.	Coupe	4,000	5,000	8,500
1935	Austin	4 cyl.	Coupe	4,000	5,000	8,500
1936	Austin	4 cyl.	Coupe	4,000	5,000	8,500
1938	Bantam	4 cyl.	Coupe	3,000	4,000	7,500

YEAR	MODEL	ENGINE	BODY	F	G	E
AUSTIN-AMERICAN;BANTAM *(United States, 1931–1940) (continued)*						
1938	Bantam	4 cyl.	Roadster	4,000	5,000	10,000

American Austin – 1938 "Bantam Roadster"

YEAR	MODEL	ENGINE	BODY	F	G	E
1939	Bantam	4 cyl.	Roadster	4,000	6,000	11,000
1940	Bantam	4 cyl.	Roadster	4,000	6,000	11,000
AUSTIN-HEALEY *(Great Britain, 1953–71)*						
1953	100	4 cyl.	Roadster	10,000	12,000	20,000
1954	100	4 cyl.	Roadster	7,000	9,000	18,000
1955	100	4 cyl.	Roadster	7,000	9,000	18,000
1956	100	4 cyl.	Roadster	7,000	9,000	18,000
1957	100-6	6 cyl.	Roadster	8,000	10,000	20,000
1958	100-6	6 cyl.	Roadster	8,000	10,000	20,000
1958	Sprite	4 cyl.	Roadster	4,000	5,000	10,000
1959	100-6	6 cyl.	Roadster	8,000	10,000	20,000
1959	Sprite	4 cyl.	Roadster	4,000	5,000	10,000
1960	3000	6 cyl.	Roadster	10,000	12,000	25,000

YEAR	MODEL	ENGINE	BODY	F	G	E
AUSTIN-HEALEY *(Great Britain, 1953–71) (continued)*						
1960	Sprite	4 cyl.	Roadster	4,000	5,000	10,000

Austin Healey – 1960 "Sprite"

1961	3000 MK I	6 cyl.	Roadster	8,000	10,000	20,000
1961	3000 MK II	6 cyl.	Roadster	10,000	12,000	22,000
1961	Sprite MK I	4 cyl.	Roadster	4,000	5,000	10,000
1961	Sprite MK II	4 cyl.	Roadster	3,000	4,000	8,000
1962	3000 MK II	6 cyl.	Roadster	8,000	10,000	21,000
1962	Sprite MK II	4 cyl.	Convertible	4,000	5,000	9,000
1963	3000 MK II	6 cyl.	Roadster	8,000	10,000	21,000
1963	Sprite MK II	4 cyl.	Convertible	4,000	5,000	9,000
1964	3000 MK II	6 cyl.	Convertible	9,000	12,000	21,000
1964	3000 MK III	6 cyl.	Convertible	7,000	10,000	22,000
1964	Sprite MK II	4 cyl.	Roadster	4,000	5,000	9,000
1964	Sprite MK III	4 cyl.	Convertible	3,000	4,000	8,000
1965	3000 MK III	6 cyl.	Convertible	8,000	10,000	22,000
1965	Sprite MK III	4 cyl.	Convertible	3,000	4,000	8,000
1966	3000 MK III	6 cyl.	Convertible	8,000	10,000	22,000
1966	Sprite MK III	4 cyl.	Convertible	3,000	4,000	8,000
1967	3000 MK III	6 cyl.	Convertible	10,000	15,000	25,000
1967	Sprite MK III	4 cyl.	Convertible	3,000	4,000	8,000
AUSTRALIS *(Australia, 1901–06)*						
1901		1 cyl.	2 Passenger	2,500	5,000	14,000
1906		2 cyl.	Tonneau	2,500	5,000	14,000

YEAR	MODEL	ENGINE	BODY	F	G	E
AUSTRO-DAIMLER *(Austria, 1899–1936)*						
1899			Runabout	3,500	6,500	14,000
1910	22/80	4 cyl.	Touring	4,500	9,500	18,000
1914	ADV	6 cyl.	Town	4,500	9,500	18,000
1932	ADR-8	8 cyl.	Drop Head			
			Coupe	10,000	20,000	36,000
AUSTRO-FIAT *(Austria, 1921–36)*						
1922	C1	4 cyl.	Touring	2,500	4,500	10,000
AUTOCAR *(United States, 1901–11)*						
1901	4	2 cyl.	Buggy	2,600	6,000	15,000
1905	4	4 cyl.	Buggy	2,800	6,000	16,000
AUTOCRAT *(Great Britain, 1913–26)*						
1913		2 cyl.	Coupe	1,500	3,000	6,000
1919		4 cyl.	Coupe	2,000	5,000	7,000
AUTODYNAMICS *(United States, 1964)*						
1964	D-7	Hustler VW	Sport	2,800	5,000	8,000
AUTOETTE *(United States, 1913)*						
1926	Closed	Electric	Sedan	3,000	7,000	14,000
AUTOTRIX *(Great Britain, 1913)*						
1913		2 cyl.	Open	900	3,000	8,000
1913	3-Wheel	1 cyl.	Open	800	2,600	6,200
A.V. *(Great Britain, 1919–26)*						
1919	Mono	Motorcycle	1 Passenger	1,700	4,000	6,000
1920	Bicar		2 Passenger	1,000	3,000	6,000
AVANTI *(United States, 1963–64)*						
1963	Avanti	V-8 R1	Coupe	5,000	10,000	21,000
1963	Avanti	V-8 R2	Coupe	5,500	12,500	22,500
1964	Avanti	V-8 R1	Coupe	4,500	9,000	20,000
1964	Avanti	V-8 R2	Coupe	5,000	10,000	21,000
AVANTI II *(United States, 1965–81)*						
1966		V 8 cyl.	Coupe	5,000	10,000	22,000
1981		V 8 cyl.	Coupe	6,500	12,000	25,000
AVERAGE MAN'S RUNABOUT *(United States, 1907–08)*						
1907		Air-cooled	Runabout	7,000	9,000	18,000
AVERIES *(Great Britain, 1911–15)*						
1911		1 cyl.	Runabout	800	3,400	6,600
1913		4 cyl.	Runabout	2,000	4,000	8,000
AVIETTE *(Great Britain, 1914–16)*						
1914		1 cyl.	Cycle	1,800	3,800	8,600
1915		1 cyl.	Cycle	2,000	4,000	9,000

YEAR	MODEL	ENGINE	BODY	F	G	E
AVON *(Great Britain, 1903–12)*						
1903	3-Wheel	1 cyl.		2,000	3,800	8,250
1905		1 cyl.		2,200	4,000	8,500

B

YEAR	MODEL	ENGINE	BODY	F	G	E
BABCOCK *(United States, 1909–13)*						
1909	A	2 cyl.	Buggy	4,000	6,000	12,000
1910	30	4 cyl.	Touring	6,000	8,000	16,000
BADGER *(United States, 1910–12)*						
1910	B	4 cyl.	Touring	6,000	8,000	15,000
1911	C	4 cyl.	Roadster	6,000	7,000	12,000
BAGULEY *(Great Britain, 1911–21)*						
1911	16/20	4 cyl.	Coupe	2,200	4,000	7,000
1914	16/20	4 cyl.	Limousine	2,400	5,800	8,800
BAILEY *(United States, 1907–15)*						
1911	Victoria	Electric	Touring	4,600	9,200	18,000
1913	Victoria	Electric	Roadster	4,000	8,200	17,000
BAILLE-LEMAIRE *(France, 1898–1902)*						
1898		2 cyl.	Runabout	1,800	4,700	9,250
BAKER ELECTRIC *(United States, 1899–1916)*						
1903		Electric	Runabout	5,800	8,800	16,000
1910		Electric	Phaeton	8,800	14,000	28,000
1913		Electric	Coupe	6,600	8,700	14,000
BALBOA *(United States, 1924–25)*						
1924		Rotary Valve	Touring		RARE	
1925		Rotary Valve	Brougham		RARE	
BALL STEAM *(United States, 1868–1902)*						
1902		Steam	Touring		RARE	
BAMBINO *(Netherlands, 1955–56)*						
1955	3-Wheel	1 cyl.	Minicar	2,000	4,000	9,000
BANKER *(United States, 1905)*						
1905		4 cyl.	Tonneau	5,000	7,000	12,000
1905		4 cyl.	Limousine	6,000	8,000	12,500
BANKER JUVENILE ELECTRIC *(United States, 1905)*						
1905		Electric	Roadster	3,000	3,500	4,500
BARDON *(France, 1899–1903)*						
1899		1 cyl.	Runabout	1,700	4,600	9,500
1902		1 cyl.	Tonneau	2,100	4,200	9,000

YEAR	MODEL	ENGINE	BODY	F	G	E
BARLEY *(United States, 1923–24)*						
1923	6-50	6 cyl.	Touring	12,000	15,000	20,000
1924	6-50	6 cyl.	Sedan	8,000	10,000	15,000
BARRE *(France, 1900–30)*						
1902		2 cyl.	Tonneau	2,000	4,000	8,500
1924		4 cyl.	Touring	2,200	4,500	10,000
BARRON-VIALLE *(France, 1923–29)*						
1923		2 cyl.	Open	1,800	4,800	7,000
BARTLETT *(Canada, 1914–17)*						
1914		(LeRoi)	Touring	2,200	4,800	11,000
1917		(LeRoi)	Roadster	2,600	5,200	14,500
BAY STATE *(United States, 1922–24)*						
1922	1	6 cyl.	Coupe	4,200	7,700	17,000
1924	2	8 cyl.	Sedan	3,000	6,000	11,500
BEACON *(Great Britain, 1912–24)*						
1912	Mark VI	V 2 cyl.	Sport Roadster	4,200	8,000	16,500
BEAN *(Great Britain, 1919–29)*						
1922		4 cyl.	2 Sport	2,000	4,800	10,000
1924		4 cyl.	Saloon Sedan	1,200	4,200	10,500
1927	18/50	4 cyl.	Saloon Sedan	1,400	4,500	9,000
1929	14/70	4 cyl.	Saloon Sedan	1,600	5,000	10,000
BEARDMORE *(Great Britain, 1920–28)*						
1920			Touring	2,200	5,200	12,500
1923	Type D		Touring	2,300	5,400	11,500
BEATRIX *(France, 1907)*						
1907	30/40	6 cyl.	Touring	2,000	5,000	12,750
BEATTIE *(Great Britain, 1969)*						
1969			Sport	2,400	4,900	9,500
BEAUFORD *(Germany, 1901–06)*						
1901		2 cyl.	Runabout	1,800	4,700	8,900
1902		2 cyl.	Touring	2,200	4,900	9,900
1903		2 cyl.	Touring	2,600	5,700	10,500
BEAVER *(United States, 1912)*						
1912		6 cyl.	Touring		RARE	
BECKMANN *(Germany, 1900–26)*						
1900		1 cyl. (DeDion)	Voiturette	2,000	4,000	10,000
1901		4 cyl.	Tonneau Limousine	2,400	4,600	11,000
BEDFORD *(Great Britain, 1904)*						
1904		4 cyl.	Tonneau	1,900	4,000	9,000

YEAR	MODEL	ENGINE	BODY	F	G	E
BEESTON *(Great Britain, 1899)*						
1899			Open	1,800	3,800	10,000
B.E.F. *(Germany, 1907–13)*						
1907	3-Wheel	Electric	Touring	2,100	4,600	9,800
BELLANGER *(France, 1912–25)*						
1912		4 cyl.	Touring	1,000	2,000	4,800
BELSIZE *(Great Britain, 1897–1925)*						
1913	18/22	4 cyl.	Cabriolet	2,000	4,000	8,000
1924		4 cyl.	Sedan	1,800	3,800	5,000
BENOIS et DAMAS *(France, 1903–04)*						
1903		2 cyl.	Coupe	1,000	2,000	4,800
1904		4 cyl.	Coupe	1,400	2,800	5,800
BENTLEY *(Great Britain, 1920 to date)*						
1920		3 Litre	Touring	12,500	18,000	75,000
1924	Speed Model	3 Litre	Sport Roadster Touring	35,000	45,000	80,000
1925	Red Label	3 Litre	Roadster	40,000	50,000	85,000
1925		3 Litre	Sport Touring	35,000	45,000	80,000
1926		3 Litre	Convertible Coupe	20,000	25,000	40,000
1926		3 Litre	Coupe	20,000	25,000	45,000
1927		3 Litre	Touring	30,000	40,000	80,000
1929		4.5 Litre	Speedster	50,000	60,000	120,000
1929		4.5 Litre	Touring	50,000	60,000	120,000
1929		4.5 Litre	Sedan	15,000	20,000	40,000
1930	Speed 6	4.5 Litre	Sedan	15,000	20,000	40,000
1931		6 cyl. 8 Litre	Cabriolet	55,000	70,000	125,000
1931		4.5 Litre	Touring	30,000	40,000	70,000
1934		4.5 Litre	Dual Cowl Phaeton	45,000	60,000	120,000
1934		4.5 Litre	Convertible Coupe	40,000	50,000	90,000
1934		4.5 Litre	Sedan	15,000	20,000	35,000
1934		4.5 Litre	Sedan	15,000	20,000	35,000
1934		3.5 Litre	Dual Cowl Phaeton	10,500	21,000	80,000
1934		3.5 Litre	Drop Head Coupe	20,000	30,000	60,000
1935		4.5 Litre	Cabriolet	30,000	40,000	80,000
1935	Speed 6	4.5 Litre	Touring	30,000	40,000	80,000
1935		3.5 Litre	Coupe	20,000	30,000	60,000

YEAR	MODEL	ENGINE	BODY	F	G	E

BENTLEY *(Great Britain, 1920 to date) (continued)*

YEAR	MODEL	ENGINE	BODY	F	G	E
1936		4.5 Litre	Sedanca Coupe	30,000	45,000	75,000

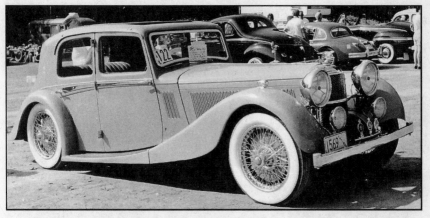

Bentley – 1936 "Speed 20" Four-door saloon, body by Charlesworth

YEAR	MODEL	ENGINE	BODY	F	G	E
1936		4.5 Litre	Sport Sedan	15,000	20,000	40,000
1936		4.5 Litre	Cabriolet	15,000	20,000	40,000
1936		4.5 Litre	Convertible Victoria	8,000	18,000	55,000
1937		4.5 Litre	Sedan	4,000	8,000	35,000
1937		4.5 Litre	Cabriolet	6,000	15,000	60,000
1937	Continental	4.5 Litre	Cabriolet	5,000	16,000	65,000
1937		4.5 Litre	Sport Sedan	4,000	9,000	35,000
1937		4.5 Litre	Coupe	4,200	6,500	30,000
1938		4.5 Litre	Sedan	4,200	8,000	30,000
1938		4.5 Litre	Drop Head Coupe	30,000	40,000	80,000
1939		4.5 Litre	Coupe	15,000	20,000	40,000
1939		4.5 Litre	Cabriolet	20,000	30,000	60,000
1940	MK-V	4.5 Litre	Convertible	30,000	40,000	75,000

Postwar Models

YEAR	MODEL	ENGINE	BODY	F	G	E
1947	Frannay	4.5 Litre	Convertible	15,000	20,000	35,000
1948	MK-VI	4.5 Litre	Sedan	7,000	10,000	20,000
1949	Park Ward	4.5 Litre	Convertible	35,000	50,000	95,000
1951	MK-VI	4.5 Litre	Sedan	7,000	10,000	20,000
1951	Abbott	6 cyl.	Coupe	10,000	12,000	25,000
1952	James Young	6 cyl. 4.6 Litre	Coupe	10,000	15,000	28,000
1952	James Young	6 cyl. 4.6 Litre	Saloon	10,000	12,000	25,000
1952	MK-VI	4.6 Litre	Sedan	7,000	10,000	20,000

YEAR	MODEL	ENGINE	BODY	F	G	E
BENTLEY *(Great Britain, 1920 to date) (continued)*						
1952	Park Ward Left-Hand Drive	4.6 Litre	Coupe	10,000	15,000	30,000
1952	Park Ward Right-Hand Drive	4.6 Litre	Coupe	7,000	10,000	20,000
1952	Park Ward	4.6 Litre	Saloon	10,000	15,000	30,000
1953	Sun Roof	4.6 Litre	Sedan	7,000	9,000	18,000
1953	Park Ward	4.6 Litre	Convertible	35,000	45,000	80,000
1954	R Type	4.6 Litre	Sedan	8,000	10,000	20,000

Bentley – 1954 "R Type" sedan

YEAR	MODEL	ENGINE	BODY	F	G	E
1954		4.6 Litre	Convertible	20,000	30,000	60,000
1954	R Type	4.6 Litre	2 Door Continental	15,000	18,000	35,000
1954	Bertone	6 cyl.	Saloon	15,000	18,000	35,000
1954	Mulliner	6 cyl.	Coupe	15,000	18,000	35,000
1955	S-1 Continental	4.9 Litre	Fastback	15,000	25,000	45,000
1955	R Type	4.9 Litre	Special Sedan	10,000	15,000	25,000
1955	R Type	4.9 Litre	Sedan	8,000	15,000	25,000
1956		4.9 Litre	Sedan	8,000	15,000	30,000
1956	Freestone & Webb	6.2 Litre	Sedan	15,000	20,000	35,000
1956	Hooper	6.2 Litre	Sedan	10,000	15,000	30,000

YEAR	MODEL	ENGINE	BODY	F	G	E
BENTLEY *(Great Britain, 1920 to date) (continued)*						
1957	Mulliner	6.2 Litre	Sedan	15,000	20,000	35,000
1957	Park Ward	6 cyl.	Fixed Head			
			Coupe	15,000	20,000	45,000
1958	James Young	6 cyl.	Saloon	7,500	15,000	30,000
1958	S I	6 cyl.	Convertible	12,000	36,000	50,000
1958	S I	6 cyl.	Sedan	7,200	12,000	30,000
1958	S I		Continental			
	Park Ward	6 cyl.	Coupe	7,200	13,000	35,000
1959	Park Ward	6 cyl.	Coupe	15,000	30,000	45,000
1959	S I	6 cyl.	Limousine	8,600	18,000	35,000
1959	S I	6 cyl.		7,500	15,000	30,000
1960	S II	8 cyl.	Sedan	5,900	15,000	25,000
1960	S II	8 cyl.	Continental			
			Convertible	12,000	36,000	70,000
1960	S II	8 cyl.	Coupe	15,000	30,000	50,000
1961	S II	8 cyl.	Coupe	17,500	35,000	55,000
1961	S II					
	Left-Hand					
	Drive	8 cyl.	Convertible	12,000	21,000	50,000
1962	S II	8 cyl.	Sedan	7,600	11,000	30,000
1962	S II	8 cyl.	Drop Head			
			Coupe	11,500	21,000	50,000
1962	S III					
	Left-Hand					
	Drive	8 cyl.	Sedan	8,700	12,000	30,000
1963	S III					
	Right-Hand					
	Drive	8 cyl.	Sedan	7,600	11,000	26,000
1964	S III	8 cyl.	Convertible	9,700	36,000	70,000
1964	S III	8 cyl.	Sedan	7,600	18,000	35,000
1965	S III	8 cyl.	Sedan	7,600	19,800	38,000
1965	James Young	8 cyl.	Coupe	7,500	15,000	30,000
1965	Mulliner-Park					
	Ward	8 cyl.	Flying Spur	15,000	30,000	45,000
1966	T1	V-8	Sedan	5,000	10,000	28,000
1966	Mulliner-Park					
	Ward	V-8	Coupe	15,000	25,000	70,000
1966	Mulliner-Park					
	Ward	V-8	Convertible	17,500	35,000	90,000
1966	James Young	V-8	Sedan	7,500	12,500	40,000
1967	T1	V-8	Sedan	5,000	10,000	28,000
1967	Mulliner-Park					
	Ward	V-8	Coupe	15,000	25,000	70,000

YEAR	MODEL	ENGINE	BODY	F	G	E

BENTLEY *(Great Britain, 1920 to date) (continued)*

YEAR	MODEL	ENGINE	BODY	F	G	E
1967	Mulliner-Park Ward	V-8	Convertible	17,500	35,000	90,000
1967	James Young	V-8	Sedan	7,500	12,500	40,000
1968	T1	V-8	Sedan	5,000	10,000	28,000
1968	Mulliner-Park Ward	V-8	Coupe	15,000	25,000	70,000
1968	Mulliner-Park Ward	V-8	Convertible	17,500	35,000	90,000
1969	T1	V-8	Sedan	5,000	10,000	28,000
1969	Mulliner-Park Ward	V-8	Coupe	15,000	25,000	70,000
1969	Mulliner-Park Ward	V-8	Convertible	17,500	35,000	90,000
1970	T1	V-8	Sedan	5,000	10,000	28,000
1970	Mulliner-Park Ward	V-8	Coupe	15,000	25,000	70,000
1970	Mulliner-Park Ward	V-8	Convertible	17,500	35,000	90,000
1971	T1	V-8	Sedan	10,000	17,500	25,000
1972	T1	V-8	Sedan	10,000	17,500	25,000
1973	T1	V-8	Sedan	10,000	17,500	25,000
1974	T1	V-8	Sedan	10,000	17,500	25,000
1975	T1	V-8	Sedan	10,000	17,500	25,000
1976	T1	V-8	Sedan	10,000	17,500	25,000
1977	T2	V-8	Sedan	12,500	17,500	25,000
1977	Corniche	V-8	Coupe	15,000	20,000	30,000
1977	Corniche	V-8	Convertible	20,000	30,000	40,000
1978	T2	V-8	Sedan	12,500	17,500	25,000
1978	Corniche	V-8	Coupe	15,000	20,000	30,000
1978	Corniche	V-8	Convertible	20,000	30,000	40,000
1979	T2	V-8	Sedan	12,500	17,500	25,000
1979	Corniche	V-8	Coupe	15,000	20,000	30,000
1979	Corniche	V-8	Convertible	20,000	30,000	40,000

YEAR	MODEL	ENGINE	BODY	F	G	E
BENZ *(Germany, 1885–1926)*						
1885	3-Wheel	1 cyl.	Vis-a-vis	11,500	22,000	36,000
1893	Sociable	1 ½ hp	Velo	32,000	50,000	78,000

Benz – "1 ½ HP Velo Sociable"

1903	Parsifal	2 cyl.	Tonneau	11,000	19,000	36,000
1906	Daimler Benz		Touring	40,000	80,000	120,000
1908	Racer	12 Litre	Race Car	35,000	70,000	100,000
1910	8/20	2 Litre	Tonneau	9,800	15,000	30,000
1911	39/100	10.1 Litre	Touring	40,000	86,000	155,000
1912		4 cyl.	Touring	15,000	30,000	45,000
1914		4 cyl.	Touring	16,000	28,000	36,000
1914	25/55	6 cyl.	Limousine	16,000	35,000	65,000
1914	Racer	6 cyl.	Race Car	36,000	35,000	65,000
BENZ SOHNE *(Germany, 1906–26)*						
1906	10/22	4 cyl.	Tonneau	3,000	6,000	16,000
BERG *(United States, 1902–05)*						
1902	15	4 cyl.	Runabout	3,250	6,000	14,000
BERGE *(France, 1923)*						
1923			Sport	2,000	4,000	6,000

YEAR	MODEL	ENGINE	BODY	F	G	E
BERGMANN *(Germany, 1907–22)*						
1907		4 cyl.	Open	1,800	4,900	9,600
BERGOOLL *(United States, 1908–13)*						
1910		4 cyl.	Touring	3,800	8,000	16,000
1913	30	4 cyl.	Limousine	2,500	7,500	14,000
BERLIET *(France, 1895–1939)*						
1902		4 cyl.	Touring	1,900	3,900	9,900
1906	60	4 cyl.	Roadster	2,000	3,200	12,000
1923	VL	6 cyl.	Touring	1,900	3,750	10,000
1932		6 cyl.	Coupe	1,600	3,500	10,000
1933	944	6 cyl.	Sedan	1,500	3,250	10,000
BERNADET *(France, 1946–50)*						
1946	5 CV	4 cyl.	2 Passenger	1,800	3,800	8,900
BERRET *(France, 1899–1903)*						
1899		3 cyl.	Open	2,000	4,200	11,000
BERTOLET *(United States, 1908–10)*						
1908	X	4 cyl.	Roadster	4,000	9,500	18,000
1910	40	4 cyl.	Touring	4,000	9,500	17,000
BERWICK *(United States, 1904)*						
1904		Electric	Runabout	4,400	8,000	18,000
BEVERLY-BARNES *(Great Britain, 1924–31)*						
1924	24/80	8 cyl.	Vanden Plas Touring	3,500	8,500	24,000
B.G.S. *(France, 1899–1906)*						
1899		Electric	Phaeton	3,400	5,800	16,000
BIANCHI *(Italy, 1899–1939;1957)*						
1899		1 cyl. (DeDion)		2,100	6,000	13,000
1907	E	1.4 Litre	Sport	2,800	5,750	12,000
1916	42-70	4 cyl.	Sport Touring	2,500	3,750	12,000
1922	GP	4 cyl.	Sport	2,100	3,250	11,000
1923	16	4 cyl.	Sport	1,750	3,400	10,000
1928		8 cyl.	Touring	1,750	6,500	13,000
1930		2.9 Litre	Touring	1,750	6,500	13,000
1933	S8 bis	2.9 Litre	Sport Sedan	1,650	6,250	8,800
1934	S9	1.5 Litre	Sport Sedan	1,650	2,250	6,000
1939		4 cyl.	7 Passenger	2,100	3,250	6,800
1955		2 cyl. (Fiat)	Convertible	1,350	2,700	4,500
1957		4 cyl.	Convertible	1,350	4,700	7,800
BIFORT *(Great Britain, 1914–15)*						
1914			Duplex	2,000	3,200	9,800

YEAR	MODEL	ENGINE	BODY	F	G	E
BIGNAN *(France, 1918–30)*						
1918	17 CV	3.5 Litre	Sport	1,400	2,800	6,200
1921	50	4 cyl.	Voiturette	1,700	3,400	7,000
1924	11 CV	2 Litre	Sedan	1,200	2,600	5,500
1927	60	8 cyl.	Touring	3,000	8,000	12,000
BIJI T VUUP *(Netherlands, 1902–05)*						
1902	6.5	2 cyl.	Tonneau	1,000	4,800	8,800
BIJOU *(Great Britain, 1901–04)*						
1901	5	1 cyl.	Open	1,800	3,000	8,000
BINNEY & BURNHAM *(United States, 1901–02)*						
1901		Steam	Tonneau		RARE	
BLACKBURN *(Great Britain, 1919–25)*						
1919		4 cyl.	Touring	2,000	4,000	10,000
BLACKHAWK *(United States, 1902–03)*						
1902		2 Litre	Phaeton	4,000	7,250	13,000
BLAKE *(Great Britain, 1900–03)*						
1900		1 cyl.	Vis-a-vis	6,000	8,000	13,000
1901		2 cyl.	Tonneau	8,000	10,000	15,000
B.M.W. *(Germany, 1928 to date)*						
1953	501	6 cyl.	Sedan	3,000	5,000	9,500
1954	501	6 cyl.	Sedan	3,000	5,000	8,500
1954	502	8 cyl.	Sedan	4,000	6,000	11,000
1955	501A	6 cyl.	Sedan	3,000	5,000	8,000
1955	502	8 cyl.	Sedan	4,000	6,000	10,000
1956	501	6 cyl.	Sedan	3,000	5,000	8,000
1956	502	8 cyl.	Sedan	4,000	6,000	10,000
1957	501	6 cyl.	Sedan	3,000	5,000	8,000
1957	502	8 cyl.	Sedan	4,000	6,000	10,000
1957	503	8 cyl.	Coupe	8,000	19,000	25,000
1957	507	8 cyl.	Roadster	20,000	40,000	75,000
1958	501	6 cyl.	Sedan	3,000	5,000	8,000
1958	502	8 cyl.	Sedan	4,000	6,000	10,000
1958	503	8 cyl.	Convertible	10,000	20,500	35,000
1959	501	8 cyl.	Sedan	4,000	6,000	9,500
1959	502	8 cyl.	Sedan	4,400	6,600	10,000
1959	503	8 cyl.	Convertible	10,000	20,500	35,000
1959	503	8 cyl.	Coupe	8,000	19,000	27,000
1959	600	2 cyl.	Sedan	1,400	2,500	3,900
1960	501	8 cyl.	Sedan	4,000	6,000	10,000
1960	502	8 cyl.	Sedan	4,000	6,000	10,000
1961	300	1 cyl.	1 Door Sedan	1,500	2,800	6,000
1961	501	8 cyl.	Sedan	4,000	6,000	10,000

YEAR	MODEL	ENGINE	BODY	F	G	E
B.M.W. *(Germany, 1928 to date) (continued)*						
1961	502	8 cyl.	Sedan	4,000	6,000	10,000
1961	2600	8 cyl.	Sedan	5,000	7,200	11,000
1962	300	1 cyl.	1 Door Sedan	1,500	2,800	6,000
1962	1500	4 cyl.	Sedan	2,500	4,000	6,000
1962	2600	8 cyl.	Sedan	4,000	6,000	8,500
1962	3200 (both styles)	8 cyl.	Sedan	4,000	6,000	10,000
1963	700	2 cyl.	Coupe	1,500	2,800	4,400
1963	700	2 cyl.	Sedan	1,200	2,300	3,200
1963	1500	4 cyl.	Sedan	2,500	4,000	6,000
1964	1800	4 cyl.	Sedan	3,000	4,000	7,500
1965	1600	4 cyl.	Sedan	3,000	5,000	7,500
1965	2000	4 cyl.	Coupe	5,000	7,200	9,500
1966	2000	4 cyl.	Sedan	3,500	5,400	8,000
1966	2000	4 cyl.	Coupe	5,000	7,200	9,500
1967	3000	8 cyl.	Coupe	7,000	11,000	15,000
1968	1600	4 cyl.	Sedan	3,000	5,000	7,500
1968	1600	4 cyl.	Cabriolet	6,500	10,000	13,000
1968	1800	4 cyl.	Sedan	3,000	5,000	7,500
1968	2000	4 cyl.	Sedan	3,000	5,000	7,500
1968	2002	4 cyl.	2 Door Sedan	4,000	6,000	8,500
1969	2800	6 cyl.	Sedan	2,750	4,600	7,000
1969	2800	6 cyl.	Coupe	5,600	7,700	10,100
1970	2000	4 cyl.	Coupe	5,600	7,700	10,100
1970	3.0CS	6 cyl.	Coupe	8,000	13,400	17,000
1970	3.0CSL	6 cyl.	Coupe	9,000	15,000	21,500
1971	1600	4 cyl.	Cabriolet	6,500	10,000	13,000
1971	2002	4 cyl.	Cabriolet	8,000	13,400	17,000
1971	Bavaria	6 cyl.	Sedan	3,000	5,000	7,500
1971	3.0S	6 cyl.	Sedan	3,000	4,000	7,500
1972	2000	4 cyl.	Touring	3,000	5,000	7,500
1972	2002ti	4 cyl.	Sedan	3,000	5,000	7,500
1972	2002tii	4 cyl.	Sedan	3,500	5,400	8,000
1973	2002 turbo	4 cyl.	Sedan	7,000	11,000	15,000
1973	3.0CSA	6 cyl.	Coupe	6,500	10,000	13,000
1973	3.0CSi	6 cyl.	Coupe	8,000	13,400	17,000
1973	3.0CSL	6 cyl.	Coupe	9,000	15,000	21,000
1974	2002	4 cyl.	Sedan	3,500	5,400	8,000
1974	2800	6 cyl.	Sedan	3,000	5,000	7,500
1974	3.0CS	6 cyl.	Sedan	8,000	13,400	17,000
1975	530i	6 cyl.	Sedan	3,500	5,400	8,000
1976	3.0Si	6 cyl.	Sedan	4,500	6,600	9,100
1976	630CS	6 cyl.	Sedan	7,000	11,000	15,000

YEAR	MODEL	ENGINE	BODY	F	G	E
B.M.W. *(Germany, 1928 to date) (continued)*						
1977	320i	4 cyl.	2 Door Sedan	2,000	4,000	6,000
1977	530i	6 cyl.	Sedan	2,250	4,500	6,500
1977	630CS	6 cyl.	Coupe	3,000	5,500	8,000
1977	630CSi	6 cyl.	Coupe	3,500	6,000	9,000
1977	633CSi	6 cyl.	Coupe	4,500	7,000	10,000
1978	320i	4 cyl.	2 Door Sedan	2,000	4,000	6,000
1978	530i	6 cyl.	Sedan	2,250	4,500	6,500
1978	630CSi	6 cyl.	Coupe	3,500	6,000	9,000
1978	633CSi	6 cyl.	Coupe	4,500	7,000	10,000
1978	733i	6 cyl.	Sedan	3,000	5,000	9,000
1979	320i	4 cyl.	2 Door Sedan	1,500	3,500	6,500
1979	528i	6 cyl.	Sedan	1,500	3,500	7,000
1979	633CSi	6 cyl.	Coupe	5,000	7,500	12,500
1979	635CSi	6 cyl.	Coupe	6,000	8,000	14,000
1979	733i	6 cyl.	Sedan	2,500	4,500	10,000
1979	MI	6 cyl.	Coupe	40,000	60,000	110,000
B.N.C. *(France, 1923–31)*						
1923		4 cyl.	Voiturette	2,100	4,400	9,900
1925		4 cyl.	Touring	2,200	4,400	12,000
1927	ST Hubert	1100cc	Sport	2,400	4,800	13,000
BOBBI-KAR *(United States, 1945–47)*						
1945		Air-cooled	Minicar	2,600	4,600	11,000
BOCAR *(United States, 1958–60)*						
1958	SP-4	V 8 cyl. (Corvette)	Roadster	3,800	6,900	14,000
BOLIDE *(United States, 1969–70)*						
1969		V 8 cyl.	Coupe	3,600	6,900	9,800
BOLWELL *(Australia, 1963–64)*						
1963		V 8 cyl. (Ford)	Coupe	2,200	4,800	10,000
BON-CAR *(Great Britain, 1905–07)*						
1905		Steam	Open	4,800	9,800	20,000
BOND *(Great Britain, 1922–28)*						
1922		4 cyl.	Touring	2,200	4,200	12,000
BOND *(Great Britain, 1949–71)*						
1949	3-Wheel	1 cyl.	Minicar	1,000	2,400	7,000
1951	3-Wheel	197cc	Minicar	1,000	2,400	7,000
1963	GT	875cc	Coupe	1,000	2,400	7,000
1970	Bug	4 cyl.	Coupe	1,000	2,400	7,000
BORCHARDING *(Germany, 1925)*						
1925			Cycle	1,800	2,700	6,500

YEAR	MODEL	ENGINE	BODY	F	G	E
BORDEREL-CAIL *(France, 1905–08)*						
1905	15/18	4 cyl.	Limousine	2,800	6,200	12,000
BORGWARD *(Germany, 1939–61)*						
1939	Hansa 1100	6 cyl.		3,250	8,000	14,500
1951	Hansa	1.5 Litre	Cabriolet	1,400	3,600	7,500
1953	1500 Renn					
	Sport	1.5 Litre	Coupe	1,000	2,400	5,300
1957	Isabella	1.5 Litre	Coupe	800	1,800	4,700
1960		6 cyl.	Limousine	2,000	4,000	9,250
BORITTIER *(France, 1899)*						
1899		(DeDion)	Voiturette	3,100	7,600	16,000
BOSTON HIGH WHEEL *(United States, 1907)*						
1907	High-wheel	2 cyl.		3,200	6,400	11,000
BOTY'S *(France, 1907)*						
1907		1 cyl.	Voiturette	2,000	3,000	6,500
BOUR-DAVIS *(United States, 1915–22)*						
1915		6 cyl.	Touring	4,500	8,800	17,000
BOURGEOIS-MAGNIN *(France, 1920)*						
1920			Runabout	1,800	2,800	8,500
1920			Touring	2,400	3,800	9,500
BOURGUIGNONNE *(France, 1899–1901)*						
1899		1 cyl.	Voiturette	1,850	2,900	9,000
BOWEN *(Great Britain, 1905–06)*						
1905		1 cyl.	Runabout	2,000	3,200	7,500
BOYER *(France, 1898–1906)*						
1898		1 cyl.	Tonneau	2,800	4,800	9,600
1901		1 cyl.	Voiturette	2,000	4,000	9,000
1902		4 cyl.	Phaeton	2,400	5,000	13,000
1903		4 cyl.	Touring	2,200	5,400	14,000
BOZIER *(France, 1906–20)*						
1906		1 cyl. (DeDion)	Voiturette	2,200	4,400	10,000
1911–24		4 cyl. (DeDion)	Voiturette	4,600	8,000	16,000
BRADBURY *(Great Britain, 1901–02)*						
1901		1 cyl.	Voiturette	2,400	4,200	7,300
BRADLEY *(United States, 1920–21)*						
1920	H	4 cyl.	Touring	4,900	10,400	20,000
BRAMWELL *(United States, 1904–05)*						
1904		1 cyl.	Runabout	2,000	4,200	12,000
BRANDT *(France, 1948)*						
1948		4 cyl.	Sedan	1,650	3,600	7,000

YEAR	MODEL	ENGINE	BODY	F	G	E
BRASIE *(United States, 1914–17)*						
1914		4 cyl.	Roadster	2,400	6,800	13,000
BRASIER *(France, 1897–1930)*						
1897		1 cyl.		1,800	2,600	10,000
1900		2 cyl.	Voiturette	2,000	4,000	11,000
1905		4 cyl.	Touring	3,200	6,400	16,000
BRAZIER *(United States, 1902–04)*						
1902		2 cyl.	Waggonette	3,000	7,800	11,750
BREMS *(Denmark, 1900–07)*						
1900		2 cyl.	Vis-a-vis	1,800	2,800	9,000
BRENNABOR *(Germany, 1908–34)*						
1908		(Fafnir)		1,850	2,900	8,000
1909	3-Wheel	4 cyl.	2 Passenger	2,900	3,900	9,000
1914	3/16	1.5 Litre	3 Passenger	2,950	4,000	9,000
1931	Juwel 6	6 cyl.	Sedan	2,200	4,600	10,000
BREWSTER *(United States, 1915–25; 1934–36)*						
1914	Town Car	4 cyl.	Limousine	12,000	27,000	36,000
1915		4 cyl.	Town-Carriage	9,000	18,000	30,000
1917		4 cyl.	Roadster	9,000	18,000	30,000
1934		4 cyl.	4 Door Convertible	9,000	19,000	25,000
1934	Limousine	V 8 cyl. (Ford)	Town	9,500	28,000	40,000

Bricklin – "SV-1 Gullwing Coupe"

YEAR	MODEL	ENGINE	BODY	F	G	E
BRICKLIN (United States, 1968–76)						
1971			Gullwing			
			Coupe	3,000	7,000	10,000
1975	SV-1		Gullwing			
			Coupe	4,000	8,000	12,000
BRILLIE (France, 1904–07)						
1904	18/24	4 cyl.	Touring	1,850	2,800	8,900
1906	35/45		Touring	2,250	6,800	9,000
BRISCO (United States, 1914–21)						
1912		4 cyl.	Touring	8,000	13,000	18,000
1913		4 cyl.	Touring	8,000	13,000	18,000
1914		4 cyl.	Roadster	9,000	14,000	19,000
1916		4 cyl.	Touring	8,000	13,000	18,000
1917		4 cyl.	Touring	7,000	12,000	17,000
1918		4 cyl.	Touring	7,000	12,000	17,000
1919		4 cyl.	Touring	7,000	12,000	17,000
1920		8 cyl.	Roadster	8,000	13,000	18,000
BRISTOL (Great Britain, 1902–08)						
1902	10	2 cyl.	Tonneau	2,000	4,000	10,000
1905	16/20	4 cyl.	Tonneau	3,250	5,500	14,000
BRISTOL (Great Britain, 1947–82)						
1947	400	6 cyl.	Coupe	2,250	4,400	8,800
1947	401	6 cyl.	Sedan	2,350	4,900	9,900
1947	402	6 cyl.	Cabriolet	2,400	5,000	10,500
1955	405	6 cyl.	Sedan	2,200	4,200	9,900
1955	405	4 cyl.	Convertible	3,500	5,500	11,500
BRITANNIA (Great Britain, 1896–1908)						
1896		Electric	Landau	5,000	12,000	22,000
1907	24/40	4 cyl.	Limousine	2,200	4,400	11,000
BRITISH ENSIGN (Great Britain, 1913–23)						
1919		6.7 Litre	Touring	4,200	8,400	29,000
1921			Touring	2,400	6,000	12,000
1926		4 cyl.	Runabout	2,200	5,500	11,000
BRITISH SALMSON (Great Britain, 1934–39)						
1934	S4C	4 cyl.	Touring	2,100	4,200	9,500
1934	12/70	4 cyl.	Sport	2,200	4,600	10,000
1939	20/90	4 cyl.	Drop Head Coupe	2,000	4,000	9,000
BRITON (Great Britain, 1908–28)						
1910		4 cyl.	2 Passenger	2,000	5,000	10,000

YEAR	MODEL	ENGINE	BODY	F	G	E
BRM	*(Great Britain, 1954–74)*					
1954	P-30	V 16 cyl. 1.5 Litre	Racing	60,000	120,000	320,000
1955	P-30	V 16 cyl. 1.5 Litre	Racing	60,000	120,000	320,000
1958	P-25	4 cyl. 2.5 Litre	Racing	20,000	80,000	165,000
1960	P-48	4 cyl. 2.5 Litre	Racing	10,000	25,000	50,000
1961	P-578	V 8 cyl. 1.5 Litre	Racing	25,000	50,000	100,000
1967	P-109	3 Litre	Racing	10,000	20,000	30,000
1969	P-139	V 12 cyl. 3 Litre	Racing	10,000	20,000	30,000
1972	P-180	V 12 cyl. 3 Litre	Racing	10,000	20,000	30,000
1974	P-160	V 12 cyl. 3 Litre	Racing	10,000	20,000	30,000
BROC	*(United States, 1909–16)*					
1909	D	Electric	Coupe	5,000	10,600	20,000
BROCK SIX	*(Canada, 1921)*					
1921		6 cyl. (Continental)	Touring	2,400	5,000	13,000
BROOKE	*(Great Britain, 1901–13)*					
1901		3 cyl.	Open	2,000	5,000	14,000
1905		4 cyl.	Runabout	2,500	6,000	12,000
1906		6 cyl.	Touring	3,200	7,400	16,000
BROOKS	*(Great Britain, 1902)*					
1902		2 cyl.	Tonneau	1,000	3,000	8,000
BROOKS	*(Canada, 1923–26)*					
1923		Steam	Sedan	6,000	12,500	20,000
BROOKS AND WOOLAN	*(Great Britain, 1907–10)*					
1907	15.9	(White & Poppe)	Custom Touring	2,000	4,000	12,000
BROUGH	*(Great Britain, 1899–1908; 1913)*					
1900		(DeDion)	Tonneau	2,000	4,000	10,000
1913		V 2 cyl.	Cycle	1,000	4,000	10,000
BROUGH SUPERIOR	*(Great Britain, 1935–39)*					
1935		V 8 cyl.	Drop Head Coupe	3,200	6,200	13,000
1936		6 cyl.	Sedan	2,000	4,000	8,000
1936		6 cyl.	2 Passenger			

YEAR	MODEL	ENGINE	BODY	F	G	E
BROUGH SUPERIOR *(Great Britain, 1935–39) (continued)*						
1936		6 cyl.	2 Passenger Sport	2,400	4,800	11,000
1938	Zephyr	V 12 cyl.	Sport	4,800	8,800	27,000
BROWN *(Great Britain, 1901–11)*						
1901		1 cyl.	Tonneau	1,800	3,600	9,200
1905		4 cyl.	Touring	2,200	4,400	12,000
1906		2 cyl.	Coupe	1,700	3,400	9,000
BROWNIE *(United States, 1916–17)*						
1916		4 cyl.	Touring	2,800	6,000	14,000
BRUNSWICK *(United States, 1916)*						
1916		4 cyl.	Touring	3,200	7,400	15,000
BRUSH *(United States, 1906–12)*						
1907	A	1 cyl.	Runabout	3,000	8,800	15,000
1908	A	1 cyl.	Runabout	3,500	7,000	11,000
1909	B	1 cyl.	Runabout	3,500	7,000	11,000
1911	E	1 cyl.	Runabout	4,000	9,000	16,000

Brush – 1911 "Runabout"

BRUTSCH *(Germany, 1951–57)*						
1951	3-Wheel	49cc	Open	2,000	3,700	9,300

YEAR	MODEL	ENGINE	BODY	F	G	E
B.S.A. *(Great Britain, 1907–26; 1933–36)*						
1922		V 2 cyl.	Coupe	2,900	4,800	12,000
1935	Light Six	6 cyl.	Coupe	3,000	6,000	13,000
B.S.A. *(Great Britain, 1929–40)*						
1929	3-Wheel	1 Litre		2,000	5,000	13,500
1935	Scout		Sport	3,100	6,400	13,500
1936	Sports		Roadster	4,200	9,900	18,500
BUCKINGHAM *(Australia, 1933)*						
1933		4 cyl.	Coupe	1,650	3,200	8,700
1933		4 cyl.	Sedan	1,650	3,100	8,400
BUCKLER *(Great Britain, 1947–62)*						
1947	Mark VI	1098cc	Coupe	2,200	4,400	9,000
1955	Mark X	2 Litre	Sport	2,400	4,800	9,500
BUFFALO *(United States, 1901–06)*						
1901		Electric	Touring	6,800	10,500	25,000
1904		Electric	Runabout	6,000	11,000	27,000
1904		Electric	Touring	6,800	10,500	26,000
BUGATTI *(Italy, 1909–56)*						
1910	Type 13	4 cyl. 1327cc	Sport	9,200	17,500	40,000
1913	Black Bess	4 cyl. 5 Litre	Sport	13,100	23,000	39,500
1919	Type 22/23	4 cyl.	Bresica	35,000	50,000	90,000
1922	Type 30	4 cyl. 2 Litre	Racing Saloon	14,200	31,250	45,000
1922	Type 30	4 cyl.	Touring	60,000	75,000	90,000
1922	Type 28	8 cyl. 3.1 Litre	Sport	25,750	51,500	91,200
1922	Type 29/30	8 cyl. 2.1 Litre	Sport	23,000	34,000	53,800
1923	Type 30	8 cyl. 2.1 Litre	Touring	13,100	27,750	60,000
1924	Type 33	8 cyl. 2.1 Litre	Touring	14,200	26,300	65,000
1924	Type 35	8 cyl. 2 Litre	4 Passenger Touring	13,100	23,750	60,000
1925	Type 30	8 cyl.	Sedan	12,000	24,000	53,800
1925	Type 23	8 cyl.	Sedan	1,000	21,350	42,800
1926	Type 38	8 cyl. 2 Litre	Touring	14,200	27,300	50,000
1926	Type 39-C	8 cyl. 1.5 Litre	Touring	30,000	40,000	70,000
1926	Type 39-D	8 cyl. 1.5 Litre	Touring	30,000	40,000	70,000
1927	Type 44	8 cyl. 3 Litre	Touring	70,000	90,000	125,000
1927	Type 43	8 cyl. 2.3 Litre	Roadster	75,000	100,000	150,000
1927	Type 35-C	8 cyl. 2 Litre	Convertible	75,000	100,000	150,000
1927	Type 38-A	8 cyl. 2 Litre	Touring	40,000	60,000	98,000
1927	Type 38-A	8 cyl. 2 Litre	Grand Sport	30,000	50,000	90,000
1927	Type 39-A	8 cyl. 1.5 Litre	Grand Prix	35,000	45,000	65,000
1928	Type 40	8 cyl. 2.3 Litre	Roadster	70,000	90,000	125,000
1928	Type 40	4 cyl. 1.5 Litre	Coupe	16,400	28,500	65,000

YEAR	MODEL	ENGINE	BODY	F	G	E
BUGATTI *(Italy, 1909–56) (continued)*						
1928	Type 44	8 cyl. 3 Litre	Touring	70,000	90,000	125,000
1928	Type 44	8 cyl. 3 Litre	Roadster	100,000	125,000	165,000
1928	Type 44	8 cyl. 3 Litre	Sport Speedster	90,000	135,000	175,000
1929	Type 46	8 cyl. 5.3 Litre	Touring	100,000	150,000	250,000
1929	Type 46-S	5.3 Litre (Supercharged)	Touring	50,000	75,000	95,000
1930	Type 35C	2 Litre	Grand Prix	150,000	200,000	300,000
1930	Type 46	5.3 Litre	Sedan	15,000	25,000	35,000
1930	Type 49	3.3 Litre	Touring	35,000	45,000	65,000
1930	Type 50	8 cyl. 5 Litre	Coupe	100,000	175,000	225,000

Bugatti – 1930 "Type 50 Sport Roadster"

1930	Type 40-A	4 cyl. 1.6 Litre	Touring	30,000	40,000	50,000
1931	Type 50	8 cyl. 3 Litre	Super Sport Roadster	75,000	100,000	175,000
1931	Type 40-A	4 cyl. 1.5 Litre	2 Passenger	20,000	30,000	50,000
1931	Type 40-A	4 cyl. 1.6 Litre	Touring	20,000	30,000	55,000
1931	Type 46-S	8 cyl. 5 Litre	Touring	75,000	125,000	200,000
1932	Type 46	8 cyl. 5 Litre	Sport Saloon Sedan	50,000	75,000	100,000
1932	Type 50-T	8 cyl. 4.9 Litre	Touring	100,000	150,000	225,000
1932	Type 53	8 cyl. 4.9 Litre	Touring	125,000	175,000	250,000
1932	Type 55	8 cyl. 2.3 Litre	2 Passenger Roadster	125,000	175,000	250,000

YEAR	MODEL	ENGINE	BODY	F	G	E
BUGATTI *(Italy, 1909–56) (continued)*						
1932	Type 50	8 cyl. 5 Litre	Coupe	100,000	150,000	225,000
1932	Type 57	8 cyl. 3 Litre	Touring	125,000	175,000	250,000
1934	Type 57	8 cyl. 3.3 Litre	Roadster	100,000	150,000	230,000
1934	Type 57	8 cyl. 3.3 Litre	Sport Sedan	40,000	50,000	85,000
1934	Type 57	8 cyl. 3.3 Litre	Cabriolet	50,000	75,000	150,000
1934	Type 57	8 cyl. 3.3 Litre	Sport Coupe	75,000	100,000	175,000
1934	Type 57-S	8 cyl. 3.3 Litre	Speedster	750,000	1000000	2000000
1935	Type 57	8 cyl. 3 Litre	Sedan Convertible	50,000	75,000	100,000
1935	Type 57 Ventoux	8 cyl. 3.3 Litre	Coupe	75,000	100,000	175,000
1935	Type 57-S	8 cyl. 3.3 Litre	Coupe	750,000	1000000	1750000
1936	Type 57-SC	8 cyl. 3.3 Litre	Sport Coupe	75,000	100,000	175,000
1936	Type 57-C	8 cyl. 3.3 Litre	Coupe	75,000	100,000	175,000
1936	Type 57-SC	8 cyl. 3.3 Litre	Roadster	75,000	100,000	200,000
1937	Type 57-S	8 cyl. 3.3 Litre	Atalante Coupe	750,000	1000000	1500000
1937	Type 57	8 cyl. 3.3 Litre	Speedster	100,000	150,000	250,000
1937	Type 44	8 cyl. 3.3 Litre	Speedster	75,000	100,000	150,000
1937	Electron	8 cyl. 3.3 Litre	Coupe	100,000	125,000	175,000
1938	Type 57-C	8 cyl. 3 Litre (Supercharged)	Touring	75,000	125,000	200,000
1939	Type 57	8 cyl. 3.3 Litre	Coupe	75,000	100,000	175,000
1939	Type 57	8 cyl. 3.3 Litre	Sport Sedan	30,000	40,000	75,000
1940	Type 57	8 cyl. 3.3 Litre	Sedan	25,000	35,000	60,000
1940	Type 57	8 cyl. 3.3 Litre	Cabriolet	75,000	100,000	150,000
1940	Type 57-C	8 cyl. 3.3 Litre	Grand Touring	100,000	125,000	200,000
1940	Type 57-C	8 cyl. 3.3 Litre	Grand Sport	500,000	750,000	1200000
1946	Type 101	8 cyl. 3.3 Litre	Convertible	20,000	35,000	50,000
1947	Type 101	8 cyl. 3.3 Litre	Convertible Coupe	30,000	40,000	65,000
1947	Type 101	8 cyl. 3.3 Litre	Close-Coupled Sedan	25,000	35,000	60,000
1948	Type 102	1.5 Litre	Sedan	12,000	20,000	35,000
1949	Type 101	8 cyl. 3.3 Litre	Convertible Coupe	50,000	60,000	80,000
1951	Type 101	8 cyl. 3.3 Litre	Convertible Coupe	55,000	65,000	85,000
1951	Type 101-C	8 cyl. 3.3 Litre	Roadster Convertible	60,000	75,000	95,000
1952	Type 101	8 cyl. 3.3 Litre	Convertible Coupe	30,000	40,000	75,000

YEAR	MODEL	ENGINE	BODY	F	G	E
BUGATTI (Italy, 1909–56) (continued)						
1952	Type 101-C	8 cyl. 3.3 Litre	Roadster	50,000	75,000	125,000
1956	2-Door	8 cyl. 3.3 Litre	Convertible	750,000	1500000	2225000
BUGATTI-GULINELLI (Italy, 1901–03)						
1901	Closed	4 cyl.	Coupe	5,500	9,750	22,500
BUICK (United States, 1903 to date)						
1904	Model B	2 cyl.	Touring		RARE	
1905	Model C	2 cyl.	Touring	7,000	10,200	24,200
1906	Model G	2 cyl.	Runabout	4,940	11,100	30,700
1906	Model F	2 cyl.	Touring	5,100	9,200	19,500
1907	Model F or G	4 cyl.	Runabout	5,500	9,450	24,000
1907	Model D or S	4 cyl.	Touring	7,000	14,000	21,000
1908	Model S	4 cyl.	Roadster	7,000	11,300	26,000
1908	Model F	2 cyl.	Touring	4,500	11,700	30,000
1909	Model F or G	2 cyl.	Touring	8,000	16,000	24,000
1909	Model F or G	2 cyl.	Roadster	8,500	17,000	25,500
1909	Model 10	4 cyl.	Roadster	3,525	6,770	15,200
1909	Model 17	4 cyl.	Touring	8,350	17,000	40,000
1910	Model 14	2 cyl.	Roadster	7,000	11,300	26,000
1910	Model 10	4 cyl.	Surrey	5,000	11,400	31,000
1910	Model 10	4 cyl.	Touring	3,525	6,770	15,200
1910	Model F	2 cyl.	Runabout	2,900	9,600	24,500
1910	Model 16 or 17	4 cyl.	Roadster	8,000	16,000	24,000
1911	Model 33	4 cyl.	Touring	4,450	7,500	12,500
1911	Model 33	4 cyl.	Roadster	4,650	7,250	12,375
1911	Model 21	4 cyl.	Touring	3,525	6,770	15,200
1911	Model 38	4 cyl.	Touring	7,000	10,200	24,200
1911	Model 38	4 cyl.	Roadster	7,000	11,300	26,000
1912	Model 35	4 cyl.	Touring	7,000	11,300	26,000
1912	Model 34	4 cyl.	Roadster	3,600	8,900	29,000
1912	Model 28 or 29	4 cyl.	Touring	6,000	9,550	14,550
1912	Model 28 or 29	4 cyl.	Roadster	6,550	10,000	15,000
1913	McLaughlin	4 cyl.	Touring	2,800	9,450	24,000
1914	Model 24	4 cyl.	Roadster	5,100	9,200	19,500
1914	B-25	4 cyl.	Touring	2,900	9,600	24,700
1914	B-37	4 cyl.	Touring	2,900	9,600	24,500
1914	B-55	6 cyl.	Touring	4,000	9,500	16,200
1915	C-55	6 cyl.	7 Passenger Touring	3,900	12,500	27,000

YEAR	MODEL	ENGINE	BODY	F	G	E
BUICK *(United States, 1903 to date) (continued)*						
1915	C-54	4 cyl.	Roadster	6,550	9,550	16,550

Buick – 1915 "C-54 Roadster"

1915	C-25	4 cyl.	Touring	6,000	9,550	14,550
1916	D-35	6 cyl.	Touring	4,500	10,900	26,600
1916	D-45	6 cyl.	Touring	4,500	6,575	13,000
1916	D-49	6 cyl.	Touring	4,500	10,900	26,600
1916	D-55	6 cyl.	Roadster	6,550	10,000	16,500
1916	D-45	6 cyl.	Sedan	4,000	9,800	16,500
1917	D-45	6 cyl.	Touring	4,300	7,000	13,575
1917	D-34	4 cyl.	Roadster	4,300	7,000	13,500
1917	D-34	4 cyl.	Touring	4,000	7,000	12,575
1917	D-44	6 cyl.	Roadster	4,300	7,500	13,500
1918	E-34 or E-35	4 cyl.	Touring	4,000	9,800	16,500
1918	E-34 or E-35	4 cyl.	Roadster	3,000	6,000	17,100
1918	G-47	6 cyl.	Sedan	4,000	7,000	13,000
1918	E-49	6 cyl.	7 Passenger Touring	4,000	7,000	13,000
1918	E-44	6 cyl.	Roadster	4,000	9,800	16,500
1919	H-45	6 cyl.	Touring	4,000	6,500	12,700
1919	H-44	6 cyl.	Roadster	4,000	6,575	13,000
1919	H-46 or H-50	6 cyl.	Sedan	4,450	7,500	12,500
1919	H-46 or H-50	6 cyl.	Coupe	4,000	9,500	16,200
1919	H-46 or H-50	6 cyl.	7 Passenger Sedan	4,450	7,500	12,500

YEAR	MODEL	ENGINE	BODY	F	G	E
BUICK *(United States, 1903 to date) (continued)*						
1920	K-50	6 cyl.	Touring	4,000	6,575	13,000
1920	K-45	6 cyl.	Touring	4,000	6,575	13,000
1920	K-46	6 cyl.	Coupe	3,400	5,000	11,500
1920	K-47	6 cyl.	Sedan	3,400	5,000	11,500
1920	K-44	6 cyl.	Roadster	4,000	9,800	16,500
1921	21-49	6 cyl.	7 Passenger Touring	4,300	7,500	13,500
1921	21-44	6 cyl.	Roadster	3,900	10,000	25,200
1921	21-46	6 cyl.	Coupe	3,400	9,200	14,500
1921		6 cyl.	Sedan	2,300	3,600	9,000
1922	40	6 cyl.	Sport Roadster	5,000	11,400	28,500
1922	22-36	4 cyl.	4 Passenger Opera Coupe	3,700	8,500	15,000
1922	30	4 cyl.	Touring	3,525	6,770	15,200
1922	30	4 cyl.	Roadster	4,000	9,500	16,200
1922	40	6 cyl.	Touring	5,100	9,200	19,500
1922	40	6 cyl.	Roadster	5,500	9,800	20,500
1922	40	6 cyl.	Sedan	2,300	3,600	9,000
1922	40	6 cyl.	Coupe	2,300	3,600	9,000
1923	23-44	4 cyl.	Roadster	3,900	10,000	28,000
1923	23-54	6 cyl.	Sport Touring	5,000	11,400	28,500
1923	23-44	6 cyl.	Sport Roadster	4,200	11,700	24,500
1923	23-35	4 cyl.	Touring	3,150	6,900	14,500
1923	23-36	4 cyl.	3 Passenger Coupe	2,800	6,700	12,900
1923	40	6 cyl.	Touring	3,000	6,000	17,100
1923	40	6 cyl.	Roadster	4,700	9,400	18,000
1923	40	6 cyl.	Sedan	1,400	3,300	6,300
1923	40	6 cyl.	Coupe	1,800	4,000	7,300
1924	Master	6 cyl.	Touring	4,700	13,500	29,500
1924	24-35	4 cyl.	Touring	3,400	7,200	16,000
1924	24-33	4 cyl.	Coupe	2,500	4,500	13,500
1924	24-48	6 cyl.	4 Passenger Coupe	2,500	5,300	13,900
1924	50	6 cyl.	Sport Touring	4,700	10,000	29,500
1924	50	6 cyl.	Sport Roadster	5,300	14,000	30,500
1924	50	6 cyl.	Cabriolet	5,100	9,200	19,500

YEAR	MODEL	ENGINE	BODY	F	G	E
BUICK *(United States, 1903 to date) (continued)*						
1924	50	6 cyl.	Brougham Sedan	2,300	3,600	9,000
1925	Standard 20	6 cyl.	Coach	3,900	7,100	22,000
1925	Standard 20	6 cyl.	Sedan	3,200	6,900	14,800
1925	Standard 20	6 cyl.	Touring	4,500	8,300	20,800
1925	Standard 20	6 cyl.	Coupe	2,900	6,700	14,500
1925	Master 50	6 cyl.	Sport Touring	5,100	9,200	19,500
1925	Master 50	6 cyl.	Sport Roadster	5,500	9,900	20,500
1925	Master 50	6 cyl.	Cabriolet	4,700	9,400	18,000
1925	Master 50	6 cyl.	Brougham Sedan	2,600	5,600	11,900
1925	Master 50	6 cyl.	Limousine	2,600	5,600	11,900
1926	Standard	6 cyl.	Touring	3,700	6,700	15,200
1926	Standard	6 cyl.	Roadster	4,000	9,500	16,200
1926	Standard	6 cyl.	Sedan	2,300	3,600	9,000
1926	Standard	6 cyl.	Coupe	2,500	3,900	10,000
1926	Master	6 cyl.	Sedan	3,000	7,500	15,700
1926	Master	6 cyl.	Sedan	3,400	7,200	16,500
1926	Master	6 cyl.	Sport Roadster	5,700	13,000	30,500
1926	Master	6 cyl.	Coupe	4,000	8,000	20,200
1926	Master	6 cyl.	Touring	4,800	11,400	28,500
1927	Master 6	6 cyl.	Roadster	5,300	10,000	29,000
1927	27-47	6 cyl.	Sedan	3,100	7,200	16,500
1927	27-54-C	6 cyl.	Convertible Coupe	4,700	10,000	28,500
1927	27-54	6 cyl.	Sport Roadster	5,300	12,000	22,000
1927	128	6 cyl.	Sport Touring	5,200	11,000	21,000
1927	128	6 cyl.	Brougham	2,300	3,600	9,000
1928	28-24	6 cyl.	Roadster	5,200	10,000	27,500
1928	28-26S	6 cyl.	Club Coupe	3,600	7,500	15,500
1928	28-47	6 cyl.	Club Sedan	3,600	7,500	15,200
1928	28-26	6 cyl.	Coupe	4,000	6,700	12,200
1928	28-54	6 cyl.	Sport Roadster	4,500	13,500	30,600
1929	Big Six	6 cyl	Cabriolet	4,700	13,200	30,700
1929	Big Six	6 cyl.	Coupe	3,800	8,100	13,500
1929	Standard	6 cyl.	2 Door Sedan	3,700	7,000	13,500

YEAR	MODEL	ENGINE	BODY	F	G	E
BUICK *(United States, 1903 to date) (continued)*						
1929	Master Six	6 cyl.	7 Passenger Sedan	3,700	7,000	13,500
1929	Standard	6 cyl.	Roadster	4,500	11,700	29,500
1929	Big Six	6 cyl.	Phaeton	5,000	15,000	30,000
1929	Master Six	6 cyl.	Roadster	5,700	14,000	32,000
1929	129	6 cyl.	Limousine	2,600	5,600	11,900
1930	Marquette	6 cyl.	2 Door Sedan	3,600	7,100	13,000
1930	30-60	6 cyl.	Sedan	2,800	5,600	13,000
1930	30-64	6 cyl.	R S Coupe	3,400	6,700	14,000
1930	30-64	6 cyl.	Sport Roadster	5,600	16,000	32,000
1930	60-69	6 cyl.	7 Passenger Phaeton	6,100	16,000	38,000
1930	30-46S	6 cyl.	Sport Coupe	3,200	6,400	13,000
1930	40	6 cyl.	Roadster	7,000	11,300	26,000
1930	40	6 cyl.	Coupe 2 styles	3,300	6,000	13,000
1930	40	6 cyl.	Phaeton	7,400	11,700	27,100
1931	94	8 cyl.	Roadster	8,900	23,000	42,000
1931	8-50	8 cyl.	Sedan	3,400	6,700	13,000
1931	67	8 cyl.	Sedan	3,600	7,200	16,000
1931	56-C	8 cyl.	Rumble Seat Coupe	4,700	9,400	18,000
1931	8-50	8 cyl.	2 Door Sedan	3,400	6,700	13,000
1931	56-C	8 cyl.	Cabriolet	4,200	10,500	25,000
1931	90	8 cyl.	7 Passenger Sedan	3,400	6,700	18,000
1931	80	8 cyl.	Sedan	2,575	6,200	15,200
1931	90-L	8 cyl.	Limousine	4,700	12,000	28,000
1932	56-C	8 cyl.	Convertible Coupe	5,600	11,000	32,000
1932	90	8 cyl.	Phaeton	6,700	14,000	34,000
1932	67	8 cyl.	Sport Sedan	3,500	7,500	18,000
1932	91	8 cyl.	Sedan	3,400	7,200	17,000
1932	96	8 cyl.	Victoria	3,000	6,900	17,000
1932	80	8 cyl.	Victoria Coupe	5,100	9,200	19,500
1932	87	8 cyl.	Sedan	3,000	6,800	16,000
1932	96-S	8 cyl.	Rumble Seat Coupe	3,600	8,600	19,000
1932	96-C	8 cyl.	Cabriolet	4,700	12,000	23,000
1933	50	8 cyl.	Sedan	2,100	4,100	10,100
1933	98	8 cyl.	Victoria	4,200	8,300	16,000

YEAR	MODEL	ENGINE	BODY	F	G	E
BUICK	_(United States, 1903 to date) (continued)_					
1933	68-C	8 cyl.	Phaeton	5,500	13,000	29,000
1933	66-C	8 cyl.	Cabriolet	5,000	11,000	20,000
1933	66-S	8 cyl.	Coupe	4,400	7,800	16,000
1933	90	8 cyl.	7 Passenger Sedan	3,000	6,000	18,000
1933	80	8 cyl.	Sport Coupe	3,300	6,000	13,000
1933	80	8 cyl.	Sedan	2,600	5,600	11,900
1933	80	8 cyl.	Phaeton	5,500	13,000	29,000
1934	40	8 cyl.	2 Door Sedan	2,500	5,000	13,000
1934	50	8 cyl.	Sedan	3,000	5,000	12,000
1934	98-C	8 cyl.	Convertible Sedan	7,800	19,000	42,500
1934	46	8 cyl.	2 Passenger Coupe	2,700	6,400	13,000
1934	50	8 cyl.	Victoria Coupe	2,000	3,000	11,000
1934	60	8 cyl.	Sedan	2,600	5,600	11,900
1934	60	8 cyl.	Sport Coupe	3,300	6,000	13,000
1934	60	8 cyl.	Phaeton	5,500	13,000	29,000
1934	60	8 cyl.	Victoria	2,600	5,600	11,900
1934	90	8 cyl.	Sedan	3,000	6,000	13,000
1935	98-C	8 cyl.	Convertible Sedan	8,300	20,000	45,000
1935	46	8 cyl.	Coupe	2,700	6,400	13,000
1935	50	8 cyl.	Sedan	2,500	4,500	10,000
1935	50	8 cyl.	Coupe 2 styles	2,500	4,500	10,000
1935	50	8 cyl.	Victoria	2,600	5,600	11,900
1935	66-C	8 cyl.	Cabriolet	3,700	8,900	16,000
1935	96-C	8 cyl.	Convertible Coupe	7,800	18,000	38,000
1935	66	8 cyl.	Sport Coupe Rumble Seat	3,900	8,200	15,500
1936	Special	8 cyl.	Sport Coupe	4,200	7,200	14,000
1936	Century	8 cyl.	Convertible Coupe	6,200	7,700	27,000
1936	Special	8 cyl.	Convertible	7,200	13,000	30,000
1936	Limited	8 cyl.	Sedan	3,100	6,000	13,000
1936	Century	8 cyl.	4 Door Sedan	2,100	4,400	10,200
1936	Century	8 cyl.	4 Door Convertible	4,100	8,000	21,000
1936	Century	8 cyl.	Opera Coupe	2,300	5,000	11,500

YEAR	MODEL	ENGINE	BODY	F	G	E
BUICK *(United States, 1903 to date) (continued)*						
1936	Roadmaster	8 cyl.	Convertible Sedan	2,600	5,600	11,900
1936	Roadmaster	8 cyl.	Phaeton	5,100	9,200	19,500
1937	Limited	8 cyl.	Limousine	2,500	4,200	12,600
1937	Century	8 cyl.	Sedan	1,500	4,200	10,500
1937	Special	8 cyl.	Convertible Sedan	4,500	8,500	24,500
1937	Roadmaster	8 cyl.	Convertible Sedan	3,000	5,300	12,000
1937	Roadmaster	8 cyl.	Sedan	2,000	4,300	10,575
1937	Century	8 cyl.	Convertible Sedan	4,800	7,000	15,000
1937	Century	8 cyl.	Convertible Coupe	4,600	7,000	16,500
1937	Special	8 cyl.	2 Door Sedan	1,500	3,300	10,000
1938	Roadmaster	8 cyl.	Sedan	1,575	3,250	10,500
1938	Roadmaster	8 cyl.	Convertible Sedan	4,000	10,000	15,000
1938	Special	8 cyl.	Sedan	1,500	3,250	9,500

Buick – 1938 "Special Coupe"

1938	Century	8 cyl.	Convertible Sedan	5,000	10,000	15,000
1938	Century	8 cyl.	Sedan	1,600	4,000	10,000

YEAR	MODEL	ENGINE	BODY	F	G	E
BUICK (United States, 1903 to date) (continued)						
1938	Special	8 cyl.	Convertible Coupe	4,300	7,000	16,000
1938	Special	8 cyl.	2 Passenger Coupe	2,200	4,500	7,000
1939	Century	8 cyl.	Sedan	2,500	6,000	9,500
1939	Century	8 cyl.	Convertible Coupe	5,000	7,000	13,000
1939	Century	8 cyl.	Club Coupe	3,000	5,000	10,000
1939	Special	8 cyl.	Sedan	1,400	2,650	9,000

Buick – 1939 "Special"

YEAR	MODEL	ENGINE	BODY	F	G	E
1939	Special	8 cyl.	Convertible Phaeton	5,000	8,000	16,500
1939	Roadmaster	8 cyl.	Sedan 2 styles	3,300	6,000	13,000
1939	Roadmaster	8 cyl.	Phaeton 2 styles	4,500	11,700	30,000
1940	Super	8 cyl.	Coupe	2,200	4,200	10,200
1940	Super	8 cyl.	Convertible Coupe	3,500	7,000	10,000
1940	Super	8 cyl.	Station Wagon	3,100	6,100	22,100
1940	Super	8 cyl.	Sedan	1,200	1,700	10,000
1940	Special	8 cyl.	Coupe	2,000	4,000	8,000
1940	Special	8 cyl.	Sedan Dyna Flash	2,600	5,600	11,900
1940	Special	8 cyl.	Phaeton	4,500	11,700	30,000
1940	Century	8 cyl.	Convertible	5,575	10,500	28,500

YEAR	MODEL	ENGINE	BODY	F	G	E
BUICK *(United States, 1903 to date) (continued)*						
1940	Century	8 cyl.	Sedan	3,300	6,000	13,000
1940	Century	8 cyl.	Coupe			
			2 styles	4,000	9,500	16,200
1940	Century	8 cyl.	Phaeton	8,300	17,000	32,000
1940	Limited	8 cyl.	Convertible			
			Sedan	6,700	18,900	45,500
1940	Limited	8 cyl.	6 Passenger	2,900	6,000	13,000
1941	Limited		Formal			
	(90L)	8 cyl.	Limousine	5,000	9,400	20,000
1941	Limited (91)	8 cyl.	Formal Sedan	2,800	6,000	12,500
1941	Limited	8 cyl.	Sedan			
			2 styles	4,000	9,200	16,200
1941	Roadmaster	8 cyl.	Convertible			
			Sedan	8,300	17,000	32,000
1941	Special	8 cyl.	Convertible			
			Coupe	3,300	6,000	13,000
1941	Special	8 cyl.	Sedan	1,200	3,200	8,600
1941	Super	8 cyl.	Sedan	1,800	4,100	11,000

Buick – 1941 "Super 8 Sedan"

1941	Super	8 cyl.	Coupe	3,300	6,000	13,000
1941	Super	8 cyl.	Phaeton	3,600	8,900	29,000
1941	Roadmaster	8 cyl.	Sedan	2,400	5,200	13,000
1941	Special					
	(44-S)	8 cyl.	Coupe	2,300	6,200	13,000
1942	Roadmaster	8 cyl.	Sedan	2,300	6,200	13,000
1942	Special	8 cyl.	Sedan	2,300	4,700	11,100

YEAR	MODEL	ENGINE	BODY	F	G	E
BUICK *(United States, 1903 to date) (continued)*						
1942	Roadmaster	8 cyl.	Convertible	5,100	13,000	31,800
1942	Roadmaster	8 cyl.	Sedanet	2,500	4,500	11,400
1942	Super	8 cyl.	Sedan	2,800	5,900	12,200
1942	Super	8 cyl.	Convertible	5,100	9,200	19,500
Postwar Models						
1946	Super	8 cyl.	Convertible	10,000	15,000	30,000
1946	Roadmaster	8 cyl.	Convertible	15,000	20,000	35,000
1946	Roadmaster	8 cyl.	Sedanet	4,000	8,000	15,000
1946	Super	8 cyl.	2 Door Sedan	4,000	7,000	12,000
1946	Special	8 cyl.	Sedan 2 styles	4,000	7,000	12,000
1947	Super	8 cyl.	Convertible	9,000	15,000	30,000
1947	Roadmaster	8 cyl.	Sedanet	6,000	9,000	17,000
1947	Roadmaster	8 cyl.	Convertible	15,000	20,000	35,000
1947	Special	8 cyl.	2 Door Sedan	4,000	6,000	12,000
1948	Roadmaster	8 cyl.	Convertible	10,000	20,000	35,000
1948	Roadmaster	8 cyl.	Sedan	7,000	10,000	16,000
1948	Super	8 cyl.	Convertible	10,000	20,000	30,000
1948	Roadmaster	8 cyl.	Station Wagon	6,000	15,000	28,000
1949	Super	8 cyl.	Sedanet	4,000	6,000	14,000
1949	Roadmaster	8 cyl.	Hardtop Coupe	4,000	12,000	20,000
1949	Roadmaster	8 cyl.	Convertible Coupe	10,000	20,000	35,000
1949	Super	8 cyl.	Convertible	10,000	20,000	30,000
1949	Super	8 cyl.	Estate Wagon	10,000	17,000	25,000
1949	Special	8 cyl.	Sedan	3,000	6,000	12,000

Buick – 1951 "Roadmaster Riviera"

YEAR	MODEL	ENGINE	BODY	F	G	E
BUICK *(United States, 1903 to date) (continued)*						
1950	Special	8 cyl.	Sedan			
			Fastback	3,000	5,000	10,000
1950	Super	8 cyl.	Convertible	8,000	15,000	25,000
1950	Roadmaster	8 cyl.	Hardtop	4,000	8,000	18,000
1950	Roadmaster	8 cyl.	Convertible	6,000	12,000	27,000
1950	Roadmaster	8 cyl.	Station			
			Wagon	6,000	12,000	26,000
1951	Super	8 cyl.	Convertible	7,000	14,000	25,000
1951	Roadmaster	8 cyl.	Sedan	2,000	5,000	10,000
1951	Roadmaster	8 cyl.	Convertible	6,000	12,000	22,000
1951	Roadmaster	8 cyl.	Station			
			Wagon	5,000	14,000	25,000
1952	Special	8 cyl.	Sedan	1,000	4,000	8,000
1952	Special	8 cyl.	Coupe	2,000	4,000	8,000
1952	Super	8 cyl.	Convertible	5,000	10,000	20,000
1952	Super	8 cyl.	Hardtop	3,000	7,000	15,000
1952	Roadmaster	8 cyl.	Hardtop	4,000	8,000	17,000
1952	Roadmaster	8 cyl.	Convertible	4,000	10,000	22,000
1952	Roadmaster	8 cyl.	Station			
			Wagon	5,000	12,000	25,000
1953	Special	8 cyl.	Hardtop	3,000	6,000	12,000
1953	Super	8 cyl.	Sedan	2,000	4,000	8,000
1953	Super	8 cyl.	Hardtop	2,000	6,000	13,000
1953	Roadmaster	8 cyl.	Hardtop	3,000	9,000	18,000
1953	Roadmaster	8 cyl.	Convertible	4,000	12,000	25,000

Buick – 1954 "Skylark"

YEAR	MODEL	ENGINE	BODY	F	G	E
BUICK (United States, 1903 to date) (continued)						
1954	Special	8 cyl.	Sedan	1,000	3,000	7,000
1954	Skylark	8 cyl.	Convertible	7,000	20,000	45,000
1954	Super	8 cyl.	Sedan	1,000	4,000	8,000
1954	Century	8 cyl.	Convertible	5,000	15,000	30,000
1954	Century	8 cyl.	Station Wagon	2,000	4,000	10,000
1954	Century	8 cyl.	Coupe	2,000	5,000	13,000
1954	Roadmaster	8 cyl.	Sedan	1,000	4,000	9,000
1954	Roadmaster	8 cyl.	Convertible	6,000	15,000	30,000
1954	Roadmaster	8 cyl.	Coupe	3,000	8,000	17,000
1955	Special	8 cyl.	Convertible	5,000	12,000	25,000
1955	Special	8 cyl.	4 Door Hardtop	2,000	4,000	10,000
1955	Century	8 cyl.	Convertible	6,000	17,000	35,000

Buick – 1955 "Century"

YEAR	MODEL	ENGINE	BODY	F	G	E
1955	Century	8 cyl.	Sedan	1,000	3,000	6,000
1955	Century	8 cyl.	4 Door Hardtop	1,000	4,000	10,000
1955	Century	8 cyl.	Station Wagon	2,000	4,000	9,000
1955	Super	8 cyl.	Sedan	1,000	3,000	7,000
1955	Super	8 cyl.	Convertible	5,000	15,000	35,000
1955	Super	8 cyl.	Coupe	3,000	8,000	18,000
1955	Roadmaster	8 cyl.	Hardtop	3,000	8,000	18,000
1955	Roadmaster	8 cyl.	Convertible	6,000	15,000	35,000

YEAR	MODEL	ENGINE	BODY	F	G	E
BUICK	*(United States, 1903 to date)*	*(continued)*				
1956	Special	8 cyl.	4 Door Hardtop	3,000	5,000	11,000
1956	Special	8 cyl.	Convertible	7,000	15,000	30,000
1956	Century	8 cyl.	Sedan	1,000	3,000	7,000
1956	Century	8 cyl.	Convertible	5,000	15,000	35,000
1956	Super	8 cyl.	4 Door Hardtop	2,000	6,000	13,000
1956	Roadmaster	8 cyl.	Hardtop	3,000	7,000	13,000
1956	Roadmaster	8 cyl.	Convertible	7,000	15,000	35,000
1957	Special	8 cyl.	Hardtop	4,000	6,000	17,000
1957	Special	8 cyl.	Convertible	6,000	15,000	30,000
1957	Century	8 cyl.	4 Door Hardtop	2,000	5,000	11,000
1957	Century	8 cyl.	Callabero Station Wagon	3,000	8,000	18,000
1957	Super	8 cyl.	Convertible	6,000	15,000	32,000
1957	Super	8 cyl.	Sedan	3,000	5,000	12,000
1957	Super	8 cyl.	Coupe	4,000	10,000	20,000
1957	Roadmaster	8 cyl.	2 Door Hardtop	3,000	10,000	22,000
1957	Roadmaster	8 cyl.	Convertible	6,000	15,000	35,000
1958	Special	8 cyl.	Sedan	1,000	2,000	6,000
1958	Century	8 cyl.	4 Door Hardtop	2,000	5,000	11,000
1958	Century	8 cyl.	Station Wagon	2,000	6,000	15,000
1958	Century	8 cyl.	Convertible	5,000	10,000	22,000
1958	Century	8 cyl.	Coupe	3,000	7,000	15,000
1958	Super	8 cyl.	4 Door Hardtop	1,000	3,000	8,000
1958	Roadmaster	8 cyl.	4 Door Hardtop	2,000	4,000	9,000
1958	Roadmaster	8 cyl.	Convertible	5,000	12,000	25,000
1958	Roadmaster	8 cyl.	Coupe	2,000	6,000	17,000
1958	Limited	8 cyl.	Hardtop Coupe	3,000	7,000	18,000
1958	Limited	8 cyl.	4 Door Hardtop	2,000	6,000	14,000
1958	Limited	8 cyl.	Convertible	6,000	15,000	37,000
1959	LeSabre	8 cyl.	4 Door Hardtop	1,000	2,000	6,000
1959	Invicta	8 cyl.	Convertible	4,000	10,000	22,000

YEAR	MODEL	ENGINE	BODY	F	G	E
BUICK (United States, 1903 to date) (continued)						
1959	Electra	8 cyl.	4 Door Hardtop	1,000	3,000	8,000
1959	Electra	8 cyl.	2 Door Hardtop	2,000	4,000	10,000
1959	Electra 225	8 cyl.	Sedan	1,000	3,000	8,000
1959	Electra 225	8 cyl.	4 Door Hardtop	1,000	4,000	9,000
1959	Electra 225	8 cyl.	Convertible	4,000	12,000	25,000
1960	LeSabre	8 cyl.	Station Wagon	1,000	2,000	5,000
1960	LeSabre	8 cyl.	Convertible	5,000	10,000	20,000
1960	Invicta	8 cyl.	Sedan	1,000	3,000	5,000
1960	Invicta	8 cyl.	2 or 4 Door Hardtop	2,000	4,000	8,000
1960	Invicta	8 cyl.	Station Wagon	1,000	2,000	5,000
1960	Invicta	8 cyl.	Convertible	5,000	12,000	25,000
1960	Electra 225	8 cyl.	Convertible	5,000	12,000	25,000

Buick – 1960 "Electra 225 Convertible"

YEAR	MODEL	ENGINE	BODY	F	G	E
1961	Special	8 cyl.	Sedan	1,000	2,000	5,000
1961	Special	8 cyl.	Coupe	2,000	3,000	6,000
1961	Special	8 cyl.	Station Wagon	1,000	2,000	5,000
1961	Deluxe	8 cyl.	Sedan	1,000	2,000	5,000
1961	Deluxe	8 cyl.	Coupe (Skylark)	2,000	3,000	6,000
1961	LeSabre	8 cyl.	Sedan 2 styles	1,100	2,100	6,000

YEAR	MODEL	ENGINE	BODY	F	G	E
BUICK	*(United States, 1903 to date) (continued)*					
1961	LeSabre	8 cyl.	Hardtop			
			2 styles	1,400	3,300	7,000
1961	Invicta	8 cyl.	Hardtop			
			2 styles	1,200	2,400	8,000
1961	Invicta	8 cyl.	Convertible	2,800	4,100	19,000
1961	Electra	8 cyl.	Sedan	1,200	2,400	6,000
1961	Electra	8 cyl.	Hardtop			
			2 styles	1,200	3,100	8,000
1961	Electra	8 cyl.	Sedan	1,200	2,400	7,000
1961	Electra 225	8 cyl.	Convertible	1,400	3,200	20,000
1962	Wildcat	8 cyl.	Hardtop	1,200	2,800	10,000
1962	Invicta	8 cyl.	Convertible	1,300	3,300	20,000
1962	Electra 225	8 cyl.	2 Door			
			Hardtop	1,200	2,900	9,000
1962	Electra 225	8 cyl.	Convertible	1,650	2,650	20,000
1962	Special	6 cyl.	Convertible	1,000	2,000	30,000
1962	Skylark	8 cyl.	Hardtop	1,200	2,500	6,000
1963	Deluxe	6 cyl.	Sedan	1,100	2,100	5,000
1963	Deluxe	8 cyl.	Sedan	1,200	2,400	5,500
1963	LeSabre	8 cyl.	Sedan			
			2 styles	1,100	2,100	5,000
1963	LeSabre	8 cyl.	2 Door			
			Hardtop	1,200	2,400	6,000
1963	Skylark	8 cyl.	Hardtop	1,400	2,500	7,000
1963	Skylark	8 cyl.	Convertible	1,200	3,100	10,000
1963	Special	6 cyl.	Sedan	1,100	2,100	5,000
1963	Special	8 cyl.	Coupe	1,100	2,100	5,500
1963	Wildcat	8 cyl.	Coupe	1,300	3,300	8,000
1963	Wildcat	8 cyl.	4 Door			
			Hardtop	1,200	2,400	7,000
1963	Wildcat	8 cyl.	Convertible	1,400	3,000	17,000
1963	Riviera	8 cyl.	Hardtop	1,200	2,800	12,000
1964	Skylark	8 cyl.	Convertible	1,000	2,000	12,000
1964	LeSabre	8 cyl.	Convertible	1,300	4,200	15,000
1964	Electra 225	8 cyl	2 Door			
			Hardtop	1,200	2,600	9,000
1964	Electra 225	8 cyl.	Convertible	1,300	3,200	17,000
1964	Riviera	8 cyl.	Hardtop	1,200	3,100	12,000
1965	Wildcat	8 cyl.	Convertible	1,400	3,100	12,000
1965	Electra 225	8 cyl.	Convertible	1,500	3,200	12,000
1965	Riviera GS	8 cyl.	Hardtop	1,300	3,100	12,000
1965	Skylark GS	8 cyl.	Convertible	1,200	3,400	12,000
1966	Wildcat	8 cyl.	Convertible	1,200	3,200	13,000

YEAR	MODEL	ENGINE	BODY	F	G	E
BUICK	*(United States, 1903 to date) (continued)*					
1966	Electra 225	8 cyl.	Convertible	1,200	2,800	15,000
1967	Riviera GS	8 cyl.	Coupe	1,200	2,800	9,000
1967	GS 400	8 cyl.	Convertible	1,200	2,800	13,000
1968	Electra 225	8 cyl.	Convertible	1,200	2,700	15,000
1968	Wildcat	8 cyl.	Convertible	1,200	2,700	13,000
1969	Deluxe	6 cyl.	Sedan 2 styles	900	1,700	3,500
1969	Skylark	6 cyl.	Sedan	900	1,700	3,500
1969	Skylark	8 cyl.	2 Door Hardtop	900	1,700	4,500
1969	GS	8 cyl.	2 Door Hardtop	900	1,700	11,000
1969	LeSabre	8 cyl.	Hardtop 2 styles	900	1,700	4,500
1969	Wildcat	8 cyl.	Hardtop 2 styles	900	1,700	5,000
1969	Electra 225	8 cyl.	Sedan	900	1,700	4,000
1969	Electra	8 cyl.	2 Door Hardtop	900	1,700	6,000
1969	Riviera GS	8 cyl.	Coupe	1,200	2,500	8,000
1969	Riviera	8 cyl.	Hardtop	1,200	2,500	7,000
1970	Wildcat	8 cyl.	Convertible	1,200	3,100	12,000
1970	Electra 225	8 cyl.	Convertible	900	1,700	15,000
1970	GSX	8 cyl.	Coupe	1,400	1,900	15,000
1972	Skylark	8 cyl.	Convertible	1,200	1,600	15,000
BURG	*(United States, 1910–13)*					
1910	K	4 cyl.	Touring	2,400	8,000	16,500
1910	L	4 cyl.	Roadster	2,800	8,600	22,000
BUSH	*(United States, 1916–24)*					
1916	4-18	6 cyl. (Continental)	Touring	4,000	12,000	20,000
1920	6	4 cyl. (Lycoming)	Speedster	6,000	15,000	25,000

YEAR	MODEL	ENGINE	BODY	F	G	E

C

CADILLAC *(United States, 1903 to date)*

YEAR	MODEL	ENGINE	BODY	F	G	E
1903	A	1 cyl.	Runabout	8,000	15,000	30,000
1903	A	1 cyl.	Touring	8,000	15,000	30,000
1904	A	1 cyl.	Runabout	3,350	9,000	26,000
1905	B	1 cyl.	Runabout	3,350	9,000	26,000

Cadillac – 1905 "Roadster"

YEAR	MODEL	ENGINE	BODY	F	G	E
1906	K	1 cyl.	Runabout	3,350	9,000	26,000
1906	H	4 cyl.	Runabout	3,350	9,000	26,000
1906	L	4 cyl.	7 Passenger Touring	4,000	12,000	27,000
1907	G	4 cyl.	Roadster	3,350	9,000	26,000
1907	K	1 cyl.	Roadster	4,000	9,500	26,100
1907	M	1 cyl.	Roadster	4,000	10,000	21,000
1909	30	4 cyl.	Touring	4,000	6,000	21,000
1909	30	4 cyl.	Roadster	4,000	9,500	26,100
1910	30	4 cyl.	Roadster	6,000	12,000	28,000
1910	30	4 cyl.	Limousine	4,300	11,200	28,600

YEAR	MODEL	ENGINE	BODY	F	G	E
CADILLAC	*(United States, 1903 to date) (continued)*					
1910	30	4 cyl.	Touring	5,240	12,000	31,140
1911	30	4 cyl.	Touring	4,000	5,800	20,500
1911	30	4 cyl.	Roadster	4,100	6,100	21,500
1912	30	4 cyl.	Opera Coupe	3,450	9,200	15,700
1912	30	4 cyl.	Torpedo Roadster	4,600	9,200	31,300
1912	30	4 cyl.	Limousine	3,500	5,000	18,000
1912	30	4 cyl.	Phaeton	4,600	8,500	25,000
1913	30	4 cyl.	5 Passenger Touring	4,400	6,600	24,000
1913	30	4 cyl.	6 Passenger Touring	4,400	6,600	24,000
1913	30	4 cyl.	Roadster	4,300	6,500	22,100
1913	30	4 cyl.	Coupe	3,500	5,000	18,000
1913	30	4 cyl.	Phaeton	4,400	6,600	24,000
1914	30	4 cyl.	Touring	4,200	7,000	29,300
1914	30	4 cyl.	7 Passenger Touring	4,100	6,100	21,500
1914	30	4 cyl.	Roadster	4,100	6,100	21,500
1914	30	4 cyl.	Coupe	3,750	5,400	19,500
1914	30	4 cyl.	Phaeton	4,000	5,900	19,900
1915	51	V 8 cyl.	7 Passenger Touring	4,100	6,100	21,500
1915	51	V 8 cyl.	Sport Phaeton	5,750	12,000	34,500
1915	51	V 8 cyl.	Roadster	4,600	8,500	25,000
1915	51	V 8 cyl.	Coupe	3,700	5,000	18,000
1915	51	V 8 cyl.	Touring	4,500	11,300	29,300
1916	53	V 8 cyl.	Touring	4,500	11,300	29,300
1916	53	V 8 cyl.	Roadster	4,400	6,800	24,000
1916	53	V 8 cyl.	Coupe	3,700	5,000	18,000
1916	53	V 8 cyl.	Brougham	3,700	5,000	18,000
1916	53	V 8 cyl.	Limousine	3,800	8,000	21,500
1917	55	V 8 cyl.	Touring	4,200	8,900	23,000
1917	55	V 8 cyl.	Roadster	4,100	6,100	21,500
1917	55	V 8 cyl.	Coupe	3,750	5,000	19,500
1917	55	V 8 cyl.	Brougham	3,950	8,000	17,800
1917	55	V 8 cyl.	Victoria	3,750	7,700	16,200
1918	57	V 8 cyl.	7 Passenger Touring	4,200	8,900	23,000
1918	57	V 8 cyl.	Roadster	4,400	6,600	24,000
1918	57	V 8 cyl.	Brougham	3,450	9,200	15,700
1919	57	V 8 cyl.	Touring	3,700	5,000	18,000

YEAR	MODEL	ENGINE	BODY	F	G	E
CADILLAC *(United States, 1903 to date) (continued)*						
1919	57	V 8 cyl.	Roadster	4,400	6,600	24,000
1919	57	V 8 cyl.	Phaeton	4,800	7,200	27,000
1919	57	V 8 cyl.	Brougham	3,450	9,200	15,700
1920	59	V 8 cyl.	7 Passenger Touring	3,700	7,900	22,000
1920	59	V 8 cyl.	Roadster	3,750	5,400	19,500
1920	59	V 8 cyl.	Touring	3,500	5,000	18,000
1921	59	V 8 cyl.	7 Passenger Touring	3,900	8,200	22,000
1921	59	V 8 cyl.	Roadster	4,100	6,100	21,500
1921	59	V 8 cyl.	Sedan	2,300	4,800	14,700
1921	59	V 8 cyl.	Coupe	3,000	5,200	15,200
1921	59	V 8 cyl.	Victoria	3,450	9,200	15,700
1922	61	V 8 cyl.	7 Passenger Phaeton	4,600	8,500	25,000
1922	61	V 8 cyl.	Limousine	3,700	8,300	23,000
1922	61	V 8 cyl.	7 Passenger Touring	4,100	8,700	26,000
1922	61	V 8 cyl.	Club Sedan	3,700	5,600	19,900
1922	61	V 8 cyl.	Touring	3,500	5,000	18,000
1922	61	V 8 cyl.	Roadster	3,800	5,400	18,600
1922	61	V 8 cyl.	Sedan	1,900	4,000	11,000
1922	61	V 8 cyl.	Coupe	2,000	4,200	11,500
1922	61	V 8 cyl.	Victoria	2,500	4,700	12,500
1923	61	V 8 cyl.	Sport Phaeton	4,600	8,500	30,000
1923	61	V 8 cyl.	Suburban	3,450	9,200	15,700
1924	V-63	V 8 cyl.	Phaeton	6,600	11,500	34,500
1924	V-63	V 8 cyl.	Touring	5,700	9,300	31,500
1924	V-63	V 8 cyl.	Limousine	3,650	5,000	16,000
1924	V-63	V 8 cyl.	Sport Roadster	6,250	22,000	34,500
1924	V-63	V 8 cyl.	Sport Phaeton	6,400	23,400	37,500
1925	V-63	V 8 cyl.	Sport Touring	5,150	16,200	33,500
1925	V-63	V 8 cyl.	Roadster	5,150	16,200	35,000
1925	V-63	V 8 cyl.	Coupe	4,400	8,250	22,400
1925	V-63	V 8 cyl.	Sedan	3,870	8,050	14,650
1925	V-63	V 8 cyl.	Limousine	3,950	8,000	17,800
1925	V-63	V 8 cyl.	7 Passenger Touring	6,250	15,000	32,500

YEAR	MODEL	ENGINE	BODY	F	G	E
CADILLAC *(United States, 1903 to date) (continued)*						
1925	V-63	V 8 cyl.	Dual Cowl Phaeton	8,450	20,950	41,000
1926	314	V 8 cyl.	Sedan	3,650	8,400	16,750
1926	314	V 8 cyl.	Roadster	8,300	21,900	42,000
1926	314	V 8 cyl.	7 Passenger Touring	7,800	17,600	37,500
1926	314	V 8 cyl.	Dual Cowl Phaeton	8,900	21,900	46,000
1926	314	V 8 cyl.	Limousine	4,000	8,300	17,800
1926	314	V 8 cyl.	2 Door Sedan	3,750	7,700	16,200
1926	314	V 8 cyl.	Touring	20,000	40,000	70,000
1926	314	V 8 cyl.	Roadster	24,000	43,000	76,000
1927	314	V 8 cyl.	Dual Cowl Phaeton	10,000	30,000	65,500
1927	314	V 8 cyl.	7 Passenger Touring	9,200	21,500	45,000
1927	314	V 8 cyl.	Victoria Coupe	5,750	10,450	18,900
1927	314	V 8 cyl.	Sedan	4,600	9,200	17,800
1927	314	V 8 cyl.	Town Sedan	4,700	9,900	22,000
1927	314	V 8 cyl.	Sedan	8,500	16,400	32,000
1927	314	V 8 cyl.	Coupe	8,900	17,000	36,000
1927	314	V 8 cyl.	Suburban	8,500	16,400	32,000
1928	341-A	V 8 cyl.	Cabriolet	8,600	16,800	33,500
1928	341-A	V 8 cyl.	Dual Cowl Phaeton	15,000	32,000	66,000
1928	341-A	V 8 cyl.	Sedan	7,800	17,600	37,500
1928	341-A	V 8 cyl.	Brougham Limousine	18,000	38,000	66,000
1928	341-A	V 8 cyl.	Touring	25,000	45,000	79,000
1928	341-A	V 8 cyl.	Phaeton	26,000	47,500	81,000
1928	341-A	V 8 cyl.	7 Passenger Touring	8,250	19,900	41,500
1928	341-A	V 8 cyl.	Sedan	7,000	11,500	36,500
1928	341-A	V 8 cyl.	Sport Roadster	9,950	29,500	65,500
1928	341-A	V 8 cyl.	Town Sedan	6,600	9,900	23,000
1929	341-B	V 8 cyl.	Sport Roadster	9,900	22,800	65,500
1929	341-B	V 8 cyl.	Cabriolet	8,700	15,900	36,500
1929	341-B	V 8 cyl.	Dual Cowl Phaeton	17,000	35,500	85,500

YEAR	MODEL	ENGINE	BODY	F	G	E

CADILLAC *(United States, 1903 to date) (continued)*

YEAR	MODEL	ENGINE	BODY	F	G	E
1929	341-B	V 8 cyl.	Coupe Roadster	8,000	12,000	40,000
1929	341-B	V 8 cyl.	7 Passenger Sedan	8,400	13,000	41,500
1929	341-B	V 8 cyl.	Victoria	5,800	12,000	31,400
1929	341-B	V 8 cyl.	Sedan	4,900	10,400	24,000
1929	341-B	V 8 cyl.	Touring	20,500	30,500	80,500
1929	341-B SM		Town Sedan	8,575	13,500	42,500
1929	341-B	V 8 cyl.	Roadster	25,000	45,000	79,000
1929	341-B	V 8 cyl.	5 Passenger Sedan	8,500	13,000	43,400
1930	353	V 8 cyl.	Coupe Roadster	7,000	12,500	29,800
1930	353	V 8 cyl.	Sedan	5,500	12,300	24,000
1930	353	V 8 cyl.	Dual Cowl Phaeton	16,800	42,900	80,300
1930	353	V 8 cyl.	Cabriolet	9,200	24,000	37,700
1930	353	V 8 cyl.	7 Passenger Touring	12,500	31,300	60,000
1930	353	V 8 cyl.	Sport Roadster	14,700	44,900	71,500
1930	353	V 8 cyl.	7 Passenger Sedan	10,500	16,500	48,575
1930	452	V 16 cyl.	Sedan Club	13,600	29,300	53,300
1930	452	V 16 cyl.	Dual Cowl Phaeton	32,500	104,000	255,000
1930	Madam X	V 16 cyl.	Imperial Limousine	17,800	57,500	104,000
1930	Fisher Body	V 16 cyl.	Phaeton	54,500	240,000	293,000
1930	452	V 16 cyl.	Coupe	14,700	31,400	57,500
1930	452	V 16 cyl.	Convertible Sedan	36,000	74,000	125,000
1930	452	V 16 cyl.	7 Passenger Sedan	12,500	32,500	62,500
1930	452	V 16 cyl.	Sport Roadster	32,500	92,000	151,000

YEAR	MODEL	ENGINE	BODY	F	G	E
CADILLAC *(United States, 1903 to date)* *(continued)*						
1931	355	V 8 cyl.	Convertible Coupe	21,900	52,000	92,000

Cadillac – 1931 "Fleetwood Roadster"

YEAR	MODEL	ENGINE	BODY	F	G	E
1931	355	V 8 cyl.	Phaeton	28,300	54,300	94,000
1931	355	V 8 cyl.	Roadster	26,700	44,250	96,000
1931	355	V 8 cyl.	Convertible Sedan	23,000	49,000	101,000
1931	355	V 8 cyl.	Rumble Seat Coupe	9,200	16,700	33,400
1931	355	V 8 cyl.	Club Sedan	8,200	13,600	30,300
1931	370	V 12 cyl.	Roadster	36,500	61,000	121,000
1931	370	V 12 cyl.	7 Passenger Touring	19,900	46,000	101,000
1931	370	V 12 cyl.	Dual Cowl Phaeton	28,300	69,000	135,000
1931	370	V 12 cyl.	Cabriolet	18,800	46,000	69,000
1931	370	V 12 cyl.	Phaeton	38,000	63,000	126,000
1931	370	V 12 cyl.	Sedan	9,500	15,000	45,500
1931	370	V 12 cyl.	7 Passenger Sedan	11,100	18,900	39,800
1931	452	V 16 cyl.	Dual Cowl Phaeton	39,800	110,000	225,000
1931	452	V 16 cyl.	Roadster	36,600	85,000	157,000
1931	452	V 16 cyl.	Convertible Sedan	28,200	85,500	125,000
1931	452	V 16 cyl.	Convertible Coupe	28,200	112,700	125,000

YEAR	MODEL	ENGINE	BODY	F	G	E
CADILLAC *(United States, 1903 to date) (continued)*							
1931	452	V 16 cyl.	Town Sedan	28,800	39,700	64,000
1931	452	V 16 cyl.	7 Passenger Sedan	13,600	26,100	52,100
1931	452	V 16 cyl.	Sedan	12,600	22,000	46,000
1932	355B	V 8 cyl.	Club Sedan	6,400	16,700	26,200
1932	355B	V 8 cyl.	Cabriolet	13,600	25,200	50,000
1932	355B	V 8 cyl.	Roadster	21,000	31,400	81,500
1932	355B	V 8 cyl.	Phaeton	19,900	35,600	92,000
1932	355B	V 8 cyl.	Sedan	8,050	12,575	41,000
1932	355B	V 8 cyl.	Rumble Seat Coupe	8,600	16,700	29,300
1932	370B	V 12 cyl.	Dual Cowl Phaeton	22,000	62,500	130,000
1932	370B	V 12 cyl.	Roadster	32,000	53,000	106,000

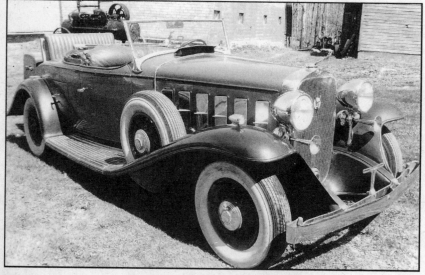

Cadillac 1932 "V-12 Roadster"

YEAR	MODEL	ENGINE	BODY	F	G	E
1932	370B	V 12 cyl.	Phaeton	22,000	61,000	120,000
1932	370B	V 12 cyl.	Sedan	11,500	19,900	40,800
1932	370B	V 12 cyl.	Cabriolet	15,700	25,100	57,100
1932	452B	V 16 cyl.	Cabriolet	17,800	38,800	104,000
1932	452B	V 16 cyl.	Convertible Sedan	22,000	64,000	145,000
1932	452B	V 16 cyl.	Roadster	33,100	56,000	112,000

YEAR	MODEL	ENGINE	BODY	F	G	E
CADILLAC *(United States, 1903 to date) (continued)*						
1932	352B	V 16 cyl.	Dual Cowl Phaeton	46,000	130,000	245,000
1932	452A	V 16 cyl.	7 Passenger Sedan	13,600	37,500	70,000
1933	355C	V 8 cyl.	Convertible Sedan	13,600	37,500	70,000
1933	355C	V 8 cyl.	Sedan	11,500	17,800	51,000
1933	355C	V 8 cyl.	Convertible Coupe	11,500	27,200	46,000
1933	370C	V 12 cyl.	Rumble Seat Coupe	7,650	15,700	28,000
1933	370C	V 12 cyl.	Town Sedan	10,400	15,700	33,500
1933	370C Fleetwood	V 12 cyl.	Convertible Sedan	22,000	34,000	88,000
1933	370C	V 12 cyl.	Sedan	7,950	16,000	28,000
1933	452C	V 16 cyl.	Coupe	17,800	37,700	65,700
1933		V 16 cyl.	Phaeton	23,000	85,700	178,000
1934	355D	V 8 cyl.	Convertible Sedan	20,000	40,000	70,000
1934	355D	V 8 cyl.	Cabriolet	9,900	15,700	46,000
1934	355D	V 8 cyl.	Rumble Seat Coupe	8,500	21,100	32,500
1934	355D	V 8 cyl.	Sedan	8,500	14,000	42,500
1934	355D	V 8 cyl.	Sport Sedan	9,975	16,000	47,000
1934	355D	V 8 cyl.	Sport Limousine	9,975	16,000	47,000
1934	370D	V 12 cyl.	Convertible Sedan	22,000	42,000	100,000
1934	370D	V 12 cyl.	Sedan	9,975	16,000	47,000
1934	452D	V 16 cyl.	Cabriolet	17,800	46,000	115,000
1934	452D	V 16 cyl.	Side Mount Sedan	10,450	29,300	57,000
1935	355E	V 8 cyl.	Convertible Coupe	8,400	33,500	64,700
1935	355E	V 8 cyl.	Club Sedan	6,400	15,700	24,100
1935	355E	V 8 cyl.	Cabriolet	9,700	19,900	48,100
1935	355E	V 8 cyl.	Rumble Seat Coupe	12,400	19,500	56,000
1935		V 12 cyl.	Victoria	11,000	32,500	50,200
1935	370E	V 12 cyl.	Convertible Sedan	17,800	69,000	93,500
1935	370E	V 12 cyl.	Sports Roadster	17,800	85,700	130,000

YEAR	MODEL	ENGINE	BODY	F	G	E
CADILLAC	*(United States, 1903 to date) (continued)*					
1935	370E	V 16 cyl.	Convertible			
			Sedan	29,500	97,000	141,000
1935	370E	V 12 cyl.	Rumble Seat			
			Coupe	11,000	32,400	45,000
1935	370E	V 12 cyl.	Sedan	8,570	19,900	38,600
1935	370E					
	Fleetwood	V 12 cyl.	Limousine	10,350	29,200	42,000
1935	452D	V 16 cyl.	Town Sedan	20,000	30,000	80,000
1936	70	V 8 cyl.	Convertible			
			Coupe			
			Side Mount	9,700	25,500	49,000
1936	70	V 8 cyl.	Rumble Seat			
			Coupe	5,450	17,400	27,500
1936	70	V 8 cyl.	Side Mount			
			Sedan	6,400	15,100	24,000
1936	70	V 8 cyl.	Convertible			
			Sedan	13,000	20,000	60,000
1936	60	V 8 cyl.	Convertible			
			Sedan	14,000	46,500	90,000
1936	60	V 8 cyl.	Convertible			
			Coupe	12,000	37,500	77,500
1936	60	V 8 cyl.	Club Coupe	6,600	9,700	15,200
1936	80	V 12 cyl.	Rumble Seat			
			Coupe	7,200	14,700	35,000
1936	80		Convertible			
	Fleetwood	V 12 cyl.	Sedan	15,500	23,000	67,500
1936	80	V 12 cyl.	Limousine	8,050	24,000	40,800
1936	80	V 16 cyl.	Convertible			
			Sedan	40,000	70,000	133,000
1937	60	V 8 cyl.	Rumble Seat			
			Coupe	7,000	11,000	25,000
1937	60	V 8 cyl.	Cabriolet	6,900	14,100	33,000
1937	60	V 8 cyl.	Sedan	4,400	8,400	15,900
1937	60	V 8 cyl.	Convertible			
			Sedan	12,000	18,200	52,000
1937	65	V 8 cyl.	Touring			
			Sedan	4,200	7,000	29,300
1937	70	V 8 cyl.	Touring			
			Sedan	4,200	7,000	29,300
1937	70	V 8 cyl.	Sport Coupe	4,500	7,600	31,000
1937	75	V 8 cyl.	Touring			
			Sedan	4,200	7,000	29,300
1937	75	V 8 cyl.	Town Sedan	4,500	7,600	31,000

YEAR	MODEL	ENGINE	BODY	F	G	E
CADILLAC (United States, 1903 to date) (continued)						
1937	75	V 8 cyl.	Formal Sedan	5,000	8,100	33,500
1937	75	V 8 cyl.	Convertible Sedan	7,000	17,000	45,500
1937	85	V 12 cyl.	Town Sedan	6,900	12,000	37,500
1937	85	V 12 cyl.	Convertible Sedan	14,500	21,000	64,500
1937	85	V 12 cyl.	Formal Sedan	9,700	23,000	45,500
1937	85	V 16 cyl.	Convertible Sedan	9,700	66,500	132,500
1937	90	V 16 cyl.	Coupe	25,000	50,000	90,000

Cadillac – 1937 "V-12 Coupe"

YEAR	MODEL	ENGINE	BODY	F	G	E
1937	90	V 16 cyl.	Convertible Sedan	10,000	20,000	53,000
1937	90	V 16 cyl.	Aero Coupe	25,000	50,000	90,000
1937	90	V 16 cyl.	5 or 7 Passenger Cabriolet 4 styles	30,000	55,000	100,000
1937	90	V 16 cyl.	Town Sedan	20,000	40,000	79,000
1938	61	V 8 cyl.	2 Passenger Coupe	5,100	9,300	17,500
1938	61	V 8 cyl.	Convertible Coupe	6,900	17,800	33,000

YEAR	MODEL	ENGINE	BODY	F	G	E
CADILLAC *(United States, 1903 to date) (continued)*						
1938	65	V 8 cyl.	Convertible Sedan	11,500	18,000	51,000
1938	61	V 8 cyl.	4 Door Sedan	5,550	12,000	17,800
1938	90	V 16 cyl.	Convertible Sedan	26,000	56,000	96,000
1938	90	V 16 cyl.	Sedan	8,700	16,700	39,800
1938	75	V 8 cyl.	2 or 5 Passenger Coupe	8,500	13,000	43,400
1938	75	V 8 cyl.	Touring Sedan	6,000	9,000	37,000
1938	75	V 8 cyl.	Town Sedan	6,000	9,000	37,000
1938	75	V 8 cyl.	7 Passenger Formal Sedan	6,400	9,700	41,000
1938	75	V 8 cyl.	7 Passenger Touring Sedan	6,000	9,000	37,000
1938	75	V 8 cyl.	Town Car	7,300	19,100	48,500
1938	75	V 8 cyl.	Convertible	13,000	24,000	58,000
1938	75	V 8 cyl.	Convertible Sedan	15,000	22,000	65,500
1938	60 Special	V 8 cyl.	Sedan	4,200	8,050	15,700
1939	75	V 8 cyl.	Limousine	4,700	9,400	22,500
1939	75 Formal	V 8 cyl.	4 Door Sedan	4,450	7,400	19,000
1939	61	V 8 cyl.	Sedan	3,700	10,000	16,200
1939	90	V 16 cyl.	Convertible Sedan	24,500	69,000	136,000
1939	90	V 16 cyl.	Formal Sedan	12,000	32,400	67,500
1939	90	V 16 cyl.	Limousine	11,000	28,200	57,500
1939	90	V 16 cyl.	Coupe	12,000	30,400	63,000
1940	75	V 8 cyl.	Sedan	4,600	9,200	15,500
1940	75	V 8 cyl.	Convertible Sedan	14,500	17,000	45,000
1940	75	V 8 cyl.	Formal Sedan	4,600	8,300	18,200
1940	72	V 8 cyl.	Sedan	3,350	9,000	26,000
1940	72	V 8 cyl.	7 Passenger Sedan 5 styles	5,000	10,000	32,000
1940	72	V 8 cyl.	2 or 5 Passenger Coupe	6,000	9,000	37,000
1940	75	V 8 cyl.	Town Car	7,300	19,100	48,500
1940	90	V 16 cyl.	Coupe	14,100	29,300	62,500

YEAR	MODEL	ENGINE	BODY	F	G	E
CADILLAC *(United States, 1903 to date) (continued)*					
1940	90	V 16 cyl.	7 Passenger Limousine	14,700	35,000	57,500
1940	62	V 8 cyl.	Sedan	4,200	8,800	14,100
1940	60 Special	V 8 cyl.	4 Door Sedan	5,500	9,200	15,500
1940	62	V 8 cyl.	Convertible Sedan	8,600	21,100	46,000
1940	62	V 8 cyl.	Club Coupe	4,600	9,000	15,000
1941	75	V 8 cyl.	Sedan	2,800	7,800	15,200
1941	Fleetwood	V 8 cyl.	Limousine	4,000	11,300	20,200
1941	61	V 8 cyl.	Convertible Coupe	7,300	16,200	35,000
1941	60 Special	V 8 cyl.	Sedan	5,000	8,000	28,000

Cadillac – 1941 "60 Special" Convertible

1941	63	V 8 cyl.	Sedan	3,400	7,500	19,000
1941	61	V 8 cyl.	Fast Back	3,300	6,700	14,100
1942	75	V 8 cyl.	Imperial Sedan	3,700	12,000	16,700
1942	75	V 8 cyl.	Formal Sedan	2,800	7,400	15,500

YEAR	MODEL	ENGINE	BODY	F	G	E
CADILLAC *(United States, 1903 to date) (continued)*						
1942	75					
	Fleetwood	V 8 cyl.	Limousine	4,400	9,010	15,500

Cadillac – 1942 "Fleetwood Limousine"

1942	61	V 8 cyl.	Sedan	1,500	2,600	6,100
1942	62	V 8 cyl.	Sedanet Fast Back	3,700	7,200	16,700
1942	62	V 8 cyl.	Sedan Fast Back	3,700	8,500	16,500
Postwar Models						
1946	61	V 8 cyl.	Fast Back Coupe	5,000	10,000	20,000
1946	62	V 8 cyl.	Coupe	6,000	11,000	21,000
1946	62	V 8 cyl.	Convertible	7,000	15,000	32,000
1946	60 Special	V 8 cyl.	Sedan	5,000	10,000	22,000
1946	75	V 8 cyl.	5 or 7 Passenger Sedan	3,000	10,000	24,000
1946	75	V 8 cyl.	5 or 7 Passenger Imperial Sedan	6,000	12,000	28,000
1946	75	V 8 cyl.	Business Sedan	5,000	12,000	25,000
1947	62	V 8 cyl.	Sedan	4,000	10,000	21,000
1947	62	V 8 cyl.	Sedanet	5,000	10,000	21,000
1947	62	V 8 cyl.	Convertible	7,000	15,000	32,000
1947	61	V 8 cyl.	Coupe	3,000	8,000	20,000
1947	61	V 8 cyl.	Sedan	3,000	7,000	19,000
1948	75		Imperial Sedan			
	Fleetwood	V 8 cyl.	Sedan	5,000	12,000	28,000

YEAR	MODEL	ENGINE	BODY	F	G	E
CADILLAC *(United States, 1903 to date) (continued)*						
1948	62	V 8 cyl.	Convertible	7,000	15,000	33,000
1948	61	V 8 cyl.	Sedan	3,000	10,000	22,000
1948	60 Special	V 8 cyl.	Sedan	4,000	10,000	22,000
1949	62	V 8 cyl.	Convertible	7,000	15,000	32,000
1949	62	V 8 cyl.	Hardtop Coupe de Ville	6,000	14,000	28,000
1949	75	V 8 cyl.	9 Passenger Business Imperial	6,000	12,000	27,000
1950	62	V 8 cyl.	Convertible	10,000	18,000	31,000
1950	62	V 8 cyl.	Coupe de Ville	5,000	10,000	23,000
1950	62	V 8 cyl.	Hardtop Coupe	3,000	8,000	21,000
1950	60 Special Fleetwood	V 8 cyl.	Sedan	4,000	9,000	22,000
1951	61	V 8 cyl.	2 Door Hardtop	5,000	10,000	20,000
1951	62	V 8 cyl.	Coupe de Ville	6,000	11,000	22,000
1951	75 Fleetwood	V 8 cyl.	8 Passenger Imperial Sedan	6,000	12,000	25,000
1952	62	V 8 cyl.	Coupe de Ville	6,000	12,000	23,000
1953	Fleetwood	V 8 cyl.	Sedan	5,000	10,000	22,000
1953	Eldorado	V 8 cyl.	Convertible	20,000	50,000	80,000
1953	62	V 8 cyl.	Coupe de Ville	7,000	16,000	34,000
1954	Eldorado	V 8 cyl.	Convertible	15,000	35,000	65,000
1954	Fleetwood	V 8 cyl.	4 Door Sedan	5,000	12,000	25,000
1954	62	V 8 cyl.	Hardtop	7,000	14,000	25,000
1954	62	V 8 cyl.	Coupe de Ville	7,000	14,000	26,000
1954	62	V 8 cyl.	Sedan	3,000	7,000	16,000
1955	75	V 8 cyl.	7 Passenger Imperial Sedan	6,000	12,000	27,000
1955	75 Fleetwood	V 8 cyl.	Sedan	4,000	12,000	25,000

YEAR	MODEL	ENGINE	BODY	F	G	E
CADILLAC *(United States, 1903 to date) (continued)*							
1955	62	V 8 cyl.	Eldorado Convertible	7,000	18,000	37,000
1955	62	V 8 cyl.	Coupe de Ville	5,000	10,000	22,000
1955	62	V 8 cyl.	2 Door Hardtop	4,000	10,000	21,000
1956	60-S	V 8 cyl.	Sedan	3,000	8,000	20,000
1956	62	V 8 cyl.	Convertible	10,000	25,000	40,000
1956	Coupe de Ville	V 8 cyl.	Hardtop	5,000	12,000	25,000
1956	Sedan de Ville	V 8 cyl.	4 Door Hardtop	3,000	8,000	18,000
1956	Eldorado	V 8 cyl.	Hardtop	6,000	15,000	32,000
1956	Eldorado	V 8 cyl.	Convertible	5,000	12,500	37,000
1956	75	V 8 cyl.	Imperial Sedan	6,000	13,000	27,000
1957	Coupe de Ville	V 8 cyl.	Hardtop	5,000	12,000	25,000
1957	60-S Fleetwood	V 8 cyl.	4 Door Hardtop	3,000	8,000	18,000
1957	Eldorado	V 8 cyl.	Brougham	6,000	13,000	27,000
1957	Eldorado	V 8 cyl.	Hardtop	6,000	12,000	25,000
1957	Eldorado	V 8 cyl.	Convertible	8,000	15,000	34,000
1957	75	V 8 cyl.	8 Passenger Sedan	3,000	8,000	18,000
1958	62	V 8 cyl.	4 Door Hardtop	2,000	5,000	12,000
1958	62	V 8 cyl.	2 Door Hardtop	4,000	10,000	22,000
1958	60-S Fleetwood	V 8 cyl.	4 Door Hardtop	3,000	8,000	18,000
1958	Eldorado	V 8 cyl.	Brougham	6,000	12,000	26,000
1958	62	V 8 cyl.	Convertible	8,000	16,000	28,000
1958	Eldorado	V 8 cyl.	Hardtop	4,000	10,000	22,000
1958	Eldorado	V 8 cyl.	Biarritz Convertible	8,000	16,000	30,000
1959	62	V 8 cyl.	Hardtop Coupe	3,000	8,000	18,000
1959	60-S	V 8 cyl.	6 Passenger Sedan	4,000	10,000	22,000
1959	62	V 8 cyl.	Convertible	15,000	25,000	42,000
1959	Eldorado	V 8 cyl.	Brougham	5,000	13,000	29,000
1959	Eldorado	V 8 cyl.	Convertible	15,000	35,000	65,000

YEAR	MODEL	ENGINE	BODY	F	G	E
CADILLAC (United States, 1903 to date) (continued)						
1959	Eldorado	V 8 cyl.	Hardtop	6,000	14,000	31,000
1959	75					
	Fleetwood	V 8 cyl.	Limousine	5,000	12,000	27,000
1960	62	V 8 cyl.	Hardtop			
			Coupe	4,000	9,000	20,000
1960	62	V 8 cyl.	Hardtop			
			Sedan	2,000	5,000	12,000

Cadillac – 1960 "62 Sedan"

1960	62	V 8 cyl.	Convertible	10,000	25,000	42,000
1960	60-S	V 8 cyl.	Hardtop			
			Sedan	4,000	8,000	22,000
1960	Eldorado	V 8 cyl.	Brougham	7,000	15,000	30,000
1960	Eldorado	V 8 cyl.	Hardtop	9,000	17,000	32,000
1960	Eldorado	V 8 cyl.	Convertible	20,000	40,000	65,000
1960	75		9 Passenger			
	Fleetwood	V 8 cyl.	Sedan	5,000	10,000	21,000
1961	62	V 8 cyl.	Convertible	8,000	16,000	28,000
1961	62	V 8 cyl.	Sedan	2,000	4,000	9,000
1961	Eldorado	V 8 cyl.	Convertible	8,000	16,000	36,000
1961	60-S					
	Fleetwood	V 8 cyl.	Sedan	2,000	6,000	13,000
1962	62	V 8 cyl.	Hardtop			
			Coupe	3,000	7,000	15,000
1962	62 Park					
	Avenue	V 8 cyl.	Short Sedan	3,000	5,000	10,000
1962	62	V 8 cyl.	Convertible	8,000	17,000	32,000
1962	Eldorado	V 8 cyl.	Convertible	10,000	20,000	38,000
1962	75					
	Fleetwood	V 8 cyl.	Limousine	2,000	8,000	20,000

YEAR	MODEL	ENGINE	BODY	F	G	E
CADILLAC *(United States, 1903 to date) (continued)*						
1963	62	V 8 cyl.	Hardtop Coupe	2,000	4,000	10,000
1963	60-S Fleetwood	V 8 cyl.	6 Passenger Sedan	3,000	8,000	20,000
1963	Eldorado	V 8 cyl.	Convertible	7,000	14,000	28,000
1963	62	V 8 cyl.	Convertible	6,000	14,000	26,000
1963	75 Fleetwood	V 8 cyl.	Limousine	2,000	6,000	18,000
1964	62	V 8 cyl.	Hardtop Sedan	1,000	3,000	7,000
1964	60-S Fleetwood	V 8 cyl.	Sedan	2,000	5,000	12,000
1964	Eldorado	V 8 cyl.	Convertible	8,000	15,000	29,000
1965	Calais	V 8 cyl.	Hardtop	2,000	4,000	9,000
1965	62 Coupe de Ville	V 8 cyl.	Convertible	6,000	11,000	21,000
1965	Eldorado	V 8 cyl.	Convertible	5,000	10,000	20,000
1966	Coupe de Ville	V 8 cyl.	Hardtop	2,000	4,000	10,000
1966	Coupe de Ville	V 8 cyl.	Convertible	5,000	11,000	21,000
1966	Eldorado	V 8 cyl.	Convertible	6,000	12,000	23,000
1967	Fleetwood	V 8 cyl.	Sedan	1,000	4,000	9,000
1967	Eldorado FWD	V 8 cyl.	Coupe	3,000	6,000	10,000
1967	Coupe de Ville	V 8 cyl.	Convertible	5,000	11,000	21,000

Cadillac – 1970 "Fleetwood Eldorado"

YEAR	MODEL	ENGINE	BODY	F	G	E
CADILLAC (United States, 1903 to date) (continued)						
1968	Coupe de Ville	V 8 cyl.	Convertible	4,000	9,000	18,000
1969	Coupe de Ville	V 8 cyl.	Convertible	4,000	8,000	18,000
1969	Fleetwood	V 8 cyl.	Limousine	1,000	3,000	7,000
1970	Eldorado	V 8 cyl.	Convertible	4,000	9,000	17,000
1971	Eldorado	V 8 cyl.	Convertible	4,000	9,000	17,000
1972	Eldorado	V 8 cyl.	Convertible	4,000	9,000	17,000
1973	Eldorado	V 8 cyl.	Convertible	4,000	9,000	17,000
1974	Eldorado	V 8 cyl.	Convertible	5,000	10,000	18,000
1975	Eldorado	V 8 cyl.	Convertible	5,000	10,000	18,000
1976	Eldorado	V 8 cyl.	Convertible	6,000	12,000	20,000

Cadillac – 1976 "Eldorado with Tumble Seat"

YEAR	MODEL	ENGINE	BODY	F	G	E
1976	Eldorado	V 8 cyl.	Convertible	8,000	15,000	25,000
CAMERON (United States, 1902–21)						
1904		1 cyl.	Runabout	6,000	16,400	32,500
1909	11	6 cyl.	Touring	6,600	16,200	31,000
1912	32	6 cyl.	Touring	7,000	14,000	28,000
1919	45	6 cyl.	Touring	6,000	12,000	27,000
1920	55	6 cyl.	Touring	6,000	12,000	27,000
CANTERBURY (Great Britain, 1903–06)						
1903		(Aster)	Tonneau	2,000	8,000	18,250
1904		4 cyl.	Tonneau	3,500	8,200	19,000
C.A.R. (Italy, 1906)						
1906			Touring	1,500	3,600	8,700
1906			Voiturette	1,600	3,800	8,000
C.A.R. (Italy, 1927–29)						
1927		1095cc	Touring	2,400	6,200	13,200

YEAR	MODEL	ENGINE	BODY	F	G	E
CARDEN; NEW CARDEN *(Great Britain, 1913–25)*						
1913		1 cyl.	2 Passenger	1,500	3,600	9,750
1920		2 cyl.	2 Passenger	1,800	4,400	10,000
1924			Touring	2,000	4,800	12,000
CARHARTT *(United States, 1911–12)*						
1911	C	4 cyl.	Runabout	5,000	10,500	20,000
1911	H	4 cyl.	Limousine	5,000	9,000	17,000
CARON *(France, 1900–01)*						
1900		2 cyl.	Voiturette	2,250	3,800	9,500
1900		2 cyl.	Vis-a-vis	3,250	5,800	15,500
CARROW *(Great Britain, 1919–23)*						
1919		4 cyl.	Roadster	1,600	3,500	11,750
1920		4 cyl.	Touring	1,800	4,000	13,800
CARTERCAR *(United States, 1905–15)*						
1905	C	2 cyl.	Runabout	3,950	13,500	21,000
1912	R	4 cyl.	Roadster	8,000	16,000	34,000
1912	R	4 cyl.	Touring	6,000	12,000	25,000
1915	9	4 cyl.	Touring	6,000	12,000	25,000
CASE *(Canada, 1907)*						
1907	A	4 cyl. 20		3,700	8,800	14,800
CASE *(United States, 1911–27)*						
1911	U	4 cyl.	Touring	7,000	15,000	27,000
1914	O.R.S. 35	4 cyl.	Touring	8,000	16,000	28,000
1916	T	4 cyl.	Touring	9,000	18,000	30,000
1926	Y	6 cyl.	Touring	10,000	19,000	31,000
C.C.C. *(Great Britain, 1906–07)*						
1906		1 cyl.		1,500	2,500	9,000
1907		4 cyl.		1,700	3,000	10,000
CEGGA *(China, 1960–67)*						
1960			Coupe	1,450	2,800	5,000
1960		V 12 cyl. (Ferrari)	Sport	3,600	8,250	14,500
CENTURY *(Great Britain, 1899–1907)*						
1900		1 cyl.	Tri-car	1,500	3,550	9,500
1904			Runabout	1,600	3,650	10,000
CENTURY *(United States, 1899–1903; 1911–15)*						
1901		Steam	Runabout	6,000	12,000	20,000
1903		Gasoline	Touring	5,000	10,000	18,000
CHABOCHE *(France, 1901–06)*						
1901	Open	Steam	Vis-a-vis	5,000	15,000	30,000
1903	Sedan	Steam	Limousine	3,000	8,500	25,500

YEAR	MODEL	ENGINE	BODY	F	G	E
CHABOCHE *(France, 1901–06) (continued)*						
1904	Closed	Steam	Coupe de Ville	3,100	8,600	20,000
1905	Open	Steam	Phaeton	6,100	17,600	35,000
1906	Open	Steam	Racing	6,500	17,800	35,000
CHADWICK *(United States, 1904–16)*						
1904	9	4 cyl.	Touring	10,000	25,000	55,000
1907	Great Six	11.2 Litre	Touring	12,000	30,000	75,000
1911	Great Six	11.2 Litre	Touring	15,000	35,000	79,000
CHALMERS; CHALMERS-DETROIT *(United States, 1908–24)*						
1909	30	4 cyl.	Touring	5,000	12,000	26,000
1910	30	4 cyl.	Roadster	6,000	14,000	29,000
1910	40	4 cyl.	Touring	6,000	13,000	27,000
1911	30	4 cyl.	Limousine	4,000	10,000	21,000
1911	30	4 cyl.	Touring	6,000	13,000	28,000
1911	30	4 cyl.	Roadster	6,000	14,000	30,000
1912	10	4 cyl.	Touring	5,000	13,000	29,000
1913	18	6 cyl.	Roadster	4,500	15,000	35,000
1915	Light Six	6 cyl.	5 Passenger Touring	3,750	14,000	29,000
1917	Six-30	6 cyl.	7 Passenger Touring	3,500	11,500	22,000
1918	Six-30	6 cyl.	7 Passenger Touring	3,400	11,200	21,800
1921	35-C	6 cyl.	Touring	3,250	10,500	25,000
1923	Y	6 cyl.	Roadster	3,200	7,250	25,000
CHAMBERS *(Great Britain, 1904–25)*						
1908		2 cyl.	Touring	2,200	4,250	11,500
1920		4 cyl.	Touring	2,250	6,500	14,800
CHAMPION *(United States, 1919–24)*						
1919	KO	4 cyl.	Touring	3,500	7,500	20,000
1921	KO	4 cyl.	Touring	3,000	7,000	21,000
1922	KO	4 cyl.	Touring	2,400	7,500	18,000
1924	KO	4 cyl.	Touring	2,200	7,200	16,600
CHAMPROBERT *(France, 1902–05)*						
1902		(DeDion)		2,000	4,250	10,500
1904		(DeDion-Aster)		2,250	4,500	10,900
CHANDLER *(United States, 1914–29)*						
1914	14	6 cyl.	Coupe	3,000	6,000	13,000
1918	Series 25	6 cyl.	Roadster	4,000	9,500	23,500
1922	Series 29	6 cyl.	Touring	3,500	9,000	20,000

YEAR	MODEL	ENGINE	BODY	F	G	E
CHANDLER (United States, 1914–29) (continued)						
1924	Series 32-A	6 cyl.	7 Passenger			
			Touring	3,200	8,800	19,500
1926	35	6 cyl.	7 Passenger			
			Touring	4,200	8,800	21,500
1927	Big Slx	6 cyl.	Sedan	2,900	5,100	14,300
1928	Royal 8	8 cyl.	7 Passenger			
			Touring	7,500	19,500	35,000
1929	Royal 85	8 cyl.	Sedan	2,800	8,200	27,000
CHATEL-JEANNIN (Germany, 1902–03)						
1902		1 cyl.	Runabout	1,500	3,600	9,000
1902		1 cyl.	Convertible	2,000	3,800	10,000
CHATHAM (Canada, 1907–08)						
1907		2 cyl.	Touring	1,500	3,850	9,000
1908		4 cyl. (Reeves)	Touring	2,000	4,400	11,500
CHECKER (United States, 1922–82)						
1920	C	(Lycoming)	4 Door			
			Taxicab	2,000	6,000	11,000
1939	Y-8	(Lycoming)	4 Door			
			Taxicab	2,000	6,000	12,000
CHELSEA (United States, 1914)						
1914		4 cyl.	Cycle		RARE	
CHELSEA (Great Britain, 1922)						
1922		Electric	Coupe	3,000	7,000	14,500
CHENU (France, 1903–07)						
1903		1 cyl.	Open	1,500	2,750	9,000
1905		2 cyl.	Open	2,000	3,500	13,800
1907		4 cyl.	Open	2,500	5,400	20,000
CHESWOLD (Great Britain, 1911–15)						
1911		4 cyl.	Touring	1,500	4,000	11,000
CHEVROLET (United States, 1911 to date)						
1912	Classic Six	6 cyl.	Touring	5,700	9,300	32,000
1913	Baby Grand	4 cyl.	Roadster	4,100	10,900	27,000
1913	Baby Grand	4 cyl.	Touring	3,900	11,400	24,000
1914	Baby Grand	4 cyl.	Touring	4,100	10,900	26,000
1914	C	6 cyl.	Touring	4,700	11,500	22,700
1914	L	6 cyl.	Touring	4,700	11,500	22,700
1915	Baby Grand	4 cyl.	Touring	3,400	11,400	26,000
1915	Baby Grand	4 cyl.	Touring	3,400	11,400	26,000
1915	Amesbury	4 cyl.	Roadster	7,000	15,500	32,000
1915	Baby Grand	4 cyl.	Roadster	3,700	11,400	24,000
1915	L	6 cyl.	Touring	5,200	10,400	18,000

YEAR	MODEL	ENGINE	BODY	F	G	E
CHEVROLET *(United States, 1911 to date) (continued)*						
1915	L	6 cyl.	Roadster	5,500	11,000	19,000
1916	490	4 cyl.	Touring	3,400	4,700	16,100
1916	Special	6 cyl.	Roadster	4,700	11,500	22,700
1916	H4	4 cyl.	Touring	5,400	10,900	18,800
1917	D	V 8 cyl.	Roadster	2,800	6,000	18,000
1917	D	V 8 cyl.	Touring	2,500	5,400	17,000
1917	490	4 cyl.	Touring	5,200	8,100	15,200
1917	490	4 cyl.	Roadster	5,500	8,500	16,000
1918	490	4 cyl.	Touring	3,400	4,700	17,100
1918	490	4 cyl.	Roadster	3,300	4,500	15,100
1918	490	4 cyl.	Coupe	1,900	3,200	7,600
1918	D	8 cyl.	Touring	3,400	11,400	26,000
1918	D	8 cyl.	Roadster	3,400	11,400	26,000
1919	490	4 cyl.	Touring	3,300	4,500	15,100
1919	490	4 cyl.	Roadster	3,100	4,300	14,500
1919	490	4 cyl.	Sedan	2,000	3,400	7,400
1919	490	4 cyl.	Coupe	2,000	3,400	7,400
1920	490	4 cyl.	Touring	3,200	4,500	15,500
1920	490	4 cyl.	Roadster	3,100	4,300	14,500
1920	490	4 cyl.	Sedan	1,900	3,000	7,900
1920	490	4 cyl.	Coupe	2,100	3,100	8,400
1920	FB	4 cyl.	Touring	3,400	4,500	16,000
1920	FB	4 cyl.	Roadster	3,200	4,000	15,200
1920	FB	4 cyl.	Sedan	2,300	3,300	9,200
1920	FB	4 cyl.	Coupe	2,500	3,600	9,700
1921	490	4 cyl.	Touring	3,300	4,500	15,100
1921	490	4 cyl.	Roadster	3,100	4,300	14,100
1921	490	4 cyl.	Coupe	2,700	5,300	11,500
1921	FB	4 cyl.	Touring	4,300	8,300	18,000
1921	FB	4 cyl.	Roadster	4,000	8,000	17,500
1921	FB	4 cyl.	Sedan	2,300	3,300	9,100
1921	FB	4 cyl.	Coupe	2,300	3,300	9,100
1922	FB	4 cyl.	Sport Touring	4,100	10,600	18,800
1922	490	4 cyl.	Touring	4,300	8,300	18,000
1922	490	4 cyl.	Roadster	4,000	8,000	17,500
1922	490	4 cyl.	Sedan	2,300	3,300	9,100
1922	490	4 cyl.	Coupe	2,300	3,300	9,100
1923	B	4 cyl.	Sedan	1,800	5,200	10,900
1923	B	4 cyl.	Coupe	2,300	5,200	12,900
1923	B	4 cyl.	Touring	2,400	3,400	10,500
1924	Superior	4 cyl.	Roadster	4,000	8,000	16,000
1924	Superior	4 cyl.	Coupe	3,000	4,000	6,000

YEAR	MODEL	ENGINE	BODY	F	G	E
CHEVROLET *(United States, 1911 to date) (continued)*						
1924	Superior	4 cyl.	Touring	4,000	8,000	17,000
1924	Superior	4 cyl.	Sedan	1,000	3,000	6,000
1925	Superior	4 cyl.	Roadster	4,000	8,000	16,000
1925	Superior K	4 cyl.	Touring	4,000	10,000	24,000
1925	Superior K	4 cyl.	Sedan	1,000	3,000	8,000
1926	Superior V	4 cyl.	Roadster	5,000	11,000	22,000
1926	Superior V	4 cyl.	Coupe	2,000	4,000	9,000
1926	Superior V	4 cyl.	Touring	4,300	6,600	24,000
1926	Superior V	4 cyl.	Sedan	1,000	3,000	7,000
1927	AA	4 cyl.	Roadster	5,000	12,000	23,000
1927	AA	4 cyl.	2 Door Sedan	1,000	3,000	8,000
1927	AA	4 cyl.	Touring	5,000	10,000	24,000
1928	AB	4 cyl.	Sedan	1,000	3,000	7,000
1929	AC	6 cyl.	Touring	4,000	12,000	27,000
1929	AC	6 cyl.	Landau Convertible	6,000	12,000	20,000
1929	AC	6 cyl.	Roadster	5,000	12,000	26,000
1929	AC	6 cyl.	Sedan	2,000	5,000	12,000
1929	AC	6 cyl.	Cabriolet	7,000	14,000	24,000
1930	AD	6 cyl.	Sport Coupe	3,100	7,500	17,000
1930	AD	6 cyl.	Roadster	6,000	14,000	27,000
1930	AD	6 cyl.	Coupe	3,300	4,500	15,000
1930	AD	6 cyl.	Phaeton	7,000	14,000	28,000
1930	AD	6 cyl.	Sedan	3,200	4,400	14,600
1930	AD	6 cyl.	Club Coach Sedan	3,500	6,000	14,000
1930	AD	6 cyl.	Sport Roadster	5,100	11,100	29,900
1931	AE	6 cyl.	Special Sedan	3,300	7,000	14,900
1931	AE	6 cyl.	Sport Roadster	6,000	14,000	36,000
1931	AE	6 cyl.	Cabriolet	8,000	16,000	32,000
1931	AE	6 cyl.	Special Coach Sedan	4,000	7,500	15,500
1931	AE	6 cyl.	Sport Coupe	3,000	8,000	18,000
1931	AE	6 cyl.	2 Door Sedan	3,300	4,500	15,200
1932	BA Deluxe	6 cyl.	5 Window Coupe	4,300	6,400	22,500
1932	BA Deluxe	6 cyl.	Sedan	2,000	7,000	16,000
1932	BA Deluxe	6 cyl.	Sport Roadster	5,500	8,800	31,000
1932	BA Standard	6 cyl.	Roadster	5,000	8,500	29,000

YEAR	MODEL	ENGINE	BODY	F	G	E
CHEVROLET *(United States, 1911 to date)* *(continued)*						
1932	BA Deluxe	6 cyl.	Sport Coupe	4,000	12,000	23,000
1932	BA Deluxe	6 cyl.	Landau Phaeton	6,000	15,000	35,000
1933	Eagle	6 cyl.	Sport Roadster	5,000	12,000	30,000
1933	Eagle	6 cyl.	Phaeton	6,800	19,000	36,000
1933	Eagle	6 cyl.	2 Door Sedan	2,000	4,000	8,000
1933	Eagle	6 cyl.	Sedan	2,000	4,000	8,000
1933	Eagle	6 cyl.	Cabriolet	6,000	12,000	25,000
1933	Eagle	6 cyl.	Rumble Seat Coupe	3,200	6,500	15,000
1934	Standard	6 cyl.	Coupe	2,000	4,000	10,000
1934	Standard	6 cyl.	Sport Roadster	4,000	12,000	28,000
1934	Standard	6 cyl.	Phaeton	6,000	12,000	30,000
1934	Master	6 cyl.	2 Door Sedan	2,000	3,000	8,000
1934	Master	6 cyl.	Sedan	1,000	3,000	8,000
1935	Standard	6 cyl.	Roadster	5,000	12,000	25,000
1935	Standard	6 cyl.	Coupe	2,000	4,000	10,000
1935	Standard	6 cyl.	Phaeton	5,000	12,000	27,000
1935	Standard	6 cyl.	Sedan	1,000	3,000	8,000
1936	Standard	6 cyl.	2 Door Sedan	2,000	4,000	9,000
1936	Standard	6 cyl.	Coupe	1,900	4,100	11,200
1936	Master	6 cyl.	Sedan	1,000	3,000	9,000
1937	Master	6 cyl.	Convertible	8,000	14,000	28,000
1937	Master Deluxe	6 cyl.	Coupe	2,000	4,000	9,000
1937	Master Deluxe	6 cyl.	2 Door Sedan	1,000	3,000	8,000
1937	Master Deluxe	6 cyl.	Sport Coupe	2,000	4,000	10,000
1937	Master	6 cyl.	Sedan	1,000	3,000	8,000
1938	Master	6 cyl.	Coupe	1,700	4,300	9,200
1938	Master	6 cyl.	Convertible	8,000	17,000	30,000
1938	Master	6 cyl.	Town Sedan	1,700	4,100	8,100
1938	Master	6 cyl.	2 or 4 Door Sedan	1,800	4,500	8,500
1938	Master Deluxe	6 cyl.	Coupe	1,900	5,900	10,000
1938	Master Deluxe	6 cyl.	Sport Coupe	2,000	5,000	11,000
1939	Master 85	6 cyl.	2 Door Sedan	1,000	3,000	8,000

YEAR	MODEL	ENGINE	BODY	F	G	E
CHEVROLET	*(United States, 1911 to date) (continued)*					
1939	Master Deluxe	6 cyl.	Sport Coupe	2,000	5,000	11,000
1939	Master Deluxe	6 cyl.	Sedan	1,700	3,000	10,000
1939	Master Deluxe	6 cyl.	2 Door Sedan	2,000	4,000	10,000
1940	Special Deluxe	6 cyl.	Convertible	5,000	15,000	25,000
1940	Master Deluxe	6 cyl.	Coupe	1,000	4,000	10,000
1940	Master 85	6 cyl.	Coupe	1,000	4,000	10,000
1940	Special Deluxe	6 cyl.	2 Door Sedan	2,000	4,000	10,000
1941	Special Deluxe	6 cyl.	Convertible	8,000	16,000	30,000
1941	Special Deluxe	6 cyl.	Sedan	1,000	4,000	9,000
1941	Special Deluxe	6 cyl.	4 Passenger Coupe	2,000	4,000	10,000
1941	Master Deluxe	6 cyl.	2 Passenger Coupe	2,000	4,000	10,000
1942	Fleetline	6 cyl.	2 Door Aero	1,000	3,000	7,000
1942	Master Deluxe	6 cyl.	Coupe	2,000	4,000	8,000
1942	Special Deluxe	6 cyl.	4 Door Sedan	1,000	2,000	6,000
1942	Special Deluxe	6 cyl.	Convertible	8,000	15,000	28,000
1942	Special Deluxe	6 cyl.	2 or 5 Passenger Coupe	1,900	3,000	7,900
1942	Special Deluxe	6 cyl.	Sedan 2 styles	1,500	3,300	6,300
Postwar Models						
1946	Fleetmaster	6 cyl.	Convertible	6,000	15,000	30,000
1946	Fleetmaster	6 cyl.	Sport Coupe	3,000	4,000	10,000
1946	Fleetmaster	6 cyl.	Sedan 2 styles	1,000	3,000	8,000
1946	Fleetmaster	6 cyl.	Station Wagon	4,000	12,000	24,000
1946	Fleetline	6 cyl.	Aero Sedan	1,700	3,400	8,700
1946	Stylemaster	6 cyl.	2 Door Sedan	1,700	4,000	8,250
1946	Stylemaster	6 cyl.	4 Door Sedan	1,700	4,000	8,400

YEAR	MODEL	ENGINE	BODY	F	G	E
CHEVROLET *(United States, 1911 to date) (continued)*						
1946	Stylemaster	6 cyl.	Sport Coupe	2,000	4,000	10,000
1947	Fleetmaster	6 cyl.	Convertible	6,000	15,000	30,000
1947	Fleetmaster	6 cyl.	2 Door Sedan	1,700	4,500	8,400
1948	Stylemaster	6 cyl.	Sedan	2,000	3,500	9,000
1948	Fleetmaster	6 cyl.	Town Sedan	1,000	3,000	8,000
1948	Fleetmaster	6 cyl.	Sport Coupe	2,000	5,000	10,000
1948	Fleetmaster	6 cyl.	Sport Sedan	1,900	3,200	7,000
1949	Styleline Deluxe	6 cyl.	Convertible	6,000	12,000	25,000
1949	Styleline Deluxe	6 cyl.	Sedan	1,000	3,000	8,000
1949	Styleline Deluxe	6 cyl.	"Woodie" Station Wagon	3,000	8,000	20,000
1950	Bel Air	6 cyl.	Hardtop	4,000	7,000	14,000
1950	Fleetline Deluxe	6 cyl.	2 Door Sedan	2,000	4,000	8,000
1950	Fleetline Deluxe	6 cyl.	4 Door Sedan	1,000	3,000	8,000
1950	Deluxe	6 cyl.	Convertible	5,000	12,000	26,000
1950	Styleline Deluxe	6 cyl.	Sedan	1,000	3,000	8,000
1950	Styleline Deluxe	6 cyl.	Sport Coupe	2,000	5,000	9,000
1950	Styleline Deluxe	6 cyl.	Station Wagon	1,000	4,000	10,000
1951	Fleetline Deluxe	6 cyl.	4 Door Sedan	1,000	3,000	8,000
1951	Styleline Deluxe	6 cyl.	Convertible	4,000	12,000	25,000
1951	Fleetline Special	6 cyl.	Station Wagon	2,000	5,000	11,000
1951	Bel Air	6 cyl.	Hardtop Coupe	3,000	6,000	14,000
1952	Deluxe	6 cyl.	Convertible	4,000	12,000	25,000
1952	Deluxe	6 cyl.	Hardtop Coupe	2,000	4,000	10,000
1952	Fastback	6 cyl.	2 Door Sedan	1,700	3,000	8,200
1953	Corvette	6 cyl.	Roadster	40,000	75,000	125,000
1953	210	6 cyl.	Convertible	5,000	12,000	28,000

YEAR	MODEL	ENGINE	BODY	F	G	E
CHEVROLET *(United States, 1911 to date) (continued)*						
1953	Bel Air	6 cyl.	Hardtop	3,000	6,000	15,000

Chevrolet – 1953 "Bel Air"

YEAR	MODEL	ENGINE	BODY	F	G	E
1953	Bel Air	6 cyl.	4 Door Sedan	1,500	3,400	9,500
1953	Bel Alr	6 cyl.	2 Door Sedan	1,000	4,000	10,000
1953	Bel Alr	6 cyl.	Convertible	6,000	18,000	30,000
1954	Corvette	6 cyl.	Roadster	25,000	50,000	75,000
1954	Bel Air	6 cyl.	Convertible	6,000	15,000	30,000
1954	Bel Air	6 cyl.	Hardtop	3,000	4,000	15,000
1954	Bel Air	6 cyl.	2 Door Sedan	2,000	4,000	10,000
1954	Bel Air	6 cyl.	Station Wagon	1,000	4,000	12,000
1955	210	8 cyl.	Hardtop	3,000	6,000	15,000
1955	210 Del Rey	V 8 cyl.	2 Door Sedan	2,000	4,000	10,000
1955	Bel Air	V 8 cyl.	2 Door Sedan	2,400	7,000	12,000
1955	Bel Air	V 8 cyl.	Hardtop	4,000	10,000	23,000
1955	Bel Air	V 8 cyl.	Station Wagon	2,000	5,000	12,000
1955	Bel Alr	V 8 cyl.	Convertible	8,000	18,000	30,000
1955	Nomad	V 8 cyl.	2 Door Wagon	6,000	12,000	20,000
1955	Corvette	6 cyl.	Roadster	25,000	50,000	95,000
1955	Corvette	V 8 cyl.	Roadster	20,000	40,000	85,000
1956	150	8 cyl.	Sedan	1,000	3,000	7,000
1956	150	8 cyl.	Station Wagon	2,000	4,000	9,000
1956	210	V 8 cyl.	4 Door Hardtop	2,000	4,000	9,000
1956	210	V 8 cyl.	Hardtop	3,000	6,000	14,000

YEAR	MODEL	ENGINE	BODY	F	G	E
CHEVROLET *(United States, 1911 to date) (continued)*						
1956	Bel Air	V 8 cyl.	2 Door Sedan	2,000	4,000	10,000
1956	Bel Air	V 8 cyl.	2 Door Hardtop	2,000	8,000	20,000
1956	Bel Air	V 8 cyl.	Sedan	1,000	4,000	10,000
1956	Bel Air	V 8 cyl.	Convertible	7,000	15,000	31,000
1956	Nomad	V 8 cyl.	2 Door Wagon	3,000	8,000	18,000
1956	Corvette	V 8 cyl.	Roadster	15,000	35,000	65,000
1957	150	8 cyl.	Sedan	1,000	4,000	8,000
1957	150	8 cyl.	2 Door Sedan	2,000	4,000	8,000
1957	150	8 cyl.	Station Wagon	1,000	4,000	10,000
1957	210	V 8 cyl.	Sedan	1,000	4,000	9,000
1957	210	V 8 cyl.	2 Door Hardtop	2,000	5,000	12,000
1957	Bel Air	V 8 cyl.	Sedan	2,000	5,000	11,000
1957	Bel Air	V 8 cyl.	2 Door Sedan	2,000	6,000	12,000
1957	Bel Air	V 8 cyl.	2 Door Hardtop	6,000	12,000	25,000
1957	Bel Air	V 8 cyl.	Convertible	15,000	25,000	45,000
1957	Nomad	V 8 cyl.	2 Door Wagon	4,000	8,000	20,000
1957	Corvette	V 8 cyl.	Roadster	25,000	35,000	60,000
1957	Corvette	V 8 cyl. (Fuel Injection)	Roadster	30,000	45,000	80,000
1957	Bel Air	V 8 cyl. (Fuel Injection)	Hardtop	6,000	12,000	30,000
1958	Bel Air	V 8 cyl.	Hardtop Coupe	2,000	5,000	12,000
1958	Del Ray	8 cyl.	Sedan	1,000	2,000	6,000
1958	Impala	V 8 cyl.	Hardtop Coupe	6,000	12,000	25,000
1958	Impala	V 8 cyl.	Convertible	10,000	25,000	40,000
1958	Nomad	V 8 cyl.	Station Wagon 4 Door	2,900	5,300	12,000
1958	Corvette	V 8 cyl.	Roadster	15,000	25,000	50,000
1958	Corvette	V 8 cyl. (Fuel Injection)	Roadster	20,000	35,000	65,000
1959	Bel Air	8 cyl.	2 Door Sedan	2,000	3,000	6,000
1959	Biscayne	8 cyl.	Sedan	1,000	2,000	6,000
1959	Impala	V 8 cyl.	Sport Coupe	3,000	8,000	16,000
1959	Impala	V 8 cyl.	Convertible	7,000	15,000	27,000
1959	Nomad	V 8 cyl.	Station Wagon 4 Door	2,300	3,700	9,500
1959	Corvette	V 8 cyl.	Roadster	15,000	25,000	45,000

YEAR	MODEL	ENGINE	BODY	F	G	E
CHEVROLET (United States, 1911 to date) (continued)						
1959	Corvette	V 8 cyl. (Fuel Injection)	Roadster	20,000	30,000	55,000
1960	Bel Air	V 8 cyl.	Hardtop Coupe	1,700	3,600	8,400
1960	Impala	V 8 cyl.	Sport Coupe	2,000	6,000	14,000
1960	Impala	V 8 cyl.	Convertible	8,000	15,000	25,000
1960	Corvette	V 8 cyl.	Roadster	5,700	25,000	45,000

Chevrolet –1960 "Corvette Roadster"

YEAR	MODEL	ENGINE	BODY	F	G	E
1960	Corvette	V 8 cyl. (Fuel Injection)	Roadster	20,000	30,000	55,000
1960	Corvair	6 cyl.	Coupe	1,500	3,300	6,500
1960	Corvair Monza	6 cyl.	Coupe	1,900	3,700	7,200
1960	Corvair	6 cyl.	Sedan	500	2,000	5,000
1961	Impala	V 8 cyl.	2 Door Sedan	2,000	5,000	12,000
1961	Bel Air	V 8 cyl.	Hardtop Coupe	3,000	6,000	13,000
1961	Impala	V 8 cyl.	Sport Coupe	3,000	6,000	12,000
1961	Impala SS	V 8 cyl. 409	Sport Coupe	6,000	12,000	20,000
1961	Impala	V 8 cyl.	Convertible	5,000	12,000	20,000
1961	Impala SS	V 8 cyl. 348	Convertible	6,000	12,000	25,000
1961	Corvair Monza	6 cyl.	Coupe	1,000	3,000	7,000
1961	Corvair	6 cyl.	Sedan	500	2,000	5,000
1961	Corvette	V 8 cyl.	Roadster	15,000	25,000	45,000
1961	Corvette	V 8 cyl. (Fuel Injection)	Roadster	25,000	25,000	50,000
1962	Bel Air	V 8 cyl.	Sport Coupe	3,000	6,000	12,000

YEAR	MODEL	ENGINE	BODY	F	G	E
CHEVROLET *(United States, 1911 to date) (continued)*						
1962	Impala	V 8 cyl.	Sport Coupe	3,000	7,000	15,000
1962	Impala SS	V 8 cyl. 327	Sport Coupe	3,000	8,000	17,000
1962	Impala SS	V 8 cyl. 409	Convertible	8,000	15,000	25,000
1962	Corvette	V 8 cyl.	Roadster	15,000	25,000	47,000
1962	Corvette	V 8 cyl. (Fuel Injection)	Roadster	15,000	27,000	52,000
1962	Corvair Monza	6 cyl.	Coupe	1,000	3,000	8,000
1962	Corvair Monza	6 cyl.	Convertible	3,000	6,000	11,000
1962	Corvair Greenbrier	6 cyl.	Station Wagon	1,000	2,000	6,000
1962	Chevy II	6 cyl.	Sport Coupe	2,000	4,000	9,000
1963	Impala	V 8 cyl. 283	Sport Coupe	3,000	7,000	15,000
1963	Impala SS	V 8 cyl. 409	Sport Coupe	5,000	10,000	20,000
1963	Impala	V 8 cyl. 327	Convertible	6,000	11,000	23,000
1963	Impala SS	V 8 cyl. 327	Convertible	8,000	14,000	28,000
1963	Corvette	V 8 cyl. (Fuel Injection)	Coupe	12,000	20,000	40,000
1963	Corvette	V 8 cyl.	Roadster	10,000	18,000	38,000
1963	Corvair Monza	6 cyl.	Coupe	1,000	3,000	8,000
1963	Corvair Monza	6 cyl.	Convertible	3,000	5,000	10,000
1963	Nova SS	6 cyl.	Sport Coupe	3,000	5,000	10,000
1963	Nova SS	6 cyl.	Convertible	4,000	7,000	12,000
1964	Chevelle	8 cyl.	Sedan	2,000	3,000	5,000
1964	Chevelle	8 cyl.	4 Door Station Wagon	1,000	2,000	6,000
1964	Impala	V 8 cyl.	Convertible	7,000	12,000	22,000
1964	Impala SS	V 8 cyl. 327	Convertible	8,000	14,000	25,000
1964	Impala SS	V 8 cyl. 409	Sport Coupe	5,000	11,000	23,000
1964	Corvette	V 8 cyl.	Coupe	10,000	15,000	30,000
1964	Corvette	V 8 cyl.	Roadster	8,000	14,000	28,000
1964	Corvair Monza	6 cyl.	Coupe	1,500	3,000	8,000
1964	Corvair Monza	6 cyl.	Convertible	2,000	5,000	10,000
1964	Corvair Spyder	6 cyl. (Turbo)	Coupe	2,000	3,000	8,000
1964	Corvair Spyder	6 cyl. (Turbo)	Convertible	3,000	6,000	11,000

YEAR	MODEL	ENGINE	BODY	F	G	E
CHEVROLET *(United States, 1911 to date) (continued)*						
1964	Nova SS	V 8 cyl. 283	Sport Coupe	2,000	5,000	12,000
1965	Impala SS	V 8 cyl. 327	Convertible	8,000	12,000	25,000
1965	Impala SS	V 8 cyl. 327	Sport Coupe	5,000	10,000	20,000
1965	Corvette	V 8 cyl.	Roadster	8,000	18,000	35,000
1965	Corvette	V 8 cyl. (Fuel Injection)	Coupe	7,000	15,000	33,000
1965	Corvair Monza	6 cyl.	Convertible	3,000	5,000	9,500
1965	Corvair Monza	6 cyl.	Sport Coupe	2,000	3,000	7,000
1965	Malibu	8 cyl.	Sedan	1,000	2,000	5,000
1965	Malibu	8 cyl.	Hardtop	2,000	5,000	11,000
1965	Malibu SS	8 cyl.	Hardtop	3,000	7,000	15,000
1965	Malibu SS	8 cyl.	Convertible	5,000	12,000	20,000
1965	Nova SS	V 8 cyl. 327	Sport Coupe	2,000	4,000	10,000
1966	Impala SS	V 8 cyl. 427	Sport Coupe	2,000	5,000	12,000
1966	Impala SS	V 8 cyl. 327	Convertible	3,000	8,000	17,000
1966	Corvette	V 8 cyl. 427	Coupe	7,000	18,000	35,000
1966	Corvette	V 8 cyl. 327	Roadster	6,000	15,000	33,000
1966	Corvair Monza	6 cyl.	Convertible	2,000	4,000	9,500
1966	Corvair Monza	6 cyl.	Coupe	1,000	3,000	7,000
1966	Nova SS	V 8 cyl. 327	Sport Coupe	2,000	4,000	9,000
1966	Caprice	V 8 cyl. 396	2 Door Hardtop	3,000	7,000	15,000
1967	Impala	8 cyl.	Sedan	1,500	4,000	9,000
1967	Impala	8 cyl.	Station Wagon	1,500	3,000	7,000
1967	Impala	8 cyl.	Convertible	4,000	8,000	17,000
1967	Impala SS	V 8 cyl. 327	Convertible	4,000	10,000	20,000
1967	Impala SS	V 8 cyl. 427	Convertible	4,000	10,000	25,000
1967	Corvette	V 8 cyl. 427	Roadster	9,000	20,000	45,000
1967	Corvette	V 8 cyl. 327	Coupe	7,000	15,000	35,000
1967	Corvair Monza	6 cyl.	Convertible	2,000	4,000	10,000
1967	Corvair Monza	6 cyl.	Coupe	1,000	3,000	7,000
1967	Camaro SS	V 8 cyl. 327	Sport Coupe	2,000	6,000	12,000

YEAR	MODEL	ENGINE	BODY	F	G	E
CHEVROLET *(United States, 1911 to date) (continued)*						
1967	Camaro SS	V 8 cyl. 327	Convertible	3,000	8,000	18,000

Chevrolet – 1967 "Camaro SS Convertible"

YEAR	MODEL	ENGINE	BODY	F	G	E
1967	Camaro Z-28	V 8 cyl. 302	Sport Coupe	6,000	15,000	30,000
1967	Nova SS	V 8 cyl. 327	Sport Coupe	2,000	4,000	9,000
1968	Chevelle Malibu	8 cyl.	Sedan	1,400	2,400	4,600
1968	Chevelle Malibu	8 cyl.	2 Door Hardtop	2,000	4,000	9,000
1968	Chevelle Malibu	8 cyl.	Convertible	4,000	6,000	12,000
1968	Impala	V 8 cyl. 427	Convertible	8,000	10,000	20,000
1968	Camaro Z-28	V 8 cyl. 302	Sport Coupe	4,000	9,000	18,000
1968	Caprice	V 8 cyl. 427	Coupe	2,000	5,000	12,000
1969	Impala SS	V 8 cyl. 427	Convertible	4,000	12,000	22,000
1969	Impala	V 8 cyl. 327	Convertible	3,000	7,000	15,000
1969	Camaro Z-28	V 8 cyl. 302	Sport Coupe	4,000	8,000	18,000
1969	Camaro SS	V 8 cyl. 350	Convertible	4,000	8,000	16,000
1969	Corvette	V 8 cyl. 350	Convertible	8,000	15,000	30,000
1969	Corvette	V 8 cyl. 427	Coupe	9,000	16,000	35,000
1969	Corvair	6 cyl.	Coupe	1,000	2,000	6,000
1969	Corvair	6 cyl.	Convertible	2,000	4,000	10,000
1970	Nova	4 cyl.	Sedan	900	1,600	3,500
1970	Nova	6 cyl.	Coupe	1,000	2,000	4,000
1970	Biscayne	8 cyl.	Sedan	900	1,500	3,500
1970	Biscayne	8 cyl.	Station Wagon	600	1,500	3,500
1970	Chevelle	8 cyl.	Sedan	800	1,500	4,000
1970	Chevelle	8 cyl.	Coupe	1,000	3,000	5,500

YEAR	MODEL	ENGINE	BODY	F	G	E
CHEVROLET *(United States, 1911 to date) (continued)*						
1970	Malibu	8 cyl.	Sedan	1,000	2,000	4,000
1970	Malibu	8 cyl.	Sport Coupe	2,000	4,000	9,000
1970	Malibu	8 cyl.	Convertible	4,000	6,000	11,000
1970	Malibu	8 cyl.	Estate	1,000	3,000	5,000
1971	Corvette	V 8 cyl. 350	Coupe T-Top	6,000	10,000	22,000
1971	Corvette 454	V 8 cyl.	Convertible	8,000	17,000	30,000
1971	Monte Carlo SS 454	V 8 cyl.	Coupe	3,000	6,000	14,000
1972	Chevelle SS 454	V 8 cyl.	Convertible	3,000	7,000	15,000
1974	Caprice Classic	V 8 cyl.	Convertible	3,000	5,000	10,000
1975	Caprice Classic	V 8 cyl.	Convertible	4,000	6,000	12,000
1975	Corvette	V 8 cyl.	T-Top	4,000	6,500	20,000
1975	Corvette	V 8 cyl.	Convertible	4,200	6,700	28,000
1978	Corvette Pace 350	V 8 cyl.	T-Top	6,200	9,000	22,000
1978	Corvette L-82	V 8 cyl.	T-Top	9,000	12,500	22,000
CHEVRON *(Great Britain, 1961–73)*						
1961		(Holbay-Ford)	Racing	2,500	4,900	10,500
1966	GT	(B.M.W.)	Coupe	1,800	4,500	9,000
1967	SP	V 8 cyl.	1 Passenger	1,500	4,000	8,000
1971	B-19 Spyder	V 8 cyl. (Repco)	Racing	2,500	4,200	10,000
1973	B-23	2 Litre	Sport Racing	2,700	4,200	10,000
CHIYODA *(Japan, 1932–35)*						
1932	HF		7 Passenger Touring	1,000	3,400	7,000
1933	H4		Sedan	800	1,700	4,000
1933	HS		7 Passenger Touring	1,500	3,800	9,000
CHRISTIE *(United States, front-wheel drive, 1904–10)*						
1904	30	4 cyl.	Racing	8,000	27,000	45,000
1905	50	4 cyl.	Touring	7,000	20,000	40,000
1907	60	V 4 cyl.	Racing	10,000	30,000	60,000
CHRYSLER *(United States, 1924 to date)*						
1924	B-70	6 cyl.	Touring	3,200	8,000	16,200
1924	B-70	6 cyl.	Roadster	4,000	9,000	17,500
1924	B-70	6 cyl.	Brougham	2,600	4,000	8,300

YEAR	MODEL	ENGINE	BODY	F	G	E
CHRYSLER *(United States, 1924 to date) (continued)*						
1924	B-70	6 cyl.	Town Car	3,500	6,500	13,000
1924	B-70	6 cyl.	Phaeton	5,000	10,000	18,700
1924	B-70	6 cyl.	Sedan	3,100	7,600	15,000
1925	B-70	6 cyl.	Sport Phaeton	4,900	12,000	26,000
1925	B-70	6 cyl.	Sedan	2,800	5,400	13,000
1925	B-70	6 cyl.	Touring	4,500	11,000	21,000
1925	B-70	6 cyl.	Touring	4,000	9,000	17,500
1925	B-70	6 cyl.	Roadster	5,000	10,000	18,700
1925	B-70	6 cyl.	Brougham	3,400	6,000	10,000
1926	80	6 cyl.	Victoria Coupe	3,000	5,800	13,000
1926	80	6 cyl.	Sedan	2,600	7,000	12,000
1926	50	6 cyl.	Coupe	1,900	3,800	7,500
1926	70	6 cyl.	Phaeton	5,500	11,000	24,000
1926	60	6 cyl.	Roadster	6,100	12,000	29,000
1926	58	4 cyl.	Touring	4,000	9,000	17,500
1926	58	4 cyl.	Roadster	5,000	10,000	18,700
1926	58	4 cyl.	2 or 4 Door Sedan	2,200	5,900	7,400
1926	58	4 cyl.	Coupe	2,500	3,800	8,000
1927	50	6 cyl.	Roadster Rumble Seat	5,800	13,000	26,000
1927	60	6 cyl.	Touring	4,000	9,000	17,500
1927	60	6 cyl.	Roadster 2 styles	5,000	10,000	18,700
1927	60	6 cyl.	Coupe 2 styles	2,700	4,300	8,600
1927	70	6 cyl.	Coupe Rumble Seat	2,500	6,200	16,000
1927	52	6 cyl.	Sedan	2,200	5,500	13,000
1927	70	6 cyl.	Roadster	5,500	14,000	27,000
1927	Imperial	6 cyl.	7 Passenger Touring	7,800	29,000	52,000
1927	Imperial	6 cyl.	Sport Roadster	6,100	21,000	35,000
1927	Imperial	6 cyl.	Victoria Coupe	4,200	12,000	17,000
1928	62	6 cyl.	Coupe Rumble Seat	3,500	6,500	13,000
1928	62	6 cyl.	Business Coupe	2,200	5,500	11,000
1928	62	6 cyl.	2 Door Sedan	1,800	5,200	10,000

YEAR	MODEL	ENGINE	BODY	F	G	E
CHRYSLER *(United States, 1924 to date) (continued)*						
1928	72	6 cyl.	Coupe	3,800	7,800	13,000
1928	72	6 cyl.	Roadster	5,200	18,000	33,000
1928	Imperial	6 cyl.	Touring	8,300	22,000	42,000
1928	Imperial	6 cyl.	Sport Roadster	8,500	30,000	52,000
1928	Imperial	6 cyl.	Club Sedan	5,200	11,000	22,000
1928	Imperial	6 cyl.	Victoria Coupe	5,100	11,000	22,000
1928	Imperial	6 cyl.	Sedan	5,100	11,000	21,000
1929	65	6 cyl.	Roadster	6,700	13,000	33,000
1929	75	6 cyl.	Roadster	7,400	16,000	37,000
1929	75	6 cyl.	Sedan	3,200	6,200	16,000
1929	65	6 cyl.	Rumble Seat Coupe	3,400	7,200	16,000
1929	75	6 cyl.	Club Sedan	3,300	6,800	16,000
1929	75	6 cyl.	Cabriolet	4,000	10,400	19,000
1929	80	8 cyl.	Sedan	5,100	11,000	19,000
1929	Imperial 80	8 cyl.	Sport Roadster	19,000	47,000	56,000
1930	77	6 cyl.	Coupe	3,700	6,800	16,000
1930	77	6 cyl.	Roadster	7,000	18,000	37,000
1930	77	6 cyl.	Phaeton	6,100	17,000	35,000
1930	Imperial 80	6 cyl.	Formal Sedan	9,200	19,000	38,000
1930	Imperial 80	6 cyl.	Sport Roadster	30,000	60,000	105,000
1930	66	6 cyl.	Sport Phaeton	6,500	18,000	37,500
1930	70	6 cyl.	Roadster	4,200	11,000	27,000
1930	70	6 cyl.	Phaeton	6,100	17,000	35,500
1930	70	6 cyl.	Coupe 2 styles	3,000	5,100	10,000
1930	Imperial 80	6 cyl.	Rumble Seat Coupe	6,700	13,000	30,000
1930	66	6 cyl.	Sedan	3,200	7,200	16,000
1930	77	6 cyl.	Sedan	3,400	7,600	17,000
1931	CD	8 cyl.	Roadster	11,000	27,000	48,000
1931	CM	6 cyl.	Town Cabet	6,200	11,000	26,000
1931	Imperial CG	8 cyl.	Limousine	9,200	22,000	38,000
1931	Imperial CG	8 cyl. (Close Couple)	Coupe	9,300	22,000	43,000
1931	Imperial CG	8 cyl.	LeBaron Dual Cowl Phaeton	41,000	80,000	140,000
1931	Imperial CG	8 cyl.	Cabriolet	8,600	23,000	37,000

YEAR	MODEL	ENGINE	BODY	F	G	E
CHRYSLER *(United States, 1924 to date) (continued)*						
1931	Imperial CG	8 cyl.	Convertible Sedan	30,000	60,000	105,000
1931	Imperial CG	8 cyl.	Rumble Seat Coupe	8,500	19,000	38,000
1931	Imperial	8 cyl.	LeBaron Roadster	3,700	11,000	18,000
1931	CM	6 cyl.	Roadster	6,800	16,000	37,000
1931	CD	8 cyl.	Sport Sedan	3,700	8,400	19,000
1932	CP	8 cyl.	Convertible Coupe	6,800	15,000	38,000
1932	Imperial CL	8 cyl.	8 Passenger Sedan	8,200	18,000	40,000
1932	Imperial CL	8 cyl.	Phaeton	31,000	67,000	130,000
1932	Imperial CL	8 cyl.	Roadster	33,000	50,000	90,000
1932	Imperial CQ	8 cyl.	Convertible Sedan	34,000	62,000	110,000
1932	Imperial CL	8 cyl.	Waterhouse Convertible Victoria	41,000	80,000	140,000
1932	Royal CT	8 cyl.	Sedan	6,800	12,000	22,000
1932	CL	6 cyl.	Rumble Seat Coupe	3,600	7,800	16,000
1933	CO	8 cyl.	Convertible Coupe	11,000	22,000	50,000
1933	CO	6 cyl.	Coupe	3,600	7,800	20,000
1933	CO	6 cyl.	Sedan	3,600	7,800	18,000
1933	CO	6 cyl.	Cabriolet	4,200	11,000	26,000
1933	CT	8 cyl.	Sedan	4,400	9,600	18,000
1934	CA	6 cyl.	Cabriolet	3,300	6,500	14,000
1934	CA	6 cyl.	Sedan	3,300	5,200	14,000
1934	CW Airflow	8 cyl.	Sedan	10,400	20,000	35,000
1934	CA	6 cyl.	Coupe	2,800	6,400	10,000
1934	CW Airflow	8 cyl.	Club Sedan	3,200	9,500	18,000
1934	CU Airflow	8 cyl.	Sedan	3,100	6,400	16,000
1935	Airstream	6 cyl.	Sedan	2,500	6,200	13,000
1935	Airflow	8 cyl.	Sedan	3,700	6,300	15,000
1936	Airstream	6 cyl.	Sedan	2,500	6,000	15,000
1936	Airstream	6 cyl.	Coupe	2,600	6,200	16,000
1936	C-10 Airflow	8 cyl.	Sedan	3,800	8,400	19,000
1936	C-8	8 cyl.	Cabriolet	3,700	11,000	19,000
1937	Imperial Airflow	8 cyl.	Sedan	4,200	7,500	16,000

YEAR	MODEL	ENGINE	BODY	F	G	E
CHRYSLER *(United States, 1924 to date) (continued)*						
1937	Imperial Airflow	8 cyl.	Coupe	5,000	11,000	20,000
1937	Royal	6 cyl.	Convertible Sedan	5,500	14,000	25,000
1937	Royal	6 cyl.	Sedan	1,800	3,200	7,400
1938	Imperial	8 cyl.	Convertible Sedan	6,200	16,000	34,000
1938	Imperial	8 cyl.	Sedan	2,200	4,300	8,500
1939	Imperial	8 cyl.	Opera Coupe	1,900	3,800	9,200
1939	New Yorker	8 cyl.	Opera Coupe	1,800	3,700	9,400
1939	New Yorker	8 cyl.	Hayes Coupe	4,300	8,500	19,000
1939	Imperial	8 cyl.	Limousine	3,200	7,300	15,000
1939	Royal	6 cyl.	Sedan	1,500	3,200	7,200
1940	Windsor	6 cyl.	2 Door Sedan	1,500	3,200	7,200
1940	Thunderbolt	8 cyl.	Convertible	32,000	62,000	120,000
1940	Windsor	6 cyl.	Sedan	1,600	2,800	7,200
1940	New Yorker	8 cyl.	Sedan	2,000	2,900	8,000
1941	Highlander	6 cyl.	Sedan	1,600	3,600	7,000
1941	Imperial	8 cyl.	Sedan	2,000	4,200	8,200
1941	Newport	8 cyl.	Dual Cowl Phaeton	49,000	120,000	210,000

Chrysler – 1941 "Newport Dual Phaeton"

1941	New Yorker	8 cyl.	Club Coupe	1,900	4,200	7,800
1941	Saratoga	6 cyl.	Sedan	1,500	2,800	4,000
1941	Royal	6 cyl.	Coupe	1,500	2,800	7,000
1942	Royal	6 cyl.	Sedan	1,500	2,800	7,000
1942	Saratoga	8 cyl.	Coupe	1,500	2,800	7,000
1942	Imperial Crown	8 cyl.	Limousine	3,300	7,300	13,000

YEAR	MODEL	ENGINE	BODY	F	G	E
CHRYSLER *(United States, 1924 to date) (continued)*						
1942	Town & Country	8 cyl.	Station Wagon	4,200	10,400	17,000
Postwar Models						
1946	Royal	6 cyl.	Sedan	1,500	3,000	7,500
1946	Town & Country	8 cyl.	Sedan	7,000	15,000	35,000
1946	Imperial	8 cyl.	8 Passenger Sedan	2,500	6,200	13,000
1947	Town & Country	6 cyl.	Convertible	15,000	35,000	75,000
1947	Town & Country	8 cyl.	Sedan	6,000	15,000	35,000
1947	New Yorker	8 cyl.	2 Passenger Coupe	2,000	5,000	12,000
1947	Royal	6 cyl.	Sedan	2,000	4,000	10,000
1947	Saratoga	8 cyl.	Club Coupe	3,000	5,000	11,000
1948	Royal	6 cyl.	2 Passenger Coupe	2,000	4,000	9,500

Chrysler – 1948 "Town and Country Sedan"

1948	Town & Country	6 cyl.	Convertible	20,000	40,000	75,000
1948	Windsor	6 cyl.	Sedan	2,000	4,000	10,000
1948	New Yorker	8 cyl.	Sedan	1,500	3,000	8,000
1949	Town & Country	V 8 cyl.	Convertible	8,000	20,000	45,000
1949	New Yorker	V 8 cyl.	Convertible	5,000	12,000	20,000
1949	New Yorker	V 8 cyl.	Sedan	1,500	3,000	8,000
1949	New Yorker	V 8 cyl.	Club Coupe	1,900	4,000	9,000
1949	Imperial	V 8 cyl.	Limousine	3,000	7,000	16,000

162 / CHRYSLER

CHRYSLER *(United States, 1924 to date) (continued)*

YEAR	MODEL	ENGINE	BODY	F	G	E
1950	Royal	V 8 cyl.	Station Wagon	3,000	8,000	20,000
1950	Windsor	V 8 cyl.	Convertible	3,000	8,000	18,000
1950	New Yorker	V 8 cyl.	Convertible	6,000	12,000	20,000
1950	Town & Country	V 8 cyl.	Hardtop	7,000	15,000	35,000
1951	Windsor	V 8 cyl.	2 Door Hardtop	1,600	5,000	11,000
1951	New Yorker	V 8 cyl.	Club Coupe	2,000	5,000	11,000
1951	New Yorker	V 8 cyl.	Town & Country Station Wagon	4,000	9,000	18,000
1952	New Yorker	V 8 cyl.	Convertible	5,000	10,000	20,000
1952	Imperial	V 8 cyl.	4 Door Sedan	1,900	3,000	8,000
1952	Windsor	V 8 cyl.	Convertible	4,000	9,000	18,000
1953	Imperial	V 8 cyl.	2 Door Hardtop	4,000	10,000	22,000
1953	Windsor	V 8 cyl.	Convertible	6,000	12,000	20,000
1953	Windsor	V 8 cyl.	Sedan	2,000	3,000	7,000
1954	Imperial	V 8 cyl.	Crown Sedan	3,000	5,000	12,000
1954	New Yorker	V 8 cyl.	Hardtop	4,000	10,000	21,000
1954	New Yorker	V 8 cyl.	Convertible	5,000	12,000	25,000
1955	Newport	V 8 cyl.	2 Door Hardtop	3,000	7,000	16,000
1955	Imperial	V 8 cyl.	Custom Sedan	2,000	4,000	10,000
1955	300	V 8 cyl.	Coupe	5,000	15,000	35,000
1955	Nassau	V 8 cyl.	2 Door Hardtop	2,000	6,000	15,000
1955	New Yorker	8 cyl.	Sedan	1,500	3,000	8,000
1955	New Yorker	8 cyl.	Convertible	4,000	12,000	26,000
1955	New Yorker	8 cyl.	Hardtop 2 styles	3,000	7,000	18,000
1956	300-B	V 8 cyl.	Coupe	6,000	15,000	35,000
1956	Windsor	V 8 cyl.	Sedan	1,500	3,000	7,000
1956	New Yorker	V 8 cyl.	Convertible	5,000	12,000	28,000

YEAR	MODEL	ENGINE	BODY	F	G	E
CHRYSLER *(United States, 1924 to date)* *(continued)*						
1957	300-C	V 8 cyl.	Convertible	10,000	25,000	50,000

Chrysler – 1957 "Sport Coupe"

YEAR	MODEL	ENGINE	BODY	F	G	E
1957	300-C	V 8 cyl.	Hardtop	8,000	20,000	40,000
1957	New Yorker	V 8 cyl.	Convertible	5,000	12,000	28,000
1957	Imperial	V 8 cyl.	Convertible	6,000	13,000	30,000
1957	New Yorker	V 8 cyl.	Sedan	2,000	4,000	9,000
1958	300-D	V 8 cyl.	2 Door Hardtop	6,000	18,000	40,000
1958	Imperial	V 8 cyl.	2 Door Hardtop	3,000	7,000	18,000
1958	Windsor	V 8 cyl.	Town & Country Station Wagon	1,500	3,000	7,000
1959	Windsor	V 8 cyl.	Sedan	1,500	3,000	7,000
1959	300-E	V 8 cyl.	2 Door Hardtop	6,000	18,000	40,000
1959	300-E	V 8 cyl.	Convertible	10,000	25,000	55,000
1959	New Yorker	V 8 cyl.	2 Door Hardtop	3,000	7,000	17,000
1959	Imperial Crown	V 8 cyl.	4 Door Hardtop	2,500	4,000	10,000
1959	Saratoga	V 8 cyl.	Sedan	1,600	2,000	5,000
1959	Town & Country	8 cyl.	Station Wagon	1,500	2,500	6,000
1961	300-G	V 8 cyl. 413	2 Door Hardtop	6,000	15,000	35,000
1961	300-G	V 8 cyl.	Convertible	8,000	20,000	45,000
1962	300-H	V 8 cyl.	Hardtop	6,000	14,000	31,000

YEAR	MODEL	ENGINE	BODY	F	G	E
CHRYSLER *(United States, 1924 to date) (continued)*						
1962	300-H	V 8 cyl.	Convertible	8,000	20,000	42,000
1962	300	V 8 cyl.	Convertible	3,400	6,000	12,000
1962	Imperial		2 Door			
	Crown	V 8 cyl.	Hardtop	1,900	4,000	8,000
1962	Imperial		4 Door			
	LeBaron	V 8 cyl.	Hardtop	2,000	4,000	9,000
1962	Newport	8 cyl.	Sedan	800	1,800	3,200
1962	Newport	8 cyl.	Hardtop			
			2 styles	800	1,800	3,200
1962	Newport	8 cyl.	Convertible	1,600	4,000	9,500
1963	300-J	V 8 cyl.	2 Door			
			Hardtop	4,000	10,000	24,000
1963	Imperial	V 8 cyl.	Convertible	3,400	6,800	14,000
1964	Imperial	V 8 cyl.	Convertible	3,400	4,400	15,000
1964	300-K	V 8 cyl.	2 Door			
			Hardtop	4,000	10,000	24,000
1965	Imperial					
	Crown	V 8 cyl.	Convertible	3,500	7,000	14,000
1967	300	V 8 cyl.	Convertible	3,400	6,400	13,000
1970	300-Hurst	V 8 cyl. 440	2 Door			
			Hardtop	2,000	3,700	9,500
1970	300	V 8 cyl.	Convertible	2,200	4,000	10,000
C.I.E.M. *(China, 1904–06)*						
1904		V 2 cyl.	Runabout	1,100	2,600	6,250
1904		V 4 cyl.	Tonneau	1,100	2,800	6,600
1905		V 2 cyl.	Tonneau	1,100	2,000	5,000
CINO *(United States, 1910–13)*						
1910	A	4 cyl.	Touring	4,200	8,800	18,000
1913	450A	4 cyl.	Roadster	6,000	12,000	28,000
CISITALIA *(Italy, 1946–65)*						
1946	CP		1 Passenger	1,200	3,500	7,000
1948			Coupe	900	1,800	3,600
1948			Touring	1,400	3,000	7,000
1950			Coupe	900	1,800	3,600
1952		(DeDion)	Sport Sedan	1,200	2,400	4,800
1961	Tourism	400 (Fiat)	Coupe	950	2,100	4,200
CITROEN *(France, 1919 to date)*						
1919	Type A	10hp	Touring	1,200	3,000	8,500
1922	Type B	1.5 Litre	Clover Leaf	1,100	2,500	7,500
1924		5 cyl.	Town Coupe	1,100	2,250	6,500
1925		4 cyl.	Saloon Sedan	1,000	2,250	6,500
1927		4 cyl.	Touring	1,200	3,500	8,500

YEAR	MODEL	ENGINE	BODY	F	G	E
CITROEN *(France, 1919 to date) (continued)*						
1930	C-6	4 cyl.	Sedan	1,000	2,250	6,500
1931		4 cyl.	Sedan	1,000	2,250	6,500
1932	Ten	4 cyl.	Sedan	1,200	2,700	6,500
1934	Four	4 cyl.	Sedan	1,100	2,500	6,000
1935	Six	6 cyl.	Sport			
			Roadster	1,500	3,600	9,300
1936		V 8 cyl.	Sedan	1,200	2,250	6,500
1936		V 8 cyl.	Sport			
			Roadster	1,300	3,500	9,000
1936		11 CV	7 Passenger			
			Sedan	1,100	2,250	6,500
1939		6 cyl.	Sport			
			Roadster	1,500	3,500	9,000

Citroen – 1939 "Sport"

YEAR	MODEL	ENGINE	BODY	F	G	E
1949		2 CV	Sedan	1,000	1,750	4,500
1951		2 CV	Sedan	1,000	1,750	4,500
1955	11 CV	4 cyl.	Sedan	1,200	2,000	6,000
1959	D519	6 cyl.	Sedan	1,200	2,200	6,250
1971	SM		Coupe	1,750	4,500	9,500
CITY & SUBURBAN *(Great Britain, 1901–05)*						
1901		Electric	Brougham			
			Voiturette	4,000	10,000	19,000
1903		Electric	Runabout	4,900	11,300	20,250
1903		Electric	Landaulet	4,100	11,500	20,000
1903		Electric	Shooting-Brake	4,500	12,000	24,250

YEAR	MODEL	ENGINE	BODY	F	G	E
CIVELLI DE BOSCH *(France, 1907–09)*						
1907		2 cyl.	Touring	1,200	2,800	7,500
1908		4 cyl.	Touring	1,500	3,000	8,000
1909		6 cyl.	Touring	1,700	3,800	9,000
CLARIN MUSTAD *(New Foundland, 1916–35)*						
1916		4 cyl.	Limousine	2,000	6,000	12,000
1916		4 cyl.	Touring	1,000	3,000	9,000
1917		6 cyl.	Limousine	1,000	3,200	9,200
1935		6 cyl.	Coupe	1,000	2,400	8,000
CLARK *(United States, 1910–12)*						
1910	A	4 cyl.	Touring	3,000	7,000	15,000
1911	B	4 cyl.	Roadster	3,500	8,500	16,000
1912	X	4 cyl.	Touring	4,000	9,000	20,000
1912	Y	4 cyl.	Roadster	5,000	10,000	21,000
CLARKSON *(Great Britain, 1899–1902)*						
1899		Steam	Baroche	4,200	9,000	16,500
1899		Steam	Victoria	4,000	8,600	15,800
1900	Clemsford	2 cyl.	Station Hack	1,000	3,000	8,000
CLASSIC *(France, 1925–29)*						
1925			Touring	1,200	3,600	9,750
1925			Touring	1,300	3,800	8,200
CLAVEAU *(France, 1926–50)*						
1926		4 cyl.	Tonneau	1,100	2,600	7,200
1927		1.5 Litre	Sedan	1,000	2,400	7,800
1932		V 2 cyl.	Roadster	1,250	3,250	9,700
1946	5S	V 4 cyl.	Sedan	1,100	2,400	7,900
CLEM *(France, 1912–14)*						
1912		4 cyl.	Runabout	1,100	2,400	7,750
1914		1320cc	Touring	1,200	2,500	8,000
CLEMENT; CLEMENT-BAYARD *(France, 1899–1922)*						
1899			Dos-a-dos	2,750	5,500	13,000
CLEMENT *(Great Britain, 1908–14)*						
1908		2 cyl.	Tonneau	2,000	4,000	9,000
1908	18-28	4 cyl.	Runabout	2,200	4,400	10,200
1913	All-weather	4 cyl.	Touring	2,400	5,000	11,000
CLEMENT-ROCHELLE *(France, 1927–30)*						
1927		1100cc (Ruby)	2 Door Sedan	1,000	4,500	9,500
1927	DH	1100cc (Ruby)	Coupe	1,200	2,800	10,800
1927	Sport	1100cc (Ruby)	Doorless	2,000	4,000	14,000
CLEVELAND *(United States, 1899–1926)*						
1899		Electric	Stanhope	4,500	11,500	22,000
1914		4 cyl.	Cycle	1,200	2,400	8,000

YEAR	MODEL	ENGINE	BODY	F	G	E
CLEVELAND *(United States, 1899–1926) (continued)*						
1920		6 cyl.	Roadster	2,900	7,900	17,800
1922		6 cyl.	Roadster	2,800	7,700	17,600
1923		6 cyl.	Sedan	1,200	3,000	9,000
1924		6 cyl.	Touring	2,000	7,500	16,500
1925		6 cyl.	Touring	2,000	7,600	16,800
1926		6 cyl.	Sedan	1,200	3,000	9,000
CLIMAX *(Great Britain, 1905–07)*						
1905		2 cyl.	Tonneau	1,200	3,000	11,000
1906		4 cyl.	Touring	2,000	5,200	12,500
CLINTON *(Canada, 1912)*						
1912		4 cyl.	Touring	2,000	5,200	12,000
1912		4 cyl.	Convertible	2,000	5,400	12,500
CLIPPER *(United States, Packard-built, 1955–56)*						
1955	Deluxe	V 8 cyl.	Sedan	1,250	3,500	7,200
1956	Super Deluxe	V 8 cyl.	Sedan	1,300	3,500	7,500
1956	Custom	V 8 cyl.	Sedan	1,200	3,400	7,200
CLUB CAR *(United States, 1910–11)*						
1910	A-E	4 cyl.	Limousine	4,000	8,800	26,000
1910	A-A	4 cyl.	Touring	4,500	8,500	22,000
1910	B-B	4 cyl.	Torpedo	4,400	8,500	27,500
1910	B-C	4 cyl.	Runabout	3,200	7,800	20,000
CLULEY *(Great Britain, 1922–28)*						
1922		4 cyl.	Roadster	1,500	2,800	8,000
1923		4 cyl.	Touring	1,200	4,000	10,200
CLYDE *(Great Britain, 1901–30)*						
1901		(Simms)		1,000	2,600	9,500
1908	12/14	3 cyl.	Touring	1,200	3,200	10,000
1924		2 cyl.	Roadster	1,100	2,700	9,600
CLYNO *(Great Britain, 1922–30)*						
1922	Royal	4 cyl. (Coventry-Climax)	Sport	1,100	3,650	9,000
1927			Touring	1,300	3,800	9,500
1928	Olympic		Sedan	1,000	2,500	6,800
C.M. *(France, 1924–30)*						
1929		1 cyl.	Cycle	1,000	2,400	6,500
COATES-GOSHEN *(United States, 1909–10)*						
1910	32	4 cyl. (Rutenber)	5 Passenger Touring	3,200	9,000	16,000

YEAR	MODEL	ENGINE	BODY	F	G	E
COEY *(United States, 1913–17)*						
1914	Bear	4 cyl.	Roadster	6,000	15,000	30,000
1917	Flyer A	4 cyl.	Touring	4,000	13,500	27,000
COHENDET *(France, 1898–1914)*						
1898	3	2 cyl.	Runabout	1,500	3,000	7,000
1903		4 cyl.	Tonneau	2,200	4,100	9,250
1906		1 cyl.	Voiturette	2,000	3,900	8,000
COLANI *(Germany, 1964–68)*						
1964		1.2 Litre	Sport	1,000	2,600	7,200
1964		1.2 Litre	Roadster	1,100	2,700	8,000
1964		1.2 Litre	Coupe	1,000	2,400	7,000
COLE *(United States, 1909–25)*						
1909	30	2 cyl.	Runabout	2,000	5,500	12,200
1916	8-50	V 8 cyl.	Touring	6,000	14,000	29,000
1917	860	V 8 cyl.	Touring	6,000	14,000	29,000
1917	860	V 8 cyl.	Roadster	7,000	15,000	31,000
1919		V 8 cyl.	Sport Touring	8,000	16,000	32,000
1920	Aero Eight	V 8 cyl.	Sportster Touring	7,000	15,000	30,000
1921	Aero Eight	V 8 cyl.	7 Passenger Touring	6,000	14,000	28,000
COLIBRI *(Germany, 1908–11)*						
1908		2 cyl.	Roadster	1,200	3,600	8,200
1910		4 cyl.	Roadster	1,400	3,800	9,500
COLLINET *(United States, 1921)*						
1921		4 cyl. (Wisconsin)	Open	2,800	5,500	11,000
COLOMBO *(Italy, 1922–24)*						
1922		4 cyl.	Open	1,000	2,000	5,100
COLONIAL *(United States, 1912–22)*						
1912		Electric	Brougham		RARE	
1912		Electric	Roadster		RARE	
1917		6 cyl.	Touring	3,500	8,000	17,000
1920		8 cyl.	Touring	4,250	9,500	24,000
1922		6 cyl. (Beaver)	Roadster	5,000	13,000	28,000
COLT *(United States, 1907)*						
1907		6 cyl.	Runabout	3,750	8,400	17,000
COLTMAN *(Great Britain, 1907–13)*						
1907	Side Entrance	4 cyl.	Touring	2,000	3,900	10,000

YEAR	MODEL	ENGINE	BODY	F	G	E

COLUMBIA *(United States, 1897–1913)*

YEAR	MODEL	ENGINE	BODY	F	G	E
1901	Mark VIII	1 cyl.	Runabout	3,900	7,800	16,500
1901	Mark XXXI	Electric	Brougham	5,200	12,500	28,000
1904	Mark XXXV	Electric	Victoria	5,500	12,000	28,000
1905	Mark LX	Electric	Runabout	6,500	13,500	29,000
1905	Mark XLIII	2 cyl.	Tonneau	5,000	9,000	19,000
1911	Mark 48	4 cyl	Touring	3,500	8,000	17,000
1911	Mark 85	4 cyl.	Touring	3,750	9,500	18,000

COLUMBIA SIX *(United States, 1916–24)*

YEAR	MODEL	ENGINE	BODY	F	G	E
1919	Six	6 cyl. (Continental)	Touring	4,200	10,400	22,000
1921	Six-20	6 cyl. (Continental)	Touring	4,200	10,400	22,000
1923	Light Six	6 cyl. (Continental)	Roadster	7,000	14,000	29,000
1924	Six	6 cyl. (Continental)	Tiger Sport	6,000	12,000	25,000

COLUMBUS *(United States, 1903–13)*

YEAR	MODEL	ENGINE	BODY	F	G	E
1903		Electric	Runabout	4,500	8,000	21,000
1907		Electric	Surrey	2,400	6,800	16,000
1908		Electric	Surrey	4,200	8,400	20,000

COMET *(United States, 1907–22)*

YEAR	MODEL	ENGINE	BODY	F	G	E
1906		4 cyl.	Runabout	3,500	6,800	14,000
1908		4 cyl.	Roadster	5,000	15,000	30,000
1914	Tandem	2 cyl. (Air-cooled)	Cycle	2,500	4,200	10,400
1914		4 cyl.	Roadster	4,000	8,500	18,500
1914		4 cyl.	Touring	3,500	7,000	17,000
1917	Six-50	6 cyl.	Touring	4,200	13,000	25,000

COMET *(Great Britain, 1921–37)*

YEAR	MODEL	ENGINE	BODY	F	G	E
1921		4 cyl.	Sport	1,300	3,750	9,500
1935		4 cyl.	Sport	1,300	3,750	9,500
1935		4 cyl.	Sedan	1,000	2,400	7,800
1935		4 cyl.	Drop Head Coupe	1,100	2,500	8,250

COMMONWEALTH *(United States, 1903–22)*

YEAR	MODEL	ENGINE	BODY	F	G	E
1903		1 cyl.	Tonneau	2,200	5,400	14,000
1903		1 cyl.	Runabout	2,250	5,500	13,000
1917		4 cyl.	Touring	2,100	3,250	13,500
1919	Victory Six	6 cyl.	Touring	3,500	9,000	19,000
1920		4 cyl.	Touring	2,100	5,250	13,500

CONDOR *(Great Britain, 1960)*

YEAR	MODEL	ENGINE	BODY	F	G	E
1960	Formula Jr.	Triumph-Herald Open		1,000	1,900	6,000

CONNAUGHT *(Great Britain, 1949–57)*

YEAR	MODEL	ENGINE	BODY	F	G	E
1949	L-Series		Sport	2,100	5,250	11,000
1953	A-Series	(Lea-Francis)	Racing	3,000	7,900	14,000

YEAR	MODEL	ENGINE	BODY	F	G	E
CONOVER *(United States, 1907–12)*						
1906		4 cyl.	Tonneau	3,100	7,250	12,500
1906		4 cyl.	Runabout	4,250	8,500	15,000
CONRERO *(Italy, 1953–60)*						
1953		(Fiat)	Michelotti	1,000	1,900	4,800
1953		(Peugeot 203)	Michelotti	1,000	2,000	5,000
1953	GT	(Alfa Romeo)	Coupe	1,000	2,000	5,900
CONTINENTAL *(United States, 1907–33)*						
1907	C	4 cyl.	Touring	3,650	9,300	17,000
1907	A	4 cyl.	Runabout	3,250	9,500	18,200
1907	B	4 cyl.	Tonneau	4,250	10,500	20,000
1914	XXX	4 cyl.	Touring	5,000	9,000	18,000
1933	Beacon	4 cyl.	Roadster	3,500	9,000	18,500
1933	Flyer	6 cyl.	Coupe	4,000	8,000	19,000
CONY *(Japan, 1952–67)*						
1952		2 cyl.	2 Door Sedan	750	1,500	3,000
1952		2 cyl.	Station Wagon	750	1,500	3,000
COOPER *(Great Britain, 1909–69)*						
1909		4 cyl.	Touring	2,100	4,250	10,500
1911		4 cyl.	Limousine	2,750	5,250	11,500
1919		3 cyl.	2 Passenger	2,000	3,900	10,000
1933		4 cyl.	Runabout	2,900	6,750	10,500
1938		4 cyl.	Sport	2,900	6,750	11,000
1957		1100cc	Sport	4,250	8,500	16,000
CORBIN *(United States, 1905–12)*						
1905	D	4 cyl. (Air-cooled)	5 Passenger Touring	4,000	7,000	15,000
1910	18	4 cyl.	5 Passenger Touring	8,000	18,000	40,000
CORBITT *(United States, 1907–14)*						
1912	A	4 cyl.	Roadster	5,000	12,000	25,000
1912	C	4 cyl.	Touring	4,000	10,000	22,000

YEAR	MODEL	ENGINE	BODY	F	G	E
CORD *(United States, 1929–37)*						
1929	L-29	8 cyl.	Cabriolet	38,000	95,000	180,000
1930	L-29	8 cyl.	Brougham	15,000	25,000	55,000

Cord – 1930 "Phaeton"

YEAR	MODEL	ENGINE	BODY	F	G	E
1930	L-29	8 cyl.	Sedan	12,000	23,000	53,000
1930	L-29	8 cyl.	Convertible Phaeton	35,000	65,000	125,000
1930	L-29	8 cyl.	Cabriolet	20,000	45,000	95,000
1931	L-29	8 cyl.	Phaeton	33,000	60,000	120,000
1931	L-29	8 cyl.	Town Limousine	26,000	55,000	110,000
1931	L-29	8 cyl.	Brougham	16,000	25,000	52,000
1931	L-29	8 cyl.	Cabriolet	26,000	50,000	100,000
1931	L-29	8 cyl.	5 Passenger Sedan	10,000	25,000	50,000
1931	L-29	8 cyl.	Coupe	19,000	39,000	79,000
1932	L-29	8 cyl.	Speedster Roadster	48,000	85,000	160,000
1932	L-29	8 cyl.	Sedan	13,000	33,000	52,000
1932	L-29	8 cyl.	Club Sedan	22,000	46,000	68,000
1932	L-29	8 cyl.	Sedanca de Ville	22,000	59,000	104,000
1932	L-29	8 cyl.	Brougham	15,500	23,000	67,500
1932	L-29	8 cyl.	Phaeton	33,000	79,000	140,000
1936	810	V 8 cyl.	Phaeton	21,000	33,000	90,000
1936	Sportsman 810	V 8 cyl.	Coupe	22,000	36,000	91,000

YEAR	MODEL	ENGINE	BODY	F	G	E
CORD *(United States, 1929–37) (continued)*						
1936	Westchester					
	810	V 8 cyl. LC	Coupe	11,000	32,000	39,000
1936	Beverly					
	810	V 8 cyl. LC	4 Door Sedan	7,000	11,500	40,000
1937	Beverly					
	812	V 8 cyl.	Coupe	13,000	27,000	40,000
1937	Sportsman		Convertible			
	812	V 8 cyl.	Coupe	19,000	75,000	120,000
1937	812	V 8 cyl. SC	Convertible			
			Coupe	22,000	79,000	190,000

Cord – 1937 "812 Convertible"

1937	Beverly					
	812	V 8 cyl. SC	Sedan	14,000	27,000	40,000
1937	Custom	8 cyl.	Berline	9,000	14,500	44,500
CORNILLEAU *(France, 1912–14)*						
1912	8/10	2 cyl.	Convertible	1,500	3,600	7,250
1912	12	4 cyl.	Convertible	1,800	4,750	9,500
CORNISH-FRIEDBERG; C.F. *(United States, 1908–09)*						
1908		4 cyl.	Roadster	4,250	8,500	16,000
1908		4 cyl.	Touring	4,200	8,400	15,800
CORONA *(Germany, 1904–09)*						
1904	3-Wheel	1 cyl. (Fafnir)		1,000	3,900	6,800
1905	6/8	1 cyl.	Voiturette	3,100	4,000	8,000
1907	9/11	2 cyl.	Tonneau	2,200	4,250	9,500

YEAR	MODEL	ENGINE	BODY	F	G	E
CORONET *(Great Britain, 1904–06)*						
1904		4 cyl.	Tonneau	1,300	3,500	8,000
CORRE LALICORNE *(France, 1901–50)*						
1901		1 cyl. (DeDion)	Voiturette	3,250	6,500	11,000
1904		1 cyl.	Touring	2,200	5,400	10,800
1905	10	2 cyl.	Touring	2,000	5,100	9,200
1906	16	4 cyl.	Runabout	2,200	5,000	9,000
1906		10.6 Litre	Racing	5,000	15,000	42,000
1906		2 cyl.	Tonneau	2,000	4,000	8,000
1909	R	4 cyl.	Landaulet	2,250	4,500	9,000
1910		1 cyl.	Roadster	1,850	3,650	7,250
1914		2 cyl.	Roadster	2,100	4,250	9,500
1917		5.5 Litre	Racing	3,500	6,000	13,000
1919	7 CV		Racing	2,750	6,250	13,500
1923	9/12 CV		Racing	4,250	8,500	16,000
1925		6 cyl.	Sport	3,500	7,000	15,000
1926		4 cyl.	Touring	2,100	5,250	9,500
1929	Femina		Cabriolet	2,000	4,750	8,500
1930			Sedan	1,000	2,250	5,500
1931	6/8 CV		Racing	3,250	5,500	13,000
1937	DV-4	2.2 Litre	Racing	3,000	5,000	12,000
1939	6 CV		Saloon Sedan	1,200	3,250	8,500
1949	14 CV		Sport	2,500	5,500	13,900
C.O.S. *(Germany, 1907)*						
1907		4 cyl.		1,250	3,600	9,200
1907		6 cyl.		2,100	6,250	14,500
COTAY *(United States, 1920–21)*						
1920		4 cyl. (Cameron Air-cooled)	Roadster	3,100	6,250	13,500
COTE *(France, 1900–13)*						
1900		2 cyl.	Voiturette	2,000	3,900	9,000
1908		4 cyl.	Voiturette	3,000	5,150	11,000
COTTEREAU *(France, 1898–1910)*						
1898		2 cyl.	Voiturette	1,250	5,600	7,200
1900		2 cyl.	Racing	3,100	7,250	14,500
1903		1 cyl.	Tonneau	1,100	2,250	6,500
1910		1 cyl.	Voiturette	1,100	2,100	6,250
COTTIN-DESGOUTTES *(France, 1905–33)*						
1905	20/40	4 cyl.	Open	1,200	3,600	7,250
1911	40	6 cyl.	Touring	3,100	7,250	13,500
1920	14 CV		Touring	2,100	3,750	7,250

YEAR	MODEL	ENGINE	BODY	F	G	E
COTTIN-DESGOUTTES *(France, 1905–33) (continued)*						
1927	San					
	Secousses		Sedan	1,100	1,900	5,000
COURIER *(United States, 1904–24)*						
1904	D	1 cyl.	Runabout	3,000	7,000	15,000
1910	10-A-3	4 cyl.	5 Passenger			
			Touring	5,000	10,000	20,000
1912	Clermont	4 cyl.	4 Door			
			Roadster	6,000	12,000	22,000
1923	D	6 cyl. (Falls)	3 Passenger			
			Roadster	6,000	14,000	28,000
COURIER *(France, 1906–08)*						
1906		2 cyl. (Gnome)		1,000	3,100	7,250
1908		6 cyl. (Mutel)		3,200	5,250	10,500
COVENTRY-PREMIER *(Great Britain, 1919–23)*						
1919	3-Wheel	V 2 cyl.	Cycle	1,250	2,500	6,000
1921	8	4 cyl. (Singer)	Racing	3,500	6,600	14,250
COVENTRY-VICTOR *(Great Britain, 1926–38)*						
1926	3-Wheel		Cycle	1,100	2,600	6,250
1932	Luxury Sport	1000cc	Open	4,000	7,750	18,500
CRANE-SIMPLEX *(United States, 1912–22)*						
1912	3	4 cyl.	Touring	8,000	20,000	50,000
1913	4	4 cyl.	Touring	8,000	20,000	50,000
1915	5	6 cyl.	Touring	10,000	30,000	70,000
1916	5	6 cyl.	Town	8,500	17,000	24,000
1916	5	6 cyl.	Underslung			
			Touring	14,000	38,000	88,000
CRAWFORD *(United States, 1904–23)*						
1905	A	2 cyl.	Runabout	3,600	6,250	13,500
1922	6-40	6 cyl. (Continental)	Touring	4,100	8,250	19,500
CRENMORE *(Great Britain, 1903–04)*						
1903		2 cyl.		2,100	4,250	9,500
1904		Steam	Limousine	4,650	8,250	17,500
CRESCENT *(United States, 1907; 1913–14)*						
1907		4 cyl.	Touring	3,650	7,250	13,500
1907		4 cyl.	Runabout	3,750	7,500	13,000
1913	Ohio	4 cyl.	Touring	3,650	7,250	12,500
1913	Royal	6 cyl.	Touring	4,750	9,500	17,000
CRESCENT *(Great Britain, 1911–15)*						
1911		2 cyl.	Cycle	1,200	2,750	6,250
1913		V 2 cyl.	Cycle	1,300	2,900	6,500

YEAR	MODEL	ENGINE	BODY	F	G	E
CRESPELLE *(France, 1906–23)*						
1906		1 cyl. (Aster)	Sport	1,750	3,500	7,000
CROESUS *(United States, 1906)*						
1906	Junior	4 cyl.	Runabout	4,100	8,250	15,500
1906	Four	4 cyl.	7 Passenger			
			Touring	4,050	8,100	15,250
CROISSANT *(France, 1920–22)*						
1920		2 cyl.	Cycle	1,200	2,800	4,250
1921		4 cyl.	Touring	1,600	5,400	11,000
CROMPTON *(Great Britain, 1914)*						
1914		2 cyl. (J.A.P.)	Cycle	1,200	2,650	6,250
1914		2 cyl. (J.A.P.)	Monocar	1,400	3,300	7,500
CROSLEY *(United States, 1939–52)*						
1939		2 cyl. (Waukesha)	Convertible	1,200	3,100	6,000
1940		2 cyl.	Station			
			Wagon	1,200	3,000	5,100
1948		4 cyl.	Convertible	1,000	1,200	3,000
1950	SS	4 cyl.	Sport	1,400	4,100	8,000
1950	Hot Shot	4 cyl.	Doorless			
			Sport	1,400	3,900	7,750
1950	Standard	4 cyl.	Station			
			Wagon	900	1,300	3,100
CROSSLE *(Great Britain, 1959–72)*						
1959		V 8 cyl. (Ford)	Racing	2,800	5,250	14,500
1967		(Ford)	Sport	1,200	2,500	5,000
1969	16 F		Sport	1,200	2,600	5,250
1969	20 F		Sport	1,300	2,750	5,500
1972	22 F 2		Sport	1,400	3,250	5,500
1972	23 F		Sport	1,400	3,250	5,500
CROSSLEY *(Great Britain, 1904–37)*						
1904	22	4 cyl.	Runabout	2,800	5,500	10,000
1906	28	4 cyl.	Coupe	2,500	5,000	10,000
1910	40	4 cyl.	Touring	2,800	5,500	10,000
1912	15	4 cyl.	Coupe	2,500	5,000	10,000
1920	25/30	4 cyl.	Touring	2,800	5,500	10,000
1921		4 cyl.	Sport	2,600	5,200	10,400
1923		4 cyl.	Sport	1,800	2,600	7,200
1926		2.6 Litre	Sedan	1,000	2,400	4,800
1928	20.9	3.2 Litre	Sport	1,700	3,500	6,000
1934		2 Litre	Sedan	1,000	2,100	4,200
1936	Regis Ten	2.6 Litre	Sedan	1,000	2,100	4,200
1937	Ten	1100cc	Coupe	1,200	2,750	7,500

YEAR	MODEL	ENGINE	BODY	F	G	E
CROUAN *(France, 1897–1904)*						
1897		2 cyl.	Voiturette	2,200	4,400	8,800
1900		2 cyl.	Voiturette	2,150	4,300	8,600
1901		1 cyl.	Voiturette	2,000	3,900	7,800
1903		2 cyl.	Voiturette	2,000	4,000	8,000
1903		4 cyl.	Voiturette	2,000	4,100	8,250
CROUCH *(Great Britain, 1912–28)*						
1912	3-Wheel (Carette)		Cycle	1,000	2,150	6,300
1913	Snub-nose	V 2 cyl.	Open	1,250	2,650	7,250
1922		V 2 cyl.	Open	1,000	2,700	7,400
1924	Super Sport	4 cyl.	Sport	1,300	3,300	8,600
CROWDY *(Great Britain, 1909–12)*						
1909	10/30	4 cyl.	Touring	1,250	3,800	8,500
1910	39	4 cyl.	Touring	1,500	3,850	8,600
1910	29	6 cyl.	Touring	2,200	6,000	12,000
CROW-ELKHART *(United States, 1911–23)*						
1911	12	4 cyl.	Touring	4,000	9,000	16,000
1913	C-1	4 cyl.	Roadster	3,750	8,500	15,000
1913	C-6-8	6 cyl.	7 Passenger Touring	4,250	9,500	18,000
1915	E-25	4 cyl.	Touring	3,250	7,500	13,500
1918	E-42	4 cyl.	Roadster	5,000	13,000	22,500
CROWN *(United States, 1905–14)*						
1905	Side Entry	4 cyl.	5 Passenger	3,200	7,350	16,750
1908	High-wheel	2 cyl.	2 Passenger	2,500	6,000	15,000
1913	Model A Cyclecar	4 cyl.	Roadster	3,000	7,000	14,000
CROXTED *(Great Britain, 1904–05)*						
1904		2 cyl.	Roadster	1,900	3,800	8,500
1905		4 cyl.	Roadster	3,200	5,300	10,600
CROXTON *(United States, 1911–14)*						
1911	German 45	4 cyl. (Rutenber)	Touring	7,000	15,000	30,000
1911	French Six	6 cyl.	Touring	6,000	12,000	25,000
1911	French Thirty	4 cyl.	Touring	5,000	11,000	22,000
CRUISER *(United States, 1917–19)*						
1917			Roadster	5,000	10,000	21,000
CSONKA *(Hungary, 1906–12)*						
1906		1 cyl.		1,150	2,300	6,650
1906		4 cyl.		1,100	2,250	6,500
1908		4 cyl.		1,200	2,400	6,800

YEAR	MODEL	ENGINE	BODY	F	G	E
CUBITT *(Great Britain, 1920–25)*						
1920	16/20	4 cyl.	Touring	1,500	3,800	7,500
CUDELL *(Germany, 1898–1908)*						
1898	3-Wheel	(DeDion)		2,000	5,000	9,000
1901		(DeDion)	Voiturette	2,200	5,400	9,800
1905	Phoenix		Limousine	2,200	5,400	9,800
CULVER *(United States, 1905–16)*						
1905	High-wheel	2 cyl. (Air-cooled)	Buggy	3,200	6,500	14,000
1916	Youth	1 cyl. (Air-cooled)	Two-Seater	2,000	4,000	8,000
CUMBRIA *(Great Britain, 1913–14)*						
1913		V 2 cyl. (J.A.P.)	Cycle	1,000	2,600	5,250
1913		(J.A.P.)	Cycle	1,000	2,600	5,250
1914		4 cyl.	Light	1,100	2,750	5,500
CUNNINGHAM *(United States, 1907–36; 1951–55)*						
1911	J	4 cyl.	Runabout	12,000	25,000	50,000
1912	J	4 cyl.	7 Passenger Limousine	9,000	20,000	42,000
1914	R	4 cyl.	7 Passenger Touring	10,000	22,000	46,000
1925	V6	V 8 cyl.	4 Passenger Sport Touring	12,000	24,000	48,000
1927	V6	V 8 cyl.	Roadster	12,000	25,000	55,000
1928	V7	V 8 cyl.	Limousine	4,500	6,800	61,000
1928	V7	V 8 cyl.	6 Passenger Touring	12,000	26,000	65,000
1929	V7	V 8 cyl.	Roadster	11,000	25,000	61,000
CUTTING *(United States, 1909–13)*						
1910	A-40	4 cyl.	Tourabout	4,200	9,400	23,000
1912	T-55	4 cyl. (Wisconsin)	Torpedo Touring	3,400	7,000	21,000
C.W.S. *(Poland, 1922–29)*						
1922		4 cyl.	Touring	800	2,600	6,200
1923		8 cyl.	Sedan	750	2,400	5,800
1924		8 cyl.	Sport	1,500	3,750	6,400
CYKLON *(Germany, 1902–29)*						
1904	Cyklonette	1 cyl.		1,500	3,500	7,100
1905		2 cyl.		1,600	3,750	7,500
1926	Schebera			1,700	3,800	7,600

YEAR	MODEL	ENGINE	BODY	F	G	E

D

D.A.F. *(Netherlands, 1958–75)*

YEAR	MODEL	ENGINE	BODY	F	G	E
1958		600cc	Flat-twin	1,200	2,500	4,000
1965	Formula 3		Racing	2,800	6,900	12,750
1966	Daffodil	764cc	Sedan	1,000	2,500	5,000
1969	Sport	4 cyl. (Renault)	Coupe	1,100	2,700	5,400
1972	Marathon 65	1440cc	Coupe	1,300	3,900	7,800
1973	Marathon 65	(Renault)	Sedan	1,100	2,250	6,500

DAGMAR *(United States, 1922–26)*

YEAR	MODEL	ENGINE	BODY	F	G	E
1923	6-70	6 cyl.	Roadster	10,000	20,000	42,000
1924	6T 6-70	6 cyl.	Sport Victoria	9,000	18,000	40,000
1924	6-70	6 cyl.	Brougham	6,000	12,000	28,000
1925	6-60	(Continental)	5 Passenger Sedan	5,000	10,000	23,000
1926	6-80	6 cyl.	Sport Victoria	10,000	20,000	42,000
1926	6-80	6 cyl. (Continental)	5 Passenger Sedan	6,000	13,000	28,000

DAIHATSU *(Japan, 1954 to date)*

YEAR	MODEL	ENGINE	BODY	F	G	E
1954	Bee 3-Wheel	2 cyl.		350	750	1,500
1954		2 cyl.	Sedan	175	350	750
1963		4 cyl.	Sedan	200	400	800
1966	Campagno Berlina	958cc	Sedan	1,250	2,400	3,750
1967		4 cyl.	Racing	2,300	3,750	8,500

DAIMLER *(Germany, 1886–90)*

YEAR	MODEL	ENGINE	BODY	F	G	E
1886		1 cyl.	Racing	15,250	35,500	75,000
1893		V 2 cyl.	Voiturette	7,250	15,500	28,000
1899		4 cyl.	Victoria	6,750	12,500	35,500

DAIMLER *(Great Britain, 1896–1965)*

YEAR	MODEL	ENGINE	BODY	F	G	E
1896	Crawford	2 cyl.	Waggonette	2,500	6,000	15,500
1899		4 cyl.	Phaeton	3,000	9,500	26,000
1904		4 cyl.	Laundaulet	2,500	6,000	15,000
1909		(Knight)	Touring	3,000	9,000	30,000
1920		6 cyl.	Touring	3,000	9,000	30,000
1921	45	6 cyl.	Touring	3,250	9,500	30,000
1922	20	4 cyl.	Sedan	1,500	3,000	8,500
1923		6 cyl.	Touring	3,000	9,000	28,000
1924		6 cyl.	Touring	3,000	9,000	28,000
1925		6 cyl.	Limousine	2,500	7,500	19,500

YEAR	MODEL	ENGINE	BODY	F	G	E
DAIMLER *(Great Britain, 1896–1965) (continued)*						
1927	Double Six	12 cyl.	Touring	9,000	22,000	42,000
1930	25/85	6 cyl.	Saloon Sedan	2,500	6,500	13,500
1932		V 12 cyl.	Limousine	10,500	20,000	30,000

Daimler – 1932 "Limousine"

YEAR	MODEL	ENGINE	BODY	F	G	E
1933	15	6 cyl.	Touring	5,500	13,000	39,000
1936		6 cyl.	Limousine	2,700	5,500	11,750
1938		8 cyl.	Limousine	3,700	7,500	13,750
1949		8 cyl.	Limousine	3,800	7,600	13,000
1950	Conquest	8 cyl.	Sedan	2,800	5,600	10,000
1951	Conquest Century	8 cyl.	Sedan	2,900	5,800	10,000
1951	Small	6 cyl.	Convertible	6,000	16,000	25,000
1951	Lady Daimler	8 cyl.	Large Convertible	22,000	45,000	90,000
1952		6 cyl.	Convertible	6,900	19,000	36,000
1952		6 cyl.	Limousine	3,800	7,600	13,000
1954		8 cyl.	Sedan	2,400	4,800	12,500
1955		V 8 cyl.	Sport Convertible	14,600	31,900	41,500
1959		V 8 cyl.	Roadster	8,600	16,900	28,500
DALHOUSIE *(Great Britain, 1906–10)*						
1906		4 cyl.	Racing	3,000	5,900	13,750
1906		4 cyl.	Runabout	1,500	4,000	9,000
1907		4 cyl.	Tonneau	1,500	4,000	9,000

YEAR	MODEL	ENGINE	BODY	F	G	E
DANIELS *(United States, 1916–24)*						
1916	A	V 8 cyl. (Herschell Spillman)	Roadster	12,000	25,000	55,000
1917	B	V 8 cyl. (Herschell Spillman)	Sedan	7,000	15,000	34,000
1920	Submarine	V 8 cyl.	Roadster	12,000	30,000	65,000
1922	D	V 8 cyl.	Sedan	5,000	15,000	34,000
DAREN *(Great Britain, 1968–73)*						
1968	Mark 2		Sport	1,000	2,100	4,250
1970	Mark 3		Sport	1,100	2,250	4,500
1972	Mark 4		Sport	1,200	2,400	4,800
1973	Mark 5	(BDA)	Sport	1,200	2,500	5,000
DARMONT *(France, 1924–39)*						
1924	Etoile de France	Air-cooled		1,000	2,000	4,250
1936	Speciale	V 2 cyl.	Sport	1,500	3,100	5,100
DARRACQ; TALBOT *(France, 1896–1959)*						
1896		Electric	Coupe	3,250	7,500	13,000
1900		1 cyl.	Voiturette	1,250	4,500	8,000
1901		1 cyl.	Tonneau	1,300	3,600	7,500
1902		1 cyl.	Runabout	1,300	3,750	7,500
1903		2 cyl.	Racing	2,500	4,750	11,500
1905		4 cyl.	Racing	3,200	7,400	13,800
1907		2 cyl.	Runabout	2,000	3,250	5,500
1913	70	8 cyl.	Sport Roadster	4,000	9,000	18,000
1914	12/16	4 cyl.	Runabout	2,250	4,500	9,000
1920		8 cyl.	Racing	4,750	9,500	18,500
1921	15	3.2 Litre	Touring	2,750	4,500	9,500
1924	15/40	6 cyl.	Sport	2,750	4,500	9,500
1928	12/32	6 cyl.	Sedan	1,000	2,000	6,000
1930	TL 20/98	8 cyl.	Sedan	2,000	4,000	9,000
1935	17 CV	3 Litre	Touring	2,250	4,500	10,000
1938		4.5 Litre	Grand Prix Racing	4,100	9,250	21,500
1949		4.5 Litre	Sport Sedan	3,000	6,000	12,000
1955	Lago	2.5 Litre	Coupe	3,000	6,000	12,500
1956		(Maserati 250)	Racing	3,750	5,500	12,500
1959		V 8 cyl. (Ford)	Coupe	2,000	4,000	8,000
DARRIN *(United States, 1946; 1953–58)*						
1946	Prototype	6 cyl. (Willys)	Convertible	4,000	8,500	25,000
1954	Kaiser	6 cyl. (Willys)	Sport Roadster	4,500	9,800	27,000

YEAR	MODEL	ENGINE	BODY	F	G	E
DARRIN *(United States, 1946; 1953–58) (continued)*						
1958	Flintridge	V 8 cyl. (Cadillac)	Sport			
			Roadster	4,800	10,200	30,000
DASSE *(Brazil, 1894–1924)*						
1894	3-Wheel	1 cyl.	Cycle	1,600	3,250	6,500
1896		2 cyl.	Cabriolet	2,250	3,500	7,000
1922		4 cyl.	Cabriolet	2,500	4,000	8,000
DAT; DATSUN; DATSON *(Japan, 1912–30; 1931/32 to date)*						
1912		4 cyl.	2 Passenger	1,500	3,300	7,600
1915	31	4 cyl.	2 Passenger	1,500	3,250	7,500
1916	41	4 cyl.	Sedan	1,400	3,000	7,000
1920	41	4 cyl.	Sedan	1,400	3,000	7,750
1930	91	4 cyl.	Sedan	1,400	3,000	17,800
1932		4 cyl.	Phaeton	2,800	7,250	15,500
1933		4 cyl.	Coupe	1,400	3,050	6,500
1934		4 cyl.	Roadster	2,000	6,250	13,500
1935		4 cyl.	Phaeton	2,800	7,000	14,000
1936	15	4 cyl.	Sedan	1,400	2,625	4,250
1938	7	4 cyl.	Sedan	1,400	2,625	4,250
1941		4 cyl.	Sport			
			Roadster	2,800	7,000	12,000
1950		4 cyl.	Sedan	1,000	2,500	4,000
1952		4 cyl.	Sport Coupe	1,500	3,000	6,000
1953		4 cyl.	Sport			
			Roadster	2,000	6,000	11,000
1956		4 cyl.	Sedan	1,000	2,500	4,000
1959		4 cyl.	Sedan	1,000	2,500	4,000
1967	2000	4 cyl.	Roadster	1,700	3,800	7,200
1972	240-Z	6 cyl.	Coupe	1,700	2,200	5,500
DAVID *(Spain, 1913–22; 1950–56)*						
1914		4 cyl.	Cycle	1,000	2,600	4,250
1918		(Hispano Suiza)	Sedan	2,000	4,400	8,800
1918		(Hispano Suiza)	Sport			
			Roadster	4,000	8,500	28,000
1950	3-Wheel	1 cyl.	Cycle	1,000	2,650	3,250
DAVIS *(United States, 1908–29)*						
1911		4 cyl.	Touring	3,400	6,800	15,000
1914	Six 50	6 cyl.	Touring	2,800	6,600	39,000
1914	35-K	4 cyl.	Cycle			
			Roadster	2,000	3,800	18,000
1918	6-H	6 cyl.	4 Passenger			
			Touring	3,500	7,000	18,000

YEAR	MODEL	ENGINE	BODY	F	G	E
DAVIS *(United States, 1908–29) (continued)*						
1920	50	6 cyl.	Special Roadster 4 Passenger Sport	3,600	7,250	20,000
DAWSON *(Great Britain, 1897–1921)*						
1897		1 cyl.	Voiturette	1,100	3,250	6,500
1920		4 cyl.	Sedan	1,200	2,400	4,800
DAWSON *(United States, 1900–05)*						
1900		Steam	Runabout	4,250	9,500	18,900
1904		2 cyl.	Touring	2,100	5,250	9,500
DAY-LEEDS *(Great Britain, 1913–24)*						
1913		2 cyl.	Cycle	1,000	2,600	4,400
1920		4 cyl.	Coupe	1,000	2,600	4,400
DAYTON *(United States, 1909–15)*						
1909	High-wheel	2 cyl.	Buggy	2,900	6,750	13,000
1911		Electric	Brougham	4,800	11,500	22,000
1913	Side-by-Side	2 cyl. (Spacke)	Cycle	1,600	3,750	8,500
1913	Tandem	2 cyl. (Spacke)	Cycle	1,300	3,800	6,600
D.B. *(France, 1938–61)*						
1938	11 CV		Touring	1,000	2,250	4,500
1947		2 Litre	Sedan	1,000	2,200	4,400
1949	Formula III	(Panhard)	Racing	2,550	4,100	9,200
1952	G.P. Formula	750cc	Coupe	1,500	2,400	6,800
1958	Rallye	850cc (Panhard)	Coupe	1,800	3,800	8,500
DEASY *(Great Britain, 1906–11)*						
1906		4 cyl.	Open	1,000	4,000	9,000
1908	"45"	12 Litre	Cabriolet	4,800	16,600	25,000
1911	"12"	1944cc	Cabriolet	3,750	11,500	18,000
DE BAZELAIRE *(France, 1907–28)*						
1907		2 cyl.	Racing	2,050	6,000	12,000
1908		2 cyl.	Racing	2,100	6,100	12,200
1910		6 cyl.	Racing	4,250	14,300	28,600
1925		4 cyl.	Racing	3,000	7,800	13,500
DE BRUYNE *(Great Britain, 1968)*						
1968	GT	V 8 cyl. (Chev)	Saloon Sedan	1,200	2,400	5,800
1968		V 8 cyl. (Chev)	Coupe	1,650	3,250	7,500
DECAUVILLE *(France, 1898–1910)*						
1898		2 cyl.	Voiturette	2,100	4,250	10,500
1900		2 cyl.	Voiturette	2,000	4,100	10,000
1909	60	2 cyl.	Voiturette	2,200	4,400	11,000
1909	16/20	2 cyl.	Touring	2,100	4,250	10,500

YEAR	MODEL	ENGINE	BODY	F	G	E
DE CEZAC *(France, 1925–27)*						
1925		1685cc (Ballot)	Open	3,000	4,800	10,600
1925		1200cc (C.I.M.A.)	Open	2,000	3,600	8,250
DECHAMPS *(Brazil, 1899–1906)*						
1899		2 cyl.	Vis-a-vis	1,500	3,700	9,500
1901	20	4 cyl.	Racing	2,500	4,800	11,500
1902		2 cyl.	Tonneau	1,500	3,800	9,600
1904	25	4 cyl.	Tonneau	2,000	3,900	11,750
DECKERT *(France, 1901–06)*						
1901		1 cyl.	Runabout	1,200	3,700	8,500
1901		2 cyl.	Runabout	1,500	3,900	8,800
1901		4 cyl.	Racing	2,000	4,900	11,800
DE DIETRICH; LORRAINE-DETRICH; LORRAINE *(France, 1897–1934)*						
1897		2.3 Litre	Petit Duc	2,700	6,250	10,500
1902		4 cyl.	Touring	3,100	6,250	10,500
1904		12.8 Litre	Racing	5,400	19,800	49,000
1906	DH	3 Litre	Racing	3,000	8,000	16,000
1907	GO		2 Passenger	2,100	6,250	11,500
1907		4 cyl.	Touring	2,750	7,500	13,000
1911		8.3 Litre	Racing	4,250	11,500	28,000
1919		6 cyl.	Racing	4,200	9,400	19,800
1923	15 CV		Touring	2,950	7,900	15,800
1929	12 CV	4 cyl.	Racing	2,900	7,750	15,500
1934	20 CV	4.1 Litre	Touring	4,200	11,400	28,800
1934	20 CV	4.1 Litre	Sport			
			Roadster	7,500	19,500	54,000
DE DION-BOUTON *(France, 1883–1932)*						
1883	3-Wheel	Steam	Open	6,500	16,000	30,000
1900		1 cyl.	Voiturette	3,250	9,500	16,000
1901		1 cyl.	Roadster	6,000	14,000	24,000
1901		1 cyl.	Touring	3,500	7,000	19,500
1902		1 cyl.	Touring	4,750	9,500	21,000
1903	Rear Entry	1 cyl.	Touring	5,000	11,000	28,000
1905		4.4 Litre	Touring	3,500	7,000	18,000
1910		1.8 Litre	Roadster	2,900	6,750	16,500
1914			Limousine	2,750	6,250	16,500
1915	EZ	14.8 Litre	Roadster	7,100	18,250	34,500
1923		8 cyl.	Touring	4,900	13,750	28,500
1924	JK	4 Litre	Roadster	3,500	9,000	19,000
1926	JP	1328cc	Touring	4,100	10,250	20,500
1930	LA		Coupe	2,000	4,000	9,000

YEAR	MODEL	ENGINE	BODY	F	G	E
DELAGE (France, 1905–54)						
1905		1 cyl.	Runabout	4,000	8,000	16,000
1906	6	1 cyl.	Touring	4,000	8,000	16,000
1907	8	2 cyl.	Racing	4,250	8,500	16,500
1908	9	4 cyl.	Coupe	3,750	6,250	11,500
1909	"12"	1.4 Litre	Touring	4,000	8,000	16,000
1912		6 cyl.	Touring	4,250	8,500	18,500
1914		Electric	Town	6,900	12,750	25,500
1919		6 cyl.	Racing	7,500	14,000	30,000
1921	CO	4 cyl.	Sedan	2,100	4,250	8,500
1923	GL		Sedan	2,100	4,250	8,500
1924	1	6 cyl.	Sprint	5,750	9,500	25,000
1924	11	6 cyl.	Sprint	5,750	9,500	25,000
1925		V 12 cyl.	Racing	12,000	28,000	60,000
1926	DI	4 cyl.	Touring	6,500	12,000	25,000
1927	DM	3.2 Litre	Coupe	4,750	7,500	15,000
1928	DR	2.5 Litre	Sedan	3,000	6,000	12,000
1932	D8	4 Litre	Convertible Coupe	5,750	9,500	25,000
1933	D6-11	6 cyl.	Drop Head Coupe	4,000	8,000	14,500
1934	D8-15	8 cyl.	Racing	5,500	16,000	30,000
1934	D8-15	8 cyl.	Roadster	9,000	22,000	66,000
1936	DI-12	4 cyl.	Cabriolet	3,250	6,500	13,000
1937		4 cyl.	Cabriolet	4,500	9,500	18,000
1943	D8-100	8 cyl.	Sedan	1,750	3,500	7,000
1946	D8-120	8 cyl.	Drop Head Coupe	2,000	4,250	8,500
1949	D6	3 Litre	Sedan	1,100	2,250	4,500
DELAHAYE (France, 1894–1954)						
1894		1 cyl.	Touring	3,500	8,200	23,000
1900		1 cyl.	Tonneau	3,400	7,900	24,000
1902		2 cyl.	Roadster	4,900	9,900	26,400
1903	Type 10-B	4 cyl.	Roadster	6,000	11,000	33,000
1904	Type 15-B	2.7 Litre	Roadster	4,600	10,250	23,600
1907		8 Litre	Roadster	5,300	17,750	42,000
1908	Type 32	1.9 Litre	Touring	4,500	6,850	15,000
1911	Type 44	V 6 cyl.	Touring	6,250	10,050	22,600
1914		1.6 Litre	Coupe	2,300	5,750	10,400
1916		5.7 Litre	Phaeton	6,250	13,750	26,000
1917		4 cyl.	Convertible	5,150	11,250	23,500
1925	Type 87	1.8 Litre	Sedan	2,300	4,650	9,300
1927	Type 82	4 cyl.	Roadster	4,500	10,150	21,000
1928		6 cyl.	Convertible	7,350	14,500	31,000

YEAR	MODEL	ENGINE	BODY	F	G	E
DELAHAYE *(France, 1894–1954) (continued)*						
1930	TY 109	6 cyl.	Roadster	6,700	14,250	30,500
1932	126	6 cyl.	Drop Head Coupe	6,250	13,500	27,500
1933			Drop Head Coupe	4,500	11,250	20,000
1934	Super 12	4 cyl.	Roadster	5,750	12,500	23,000
1935	Superlux	6 cyl.	Roadster	7,400	14,750	24,700
1935		6 cyl.	Convertible Coupe	6,850	16,050	40,000
1936	Dragonfly	12 cyl.	Convertible	33,000	104,000	220,000
1936	Type 135	6 cyl.	Town	6,000	12,000	29,000
1936	Type 135	6 cyl.	Cabriolet	6,850	15,750	37,000
1937	Competition	6 cyl.	Roadster	12,250	33,750	77,500
1937	Type 148	6 cyl.	Cabriolet	10,400	20,000	41,000
1937	Des Alpes	6 cyl.	Convertible Coupe	13,000	28,000	55,000
1938	Type 145	V 12 cyl. 4.5 Litre	Roadster	31,000	104,500	220,000

Delahaye – 1938 "Type 145 Roadster"

1939		V 12 cyl.	Roadster	27,000	99,000	190,000
1939	Type 165	V 12 cyl.	Roadster	30,000	100,000	200,000
1939	Type 135	3.5 Litre	Drop Head Coupe	4,050	8,200	16,500
1939	Type 135 M	V 12 cyl.	Roadster	27,000	100,000	200,000
1940		6 cyl.	Convertible	14,750	44,000	77,000

YEAR	MODEL	ENGINE	BODY	F	G	E
DELAHAYE (France, 1894–1954) (continued)						
1940		6 cyl.	Convertible	9,550	29,500	71,000
1943	Type 135 SM	6 cyl.	Roadster	8,900	20,250	46,500
1946		6 cyl.	Roadster	8,050	19,750	39,500
1947		6 cyl.	Convertible	6,000	16,000	26,000
1948	Type 175	6 cyl.	Sport Roadster	5,850	15,950	25,000
1949		6 cyl.	Roadster	5,600	15,650	27,400
1950		6 cyl.	Convertible	5,600	15,650	24,700
1951	Type 235	3.5 Litre	Drop Head Coupe	4,500	14,250	22,000
1951	Type 178	6 cyl.	Roadster	6,600	17,000	27,500
1952	Type 180	6 cyl.	Roadster	6,400	16,950	23,500
DELAUGERE (France, 1901–26)						
1901		1 cyl.	Runabout	1,000	3,800	10,000
1905		4 cyl.	Runabout	2,000	4,800	13,500
1912		6 cyl.	Open	3,000	4,900	17,000
1920		4 cyl.	Open	2,000	3,600	11,250
DELAUNAY-BELLEVILLE (France, 1904–50)						
1904		T-head	Roadster	3,100	6,250	12,500
1909	10 CV	6 cyl.	Touring	3,000	7,000	13,000
1912			Limousine	3,100	6,250	11,500
1924		6 cyl.	Drop Head Coupe	3,500	6,750	12,500
1928	Greyhound	6 cyl.	Sedan	2,000	4,000	9,000
DELLOW (Great Britain, 1949–59)						
1949	Ten	(Ford)	Sport Doorless	1,000	2,250	6,500
1952	Mark II		Sport	1,000	2,300	6,600
1956	Mark VI		Sport	1,000	2,400	6,800
DELTA (France, 1905–15)						
1905		2 cyl.	Runabout	1,000	2,400	5,800
1905		2 cyl.	Runabout	1,000	2,750	6,000
1913		4 cyl.	Runabout	1,000	2,650	6,250
DE MONTE (United States, 1904)						
1904		2 cyl.	Runabout	3,000	7,000	15,000
1904		4 cyl.	5 Passenger Touring	4,000	8,000	17,000
DENNIS (Great Britain, 1899–1915)						
1899		(DeDion)		2,000	4,900	9,800
1901		(DeDion)		1,900	4,800	9,600
1903		2 cyl.		2,000	4,950	8,900

YEAR	MODEL	ENGINE	BODY	F	G	E
DENNIS *(Great Britain, 1899–1915) (continued)*						
1906	30/35	(White & Poppe)	Touring	2,100	4,100	9,250
1912	24	V 2 cyl.	Landaulet	1,000	2,750	4,500
DERBY *(France, 1921–36)*						
1921		V 2 cyl.	Open	1,000	2,400	5,750
1923		4 cyl.	Roadster	1,500	3,500	10,000
1925		8 hp (Ruby)	Roadster	3,000	6,500	18,000
1928		6 cyl.	Touring	2,000	4,750	16,500
1931	L2	4 cyl.	Touring	1,800	3,500	11,000
1933	L8	4 cyl.	Open	1,500	3,250	8,500
1934		V 8 cyl.	Touring	2,500	5,000	14,100
DEREK *(Great Britain, 1925–26)*						
1925	10/20	(Chapuis-Dornier)	Coupe	1,200	3,600	7,250
1925	10/20	(Chapuis-Dornier)	Sedan	1,000	3,500	6,400
DESANCTIS *(Italy, 1958–66)*						
1958		750cc (Fiat)	Convertible	1,000	2,600	4,200
1959		1100cc (Fiat)	Convertible	1,000	3,600	5,200
1960	FJ	1100cc	Convertible	1,000	3,500	5,000
DESOTO *(United States, 1929–61)*						
1929	K	6 cyl.	Sedan	1,900	3,000	8,000
1929	K	6 cyl.	Roadster	5,700	14,000	28,000
1929		6 cyl.	2 Door Sedan	1,750	2,750	7,750
1929	K	6 cyl.	Phaeton	6,000	14,000	29,000
1929	K	6 cyl.	Deluxe Coupe	2,200	4,800	10,500
1929	K	6 cyl.	Business Coupe	3,000	4,000	8,000
1930	CK	6 cyl.	Touring	7,000	15,500	31,000
1930	CK	6 cyl.	Roadster	6,800	15,000	30,000
1930	CK	6 cyl.	Deluxe Coupe	2,000	3,000	8,000
1930	CF	8 cyl.	Roadster	7,000	15,000	33,000
1930	CF	8 cyl.	Rumble Seat Coupe	4,500	5,200	11,000
1930	CF	6 cyl.	Sedan	4,200	5,200	8,400
1931	SA	6 cyl.	Roadster	6,000	12,000	24,000
1931	SA	6 cyl.	Convertible	7,000	14,000	23,000
1931	SA	6 cyl.	Phaeton	5,000	12,000	26,000
1931	CF	8 cyl.	Roadster	5,000	11,000	22,000
1931	CF	8 cyl.	Deluxe Coupe	2,200	3,700	9,250
1931	CF	8 cyl.	Convertible	6,000	12,000	26,000
1932	SC	6 cyl.	Rumble Seat Sport Roadster	6,600	15,000	31,000
1932	SC	6 cyl.	Town Sedan	3,300	5,500	10,400

YEAR	MODEL	ENGINE	BODY	F	G	E
DESOTO *(United States, 1929–61) (continued)*						
1932	SC	6 cyl.	Rumble Seat Coupe	3,000	4,900	11,200
1932	SC	6 cyl.	Roadster	6,900	15,000	32,000
1932	SC	6 cyl.	Convertible Sedan	6,900	16,000	33,000
1932	SC	6 cyl.	Convertible	5,800	9,600	25,600
1932	Custom SC	6 cyl.	Roadster	7,100	15,000	32,000
1932	SA	6 cyl.	Touring	5,500	11,000	25,000
1932	SA	6 cyl.	Roadster	5,250	10,000	23,000
1932	SA	6 cyl.	Sedan	1,600	4,200	7,500
1932	SA	6 cyl.	Coupe	1,600	4,500	8,000
1932	SA	6 cyl.	Phaeton	6,000	12,000	27,000
1933	SD	6 cyl.	Sport Coupe	4,900	6,700	10,400
1933	SD	6 cyl.	Sedan	2,700	4,200	7,600
1933	SD	6 cyl.	Cabriolet	6,000	12,000	26,000
1933	SD	6 cyl.	Brougham	1,600	4,200	7,500
1933	SD	6 cyl.	Convertible	5,250	10,000	23,000
1934	Airflow SE	6 cyl.	Sedan	2,000	3,100	8,000
1934	Airflow SE	6 cyl.	Coupe	2,600	3,600	8,600
1935	Airflow SE	6 cyl.	Sedan	2,000	3,100	8,000
1935	Airstream	6 cyl.	Sedan	1,200	1,800	5,000
1935	Airstream	6 cyl.	Coupe	1,500	2,300	5,750
1935	Airstream	6 cyl.	Convertible	5,350	10,000	23,000
1936	S1 Custom	6 cyl.	Coupe	2,400	4,600	9,500
1936	S1 Custom	6 cyl.	Sedan	2,200	4,400	8,500
1936	S1 Custom	6 cyl.	Convertible Sedan	6,800	13,000	18,000
1936	S1 Deluxe	6 cyl.	Sedan	1,500	2,300	5,750
1936	S1 Deluxe	6 cyl.	Coupe	1,500	2,500	6,000
1936	Airflow III	6 cyl.	Sedan	4,400	9,000	15,000
1937	S3	6 cyl.	Convertible	5,700	7,500	16,000
1937	S3	6 cyl.	Sedan	1,600	5,200	9,600
1937	S3	6 cyl.	Brougham	1,200	1,800	5,000
1937	S3	6 cyl.	Rumble Seat Coupe	2,200	5,700	10,400
1938	S5	6 cyl.	Coupe	1,600	3,500	6,750
1938	S5	6 cyl.	Touring Brougham	1,600	2,500	6,000
1938	S5	6 cyl.	Touring Sedan	1,600	2,500	6,000
1938	S5	6 cyl.	Sedan	1,600	5,200	9,200
1938	S5	6 cyl.	Convertible	5,700	7,600	17,000
1939	S6 Custom	6 cyl.	Coupe	1,500	2,300	5,750

YEAR	MODEL	ENGINE	BODY	F	G	E
DESOTO *(United States, 1929–61) (continued)*						
1939	S6 Custom	6 cyl.	Club Coupe	1,750	3,000	6,250
1939	S6 Custom	6 cyl.	2 Door Sedan	1,500	2,300	5,750
1939	S6 Deluxe	6 cyl.	7 Passenger	2,300	5,700	10,400
1940	S7 Custom	6 cyl.	Coupe	1,600	5,200	8,250
1940	S7 Custom	6 cyl.	Sedan	1,200	1,950	5,600
1940	S7 Deluxe	6 cyl.	Sedan	1,600	2,500	6,000
1940	S7 Deluxe	6 cyl.	Coupe	1,600	3,500	6,750
1941	S8 Custom	6 cyl.	Sedan	1,600	2,500	6,000
1941	S8 Custom	6 cyl.	Coupe	1,600	3,500	6,750
1941	S8 Custom	6 cyl.	Brougham	1,600	2,500	6,000
1941	S8 Deluxe	6 cyl.	Coupe	1,250	2,150	5,850
1941	S8 Deluxe	6 cyl.	Sedan	1,300	2,200	5,900
1942	S10 Custom	6 cyl.	Sedan	1,600	5,200	8,250
1942	S10 Custom	6 cyl.	Coupe	1,600	4,400	7,900
1942	S10 Custom	6 cyl.	Club Coupe	1,600	4,300	7,700
1942	S10 Custom	6 cyl.	4 Door Sedan	1,600	4,400	7,900
1942	S10 Deluxe	6 cyl.	Coupe	1,600	3,900	6,750
1942	S10 Deluxe	6 cyl.	Town Sedan	1,600	2,500	6,000
1942	S10 Deluxe	6 cyl.	Convertible	6,000	12,000	23,000
Postwar Models						
1946	S-11	6 cyl.	2 Door Sedan	1,600	4,700	6,500
1946	S-11	6 cyl.	Coupe	1,600	4,900	7,000
1947	S-11	6 cyl.	8 Passenger Suburban	2,200	5,800	10,500
1947	S-11	6 cyl.	Convertible	4,000	10,000	20,000
1947	S-11	6 cyl.	Club Coupe	1,600	3,800	7,900
1948	S-11	6 cyl.	Suburban	3,100	6,100	10,500
1948	S-11	6 cyl.	Sedan	1,200	1,800	5,000
1948	S-11 Deluxe	6 cyl.	Coupe	1,500	3,000	6,500
1948	S-11 Custom	6 cyl.	Convertible	4,000	10,000	20,000
1948	S-11	6 cyl.	Limousine	2,800	4,000	8,000
1949	S-13	6 cyl.	Club Coupe	1,100	3,000	7,000
1949	S-13 Custom	6 cyl.	Convertible	3,500	7,100	14,000
1949	S-13	6 cyl.	Sedan	1,600	4,400	8,100
1949	S-13 Deluxe	6 cyl.	Club Coupe	1,600	4,700	8,300
1949	S-13 Custom	6 cyl.	Suburban	1,600	4,000	8,400
1950	S-14 Custom	6 cyl.	Sedan	900	4,000	7,300
1950	S-14 Custom	6 cyl.	Convertible	4,000	8,000	15,000
1950	S-14 Custom	6 cyl.	6 Passenger Station Wagon	1,600	4,600	9,400
1950	S-14 Deluxe	6 cyl.	Sedan	1,500	3,000	6,500
1950	S-14 Deluxe	6 cyl.	Club Coupe	2,000	3,000	7,000

YEAR	MODEL	ENGINE	BODY	F	G	E
DESOTO	*(United States, 1929–61) (continued)*					
1951	Custom	6 cyl.	Sedan	1,500	3,200	6,500
1952	Firedome	V 8 cyl.	Convertible	4,000	9,000	18,000

Desoto – 1952 "Firedome"

YEAR	MODEL	ENGINE	BODY	F	G	E
1952	Firedome	V 8 cyl.	Sportsman	3,000	5,000	11,000
1952	Firedome	V 8 cyl.	Station Wagon	2,000	5,000	10,000
1953	Firedome	V 8 cyl.	Convertible	6,000	12,000	20,000
1953	Powermastr	V 8 cyl.	Sportsman	2,500	5,000	9,000
1954	Firedome	V 8 cyl.	Sportsman	3,000	6,000	11,000
1954	Firedome	8 cyl.	Sedan	1,600	2,500	6,000
1954	Firedome	8 cyl.	Club Coupe	1,750	3,000	6,250
1954	Firedome	8 cyl.	Convertible	4,000	10,000	20,000
1954	Powermaster	6 cyl.	Sedan	1,000	1,600	5,250
1954	Powermaster	6 cyl.	Club Coupe	1,200	1,850	5,500
1955	Fireflite	V 8 cyl.	4 Door Sedan	1,600	2,500	6,000
1955	Fireflite	V 8 cyl. 4.8 Litre	2 Door Hardtop Sportsman	3,000	7,000	16,000
1955	Fireflite	V 8 cyl.	Convertible	6,000	12,000	23,000
1956	Fireflite	V 8 cyl.	Convertible	5,000	11,000	22,000
1956	Sportsman	V 8 cyl	4 Door Hardtop	3,000	6,000	13,000
1956	Fireflite	V 8 cyl. 4.8 Litre	4 Door Sedan	1,600	3,400	6,750
1956	Adventurer	V 8 cyl.	Hardtop	2,000	5,000	12,000
1957	Adventurer	V 8 cyl.	Hardtop	4,000	10,000	22,000
1957	Fireflite	V 8 cyl.	Convertible	8,000	18,000	35,000
1957	Fireflite	V 8 cyl.	Sedan	1,500	3,000	6,500

YEAR	MODEL	ENGINE	BODY	F	G	E
DESOTO *(United States, 1929–61) (continued)*						
1957	Firedome	8 cyl.	2 Door Hardtop Sportsman	3,000	7,000	16,000
1957	Firesweep	8 cyl.	Sedan	1,500	2,500	5,000
1957	Firesweep	8 cyl.	2 Door Hardtop	2,500	6,000	14,000
1958	Fireflite	V 8 cyl. 4.8 Litre	Convertible	5,000	14,000	27,000
1958	Adventurer	V 8 cyl.	2 Door Hardtop	4,000	10,000	22,000
1958	Firesweep	8 cyl.	Sedan	1,000	2,000	5,500
1958	Firesweep	8 cyl.	2 Door Hardtop	500	1,400	12,000
1958	Firesweep	8 cyl.	Station Wagon 3S	800	2,000	5,000
1959	Fireflite	V 8 cyl.	Convertible	4,000	10,000	20,000
1959	Fireflite	V 8 cyl.	4 Door Hardtop	1,600	4,000	9,000
1959	Fireflite	V 8 cyl.	Station Wagon 2S	1,600	2,400	4,500
1959	Firedome	V 8 cyl.	4 Door Sportsman	2,000	5,000	12,000
1960	Fireflite	V 8 cyl.	2 Door Hardtop	2,200	3,700	9,250
1961	Fireflite	V 8 cyl.	2 Door Hardtop	1,800	4,000	10,000
DeTOMASO *(Italy, 1959 to date)*						
1959	Isis Formula Jr.	(Fiat)	Racing	2,000	4,900	9,800
1965	Vallelunga	(British Ford Cortina)	Gran Turismo Coupe	2,000	3,750	8,500
1966	Panpero	(British Ford Cortina)		1,500	2,750	5,500
1968	Mangusta	V 8 cyl. (Ford)	Gran Turismo Coupe	3,500	7,000	17,000
1969	Mustela	V 6 cyl. (Ford)	Racing	2,100	5,250	9,500
1970	4 Door	(Cosworth Ford)	Sport Saloon Sedan	2,000	5,000	8,500
1971	Pantera	V 8 cyl. (Ford)	Gran Turismo Coupe	4,500	8,000	17,500
1973	Longchamp	V 8 cyl.	Gran Turismo Sport Coupe	5,500	11,000	23,500

YEAR	MODEL	ENGINE	BODY	F	G	E
DETROIT *(United States, 1899–1914)*						
1901		2 cyl.	Touring	5,500	10,500	23,000
1904		2 cyl.	Tonneau	3,500	9,000	16,000
1905		2 cyl.	Runabout	3,400	8,700	15,800
1907		2 cyl.	Touring	3,400	8,800	15,500
1914	Little Detroit	4 cyl.	Cycle	2,200	5,000	8,000
DETROIT ELECTRIC *(United States, 1907–39)*						
1909	L	Electric	Runabout	5,000	10,000	22,000
1914	48	Electric	Brougham	4,500	10,000	21,000
1915	51	Electric	Brougham	4,500	10,000	20,000
1916	57	Electric	Brougham Coupe	3,850	8,750	17,500
1920	72-A	Electric	Brougham Coupe	3,850	8,750	17,500
1923	90	Electric	Brougham	4,100	9,250	18,500
DETROITER; BRIGGS-DETROITER *(United States, 1912–17)*						
1913	A	4 cyl.	Touring	4,500	8,000	17,000
1917	6-45	6 cyl.	Touring	5,000	10,000	22,500
DEUTZ *(Germany, 1907–11)*						
1907		4 cyl.	Touring	2,400	6,250	12,500
1910	"21"	4 cyl.	Touring	3,200	7,400	13,800
DE VECCHI *(Italy, 1905–17)*						
1905		4 cyl.	Open	1,800	3,600	8,200
1914	20/30	4 cyl.	Open	1,750	4,300	7,600
1914	25/30	4 cyl.	Open	1,750	4,500	7,900
DE WANDRE *(Brazil, 1922–25)*						
1922		4 cyl.	Roadster	1,400	4,800	8,600
1922		4 cyl.	Touring	1,200	4,400	7,800
1922		4 cyl.	Sedan	1,000	3,600	6,200
1922		4 cyl.	Town Landaulet	1,400	3,750	8,500
D.F.P. *(France, 1906–26)*						
1906		1 cyl.	Voiturette	1,000	3,900	7,750
1908		4 cyl.	Voiturette	1,050	4,000	8,000
1910	10/12	4 cyl.	Voiturette	1,100	4,100	8,000
1911	25/30	6 cyl.	Voiturette	2,200	6,200	12,250
1914	12/40	4 cyl.	Sport	1,700	4,300	8,400
1924		8 cyl.	Touring	3,000	6,900	13,800
DHUMBERT *(France, 1920–30)*						
1920		4 cyl.	Open	1,000	2,400	5,750
1930		6 cyl.	Open	1,400	2,500	6,000

YEAR	MODEL	ENGINE	BODY	F	G	E
DIANA	*(United States, 1925–28)*					
1926		8 cyl. (Continental)	Roadster	3,000	8,000	23,000
1926		8 cyl. (Continental)	Town Touring	2,400	4,800	21,000
1927		8 cyl. (Continental)	7 Passenger Sedan	2,200	3,400	12,000
1928		8 cyl. (Continental)	Brougham	2,250	6,500	16,000
DIATTO	*(Italy, 1905–27)*					
1905		2 cyl. (T-head)	Open	1,000	2,900	7,800
1905		4 cyl. (T-head)	Open	1,000	3,000	8,000
1910	12/15	4 cyl.		1,000	2,900	7,800
1920	16	4 cyl.	Touring	1,000	3,000	8,000
1925		8 cyl.	Racing	3,250	6,500	14,000
DIAZ Y GRILLO	*(Spain, 1917–22)*					
1917		2 cyl.	Sport	1,000	2,650	5,250
1917		4 cyl.	Sport	1,200	2,800	6,600
DICKINSON MORETTE	*(Great Britain, 1903–05)*					
1903	3-Wheel	1 cyl.		1,000	2,500	4,000
1903	3-Wheel	2 cyl.		1,200	2,600	5,000
DISPATCH	*(United States, 1910–19)*					
1911	E	2 cyl. (Wisconsin)	Roadster	5,000	12,000	25,000
1913	G-2	4 cyl. (Wisconsin)	Touring	6,000	13,000	26,000
1913	G	4 cyl. (Wisconsin)	2 Passenger Coupe	3,000	7,000	15,000
DI TELLA	*(Romania, 1959–66)*					
1959	Morris	4 cyl.	Sedan	300	1,000	2,200
1959	MG	4 cyl.	Station Wagon	400	1,200	2,350
DIVA	*(Great Britain, 1962–68)*					
1962	Sport	(Coventry-Climax)	Gran Turismo Coupe	1,000	3,000	6,750
DIXI	*(Germany, 1904–28)*					
1904	28/32	4 cyl.	Touring	1,150	3,250	8,500
1914	B I	4 cyl.	Touring	1,100	3,200	8,400
1924	6/24	6 cyl.	Touring	1,000	3,000	8,000
1928		6 cyl.	Roadster	1,100	3,100	8,200
1928		6 cyl.	Roadster	1,150	3,300	8,500
DIXIE; DIXIE JR.	*(United States, 1908–10)*					
1908	Flier	4 cyl.	Runabout	4,000	9,000	19,000
1908	High-Wheel		Runabout			
	Dixie Jr.	2 cyl.	Buggy	3,000	8,000	17,000

YEAR	MODEL	ENGINE	BODY	F	G	E
D.K.W. *(Germany, 1928–66)*						
1928		2 cyl.	Sport	1,200	3,300	6,000
1928	Type F. 1	490cc	Cabriolet	1,150	3,100	5,200
1934	Reichsklasse	2 cyl.	Open	1,250	3,200	5,400
1937	Meisterklasse	2 cyl.	Drop Head Coupe	1,000	2,250	4,500
1953	Sokerklasse	V 2 cyl.	Drop Head Coupe	1,000	2,000	4,000
1957	Monza	3 cyl. 981cc	Sport	1,000	2,700	4,400
1960		3 cyl.	2 Door Hardtop	800	1,500	3,200
DOBLE *(United States, 1914–31)*						
1923	E	4 cyl.	Phaeton Deluxe	8,000	20,000	45,000
1924	E	4 cyl.	Sedan	3,000	8,000	21,000
1925	E	4 cyl.	Runabout	9,000	10,000	22,000
1925	E	4 cyl.	Limousine	5,000	12,000	23,000
1931	E	4 cyl.	Vestibule Sedan	4,000	8,000	21,000

Doble – 1931 "Steam Car"

YEAR	MODEL	ENGINE	BODY	F	G	E
DOCTORESSE *(France, 1899–1902)*						
1899	Gaillardet	2 cyl.	Open	1,000	3,600	5,250
1900		2 cyl.	Voiturette	1,000	3,700	5,400
DODGE *(United States, 1914 to date)*						
1914	30-35	4 cyl.	Touring	3,900	5,600	11,000
1915	30-35	4 cyl.	Touring	2,500	4,000	8,000
1916	30-35	4 cyl.	Touring	2,600	4,000	9,000
1916	30-35	4 cyl.	Roadster	2,600	4,000	9,000
1917	30	4 cyl.	Coupe	3,000	5,000	7,000

YEAR	MODEL	ENGINE	BODY	F	G	E
DODGE *(United States, 1914 to date) (continued)*						
1917	30	4 cyl.	Touring	2,600	4,500	9,000
1917	30	4 cyl.	Roadster	2,600	4,500	9,000
1917	30	4 cyl.	Sedan	2,200	4,000	5,700
1918	30	4 cyl.	Roadster	3,500	5,300	9,600
1919	30	4 cyl.	Sedan	2,000	4,500	9,600
1919	30	4 cyl.	Touring	3,000	4,000	9,000
1919	30	4 cyl.	Coupe	2,200	4,000	5,700
1920	30	4 cyl.	Touring	2,600	4,000	9,000
1921	30	4 cyl.	Touring	3,000	4,000	9,000
1921	30	4 cyl.	Sport Roadster	3,000	4,000	9,000
1921	30	4 cyl.	Sedan	1,800	3,500	5,100
1921	30	4 cyl.	Coupe	2,100	3,900	5,500
1922	5/1	4 cyl.	Roadster	3,400	4,700	9,000
1922	5/1	4 cyl.	Touring	3,300	4,700	9,000
1922	5/1	4 cyl.	Sedan	2,000	3,700	5,300
1922	5/1	4 cyl.	Coupe	2,100	3,900	5,500
1923	A	4 cyl.	Touring	3,000	4,400	8,500
1924	24	4 cyl.	Coupe	3,000	5,000	7,000
1924	24	4 cyl.	Touring	3,000	5,000	7,000
1924	24	4 cyl.	Touring Sport	3,000	6,000	9,000
1924	23	4 cyl.	Sedan 2 styles	2,100	3,900	5,500
1924	23	4 cyl.	Coupe 3 styles	2,400	4,200	5,700
1925	25	4 cyl.	Coach	2,000	3,000	5,000
1925	25	4 cyl.	Sport Roadster	2,500	4,000	6,000
1925	25	4 cyl.	Sedan	2,250	3,400	5,800
1925	25	4 cyl.	Touring	3,600	5,000	9,000
1926	26	4 cyl.	Sedan	2,000	5,000	7,000
1926	26	4 cyl.	Sport Touring	4,000	5,100	10,200
1926	26	4 cyl.	Coupe	2,100	3,400	5,600
1926	Special	4 cyl.	Roadster	4,100	5,100	9,600
1927	124	6 cyl.	Business Coupe	2,000	4,000	6,000
1927	124	6 cyl.	Sport Phaeton	3,000	5,000	10,000
1927	124	6 cyl.	Sedan	2,100	2,100	5,600
1928	Fast Four	4 cyl.	Sedan	2,000	3,000	5,600
1928	Fast Four	4 cyl.	Sedan	2,200	4,000	5,700

YEAR	MODEL	ENGINE	BODY	F	G	E
DODGE *(United States, 1914 to date) (continued)*						
1928	Fast Four	4 cyl.	Coupe	2,400	4,300	6,000
1928	Victory	6 cyl.	Sedan	2,000	3,500	6,100
1928	Victory	6 cyl.	Rumble Seat Coupe	2,600	4,000	7,500
1928	Victory	6 cyl.	Phaeton	4,000	6,000	8,000
1928	Victory	6 cyl.	Roadster	3,500	6,000	10,000
1928	Senior Six	6 cyl.	Sedan	2,000	4,000	10,000
1928	Senior Six	6 cyl.	Roadster	4,000	6,000	10,000
1928	Senior Six	6 cyl.	Victoria	3,500	6,000	9,000
1929	Victory	6 cyl.	Touring	7,000	10,000	24,000
1929	Victory	6 cyl.	Roadster	7,400	11,000	26,000
1929	Victory	6 cyl.	Sport Touring	7,200	10,500	24,500
1929	Victory	6 cyl.	Sport Sedan	4,000	6,000	8,000
1929	Victory	6 cyl.	Coupe	3,000	4,500	9,000
1929	Victory	6 cyl.	Sedan	2,000	3,300	6,000
1929	Senior Six	6 cyl.	Roadster	6,600	9,600	22,000
1929	Senior Six	6 cyl.	Victoria	4,000	7,000	14,000
1929	Senior Six	6 cyl.	Rumble Seat Coupe	4,000	6,500	13,500
1930	DA	6 cyl.	Roadster	8,100	12,500	31,000
1930	DA	6 cyl.	Sedan 3 styles	3,000	5,000	7,000
1930	DA	6 cyl.	Coupe 2 styles	3,100	5,400	7,300
1930	DA	6 cyl.	Victoria	3,000	5,000	7,000
1930	DA	6 cyl.	Brougham	3,100	5,400	7,300
1930	DD	6 cyl.	Sedan	2,000	3,600	6,500
1930	Senior	8 cyl.	Sport Coupe	4,000	6,500	10,000
1930	DC	8 cyl.	Sport Roadster	4,000	6,000	10,000
1930	DC	8 cyl.	Sedan	2,500	4,300	7,000
1931	DG	8 cyl.	Sport Roadster	2,600	4,400	8,000
1931	DG	8 cyl.	Rumble Seat Coupe	3,500	5,300	9,100
1931	DH	6 cyl.	Sedan	2,300	3,700	6,300
1932	DK	8 cyl.	Sedan	3,000	5,000	9,000
1932	DL	6 cyl.	Sedan	2,300	3,700	7,600
1932	DL	8 cyl.	Rumble Seat Coupe	3,000	4,600	8,500
1932	DL	8 cyl.	Cabriolet	5,000	10,000	22,000
1933	DP	6 cyl.	Sedan	2,400	4,300	6,000

YEAR	MODEL	ENGINE	BODY	F	G	E
DODGE	*(United States, 1914 to date) (continued)*					
1933	DP	6 cyl.	Coupe			
			2 styles	3,000	5,000	7,000
1933	DP	6 cyl.	Brougham			
			2 styles	2,100	3,900	5,500
1933	DP	6 cyl.	Convertible	6,000	12,000	24,000
1933	DO	8 cyl.	Sport Coupe	3,800	5,000	9,000
1933	DO	8 cyl.	Sedan	3,800	5,000	8,500
1934	DR	6 cyl.	Cabriolet	5,000	10,000	22,000
1934	DR	6 cyl.	Coupe	2,000	3,000	8,200
1934	DS	6 cyl.	Convertible	6,000	12,000	25,000
1935	DU	6 cyl.	2 Door Sedan	1,500	2,100	5,500
1935	DU	6 cyl.	Sedan	2,100	3,900	5,500
1935	DU	6 cyl.	Coupe			
			2 styles	2,400	4,200	5,700
1935	DU	6 cyl.	Touring			
			Sedan	2,400	4,300	6,000
1935	DU	6 cyl.	Convertible	5,000	10,000	22,000
1936	D2	6 cyl.	Convertible			
			Sedan	6,000	12,000	24,500
1936	D2	6 cyl.	Sedan	1,000	4,000	7,000
1936	D2	6 cyl.	2 Door Sedan	1,000	4,000	9,000
1937	D5	6 cyl.	Touring			
			Sedan	2,000	3,700	5,300
1937	D5	6 cyl.	Sedan	1,000	3,000	8,000
1937	D5	6 cyl.	Coupe	1,000	4,000	8,000
1938	D8	6 cyl.	Convertible	5,000	12,000	20,000
1938	D8	6 cyl.	Sedan	1,000	3,875	7,000
1938	D8	6 cyl.	Convertible			
			Sedan	5,000	12,000	22,000
1938	D8	6 cyl.	Business			
			Coupe	2,400	4,200	5,700
1938	D8	6 cyl.	Station			
			Wagon	2,400	4,300	6,500
1939	D11	6 cyl.	Town Coupe	2,000	5,000	10,000
1939	D11	6 cyl.	2 Door Sedan	1,000	3,500	7,000
1939	D11	6 cyl.	Coupe	2,400	4,300	6,000
1939	D11	6 cyl.	Coupe	3,000	5,000	7,000
1939	D11	6 cyl.	4 Door Sedan	2,200	4,000	5,700
1939	D11	6 cyl.	Limousine	4,000	6,000	8,000
1940	D17	6 cyl.	Sedan	1,500	2,300	5,500
1940	D17	6 cyl.	Cabriolet	5,000	12,000	22,000
1941	D19	6 cyl.	Sedan	800	1,400	4,800
1941	D19	6 cyl.	2 Door Sedan	800	1,400	5,000

YEAR	MODEL	ENGINE	BODY	F	G	E
DODGE *(United States, 1914 to date) (continued)*						
1941	D19	6 cyl.	Convertible	6,000	12,000	24,000
1941	D19	6 cyl.	Town Sedan	2,000	3,200	6,700
1942	D22 Custom	6 cyl.	Sedan	2,200	4,000	5,700
1942	D22 Custom	6 cyl.	Coupe	2,400	4,300	6,000
1942	D22 Custom	6 cyl.	Brougham	2,800	4,700	6,500
1942	D22 Custom	6 cyl.	Limousine	4,000	6,000	8,000
1942	D22	6 cyl.	2 Door Sedan	1,300	1,900	5,500
1942	D22	6 cyl.	Town Sedan	1,900	3,100	6,700
Postwar Models						
1946	D24	6 cyl.	Town Sedan	1,200	2,000	5,300
1946	D24	6 cyl.	2 Passenger Coupe	1,500	2,500	7,000
1946	D24	6 cyl.	Cabriolet	5,000	1,000	20,000
1947	D24 Custom	6 cyl.	Sedan	2,500	4,600	6,400
1947	D24 Custom	6 cyl.	Coupe	2,800	5,000	6,800
1947	D24 Custom	6 cyl.	Convertible	5,700	10,000	20,000
1947	D24	6 cyl.	Sedan	1,500	2,500	7,000
1948	D24	6 cyl.	Convertible Coupe	5,000	10,000	20,000
1948	D24 Custom	6 cyl.	Sedan	2,300	4,100	5,800
1948	D24 Custom	6 cyl.	Town Sedan	2,400	4,300	6,000
1948	D24 Custom	6 cyl.	Coupe	3,000	5,000	7,200
1948	D24 Custom	6 cyl.	Convertible	5,700	10,000	20,000
1949	Wayfarer	6 cyl.	Roadster	4,000	8,000	19,000

Dodge – 1949 "Wayfarer Roadster"

1949	Meadowbrook	6 cyl.	Sedan	2,200	4,000	5,500
1949	Coronet	6 cyl.	Sedan	2,100	3,900	5,500
1949	Coronet	6 cyl.	Coupe	2,400	4,300	6,000
1949	Coronet	6 cyl.	Station Wagon	5,000	8,000	10,000

YEAR	MODEL	ENGINE	BODY	F	G	E
DODGE *(United States, 1914 to date) (continued)*						
1950	Coronet	6 cyl.	Sedan	2,200	4,000	5,700
1950	Coronet	6 cyl.	Town Sedan	1,500	2,750	7,000
1950	Coronet	6 cyl.	Hardtop	3,100	4,700	10,000
1950	Coronet	6 cyl.	Station Wagon	4,400	6,500	8,600
1950	Coronet	6 cyl.	Convertible	5,100	9,000	18,000
1950	Wayfarer	6 cyl.	Roadster	2,800	7,000	19,000
1951	Meadowbrook	6 cyl.	2 Door Sedan	1,500	2,500	6,000
1952	Coronet	6 cyl.	Convertible	4,000	9,000	18,000
1953	Coronet	V 8 cyl.	Convertible	3,000	8,000	16,000
1954	Coronet	V 8 cyl.	Club Coupe	1,500	3,500	7,000
1955	Royal	V 8 cyl.	4 Door Sedan	2,000	3,550	7,000
1956	Custom Royal	6 cyl.	Sedan	1,000	3,000	6,000
1957	Royal Lancer	V 8 cyl.	Convertible	7,000	14,000	28,000
1958	Royal Lancer	V 8 cyl.	4 Door Sedan	1,500	3,000	7,000
1959	Custom Royal	V 8 cyl.	4 Door Sedan	1,000	2,500	4,750
1960	Phoenix	8 cyl.	2 or 4 Door Hardtop	2,000	4,000	9,000
1960	Pioneer	8 cyl.	2 or 4 Door Sedan	1,500	2,000	4,500
1960	Seneca	8 cyl.	2 or 4 Door Sedan	1,000	2,000	4,000
1961	Lancer	6 cyl.	Sedan	850	2,000	3,300
1961	Polara	8 cyl.	2 or 4 Door Sedan	850	2,000	3,300
1961	Pioneer	8 cyl.	Sedan	850	2,000	3,300
1961	Pioneer	8 cyl.	Hardtop	1,000	2,300	3,700
1962	Lancer 770	6 cyl.	2 or 4 Door Sedan	850	2,000	3,300
1962	Dart 440	8 cyl.	2 or 4 Door Sedan	900	2,100	3,200
1962	Dart 440	8 cyl.	Station Wagon	850	2,000	3,300
1962	Polara	8 cyl.	Convertible	3,000	7,000	9,000
1962	880	8 cyl.	Sedan	900	2,100	3,200
1962	880	8 cyl.	Hardtop	1,000	2,300	3,700
1963	Polara	V 8 cyl.	2 Door Hardtop	900	1,200	4,500
1964	Dart 170	6 cyl.	2 or 4 Door Sedan	850	2,000	3,300

YEAR	MODEL	ENGINE	BODY	F	G	E
DODGE *(United States, 1914 to date) (continued)*						
1964	Dart 270	6 cyl.	2 or 4 Door Sedan	850	2,200	3,300
1964	Dart 270	6 cyl.	Convertible	2,400	4,300	6,000
1964	Dodge	8 cyl.	2 or 4 Door Sedan	1,000	2,200	3,700
1964	Dodge	8 cyl.	Hardtop	1,200	2,600	4,300
1964	Polara	8 cyl.	Sedan	1,100	2,300	4,200
1964	880	8 cyl.	Sedan	1,200	2,600	4,300
1964	880	8 cyl.	Station Wagon	1,200	2,600	4,300
1966	Charger	V 8 cyl. (Hemi)	Coupe	4,000	8,000	15,000
1968	Coronet Deluxe	8 cyl.	2 or 4 Door Sedan	850	2,200	3,300
1968	Coronet Super Bee	8 cyl.	Hardtop	4,000	7,000	14,000
1968	Coronet 500	8 cyl.	Convertible	2,400	4,300	6,100
1968	Dart	6 cyl.	2 or 4 Door Sedan	850	2,200	3,300
1968	Dart	8 cyl.	Sedan	850	2,200	3,300
1968	Polara	8 cyl.	2 or 4 Door Hardtop	1,100	2,300	4,200
1968	Monaco	8 cyl.	Sedan	850	2,200	3,300
1969	Charger R/T	8 cyl.	Hardtop	8,000	14,000	28,000
1969	Charger 500	8 cyl.	Hardtop	8,000	16,000	32,000
1969	Charger Daytona	8 cyl.	Hardtop	12,000	25,000	55,000
1969	Coronet R/T	8 cyl.	Hardtop	7,000	14,000	27,000
1969	Coronet R/T	8 cyl.	Convertible	8,000	15,000	29,000
1969	Dart GT	8 cyl.	Hardtop	2,400	4,300	6,100
1969	Dart Custom	8 cyl.	Sedan	850	2,200	3,300
1969	Dart Swinger	8 cyl.	Hardtop	1,200	2,600	4,300
1970	Charger 500	V 8 cyl. (Hemi)	Hardtop	7,000	15,000	35,000
1970	Polara 500	V 8 cyl.	Convertible	3,000	5,000	8,000
1971	Charger R/T	8 cyl.	Hardtop	8,000	15,000	32,000
1971	Coronet Brougham	8 cyl.	Sedan	600	1,500	2,600
1971	Demon	8 cyl.	Coupe	850	2,200	3,300
1972	Dart	8 cyl.	Sedan	850	2,200	3,300
1972	Monaco	8 cyl.	2 or 4 Door Hardtop	850	2,200	3,300
1973	Challenger	8 cyl.	Rallye	3,000	5,000	10,000

YEAR	MODEL	ENGINE	BODY	F	G	E
DODGE *(United States, 1914 to date) (continued)*						
1973	Coronet Custom	8 cyl.	Station Wagon	700	2,000	3,000
1973	Monaco	8 cyl.	Brougham	850	2,200	3,300
1973	Polara	8 cyl.	Sedan	850	2,200	3,300
1974	Dart 360	8 cyl.	Coupe	850	2,200	3,300
1974	Swinger	8 cyl.	Hardtop	850	2,200	3,300
1974	Monaco Brougham	8 cyl.	Sedan	850	2,200	3,300
1975	Dart	8 cyl.	Sedan	700	2,000	3,000
1975	Dart Custom	8 cyl.	Coupe	1,100	2,300	4,200
1975	Royal Monaco	8 cyl.	Sedan	850	2,200	3,300
DODSON *(Great Britain, 1910–14)*						
1910		2 cyl.	Open	1,000	3,000	5,750
1911		2 cyl.	Open	1,100	3,200	6,000
DOLORES *(France, 1906)*						
1906	10		Tonneau	1,000	2,700	7,500
1906	24		Tonneau	1,200	3,800	8,600
1906	60		Tonneau	1,700	5,400	9,800
DOMMARTIN *(France, 1949–50)*						
1949		4 cyl.	Racing	2,000	5,150	11,500
1950		2 cyl.	Convertible	1,000	1,900	4,800
DONNET; DONNET-ZEDEL *(France, 1924–34)*						
1924	Type G	4 cyl.	Coupe	1,100	2,700	6,500
1932	11 CV	4 cyl.	Sedan	1,000	2,600	6,250
DONOSTI *(Spain, 1922–23)*						
1922		6 cyl.	Sport	1,500	3,900	7,750
1922		4 cyl.	Sport	1,000	2,600	6,250
DOREY *(France, 1906–07; 1912–13)*						
1906		1 cyl. (DeDion)	Voiturette	2,000	4,000	7,750
1906		4 cyl.	Voiturette	2,000	4,800	8,650
1912		2 cyl.	Cycle	1,000	2,600	4,250
DORRIS *(United States, 1906–26)*						
1906	A	4 cyl.	Touring	3,500	7,000	18,000
1923	6-80	6 cyl.	Pasadena	4,000	10,000	25,000
1923	6-80	6 cyl.	Sedan	3,000	6,000	11,000
1923	6-80	6 cyl.	4 Passenger Sport Touring	3,700	8,000	18,000
1925	6-80	6 cyl.	7 Passenger Touring	3,500	6,500	14,000

YEAR	MODEL	ENGINE	BODY	F	G	E
DORT	*(United States, 1915–24)*					
1915	5	4 cyl.	Touring	1,100	5,250	13,500
1915	Fleur de lis	4 cyl.	Roadster	1,700	5,300	13,600
1915	Centre-door	4 cyl.	Sedan	1,700	3,400	8,750
1915	5	4 cyl.	Touring	1,900	5,800	13,600
1917	5 A	4 cyl.	Touring	1,900	5,800	13,600
1918	8-11	4 cyl.	Coupe	1,750	3,500	8,000
1919	8-11	4 cyl.	Touring	1,900	5,800	13,800
1919	8-11	4 cyl.	Roadster	1,300	5,600	13,200
1919	8-11	4 cyl.	Sedanette	1,400	3,800	9,750
1922	19-14	4 cyl.	Sedan	1,200	2,500	8,000
1924	27	6 cyl.	Sport Touring	3,200	6,400	14,500
1924	27	6 cyl.	Touring	2,400	4,800	12,500
DOUGLAS	*(United States, 1918–19)*					
1918		V-8 (Herschell-Spillman)	Roadster	5,000	9,000	19,000
1918		V-8 (Herschell-Spillman)	Sportster Special	5,000	10,000	22,000
DRAGON	*(United States, 1906–21)*					
1906	25	4 cyl.	Touring	2,800	7,000	15,000
1906	35	4 cyl.	Touring	3,000	6,000	14,000
1908	35	4 cyl.	Roadster	4,500	9,000	20,000
1921		4 cyl.	Roadster	6,000	14,000	25,000
1921		4 cyl.	Victoria	7,000	12,000	25,000
1921		4 cyl.	Touring	8,000	14,000	26,000
DREXEL	*(United States, 1916–17)*					
1916	5-40	4 cyl. (Farmer)	Touring	5,000	12,000	24,000
1916	4-60	4 cyl.	Roadster	8,000	14,000	26,000
1916	R-30	4 cyl.	5 Passenger Touring	5,000	12,000	24,000
DRUMMOND	*(United States, 1915–18)*					
1915		6 cyl.	Roadster	8,000	14,000	27,000
1915		4 cyl.	Touring	6,000	12,000	23,000
1917	17	8 cyl.	3 Passenger Roadster	7,000	14,000	29,000
DUAL E TURCONI	*(Italy, 1899–01)*					
1899	3-Wheel	1 cyl.	Voiturette	1,000	2,900	5,750
1899		1 cyl.	Voiturette	1,100	3,000	6,000
DUAL-GHIA	*(United States, 1955–67)*					
1955	Firebomb	V 8 cyl. (Dodge)	Convertible	5,200	13,650	28,500
1962	L 6.4	V 8 cyl. (Chrysler)	Coupe	3,000	9,900	16,500

YEAR	MODEL	ENGINE	BODY	F	G	E
DUAL-GHIA *(United States, 1955–67) (continued)*						
1962	L 6.4	V 8 cyl. (Chrysler)	Convertible	5,100	13,000	26,000
DUBONNET *(France, 1933–36)*						
1933		6 cyl.	Saloon	1,600	3,250	7,000
1934		8 cyl. (Hispano Suiza)	Sedan	5,000	14,000	28,000
1936		V 8 cyl. (Ford)	Teardrop	4,000	8,000	13,000
DUCOMMUN *(Germany, 1903–04)*						
1903		2 cyl.	Open	1,000	2,900	6,000
1904		4 cyl.	Open	1,100	3,000	63,000
DUESENBERG *(United States, 1920–37)*						
1920	A	8 cyl.	Roadster		RARE	
1920	A	8 cyl. (Straight)	Cabriolet		RARE	
1920	A	8 cyl.	Racing		RARE	
1921	A	8 cyl.	Dual Cowl Phaeton		RARE	
1921	A	8 cyl.	Sedan		RARE	
1922	A	8 cyl.	Sedan	8,900	18,000	34,000
1922	A	8 cyl.	Touring	16,000	29,000	80,000
1922	A	8 cyl.	Roadster	13,000	26,000	75,000
1923	A	8 cyl.	Dual Cowl Phaeton	16,000	33,000	83,000
1923	A	8 cyl.	Town Car	10,900	18,000	33,000
1923	A	8 cyl.	Touring	16,000	32,000	86,000
1924	A	8 cyl.	Phaeton	40,000	65,000	115,000
1924	A	8 cyl.	Sedan Limousine	15,000	25,000	50,000
1924	A	8 cyl.	Roadster Racing	40,000	70,000	120,000
1925	A 5 Ps	8 cyl.	Brougham	20,000	30,000	55,000
1925	A	8 cyl.	Phaeton	40,000	65,000	115,000
1925	A	8 cyl.	Roadster	45,000	70,000	125,000
1926	A	8 cyl.	Touring	40,000	65,000	115,000
1926	A	8 cyl.	Sport Touring	45,000	75,000	130,000
1926	A	8 cyl.	4 Passenger Roadster	40,000	65,000	120,000
1926	A	8 cyl.	5 Passenger Sedan	15,000	26,000	75,000
1927	A	8 cyl.	Sport Touring	40,000	70,000	130,000
1927	A	8 cyl.	7 Passenger Phaeton	50,000	90,000	175,000

YEAR	MODEL	ENGINE	BODY	F	G	E
DUESENBERG	*(United States, 1920–37)*	*(continued)*				
1927	A	8 cyl.	Roadster Racing	40,000	75,000	125,000
1927	A	8 cyl.	Sedan	30,000	50,000	85,000
1928	Holbrook-J	8 cyl.	Sedan	29,000	72,000	160,000
1928	Holbrook-J	8 cyl.	Town Cabriolet	50,000	96,000	220,000
1928	J	8 cyl.	Touring	46,000	86,000	220,000
1928	Murphy-J	8 cyl.	Convertible Roadster	72,000	160,000	320,000
1928	J	8 cyl.	Dual Cowl Sport Phaeton	86,000	150,000	300,000
1928	J	8 cyl.	Brougham	50,000	104,000	190,000
1928	J	8 cyl.	Berline	50,000	105,000	220,000
1928	J	8 cyl.	Limousine	40,000	105,000	220,000
1928	Derham-J	8 cyl.	2 Window Sedan	50,000	90,000	190,000
1928	Rollston-J	8 cyl.	Town Sedan	50,000	110,000	220,000
1928	LeBaron-J	8 cyl.	Phaeton	86,000	120,000	290,000
1929	Murphy-J	8 cyl.	Convertible Roadster	86,000	120,000	300,000
1929	Derham-J	8 cyl.	Dual Cowl Phaeton	96,000	170,000	320,000
1929	J	8 cyl.	Roadster	86,000	130,000	280,000
1929	Murphy-J	8 cyl.	Convertible Sedan	86,000	130,000	320,000
1929	Rollston-J	8 cyl.	Limousine	72,000	120,000	220,000
1929	J	8 cyl.	Berline	72,000	105,000	220,000
1929	J	8 cyl.	Brougham	72,000	105,000	220,000
1929	J	8 cyl.	Sport Phaeton	86,000	160,000	320,000
1929	Derham-J	8 cyl.	Phaeton	86,000	150,000	320,000
1929	J	8 cyl.	Cabriolet	74,000	140,000	260,000
1929	J	8 cyl.	Sport Coupe	74,000	140,000	360,000
1929	J	8 cyl.	Cabriolet	74,000	140,000	280,000
1929	J	8 cyl.	Sedan	47,000	92,000	170,000
1929	J	8 cyl.	Enclosed Sedan	47,000	101,000	190,000
1929	Rollston-J	8 cyl.	Town Sedan	70,000	120,000	190,000
1929	Rollston-J	8 cyl.	All Weather Cabriolet	79,000	130,000	220,000
1929	Murphy-J	8 cyl.	Convertible Berline	86,000	160,000	320,000

YEAR	MODEL	ENGINE	BODY	F	G	E
DUESENBERG *(United States, 1920–37) (continued)*						
1929	Holbrook-J	8 cyl.	Sport Sedan	81,000	140,000	210,000
1929	Holbrook-J	8 cyl.	French Cabriolet	87,000	160,000	320,000
1929	Derham-J	8 cyl.	Close Coupe Town	81,000	140,000	210,000
1929	J	8 cyl.	Convertible Touring	87,000	160,000	300,000
1930	J	8 cyl.	Convertible Sedan	87,000	140,000	280,000
1930	Beverly-J	8 cyl.	Sedan	54,000	96,000	220,000
1930	Rollston-J	8 cyl.	Town Sedan	59,000	103,000	220,000
1930	J	8 cyl.	Cabriolet	70,000	140,000	250,000
1930	Derham-J	8 cyl.	Touring	87,000	160,000	320,000
1930	Murphy-J	8 cyl.	Boattail Speedster	98,000	190,000	380,000
1930	J	8 cyl.	Convertible	87,000	160,000	300,000
1930	Murphy-J	8 cyl.	Convertible Roadster	87,000	160,000	310,000
1930	Rollston-J	8 cyl.	Convertible Victoria	87,000	160,000	310,000
1930	Murphy-J	8 cyl.	Sedan	54,000	87,000	190,000
1930	Derham-J	8 cyl.	Close Coupe	54,000	87,000	200,000
1930	Brunn-J	8 cyl.	Town Brougham	54,000	87,000	200,000
1930	Judkins-J	8 cyl.	2 Passenger Coupe	54,000	87,000	200,000
1930	LeBaron-J	8 cyl.	Dual Cowl Phaeton	92,000	160,000	320,000
1930	Murphy-J	8 cyl.	Town Sedan	54,000	87,000	210,000
1930	Murphy-J	8 cyl.	Club Sedan	54,000	87,000	210,000
1930	J	8 cyl.	Roadster	87,000	150,000	320,000
1930	J	8 cyl.	Convertible Coupe	77,050	130,000	300,000
1930	J	8 cyl.	Sport Phaeton	87,000	150,000	320,000
1930	J	8 cyl.	Limousine	54,000	87,000	180,000
1931	J	8 cyl.	Convertible	87,000	150,000	290,000
1931	J	8 cyl.	Phaeton	92,000	160,000	320,000
1931		8 cyl.	Dual Cowl Phaeton	94,000	160,000	320,000
1931	J	8 cyl.	Convertible Sedan	87,000	160,000	300,000
1931	Franay-J	8 cyl.	Limousine	59,000	98,000	200,000

YEAR	MODEL	ENGINE	BODY	F	G	E
DUESENBERG (United States, 1920–37) (continued)						
1931	J	8 cyl.	Convertible Roadster	81,000	160,000	290,000
1931	J	8 cyl.	Town Brougham	54,000	92,000	200,000
1931	J	8 cyl.	Town Sedan	54,000	87,000	190,000
1931	Derham-J	8 cyl.	Touring	87,000	160,000	320,000
1931	LeBaron-J	8 cyl.	Convertible Berline	87,000	160,000	320,000
1931	Derham-J	8 cyl.	Convertible Sedan	87,000	160,000	320,000
1931	Murphy-J	8 cyl.	Convertible Roadster	87,000	160,000	320,000
1931	Rollston-J	8 cyl.	Convertible Victoria	87,000	160,000	320,000
1931	French-J	8 cyl.	Speedster	92,000	170,000	320,000
1931	Murphy-J	8 cyl.	Town Car	59,000	98,000	220,000
1931	Rollston-J	8 cyl.	Town Car	59,000	92,000	220,000
1931	Judkins-J	8 cyl.	4 Passenger Coupe	50,000	87,000	180,000
1931	Judkins-J	8 cyl.	Berline Coupe	50,000	87,000	190,000
1931	Murphy-J	8 cyl.	Limousine	54,000	92,000	220,000
1931	J	8 cyl.	Formal Sport Sedan	54,000	92,000	220,000
1932	SJ	8 cyl. (Supercharged)	Roadster	98,000	120,000	370,000
1932	J	8 cyl.	Convertible Sedan	87,000	170,000	320,000
1932	LeGrande SJ	8 cyl. (Supercharged)	Phaeton	105,000	200,000	390,000
1932	Beverly SJ	8 cyl. (Supercharged)	Sedan	76,000	160,000	260,000
1932	Weymann SJ	8 cyl. (Supercharged)	Fishtail Speedster	110,000	240,000	450,000
1932	Murphy-J	8 cyl.	Town Car	59,000	104,000	220,000
1932	Murphy	8 cyl.	Convertible	78,000	150,000	320,000
1932	Brunn-SJ	8 cyl. (Supercharged)	Torpedo Phaeton	98,000	220,000	320,000
1932	Murphy-J	8 cyl.	Roadster	78,000	160,000	310,000
1932	Rollston-J	8 cyl.	Town Car	59,000	104,000	200,000
1932	Murphy-J	8 cyl.	Limousine	51,250	89,500	195,000
1932	LeBaron-J	8 cyl.	Phaeton	87,000	158,500	330,000
1932	Judkins-J	8 cyl.	Berline Coupe	54,250	84,500	202,000
1932	Willoughby-J	8 cyl.	Limousine	54,250	84,500	197,000

YEAR	MODEL	ENGINE	BODY	F	G	E
DUESENBERG *(United States, 1920–37) (continued)*						
1932	LeBaron-J	8 cyl.	Dual Cowl Phaeton	85,750	174,500	325,000

Duesenberg – 1932 "Model J Dual Cowl Phaeton"

YEAR	MODEL	ENGINE	BODY	F	G	E
1933	Twenty Grand-SJ	8 cyl.	Sedan	76,000	185,000	360,000
1933	SJ	8 cyl. (Supercharged)	Roadster	106,500	228,000	330,000
1933	Weymann-J	8 cyl.	Phaeton	117,500	158,500	300,000
1933	Brunn-SJ	8 cyl. (Supercharged)	Phaeton	98,000	212,500	322,500
1933	Brunn-SJ	8 cyl. (Supercharged)	Sport Convertible	98,000	217,000	330,000
1933	Rollston-J	8 cyl.	Convertible Torpedo Victoria	87,000	170,000	315,000
1933	Special-SJ	8 cyl. (Supercharged)	Racing	103,000	215,800	325,000
1933	Murphy-SJ	8 cyl. (Supercharged)	Roadster	109,500	213,500	328,800
1933	Murphy-J	8 cyl.	Town Car	59,000	104,000	223,500
1933	Rollston-J	8 cyl.	Town Car	59,000	104,000	223,000
1933	Rollston-J	8 cyl.	Closed Sedan	51,250	87,500	200,000
1933	Murphy-J	8 cyl.	Convertible	87,500	211,500	330,000
1933	Murphy-SJ	8 cyl. (Supercharged)	Boattail Speedster	109,500	239,500	325,000

YEAR	MODEL	ENGINE	BODY	F	G	E
DUESENBERG *(United States, 1920–37) (continued)*						
1933	Murphy-J	8 cyl.	Limousine	45,500	94,500	150,000

Duesenberg – 1933 "Model J Murphy Roadster

YEAR	MODEL	ENGINE	BODY	F	G	E
1933	Fernandez & Darrin-J	8 cyl.	Open Front Victoria	62,500	163,500	250,000
1934	LeBaron-SJ	8 cyl. (Supercharged)	Dual Cowl Phaeton	105,250	229,500	330,000
1934	J	8 cyl.	Roadster	87,500	168,500	292,800
1934	LeGrande-J	8 cyl.	Speedster	85,500	164,000	323,800
1934	Brunn-SJ	8 cyl. (Supercharged)	Riviera Phaeton	107,050	228,500	370,000
1934	LeGrande-J	8 cyl.	Roadster	79,000	158,500	295,000
1934	LeGrande-J	8 cyl.	Coupe	59,250	98,500	221,500
1934	J	8 cyl.	Cabriolet	55,250	101,700	227,000
1934	J	8 cyl.	Phaeton	87,500	168,500	305,000
1934	Brunn-J	8 cyl.	Convertible Sport	87,000	165,700	301,700
1934	Murphy-J	8 cyl.	Roadster	87,000	165,900	305,500
1934	Walker-J	8 cyl.	3 Passenger Coupe	49,200	85,200	205,000
1934	Murphy-SJ	8 cyl. (Supercharged)	Limousine	77,350	153,500	285,000
1934	Judkins-J	8 cyl.	Berline Coupe	52,000	94,500	191,500
1934	Judkins-J	8 cyl.	Limousine	56,450	96,000	197,000
1934	J	8 cyl.	Roadster	99,000	158,500	325,000
1934	J	8 cyl.	Town Limousine	54,000	92,000	215,000

YEAR	MODEL	ENGINE	BODY	F	G	E
DUESENBERG *(United States, 1920–37) (continued)*						
1934	J	8 cyl.	Sport Phaeton	87,000	158,500	325,000
1935	Rollston-JN	8 cyl.	Convertible Sedan	87,000	155,200	290,000
1935	Rollston-JN	8 cyl.	Sedan	45,400	92,900	191,500
1935	Rollston-JN	8 cyl.	Convertible	87,500	165,000	289,500
1935	Rollston-JN	8 cyl.	Opera Brougham	76,250	147,500	230,000
1935	Rollston-JN	8 cyl.	Convertible Coupe Long Wheel Base	87,000	168,500	295,000
1935	LeGrande-J	8 cyl.	Roadster	87,500	168,500	305,000
1935	Walker-SJ	8 cyl.	Phaeton	104,500	228,500	359,000
1935	Bohman-SJ	8 cyl.	Town Car	87,000	158,500	287,500
1935	Murphy-SJ	8 cyl.	Roadster	109,300	228,500	328,000
1935	Rollston-J	8 cyl.	Town Car	52,500	109,000	228,000
1935	J	8 cyl.	Convertible	87,500	168,500	305,000
1935	SSJ	8 cyl. (Supercharged)	Roadster	157,500	251,000	370,000
1936	SJ	8 cyl. (Supercharged)	Sedan	81,750	163,500	250,000
1936	SSJ	8 cyl. (Supercharged)	Maharaja Boattailed Speedster	194,000	275,000	500,000
1936	Y	12 cyl.	Prototype Race Car	130,000	260,000	380,000
1936	SSJ	8 cyl.	Marmon Meter Race Car	167,000	307,500	450,000
1936	JN	8 cyl.	Convertible Coupe	82,000	168,500	300,000
1936	J	8 cyl.	Convertible Sedan	79,500	168,500	325,000
1936	SSJ	8 cyl. (Supercharged)	Roadster	106,800	226,800	325,000
1936	Bohman SJ	8 cyl.	Convertible	98,200	220,700	322,500
1936	Murphy-J	8 cyl.	Roadster	87,100	168,000	326,000
1936	SJ	8 cyl. (Supercharged)	Roadster	87,000	180,000	325,000
1936	Bohman-J	8 cyl.	Airflow Coupe	59,500	109,000	210,000
1936	Bohman-J	8 cyl.	Sedan	51,200	99,200	190,000
1936	J	8 cyl.	Limousine	54,100	99,200	190,000
1936	J	8 cyl.	Sport Phaeton	76,000	157,500	305,900
1936	J	8 cyl.	Roadster	76,500	157,500	305,900
1936	J	8 cyl.	Town Car	54,100	99,700	202,500

YEAR	MODEL	ENGINE	BODY	F	G	E
DUESENBERG *(United States, 1920–37) (continued)*						
1936	J	8 cyl.	Town Limousine	54,500	99,100	200,000
1937	Bohman-J	8 cyl.	Throne	50,500	89,700	190,000
1937	Bohman-J	8 cyl.	Convertible Coupe	70,200	140,500	270,000
1937	Derham-SJ	8 cyl. (Supercharged)	Touring	107,300	228,000	326,800
1937	Derham-J	8 cyl.	Phaeton	87,000	161,800	305,000
1937	J	8 cyl.	Convertible Sedan	76,750	151,300	305,000
1937	Rollston-J	8 cyl.	Convertible Torpedo Victoria	87,000	168,500	300,000
1937	Rollston-J	8 cyl.	Hardtop Sedan	56,700	94,500	210,000
1937	Weymann-J	8 cyl.	Convertible Coupe	85,300	163,000	290,000
1937	Weymann-J	8 cyl.	Sport Sedan	52,300	92,500	185,000
1937	Brunn-J	8 cyl.	Torpedo Phaeton	85,400	161,800	320,000
1937	Rollston-J	8 cyl.	Convertible Sedan	84,800	155,700	280,000
1937	Murphy-J	8 cyl.	Roadster	87,000	164,000	305,000
1937	LeGrande-J	8 cyl.	Dual Cowl Phaeton	86,800	185,000	325,000
1937	J	8 cyl.	Limousine	46,350	92,700	220,000
DUESENBERG II *(United States, 1978–81)*						
1978	J	8 cyl.	Speedster	109,000	114,000	130,000
1979	J	8 cyl.	Speedster	89,000	95,000	100,000
1980	J	8 cyl.	Speedster	86,000	99,000	98,000
1981	J	8 cyl.	Dual Cowl Phaeton	96,000	130,000	145,000
DUO *(Great Britain, 1912–14)*						
1912		1 cyl. (Buchingham)	Cycle	1,000	2,500	4,250
1912		6 cyl. (Dorman)	Open	1,500	3,800	9,500
1913		4 cyl. (Chopuis-Domieer)	Open	1,200	2,700	4,500
DU PONT *(United States, 1919–32)*						
1920	A	4 cyl.	Touring	4,500	12,000	27,000
1924	C	6 cyl. (Herschell-Spillman)	Touring	5,000	13,000	30,000
1925	D	6 cyl. (Wisconsin)	Touring	5,500	14,000	35,000
1928	E	8 cyl.	Touring	5,500	14,000	36,000

YEAR	MODEL	ENGINE	BODY	F	G	E
DU PONT *(United States, 1919–32) (continued)*						
1928	E	8 cyl. (Continental)	Roadster	15,000	40,000	85,000
1929	G	8 cyl.	Roadster	17,000	45,000	98,000
1931	H	8 cyl.	Touring	16,000	43,000	94,000
DUQUESNE *(United States, 1904–13)*						
1903	C	4 cyl. (Air-cooled)	Side Entrance Tonneau	5,000	10,000	24,000
1912		4 cyl. (T-head)	Touring	6,000	12,000	28,000
DURANT *(United States, 1921–32)*						
1921	A22	6 cyl.	Touring	3,250	6,500	15,000
1923	B22	6 cyl.	4 Passenger Touring	3,400	7,800	15,500
1923	B22	6 cyl. (Ansted)	Touring	3,900	7,750	16,500
1924	A22	6 cyl.	Touring	3,250	7,500	16,900
1928	M	4 cyl.	2 Door	2,750	5,000	9,000
1928	M	4 cyl.	Sedan	2,750	5,200	9,400
1928	M	4 cyl.	Touring	3,700	6,200	14,000
1928	Deluxe	6 cyl.		3,900	6,500	11,000
1929	55	6 cyl.	Sedan	2,900	5,500	9,000
1929	55	6 cyl.	Roadster	3,200	8,000	19,000
1929	55	6 cyl.	Rumble Seat Coupe	2,900	7,800	9,800
1929	66	6 cyl.	Phaeton	3,500	9,500	29,000
1930	6-14	6 cyl.	Phaeton	3,700	11,000	30,000
1930	6-14	6 cyl.	Sedan	2,900	5,500	9,000
1930	6-14	6 cyl.	Coupe	3,000	5,800	9,750
1930	6-17	6 cyl.	Roadster	4,200	12,000	36,500
DUROCAR *(United States, 1907–11)*						
1907	26	2 cyl.	Surrey	2,650	7,300	13,800
1907	26	2 cyl.	Runabout	2,800	7,700	14,200
1907	26	2 cyl.	Touring	2,800	7,700	14,200
1910	26		Roadster	3,000	7,000	13,000
DURYEA *(United States, 1895–1917)*						
1895	"Motor"	1 cyl.	Buggy	2,400	7,800	16,500
1898	3-Wheel	2 cyl.	Buggy	2,000	7,000	18,800
1908	High-Wheel	3 cyl.	Buggy	3,200	7,500	17,000
DUX *(Germany, 1909–26)*						
1909	E12	2 cyl.	Open	1,000	2,900	5,750
1919	50	4 cyl.	Open	1,200	2,250	5,500
1920	60	6 cyl.	Open	1,500	4,000	6,000

YEAR	MODEL	ENGINE	BODY	F	G	E
DYNAMOBIL *(Germany, 1906)*						
1906	24	Petrol	Open	1,000	4,100	6,500
1906	12	Electric	Brougham	2,200	5,400	12,750

E

EAGLE *(Great Britain, 1901–14)*						
1901	Tandem	2 cyl.	Tri-car	1,000	1,900	4,750
1903		2 cyl.	Open	1,000	2,000	5,000
1903	16	4 cyl.	Runabout	1,000	2,000	5,000
1907	24/30	4 cyl.	Touring	1,500	3,100	7,250
1912	8/10	V 2 cyl.	Open	1,200	2,800	5,500
1914	8	4 cyl.	Touring	1,000	2,900	5,750
EAGLE *(United States, 1904–24)*						
1904		2 cyl.	Tonneau	2,800	6,000	15,000
1905		4 cyl.	Touring	2,800	7,000	18,000
1908		2 cyl.	High-Wheel	2,500	6,300	14,000
1909		2 cyl. (Air-cooled)	Roadster	2,500	6,300	14,500
1914		5 cyl. (Air-cooled)	Cycle	2,300	7,000	17,500
1923		6 cyl. (Continental)	Touring	3,800	8,800	18,500
EASTMEAD-BIGGS *(Great Britain, 1901–04)*						
1901		(Simms)	Open	1,200	2,750	5,500
1901		(Aster)	Open	1,200	2,750	5,500
ECONOMY *(United States, 1914–21)*						
1914		2 cyl. (Spacke)	Cycle	1,300	3,500	11,000
1914	G4-36	4 cyl.	Touring	2,100	4,250	13,500
1917	G4-36	8 cyl.	Roadster	3,150	8,300	17,500
1920	6-46	6 cyl. (Continental)	Touring	2,200	5,400	15,750
EDIS *(Spain, 1919–22)*						
1919	10	2 cyl.	Roadster	1,200	2,700	6,500
1919		4 cyl.	Touring	1,500	2,900	6,750
EDMOND *(Great Britain, 1920–21)*						
1920		2 cyl. (Coventry)	Cycle	1,000	2,600	5,250
1921		2 cyl.	Cycle	1,100	2,750	5,500

YEAR	MODEL	ENGINE	BODY	F	G	E

EDSEL *(United States, 1958–60)*

YEAR	MODEL	ENGINE	BODY	F	G	E
1958	Ranger	V 8 cyl.	2 Door			
			Hardtop	2,000	5,000	10,000

Edsel – 1958 "Ranger"

YEAR	MODEL	ENGINE	BODY	F	G	E
1958	Citation	V 8 cyl.	4 Door			
			Hardtop	1,500	4,000	9,500
1958	Citation	V 8 cyl.	2 Door			
			Hardtop	2,000	6,000	14,000
1958	Citation	V 8 cyl.	Convertible	5,000	14,000	28,000
1959	Ranger	V 8 cyl.	2 Door			
			Hardtop	2,100	5,000	11,000
1959	Corsair	V 8 cyl.	Convertible	3,000	5,000	22,000
1959	Corsair	V 8 cyl.	2 Door			
			Hardtop	1,100	2,200	11,000
1959	Villager	V 8 cyl.	9 Passenger Station Wagon	650	1,300	7,500
1960	Ranger	V 8 cyl.	Convertible	2,200	3,300	25,000
1960	Ranger	V 8 cyl.	6 Passenger Station Wagon	1,100	2,400	7,000
1960	Ranger	V 8 cyl.	2 Door			
			Hardtop	1,700	2,650	12,000
1960	Ranger	V 8 cyl.	Convertible	2,000	3,000	25,000

EDWARDS *(United States, 1953–55)*

YEAR	MODEL	ENGINE	BODY	F	G	E
1953		V 8 cyl. (Ford)	Sport	1,500	3,000	8,000
1953		V 8 cyl. (Lincoln)	Sport	1,800	3,500	8,800

YEAR	MODEL	ENGINE	BODY	F	G	E
EDWARDS-KNIGHT *(United States, 1913–14)*						
1913	25	4 cyl. (Knight)	Touring	2,500	7,000	14,000
EHRHARDT *(Germany, 1904–22)*						
1904	Fidelio	2 cyl.	Open	1,000	2,900	8,750
1905	31/50	4 cyl.	Racing	2,800	4,250	12,500
1907	16/24	4 cyl.	Touring	2,400	3,400	9,800
ELCAR *(United States, 1916–31)*						
1916		4 cyl. (Lycoming)	Roadster	3,000	7,500	14,750
1919	D	6 cyl. (Continental)	Touring	3,200	8,750	16,250
1925	6-50	6 cyl. (Continental)	Sport	3,500	9,000	19,000
1926	8-81	8 cyl. (Lycoming)	5 Passenger Sedan	2,900	5,000	11,750
1929		8 cyl. (Lycoming)	Sedan	2,900	5,100	11,500
1929	8-78	8 cyl. (Lycoming)	5 Passenger Sedan	2,900	5,100	11,500
ELDEN *(Great Britain, 1969–73)*						
1970	Mark 8 FF	Formula (Ford)	Racing	2,400	3,250	7,500
1972	Mark 9	Formula (Ford)	Racing	2,500	3,650	7,500
1973	Mark 10 FF	Formula (Ford)	Racing	2,700	4,250	9,000
1973	Mark II	Formula (Ford)	Sport	2,100	4,200	9,400
1973	Mark 12 F3	Formula (Ford)	Racing	2,100	4,250	10,500
ELDREDGE *(United States, 1903–06)*						
1903		2 cyl.	Runabout	2,750	8,500	16,000
1904		2 cyl.	Runabout	2,500	7,000	15,000
1906		2 cyl.	Runabout	3,000	9,000	17,000
ELECTROMOBILE *(Great Britain, 1901–20)*						
1901		Electric	Victoria	2,000	6,000	12,000
1903		Electric	Brougham	2,100	6,100	12,250
1919	Elmo	Electric	Landaulet	2,000	6,000	12,000
1919	Elmo	Electric	Limousine	2,100	6,100	12,250
ELFIN *(Australia, 1959 to date)*						
1959			Racing	2,550	4,100	9,250
1959			Sport	1,550	3,100	6,250
1965	Formula 2	Ford	Racing	1,550	3,100	6,250
1969		V 8 cyl. (Repco)	Racing	1,700	3,400	6,750
1969		Formula (Ford)	Racing	1,750	3,500	6,000
1970	Group 7		Racing	1,750	3,500	6,000
ELGIN *(United States, 1899–1925)*						
1899	5	1 cyl.	Runabout		RARE	
1899		Electric	Runabout		RARE	
1916	17	6 cyl.	Roadster	3,500	7,000	14,000
1918	17 E	6 cyl. (Falls)	Sedan	3,500	7,000	12,000

ENDURANCE / 215

YEAR	MODEL	ENGINE	BODY	F	G	E
ELGIN	*(United States, 1899–1925) (continued)*					
1919	H	6 cyl.	Touring	4,500	9,500	18,000
1924		6 cyl.	Sportsman	3,800	11,500	21,000
ELVA	*(Great Britain, 1955–68)*					
1957		1100cc (Ford)	Sport	1,000	2,100	5,250
1958	Mark 4	(Coventry-Climax)	Sport	1,100	2,200	5,500
1959	Mark 5	(D.K.W.)	Sport	1,000	2,400	5,800
1963	Mark 7	1588cc (Ford)	Sport	1,000	2,500	5,000
1965	Courier		Sport	1,000	2,400	5,750
EMANCIPATOR	*(United States, 1909)*					
1909		2 cyl.	Tonneau		RARE	
1909		4 cyl.	Tonneau		RARE	
E.M.F.	*(United States, 1908–12)*					
1909	30	4 cyl.	Touring	2,700	6,500	16,000
1910	30	4 cyl.	Touring	2,400	6,000	15,000
1911	30	4 cyl.	Roadster	2,800	6,500	16,000
1911	30	4 cyl.	Touring	3,300	7,000	16,500
1912	30	4 cyl. 30 hp	Touring	3,000	6,800	16,500
EMMS	*(Great Britain, 1922–23)*					
1922		(Coventry-Simplex)	Coupe	1,000	3,600	8,200
1922		(Coventry-Simplex)	2 Passenger	1,000	3,800	8,600
1922		(Coventry-Simplex)	Touring	1,000	3,850	8,700
1922	Pointed Tail	(Coventry-Simplex)	Sport	1,500	4,900	10,800
EMPIRE	*(United States, 1901–19)*					
1901		Steam	Buggy	3,500	8,000	17,000
1904		2 cyl. 15 hp	Tonneau	1,800	5,750	13,750
1909	20	4 cyl. (GBS)	Roadster	2,550	6,100	14,250
1912	20	4 cyl. (Teetor)	Sport Touring	2,600	6,250	14,500
1912	20	6 cyl. (Continental)	Touring	3,100	7,250	16,500
1913	31	6 cyl. (Continental)	Touring	3,250	6,500	14,000
1919	72	6 cyl.	Touring	3,250	6,500	14,000
E.M.W.	*(Germany, 1945–55)*					
1945		2 Litre	Sport	1,600	3,250	7,500
1945		2 Litre	Racing	3,500	7,000	14,000
1952	Type 327	2 Litre	Cabriolet	2,000	4,000	8,000
1952	Type 340	2 Litre	Sedan	1,100	2,250	5,500
ENDURANCE	*(Great Britain, 1899–1901)*					
1899		1 cyl.	Sport	1,000	3,750	6,400
1901		1 cyl.	Sport	1,500	3,900	6,800

YEAR	MODEL	ENGINE	BODY	F	G	E
ENFIELD *(Great Britain, 1906 to date)*						
1906		4 cyl.	Touring	2,250	5,500	11,000
1911	3-Wheel	1 cyl.	Cycle	1,100	2,250	5,500
1969	465	Electric	Sedan	1,200	3,100	5,000
1969		Electric	Convertible	2,600	4,200	8,200
ENFIELD-ALLDAY *(Great Britain, 1919–25)*						
1919	Bullet	5 cyl. (Air-cooled)		2,200	4,400	8,800
1921	10/20	4 cyl.	Sedan	1,000	2,600	4,200
1923	12/30		Sedan	1,250	2,700	4,300
ENGLISH-MECHANIC *(Great Britain, 1900–05)*						
1900		1 cyl.	Runabout	1,000	2,600	5,250
1904		2 cyl.	Tonneau	1,500	3,900	6,600
1905	3-Wheel	Steam		2,200	4,400	10,800
EOLE *(France, 1899–1901)*						
1899		(Aster)	Voiturette	1,500	4,000	8,000
1899		(Aster)	Voiturette	1,600	4,100	8,200
1906		(Buchet)	Voiturette	1,700	4,250	8,500
ERDMANN *(Germany, 1904–08)*						
1904		2 cyl. (Korting)	Open	1,000	3,800	6,600
1905		2 cyl. (Fafnir)	Open	1,000	3,900	6,800
1905		4 cyl. (Horch)	Open	2,000	5,000	12,000
ERIC-LONGDEN *(Great Britain, 1922–27)*						
1922	8	V 2 cyl. (J.A.P.)	Sport	1,100	2,600	6,250
1922	10	V 2 cyl. (J.A.P.)	Sport	1,100	2,650	6,300
1927	9	4 cyl. (Alpha)	Sport	1,200	2,750	6,500
1927	11	4 cyl. (Coventry-Simplex)	Mini Sedan	1,000	2,400	3,750
ERSKINE *(United States, 1927–30)*						
1927	50	6 cyl.	Touring	2,200	5,500	10,500
1928	51	6 cyl.	Convertible Coupe	2,200	5,800	10,750
1929	52	6 cyl.	Coupe	2,500	6,200	11,500
1930	53	6 cyl.	Sedan	2,200	5,800	10,800
1930	53	6 cyl.	Touring	2,200	5,600	10,600
1930	53	6 cyl.	Coupe	2,600	6,100	12,400
E.S.A. *(Austria, 1920–26)*						
1920		4 cyl.	Town	1,250	3,000	6,000
1926		6 cyl.	Sedan	1,000	2,700	5,250
ESHELMAN SPORTABOUT *(United States, 1953–60)*						
1953		8.4 bhp (Air-cooled)	Sport Runabout	1,000	1,700	3,500

YEAR	MODEL	ENGINE	BODY	F	G	E
ESHELMAN SPORTABOUT *(United States, 1953–60) (continued)*						
1960	Eagle	6 cyl.	2 Door			
			Hardtop	1,200	2,900	5,300
ESSEX *(United States, 1919–32)*						
1919	A	4 cyl.	Touring	3,200	4,600	12,000
1921	5A 7A	4 cyl.	Roadster	3,000	4,600	12,000
1922	5A 7A	4 cyl.	Cabriolet	2,000	4,800	10,000
1922	5A 7A	4 cyl.	Touring	3,200	7,000	13,500
1924		6 cyl.	Coupe	2,400	4,200	8,500
1925		6 cyl.	Touring	3,200	5,000	9,200
1926		6 cyl.	Touring	3,200	5,000	9,200
1927		6 cyl.	Sedan	1,700	2,700	5,500
1927		6 cyl.	Boattail			
			Speedster	5,000	7,600	25,000
1928		6 cyl.	Coupe	1,700	4,400	7,200
1928	Super Six	6 cyl.	Roadster	4,500	9,500	17,000
1929	Challenger	6 cyl.	Coupe	2,400	4,800	9,800
1929	Challenger	6 cyl.	Roadster	4,000	9,800	20,500
1929		6 cyl.	Phaeton	3,700	8,500	18,250
1929		6 cyl.	4 Door Sedan	2,500	4,300	8,500
1930	RS		Coupe	2,600	4,500	8,800
1930	SP	6 cyl.	Roadster	4,000	9,500	18,200
1930	Sun Sedan	6 cyl.	2 Door			
			Convertible	3,500	12,500	24,000
1930	Challenger	6 cyl.	Touring	2,100	5,500	10,000
1931	Challenger	6 cyl.	Coupe	2,400	5,000	9,500
1931	Challenger	6 cyl.	Boattail			
			Roadster	15,000	25,000	45,000
1932	Pacemaker	6 cyl.	Coupe	2,400	5,700	11,500
1932	Pacemaker	8 cyl.	Convertible	5,200	13,500	26,000
ESTONIA *(Soviet Union, 1958 to date)*						
1958	3	500cc	Racing	800	1,650	3,250
1967	9	3 cyl. (Wartburg)	Racing	700	1,000	2,500
1970	16 M	(Jupiter)	Racing	900	1,800	6,600
ETNYRE *(United States, 1910–11)*						
1910	N	4 cyl.	Roadster	4,000	9,000	20,000
1910	E	4 cyl.	Touring	3,000	7,000	18,000
1911	T	4 cyl.	Double			
			Rumble	3,500	8,000	19,000
EUREKA *(United States, 1899–1914)*						
1906	L	3 cyl.	Motor Buggy	2,700	6,300	13,500
1907	D	2 cyl.	Motor Buggy	2,675	6,250	13,500
1908	10	2 cyl. (Speedwell)	Runabout	2,500	6,250	13,500

YEAR	MODEL	ENGINE	BODY	F	G	E
EUREKA *(United States, 1899–1914) (continued)*						
1909	14	2 cyl.	Surrey	2,500	6,250	13,500
EUROPEENE *(France, 1899–1903)*						
1899	3-Wheel	Steam	Dos-a-dos	2,500	5,250	13,500
1899	4-Wheel	Steam	Dos-a-dos	2,500	5,250	13,500
1900	High-Wheel	Steam	Open	2,100	5,250	13,500
EXCALIBER SS *(United States, 1964 to date)*						
1964		V 8 cyl.	Roadster	6,600	11,400	21,500
1966		V 8 cyl. (Corvette)	Sport	8,000	11,400	21,500
1973	SS	V 8 cyl. (Corvette)	4 Passenger Roadster	8,000	12,000	27,000

Excaliber – 1969 "Model SS"

YEAR	MODEL	ENGINE	BODY	F	G	E
1973	SSK	V 8 cyl. (Corvette)	Roadster	7,200	13,500	28,000
EXCELSIOR *(Brazil, 1903–32)*						
1903		1 cyl. (Aster)	Sport	1,050	3,100	6,000
1903		4 cyl. (Aster)	Sport	1,050	3,300	7,300
1907	Adex	6 cyl.	Sport	1,100	4,250	8,500
1907	Adex	4 cyl.	Sport	1,000	3,100	7,250
1914	14/20	4 cyl.	Coupe	900	1,900	4,800
1921		4 cyl.	Touring	1,100	4,250	8,500
1922	Albert I	6 cyl.	Sport Touring	2,150	5,350	9,750
EXCELSIOR-MASCOT *(Germany, 1910–22)*						
1910		2 cyl.	2 Passenger	1,100	3,650	7,250
1922		4 cyl.	2 Passenger	1,500	3,800	8,600
EYSINK *(Netherlands, 1899–1920)*						
1897		Benz	Voiturette	2,100	5,250	10,500
1899		1 cyl.	Light	2,100	4,000	7,500
1902	10	2 cyl.	Light	2,200	4,150	7,750

YEAR	MODEL	ENGINE	BODY	F	G	E
EYSINK *(Netherlands, 1899–1920) (continued)*						
1914	10/30	4 cyl.	Light	2,200	4,300	8,500
1916	30/40	6 cyl.	Light	2,250	5,350	10,750

F

YEAR	MODEL	ENGINE	BODY	F	G	E
FACEL VEGA *(France, 1954–64)*						
1954		V 8 cyl. (Chrysler)	Coupe	2,650	6,250	13,500
1955		V 8 cyl.	Coupe	2,700	6,400	12,800
1957	Excellence	V 8 cyl.	Sedan	2,900	6,800	12,600
1958	500	V 8 cyl.	Coupe	2,100	6,250	12,500
1960	HK 500	V 8 cyl.	Coupe	2,150	6,350	12,750
1961		V 8 cyl.	Roadster	4,350	9,750	19,500
1961	HT	V 8 cyl.	Sedan	2,000	6,100	11,250
1962	Facellia	4 cyl.	Cabriolet	2,400	7,800	13,600
1962	HK 500	V 8 cyl.	Coupe	2,250	6,500	12,000
1964	2 Door HT	V 8 cyl.	Coupe	2,300	6,600	12,200
FAFNIR *(Germany, 1908–26)*						
1908		4 cyl.	Sport	1,800	3,600	5,250
1912	472		Sport	2,000	3,750	5,500
1913	471		Sport	2,000	3,750	5,500
FAIRTHORPE *(Great Britain, 1954–78)*						
1954	Atom	(B.S.A.)	Sedan	750	1,700	3,500
1954	Atom	(B.S.A.)	Coupe	850	1,850	3,750
1958	Electron	(Coventry-Climax)	Coupe	1,100	1,700	3,500
1959	Electron Minor	(Standard)	Coupe	1,100	2,000	4,250
1960	EM3	(Triumph Spitfire)	Coupe	850	1,700	3,500
1961	Electrina		Sedan	800	1,600	3,250
1962	Zeta	(Ford Zephyr)	Coupe	800	1,600	3,250
1963	Rockette	(Triumph Vitesse)	Coupe	800	1,900	2,800
1965	TX I		Coupe	800	1,900	2,750
1968	TX-GT	(Triumph)	Coupe	850	2,100	3,000
1970	TXF		Coupe	800	2,000	2,200
1971	TXF	(Triumph)	Coupe	800	2,000	2,200
FALCON *(Great Britain, 1958–64)*						
1958		100 E (Ford)	Coupe	800	1,700	3,500
1960	Competition	100 E (Ford)	Racing	1,400	2,800	5,600
1961	Caribbean GT	100 E (Ford)	Coupe	800	1,650	3,250
1962	Bermuda	100 E (Ford)	Sedan	800	1,600	3,200
1963	Type 515	100 E (Ford)	Coupe Gran Turismo	1,000	1,675	4,250

YEAR	MODEL	ENGINE	BODY	F	G	E
FALCON-KNIGHT *(United States, 1927–29)*						
1927	12	6 cyl. (Knight)	Sedan	2,500	6,000	11,250
1927	12 Gray Ghost	6 cyl. (Knight)	Roadster	4,300	12,800	19,000
1927	12	6 cyl. (Knight)	Brougham	2,800	6,300	11,700
FALKE *(Germany, 1899–1908)*						
1899		2 cyl.	Voiturette	1,000	3,000	9,000
1900		2 cyl. (Fafnir)	Voiturette	1,000	3,100	10,000
1900		4 cyl. (Breuer)	Voiturette	1,100	4,200	11,400
FARMAN *(France, 1902–31)*						
1902	12 CV	2 cyl.	Racing	3,500	7,500	15,000
1925	A 6 B	6 cyl.	Touring	4,500	9,500	17,000
1925		6 cyl.	Coupe	4,500	9,500	17,000
1930	NF 2	6 cyl.	Sedanca de Ville	6,500	15,000	25,000
FEDERAL *(United States, 1901–09)*						
1901		Steam	Runabout		RARE	
1907	B	2 cyl.	Runabout	2,350	7,650	12,600
1908	C	2 cyl.	Runabout	2,600	7,250	13,500
FELDMANN *(Germany, 1905–12)*						
1905	Fafnir	2 cyl.	Voiturette	1,100	3,250	7,500
1906	Fafnir	4 cyl.	Touring	1,200	3,300	7,600
1910		4 cyl.	Sport	1,100	3,200	7,400
FEND *(Germany, 1948–53)*						
1948	3-Wheel	38cc (Victor)	Open	580	1,500	3,250
1948	3-Wheel	98cc (Sachs)	Open	680	1,750	4,500
FENG-HUANG; PHOENIX *(China, 1958)*						
1958	Phoenix	4 cyl.	Coupe	350	1,000	2,500
1958	Phoenix	6 cyl.	Sedan	400	1,800	3,500
FERRARI *(Italy, 1940 to date)*						
1947	Tipo 166	V 12 cyl. 2 Litre	Sport	75,000	150,000	250,000
1947	Tipo 195	2.3 Litre	Sport	50,000	95,000	200,000
1948	Tipo 212	2.5 Litre	Sport	45,000	90,000	240,000
1948	Tipo 212	2.5 Litre	Touring	25,000	40,000	80,000
1949	Tipo 166	2 Litre	Sedan	20,000	30,000	60,000
1950	Tipo 340	4.1 Litre	Sport	75,000	125,000	250,000
1951	Tipo 212	V 12 cyl.	Roadster	75,000	125,000	230,000
1951	Tipo 342	V 12 cyl.	Touring	30,000	50,000	75,000
1952	Tipo 375	V 12 cyl.	Touring	80,000	100,000	200,000
1953	Tipo 500 Mondial	4 cyl.	Roadster	95,000	150,000	250,000
1953	Tipo 166	4 cyl.	Roadster	75,000	100,000	175,000

YEAR	MODEL	ENGINE	BODY	F	G	E
FERRARI *(Italy, 1940 to date) (continued)*						
1953	Tipo 375	V 12 cyl.	Touring	75,000	125,000	200,000
1954	Tipo 375	V 12 cyl.	Sport	100,000	150,000	275,000
1954	Tipo 342	V 12 cyl.	Touring	25,000	40,000	60,000
1955	250 GT	V 12 cyl.	Touring	25,000	40,000	60,000
1955	250 GT	V 12 cyl.	Berlinetta	50,000	90,000	175,000
1956	Tipo 375	V 12 cyl.	Touring	30,000	40,000	75,000
1956	Tipo 250	V 12 cyl.	Gran Turismo Coupe	30,000	40,000	60,000
1956	Tipo 250	V 12 cyl.	Berlinetta	75,000	100,000	175,000
1958	250 Testa Rossa	3 Litre	Roadster	2500000	3000000	4000000
1958	250 GT	V 12 cyl.	Touring	30,000	50,000	70,000
1958	250 GT	V 12 cyl.	Berlinetta	75,000	100,000	175,000
1958	250 GT	V 12 cyl.	Coupe	75,000	100,000	150,000
1959	250 GT	V 12 cyl.	G.T. Coupe	50,000	75,000	125,000
1959	250 GT	V 12 cyl.	Berlinetta	250,000	350,000	450,000
1960	Tipo 250 GT	V 12 cyl.	Cabriolet	75,000	125,000	175,000
1960	250 GT	V 12 cyl.	Coupe	50,000	75,000	100,000
1960	Tipo 250 GT	V 12 cyl.	Berlinetta	275,000	375,000	500,000
1960	Tipo 250 GT	V 12 cyl.	2 + 2	80,000	110,000	125,000
1961	250	V 12 cyl.	Berlinetta	275,000	375,000	500,000
1961	250 GT	V 12 cyl.	California Roadster	350,000	500,000	600,000
1961	Tipo 250	3 Litre	2 + 2	50,000	75,000	100,000
1961	250 GT	V 12 cyl.	Cabriolet Convertible	75,000	125,000	175,000
1961	250 GT	V 12 cyl.	Coupe Closed	10,000	15,000	25,000
1962	250 GTO	V 12 cyl.	California	2000000	2500000	3500000
1962	250	V 12 cyl.	2 + 2	50,000	75,000	125,000
1962	400 SA	V 12 cyl.	Superamerica	75,000	125,000	200,000
1962	250	V 12 cyl.	Berlinetta	80,000	90,000	110,000
1963	250 GT	V 12 cyl.	California Roadster	350,000	500,000	700,000
1963	250	V 12 cyl.	Berlinetta	300,000	400,000	550,000
1963	Tipo 250	3 Litre	Gran Turismo 2 + 2	60,000	85,000	120,000
1963	Tipo 250 GTO	3 Litre	GTO	500,000	750,000	1000000

YEAR	MODEL	ENGINE	BODY	F	G	E
FERRARI *(Italy, 1940 to date) (continued)*						
1964	250 GTE	12 cyl.	2 + 2 Coupe	50,000	80,000	120,000

Ferrari – 1964 "500 Superfast"

YEAR	MODEL	ENGINE	BODY	F	G	E
1964	Tipo 250 GT	V 12 cyl.	California Roadster	300,000	375,000	480,000
1964	Tipo 275	V 12 cyl.	GTB	50,000	90,000	140,000
1965	GT 330	V 12 cyl.	Coupe	25,000	40,000	60,000
1965	Tipo 500 SA	V 12 cyl.	Coupe	150,000	200,000	280,000
1965	Tipo 275	V 12 cyl.	Gran Turismo	75,000	100,000	160,000
1966	275 GTB	V 12 cyl.	Berlinetta	75,000	100,000	160,000
1966	Tipo 275 GT	V 12 cyl.	Convertible	75,000	100,000	180,000
1966	Tipo 330	V 12 cyl.	Gran Turismo 2 + 2	30,000	55,000	80,000
1966	365 P3	12 cyl.	Sport	150,000	250,000	350,000
1966	Tipo 206 S	V 6 cyl.	Sport	100,000	175,000	225,000
1967	275 GTB-4	12 cyl.	Coupe	125,000	200,000	280,000
1967	330 GTS	12 cyl.	Touring	75,000	100,000	150,000
1967	330 GT	V 12 cyl.	Coupe 2 + 2	20,000	35,000	48,000
1967	330 GTC	V 12 cyl.	Coupe	25,000	40,000	60,000
1968	330 GT	V 12 cyl.	Coupe 2 + 2	20,000	35,000	48,000
1968	330 GTC	V 12 cyl.	Coupe	25,000	40,000	60,000
1968	365 GT	V 12 cyl.	Coupe 2 + 2	40,000	60,000	90,000
1968	Tipo 365	V 12 cyl.	Gran Turismo 2 + 2	50,000	75,000	100,000

YEAR	MODEL	ENGINE	BODY	F	G	E
FERRARI *(Italy, 1940 to date) (continued)*						
1969	312/P	V 12 cyl.	Sport	200,000	350,000	500,000
1969	365	V 12 cyl.	Gran Turismo			
			2 + 2	15,000	40,000	60,000
1969	246	V 6 cyl.	Gran Turismo	14,000	16,000	50,000
1970	246	V 6 cyl.	Gran Turismo	20,000	30,000	50,000
1970	365	V 12 cyl.	Gran Turismo			
			2 + 2	25,000	40,000	60,000
1971	GT 365	12 cyl.	2 + 2 Coupe	25,000	40,000	60,000
1971	246	V 6 cyl.	Gran Turismo	15,000	30,000	50,000
1971	365 GTS-4	V 12 cyl.	Berlinetta	45,000	90,000	140,000
1971	312-P	V 12 cyl.	Sport	200,000	300,000	500,000
1972	Dino 246	6 cyl.	Gran Turismo			
			Coupe	20,000	35,000	50,000
1973	Dino 246	6 cyl.	Coupe	20,000	30,000	50,000
1973	Dino 246 GTS	6 cyl.	GTS Spider	25,000	45,000	65,000
1973	365 GTB-4	12 cyl.	Coupe	50,000	60,000	100,000
1973	365 GT-4	12 cyl.	2 + 2	25,000	40,000	60,000
1973	BB	12 cyl.	Berlinetta			
			Coupe	35,000	60,000	90,000
1974	Dino	6 cyl.	246 GT	25,000	40,000	60,000
1974	Dino	6 cyl.	246 GTS	25,000	50,000	75,000
1974	365 GTS-4	12 cyl.	Spider	80,000	100,000	150,000
1974	365 GT4	12 cyl.	2 + 2	25,000	40,000	60,000
1974	365 GT4 BB	12 cyl.	Boxer	35,000	60,000	90,000
1975	365 GT4	12 cyl.	2 + 2	25,000	40,000	60,000
1975	365 GT4 BB	12 cyl.	Boxer	35,000	60,000	90,000
1976	308 GTB	8 cyl.	Coupe	20,000	22,000	25,000
1976	365 GT4	12 cyl.	2 + 2	25,000	40,000	60,000
1976	365 GT4 BB	12 cyl.	Boxer	35,000	60,000	90,000
1977	308 GTB	8 cyl.	Coupe	20,000	22,000	25,000
1977	365 GT4	12 cyl.	2 + 2	25,000	40,000	60,000
1977	365 GT4 BB	12 cyl.	Boxer	35,000	60,000	90,000
1978	308 GTB	8 cyl.	Coupe	20,000	24,000	30,000
1978	308 GTS	8 cyl.	Spider	22,000	25,000	28,000
1978	400 GT, 400A	12 cyl.	2 + 2	25,000	30,000	35,000
1978	512 BB	12 cyl.	Boxer	35,000	60,000	100,000
1979	308 GTB	8 cyl.	Coupe	20,000	24,000	30,000
1979	308 GTS	8 cyl.	Spider	22,000	25,000	28,000
1979	400 GT, 400 A	12 cyl.	2 + 2	25,000	30,000	35,000
1979	512 BB	12 cyl.	Boxer	35,000	60,000	100,000
1980	308 GTBi	8 cyl.	Coupe	22,000	25,000	35,000
1980	308 GTSi	8 cyl.	Spider	30,000	35,000	45,000

YEAR	MODEL	ENGINE	BODY	F	G	E
FERRARI *(Italy, 1940 to date) (continued)*						
1980	400i	12 cyl.	2 + 2	30,000	35,000	45,000
1980	512 BBi	12 cyl.	Boxer	40,000	60,000	100,000
1981	308 GTBi	8 cyl.	Coupe	25,000	30,000	40,000
1981	308 GTSi	8 cyl.	Spider	30,000	35,000	45,000
1981	400i	12 cyl.	2 + 2	35,000	40,000	45,000
1981	512 BBi	12 cyl.	Boxer	50,000	75,000	110,000
1982	308 GTSi	8 cyl.	Spider	40,000	44,000	48,000
1982	400i	12 cyl.	2 + 2	35,000	40,000	45,000
1982	512 BBi	12 cyl.	Boxer	55,000	80,000	120,000
FERRIS *(United States, 1920–22)*						
1922	60	6 cyl. (Continental)	Roadster	3,250	8,500	20,000
F.I.A.L. *(Italy, 1906–08)*						
1906		2 cyl.	Runabout	1,000	2,900	5,800
1908		4 cyl.	Runabout	1,100	4,000	7,000
F.I.A.M. *(Italy, 1924–27)*						
1924		2 cyl.	2 Passenger	1,000	2,500	4,000
FIAT *(Italy, 1907 to date)*						
1907		2 cyl.	Phaeton	15,000	24,000	38,000
1907	16/24	4.2 Litre	Tonneau	18,000	28,000	40,000
1909	10/14	4 cyl.	Touring	12,000	25,000	35,000
1913	Tipo 3	6 cyl.	7 Passenger Touring	4,000	7,000	14,000
1919	Tipo 501	1.5 Litre	2 Passenger	6,000	10,000	14,000
1920	Tipo 519	4.8 Litre	2 Passenger	8,000	12,000	18,000
1921		V 12 cyl.	Coupe de Ville	3,100	28,000	40,000
1923		6 cyl.	Sport Roadster	3,750	7,500	25,000
1925	509	4 cyl.	Saloon Sedan	4,000	6,000	8,500
1926	509-S Barchetta	4 cyl.	2 Passenger	5,000	8,000	12,000
1928	Tipo 521	2.5 Litre	Sedan	3,000	5,000	7,500
1929	Tipo 528	3.7 Litre	Sport	4,000	7,000	15,000
1930	Tipo 514	1.4 Litre	Sport	3,000	5,000	8,000
1931	Tipo 522	6 cyl.	Sport	4,000	8,000	14,000
1932	Tipo 508	995cc	Sedan	2,000	3,000	7,000
1933		6 cyl.	Sport	3,000	5,000	8,000
1934	Tipo 518	1.7 Litre	Sedan	1,500	3,000	6,000
1934	Balilla	1.9 Litre 995 cc	Sport	2,000	4,000	7,500
1935	Balilla	1.9 Litre	Sport	4,000	7,000	12,000
1936	Tipo 527	6 cyl.	Sedan	2,000	4,000	6,500
1936	Tipo 500-A	570cc	Coupe	3,000	4,000	7,000

YEAR	MODEL	ENGINE	BODY	F	G	E
FIAT	*(Italy, 1907 to date) (continued)*					
1937	Tipo 508-C	1089cc	Rolltop			
			Convertible	3,000	6,000	9,500
1938	1100-S	6 cyl.	Coupe	2,000	4,000	7,500
1939		6 cyl.	7 Passenger	750	2,500	6,000
1940	1100-S	6 cyl.	Coupe	650	2,250	5,500
1948	Topolino	4 cyl.	Sedan	500	2,000	5,100
1950	"1400"	4 cyl.	Sport	3,000	5,000	9,500
1952	8V	V 8 cyl.	Sport Coupe	10,000	15,000	25,000
1953	1100/103	1.1 Litre	Sedan	650	2,250	4,500
1953	"1900"	V 8 cyl.	Sport	3,000	5,000	8,500
1955	"600"	633cc	Sedan	1,000	1,650	4,250
1957	"Multipla"		Station			
			Wagon	800	1,600	4,200
1957	Nuova 500	2 cyl.	Minicar	825	1,650	3,250
1959		6 cyl. 1.8 Litre	Sedan	850	1,750	3,500
1970	850 Spider	4 cyl.	Roadster	650	1,850	3,000
1971	124 Sport		Convertible			
	Coupe	4 cyl.	Coupe	1,300	2,500	4,000
1973	850 Spider	4 cyl.	Roadster	1,000	2,500	4,000
1974	124 Spider	4 cyl.	Convertible	1,500	3,000	6,000
1974	X 1/9	4 cyl.	Targa Coupe	1,000	2,500	4,000
1975	124 Spider	4 cyl.	Convertible	1,500	3,000	6,000
1975	X 1/9	4 cyl.	Targa Coupe	1,000	2,500	4,000
1976	124 Spider	4 cyl.	Convertible	1,500	3,000	6,000
1976	X 1/9	4 cyl.	Targa Coupe	1,000	2,500	4,000
1977	124 Spider	4 cyl.	Convertible	1,500	3,000	6,000
1977	X 1/9	4 cyl.	Targa Coupe	1,000	2,500	4,000
1978	124 Spider	4 cyl.	Convertible	1,500	3,000	6,000
1978	X 1/9	4 cyl.	Targa Coupe	1,000	2,500	4,000
1979	Spider 2000	4 cyl. (2.0)	Convertible	2,500	4,000	7,500
1979	X 1/9	4 cyl.	Targa Coupe	1,000	2,500	4,000
FIAT	*(United States, 1910–18)*					
1910	Tipo 54	4 cyl.	Touring	4,000	12,000	21,000
1913	7 PS	6 cyl.	Touring	5,000	13,000	27,000
1914	Tipo 55	4 cyl.	Touring	4,000	12,000	21,000
1915	53	4 cyl.	Roadster	3,500	11,000	20,500
1916	Tipo 56	6 cyl.	Touring	4,000	11,000	21,000
1917	55	4 cyl.	Runabout	4,000	11,000	21,000
1918	55	6 cyl.	Berline	3,000	10,000	20,000
FIAT	*(Romania, 1960 to date)*					
1962	600		Sport	800	1,600	2,250
1972	128		Sport	850	1,700	2,500

YEAR	MODEL	ENGINE	BODY	F	G	E
FIAT	*(Romania, 1960 to date) (continued)*					
1972	1500		Sport Coupe	1,000	2,000	3,000
1972	Spyder		Sport	900	1,800	2,600
F.I.F.	*(Brazil, 1909–14)*					
1909		4 cyl.	Sport	1,200	3,400	7,750
1912		4 cyl.	Sport	1,150	3,300	7,500
1912		4 cyl.	Sport	1,200	3,400	7,750
1913		4 cyl.	Sport	1,250	3,500	8,000
FIGINI	*(Italy, 1900–07)*					
1900		1 cyl.	Open	1,000	3,000	6,000
1904		2 cyl.	Open	1,200	3,900	7,750
1907		4 cyl.	Open	1,300	4,500	8,750
FILOQUE	*(France, 1902)*					
1902		6/8 hp	Voiturette	1,000	3,000	6,000
1902	10	4 cyl.	Voiturette	1,300	3,500	7,250
1902	20	4 cyl.	Voiturette	1,600	4,250	8,500
FIREFLY	*(Great Britain, 1902–04)*					
1902		(Aster)	Tonneau	1,000	3,000	8,000
1903		(DeDion)	Tonneau	1,000	3,000	8,000
1904		2 cyl. (Herald)	Tonneau	1,100	3,100	8,250
FIRESTONE-COLUMBUS	*(United States, 1909–15)*					
1909	5001	4 cyl.	Baby Tonneau	2,700	7,250	19,000
1910	6	4 cyl.	Family Car	3,500	8,000	16,500
1911	74	4 cyl.	Touring	3,000	8,000	17,000
1915	69D	4 cyl.	3 Passenger Roadster	3,500	9,000	18,500
FISCHER	*(China, 1909–19)*					
1909		4 cyl.	Touring	900	1,700	4,500
1915	86E	4 cyl.	Touring	4,000	9,000	21,000
FISCHER	*(United States, 1914)*					
1914	Perkin	4 cyl.	Roadster	3,750	8,500	17,000
1914	Perkin	4 cyl.	Touring	3,500	8,250	16,500
1914	Perkin	4 cyl.	Sedan	1,100	5,250	10,500
FISSON	*(France, 1895–98)*					
1895		(Benz)	Vis-a-vis	2,500	4,000	11,000
1895		(Benz)	Dos-a-dos	2,600	5,250	12,500
1895		(Benz)	Surrey	2,750	6,500	13,000
FITCH	*(United States, 1949–51; 1966)*					
1949		V 8 cyl.	Sport	1,500	4,000	9,000
1951		(Ford 60)	Sport	1,500	4,000	9,000
1966	Phoenix	(Corvair)	Sport	1,200	2,300	7,500

YEAR	MODEL	ENGINE	BODY	F	G	E
FLAC *(Denmark, 1915)*						
1915		4 cyl.	Open	1,000	2,200	7,000
F.L.A.G. *(Italy, 1905–08)*						
1905	16/24	4 cyl.	Roadster	1,000	3,100	7,250
1905	16/24	4 cyl.	Touring	1,000	3,100	7,250
1905	40	4 cyl.	Touring	1,100	4,250	9,500
FLANDERS *(United States, 1909–12)*						
1910	20	4 cyl.	Runabout	3,750	9,500	18,000
1910	20	4 cyl.	Touring	3,000	8,000	18,000
1911	20	4 cyl.	Coupe	2,600	5,200	13,250
1911	20	4 cyl.	Roadster	3,000	8,000	18,000
1912	20	4 cyl.	Roadster	3,000	8,000	18,000
1913	20	4 cyl.	Coupe	3,000	8,000	18,000
1913	20	4 cyl.	Touring	2,000	8,400	18,000
FLINT *(United States, 1923–26)*						
1923	E	6 cyl. (Continental)	Touring	2,200	7,400	16,800
1924	E	6 cyl. (Continental)	Touring	2,250	8,500	17,000
1925	H-55	6 cyl. (Continental)	4 Passenger Coupe	2,100	8,250	17,500
1926	80	6 cyl. (Continental)	Roadster	2,500	9,000	18,000
FLORENTIA *(Italy, 1903–12)*						
1903		2 cyl.	Open	1,000	3,900	6,750
1905	16	4 cyl. (T-head)	Open	900	3,800	6,750
1905	24	4 cyl. (T-head)	Open	1,000	3,900	6,750
1908	40/50	4 cyl.	Open	1,000	4,000	7,000
1912		6 cyl.	Open	1,250	4,500	9,000
F.N. *(Brazil, 1899–1935)*						
1899	3.5	2 cyl.	Voiturette	1,150	3,250	7,500
1912	2700	4 cyl.	Limousine	1,100	3,100	7,250
1924	1300		Sport	1,000	2,900	6,750
1933		8 cyl.	Sedan	900	2,800	6,500
1934	Prince Albert	8 cyl.	Sedan	900	2,800	6,500
F.N.M. *(Brazil, 1959)*						
1959		1975cc	Saloon Sedan	1,450	2,900	7,750
1959	Onca	2132cc	Coupe	1,500	3,000	8,000
FOLLIS *(France, 1968 to date)*						
1968		1440cc (Gordini)	Racing	2,500	5,000	11,000
1971		1440cc (Gordini)	Sport	1,550	4,100	9,000
FONCK *(France, 1920–25)*						
1920		4 cyl.	Sport	1,000	3,400	6,750
1922		6 cyl.	Sport	1,250	4,600	8,250

YEAR	MODEL	ENGINE	BODY	F	G	E
FONCK *(France, 1920–25) (continued)*						
1925		8 cyl.	Sport	1,600	5,750	9,500
FONLUPT *(France, 1920–21)*						
1920		4 cyl.	Convertible	1,750	3,500	8,000
1921		8 cyl.	Convertible	2,000	4,500	10,000
FORD *(United States, 1903 to date)*						
1903	A	2 cyl.	Runabout	9,600	13,000	26,000
1904	A-AC	2 cyl.	Runabout	6,900	17,650	29,250
1904	A-AC	2 cyl.	Tonneau	7,625	15,175	29,000
1904	B	4 cyl.	Touring	11,500	23,000	40,000
1904	C	2 cyl.	Runabout	9,600	12,600	26,000
1905	B	4 cyl.	Touring	12,500	23,000	40,000
1905	C	2 cyl.	Runabout	4,600	9,825	19,000
1906	F	2 cyl.	Touring	5,000	9,600	20,000
1906	N	4 cyl.	Runabout	5,000	8,600	14,500
1907	R	4 cyl.	Runabout	5,000	8,500	14,500
1907	N	4 cyl.	Runabout	5,000	8,600	14,500
1907	K	6 cyl.	Runabout	20,000	50,000	80,000
1908	T	4 cyl.	Touring	4,600	9,800	19,000

The Model T – The Worlds first "People Car"

1908	S	4 cyl.	Runabout	2,800	6,500	18,000

YEAR	MODEL	ENGINE	BODY	F	G	E
FORD *(United States, 1903 to date) (continued)*						
1908	R	4 cyl.	Runabout	2,800	6,500	18,000
1908	N	4 cyl.	Runabout	3,975	9,000	18,850
1908	K	6 cyl.	Touring	20,000	50,000	80,000
1909	T	4 cyl.	Coupe	5,000	10,000	18,000
1909	T	4 cyl.	Runabout	5,000	10,000	19,000
1909	T	4 cyl.	Touring	5,000	10,000	17,500
1909	T	4 cyl.	Town	4,600	9,725	21,000
1910	T	4 cyl.	Runabout	3,100	6,900	14,000
1910	T	4 cyl.	Touring	3,100	6,900	15,000
1910	T	4 cyl.	Town	4,400	9,200	21,000
1911	T	4 cyl.	Torpedo Roadster	3,700	8,000	16,500
1911	T	4 cyl.	Touring	5,400	8,600	19,000

Ford – 1911 "Model T Touring " Courtesy of Towe Ford Museum, Deer Lodge, Montana

1911	T	4 cyl.	Tourabout	5,000	8,500	19,000
1911	T	4 cyl.	Town Car	4,000	8,000	17,500
1911	T	4 cyl.	Van	2,800	6,400	14,000
1911	T	4 cyl.	Runabout	4,000	8,000	17,500

YEAR	MODEL	ENGINE	BODY	F	G	E
FORD *(United States, 1903 to date) (continued)*						
1912	T	4 cyl.	Roadster	3,100	6,900	15,500
1912	T	4 cyl.	Torpedo Roadster	3,800	8,000	16,500
1912	T	4 cyl.	Touring	4,000	8,000	17,500
1912	T	4 cyl.	Town	3,700	7,740	21,000
1912	T	4 cyl.	Town Car	4,300	8,400	18,500
1912	T	4 cyl.	Van	2,800	6,500	14,000
1913	T	4 cyl.	Roadster	3,600	7,300	14,250
1913	T	4 cyl.	Touring	4,000	7,200	15,500
1913	T	4 cyl.	Town	3,600	7,225	18,850
1914	T	4 cyl.	Roadster	3,500	7,200	14,500
1914	T	4 cyl.	Touring	4,000	7,500	15,000
1914	T	4 cyl.	Town	3,600	7,225	18,850
1914	T	4 cyl.	Coupelet	3,700	7,440	21,000
1914	T	4 cyl.	Coupe	3,100	4,600	10,000
1915	T	4 cyl.	Roadster	2,800	6,400	14,000
1915	T	4 cyl.	Touring	4,000	7,200	15,000
1915	T	4 cyl	Center Door Sedan	3,500	5,750	12,500
1915	T	4 cyl.	Coupelet	3,700	7,840	22,000
1916	T	4 cyl.	Roadster	2,500	4,800	15,000
1916	T	4 cyl.	Touring	3,000	4,800	13,000
1916	T	4 cyl.	Center Door Sedan	2,800	4,000	10,000
1916	T	4 cyl.	Coupe	2,600	3,600	10,500
1916	T	4 cyl.	Town Car	4,200	6,000	11,000
1917	T	4 cyl.	Coupe	2,500	4,000	7,000
1917	T	4 cyl.	Roadster	2,400	4,600	11,500
1917	T	4 cyl.	Touring	3,000	4,600	12,000
1917	T	4 cyl.	Center Door Sedan	3,600	5,400	9,000
1917	T	4 cyl.	Town Car	2,200	4,000	11,000
1918	T	4 cyl.	Roadster	2,300	3,600	11,000
1918	T	4 cyl.	Touring	2,000	4,000	14,000
1918	T	4 cyl.	Center Door Sedan	3,600	4,600	9,000
1918	T	4 cyl.	Coupe	3,600	5,000	8,200
1918	T	4 cyl.	Town Car	4,200	6,000	11,000
1919	T	4 cyl.	Roadster	2,600	3,600	10,500
1919	T	4 cyl.	Touring	2,600	4,400	10,500
1919	T	4 cyl.	Center Door Sedan	3,600	5,000	8,200
1919	T	4 cyl.	Coupe	3,600	5,000	8,200

YEAR	MODEL	ENGINE	BODY	F	G	E
FORD *(United States, 1903 to date) (continued)*						
1919	T	4 cyl.	Town Car	4,200	6,000	11,000
1920	T	4 cyl.	Touring	2,200	4,000	11,000
1920	T	4 cyl.	Roadster	1,600	3,500	10,000
1920	T	4 cyl.	Coupe	1,600	2,500	6,500
1920	T	4 cyl.	Center Door Sedan	3,600	5,000	8,200
1921	T	4 cyl.	Roadster	1,600	3,500	10,000
1921	T	4 cyl.	Touring	2,200	4,000	11,000
1921	T	4 cyl.	Coupe	2,500	4,600	13,000
1921	T	4 cyl.	Center Door Sedan	2,700	4,800	13,000
1922	T	4 cyl.	Roadster	1,600	3,000	11,500
1922	T	4 cyl.	Touring	1,600	3,000	11,500
1922	T	4 cyl.	Coupe	1,800	3,000	7,200
1923	T	4 cyl.	Roadster	1,600	3,000	11,500
1923	T	4 cyl.	Touring	1,600	3,000	11,500
1923	T	4 cyl.	Tudor	1,900	3,700	12,000
1923	T	4 cyl.	Fordor	2,095	4,000	13,000
1924	T	4 cyl.	Roadster	2,095	4,000	10,500
1924	T	4 cyl.	Touring	2,000	4,000	11,000
1924	T	4 cyl.	Coupe	1,900	2,600	7,000
1924	T	4 cyl.	Tudor	1,700	3,300	12,500
1924	T	4 cyl.	Fordor	1,700	3,700	12,000
1924	T	4 cyl.	Roadster Pickup	2,075	4,000	12,250
1925	T	4 cyl.	Roadster	1,700	3,700	11,000
1925	T	4 cyl.	Touring	1,900	3,700	11,000
1925	T	4 cyl.	Coupe	1,600	2,600	6,500
1925	T	4 cyl.	Fordor	2,000	3,800	12,250
1926	T	4 cyl.	Roadster	2,000	3,800	11,500
1926	T	4 cyl.	Touring	2,000	3,700	12,000
1926	T	4 cyl.	Coupe	1,900	3,200	11,750
1926	T	4 cyl.	Tudor	2,500	6,000	11,500
1927	T	4 cyl.	Roadster	2,000	4,800	11,000
1927	T	4 cyl.	Touring	2,000	4,800	12,250
1927	T	4 cyl.	Coupe	1,500	4,150	11,000
1927	T	4 cyl.	Fordor	1,900	3,200	5,750
1928	A AR	4 cyl.	Phaeton	4,600	10,400	24,000
1928	A AR	4 cyl.	Roadster	4,800	10,400	25,000
1928	A AR	4 cyl.	Tudor	2,000	4,800	14,000
1928	A	4 cyl.	Roadster Deluxe	4,000	9,700	24,000
1928	A	4 cyl.	Phaeton	4,200	9,900	22,500

YEAR	MODEL	ENGINE	BODY	F	G	E
FORD *(United States, 1903 to date) (continued)*						
1928	A	4 cyl.	Coupe	2,600	4,500	10,000
1928	A	4 cyl.	Sport Coupe	4,000	5,500	13,000
1928	A	4 cyl.	Tudor	2,500	4,600	7,000
1928	A	4 cyl.	Fordor	1,900	4,800	7,500
1929	A	4 cyl.	Roadster	4,000	9,400	26,000
1929	A	4 cyl.	Touring	4,600	10,400	22,500
1929	A	4 cyl.	Coupe	2,500	5,400	10,000
1929	A	4 cyl.	Sport Coupe	2,800	5,000	13,000
1929	A	4 cyl.	Cabriolet	3,000	4,750	20,500
1929	A	4 cyl.	Tudor	2,800	4,600	11,000
1929	A	4 cyl.	Town Sedan	2,000	5,100	12,000
1929	A	4 cyl.	Sedan	1,900	4,800	10,500
1930	A	4 cyl.	Roadster	3,900	7,500	26,000
1930	A	4 cyl.	Deluxe Roadster	4,600	7,600	27,500
1930	A	4 cyl.	Touring	5,500	12,350	22,500
1930	A	4 cyl.	Cabriolet	3,900	6,575	26,500
1930	A	4 cyl.	Coupe	2,600	4,600	10,000
1930	A	4 cyl.	Sport Sedan	2,500	4,600	12,000
1930	A	4 cyl.	Tudor	3,000	5,500	12,500
1930	A	4 cyl.	Fordor	2,200	4,700	12,000

Ford – 1931 "Model A Roadster"

YEAR	MODEL	ENGINE	BODY	F	G	E
FORD	*(United States, 1903 to date) (continued)*					
1930	A	4 cyl.	3 Window Fordor	2,300	4,200	9,000
1930	A	4 cyl.	Victoria	2,800	5,650	15,000
1931	A	4 cyl.	Roadster	4,300	7,400	26,500
1931	A	4 cyl.	Deluxe Roadster	4,600	8,000	27,500
1931	A	4 cyl.	Phaeton	4,800	8,500	27,000
1931	A	4 cyl.	Cabriolet	4,000	7,000	26,500
1931	A	4 cyl.	Slant w/s Cabriolet	5,100	7,950	27,500
1931	A	4 cyl.	A-400 Convertible	5,300	13,100	28,000

Ford – 1931 "A-400 Convertible"

1931	A	4 cyl.	Victoria	2,800	6,000	15,500
1931	A	4 cyl.	Coupe	2,700	5,000	12,500
1931	A	4 cyl.	Sport Coupe	3,300	6,500	13,600

YEAR	MODEL	ENGINE	BODY	F	G	E
FORD *(United States, 1903 to date) (continued)*						
1931	A	4 cyl.	Station Wagon	3,600	7,500	13,500

Ford – 1931 "Model A Station Wagon"

YEAR	MODEL	ENGINE	BODY	F	G	E
1931	A	4 cyl.	Tudor	2,300	4,800	12,350
1931	A	4 cyl.	Fordor	2,400	4,500	11,000
1931	A	4 cyl.	Deluxe Fordor	3,000	4,500	11,500
1931	A	4 cyl.	Town Sedan	2,700	6,200	13,600
1932	B	4 cyl.	Roadster	6,500	10,000	28,500
1932	B	4 cyl.	Touring	5,700	13,600	26,700
1932	B	4 cyl.	Coupe	2,800	5,500	12,500
1932	B	4 cyl.	Tudor	2,500	5,000	10,500
1932	B	4 cyl.	Fordor	2,500	6,900	13,600
1932	18	V 8 cyl.	Deluxe Roadster	6,900	11,500	34,500
1932	18	V 8 cyl.	Deluxe Touring	9,200	17,800	37,000
1932	18	V 8 cyl.	Cabriolet	6,600	9,600	22,500
1932	18	V 8 cyl.	B-400 Convertible	6,900	17,800	36,600
1932	18	V 8 cyl.	Victoria	4,000	7,000	22,500
1932	18	V 8 cyl.	Tudor	3,000	5,000	12,500
1932	18	V 8 cyl.	Fordor	3,000	5,000	11,600
1932	18	V 8 cyl.	Station Wagon	6,200	8,200	21,400
1932	18	V 8 cyl.	Pickup	2,000	5,500	14,000

YEAR	MODEL	ENGINE	BODY	F	G	E
FORD *(United States, 1903 to date) (continued)*						
1933	40	V 8 cyl.	Roadster	5,600	8,400	21,500

Ford – 1932 "Deluxe Roadster"

YEAR	MODEL	ENGINE	BODY	F	G	E
1933	40	V 8 cyl.	Phaeton	5,700	9,000	26,500
1933	40	V 8 cyl.	3 Window Coupe	2,800	5,500	11,200
1933	40	V 8 cyl.	Coupe	2,700	7,100	14,100
1933	40	V 8 cyl.	Victoria	4,000	6,200	16,000
1933	40	V 8 cyl.	Tudor	2,700	4,400	11,200
1933	40	V 8 cyl.	Fordor	2,200	5,700	12,000
1933	40	V 8 cyl.	Station Wagon	4,300	6,700	16,500
1933	40	V 8 cyl.	Cabriolet	5,600	8,200	23,500
1934	40	V 8 cyl.	Roadster	6,000	9,000	30,500
1934	40	V 8 cyl.	Phaeton	9,000	20,500	33,500
1934	40	V 8 cyl.	Cabriolet	6,000	9,000	21,500
1934	40	V 8 cyl.	3 Window Coupe	2,800	7,700	15,000
1934	40	V 8 cyl.	Coupe	2,700	6,200	12,500
1934	40	V 8 cyl.	Tudor	2,600	4,200	8,250
1934	40	V 8 cyl.	Victoria	4,000	6,500	16,000
1934	40	V 8 cyl.	Fordor	2,800	5,000	9,000
1934	40	V 8 cyl.	Station Wagon	4,100	6,500	16,000
1934	40	4 cyl.	Roadster	6,000	9,000	30,500
1934	40	4 cyl.	Sedan	2,400	6,200	13,500
1935	48	V 8 cyl.	Roadster	7,600	10,100	26,000

YEAR	MODEL	ENGINE	BODY	F	G	E

FORD *(United States, 1903 to date) (continued)*

YEAR	MODEL	ENGINE	BODY	F	G	E
1935	48	V 8 cyl.	Phaeton	7,600	11,000	26,000
1935	48	V 8 cyl.	Cabriolet	7,100	11,100	27,500
1935	48	V 8 cyl.	Convertible Sedan	7,600	11,300	27,500
1935	48	V 8 cyl.	3 Window Coupe	3,300	5,500	10,500
1935	48	V 8 cyl.	Coupe	2,500	5,600	12,000
1935	48	V 8 cyl.	Tudor	2,500	4,200	8,000
1935	48	V 8 cyl.	Fordor	1,550	3,200	7,100
1935	48	V 8 cyl.	Station Wagon	3,700	6,000	14,000
1935	48	V 8 cyl.	Sedan Delivery	2,800	7,200	14,600
1936	68	V 8 cyl.	Roadster	7,400	11,200	27,000

Ford – 1936 "Model 68 Roadster"

YEAR	MODEL	ENGINE	BODY	F	G	E
1936	68	V 8 cyl.	Phaeton	7,300	11,000	25,500
1936	68	V 8 cyl.	Cabriolet	6,600	10,200	24,500
1936	68	V 8 cyl.	Club Cabriolet	7,100	11,200	25,500
1936	68	V 8 cyl.	Convertible Sedan	9,000	12,000	30,000
1936	68	V 8 cyl.	Convertible Sedan w/Trunk	4,800	12,000	25,600
1936	68	V 8 cyl.	3 Window Coupe	3,600	5,600	10,500
1936	68	V 8 cyl.	Coupe	2,700	6,900	13,400
1936	68	V 8 cyl.	Tudor	2,300	4,000	8,100
1936	68	V 8 cyl.	Fordor	1,500	3,400	6,500

YEAR	MODEL	ENGINE	BODY	F	G	E
FORD *(United States, 1903 to date) (continued)*						
1936	68	V 8 cyl.	Deluxe Sedan	2,400	6,600	14,000
1936	68	V 8 cyl.	Station Wagon	3,600	6,600	15,000
1936	68	V 8 cyl.	Sedan Delivery	3,000	7,700	14,000
1937	74	V 8 cyl. 60 hp	Coupe	1,900	4,600	11,000
1937	74	V 8 cyl.	Coupe Pickup	1,700	4,800	9,000
1937	74	V 8 cyl.	Fordor	1,500	3,400	6,500
1937	74	V 8 cyl.	Coupe	2,000	3,000	7,400
1937	78	V 8 cyl. 85 hp	Roadster	7,400	11,200	27,250
1937	78	V 8 cyl.	Phaeton	7,300	10,600	25,500
1937	78	V 8 cyl.	Cabriolet	6,600	10,200	24,500
1937	78	V 8 cyl.	Club Cabriolet	5,600	9,400	20,000

Ford – 1937 "Club Cabriolet"

YEAR	MODEL	ENGINE	BODY	F	G	E
1937	78	V 8 cyl.	Convertible Sedan	6,100	9,600	20,500
1937	78	V 8 cyl.	Coupe	2,600	4,000	8,000
1937	78	V 8 cyl.	Club Coupe	3,000	4,500	9,000
1937	78	V 8 cyl.	Tudor	2,000	3,500	7,100
1937	78	V 8 cyl.	Station Wagon	4,000	6,000	14,500
1938	Standard	V 8 cyl.	Coupe	2,000	3,800	7,500

YEAR	MODEL	ENGINE	BODY	F	G	E
FORD *(United States, 1903 to date) (continued)*						
1938	Standard	V 8 cyl.	Sedan	1,200	3,700	8,900
1938	Standard	V 8 cyl.	Station Wagon 2500	4,600	9,200	18,000
1938	Deluxe	V 8 cyl.	Phaeton	4,000	6,700	17,500
1938	Deluxe	V 8 cyl.	Convertible	4,000	6,700	19,500
1938	Deluxe	V 8 cyl.	Club Convertible	2,600	4,200	9,500
1938	Deluxe	V 8 cyl.	Convertible Sedan	3,100	6,100	17,000
1938	Deluxe	V 8 cyl.	Coupe	2,400	4,000	8,600
1938	Deluxe	V 8 cyl.	Club Coupe	3,600	6,100	17,000
1938	Deluxe	V 8 cyl.	Tudor	1,600	3,000	7,600
1938	Deluxe	V 8 cyl.	Fordor	1,900	3,000	8,000
1939	Standard	V 8 cyl.	Coupe	1,900	3,000	6,600

Ford – 1939 "Woody Wagon"

YEAR	MODEL	ENGINE	BODY	F	G	E
1939	Standard	V 8 cyl.	Fordor	1,650	3,000	6,000
1939	Standard	V 8 cyl.	Station Wagon	3,600	6,100	12,500
1939	Standard	V 8 cyl.	Coupe	2,000	3,400	6,400
1939	Deluxe	V 8 cyl.	Convertible	5,000	8,700	25,500
1939	Deluxe	V 8 cyl.	Convertible Sedan	5,000	8,200	26,500
1939	Deluxe	V 8 cyl.	Coupe	2,000	3,700	7,000
1939	Deluxe	V 8 cyl.	Tudor Sedan	1,400	5,100	9,600
1939	Deluxe	V 8 cyl.	Fordor	1,750	3,600	6,700

YEAR	MODEL	ENGINE	BODY	F	G	E
FORD *(United States, 1903 to date) (continued)*						
1939	Deluxe	V 8 cyl.	Station			
			Wagon	3,100	6,000	13,500
1940	Standard	V 8 cyl.	Coupe	2,600	4,100	11,000
1940	Standard	V 8 cyl.	Sedan	1,600	5,100	9,600
1940	Standard	V 8 cyl.	Station			
			Wagon	4,500	8,600	19,500
1940	Deluxe	V 8 cyl.	Convertible	5,600	8,600	26,500
1940	Deluxe	V 8 cyl.	Coupe	2,700	5,000	11,500
1940	Deluxe	V 8 cyl.	Tudor	1,200	5,400	10,000
1940	Deluxe	V 8 cyl.	Sedan	1,400	5,300	10,000
1940	Deluxe	V 8 cyl.	Station			
			Wagon	3,000	7,100	16,000
1940	Deluxe	V 8 cyl.	Sedan			
			Delivery	2,700	7,200	16,000
1940	Standard	V 8 cyl.	Pickup	3,000	5,500	10,000
1941	Special	V 8 cyl.	Coupe	1,600	2,600	7,000
1941	Special	V 8 cyl.	Tudor	2,500	3,600	6,400
1941	Special	V 8 cyl.	Fordor	2,600	4,000	7,000
1941	Deluxe	V 8 cyl.	2 Passenger			
			Coupe	2,000	3,200	7,000
1941	Deluxe	V 8 cyl.	Club Coupe	2,300	5,200	10,000
1941	Deluxe	V 8 cyl.	Station			
			Wagon	4,100	6,100	13,500
1941	Deluxe	V 8 cyl.	Tudor	2,800	4,000	6,800
1941	Deluxe	V 8 cyl.	Fordor	2,900	4,200	7,100
1941	Super Deluxe	V 8 cyl.	Convertible	4,100	7,600	22,500
1941	Super Deluxe	V 8 cyl.	Club Coupe	1,800	5,200	9,400
1941	Super Deluxe	V 8 cyl.	Tudor	2,200	3,100	5,500
1941	Super Deluxe	V 8 cyl.	Fordor	2,400	3,700	6,000
1941	Super Deluxe	V 8 cyl.	Station Wagon	4,600	9,100	20,500
1941		V 8 cyl.	Pickup	1,300	4,400	8,400
1942	Special	V 8 cyl.	Coupe	2,600	3,500	6,300
1942	Special	V 8 cyl.	Tudor	1,400	2,400	5,400
1942	Special	V 8 cyl.	Fordor	2,000	3,000	5,900

YEAR	MODEL	ENGINE	BODY	F	G	E
FORD *(United States, 1903 to date) (continued)*						
1942	Deluxe	V 8 cyl.	Coupe	3,000	4,000	7,000

Ford – 1942 "Deluxe Coupe"

YEAR	MODEL	ENGINE	BODY	F	G	E
1942	Deluxe	V 8 cyl.	Tudor	2,000	3,000	6,000
1942	Deluxe	V 8 cyl.	Fordor	3,500	4,600	7,000
1942	Special	6 cyl.	Coupe	1,900	4,000	7,200
1942	Deluxe	V 8 cyl.	Coupe	1,600	2,500	6,400
1942	Deluxe	V 8 cyl.	Tudor	1,200	2,200	5,400
1942	Super Deluxe	V 8 cyl.	Convertible	5,000	12,000	24,000
1942	Super Deluxe	V 8 cyl.	Club Coupe	1,300	3,000	8,000
1942	Super Deluxe	V 8 cyl.	Tudor	1,450	2,350	5,500
1942	Super Deluxe	V 8 cyl.	Fordor	1,300	2,800	6,000
1942	Super Deluxe	V 8 cyl.	Station Wagon	4,000	9,000	18,000
Postwar Models						
1946	Deluxe	6 cyl.	Tudor	2,000	4,000	9,000
1946	Deluxe	V 8 cyl.	Coupe	3,000	5,000	10,000
1946	Deluxe	V 8 cyl.	Tudor	2,000	3,000	7,000
1946	Deluxe	V 8 cyl.	Fordor	2,100	3,700	7,500
1946	Super Deluxe	V 8 cyl.	Convertible	7,000	14,000	25,000

YEAR	MODEL	ENGINE	BODY	F	G	E
FORD *(United States, 1903 to date) (continued)*						
1946	Super Deluxe	V 8 cyl.	Sportsman Convertible	10,000	25,000	50,000
1946	Super Deluxe	V 8 cyl.	Club Coupe	1,850	4,800	11,000
1946	Super Deluxe	V 8 cyl.	Tudor	2,000	3,000	7,000
1946	Super Deluxe	V 8 cyl.	Fordor	2,000	3,000	7,000
1946	Super Deluxe	V 8 cyl.	Station Wagon	5,000	15,000	30,000
1947	Deluxe	V 8 cyl.	Coupe	2,000	3,000	6,400
1947	Deluxe	V 8 cyl.	Tudor	2,000	3,500	5,500
1947	Deluxe	V 8 cyl.	Fordor	2,400	3,800	5,800
1947	Super Deluxe	V 8 cyl.	Convertible	7,000	14,000	25,000
1947	Super Deluxe	V 8 cyl.	Club Coupe	1,700	4,000	10,000
1947	Super Deluxe	V 8 cyl.	Sportsman Convertible	10,000	23,000	45,000
1947	Super Deluxe	V 8 cyl.	Tudor	1,700	3,500	8,000
1947	Super Deluxe	V 8 cyl.	Fordor	1,700	3,500	8,000
1947	Super Deluxe	V 8 cyl.	Station Wagon	7,000	14,000	30,000
1948	Deluxe	6 cyl.	Sedan	2,000	4,000	7,000
1948	Super Deluxe	V 8 cyl.	Convertible	6,000	13,000	24,000
1948	Super Deluxe	V 8 cyl.	Sportsman Convertible	10,000	25,000	50,000
1948	Super Deluxe	V 8 cyl.	Club Coupe	1,900	5,000	10,500
1948	Super Deluxe	V 8 cyl.	Tudor	1,700	3,600	8,000
1948	Super Deluxe	V 8 cyl.	Fordor	1,700	3,600	8,000
1948	Super Deluxe	V 8 cyl.	Station Wagon	8,000	15,000	32,000
1949	Deluxe	V 8 cyl.	Sedan	2,000	4,000	7,500
1949	Deluxe	V 8 cyl.	Coupe	1,600	3,600	7,200

YEAR	MODEL	ENGINE	BODY	F	G	E
FORD *(United States, 1903 to date) (continued)*						
1949	Custom	V 8 cyl.	Convertible	5,000	9,000	18,000
1949	Custom	V 8 cyl.	Club Coupe	2,000	4,000	10,000
1949	Custom	V 8 cyl.	Sedan	2,000	4,000	7,000
1949	Custom	V 8 cyl.	Station Wagon	6,000	12,000	27,000
1949	Deluxe	V 8 cyl.	Convertible	5,000	10,000	22,000
1950	Deluxe	V 8 cyl.	Business Coupe	2,500	5,000	11,000

Ford – 1950 "Custom Convertible"

1950	Deluxe	V 8 cyl.	Sedan	2,000	4,000	7,000
1950	Deluxe	V 8 cyl.	Convertible	4,000	9,000	21,000
1950	Custom	V 8 cyl.	2 Door Sedan	1,200	2,200	5,000
1950	Custom	V 8 cyl.	Crestliner	3,000	5,000	10,000
1950	Custom	V 8 cyl.	Station Wagon	4,000	9,000	18,000
1951	Deluxe	V 8 cyl.	Business Coupe	1,000	2,000	5,000
1951	Deluxe	V 8 cyl.	Sedan	1,000	1,700	4,000
1951	Custom	V 8 cyl.	Convertible	6,000	10,000	22,000
1951	Custom	V 8 cyl.	Crestliner	3,000	5,000	11,000
1951	Custom	V 8 cyl.	Club Coupe	2,500	5,000	12,000

YEAR	MODEL	ENGINE	BODY	F	G	E
FORD	*(United States, 1903 to date) (continued)*					
1951	Custom	V 8 cyl.	Crest	1,500	2,800	14,500
1951	Custom	V 8 cyl.	Station Wagon	3,600	8,000	18,000
1952	Mainline	6 cyl.	Business Coupe	1,500	3,000	7,000
1952	Customline	V 8 cyl.	Club Coupe	2,000	4,000	8,000
1952	Customline	V 8 cyl.	Station Wagon	1,800	2,800	9,500
1952	Crestline	V 8 cyl.	Convertible	3,000	8,000	16,000
1952	Crestline	V 8 cyl.	2 Door Hardtop	1,600	5,000	11,000
1952	Crestline	V 8 cyl.	Station Wagon	1,800	3,400	8,500
1953	Mainline	V 8 cyl.	Business Coupe	1,500	3,000	7,000
1953	Mainline	V 8 cyl.	Sedan	1,000	2,000	5,000
1953	Customline	V 8 cyl.	Sedan	1,500	2,500	6,000
1953	Customline	V 8 cyl.	2 Door Sedan	1,000	1,700	5,500
1953	Customline	V 8 cyl.	Club Coupe	1,500	3,000	7,500
1953	Customline	V 8 cyl.	Sedan	1,000	3,000	7,000
1953	Crestline	V 8 cyl.	Convertible	3,000	9,000	18,000
1953	Crestline	V 8 cyl.	2 Door Hardtop	2,000	4,000	10,000
1953	Crestline	V 8 cyl.	Station Wagon	1,850	4,600	8,600

Ford – 1954 "Customline"

YEAR	MODEL	ENGINE	BODY	F	G	E
FORD *(United States, 1903 to date) (continued)*						
1954	Mainline	V 8 cyl.	Business Coupe	1,500	3,000	7,000
1954	Mainline	6 cyl.	Station Wagon	1,700	2,800	8,000
1954	Customline	V 8 cyl.	Sedan	1,700	2,800	8,000
1954	Customline	V 8 cyl.	Club Coupe	1,700	3,000	8,000
1954	Customline	V 8 cyl.	Station Wagon	1,700	3,000	8,000
1954	Crestline	V 8 cyl.	Convertible	2,600	4,600	15,000
1954	Crestline	V 8 cyl.	2 Door Hardtop	2,100	5,000	12,000
1954	Crestline	V 8 cyl.	Skyliner	2,800	6,400	18,000
1954	Crestline	V 8 cyl.	Sedan	1,700	3,500	8,500
1954	Crestline	V 8 cyl.	Station Wagon	1,700	4,000	10,000
1955	Ranch Wagon	V 8 cyl.	Station Wagon	2,000	4,000	9,500
1955	Country Squire	V 8 cyl.	Station Wagon	2,500	4,500	10,000
1955	Mainline	6 cyl.	Business Sedan	1,500	2,500	6,000
1955	Customline	V 8 cyl.	Sedan	2,000	3,000	7,000
1955	Fairlane	V 8 cyl.	Convertible	5,000	12,000	26,000
1955	Fairlane	V 8 cyl.	Crown Victoria	4,000	10,000	21,000
1955	Fairlane	V 8 cyl.	Crown Victoria w/Glass Top	4,600	10,000	24,000
1955	Fairlane	V 8 cyl.	Town Sedan	2,000	3,000	7,000
1955	Fairlane	V 8 cyl.	Club Sedan	1,500	2,500	6,500
1955	Thunderbird	V 8 cyl.	Roadster	15,000	25,000	45,000
1956	Mainline	6 cyl.	2 Door Sedan	1,500	3,000	7,000
1956	Mainline	V 8 cyl.	Business Sedan	2,000	4,000	7,500
1956	Country Squire	V 8 cyl.	Station Wagon	1,500	4,000	10,000
1956	Customline	V 8 cyl.	2 Door Sedan	1,200	3,000	7,500
1956	Customline	V 8 cyl.	2 Door Hardtop	1,700	4,000	10,000
1956	Fairlane	V 8 cyl.	Convertible	7,000	18,000	32,000
1956	Fairlane	V 8 cyl.	Victoria	3,000	7,000	16,000
1956	Fairlane	V 8 cyl.	Crown Victoria	5,000	10,000	24,000

YEAR	MODEL	ENGINE	BODY	F	G	E
FORD *(United States, 1903 to date) (continued)*						
1956	Fairlane	V 8 cyl.	Crown Victoria w/Glass Top	6,000	12,000	28,000
1956	Fairlane	V 8 cyl.	Victoria Sedan	1,850	3,500	9,000
1956	Fairlane	V 8 cyl.	Club Sedan	1,600	3,100	8,000
1956	Fairlane	V 8 cyl.	Town Sedan	1,500	4,000	8,500
1956	Parklane	V 8 cyl.	2 Door Station Wagon	3,000	5,000	12,000
1956	Thunderbird	V 8 cyl.	Roadster	17,000	27,000	47,000

Ford – 1956 "Thunderbird Roadster"

YEAR	MODEL	ENGINE	BODY	F	G	E
1956	Country Sedan	V 8 cyl.	Station Wagon	1,500	4,000	10,000
1956	City Squire	V 8 cyl.	Station Wagon	2,000	4,500	10,500

YEAR	MODEL	ENGINE	BODY	F	G	E
FORD *(United States, 1903 to date) (continued)*						
1957	Custom	6 cyl.	Sedan	800	2,500	6,000

Ford – 1956 "Thunderbird Hardtop"

YEAR	MODEL	ENGINE	BODY	F	G	E
1957	Fairlane	V 8 cyl.	Club Sedan	1,500	3,000	7,000
1957	Fairlane	V 8 cyl.	2 Door Victoria	2,100	5,000	12,000
1957	Fairlane 500	V 8 cyl.	Convertible	4,000	12,000	25,000
1957	Fairlane 500	V 8 cyl.	Skyliner Convertible	7,500	1,500	35,000
1957	Fairlane 500	V 8 cyl.	Town Sedan	1,600	3,000	8,000
1957	Fairlane 500	V 8 cyl.	Victoria Sedan	2,500	4,000	9,000
1957	Thunderbird	V 8 cyl.	Roadster	12,000	25,000	48,000
1957	Thunderbird "F"	V 8 cyl. (Supercharged)	Roadster	15,000	30,000	63,000
1957	Thunderbird "E" & "F"	V 8 cyl. (Supercharged)	Roadster	18,000	35,000	65,000
1958	Fairlane "F"	V 8 cyl. (Supercharged)	Town Sedan	2,500	4,500	9,500
1958	Fairlane "F"	V 8 cyl. (Supercharged)	4 Door Town Victoria	3,000	5,000	10,000
1958	Fairlane 500 "F"	V 8 cyl. (Supercharged)	Convertible	5,000	10,000	23,000
1958	Fairlane 500 "F"	V 8 cyl. (Supercharged)	Club Victoria	2,000	6,000	13,000

YEAR	MODEL	ENGINE	BODY	F	G	E

FORD *(United States, 1903 to date) (continued)*

YEAR	MODEL	ENGINE	BODY	F	G	E
1958	Fairlane 500 "F"	V 8 cyl. (Supercharged)	Skyliner Convertible	6,000	12,000	30,000
1958	Fairlane 500 "F"	V 8 cyl. (Supercharged)	Town Sedan	2,500	4,500	9,500
1958	Fairlane 500 "F"	V 8 cyl. (Supercharged)	Club Sedan	2,500	4,500	9,500
1958	Thunderbird	V 8 cyl. (Supercharged)	Hardtop	8,000	12,000	20,000

Ford – 1957 "Thunderbird"

YEAR	MODEL	ENGINE	BODY	F	G	E
1958	Thunderbird	V 8 cyl. (Supercharged)	Convertible	9,000	14,000	25,000
1958	Country Squire	V 8 cyl. (Supercharged)	Station Wagon	1,800	3,900	8,000
1959	Fairlane 500	V 8 cyl. (Supercharged)	Club Sedan	2,000	4,000	9,000
1959	Fairlane 500	V 8 cyl. (Supercharged)	2 Door Town Victoria	2,500	5,000	12,000
1959	Galaxie	V 8 cyl. (Supercharged)	Convertible	6,000	14,000	28,000
1959	Galaxie	V 8 cyl. (Supercharged)	Skyliner Convertible	6,000	15,000	35,000
1959	Galaxie	V 8 cyl. (Supercharged)	2 Door Victoria	1,500	5,000	14,000
1959	Thunderbird	V 8 cyl. (Supercharged)	Hardtop	3,000	9,000	20,000
1959	Thunderbird	V 8 cyl. (Supercharged)	Convertible	5,000	15,000	30,000
1960	Galaxie	V 8 cyl. (Supercharged)	Town Sedan	1,500	2,500	6,000
1960	Galaxie	V 8 cyl. (Supercharged)	Town Victoria	2,000	4,000	8,000

FORD *(United States, 1903 to date) (continued)*

YEAR	MODEL	ENGINE	BODY	F	G	E
1960	Galaxie	V 8 cyl. (Supercharged)	Club Victoria	2,500	5,000	12,000
1960	Starliner	V 8 cyl. (Supercharged)	Hardtop	3,000	6,000	14,000
1960	Starliner	V 8 cyl. (Supercharged)	Convertible	5,000	12,000	25,000
1960	Country Squire	V 8 cyl. (Supercharged)	Station Wagon	1,000	3,000	8,000
1960	Thunderbird	V 8 cyl. (Supercharged)	Convertible	6,000	14,000	28,000
1960	Thunderbird	V 8 cyl. (Supercharged)	Hardtop	2,500	7,000	18,000
1960	Thunderbird	V 8 cyl. (Supercharged)	Hardtop w/Sun Roof	4,000	10,000	20,000
1960	Falcon	6 cyl.	2 Door Sedan	500	2,000	4,500
1961	Falcon Futura	6 cyl.	Coupe	1,600	3,000	7,000
1961	Galaxie	V 8 cyl.	Victoria	1,700	4,000	10,000
1961	Galaxie	V 8 cyl.	Skyliner Hardtop	2,000	5,000	11,000
1961	Galaxie	V 8 cyl.	Town Sedan	1,500	2,500	6,000
1961	Galaxie	V 8 cyl.	Club Sedan	1,500	2,500	6,000
1961	Galaxie	V 8 cyl.	Victoria Hardtop	2,500	4,000	10,000
1961	Galaxie	V 8 cyl.	Convertible	4,000	8,000	16,000
1961	Thunderbird	V 8 cyl.	Hardtop	2,000	5,000	13,000
1961	Thunderbird	V 8 cyl.	Convertible	6,000	14,000	28,000
1962	Falcon Futura	6 cyl.	Coupe	2,500	4,000	9,000
1962	Galaxie 500	V 8 cyl.	Convertible	3,000	7,000	15,000
1962	Galaxie 500	V 8 cyl.	Hardtop	2,000	4,500	9,000
1962	Galaxie 500	V 8 cyl.	2 or 4 Door Sedan	1,100	2,200	4,000
1962	Galaxie 500	V 8 cyl.	4 Door Sedan Hardtop	1,400	2,500	4,600
1962	Galaxie XL	V 8 cyl.	Hardtop	2,000	4,000	10,000
1962	Galaxie XL	V 8 cyl. 406	Convertible	4,000	9,000	18,000
1962	Thunderbird	V 8 cyl.	Hardtop	2,500	5,000	14,000
1962	Thunderbird	V 8 cyl.	Landau Hardtop	3,000	6,000	15,000
1962	Thunderbird	V 8 cyl.	Convertible	5,000	14,000	27,000
1962	Thunderbird	V 8 cyl.	Sport Roadster	9,000	18,000	35,000
1963	Falcon Futura	6 cyl.	Hardtop	2,000	4,000	10,000

YEAR	MODEL	ENGINE	BODY	F	G	E
FORD *(United States, 1903 to date) (continued)*						
1963	Falcon Futura	6 cyl.	Convertible	2,500	7,000	13,000
1963	Falcon Sprint	V 8 cyl. 260	Sport Coupe	2,000	3,500	8,000
1963	Falcon Sprint	V 8 cyl. 260	Sport Convertible	3,000	6,000	10,000
1963	Fairlane 500	V 8 cyl. 260	Sport Coupe FBK	2,500	6,000	13,000
1963	Galaxie 500	V 8 cyl. 390	Hardtop	2,000	5,000	11,000
1963	Galaxie 500	V 8 cyl. 406	Convertible	4,000	12,000	25,000
1963	Galaxie 500 XL	V 8 cyl. 390	Convertible	3,000	8,000	20,000
1963	Galaxie 500 XL	V 8 cyl. 427	Sport Coupe	1,500	4,000	9,000
1963	Thunderbird	V 8 cyl.	Hardtop	2,500	5,000	13,000
1963	Thunderbird	V 8 cyl.	Landau Hardtop	2,500	6,000	14,000
1963	Thunderbird	V 8 cyl.	Sport Roadster	9,000	18,000	35,000
1963	Thunderbird	V 8 cyl.	Convertible	6,000	15,000	30,000
1964	Falcon Sprint	V 8 cyl.	Hardtop	1,600	3,500	8,500
1964	Falcon Sprint	V 8 cyl. 260	Convertible	2,500	6,000	12,000
1964	Fairlane	V 8 cyl. 260	Sport Coupe	2,000	4,000	9,000
1964	Fairlane	V 8 cyl. 260	Sedan	1,100	2,000	4,000
1964	Fairlane	V 8 cyl. 260	Custom	1,000	1,800	3,600
1964	Fairlane	V 8 cyl.	Hardtop	1,500	3,000	7,000
1964	Galaxie 500 XL	V 8 cyl. 390	Convertible	4,000	9,000	18,000
1964	Galaxie 500 XL	V 8 cyl. 352	Coupe	2,000	5,000	12,000
1964	Galaxie 500 XL	V 8 cyl. 427	Sport Coupe	3,000	8,000	18,000
1964	Thunderbird	V 8 cyl.	Hardtop	2,500	4,000	10,000
1964	Thunderbird	V 8 cyl.	Landau Hardtop	3,000	5,000	11,000
1964	Thunderbird	V 8 cyl.	Convertible	6,000	13,000	26,000
1964	Mustang	V 8 cyl. 260	Convertible	2,000	8,200	27,200
1964	Mustang	V 8 cyl. 260	Hardtop	3,000	6,000	14,000

YEAR	MODEL	ENGINE	BODY	F	G	E
FORD *(United States, 1903 to date) (continued)*						
1965	Galaxie 500					
	XL	V 8 cyl. 390	Hardtop	1,300	3,000	7,000
1965	Galaxie 500					
	XL	V 8 cyl. 390	Convertible	2,000	5,500	11,000
1965	Mustang	6 cyl.	Hardtop	4,000	7,000	15,000
1965	Mustang	V 8 cyl. 289	Convertible	6,000	12,000	26,000

Ford – 1965 "Mustang GT Convertible"

YEAR	MODEL	ENGINE	BODY	F	G	E
1965	Mustang	V 8 cyl. 289	Fastback 2 + 2	5,000	10,000	20,000
1965	LTD	V 8 cyl. 390	Hardtop Sedan	1,400	2,200	5,500
1966	Fairlane 500 GT	V 8 cyl. 390	Convertible	2,500	6,000	12,000
1966	Galaxie 500 XL	V 8 cyl. 428	Convertible	3,000	8,000	17,000
1966	Mustang	6 cyl.	Hardtop	4,000	6,000	13,000
1966	Mustang GT	V 8 cyl. 289	Hardtop	3,500	6,500	14,500
1966	Mustang GT	V 8 cyl. 289	Convertible	8,000	15,000	31,000
1966	Mustang GT	V 8 cyl. 289	Fastback 2 + 2	5,000	12,000	25,000
1966	Mustang	6 cyl.	Convertible	8,000	15,000	28,000
1966	Shelby GT 350	V 8 cyl. 289	Fastback	8,500	20,000	43,000
1966	Thunderbird	V 8 cyl.	Hardtop	2,500	5,000	12,000
1966	Thunderbird	V 8 cyl.	Landau	3,000	7,000	14,000
1966	Thunderbird	V 8 cyl.	Convertible	6,000	13,000	23,000
1967	Fairlane	V 8 cyl.	Sedan	1,000	1,800	3,800
1967	Fairlane	V 8 cyl.	Coupe	1,100	2,000	4,000

YEAR	MODEL	ENGINE	BODY	F	G	E
FORD *(United States, 1903 to date) (continued)*						
1967	Fairlane					
	500	V 8 cyl.	Sedan	1,000	1,800	3,800
1967	Fairlane					
	500	V 8 cyl.	Coupe	1,100	2,000	4,000
1967	Fairlane					
	500	V 8 cyl.	Convertible	2,500	4,000	10,000
1967	Galaxie 500					
	XL	V 8 cyl.	Convertible	3,000	6,000	12,000
1967	Mustang	V 8 cyl.	Hardtop	4,000	6,000	12,000
1967	Mustang GT	V 8 cyl.	Convertible	8,000	15,000	30,000
1967	Shelby GT					
	350	V 8 cyl.	Convertible	20,000	45,000	80,000
1967	Shelby GT		Fastback			
	500	V 8 cyl.	2 + 2	15,000	25,000	40,000
1967	Thunderbird	V 8 cyl.	Hardtop	3,000	5,000	9,000
1967	Thunderbird	V 8 cyl.	Sedan	2,500	4,000	7,000
1968	Fairlane	V 8 cyl.	Sedan	1,500	3,000	4,500
1968	Fairlane	V 8 cyl.	Hardtop	1,500	3,000	5,000
1968	Fairlane	V 8 cyl.	Station Wagon	1,000	1,800	4,000
1968	Thunderbird	V 8 cyl.	Sedan	1,300	4,000	7,800
1968	Galaxie 500					
	XL	V 8 cyl.	Convertible	3,000	6,000	12,000
1968	Galaxie					
	500	V 8 cyl.	Convertible	3,500	7,000	13,000
1968	Mustang	6 cyl.	Hardtop	4,000	7,000	13,000
1968	Mustang	V 8 cyl.	Convertible	6,000	14,000	24,000
1968	Mustang GT	V 8 cyl.	Fastback 2 + 2	4,000	9,000	19,000
1968	Shelby GT					
	500	V 8 cyl.	Convertible	15,000	35,000	70,000
1968	Shelby GT					
	500 KR	V 8 cyl.	Fastback	9,000	20,000	42,000
1968	Shelby GT					
	500 KR	V 8 cyl.	Convertible	20,000	50,000	90,000
1968	Torino	V 8 cyl.	Sedan	1,000	1,800	3,600
1968	Torino	V 8 cyl.	Hardtop	1,500	2,500	6,000
1968	Torino	V 8 cyl.	Station Wagon	1,000	2,000	4,200
1969	Galaxy 500					
	XL	V 8 cyl.	Convertible	1,800	5,000	9,000
1969	Mustang	V 8 cyl.	Convertible	6,000	12,000	20,000
1969	Torino GT	V 8 cyl.	Fastback	2,000	4,000	8,000

YEAR	MODEL	ENGINE	BODY	F	G	E
FORD *(United States, 1903 to date) (continued)*						
1969	Shelby GT 350	V 8 cyl.	Fastback	10,000	20,000	32,000
1969	Shelby GT 500	V 8 cyl.	Convertible	20,000	45,000	65,000
1969	Mustang Boss 302	V 8 cyl.	Fastback	8,000	15,000	26,000
1969	Mustang	V 8 cyl.	Convertible	6,000	12,000	20,000
1969	Talladega (Torino)	V 8 cyl.	Fastback	1,400	4,000	9,000
1970	Fairlane 500	V 8 cyl.	Sedan	1,000	2,000	3,800
1970	Fairlane 500	V 8 cyl.	Hardtop	1,100	2,200	4,000
1970	Galaxie XL	V 8 cyl.	Convertible	3,000	6,000	10,000
1970	Mustang Boss 302	V 8 cyl.	Fastback	8,000	15,000	26,000
1970	Mustang Boss 429	V 8 cyl.	Fastback	20,000	35,000	50,000
1970	Mustang	V 8 cyl.	Convertible	8,000	15,000	20,000
1971	LTD	V 8 cyl.	Convertible	2,000	3,500	8,300
1971	Mustang Boss 351	V 8 cyl.	Fastback	8,000	16,000	28,000
1971	Mustang	V 8 cyl.	Convertible	6,000	12,000	20,000
1972	LTD	V 8 cyl.	Convertible	1,800	5,000	8,100
1972	Mustang	V 8 cyl.	Convertible	6,000	12,000	20,000
1973	Mustang	V 8 cyl.	Convertible	6,000	12,000	20,000
FORD *(Great Britain, 1911 to date)*						
	Pre-1932	Same as U.S.				
1932	Y	933cc	Sedan	2,000	3,000	6,000
1935	C Ten	1172cc	Sedan	1,500	3,000	6,500
1939	Anglia	4 cyl.	Sedan	2,000	4,000	9,000
1939	Perfect		Sedan	1,500	3,000	8,000
1951	Consul	4 cyl.	Sedan	945	2,000	4,500
1952	Zephyr	6 cyl.	Sedan	945	2,000	5,000
1953	Pilot	V 8 cyl.	Sedan	1,100	2,000	5,000
1954	Zodiac	6 cyl.	Convertible	2,000	4,000	7,000
1965	Lotus-Cortina	4 cyl.	2 Door Sedan	1,100	2,350	4,750
FORD *(Germany, 1931 to date)*						
1931	Rheinland	4 cyl.	Coupe	1,500	3,500	7,500
1932	Eifel	V 8 cyl.	Convertible	3,000	8,000	18,000
1933		V 8 cyl.	Cabriolet	2,500	7,000	16,000
1935	Perfect	1172cc	Sedan	1,500	3,000	6,000

YEAR	MODEL	ENGINE	BODY	F	G	E
FORD *(Germany, 1931 to date) (continued)*						
1939	Taunus	V 8 cyl.	Convertible	2,000	5,000	12,000
1945	12 M	4 cyl.	Convertible	1,500	3,000	6,500
1959	17 M	4 cyl.	Sedan	1,000	2,000	4,000
FORD *(France, 1947–54)*						
1947	Vedette	V 8 cyl.	Fastback	1,000	2,500	5,000
1951	Comete	V 8 cyl.	Sport Coupe	1,500	3,000	6,000
FORMAN *(Great Britain, 1904–06)*						
1904		2 cyl.	Open	1,300	3,700	11,500
1904		4 cyl.	Open	1,950	4,950	14,250
FOSSUM *(Netherlands, 1906–07)*						
1906		1 cyl.	Runabout	1,200	4,300	10,750
1906		2 cyl.	Runabout	945	4,000	10,000
FOUILLARON *(France, 1900–14)*						
1900		10 hp	Tonneau	1,500	4,000	12,800
1902		4 cyl. (Buchet)	Tonneau	1,600	4,100	12,000
1903		4 cyl. (Buchet)	Tonneau	1,600	4,150	12,250
1904		1 cyl.	Tonneau	1,000	3,500	11,000
1905		2 cyl.	Tonneau	1,000	3,600	11,250
1906		4 cyl.	Tonneau	1,000	3,600	11,600
1908		(DeDion)	Tonneau	2,000	6,000	13,900
1914		4 cyl.	Tonneau	1,500	4,100	12,000
1914		6 cyl.	Tonneau	1,500	4,250	12,500
FOURNIER *(France, 1913–24)*						
1913		1 cyl.		1,000	4,000	11,800
1915		4 cyl. (Ballot)		1,000	4,100	12,250
1921		4 cyl.	Coupe	1,100	4,250	12,500
FOURNIER-MARCADIER *(France, 1963–71)*						
1963		(Renault)	Sport	1,000	2,000	4,000
1967	Borzoi	(Renault Gordini 1800)	Coupe	1,000	2,250	4,500
1971		(B.M.W.)		1,000	2,250	4,500
FOY-STEELE *(Great Britain, 1913–16)*						
1913		4 cyl. (Coventry-Simplex)	Roadster	1,000	3,900	12,800
1914		4 cyl. (Coventry-Simplex)	Touring	1,000	3,800	12,600
1914	Colonial	4 cyl. (Coventry-Simplex)	Touring	1,000	3,450	12,500
FRAMO *(Germany, 1932–37)*						
1932	Stromer	(D.K.W.)	Coupe	1,000	2,000	5,000

YEAR	MODEL	ENGINE	BODY	F	G	E
FRAMO *(Germany, 1932–37) (continued)*						
1932	Piccolo					
	3-Wheel	(D.K.W.)	Coupe	1,000	1,900	3,750
FRANKLIN *(United States, 1902–34)*						
1904	C	4 cyl. (Air-cooled)	5 Passenger			
			Tonneau	4,200	13,600	26,000
1905	E	4 cyl. (Air-cooled)	Runabout	3,500	12,000	22,000
1907	G	4 cyl. (Air-cooled)	2 Passenger			
			Runabout	4,000	9,000	28,000

Franklin – 1907 "Model G Runabout"

YEAR	MODEL	ENGINE	BODY	F	G	E
1910	G	4 cyl. (Air-cooled)	4 Passenger			
			Runabout	3,400	10,000	29,000
1910	G	4 cyl. (Air-cooled)	Touring	3,800	10,750	31,000
1915	Six-30	6 cyl. (Air-cooled)	2 Passenger			
			Roadster	6,000	15,000	32,000
1919	9	6 cyl. (Air-cooled)	Touring	6,500	16,000	33,000
1921	9-B	6 cyl. (Air-cooled)	Touring	6,500	16,000	33,000
1922	10-A	6 cyl. (Air-cooled)	Touring	6,500	16,000	33,000
1923	10-B	6 cyl. (Air-cooled)	Sedan	4,000	12,000	25,000
1924	10-B	6 cyl. (Air-cooled)	Sedan	4,000	12,000	25,000
1924	10-B	6 cyl. (Air-cooled)	Touring	5,000	14,000	29,000
1925	10-C	6 cyl. (Air-cooled)	4 Passenger			
			Coupe	4,000	12,000	27,000
1925	II	6 cyl. (Air-cooled)	Touring	5,500	14,000	29,000
1925	10-C	6 cyl. (Air-cooled)	Sedan	2,600	6,000	24,000

YEAR	MODEL	ENGINE	BODY	F	G	E
FRANKLIN *(United States, 1902–34) (continued)*					
1925	10-C	6 cyl. (Air-cooled)	Demi Sedan	3,500	9,000	25,000
1925	II	6 cyl. (Air-cooled)	Sedan	2,800	6,000	23,000
1925	II	6 cyl. (Air-cooled)	Coupe	3,500	12,000	30,000
1926	II A	6 cyl.	Boattail Roadster	4,800	20,000	44,000
1926	II A	6 cyl.	Phaeton	3,800	16,000	37,000
1926	II A	6 cyl.	Coupe	5,000	12,000	26,000
1927	II B	6 cyl.	Boattail Speedster	4,800	20,000	42,500
1927	II B	6 cyl.	Touring	8,000	18,000	38,000
1927	11 B	6 cyl.	Sedan	4,000	10,000	24,000
1927	11 B	6 cyl.	Cabriolet	15,000	20,000	39,000
1928	Airman	6 cyl.	Convertible	17,500	25,000	44,000
1929	135	6 cyl.	Coupe	3,500	14,800	37,500
1929	135	6 cyl.	Brougham	5,000	12,000	26,000
1929	135	6 cyl.	Sport Sedan	6,000	13,000	26,000
1929	135	6 cyl.	Convertible Coupe	7,000	17,000	38,000
1930	145	6 cyl.	Pursuit	7,000	14,000	26,000
1930	145	6 cyl.	Convertible Coupe	15,000	25,000	51,000
1930	147	6 cyl.	Convertible Sedan	10,000	25,000	55,000
1931	15	6 cyl.	Sedan	4,000	10,000	24,000
1931	15 Deluxe	6 cyl.	Touring	12,000	25,000	57,000
1931	15	6 cyl.	Roadster	12,000	35,000	68,000
1931	15 Deluxe	6 cyl.	Convertible Coupe	12,000	28,000	55,000
1932	Airman	6 cyl.	Speedster	14,000	28,000	54,000
1932	Airman	6 cyl.	Convertible Coupe	10,000	22,000	47,000
1932	Airman	6 cyl.	Coupe	3,800	12,500	25,000
1933	Olympic	6 cyl.	Sedan	2,500	9,500	18,500
1933	Airman	6 cyl.	5 Passenger Brougham	3,600	11,000	24,000
1933	Twelve	V 12 cyl.	Sedan	5,400	14,800	33,000
1933	Airman	6 cyl. (Supercharged)	Sedan	4,000	10,800	24,500
1933	Olympic	6 cyl.	Convertible Coupe	9,000	18,000	35,000
FRAYER-MILLER *(United States, 1904–08)*					
1904		4 cyl. (T-head)	Touring	2,200	8,400	16,000
1906		6 cyl.	Touring	2,600	8,250	16,500
1908	B	4 cyl.	Touring	2,500	7,000	16,000

YEAR	MODEL	ENGINE	BODY	F	G	E
FRAZER *(United States, 1947–51)*						
1947	Manhattan	6 cyl.	Sedan	1,200	2,200	5,400
1948	Manhattan	6 cyl.	Sedan	1,300	2,250	5,500
1949	Manhattan	6 cyl.	Sedan	1,500	2,600	6,000
1950	Manhattan	6 cyl.	Sedan	1,500	2,600	6,000
1951	Manhattan	8 cyl.	Convertible	4,000	6,000	20,000
1951	Manhattan	8 cyl.	Sedan	1,600	3,500	6,000
1951	Manhattan		Sedan	1,600	3,200	5,500
FRAZER NASH *(Great Britain, 1924–60)*						
1924		4 cyl.	Sport	2,000	5,000	12,000
1927		4 cyl.	Cabriolet	4,500	9,000	18,000
1932		4 cyl.	Roadster	5,000	10,000	22,500
1932	TT Replica	1.5 Litre	Sport	4,750	9,500	18,500
1935	Type 319	6 cyl.	Sport	4,100	8,250	16,500
1948	High Speed	V 8 cyl.	Racing	5,250	16,500	32,500
1953		V 8 cyl.	Coupe	1,750	3,500	7,500
1954	Sebring	2 Litre	Sport	1,750	3,500	7,000
FREIA *(Germany, 1922–27)*						
1922	5/14	1320cc	Open	1,000	2,400	7,800
1922	20		Open	1,000	3,750	6,500
1924	6/30	1472cc	Open	1,100	2,400	8,000
1924	7/35	1807cc	Open	1,000	2,500	7,000
FRISKEY *(Great Britain, 1957–64)*						
1957		328cc (Villiers)	Minicar	500	1,250	2,450
1957			Coupe	500	1,200	2,400
1957	Closed		Coupe	500	1,150	2,300
1959	Sport	Excelsior	2 Passenger	500	1,250	2,500
1964	Prince	324cc (Villiers)	4 Passenger	500	1,100	2,250
FRITCHLE *(United States, 1905–19)*						
1904		Electric	Stanhope	3,000	8,000	17,000
1904		Electric	Victoria	3,000	7,000	16,000
1909	100 Mile	Electric	Coupe	2,500	6,000	14,000
1909	100 Mile	Electric	Roadster	3,000	7,000	16,000
1916		Gas/Electric	Coupe	3,000	6,500	15,000
FRONTENAC *(United States, 1906–13)*						
1906		4 cyl.	Runabout	5,000	12,000	25,000
1906		4 cyl.	Touring	4,000	13,000	26,000
1913	C	4 cyl.	Touring	3,500	13,500	27,000
FRONTENAC *(Canada, 1931–60)*						
1931		6 cyl.	Racing	2,000	3,900	9,750
1959		4 cyl.	Coupe	1,250	2,650	3,250
1960		6 cyl.	Sedan	1,200	2,850	4,000

YEAR	MODEL	ENGINE	BODY	F	G	E

F-S *(United States, 1911–12)*

YEAR	MODEL	ENGINE	BODY	F	G	E
1911	22	4 cyl. (Beaver)	Touring			
			Parcel Car	2,300	6,000	12,000
1911	30	4 cyl. (Beaver)	Touring			
			Runabout	3,000	7,000	14,000
1911	40	4 cyl. (Beaver)	Touring			
			Torpedo	3,500	8,000	16,000

FULLER *(United States, 1908–10)*

YEAR	MODEL	ENGINE	BODY	F	G	E
1908	30	4 cyl.	Touring	3,200	6,000	13,000
1908	40	4 cyl.	Touring	3,500	7,000	15,000
1908	60	6 cyl.	Touring	4,000	8,000	17,000
1910	A-2	4 cyl.	Touring	2,500	5,500	14,000
1910	A	4 cyl.	Touring	3,500	7,000	15,000

FULMINA *(Germany, 1913–26)*

YEAR	MODEL	ENGINE	BODY	F	G	E
1913	E 10/30		Limousine	1,000	3,000	8,000
1913	B 17/55		Limousine	1,100	3,250	8,500
1914	16/45		Limousine	1,050	3,100	8,250

G

GABRIEL *(France, 1912–14)*

YEAR	MODEL	ENGINE	BODY	F	G	E
1912	9/12	4 cyl.	Coupe	1,000	2,900	7,000
1912	13/18	4 cyl.	Sedan	900	2,800	7,000
1912	20/30	4 cyl.	Coupe	1,200	3,000	10,000

GAGGENAU *(Germany, 1905–11)*

YEAR	MODEL	ENGINE	BODY	F	G	E
1905			Touring	1,000	2,900	11,000
1905			Touring	2,000	5,000	10,000
1910	35	4700cc	Sport	1,100	4,100	9,250
1910	60	8830cc	Touring	1,200	4,300	9,600

GAINSBOROUGH *(Great Britain, 1902–03)*

YEAR	MODEL	ENGINE	BODY	F	G	E
1902		4 cyl.	Runabout			
			Hardtop	1,200	4,250	8,500
1902		4 cyl.	Tonneau	1,300	4,400	10,000
1902		4 cyl.	Brougham	1,500	4,600	10,000

GALE *(United States, 1905–07)*

YEAR	MODEL	ENGINE	BODY	F	G	E
1905	A	1 cyl.	Runabout	3,000	6,000	12,000
1905	D	1 cyl.	Runabout	3,500	6,500	13,000
1906	G	2 cyl.	Runabout	3,500	6,500	13,000
1907	G-7	2 cyl.	Runabout	3,000	6,000	12,000

GALLOWAY *(United States, 1908–11; 1915–17)*

YEAR	MODEL	ENGINE	BODY	F	G	E
1908		2 cyl.	Roadster	3,500	8,800	17,000
1915	Arabian	4 cyl.	Runabout	3,600	9,000	20,000

YEAR	MODEL	ENGINE	BODY	F	G	E
GALLOWAY *(Great Britain, 1921–28)*						
1921		4 cyl.	Open	2,000	5,000	11,000
1925		4 cyl.	2 Passenger	2,250	6,500	12,000
1928		4 cyl.	Coupe	2,000	5,100	11,250
GALY *(France, 1954–57)*						
1954	Vibel	175cc (Ydral)	Coupe	450	1,300	2,750
1954	Vistand	175cc (Ydral)	Open Jeep	500	1,500	3,000
GAMAGE *(Great Britain, 1903–04; 1914–15)*						
1903		1 cyl. (DeDion)	Roadster	2,000	6,000	12,000
1903		2 cyl. (DeDion)	Roadster	2,100	6,250	12,500
1904		4 cyl.	Roadster	2,200	6,400	12,800
GARBATY *(Germany, 1924–27)*						
1924	5/25	4 cyl.	Sedan	1,500	3,600	7,000
GARDNER *(France, 1898–1900)*						
1898		1 cyl.	Phaeton	2,200	5,300	12,000
1898		1 cyl.	Voiturette	2,250	5,400	12,000
1899		2 cyl.	Racing	2,300	5,500	12,000
GARDNER *(United States, 1920–31)*						
1922	G	4 cyl.	Touring	5,000	10,000	22,000
1923	5	4 cyl.	Touring	5,000	10,000	22,000
1924	5	4 cyl.	Touring	5,000	9,000	24,000
1924	5	4 cyl.	Sedan	3,500	5,800	13,900
1926	6B	8 cyl.	Cabriolet	10,000	22,000	42,000
1926	6B	6 cyl.	Roadster	6,000	14,000	29,000
1926	6B	8 cyl.	Sedan	5,000	12,000	25,000
1927	8-80	8 cyl.	Sedan	4,500	11,000	24,000
1928	8-85	8 cyl.	Sedan	3,500	10,000	25,000
1929	125	8 cyl.	Cabriolet	8,000	20,000	36,000
1929	120	8 cyl.	Sedan	3,500	10,000	24,000
1929	130	8 cyl.	Roadster	6,500	19,000	42,000
GARFORD *(United States, 1908–13)*						
1908	A	4 cyl.	Touring	4,000	10,500	24,500
1913	G-14	6 cyl.	5 Passenger			
			Touring	5,400	16,000	29,000
GARY *(United States, 1914)*						
1914	34	6 cyl.	Speedster	5,000	14,000	29,000
1916	34	6 cyl.	Touring	3,500	12,000	27,000
GAUTHIER *(France, 1904–37)*						
1904		1 cyl.	Voiturette	1,500	3,500	11,000
GAUTHIER-WEHRLE *(France, 1894–98)*						
1894		Steam	Vis-a-vis	3,500	8,000	20,000
1896		8 hp	Vis-a-vis	2,250	6,500	14,000

YEAR	MODEL	ENGINE	BODY	F	G	E
GAUTHIER-WEHRLE *(France, 1894–98) (continued)*						
1898		1 cyl.	Runabout	2,100	5,250	13,500
1899		1 cyl.	Runabout	1,250	4,500	12,000
1899		Electric	Voiturette	2,500	8,000	19,000
1899		Electric	Dogcart	2,700	7,750	18,500
GAZ *(Soviet Union, 1932–45)*						
1932	A	4 cyl.	Touring	2,500	6,600	9,500
1936	MI		Sedan	1,500	3,000	6,000
1938	MII-40	4 cyl.	Touring	2,400	6,300	9,000
1938	67	4 cyl.	Sedan	700	1,400	2,750
1938	69	4 cyl.	Touring	650	1,300	2,500
1939	M-20	4 cyl.	Sedan	600	1,200	2,450
1940	MII-70	6 cyl.	Sedan	650	1,250	2,500
1941	M-21	6 cyl.	Limousine	700	1,400	2,750
1942	M-22	6 cyl.	Touring	650	1,300	2,500
1943	M-25	6 cyl.	Sedan	650	1,250	2,500
1944	M-12	6 cyl.	Limousine	800	1,500	3,000
1945	M-13	6 cyl.	Chaika	750	1,400	2,750
GEARLESS *(United States, 1907–09)*						
1907	50	4 cyl.	Touring	3,900	12,700	28,000
1908	Four	4 cyl.	Roadster	4,500	15,000	32,000
1908	Great Six	6 cyl.	Touring	3,800	13,800	25,000
1909	Four	4 cyl.	Roadster	2,500	11,000	20,000
1909	Six-30	6 cyl.	Touring	5,800	11,500	21,000
GELRIA *(Netherlands, 1900–02)*						
1900		1 cyl.	Phaeton	2,500	6,000	14,000
1900		1 cyl.	Touring	2,600	6,250	14,500
1900		1 cyl.	Dos-a-dos	2,550	6,100	14,200
1901	Duc	1 cyl.	3 Passenger	2,500	5,900	13,800
1902		2 cyl.	Touring	2,500	6,000	14,000
GEMINI *(Great Britain, 1959–63)*						
1959		(Cosworth-Ford)	Racing	2,500	6,000	12,000
1960	Mark 3	(Cosworth-Ford)	Racing	2,500	6,100	12,000
1961	Mark 4	(Cosworth-Ford)	Racing	2,650	6,250	12,500
GENERAL *(Great Britain, 1902–05)*						
1902		4 cyl.	Racing	3,500	8,000	16,000
1903		(Aster)	Runabout	2,350	6,750	14,500
1903		(Buchet)	Touring	2,250	6,500	14,000
1904		(Simms)	Runabout	2,200	5,400	13,750
GENESTIN *(France, 1926–29)*						
1926		4 cyl.	Sport	2,000	4,500	9,000
1926		6 cyl.	Touring	2,000	4,800	9,500

YEAR	MODEL	ENGINE	BODY	F	G	E
GENESTIN *(France, 1926–29) (continued)*						
1928		6 cyl.	Sport	2,000	4,750	9,500
GENEVA *(United States, 1901–04)*						
1901	A	Steam	Runabout	3,000	7,000	14,000
1904	F	Steam	Tonneau	3,500	7,500	15,000
GEORGES IRAT *(France, 1921–46)*						
1921		4 cyl.	Touring	1,800	3,600	8,250
1927		6 cyl.		2,000	3,900	8,750
1929		8 cyl. (Lycoming)	Touring	3,750	7,400	15,000
1935		1100cc (Ruby)	Sport	1,600	3,200	8,400
1939	11 CV	(Citroen)		1,650	3,000	7,500
GEORGES ROY *(France, 1906–29)*						
1906		2 cyl.	Open	1,750	5,500	11,000
1906		4 cyl.	Open	1,900	5,900	11,750
1907		6 cyl.	Touring	2,000	6,000	12,000
1920		4 cyl.	Touring	2,000	6,000	12,000
G.E.P. *(France, 1913–14)*						
1913		1 cyl. (Ballot)	Open	2,500	4,000	9,000
1913		2 cyl. (Ballot)	Open	2,750	4,500	9,000
1913		4 cyl. (Ballot)	Open	3,000	5,000	10,000
GERMAIN *(Brazil, 1897–1914)*						
1897		2 cyl. (Daimler)	Vis-a-vis	1,000	5,000	11,500
1897		4 cyl. (Daimler)	Limousine	1,100	5,250	11,500
1903		4 cyl.	Tonneau	1,100	5,200	11,400
1905	Chainless	14/22 hp	Tonneau	1,100	5,250	11,500
1907		6 cyl.	Limousine	1,750	6,250	12,500
1913		(Knight)	Sedan	2,000	6,500	13,000
GERONIMO *(United States, 1917–20)*						
1917	4-A-40	4 cyl.	Touring	2,900	7,900	17,000
1920	6-A-45	6 cyl.	5 Passenger			
			Touring	3,750	8,750	20,000
GHENT *(United States, 1917–18)*						
1917	6-60	6 cyl.	Touring	4,000	12,500	25,000
GIANNINI *(Italy, 1963–75)*						
1963		850cc	Coupe	800	1,600	3,400
1965		930cc	Sport	850	1,700	3,400
1965		4 cyl.	Sport	825	1,650	3,250
1967		V 8 cyl.	Sport	875	1,750	3,500
1972	Sirio	650cc	Sport			
			Cabriolet	850	1,700	3,500

YEAR	MODEL	ENGINE	BODY	F	G	E
GIAUR *(Italy, 1950–54)*						
1950		750cc (Fiat)	Racing	1,750	4,500	9,500
1950	Single S	570cc (Fiat)	Racing	1,600	4,200	9,000
GIBBONS *(Great Britain, 1921–26)*						
1921		1 cyl. (Precision)	Racing	2,000	4,750	8,500
1921		1 cyl. (Blackburne)	Racing	2,000	4,750	8,500
1921	Tandem 2 S	2 cyl. (Coventry-Victor)	Racing	2,000	5,000	11,000
GILBERN *(Great Britain, 1959–73)*						
1959	4 S	(Coventry-Climax)	Gran Turismo Coupe	1,500	3,100	5,200
1966	Genie	V 6 cyl. (Ford)	Sport	1,600	3,200	5,500
1969	Invader	V 6 cyl. (Ford)	Coupe	1,700	3,300	5,600
1972	Mark 2	(Ford)	Sport	1,800	3,750	6,500
1973	Mark 3	(Ford)	Coupe	1,900	3,800	6,500
GILCHRIST *(Great Britain, 1920–23)*						
1920		(Hotchkiss)	Touring	2,000	5,750	11,000
1920		(Hotchkiss)	Closed	1,800	5,400	9,800
GILLET-FOREST *(France, 1900–07)*						
1900		1 cyl.	Tonneau	1,900	4,900	10,750
1902		1 cyl.	Runabout	1,900	4,800	10,500
1902		1 cyl.	Voiturette	2,000	5,000	11,000
1905		2 cyl.	Runabout	1,900	4,900	10,750
1905	12	2 cyl.	Tonneau	1,900	4,900	10,700
1905	16	4 cyl.	Coupe	1,900	4,800	10,600
1905	40	4 cyl.	Coach	1,800	4,600	10,200
GINETTA *(Great Britain, 1957–73)*						
1957	G 2		Coupe	1,000	2,000	4,000
1959	G 3		Coupe	1,000	2,000	4,000
1962	G 4	(Ford) 105E	Coupe	1,100	2,400	5,800
1963	G 10	V 8 cyl. (Ford)	Coupe	1,600	3,750	6,500
1964	G 11	(M.G.B.)	Coupe	1,000	1,700	4,400
1965	G 12		Gran Turismo	1,500	2,700	5,500
1968	G 15	(Hillman Imp)	Coupe	1,000	1,900	4,000
1970	G 16		Coupe	1,000	1,750	3,500
1970	G 17		Coupe	1,000	1,750	3,500
GIRLING *(Great Britain, 1913–14)*						
1913	3-Wheel CC	1 cyl.	Open	850	2,600	5,250
GLADIATOR *(France, 1896–1920)*						
1896		1 cyl.	Voiturette	3,100	7,250	14,500
1899		1 cyl.	Racing	4,000	12,100	24,250
1900		1 cyl. (Aster)	Tonneau	3,000	7,000	14,000

YEAR	MODEL	ENGINE	BODY	F	G	E
GLADIATOR *(France, 1896–1920) (continued)*						
1903		4 cyl. (Aster)	Voiturette	3,000	6,900	13,750
1905		4 cyl. (Aster)	Tonneau	3,100	7,250	14,500
1914		6 cyl. (Aster)	Coupe	2,000	5,900	14,000
GLAS *(Germany, 1955–68)*						
1955	Goggomobil	2 cyl.	Sedan	800	1,500	3,000
1958		2 cyl.	Sedan	800	1,500	3,000
1961		4 cyl.	Sedan	850	1,650	3,250
1962	1004	993cc	Sedan	850	1,650	3,250
1963	1204	1109cc	Sedan	900	1,650	3,250
1964	1304	1289cc	Sedan	900	1,700	3,500
1965	1700	1682cc	Sedan	1,000	1,800	3,600
1966	2600	V 8 cyl.	Coupe	1,750	3,500	6,000
GLASSIC *(United States, 1966–73)*						
1966	A Replica	4 cyl. (IHC)	Phaeton	1,500	3,000	7,000
1972	A Replica	V 8 cyl. (Ford)	Roadster	2,000	5,000	9,000
GLIDE *(United States, 1903–20)*						
1903	8	1 cyl.	Runabout	4,500	8,000	17,000
1907	G	4 cyl.	5 Passenger Touring	6,000	12,000	22,000
1907	H	6 cyl. (Rutenber)	Touring	7,500	20,000	42,000
1915	30	4 cyl. (Rutenber)	5 Passenger Touring	4,000	8,000	18,000
1916	6-40	6 cyl. (Rutenber)	5 Passenger Touring	4,000	12,000	23,000
1918	6-40	6 cyl.	Touring Sedan	3,200	6,000	16,000
GLOBE *(Great Britain, 1904–16)*						
1904		1 cyl. (Hitchon)	Touring	1,500	3,900	11,000
1904		4 cyl. (White & Poppe)	Touring	2,000	6,200	14,200
1913		1 cyl. (Anzani)	Cycle	1,000	2,650	6,250
1913		1 cyl. (Aster)	Cycle	1,000	3,500	6,000
1913		2 cyl. (J.A.P.)	Cycle	1,000	3,600	7,300
GLOBE *(United States, 1921–22)*						
1921		4 cyl. (Supreme)	Touring	5,500	13,000	26,000
1922	Cloverleaf	4 cyl. (Supreme)	Roadster	5,800	17,500	34,000
G.N. *(Great Britain, 1910–25)*						
1910		V 2 cyl. (J.A.P.)	Cycle	800	2,470	4,500
1912		4 cyl.	Coupe	800	2,400	4,500
1920	Legere	4 cyl.	2 Passenger	1,000	1,900	4,750
1920	Popular	4 cyl.	Cycle	1,000	1,900	4,750

YEAR	MODEL	ENGINE	BODY	F	G	E
G.N. *(Great Britain, 1910–25) (continued)*						
1921	Vitesse	4 cyl.	Racing	1,200	3,000	8,000
1923		4 cyl.	2 Passenger	1,000	1,900	4,800
1923		4 cyl.	2 Passenger	1,000	1,900	4,800
GNESUTTA *(Italy, 1900)*						
1900		2 cyl.	Sedan	1,000	2,000	7,000
GNOME; NOMAD *(Great Britain, 1925–26)*						
1925		1 cyl. (Villiers)	2 Passenger	750	1,500	4,000
GOBRON-BRILLIE; GOBRON *(France, 1898–1930)*						
1898		2 cyl.	Tonneau	1,000	2,000	7,000
1903		4 cyl.	Touring	1,000	1,900	8,000
1908		13.5 Litre	Racing	3,000	5,950	16,500
1910	40/60	4 cyl. (T-head)	Roadster	1,000	1,950	7,500
1914	25	4 cyl.	Tonneau	1,000	2,000	7,000
1917	50	4 cyl.	Roadster	1,000	1,950	7,500
1920	20	4 cyl.	Sport Touring	1,000	1,900	7,750
1926	10	4 cyl.	Touring	850	1,750	7,500
1928	Turbo	6 cyl.	Sport	1,000	2,000	7,000
GOLIATH *(Germany, 1931–63)*						
1931	Pioiner	1 cyl.	Coupe	900	1,900	3,750
1951	GP-700	2 cyl.	Sport Coupe	875	1,800	3,750
1954	GP-900		Sport Coupe	800	1,650	3,500
1967	Hanza 1100	4 cyl.	Sport Coupe	800	1,650	3,250
GORDANO *(Great Britain, 1946–50)*						
1946		(M.G. VA)	Sport	1,500	3,000	8,000
1948		(Lea-Francis)	Sport	1,400	2,900	7,500
GORDINI *(France, 1951–57)*						
1951		1100cc (Simca)	Racing	2,000	5,750	14,500
1952		6 cyl.	Sport	1,750	3,500	8,000
1953		8 cyl.	Sport Racing	2,000	5,750	12,500
1955	Formula 1 GP	6 cyl.	Racing	2,100	5,250	12,500
1956	Formula 2	8 cyl.	Racing	2,250	6,500	14,000
GORDON *(Great Britain, 1903–58)*						
1903		1 cyl.	Voiturette	1,000	3,000	7,000
1912		V 2 cyl.	Runabout	1,000	2,800	6,500
1912		V 2 cyl. (J.A.P.)		1,000	2,700	6,400
1954	3-Wheel	1 cyl. (Villiers)		750	1,600	4,000
GORHAM *(Japan, 1920–22)*						
1920	3-Wheel	2 cyl.	Coupe	800	1,600	4,000
1921	Lila	2 cyl.	Sedan	600	1,000	3,000

YEAR	MODEL	ENGINE	BODY	F	G	E
G.R.A.C. *(France, 1963 to date)*						
1963			Racing	1,750	4,300	9,500
1965	Formula France		Racing	1,750	4,300	9,500
1967	Formula Bleu		Racing	1,800	4,500	9,000
1969	MT-8	Formula 3	Racing	1,800	4,900	9,500
1969	MT-15		Coupe	1,100	3,000	6,000
GRACIELA *(Romania, 1960–61)*						
1960	2 Door	3 cyl.	Sedan	850	1,700	4,500
1961	Wartburg 900	3 cyl.	4 Door Sedan	875	1,750	4,500
GRADE *(Germany, 1921–26)*						
1921	Type F2	2 cyl.	2 Passenger	1,000	3,900	6,800
1922		2 cyl. 980cc	4 Passenger	950	3,600	6,000
GRAF & STIFT *(Austria, 1907–38)*						
1907		1 cyl. (DeDion)	Touring	2,900	6,750	11,500
1907		4 cyl. (T-head)	Touring	4,900	9,000	16,000
1921	SR 1	4 cyl.	Touring	4,600	8,000	15,000
1930	VK	4 cyl.	Open Touring	4,600	8,000	15,000
1931	SR 4	6 cyl.	Sport Coupe	4,400	7,800	14,500
1932	SP 5	6 cyl.	6 Passenger Sedan	4,000	7,000	13,000
1933	SP 8	8 cyl.	Sedan	5,000	9,000	18,000
GRAHAME-WHITE *(Great Britain, 1920–24)*						
1920		1 cyl.	Buckboard	750	1,300	3,600
1921		1 cyl.	Cycle	900	1,600	4,200
1922		4 cyl. (Dorman)	2 Passenger	1,000	1,900	4,800
GRAHAM-PAIGE; GRAHAM *(United States, 1928–41)*						
1928	610	6 cyl.	Sedan	2,000	4,000	10,000
1929	621	6 cyl.	Touring	6,000	9,000	28,000
1929	612	6 cyl.	Coupe	3,000	4,000	8,000
1930	Standard	6 cyl.	Roadster	6,000	15,000	33,000
1930	Standard	8 cyl.	Convertible Sedan	7,000	18,000	36,000
1930	Special	8 cyl.	Rumble Seat Coupe	1,500	3,000	9,250
1930	Standard	6 cyl.	Sedan	1,700	3,200	8,500
1930	Standard	6 cyl.	Phaeton	4,000	15,000	29,000
1931	127 Custom	8 cyl.	Cabriolet	5,600	8,500	30,000
1931	56 Prosperity	6 cyl.	Sedan	1,500	3,000	9,200
1932	57	8 cyl.	Rumble Seat Coupe	2,000	4,700	9,500
1932	57	8 cyl.	Sedan	1,800	4,000	9,000

YEAR	MODEL	ENGINE	BODY	F	G	E
GRAHAM-PAIGE; GRAHAM *(United States, 1928–41) (continued)*						
1932	Graham	6 cyl.	Cabriolet	3,000	7,700	19,000
1932	Special	6 cyl.	Sedan	1,600	3,200	8,500
1933	Custom	8 cyl.	Sedan Side Mount	2,000	4,500	9,900
1933	57 A Custom	8 cyl.	Sedan	1,800	4,000	9,000
1933	58	6 cyl.	Sedan	1,600	3,500	9,500
1934	68	6 cyl.	Sedan	1,600	3,500	9,500
1935	68	6 cyl.	Cabriolet	2,200	6,000	15,500
1935	69	8 cyl.	Sedan	1,500	4,400	9,300
1935	74	6 cyl.	Sedan	1,200	4,000	9,200
1936	Crusader	6 cyl.	Coach	1,000	3,500	9,000
1936	Cavalier	6 cyl.	Sedan	1,000	3,500	9,000
1936	Cavalier	6 cyl.	Coupe	1,200	3,800	9,000
1937	116	6 cyl. (Supercharged)	Sedan	1,000	6,500	12,000
1937	116	6 cyl. (Supercharged)	Cabriolet	2,000	7,200	13,500
1938	96	6 cyl.	Sedan	1,000	3,500	9,800
1938	97	6 cyl.	Sedan	1,000	3,500	9,600
1939	96	6 cyl.	Sedan	1,000	3,500	9,600
1939	96	6 cyl.	Victoria	1,250	4,000	10,200
1941	Hollywood	6 cyl.	Sedan	2,000	4,500	12,000
1941	Hollywood	6 cyl. (Supercharged)	Sedan	3,000	7,000	15,000
GRANT *(United States, 1913–22)*						
1914	M	4 cyl.	Roadster	3,800	6,750	17,000
1915	S	6 cyl.	Touring	4,000	7,600	18,500
1917	K	6 cyl.	Sedan	3,500	7,000	17,000
1921	HX	6 cyl.	Touring	3,000	6,000	15,000
1921	HX	6 cyl.	Sedan	2,500	5,000	10,000
GRAY *(United States, 1922–26)*						
1922	N	4 cyl.	Touring	1,800	7,600	14,000
1923	N	4 cyl.	Roadster	2,000	7,000	14,600
1924	N	4 cyl.	Touring	2,400	8,600	16,000
1926	N	4 cyl.	Sedan	1,200	4,800	10,400
GRAY-DORT *(Canada, 1915–25)*						
1915		4 cyl. (Lycoming)	Touring	3,000	4,800	11,500
1918	Special	4 cyl. (Lycoming)	Sport	2,400	4,600	11,000
1922	Special	4 cyl. (Lycoming)	Touring	2,000	4,000	10,000
1923		6 cyl.	Touring	2,400	4,600	11,000
G.R.D. *(Great Britain, 1971–73)*						
1971	372		Racing	1,700	3,200	6,500
1971	B 73		Racing	1,700	3,200	6,500
1973	272		Racing	1,900	3,700	7,500
1973	S 73	2 Litre	Sport	2,000	3,900	7,800

YEAR	MODEL	ENGINE	BODY	F	G	E
GREAT WESTERN *(United States, 1910–16)*						
1910	Thirty	4 cyl.	Touring	3,000	12,800	25,000
1913	Forty	4 cyl.	Touring	2,400	8,500	19,500
1916	Six	4 cyl.	Touring	1,200	8,250	18,500
GREENLEAF *(United States, 1902)*						
1902		2 cyl.	Surrey	2,000	5,000	12,500
GREGOIRE *(France, 1903–62)*						
1903	8 CV	1 cyl.	Voiturette	1,400	3,500	9,800
1904	10 CV	4 cyl.	Sport	1,600	3,200	9,000
1905	12 CV	2 cyl.	Voiturette	1,200	3,000	8,800
1909	14 CV		Sport	900	2,750	7,500
1924	20 CV	4 cyl.	Sport	1,000	2,900	7,800
1945		2 cyl.	Sedan	750	2,250	6,500
1947		2 cyl.	Cabriolet	900	2,750	6,500
1961		2.2 Litre	Convertible	800	2,500	6,000
GREGORY *(United States, 1920–22)*						
1920		4 cyl.	Roadster	3,000	10,800	22,000
GRIFFITH-TVR; GRIFFITH *(United States, 1964–66)*						
1964	VR	V 8 cyl. (Ford)	Sport Coupe	2,500	4,000	6,000
1965	GT	V 8 cyl. (Ford)	Coupe	2,500	4,000	6,500
1966	Omega	V 8 cyl. (Ford)	Coupe	4,500	8,000	15,000
GRIFFON *(France, 1906–10; 1921–24)*						
1906		1 cyl. 7	Voiturette	1,600	3,000	8,500
1920		V 2 cyl.	Cycle	1,000	2,000	3,750
GRISWOLD *(United States, 1907)*						
1907		2 cyl.	Runabout	3,000	7,500	15,500
1907	15	2 cyl.	Tonneau	2,250	6,000	14,000
1907	20	2 cyl.	Runabout	2,500	6,500	14,500
GRONINGER *(Netherlands, 1898–99)*						
1898			Dos-a-dos	1,500	4,400	9,500
1899			Dos-a-dos	1,600	4,500	10,000
GROUT *(United States, 1900–1912)*						
1901		Steam	Standope	6,500	15,000	29,000
1904		Steam	Surrey	6,500	15,000	29,000
1912	35	4 cyl.	Touring	7,500	12,000	21,000
G.S.M. *(ZA; Great Britain, 1958–66)*						
1958		Ford 105 E	Sport Racing	1,000	1,900	5,000
1960		Ford 105 E	Sport Coupe	1,000	2,000	3,800
1962		Ford Ten	Coupe	1,000	2,200	3,000
1964	2 + 2	Cortina GT	Coupe	1,000	2,300	3,500
G.T.M. *(Great Britain, 1966)*						
1966		BMC Mini	Racing	1,000	2,500	4,000

YEAR	MODEL	ENGINE	BODY	F	G	E
GUERRAZ *(France, 1900–02)*						
1900		(Bolide)	Open	1,250	4,400	9,500
1900		(Aster)	Open	1,300	3,500	9,750
1901		(Buchet)	Open	1,300	3,500	9,750
1902		(Sonsin)	Vis-a-vis	1,300	3,500	9,750
GUILICK *(France, 1914–29)*						
1914		4 cyl. (Atlos)	Open	1,000	3,000	8,000
1914		4 cyl. (Ruby)	Open	1,200	3,200	8,200
1914		4 cyl. (CIME)	Open	1,000	3,000	8,000
GUTBROD *(Germany, 1949–54)*						
1949	Superior 600	2 cyl.	Coupe	900	1,800	3,500
1949	Superior 700	2 cyl.	Sport Roadster	1,000	2,000	3,750
1951	Superior 604	2 cyl.	Convertible	1,000	2,000	3,750
1951	Superior 704	2 cyl.	Convertible	1,000	1,900	3,700
GUY; LE GUY *(France, 1904–16)*						
1904		4 cyl.	Voiturette	1,700	4,500	10,000
1906		4 cyl.	Voiturette	1,500	4,300	9,600
1908		4 cyl.	Voiturette	1,600	4,400	9,700
1910		4 cyl.	Voiturette	1,400	4,200	9,200
GUY *(Great Britain, 1919–25)*						
1919		8 cyl.	Roadster	2,000	5,500	13,000
1920		V 8 cyl.	Touring	2,000	5,000	13,500
1921		4 cyl.	Roadster	1,500	3,800	10,000
GUYOT SPECIALE *(France, 1925–31)*						
1925	Speciale	6 cyl.	Racing	2,500	6,800	13,500
1926		6 cyl.	Touring	1,500	5,000	10,000
1927		6 cyl.	Saloon Sedan	1,000	2,900	7,000
1928		6 cyl.	Coupe de Ville	1,400	3,750	9,500
1929	Super Huit	V 8 cyl.	Racing	1,600	4,500	12,000
G.W.K. *(Great Britain, 1911–31)*						
1911		2 cyl.	Cycle	1,000	2,750	4,500
1913		2 cyl.	Cycle	1,000	2,750	4,500
1921		4 cyl. (Coventry-Simplex)	Open	1,000	3,000	8,750
GWYNNE *(Great Britain, 1922–29)*						
1922		4 cyl.	Touring	1,200	3,000	8,750
1923		1247cc	Sedan	2,000	2,600	6,250

YEAR	MODEL	ENGINE	BODY	F	G	E

H

HACKETT *(United States, 1917–19)*

YEAR	MODEL	ENGINE	BODY	F	G	E
1917		4 cyl. (G.B.&S.)	Touring	3,000	7,000	17,000
1919		4 cyl. (G.B.&S.)	Roadster	4,000	9,000	19,000

HAL *(United States, 1916–18)*

1916	12	V 12 cyl. (Weidely)	Roadster	4,400	15,400	36,000
1916	12	V 12 cyl. (Weidely)	Touring	6,000	15,000	35,000
1917	21	V 12 cyl. (Weidely)	Brougham	5,000	12,000	26,000
1918	Twelve	V 12 cyl. (Weidely)	Sedan	4,600	10,000	25,000
1918	Twelve	V 12 cyl. (Weidely)	Limousine	5,000	13,000	27,000

HALL *(United States, 1903–04)*

1903		2 cyl.	Touring	4,600	7,000	13,000
1904		2 cyl.	Touring	4,000	6,000	13,000

HALL *(Great Britain, 1918–19)*

1918		8 cyl.	Landaulet	2,200	6,200	12,000

HALLADAY *(United States, 1905–22)*

1905	B	4 cyl. (Oswald)	Touring	4,000	9,000	20,000
1910	J	4 cyl. (Rutenber)	Roadster	3,400	8,000	19,000
1912	6-50	6 cyl.	5 Passenger Touring	5,000	11,000	23,000
1914	40	4 cyl.	Touring	3,000	8,000	19,000
1922	Six-46	6 cyl.	Touring	4,000	9,000	20,000

HALLAMSHIRE *(Great Britain, 1900–05)*

1900		(Simms)	Runabout	1,200	3,200	8,000
1900		(Aster)	Runabout	1,300	3,350	8,500
1904		4 cyl. (Forman)	Runabout	1,400	3,500	8,800

HAMLIN-HOLMES; HAMLIN *(United States, 1919–29)*

1919		4 cyl. (Lycoming)	Touring	2,400	7,500	14,500
1928		(Lycoming)	Sedan	1,700	5,500	11,500

HAMPTON *(Great Britain, 1911–33)*

1911	12/16	4 cyl.	Sedan	1,000	2,750	6,500
1914		2 cyl.	Sedan	1,000	2,900	6,750
1915		2 cyl.	Cycle	900	1,800	4,500
1917			Cycle	900	1,800	4,500
1919		(Dorman 4KNO)	Sedan	1,200	2,000	6,800
1923		(Meadows)	Touring	1,300	3,500	8,800
1925	Hampton 12	(Meadows)	Sedan	1,000	1,900	5,800
1927		6 cyl.	Coupe	1,300	2,300	5,500
1928			Sedan	1,200	2,000	5,000
1929		6 cyl. (Meadows)	Touring	2,750	5,500	11,000

YEAR	MODEL	ENGINE	BODY	F	G	E
HAMPTON *(Great Britain, 1911–33) (continued)*						
1930	12/40		Sport	2,000	4,000	9,000
1931		8 cyl. (Rohr)	Touring	3,200	8,000	16,000
HANDLEY-KNIGHT; HANDLEY *(United States, 1921–22)*						
1921	A	4 cyl. (Knight)	Sedan	1,600	4,250	14,000
1922	B	4 cyl.	Sedan	1,800	4,500	15,000
1922		6 cyl. (Falls)	Sedan	1,750	4,500	15,000
HANOMAG *(Germany, 1924–39)*						
1924	Kommissbrot	1 cyl.	Coupe	1,000	2,600	6,250
1930	Garant	4 cyl.	Convertible	1,500	4,500	9,000
1930	Kurier	4 cyl.	Convertible	1,700	4,450	9,750
1931	Rekord	4 cyl.	Drop Head Coupe	1,000	3,500	8,000
1932	Sturm	6 cyl.	Sedan	1,000	3,300	6,500
1935	Sturm	6 cyl.	Touring	1,000	3,300	6,500
1939	Diesel	6 cyl. (Diesel)	Sedan	1,000	3,000	7,000
HANSA *(Germany, 1906–39)*						
1906		1 cyl. (DeDion)	Runabout	2,200	4,000	9,000
1907		4 cyl. (Fafnir)	Sedan	900	2,700	6,250
1911	D		Sedan	850	2,600	6,000
1911	E		Touring	1,900	3,700	8,250
1914	F		Sport	800	2,500	8,000
1914	Lloyd	4 cyl.	Sport	600	2,100	6,000
1929	Konsul	6 cyl. (Continental)	Sedan	700	2,300	6,500
1929	Senator	8 cyl. (Continental)	Sedan	1,000	3,800	8,500
1929	Matador	6 cyl. (Continental)	Sedan	700	3,500	7,500
1929	Imperator	8 cyl. (Continental)	Sedan	900	3,700	8,250
1934	"500"	2 cyl.	Coupe	800	1,500	3,000
1939	2000 Privat	6 cyl.	Sport	1,200	2,500	6,750
1939	3500 Privat	6 cyl.	Sport	1,200	2,500	6,750
HANSON *(United States, 1918–25)*						
1918		6 cyl. (Continental)	Touring	4,400	12,000	25,000
1925		6 cyl. (Continental)	Sedan	3,600	7,000	12,000
HANZER *(France, 1900–03)*						
1900		(DeDion)	Voiturette	1,300	3,600	9,750
1900		(Aster)	Runabout	1,200	3,200	7,500
1901		1 cyl.	Tonneau	1,000	2,900	8,750
1902		2 cyl.	Sport	1,250	2,500	7,500
HARPER *(Great Britain, 1905–26)*						
1905		1 cyl. (Cadillac)	Landaulet	2,200	4,300	8,500
1921	3-Wheel	1 cyl. (Villiers)	Cycle	900	2,750	4,500
1921		1 cyl.	Runabout	1,000	2,900	4,750

YEAR	MODEL	ENGINE	BODY	F	G	E
HARRISON *(Great Britain, 1971–72)*						
1971	Formula 2		Sport	1,700	3,400	6,750
1972	Formula 3		Sport	1,750	3,600	7,000
HARTMAN *(United States, 1914–18)*						
1914		4 cyl.	Roadster	2,600	7,000	15,000
1914		4 cyl.	Touring	2,600	7,000	15,000
HARVARD *(United States, 1915–21)*						
1915	4-20	4 cyl.	Roadster	2,800	10,500	21,000
1921		4 cyl.	Touring	3,200	13,000	26,000
HATAZ *(Germany, 1921–25)*						
1921		4 cyl. (Steudel)	Racing	2,300	5,500	10,000
HATFIELD *(United States, 1907–24)*						
1907	B	2 cyl.	Buggyabout	2,750	6,500	13,500
1908	B	2 cyl.	Buggyabout	3,000	7,000	18,000
1924	A-42	4 cyl.	Roadster			
			Touring	4,000	9,000	20,000
1924	55	6 cyl. (Herschell-Spillman)	Touring	3,600	7,800	16,500
HAUTIER *(France, 1899–1905)*						
1899		1 cyl.	Voiturette	1,500	3,500	8,500
1900		2 cyl.	Tonneau	1,500	3,500	8,500
1904		4 cyl.	Tonneau	1,600	4,500	9,000
HAWKE *(Great Britain, 1969–73)*						
1969	Formula Ford		Racing	1,650	4,300	7,500
1970	DL2		Racing	1,750	4,500	8,000
1970	DL 2 B		Racing	1,900	4,600	8,250
1971	DL 5		Racing	2,000	4,800	8,500
1971	DL 6 A/B		Racing	2,000	4,800	8,500
1971	DL 7		Racing	2,000	4,800	8,500
1971	DL 8		Racing	2,000	4,800	8,500
1972	DL 9		Racing	2,300	4,800	8,500
HAWLEY *(United States, 1906–08)*						
1907		2 cyl.	Runabout	2,600	6,800	17,000
1907		2 cyl.	Tonneau	3,000	7,000	17,500
HAYNES-APPERSON *(United States, 1898–1904)*						
1898		2 cyl.	4 Passenger Carriage	2,500	6,900	15,000
1902		2 cyl.	Surrey	2,500	6,900	28,000
1903		2 cyl.	Runabout	2,500	6,900	27,000
1904		2 cyl.	Touring	2,300	6,500	29,000
1904		4 cyl.	Touring	2,300	6,500	30,000

YEAR	MODEL	ENGINE	BODY	F	G	E
HAYNES *(United States, 1904–25)*						
1905	O	4 cyl.	Runabout	3,000	8,000	27,000
1912	Y	4 cyl.	Touring 72	4,000	11,000	28,000
1914	26	6 cyl.	Roadster	4,250	11,500	26,000
1916	40/41	V 12 cyl.	Touring	5,750	12,500	32,000
1920	45	6 cyl.	Limousine	4,500	11,900	22,500
1921	47	6 cyl.	4 Passenger Touring	5,500	13,000	28,000
1923	77	6 cyl.	Speedster	5,500	13,000	35,000
1925	60	4 cyl.	Sedan	3,800	5,500	12,000
H-B (H. BROTHERS) *(United States, 1908)*						
1908	High-Wheel	2 cyl. (Air-cooled)	Runabout	2,750	6,500	13,500
H-C *(United States, 1916)*						
1916	28	4 cyl.	Roadster		RARE	
1916	28	4 cyl.	Roadster		RARE	
H.C.S. *(United States, 1920–25)*						
1920	Series II	4 cyl. (Weidely)	Roadster	6,500	12,500	25,000
1925	Series IV	6 cyl. (Midwest)	Touring	7,000	15,000	32,000
H.E. *(Great Britain, 1920–31)*						
1920	14-20	4 cyl.	Touring	1,500	3,600	9,250
1922	14-40	4 cyl.	Sport	1,500	3,700	9,500
1927		6 cyl.	Sport	1,600	4,000	10,000
1929	16/55	6 cyl.	Sport Touring	1,500	3,900	10,000
HEALEY *(Great Britain, 1946–54)*						
1946		4 cyl. (Riley)	Sedan	1,000	2,800	6,250
1949		4 cyl. (Riley)	Touring	1,600	4,000	9,750
1951		6 cyl. (Riley)	Sport Sedan	1,800	3,750	7,000
1951	Silverstone	6 cyl. (Riley)	Sport	2,500	5,000	9,500
1952		(Austin)	Sport	1,400	3,200	8,000
HEBE *(Spain, 1920–21)*						
1920		4 cyl.	Touring	1,000	2,700	6,250
1920		4 cyl.	Sport	900	2,600	6,250
1920		4 cyl.	Sedan	850	2,500	6,750
HEIM *(Germany, 1921–26)*						
1921	8/40	4 cyl.	Touring	1,750	4,500	10,000
1922		6 cyl.	Sport	1,900	5,750	11,400
1924		6 cyl.	Touring	2,000	5,900	12,600
HEINE-VELOX *(United States, 1906; 1921–23)*						
1906	45	4 cyl.	Touring		RARE	
1921		V 12 cyl.	Touring		RARE	

YEAR	MODEL	ENGINE	BODY	F	G	E
HEINIS *(France, 1925–30)*						
1925		4 cyl. (S.C.A.P.)	Sedan	1,000	3,300	6,500
1926		8 cyl. (Lycoming)	Sedan	1,500	4,900	7,750
HEINKEL *(Germany, 1955–58)*						
1955	3-Wheel	1 cyl.	Bubble	850	1,750	3,250
HEJENSKIOLD *(Sweden, 1918)*						
1918		4 cyl.	Cycle	1,200	2,000	3,750
HELBE *(France, 1905–07)*						
1905		1 cyl. (DeDion)	Sedan	1,200	4,000	9,000
1905		1 cyl. (DeDion)	Sedan	1,000	3,800	8,600
1905		1 cyl. (DeDion)	Sedan	1,000	3,700	8,500
1907		4 cyl.	Sedan	1,200	4,000	9,000
HENDERSON *(United States, 1912–14)*						
1912		4 cyl.	2 Passenger Roadster	2,600	8,000	17,500
1913		4 cyl.	7 Passenger Touring	2,600	8,000	17,500
1914		6 cyl.	Roadster	4,000	10,000	22,000
HENNEY *(United States, 1921–31)*						
1921		6 cyl. (Continental)	Touring		RARE	
1921		6 cyl. (Continental)	Phaeton		RARE	
1931		8 cyl. (Lycoming)	Limousine		RARE	
HENROD *(France, 1898–1908)*						
1898	Simplon	1 cyl.	Voiturette	1,600	4,100	9,000
1900	12	2 cyl.	Racing	2,300	6,200	13,200
1902	24	4 cyl.	Racing	3,000	7,300	14,500
1906	32	4 cyl.	Racing	3,400	8,300	16,500
HENRY *(United States, 1910–12)*						
1910	35-L	4 cyl.	4 Passenger Touring	4,000	8,000	19,000
1911	24-K	4 cyl.	Roadster	3,000	7,000	18,000
1912	40-M	4 cyl.	5 Passenger Touring	4,000	8,000	19,000
HENRY J *(United States, 1950–54)*						
1950	Deluxe	4 cyl. (Willys)	2 Door Sedan	2,000	4,000	8,500
1951	Deluxe	6 cyl. (Willys)	2 Door Sedan	1,500	3,500	7,500
1952	Vagabond	6 cyl.	2 Door Sedan	1,400	3,500	7,500
1953	Vagabond	6 cyl.	2 Door Sedan	1,850	4,000	8,500
1954	Corsair	6 cyl. (Willys)	2 Door Sedan	2,000	4,000	8,000
HENSCHEL *(Germany, 1899–1906)*						
1899		4 cyl.	Sedan	1,250	2,500	7,750
1900		Electric	Coupe	2,100	7,250	14,500

YEAR	MODEL	ENGINE	BODY	F	G	E
HERALD *(France, 1901–06)*						
1901		1 cyl.	Voiturette	2,000	4,000	9,000
1901		2 cyl.	Voiturette	2,200	4,200	9,250
1902		2 cyl.	Voiturette	2,000	4,000	9,000
1904		4 cyl.	Voiturette	2,200	4,200	9,250
1906		4 cyl.	Voiturette	2,300	4,300	9,500
HERCULES *(China, 1902–03)*						
1902		1 cyl.	Tonneau	1,000	2,900	5,750
1902		2 cyl.	Tonneau	1,200	3,000	7,000
HERCULES *(United States, 1907)*						
1907	140	Electric	Runabout	2,900	8,500	16,000
1907	141	Electric	Landaulet	3,500	9,800	18,500
HERFF-BROOKS *(United States, 1915–16)*						
1915	4-40	4 cyl.	Roadster	4,000	8,000	19,000
1916	6-50	6 cyl.	Roadster	5,000	10,000	21,000
HERO *(Germany, 1934)*						
1934	3-Wheel	(D.K.W.)	Coupe	900	1,900	3,800
1934	3-Wheel	(D.K.W.)	Roadster	1,100	2,000	5,000
HERON *(Great Britain, 1904–65)*						
1904		2 cyl. (Aster)	Coupe	1,300	2,600	6,100
1904		2 cyl. (Aster)	Sedan	1,200	2,400	7,000
1904		2 cyl. (Aster)	Touring	1,500	3,800	8,500
1904		4 cyl. (Aster)	Coupe	1,200	2,400	6,800
1924		(Ruby)	Touring	1,700	4,250	9,400
1924		(Dorman)	Touring	1,700	4,250	9,400
1924		(Coventry-Climax)	Touring	1,650	4,300	9,500
1961	Europa	(Ford 105 E)	Gran Turismo			
			Coupe	1,750	3,400	7,000
HERRESCHOFF *(United States, 1909–14)*						
1909	20-A	4 cyl.	Touring	4,000	8,000	18,000
1911	25	4 cyl.	Touring	4,000	8,000	17,000
1914	6-40	6 cyl.	Roadster	4,200	8,500	20,000
HERTEL *(United States, 1895–1900)*						
1895	High-Wheeler	2 cyl.	Runabout		RARE	
HERTZ *(United States, 1924–27)*						
1926	D-1	6 cyl.	Sedan	3,000	7,000	16,000
1926	D-1	6 cyl.	Touring	3,800	11,000	22,000
HESELTINE *(United States, 1916–17)*						
1916	Shamrock	4 cyl. (Lycoming)	Roadster	2,300	7,500	15,000
1917	Shamrock	4 cyl. (Lycoming)	Roadster	2,300	7,500	15,000

YEAR	MODEL	ENGINE	BODY	F	G	E
HEWITT (United States, 1906–07)						
1907		V 8 cyl.	Touring	3,000	6,750	16,500
1907		1 cyl.	Open Touring	3,000	7,000	15,000
HEXE (Germany, 1905–07)						
1905		2 cyl.	Open	1,200	2,750	6,500
1905		4 cyl.	Open	1,300	3,000	7,000
1905		4 cyl.	Sedan	1,000	2,100	5,200
1906		4 cyl.	Touring	1,300	3,250	7,500
1907		6 cyl.	Touring	1,400	3,500	8,000
H.H.; HUTTIS & HARDEBECK (Germany, 1906–07)						
1906	10	(Ferna)	Sedan	900	2,400	4,750
1906	24	(Ferna)	Sedan	1,000	2,750	5,500
1906	28	(Ferna)	Sedan	1,200	3,000	6,000
HIGHGATE (Great Britain, 1903–04)						
1903		1 cyl. (Aster)	2 Passenger	1,100	4,000	8,000
1904		1 cyl. (DeDion)	2 Passenger	1,200	4,200	8,250
HIGHLANDER (United States, 1919–21)						
1921		6 cyl. (Continental)	Touring	2,000	7,750	16,500
1921		6 cyl. (Continental)	Roadster	2,200	8,000	16,800
HILLMAN (Great Britain, 1907–79)						
1907		4 cyl.	Open	1,750	3,400	8,000
1908		6 cyl.	Roadster	2,900	8,000	18,000
1913		2 cyl.	Drop Head Coupe	2,000	4,000	9,000
1914		6 cyl.	Coupe	1,900	5,000	11,000
1915		4 cyl.	Coupe	1,500	3,000	5,000
1920		4 cyl.	Sport	2,000	3,500	5,500
1923		4 cyl.	Drop Head Coupe	1,500	3,000	8,000
1925		4 cyl.	Drop Head Coupe	1,500	3,000	8,000
1926	Fourteen	4 cyl.	Drop Head Coupe	1,500	3,000	8,000
1928	Fourteen	4 cyl.	Drop Head Coupe	2,000	3,500	7,500
1931		8 cyl. 2.6 Litre	Coupe	1,500	3,000	7,000
1932	Minx	6 cyl.	Sedan	1,000	3,000	6,000
1933	Aero-Minx	6 cyl.	Sport	1,500	2,900	6,000
1936		6 cyl.	Coupe	1,500	2,500	5,500
1940	Fourteen	1.9 Litre	Sedan	1,500	3,000	5,500
1941		1.9 Litre	5 Passenger	1,000	3,000	6,000
1942		1.9 Litre	6 Passenger	1,000	3,000	6,000
1943		1.9 Litre	Coupe	1,500	2,500	5,500

YEAR	MODEL	ENGINE	BODY	F	G	E
HILLMAN *(Great Britain, 1907–79) (continued)*						
1944		1.9 Litre	Sedan	1,000	2,500	5,500
1945		1.9 Litre	Coupe	1,000	2,500	5,500
1946		1.9 Litre	Sedan	1,000	2,000	5,000
1947	Minx	1.9 Litre	Sedan	900	2,000	5,000
1948		1.9 Litre	Sedan	750	1,500	4,000
1949		1.9 Litre	5 Passenger	800	1,800	4,000
1950		1.25 Litre	Sedan	700	2,000	5,000
1951		1.25 Litre	Sedan	700	2,000	5,000
1952		1.25 Litre	Sedan	700	2,000	5,000
1953	Hardtop	1.25 Litre	Coupe	900	3,000	6,000
1954	Minx Calif.	1.25 Litre	Coupe	800	3,000	6,000
1955		1.25 Litre	Station Wagon	500	2,000	5,000
1956		1.25 Litre	Sedan	1,000	2,500	5,500
1957		1.25 Litre	Sedan	900	2,000	5,000
1958		1.25 Litre	Sedan	900	2,000	5,000
1959		1.5 Litre	Sedan	900	2,000	5,000
1960		1.5 Litre	Sedan	900	2,000	5,000
1961		1.5 Litre	Sedan	900	2,000	5,000
1962	Super	1.6 Litre	Sedan	900	2,000	5,000
1963	Super MKII	4 cyl.	Sedan	1,500	3,000	7,000
1964		4 cyl.	Sedan	900	2,000	5,000
1965		4 cyl.	Sedan	900	2,000	5,000
1966		1.7 Litre	Sedan	900	2,000	5,000
1967	Huskey	1.7 Litre	Station Wagon	900	2,000	5,000
HILTON *(United States, 1920–21)*						
1921		4 cyl. (Herschell-Spillman)	Coupe	3,000	6,000	12,000
HINDUSTHAN *(India, 1946–60)*						
1946	Ten	6 cyl. (Champion)	Sedan	375	1,750	3,500
1951	Oxford 14	6 cyl.		400	1,800	3,250
1959	Ambassador Mark 2	6 cyl.	Sedan	450	1,850	3,250
1959	Minor	6 cyl.	Sedan	425	1,825	3,200
HISPAKART *(Spain, 1966–70)*						
1966	29	(Bultaeo)	Racing	850	1,750	3,000
1966	35	(Ducati)	Racing	850	1,750	3,000
1966	40	(Montesa)	Racing	850	1,750	3,000
HISPANO-ARGENTINA *(Romania, 1940–41)*						
1940		6 cyl.	Sedan	1,750	4,200	9,250
1940		2 cyl.	Sedan	450	1,900	3,750

YEAR	MODEL	ENGINE	BODY	F	G	E
HISPANO-SUIZA	*(Spain, 1904–44)*					
1904	20	4 cyl. (T-head)	Touring	35,000	75,000	150,000
1907	30/40	6 cyl.	Voiturette	15,000	40,000	95,000
1908	60/65	6 cyl.	Touring	40,000	85,000	175,000
1910	40	6 cyl.	Sedanca de Ville	25,000	55,000	125,000
1910		6 cyl.	Touring	35,000	75,000	175,000
1914	16	4 cyl.	Sedan	15,000	30,000	60,000
1917	30	4 cyl.	Touring	30,000	75,000	150,000
1919	H 6 B	3.7 Litre	Sedan	15,000	25,000	50,000
1930	K 6 B	6 cyl.	Phaeton	60,000	150,000	300,000

Hispano-Suiza – 1925 "Model H6 Phaeton"

YEAR	MODEL	ENGINE	BODY	F	G	E
1930		3 Litre	Convertible Sedan	35,000	85,000	190,000
1935		3 Litre	Limousine	15,000	30,000	60,000
1937	K6	3.7 Litre	Cabriolet	50,000	100,000	250,000
1938		3 Litre	Touring Sedan	12,000	25,000	55,000
1940		8 Litre	Sedan	50,000	95,000	190,000
HISPARCO	*(Spain, 1925–28)*					
1925	BO	4 cyl.	Sport	1,200	3,600	7,250
1928	BO 2	4 cyl.	Sport	1,500	3,800	7,500
H.L.	*(France, 1912–14)*					
1912		4 cyl.	2 Passenger	2,000	3,900	8,800
1912		4 cyl.	4 Passenger Touring	2,000	4,000	9,000

YEAR	MODEL	ENGINE	BODY	F	G	E
H.L. *(France, 1912–14) (continued)*						
1914		4 cyl.	Landaulet	1,900	3,800	8,600
HOFFMAN *(United States, 1901–04)*						
1901		Steam	Stanhope	4,000	10,000	20,000
1903		Steam	Stanhope	4,000	10,000	20,000
1904		Steam	Stanhope	4,000	10,000	20,000
HOLCAR *(Great Britain, 1897–1905)*						
1897		2 cyl.	Runabout	1,000	4,000	10,750
1901		V 2 cyl.	Runabout	1,200	5,200	11,000
1904		V 4 cyl.	Touring	1,400	6,300	12,500
HOLDEN *(Australia, 1948 to date)*						
1948	FX	6 cyl.	Fastback Coupe	1,600	3,100	5,250
1954	FJ	6 cyl.	Coupe	850	1,750	4,500
1954	FX	6 cyl.	Sedan	850	1,750	4,500
1964	Premier	6 cyl.	Sedan	800	1,700	4,250
1964	Standard	6 cyl.	Sedan	750	1,500	4,000
1964	Special	6 cyl.	Sedan	875	1,600	4,100
1965	HD	6 cyl.	Coupe	850	1,700	4,300
1969	Torana	6 cyl.	Sedan	700	1,600	4,200
1969	Belmont	6 cyl.	Sedan	825	1,650	4,250
1970	Deluxe Kingswood	V 8 cyl.	Sedan	900	1,800	4,500
1970	Monaro	V 8 cyl.	Coupe	950	1,900	4,600
1971	Brougham	V 8 cyl.	Sedan de Ville	950	1,900	4,500
1972	Statesman	V 8 cyl.	Sedan	950	1,900	4,500
HOLDSWORTH *(Great Britain, 1903–04)*						
1903		Aster	Runabout	1,000	4,000	10,000
1904		Aster	Runabout	1,000	4,000	10,000
HOLLAND *(United States, 1898–1908)*						
1898		Steam	Runabout		RARE	
1898		1 cyl.	Runabout		RARE	
1902		1 cyl.	Touring Runabout		RARE	
HOLLIER *(United States, 1915–21)*						
1915		V 8 cyl.	Touring	4,000	12,500	25,000
1919	206	6 cyl. (Falls)	Touring	3,000	8,000	19,000
HOLMES *(United States, 1906–07)*						
1906	D	2 cyl.	Touring	3,000	7,000	16,000
1906	H	4 cyl.	Touring	3,200	11,500	22,500

YEAR	MODEL	ENGINE	BODY	F	G	E
HOLSMAN *(United States, 1903–10)*						
1903	High-Wheel	2 cyl.	Runabout	1,600	7,000	14,000
1905	High-Wheel	2 cyl.	Buggy Surrey	1,750	7,500	14,500
1910	H-11	4 cyl.	4 Passenger Touring	2,500	8,500	17,000
HONDA *(Japan, 1962 to date)*						
1962	Open	4 cyl.	2 Passenger	1,650	3,250	7,500
1964	S-600	4 cyl.	Sport Roadster	1,700	3,600	8,000
1966		Vert-twin	Roadster	1,600	3,200	7,400
1968	N 370	4 cyl.	Sedan	800	1,700	3,200
1969		4 cyl.	Coupe	800	1,750	3,500
1971	Z	356cc	Coupe	800	1,650	3,250
1973	Civic 1200	4 cyl.	Sedan	800	2,000	4,000
HONG-QI; HUNG-CH'I (RED FLAG) *(China, 1958–73)*						
1958		V 8 cyl.	Sedan	800	2,000	4,000
1958		V 8 cyl.	Convertible	1,200	3,250	7,500
1973		6 cyl.	Limousine	1,000	2,200	6,400
HOPPENSTAND *(United States, 1948–49)*						
1948		2 cyl.	Coupe	800	2,000	4,000
1949		2 cyl.	Convertible	1,000	2,300	4,500
HORBICK *(Great Britain, 1902–09)*						
1902		(M.M.C.)	Tonneau	1,000	2,400	6,750
1902		2 cyl.	Tonneau	1,000	2,600	6,500
1904			Tonneau	1,100	3,800	7,250
1904			Tonneau	1,100	3,900	7,800
1905	Minor	3 cyl.	Touring	1,200	3,750	8,500
1905	Major	4 cyl.	Touring	1,300	3,750	9,500
HORCH *(Germany, 1900–39)*						
1900		2 cyl.	Roadster	4,000	8,750	17,500
1901	10/12	2 cyl.	Sedan	2,100	3,500	9,500
1902	16/20	4 cyl.	Sedan	3,100	3,500	9,500
1904	18/22	4 cyl.	Sedan	3,100	3,500	9,500
1906		6 cyl.	Roadster	5,250	14,500	32,500
1906	6/18	4 cyl.	Touring	4,500	12,000	24,000
1924	300	8 cyl.	Sedan	3,000	7,750	17,000
1927	305	8 cyl.	Sedan	3,000	7,750	17,000
1927	306	8 cyl.	Roadster	8,500	15,000	48,000
1928	375	8 cyl.	Touring	9,000	18,000	43,000
1929	400	8 cyl.	Touring	9,500	20,000	45,000
1929	405	8 cyl.	Touring	9,500	20,000	45,000
1930	450	8 cyl.	Touring	10,000	22,000	48,000

YEAR	MODEL	ENGINE	BODY	F	G	E
HORCH *(Germany, 1900–39) (continued)*						
1932	670	V 12 cyl.	Drop Head			
			Coupe	15,000	25,000	55,000
1932		V 12 cyl.	Cabriolet	17,000	40,000	90,000
1937		V 12 cyl.	Cabriolet	12,000	37,500	85,000
1938		V 12 cyl.	Cabriolet	11,500	35,000	80,000
1939		V 12 cyl.	Sport			
			Cabriolet	10,500	25,000	70,000
HORLEY *(Great Britain, 1904–07)*						
1904		1 cyl.	Runabout	1,500	4,000	8,000
1906		1 cyl.	Runabout	1,500	4,000	7,800
1907		2 cyl.	Runabout	2,100	5,100	10,000
HORSE SHOE *(France, 1908)*						
1908		1 cyl.	2 Passenger	1,200	3,000	8,000
1908		2 cyl.	Touring	1,400	4,200	9,250
HORSTMANN *(Great Britain, 1914–29)*						
1914		4 cyl.	Sport	1,400	5,200	10,000
1919		(Coventry-Simplex)	Super Sport	1,600	5,500	11,000
1923	12/30	(Anzani)	Touring	1,600	5,000	11,000
1924	9/20	(Coventry-Simplex)	Racing	3,000	6,750	16,500
1928	9/25	(Anzani)	Racing	3,000	6,750	16,500
HOTCHKISS *(France, 1903–55)*						
1903		4 cyl. (T-head)	Racing	2,250	7,500	14,000
1904		4.6 Litre	Racing	2,250	7,500	14,750
1905		7.4 Litre	Touring	3,000	8,000	17,000
1906			Racing	3,000	8,000	17,800
1907		15.3 Litre	Racing	4,750	13,250	26,500
1908	20/30	4 cyl.	Landaulet	2,200	5,100	10,250
1910	30	4 cyl.	Brougham	1,950	4,900	9,750
1911	42	6 cyl.	Touring	2,000	6,000	13,000
1912	AB	3.7 Litre	Racing	2,000	6,000	13,800
1914	AC 6	6 cyl.	Racing	1,900	6,750	13,500
1921	AH	6 cyl.	Racing	1,900	6,750	13,500
1923	AL	6 cyl.	Racing	1,900	6,800	13,500
1924	AK	6 cyl.	Racing	1,900	6,800	13,500
1926	AM	4 cyl.	Racing	1,900	6,400	13,750
1927	AM 2	6 cyl.	Racing	1,850	6,650	13,250
1931	AM 80	6 cyl.	Touring	1,850	6,650	13,250
1934	15 CV	3 Litre	Sport	1,900	6,750	13,500
1939		3 Litre	Limousine	1,750	6,500	13,000
1940	B-67	1.3 Litre	Racing	1,500	6,000	12,000
1949	686	3.5 Litre	Racing	1,500	6,000	12,000
1951	Gregoire	2 Litre	Sedan	1,700	6,300	12,500

YEAR	MODEL	ENGINE	BODY	F	G	E
HOUPT; HOUPT-ROCKWELL *(United States, 1909–12)*						
1909	60	4 cyl.	Limousine	2,500	8,000	16,000
1909	90	6 cyl.	Landaulet	2,750	8,500	17,000
1910	90	6 cyl.	Touring	2,900	9,000	18,000
HOWARD *(United States, 1895–1908)*						
1903	1	2 cyl.	Runabout	2,400	7,750	13,500
1903	3	3 cyl.	Touring	3,000	7,000	15,000
1904	4	4 cyl.	Coupe	2,500	8,000	16,000
1904	4	4 cyl.	Tonneau	2,750	8,500	16,500
H.R.G. *(Great Britain, 1936–56)*						
1936		4 cyl. (Meadows)	Sport	2,000	5,000	8,000
1939		4 cyl. (Singer)	Coupe	1,900	4,000	7,500
1948		4 cyl. (Singer)	Racing	1,900	6,000	14,000
1950	1100	4 cyl. (Singer)	Racing	2,000	6,000	14,000
1953	12 WS	(Singer)	Sport	1,200	2,000	4,000
1955		V 12 cyl.	Sport	3,000	8,000	18,800
HUDLASS *(Great Britain, 1897–1902)*						
1897		V 2 cyl.	Dogcart	2,200	4,400	10,000
1900		1 cyl.	Doctor Coupe	1,500	3,750	7,500
1902		1 cyl.	Coupe	1,000	3,000	7,000
1902		1 cyl.	Coupe	1,100	3,200	7,100

Hudson – 1913 "Touring"

YEAR	MODEL	ENGINE	BODY	F	G	E
HUDSON *(United States, 1910–57)*						
1909	20	4 cyl.	Roadster	6,500	13,000	29,000
1910	20	4 cyl.	Roadster	7,000	15,000	28,000
1911	33	4 cyl.	Touring	5,000	12,000	26,000
1912	33	4 cyl.	Coupe	7,000	14,000	31,000
1912	33	4 cyl.	Limousine	5,000	11,000	27,000
1912	33	4 cyl.	Roadster	8,000	17,000	33,000
1912	33	4 cyl.	Touring	6,000	14,000	32,000
1913	37	4 cyl.	Touring	6,000	14,000	32,000
1913	37	4 cyl.	Roadster	9,000	16,000	30,000
1913	37	4 cyl.	Coupe	3,300	10,000	23,000
1913	37	4 cyl.	Limousine	5,000	12,000	26,000
1913	54	6 cyl.	2 Passenger Roadster	10,000	18,000	32,000
1913	54	6 cyl.	Touring Roadster	9,000	19,000	33,000
1913	54	6 cyl.	5 Passenger Roadster	10,000	18,000	32,000
1914	40	6 cyl.	Touring	5,000	14,000	29,000
1914	54	6 cyl.	7 Passenger Touring	8,000	17,000	30,000
1915	40	6 cyl.	Touring	4,500	13,000	27,000
1915	40	6 cyl.	Roadster	8,000	15,000	26,000
1915	40	6 cyl.	Phaeton	7,000	14,000	28,000
1915	54	6 cyl.	Sedan	3,300	7,000	17,000
1915	54	6 cyl.	Phaeton	8,000	15,000	30,000
1916	Super Six	6 cyl.	Touring Sedan	4,500	7,400	15,000
1916	Super Six	6 cyl.	Roadster	8,000	14,000	24,000
1917	Super Six	6 cyl.	Touring Sedan	2,900	7,000	15,000
1917	Super Six	6 cyl.	Cabriolet	8,000	15,000	25,000
1917	Super Six	6 cyl.	Roadster	6,000	12,000	22,000
1917	Super Six	6 cyl.	Phaeton	6,000	12,000	24,000
1917	Super Six	6 cyl.	Town Car	3,000	8,000	16,000
1918	Super Six	6 cyl.	Touring Sedan	4,000	8,000	16,000
1918	Super Six	6 cyl.	Roadster	5,000	10,000	20,000
1918	Super Six	6 cyl.	5 Passenger Phaeton	5,000	11,000	22,000
1918	Super Six	6 cyl.	Sedan	3,000	6,000	14,000
1918	Super Six	6 cyl.	Coupe	4,000	7,000	13,000
1919	Super Six	6 cyl.	Touring Limousine	3,000	5,000	10,000

YEAR	MODEL	ENGINE	BODY	F	G	E
HUDSON (United States, 1910–57) (continued)						
1919	Super Six	6 cyl.	Sedan	1,200	3,000	9,000
1919	Super Six	6 cyl.	7 Passenger Phaeton	4,000	9,000	19,000
1919	Super Six	6 cyl.	Cabriolet	5,000	9,000	17,000
1920	Super Six	6 cyl.	Cabriolet	3,800	8,000	14,000
1920	Super Six	6 cyl.	Coupe	1,200	3,000	9,000
1920	Super Six	6 cyl.	7 Passenger Phaeton	4,000	8,000	19,000
1921	Super Six	6 cyl.	4 Passenger Phaeton	4,500	9,000	18,000
1921	Super Six	6 cyl.	Sedan	1,200	3,000	7,000
1921	Super Six	6 cyl.	Coupe	1,500	3,500	8,000
1921	Super Six	6 cyl.	7 Passenger Phaeton	4,000	9,000	19,000
1922	Super Six	6 cyl.	Coupe	1,900	3,600	8,000
1922	Super Six	6 cyl.	Sedan	1,000	2,800	7,000
1922	Super Six	6 cyl.	2 Door Sedan	1,100	2,900	7,200
1922	Super Six	6 cyl.	Cabriolet	4,000	8,000	14,000
1923	Super Six	6 cyl.	7 Passenger Sedan	2,000	4,000	8,000
1923	Super Six	6 cyl.	Sedan	1,200	3,000	7,000
1923	Super Six	6 cyl.	Coupe	1,500	3,400	9,500
1923	Super Six	6 cyl.	Phaeton	4,000	9,000	18,000
1924	Super Six	6 cyl.	Phaeton	4,000	9,000	18,000
1924	Super Six	6 cyl.	Sedan	1,200	3,000	8,000
1924	Super Six	6 cyl.	Phaeton	4,000	8,000	16,000
1924	Super Six	6 cyl.	Speedster	5,000	9,000	17,000
1925	Super Six	6 cyl.	Sedan	1,200	3,000	9,000
1925	Super Six	6 cyl.	Phaeton	4,000	8,000	17,000
1925	Super Six	6 cyl.	Brougham	1,600	3,500	10,000
1926	Super Six	6 cyl.	Brougham	2,450	4,000	10,000
1927	Standard Six	6 cyl.	Phaeton	3,800	6,300	18,000
1927	Standard Six	6 cyl.	Brougham	1,200	3,000	9,000
1927	Super Six	6 cyl.	Sedan	2,000	4,000	11,000
1927	Super Six	6 cyl.	Brougham	3,300	7,000	15,500
1927	Standard Six	6 cyl.	7 Passenger Sedan	2,500	3,800	9,000
1928	First	6 cyl.	Roadster	5,000	10,000	21,000
1929	Greater Hudson	6 cyl.	Boattail Roadster	8,800	17,000	35,000
1930	Great Eight	8 cyl.	Dual Cowl Phaeton	8,500	19,000	39,000
1930	Great Eight	8 cyl.	Roadster	9,000	19,000	36,000

YEAR	MODEL	ENGINE	BODY	F	G	E
HUDSON *(United States, 1910–57) (continued)*						
1930	Great Eight	8 cyl.	Sedan	2,300	3,700	10,500
1930	Great Eight	8 cyl.	Brougham	3,000	7,000	14,000
1931	Greater Eight	8 cyl.	Roadster	9,600	16,000	40,000
1931	Greater Eight	8 cyl.	Sedan	1,200	3,000	9,000
1931	Greater Eight	8 cyl.	Phaeton	10,000	20,000	46,000
1931	Great Eight	8 cyl.	Touring Sedan	2,600	4,500	11,250
1931	Great Eight	8 cyl.	Phaeton	8,750	17,500	39,000
1931	Great Eight	8 cyl.	Brougham	3,000	7,000	14,000
1932	Standard	6 cyl.	Convertible	4,500	14,000	30,000
1933	Sterling	6 cyl.	Special Sedan	2,700	4,300	12,500

Hudson – 1933 "Terriplane"

1933	Major	6 cyl.	7 Passenger Sedan	3,000	5,900	13,000
1934	Special	6 cyl.	Coupe	2,000	4,000	8,000
1935	Custom	8 cyl.	Sedan Cabriolet	3,800	6,300	17,000
1936	Custom	8 cyl.	RS Coupe	1,000	2,800	7,000
1936	Custom	6 cyl.	Coupe	2,200	4,000	8,000

YEAR	MODEL	ENGINE	BODY	F	G	E
HUDSON (United States, 1910–57) (continued)						
1936	Custom	8 cyl.	Convertible	8,000	16,000	30,000
1937	Custom	6 cyl.	Sedan	2,400	4,000	7,000
1937	Custom	6 cyl.	Convertible	8,000	16,000	30,000
1937	Custom	6 cyl.	Coupe	3,000	4,000	8,000
1938	Country Club	8 cyl.	Sedan	3,000	6,000	12,000
1938	Standard 89	6 cyl.	Sedan	1,600	3,000	6,000
1938	Standard 89	6 cyl.	Brougham	1,600	3,000	6,000
1938	Standard 89	6 cyl.	Convertible	9,000	17,000	30,000
1939	Deluxe 112	6 cyl.	Sedan	2,300	3,700	8,000
1940	Deluxe 40	6 cyl.	Coupe	2,150	3,200	8,000
1940	Deluxe 45	8 cyl.	2 or 4 Door Sedan	2,500	6,000	14,000
1940	Traveler	8 cyl.	Sedan	1,600	3,000	8,000
1940	Country Club	8 cyl.	Coupe	3,000	7,000	14,000
1940	Super	8 cyl.	6 Passenger Convertible	7,000	14,000	26,000
1940	Country Club	8 cyl.	Sedan	2,000	5,000	11,000
1941	Deluxe	6 cyl.	Sedan	1,600	4,000	10,000
1941	Deluxe	6 cyl.	Convertible	7,000	15,000	26,000
1941	Super 11	6 cyl.	Sedan	1,600	4,000	10,000
1941	Super 11	6 cyl.	Coupe	2,000	5,000	12,000
1941	Commodore 14	8 cyl.	Sedan	2,150	5,000	12,000
1941	Commodore 14	8 cyl.	Convertible	9,000	17,000	30,000
1942	Commodore 22	8 cyl.	Sedan	2,500	5,000	10,000
Postwar Models						
1946	Super 6	6 cyl.	Sedan	1,200	3,000	8,000
1947	Super 6	6 cyl.	Coupe	1,200	3,000	9,000
1948	Super 6	6 cyl.	Convertible Coupe	4,000	10,000	21,000
1949	Commodore 6	6 cyl.	Sedan	2,500	5,000	12,000
1950	Pacemaker	6 cyl.	Coupe	3,000	5,000	10,000
1951	Hornet	6 cyl.	Sedan	2,000	5,000	12,000
1952	Hornet	6 cyl.	Sedan	2,000	4,000	10,000
1953	Super Jet	6 cyl.	4 Door Sedan	2,000	4,000	9,000
1954	Hornet	6 cyl.	Convertible	8,000	14,000	24,000
1954	Hornet	6 cyl.	Club Coupe	4,000	6,000	12,000
1954	Hornet	6 cyl.	Hollywood Hardtop	4,500	7,000	14,000
1955	Hornet	V 8 cyl.	Sedan	700	1,400	6,500
1955	Custom Hornet	V 8 cyl. (Hollywood)	2 Door Hardtop	2,500	5,000	11,000
1956	Hornet	8 cyl.	Sedan	1,500	4,000	9,000

YEAR	MODEL	ENGINE	BODY	F	G	E
HUDSON *(United States, 1910–57) (continued)*						
1956	Wasp	6 cyl.	Sedan	1,000	3,000	7,000
1957	Hornet Super	8 cyl.	Sedan	2,500	5,000	11,000
1957	Hornet		2 Door			
	Super	V 8 cyl.	Hardtop	3,000	8,000	15,000
HUFFMAN *(United States, 1920–25)*						
1920	R	6 cyl. (Continental)	Touring	2,500	8,000	17,000
1925		6 cyl.	Roadster	3,000	8,000	19,000
HUMBER *(Great Britain, 1898–1976)*						
1898	3-Wheel			1,100	2,100	6,250
1900	M.D.		Voiturette	1,000	2,000	6,000
1901		(DeDion)	Touring	1,000	3,000	6,750
1902		4 cyl.	Tonneau	900	2,800	6,600
1903		4 cyl.	Tonneau	1,000	2,900	6,750
1905	Humberette	3 cyl.	Runabout	600	2,200	6,400
1908	8/12	4 cyl.	Touring	750	2,400	6,750
1927	14/40	4 cyl.	Racing	1,800	5,600	10,250
1928			Sport			
			Touring	800	2,600	6,250
1929	16/50		Coupe	700	2,400	5,750
1930	Pullman		Coupe	700	2,400	5,750
1936		6 cyl.	Sedan	700	2,400	6,500
1937	Twelve	6 cyl.	Drop Head			
			Coupe	3,250	6,400	12,750
1939	Super Snipe	6 cyl.	Sedan	1,750	4,400	8,500
1952	Super Snipe	4 Litre	Sedan	1,650	3,200	7,250
1955		3 Litre	Sedan	1,500	2,900	6,750
1957		6 cyl.	Sedan	2,500	4,900	9,750
HUMPHRIS *(Great Britain, 1908–09)*						
1908	10/12		Tonneau	1,000	4,000	9,000
1908	12/14		Touring	1,100	4,200	9,750
1909	15/17		Touring	2,200	6,400	12,000
HUPMOBILE *(United States, 1908–41)*						
1909	20	4 cyl.	Runabout	3,500	11,000	22,500
1910	20	4 cyl.	Runabout	3,500	11,000	22,500
1911	20	4 cyl.	Coupe	3,500	11,500	23,000
1911	20	4 cyl.	Roadster	3,200	12,500	24,000
1911	20	4 cyl.	Touring	3,000	11,000	21,000
1911	20	4 cyl.	Torpedo	3,000	11,000	21,000
1912	20	4 cyl.	Roadster	3,200	11,400	21,500
1912	20	4 cyl.	Touring			
			Coupe	3,000	11,000	21,000
1913	32	4 cyl.	Touring	3,800	10,800	20,500

YEAR	MODEL	ENGINE	BODY	F	G	E
HUPMOBILE *(United States, 1908–41) (continued)*						
1914	32	4 cyl.	5 Passenger Touring	4,800	12,575	21,000

Hupmobile – 1910 "Model 20 Roadster"

YEAR	MODEL	ENGINE	BODY	F	G	E
1914	32	4 cyl.	Roadster	3,000	10,500	22,000
1915	K	4 cyl.	Touring	2,800	9,700	20,200
1916	N	4 cyl.	Touring	2,800	9,700	20,000
1917	N	4 cyl.	Touring	2,600	9,500	19,500
1922	R	4 cyl.	Touring	2,600	9,500	19,500
1923	R	4 cyl.	Sedan	2,200	8,500	16,000
1924	R	4 cyl.	Coupe	2,400	8,800	16,500
1924	R	4 cyl.	Touring	2,700	9,700	20,000
1925	R	4 cyl.	Touring	2,900	9,900	20,500
1925	E	8 cyl.	Sedan	2,200	6,000	12,750
1926	A	6 cyl.	Sedan	2,000	6,500	12,200
1927	E	8 cyl.	5 Passenger Sedan	2,200	6,000	12,800
1927	E	8 cyl.	Victoria	2,900	7,200	14,500
1927	E	6 cyl.	7 Passenger Sedan	2,200	5,800	11,250
1927	E	6 cyl.	Roadster	4,200	10,000	21,000
1928	A	6 cyl.	Coupe	2,500	6,500	12,500

YEAR	MODEL	ENGINE	BODY	F	G	E
HUPMOBILE *(United States, 1908–41) (continued)*						
1928	Century M	8 cyl.	Roadster	3,800	11,000	23,000
1928	Century M	8 cyl.	Sedan	2,200	4,000	11,250
1928	125	8 cyl.	Roadster	6,000	14,000	27,000
1928	125	8 cyl.	5 Passenger Touring	5,000	13,000	26,000
1929	M	8 cyl.	Roadster	5,000	13,000	28,000
1929	M	8 cyl.	Cabriolet	4,800	12,800	26,000
1929	A	6 cyl.	Sedan	2,300	4,500	11,250
1932	B-126	6 cyl.	Roadster Coupe	12,000	20,000	39,000
1933	I-326	6 cyl.	3 Passenger Cabriolet	10,000	21,000	38,000
1933	I-326	8 cyl.	4 Passenger Coupe	3,000	8,000	18,000
1934	427-T	8 cyl.	Coupe	4,000	9,000	20,000
1935	521-O	6 cyl.	Touring Sedan	2,800	3,000	6,500
1938	H	8 cyl.	Custom Sedan	2,200	5,800	12,800
1941	Skylark	6 cyl.	4 Door Sedan	3,000	5,000	9,000
HUPP-YEATS *(United States, 1911–19)*						
1911		Electric	3 Passenger Landaulet	3,750	8,500	18,500
1919	5	Electric	5 Passenger Coupe	3,750	8,500	18,500
HURST; HURMID *(Great Britain, 1900–07)*						
1900		2 cyl.		2,000	4,900	9,750
1900		4 cyl.		2,000	5,000	10,000
1906	30/40	6 cyl.		2,100	5,100	11,200
1906	10	2 cyl.		2,000	3,900	8,800
1907	15/18	4 cyl.		1,750	4,600	9,600
HURTU *(France, 1896–1930)*						
1896		1 cyl. (Benz)		2,000	5,900	12,750
1900		1 cyl. (DeDion)	Voiturette	2,000	5,000	11,000
1902		2 cyl. (Aster)	Tonneau	2,000	5,000	11,000
1906		4 cyl. (Aster)	Saloon Sedan	1,500	4,800	10,500
1914		4 cyl.	Tonneau	1,600	5,000	11,000
1920		4 cyl.	Touring	1,800	5,250	11,500
1930		4 cyl.	Sport	1,200	4,600	10,250
HUTTON *(Great Britain, 1900–05; 1908)*						
1900		(DeDion)	Voiturette	2,800	5,400	11,750
1900		(Aster)	Vis-a-vis	2,800	5,400	11,750
1904		4 cyl.	Coupe	2,200	4,400	9,500

YEAR	MODEL	ENGINE	BODY	F	G	E
HUTTON *(Great Britain, 1900–05; 1908) (continued)*						
1905		4 cyl.	Sedan	2,000	3,750	8,750
1905		4 cyl.	Touring	2,900	6,600	12,500
1908		4 cyl.	Racing	4,850	8,550	17,200
H.W.M. *(Great Britain, 1950–56)*						
1950		4 cyl. (Alta)	Sport	1,500	4,500	9,500
1950		(Jaguar D)	Racing	2,750	7,600	14,500
HYDROMOBIL *(Germany, 1903–07)*						
1903				2,300	5,400	9,750

I

YEAR	MODEL	ENGINE	BODY	F	G	E
IBIS *(France, 1907)*						
1907	8/10	2 cyl.	Open	1,200	4,000	8,000
1907	12/14	4 cyl.	Open	2,000	5,900	10,750
IDEAL ELECTRIC *(United States, 1910–11)*						
1902		Electric	Brougham	3,000	8,000	17,000
1909		Electric	Brougham	4,000	9,000	18,000
IDEN *(Great Britain, 1904–07)*						
1904		4 cyl.	Touring	1,100	4,250	9,500
1904		4 cyl.	Coupe	1,000	4,100	9,250
1905		4 cyl.	Touring	1,200	4,400	9,800
1907		V 2 cyl.	Landaulet	1,150	4,300	9,600
ILLINOIS *(United States, 1909–12)*						
1909		2 cyl.	Roadster	2,300	6,500	13,800
1912	G	4 cyl.	Tonneau Roadster	3,250	7,400	16,000
IMP *(United States, 1913–14)*						
1913		V 2 cyl.	Cycle Car	2,000	4,000	8,750
1914	11	4 cyl.	Roadster	3,000	4,000	10,000
IMPERIA *(Brazil, 1906–49)*						
1906	24/30	4 cyl.	Coupe	1,000	3,000	6,750
1909	28	4 cyl.	Limousine	900	4,800	8,600
1919		8 cyl.	Coupe	1,000	3,000	6,800
1919		4 cyl.	Racing	2,200	5,200	10,000
1947	TA-8	4 cyl.	Sport	1,750	4,250	9,400
IMPERIAL *(Great Britain, 1900–14)*						
1900	3.5 hp	1 cyl.	Vis-a-vis	1,500	4,000	9,000
1901	6 hp	2 cyl.	4 Passenger Tonneau	1,200	3,100	8,250
1904	3 hp	Electric	Landaulet	2,100	6,000	12,000
1914	8 hp	V 2 cyl.	Cycle	1,000	1,900	4,750

YEAR	MODEL	ENGINE	BODY	F	G	E
IMPERIAL *(United States, 1908–16)*						
1908		4 cyl.	Runabout	2,000	6,800	13,500
1912	51	4 cyl. (Rutenber)	4 Passenger Roadster	3,500	11,500	23,000
1913	44	4 cyl.	5 Passenger Touring	3,300	11,000	22,500
1914	33	4 cyl.	Touring Roadster	3,900	12,800	25,000
1915	56	6 cyl.	7 Passenger Touring	3,900	12,800	25,000
1916	64	4 cyl.	5 Passenger Touring	3,700	12,500	24,000
IMPETUS *(France, 1899–1903)*						
1899		(DeDion)	Voiturette	1,500	5,000	9,750
1901		(DeDion)	Voiturette	1,500	5,000	9,750
1903		2 cyl.	Voiturette	1,500	5,000	9,750
INDIAN *(United States, 1928–29)*						
1928		(Indian)	Town Car		RARE	
1929		4 cyl. (Continental)	Coupe		RARE	
INNES *(United States, 1920–21)*						
1921		4 cyl.	Touring		RARE	
1921		4 cyl.	Roadster		RARE	
INSTITEC *(Romania, 1954–55)*						
1954		2 cyl. (D.K.W.)	Sedan	750	1,200	2,500
1954		2 cyl. (D.K.W.)	Station Wagon	850	1,850	2,500
1954	Justicialista	V 8 cyl. (Porsche)	Sport Coupe	1,750	3,500	7,000
INTERMECCANICA *(Italy, 1967 to date)*						
1967	2 S	V 8 cyl. (Ford)	Convertible	2,100	4,250	8,500
1968	IMX		Coupe	3,000	6,000	10,500
1970	Murena GT	7 Litre	Station Wagon	1,900	3,800	7,000
1972	Indra	2.8 Litre		2,250	4,500	8,500
1972		5.4 Litre		2,450	5,500	10,000
INTERNATIONAL *(Great Britain, 1898–1904)*						
1898		1 cyl.	Racing	1,000	4,000	9,750
1898		2 cyl.	Racing	1,000	5,000	11,750
1899		2 cyl.	Racing	1,100	5,200	11,000
1901	Charette	6 hp (DeDion)	Phaeton	1,200	5,500	12,750
1903		4 cyl. (Aster)	Tonneau	1,150	4,300	9,500
1904	Portland	1 cyl. (Aster)	Tonneau	1,150	3,300	9,000

YEAR	MODEL	ENGINE	BODY	F	G	E
INTERNATIONAL *(United States, 1907–12)*						
1907	High-wheeler-A	2 cyl.	Runabout	3,000	7,000	15,000
1907	High-wheeler-B	2 cyl.	Farmer's Auto	3,200	7,250	15,500
1908	A	2 cyl.	Runabout	3,000	7,000	15,000
1910		2 cyl.	Buggy	3,200	7,400	15,750
1910	F	4 cyl.	Roadster	3,000	7,000	15,000
1911	J	4 cyl.	5 Passenger Touring	3,500	8,000	17,000
INTER-STATE *(United States, 1909–19)*						
1909	35	4 cyl.	5 Passenger Touring	2,900	7,600	16,000
1913	45	4 cyl. (Beaver)	5 Passenger Touring	4,000	10,000	22,000
1918	T	4 cyl. (Beaver)	5 Passenger Touring	3,200	8,500	20,000
INVICTA *(Great Britain, 1900–50)*						
1900		(Invicta)	Voiturette	2,250	4,500	9,750
1925		6 cyl. (Meadows)	Touring	3,450	6,500	13,000
1928		3 Litre	Drop Head Coupe	2,500	5,000	10,500
1930		4.5 Litre	Roadster	3,500	6,500	16,500
1930		4.5 Litre	Phaeton	3,750	7,500	18,000
1930		4.5 Litre	Low Chassis Coupe	3,500	6,500	12,500
1931	12/45	6 cyl. (Blackburne)	Sport Sedan	2,000	4,000	8,000
1933	12/90			3,500	7,500	15,000
1949	Black Prince	6 cyl. (Meadows)	Drop Head Coupe	3,000	6,000	12,000
IPE *(Germany, 1919)*						
1919	4/12	4 cyl.	Saloon Sedan	1,000	2,500	4,000
IRADAM *(Poland, 1925–39)*						
1925		600cc	4 Passenger	800	2,600	4,200
1925	Closed	600cc	4 Passenger	750	2,400	4,750
1935		2 cyl. 1000cc	Sedan	750	1,800	3,750
IRIS *(Great Britain, 1905–15)*						
1905		4 cyl.	Tonneau	1,600	4,000	9,800
1906		4 cyl.	Tonneau	1,800	4,200	10,200
1907	35	4 cyl.	Tonneau	1,800	4,200	10,200
1912		4 cyl.	Touring	1,600	4,000	9,800
1915	40	6 cyl.	Sedan	1,500	4,800	9,500

YEAR	MODEL	ENGINE	BODY	F	G	E
IROQUOIS *(United States, 1903–07)*						
1903		4 cyl.	Runabout	1,500	4,500	13,000
1905		4 cyl.	Tonneau	2,000	6,500	16,000
1907	D	4 cyl.	7 Passenger Touring	2,500	7,000	17,000
ISOTTA-FRASCHINI *(Italy, 1900–49)*						
1908		4 cyl.	Racing Voiturette	10,000	22,000	44,000
1909		4 cyl. (T-head)	Sport	12,500	25,000	50,000
1914	KM		Boattail Speedster	15,000	30,000	60,000
1914		4 cyl.	Touring	15,200	30,000	60,000
1922	Tipo 8	8 cyl.	Sport Touring	16,000	36,000	72,000
1923		8 cyl.	Touring	12,000	24,000	65,000
1925	50/100 hp	8 cyl.	Touring	14,000	33,000	70,000
1926	8 A	8 cyl.	Roadster	25,000	60,000	125,000
1926	8 A	8 cyl.	Cabriolet	27,000	74,000	140,000
1928		8 cyl.	Town	12,500	30,000	68,000
1928	8 A 4 Ps	8 cyl.	Convertible	26,000	69,000	140,000
1929	Special	8 cyl.	Convertible Coupe	35,000	85,000	200,000

Isotta-Franschini – 1929 "Convertible Coupe"

YEAR	MODEL	ENGINE	BODY	F	G	E
1929		8 cyl.	Limousine	15,000	28,000	81,000
1930	8 A	8 cyl.	Phaeton	35,000	85,000	200,000
1930	8 A	8 cyl.	Coupe	15,000	26,000	45,000

YEAR	MODEL	ENGINE	BODY	F	G	E
ISOTTA-FRASCHINI *(Italy, 1900–49) (continued)*						
1947	Tipo 8 C					
	Monerosa	V 8 cyl.	Sedan	9,000	17,000	33,000
ITALIA *(Italy, 1904–34)*						
1904		4 cyl. (T-head)		4,000	8,000	16,000
1906	Targa Florio		Touring	3,200	6,500	15,000
1908	14/20	2.6 Litre		3,000	6,000	12,000
1909	35	4 cyl.	Limousine	3,200	7,000	13,000
1921	50	4 cyl.	Sedanca de Ville	1,750	3,500	7,500
1922	51-F	6 cyl.	Racing	2,600	5,350	10,500
1925	61	6 cyl.	Sedan	1,400	2,750	5,500
1929		6 cyl.	Roadster	2,750	5,500	11,000
IVEL *(Great Britain, 1899–1906)*						
1899		(Benz)	Vis-a-vis	2,500	6,000	13,000
1900		2 cyl.	Landaulet	1,100	3,250	9,500
1906		2 cyl.	Vis-a-vis	2,200	5,400	10,800
IVERNIA *(Great Britain, 1920)*						
1920		4 cyl.	Large Touring	2,200	5,200	12,000
IZARO *(Spain, 1920)*						
1920		3 cyl.	Open	750	1,500	4,000
1920		4 cyl.	Open	950	1,750	4,500

J

YEAR	MODEL	ENGINE	BODY	F	G	E
JACK ENDERS *(France, 1914–20)*						
1914		2 cyl.	Touring	1,000	3,750	7,500
1916		4 cyl.	Sport	1,100	4,000	8,000
JACKSON *(Great Britain, 1899–1915)*						
1899		1 cyl. (DeDion)	Dogcart	2,250	4,500	10,500
1900		2 cyl. (Mytholm)	Sedan	1,500	3,000	7,800
1903		2 cyl. (DeDion)	Dos-a-dos	1,200	2,750	9,500
1905		2 cyl. (DeDion)	Dos-a-dos	1,200	2,750	9,500
1906		1 cyl. (DeDion)	Estate Wagon	1,000	2,600	7,250
1907		2 cyl.	Sport	1,000	2,750	7,500
1909	Black Demon	4 cyl.	Racing	3,000	6,000	16,750
1909		2 cyl.	Roadster	1,500	3,000	9,750
1911	12/15	4 cyl.	Touring	2,000	4,000	10,750
JACKSON *(United States, 1903–23)*						
1903	A	Steam	Runabout	4,000	11,000	22,000
1904	B	2 cyl.	Surrey	4,000	11,000	22,000

YEAR	MODEL	ENGINE	BODY	F	G	E
JACKSON *(United States, 1903–23) (continued)*						
1905	A	1 cyl.	Runabout	2,000	6,000	19,000
1906	C	4 cyl.	Touring	2,400	8,800	16,500
1913	Sultanic	6 cyl. (Northway)	7 Passenger Touring	3,000	6,500	20,000
1916	348	V 8 cyl. (Ferro)	Touring	5,000	14,000	30,000
1923	6-38	6 cyl.	Touring	4,200	9,500	23,000
JAEGER *(United States, 1932–33)*						
1933		6 cyl. (Continental)	Coupe		RARE	
JAGUAR *(Great Britain, 1922/1945 to date)*						
1935	SS90	2.7 Litre	Roadster	30,000	60,000	80,000

Jaguar – 1935 "SS 100 Convertible"

YEAR	MODEL	ENGINE	BODY	F	G	E
1935	SSI	2.7 Litre	Touring	14,000	25,000	55,000
1935	SSI	2.7 Litre	Saloon	6,000	17,000	35,000
1936	S-100	2.6 Litre	Drop Head Coupe	40,000	75,000	125,000
1936	SSI	2.7 Litre	Roadster	40,000	75,000	130,000
1936	SS-100	2.7 Litre	Touring	35,000	65,000	125,000
1937	SSII	1.6 Litre	Touring	7,000	19,000	36,000
1937	SS-100	3.4 Litre	Roadster	40,000	75,000	125,000
1938	SSI	2.6 Litre	Sedan	6,000	12,000	28,000
1938	SSI	2.6 Litre	Cabriolet	25,000	40,000	72,000
1938	SS-100	3.5 Litre (Supercharged)	Roadster	50,000	85,000	150,000

YEAR	MODEL	ENGINE	BODY	F	G	E
JAGUAR *(Great Britain, 1922/1945 to date) (continued)*						
1938	SS-100	3.5 Litre	Speedster	45,000	65,000	125,000
1939	SS-100	3.5 Litre	Drop Head Coupe	9,000	18,000	46,000
1940	SS-100	3.5 Litre	Saloon	4,000	7,900	17,000
1941	SS-100	3.5 Litre	2 Passenger	7,900	15,000	30,000
1946	Mark IV	1.8 Litre	Cabriolet	5,200	10,000	19,000
1946	Mark V	3.5 Litre	Sedan	4,000	8,000	18,000
1947	Mark V	3.5 Litre	Sedan	4,000	8,000	18,000
1948	Mark IV	3.5 Litre	Drop Head Coupe	12,000	20,000	45,000
1948	Mark IV	6 cyl.	Saloon	5,000	10,000	20,000
1949	XK 120	6 cyl. 3.4 Litre	Roadster	25,000	40,000	70,000
1949	Mark IV	6 cyl.	Drop Head Coupe	14,000	25,000	55,000
1949	Mark V	6 cyl.	Saloon	4,000	8,000	20,000
1949	Mark V	6 cyl.	Cabriolet	12,000	20,000	40,000
1950	Mark V	6 cyl.	Saloon	4,000	7,000	15,000
1950	XK 120	3.4 Litre	Roadster	25,000	40,000	70,000
1950	Mark V	6 cyl.	Convertible Coupe	20,000	35,000	60,000
1951	XK 120	6 cyl.	Coupe	10,000	20,000	45,000
1951	XK 120	3.4 Litre	Roadster	25,000	45,000	80,000
1951	Mark II	6 cyl.	Sedan	4,000	7,000	15,000
1952	XK 120	3.4 Litre	Coupe	14,000	25,000	50,000
1952	XK 120S	3.4 Litre	Roadster	30,000	45,000	85,000

Jaguar – 1953 "Newport Beach"

YEAR	MODEL	ENGINE	BODY	F	G	E
JAGUAR *(Great Britain, 1922/1945 to date)* *(continued)*						
1953	XK 120	3.4 Litre	Roadster	25,000	40,000	80,000
1953	Mark VII	6 cyl.	Saloon Sedan	6,000	12,000	22,000
1954	Mark VII	6 cyl.	4 Door Sedan	6,000	12,000	25,000
1954	XK 120-M	190 bhp	Roadster	17,500	30,000	55,000
1954	XK 120	3.4 Litre	Coupe	14,000	25,000	45,000
1954	XK 120	6 cyl.	Roadster	25,000	45,000	80,000
1954	XK 120	3.4 Litre	Drop Head Coupe	20,000	35,000	60,000
1955	XK 140	210 hp	Coupe	12,000	22,000	40,000

Jaguar – 1955 "Convertible"

1955	XK 140	6 cyl. 210 hp	Roadster	25,000	45,000	75,000
1955	Mark VII	6 cyl.	Saloon	5,000	10,000	20,000
1956	XK 140	2.4 Litre	Coupe	10,000	22,000	40,000
1956	XK 140		Roadster	25,000	50,000	80,000
1956	Mark VII	2.4 Litre	Sedan	5,000	10,000	21,000
1957	XK 140	2.4 Litre	Coupe	8,000	14,000	25,000
1958	Mark VIII M	3.4 Litre	Drop Head Coupe	6,000	10,000	18,000
1958	XK 150	3.4 Litre	Sport	15,000	28,000	50,000
1958	XK 150	3.4 Litre	Coupe	8,000	17,000	30,000
1958	XK 150	3.4 Litre	Roadster	20,000	35,000	60,000
1959	Mark IX	3.8 Litre	Sedan	6,000	12,000	25,000
1959	XK 150	3.4 Litre	Coupe	10,000	20,000	35,000
1959	XK 150	2.4 Litre	Roadster	12,000	22,000	45,000

YEAR	MODEL	ENGINE	BODY	F	G	E
JAGUAR *(Great Britain, 1922/1945 to date) (continued)*						
1959	Mark IX	3.8 Litre	Sedan	6,000	12,000	25,000
1960	Mark IX	3.8 Litre	Sedan	5,000	10,000	20,000
1960	XK 150	3.4 Litre	Convertible	15,000	25,000	45,000
1960	XK 150	3.8 Litre	Coupe	7,000	15,000	30,000
1960	XK 150	3.8 Litre	Roadster	18,000	35,000	60,000
1961	Mark IX	3.8 Litre	Sedan	6,000	12,000	25,000
1961	XKE	3.8 Litre	Coupe	6,000	12,000	25,000
1961	E Type	3.8 Litre	Roadster	10,000	20,000	40,000
1962	Mark X	3.8 Litre	Sedan	4,000	7,000	15,000
1963	Mark II	3.8 Litre	Sedan	5,000	10,000	20,000
1963	XKE	3.8 Litre	Coupe	10,000	20,000	40,000
1964	XKE	3.4 Litre	Roadster	20,000	40,000	60,000

Jaguar – 1964 "XKE"

YEAR	MODEL	ENGINE	BODY	F	G	E
1964	Mark II	3.4 Litre	Sedan	5,000	10,000	18,000
1964	XKE	3.8 Litre	Coupe	12,000	20,000	35,000
1965	Mark II	4.2 Litre	Sedan	3,000	8,000	18,000
1966	Mark II	4.2 Litre	Sedan	3,000	8,000	20,000
1966	XKE	4.2 Litre	Coupe	7,500	15,000	40,000
1967	XKE	4.2 Litre	Roadster	25,000	40,000	70,000
1967	420G	4.2 Litre	Sedan	3,000	8,000	20,000
1973	E Type	V 12 cyl.	Coupe 2 + 2	15,000	25,000	45,000
1974	E Type	V 12 cyl.	Roadster	30,000	50,000	80,000
1974	XK-E III	V-12	Convertible	20,000	30,000	50,000
1974	XJ6 II	I-6	Sedan	4,000	5,500	13,000
1974	XJ6L II	I-6	Sedan	5,000	6,500	14,000

YEAR	MODEL	ENGINE	BODY	F	G	E
JAGUAR *(Great Britain, 1922/1945 to date) (continued)*						
1974	XJ12L II	V-12	Sedan	7,500	9,000	16,000
1975	XJ6C II	I-6	Coupe	8,500	12,000	20,000
1975	XJ6L II	I-6	Sedan	6,500	10,000	16,000
1975	XJ12C II	V-12	Coupe	10,000	15,000	22,500
1975	XJ12L II	V-12	Sedan	9,000	11,000	21,000
1976	XJ6C II	I-6	Coupe	8,500	12,000	20,000
1976	XJ6L II	I-6	Sedan	6,500	10,000	16,000
1976	XJ12C II	V-12	Coupe	10,000	15,000	22,500
1976	XJ12L II	V-12	Sedan	9,000	11,000	21,000
1976	XJ-S	V-12	Coupe	9,000	12,500	20,000
1977	XJ6C II	I-6	Coupe	8,500	12,000	20,000
1977	XJ6L II	I-6	Sedan	6,500	10,000	16,000
1977	XJ12C II	V-12	Coupe	10,000	15,000	22,500
1977	XJ12L II	V-12	Sedan	9,000	11,000	21,000
1977	XJ-S	V-12	Coupe	9,000	12,500	20,000
1978	XJ6L II	I-6	Sedan	5,000	9,000	15,000
1978	XJ12L II	V-12	Sedan	10,000	16,000	23,000
1978	XJ-S	V-12	Coupe	7,500	12,500	20,000
1979	XJ6L II	I-6	Sedan	4,000	8,000	14,000
1,979	XJ12L II	V-12	Sedan	10,000	16,000	23,000
1979	XJ-S	V-12	Coupe	7,500	12,500	20,000
JAMES & BROWNE *(Great Britain, 1901–10)*						
1901		2 cyl.	Landaulet	1,250	4,250	9,500
1904		4 cyl.	Landaulet	2,000	5,000	11,000
1906	Vertex	6 cyl.	Landaulet	1,500	4,900	10,800
JAMOS *(Austria, 1964)*						
1964		2 cyl.	Gran Turismo Sport Coupe	1,100	2,250	4,250
JAN *(Denmark, 1915–18)*						
1915		4 cyl.	Sedan	950	2,900	6,750
1917		4 cyl.	Touring	1,000	4,000	10,000
JANEMIAN *(France, 1920–23)*						
1920		2 cyl.	Cycle	750	1,800	4,000
1923		V 2 cyl.	Cycle	800	1,800	4,250
JANSEN *(Netherlands, 1900–01)*						
1900		(DeDion)	Voiturette	1,000	3,000	8,000
1901		(DeDion)	Voiturette	1,000	3,000	8,750
JANVIER *(France, 1903–28)*						
1903		4 cyl.	Tonneau	1,750	3,500	9,000

YEAR	MODEL	ENGINE	BODY	F	G	E
JAWA *(Czechoslovakia, 1934–39)*						
1934	700	2 cyl. (D.K.W.)	Sport Roadster	450	1,900	4,750
1935	700	2 cyl. (D.K.W.)	Sport Coupe	350	950	2,500
1938	Minor I	2 cyl.	Roadster	450	1,900	4,750
1938		2 cyl.	Sedan	400	950	2,500
J.B. *(Great Britain, 1926)*						
1926		4 cyl. (Meadows)	Sedan	600	3,200	6,500
J.B.S. *(Great Britain, 1913–52)*						
1913		V 2 cyl. (J.A.P.)	Cycle	900	1,750	3,500
1914		V 2 cyl. (J.A.P.)	Light	900	1,750	3,500
1915		4 cyl. (Blumfield)	Roadster	1,250	2,900	6,750
1916		4 cyl. (Dorman)	Roadster	1,300	3,950	8,000
1950	Grand Prix	500cc (Norton)	Racing	4,450	9,900	21,750
JEANNIN *(United States, 1908–09)*						
1908	High-Wheel	Air-cooled	Buggy	2,650	8,250	16,500
1908	High-Wheel		Surrey	2,250	7,250	14,500
1908	High-Wheel		Runabout	2,250	7,250	14,500
JEANTAUD *(France, 1881–1906)*						
1881		Electric	Racing	2,200	7,400	14,800
1903		Electric	Coupe	1,700	4,400	11,800
1904	Petit Duc	2 cyl.	Runabout	900	2,750	6,500
1905		3 cyl.	Touring	950	2,900	6,750
1906		4 cyl.	Touring	1,000	4,000	8,000
JEECY-VEA *(Brazil, 1925–26)*						
1925		750cc (Coventry-Victor)	Touring	900	2,800	7,500
1926		750cc (Coventry-Victor)	Cabriolet	950	2,900	7,750
JEEP *(United States, 1963 to date)*						
1963		4 cyl.	Station Wagon	1,000	3,000	6,000
1963		6 cyl.	Station Wagon	2,500	3,000	6,500
1965	Wagoneer	V 8 cyl.	Station Wagon	2,500	3,000	6,500
1965	Universal	4 cyl. (Perkins) Diesel	Station Wagon	1,000	2,600	5,000
1965	Universal	V 6 cyl. (Buick)	Station Wagon	1,500	3,000	6,000
1968	Jeepster	V 6 cyl.	Convertible	2,500	3,550	7,000
1971	Jeepster	4 cyl.	Convertible	1,500	2,250	5,250

YEAR	MODEL	ENGINE	BODY	F	G	E
JEEP *(United States, 1963 to date) (continued)*						
1971	Jeepster	V 6 cyl.	Convertible	2,250	3,300	7,000
1972	Jeepster	V 6 cyl.	Station Wagon	1,250	2,250	4,000
1972	Jeepster	V 8 cyl.	Roadster	2,300	3,450	6,250
1972	Jeepster	V 6 cyl.	Convertible	1,400	2,500	6,000
JEFFERY *(Great Britain, 1968–71)*						
1968	Mark I	(Ford)	Sport Racing	1,650	3,250	6,500
1969	Mark 2	(Ford)	Sport Racing	1,650	3,250	6,500
1970	Mark 3	(Ford)	Sport Racing	1,850	3,500	7,500
JENATZY *(Brazil, 1898–1903)*						
1898		Electric	Dos-a-dos	1,150	4,250	8,500
1901	12/15	(Mors)	Racing	1,500	5,000	9,000
1903	20/28	(Mors)	Racing	1,500	5,000	9,000
JENSEN *(Great Britain, 1936–76)*						
1936	H	V 8 cyl. (Ford)	Sport Touring	7,000	15,000	35,000
1938	S	V 8 cyl. (Ford)	Sedan	3,000	8,000	20,000
1938	D C	8 cyl. (Meadows)	Phaeton	6,000	12,000	30,000
1950		6 cyl.	Sedan	2,000	4,000	10,000
1950	Interceptor	6 cyl. (Austin)	Cabriolet	4,000	7,000	15,000
1954	541	6 cyl.	Gran Turismo Sedan	4,000	8,000	16,000
1963		V 8 cyl. (Chrysler)	Coupe	3,000	7,000	16,000
1966	F F	6.3 Litre	Coupe	2,500	9,000	20,000
1969	Director	V 8 cyl.	Limousine	3,000	8,000	18,000
1974	Interceptor	V 8 cyl.	Coupe	4,000	9,000	20,000
1974	Interceptor	V 8 cyl.	Convertible	8,000	15,000	27,000

Jensen – 1974 "Interceptor"

YEAR	MODEL	ENGINE	BODY	F	G	E
JENSEN-HEALEY *(Great Britain, 1972–75)*						
1972	2 S	4 cyl. (Lotus)	Roadster	1,100	2,250	4,500
1973	JH-5		Roadster	2,000	3,550	5,500
JEWEL *(United States, 1906–09)*						
1906	B/C	1 cyl.	Runabout	2,750	6,500	13,000
1907	D	1 cyl.	Runabout	2,900	6,750	13,500
1908	40	4 cyl. (Rutenber)	Touring			
			Roadster	3,000	7,000	15,000
1909	G	4 cyl. (Rutenber)	Touring	3,150	7,250	15,500
JEWEL *(Great Britain, 1921–39)*						
1921		2 cyl. (Precision)	Cycle	700	2,400	3,750
1922		2 cyl. (Coventry-Simplex)	Cycle	700	2,400	3,750
1923		2 cyl. (Coventry-Simplex)	Sedan	1,000	2,200	4,500
1924	Meadows	4 cyl.	Touring	1,500	3,200	8,500
1935	Meadows	4 cyl.	Sedan	1,000	1,900	4,250
JEWETT *(United States, 1922–27)*						
1922		6 cyl.	Touring	2,150	7,200	16,500
1923		6 cyl.	Roadster	2,400	8,750	17,500
1924		6 cyl.	Touring	2,000	8,000	17,000
1925		6 cyl.	Sedan	1,150	3,250	8,500
1926		6 cyl.	Deluxe Touring	2,150	8,250	17,500
J.L. *(Great Britain, 1920)*						
1920		4 cyl.	Sport	1,100	3,400	6,750
JOEL *(Great Britain, 1899–1902)*						
1899		Electric	Voiturette	3,000	7,500	15,000
1900		Electric	Cabriolet	1,900	3,800	8,000
JOHNSON *(United States, 1905–12)*						
1905		Steam	Limousine	3,500	11,000	22,000
1907		Steam	Open Touring	3,500	11,000	22,000
1912	A	4 cyl.	Touring	2,150	9,250	18,500
JONES *(United States, 1914–20)*						
1914		6 cyl.	Touring	3,500	11,000	20,000
1917		6 cyl.	Roadster	3,900	12,500	18,000
1918	Sport	6 cyl.	5 Passenge Touring	4,500	8,000	18,000
1920		6 cyl.	Speedster	3,500	10,500	23,000
JONES-CORBIN *(United States, 1903–07)*						
1903		1 cyl. (DeDion)	Runabout	2,000	6,000	13,000
1904		1 cyl.	Runabout	2,150	6,250	13,500

YEAR	MODEL	ENGINE	BODY	F	G	E
JONES-CORBIN *(United States, 1903–07) (continued)*						
1905	B	2 cyl.	Tonneau	2,250	7,500	14,000
1906	L	4 cyl.	Tonneau			
			Touring	2,400	7,750	15,500
JONZ *(United States, 1909–12)*						
1909		3 cyl.	Touring	2,400	7,800	15,500
1910	O	2 cyl.	Roadster	2,500	9,000	18,000
1912	C	4 cyl.	Touring	3,250	11,000	22,000
JORDAN *(United States, 1917–31)*						
1917		4 cyl.	Touring	4,500	13,000	26,000
1919	C	6 cyl. (Continental)	Touring	5,000	14,000	27,000
1920	Playboy	6 cyl. (Continental)	Touring	5,500	14,500	30,000
1923	MX	6 cyl. (Continental)	Touring	5,000	12,000	25,000
1925	Line Eight	8 cyl. (Continental)	Playboy	5,400	14,000	28,000
1925	Line Eight	8 cyl. (Continental)	Brougham	4,400	11,750	23,500
1926	Line Eight	8 cyl. (Continental)	Sedan	4,000	9,000	20,000
1927	Great Line	8 cyl. (Continental)	Sedan	4,000	11,000	25,000
1927	Great Line	8 cyl. (Continental)	Victoria	6,000	12,000	26,000
1928	R	8 cyl. (Continental)	Cabriolet	10,000	18,000	32,000
1928	Blueboy	8 cyl. (Continental)	Roadster	7,000	14,000	28,000
1928	Series Z					
	Air Line	8 cyl. (Continental)	Roadster	5,000	11,000	22,500
1929	8JE	8 cyl. (Continental)	Sedan	4,000	8,000	19,000
1929	8JE	8 cyl. (Continental)	Coupe	6,150	13,250	28,500
1929	6RE	6 cyl. (Continental)	Blueboy			
			Cabriolet	10,000	18,000	35,000
1929	6RE	6 cyl. (Continental)	Sedan	4,000	10,000	22,000
1930	8T	8 cyl. (Continental)	Sedan	3,000	8,000	20,000
1930	8T	8 cyl. (Continental)	Coupe	5,000	10,000	25,000
1930	8G	8 cyl. (Continental)	Convertible			
			Coupe	5,000	13,000	28,000
1930	8G	8 cyl. (Continental)	Roadster	15,000	25,000	45,000
1930	90	8 cyl. (Continental)	Playboy	20,000	30,000	50,000
1931	90	8 cyl. (Continental)	Touring	6,000	15,000	35,000
JOSWIN *(Germany, 1920–26)*						
1920	25/75	(Mercedes)	Sedanca de Ville	1,900	3,750	8,500
1922	28/95	(Mercedes)	Sedanca de Ville	2,400	4,750	9,500
JOUFFRET *(France, 1920–28)*						
1920		(Ballot)	Touring	1,750	4,800	8,500
1922		(C.I.M.E.)	Touring	1,750	4,800	8,500
1925		(S.C.A.P.)	Touring	2,000	5,800	9,500

YEAR	MODEL	ENGINE	BODY	F	G	E
JOUSSET *(France, 1924–26)*						
1924	C.I.M.E.	4 cyl.	Sport Coupe	1,250	3,500	6,000
1924	Ruby	4 cyl.	Sedan	600	2,200	4,500
JOWETT *(Great Britain, 1906–54)*						
1906		V 2 cyl.	2 Passenger	1,200	2,800	7,750
1908		2 cyl.	2 Passenger	1,200	2,800	7,750
1923	Long Four		4 Passenger	1,300	3,250	8,500
1926			Sedan	1,000	2,150	4,250
1926			Touring	1,800	4,250	10,500
1929	Black Prince		Sedan	1,000	2,150	4,250
1929			Sport	1,100	2,200	5,500
1934	Kestrel		Sport Sedan	1,100	3,000	6,000
1935	Weasel		Sport	1,100	2,200	5,500
1935			Touring	1,200	4,500	11,500
1936	Ten	4 cyl.	Sedan	1,000	2,500	4,500
1937	Eight	2 cyl.	Sedan	1,000	2,100	4,250
1950	Javelin	4 cyl.	Sedan	1,000	3,500	4,000
1950	Jupiter	1.5 Litre	Sport	1,100	3,000	6,000
1954	Jupiter R4	1.5 Litre	Sport Racing	1,500	5,500	11,500
J.P. *(France, 1905)*						
1905	10/12	2 cyl. (Gnome)	Touring	1,000	3,000	8,000
1905	16/20	4 cyl. (Gnome)	Touring	1,500	4,500	9,500
1905	24/30	4 cyl. (Gnome)	Touring	1,800	5,300	10,600
J.P. WIMILLE *(France, 1946–50)*						
1946		V 6 cyl.	Sport Coupe	1,000	2,100	4,250
1949		V 8 cyl. (Ford)	Saloon Sedan	1,100	2,200	4,500
JUNIOR; F.J.T.A. *(Italy, 1905–10)*						
1905		1 cyl.	Voiturette	900	3,750	6,500
1906	12/14	2 cyl.	Voiturette	1,500	4,800	7,600
1909	16/20	4 cyl.	Voiturette	2,000	5,850	8,750
JUNIOR SPORTS *(Great Britain, 1920–21)*						
1920		4 cyl. (Peters)	Sport	1,000	2,100	4,500
1921		4 cyl. (Peters)	Sport	1,200	2,300	4,600
JUWEL *(Brazil, 1923–27)*						
1923		4 cyl.	Touring	1,500	3,100	6,750
1923		4 cyl.	Sport	1,600	3,300	7,000

YEAR	MODEL	ENGINE	BODY	F	G	E

K

K.A.C. *(Denmark, 1914)*

YEAR	MODEL	ENGINE	BODY	F	G	E
1914	6/16	4 cyl.	Roadster	950	1,900	6,750
1914	6/16	4 cyl.	Touring	850	1,800	6,500

KAISER *(Germany, 1911–35)*

YEAR	MODEL	ENGINE	BODY	F	G	E
1911		Electric	Coupe	2,900	6,750	13,500
1911		2 cyl.	Sport Coupe	1,950	3,900	8,750
1935	3-Wheel	1 cyl. (N.S.U.)	Cycle	900	1,650	3,250

KAISER *(United States, 1946–54)*

YEAR	MODEL	ENGINE	BODY	F	G	E
1947	Manhattan	6 cyl.	Sedan	1,550	4,000	9,000
1948	Custom	6 cyl.	Sedan	2,000	4,500	9,500
1949	Virginian	6 cyl.	Hardtop Sedan	5,000	12,000	24,000
1950	Deluxe	6 cyl.	4 Door Convertible	15,000	25,000	45,000
1951	Deluxe	6 cyl.	4 Door	2,000	4,000	10,000
1951	Deluxe	6 cyl.	Travel Sedan	2,500	4,500	11,000
1951	Special	6 cyl.	2 Door Sedan	2,000	4,000	10,000
1952	Manhattan	6 cyl.	Sedan	2,500	5,000	12,000
1952	Deluxe	6 cyl.	Club Sedan	2,000	5,000	11,000
1954	Manhattan	6 cyl.	Sedan	2,500	5,000	12,000
1954	Special	6 cyl.	2 Door Sedan	3,000	7,000	15,000
1954	Darrin	6 cyl.	Roadster	15,000	25,000	40,000
1955	Manhattan	6 cyl.	Sedan	2,000	5,000	12,000

KAISER CARABELA *(Romania, 1958–62)*

YEAR	MODEL	ENGINE	BODY	F	G	E
1958		6 cyl. (Willys)	2 Door Sedan	900	2,200	4,500
1960		6 cyl. (Willys)	Sedan	900	2,250	4,500

KAMPER *(Germany, 1905–06)*

YEAR	MODEL	ENGINE	BODY	F	G	E
1905		2 cyl.	Touring	1,200	3,750	7,500

KANSAS CITY *(United States, 1905–09)*

YEAR	MODEL	ENGINE	BODY	F	G	E
1905		2 cyl.	Roadster	4,500	9,000	17,000
1909		6 cyl.	Touring	8,500	18,000	30,000

KEARNS *(United States, 1909–16)*

YEAR	MODEL	ENGINE	BODY	F	G	E
1909	High-Wheel	2 cyl. (Speedwell)	Buggy	4,000	7,000	17,000
1910	L	3 cyl.	Roadster	4,000	8,000	16,000
1912	J	4 cyl.	Tourabout	4,000	8,000	16,000
1915	LuLu	4 cyl.	Speedster	2,650	6,250	13,500

KELLER *(United States, 1948–50)*

YEAR	MODEL	ENGINE	BODY	F	G	E
1948		4 cyl. (Continental)	Convertible	3,000	6,000	12,000
1948		4 cyl. (Hercules)	Sedan	2,000	4,000	8,000

YEAR	MODEL	ENGINE	BODY	F	G	E

KELLER *(United States, 1948–50) (continued)*

YEAR	MODEL	ENGINE	BODY	F	G	E
1949		4 cyl. (Hercules)	Station Wagon	1,600	2,900	7,000

KELSEY *(United States, 1920–24)*

YEAR	MODEL	ENGINE	BODY	F	G	E
1920	GW	6 cyl.	Touring	6,000	12,000	24,000
1922	GW	6 cyl. (Gray)	Coupe	4,000	8,000	16,000
1923	G	4 cyl. (Lycoming)	Sedan	2,000	5,000	12,000

KENNEDY *(Canada, 1909–10)*

YEAR	MODEL	ENGINE	BODY	F	G	E
1909	High-Wheel	(DeTamble)	Buggy	1,650	3,250	8,500
1909		(DeTamble)	Runabout	1,250	2,500	8,000
1909		(DeTamble)	Surrey	1,850	3,600	8,750

KENSINGTON *(United States, 1899–1904)*

YEAR	MODEL	ENGINE	BODY	F	G	E
1899		Electric	Stanhope	3,500	8,000	16,000
1899		Steam	Runabout	4,500	10,000	21,000
1904		2 cyl. (Kelecon)	Tonneau	3,000	7,000	16,000

KENTER *(Germany, 1924–25)*

YEAR	MODEL	ENGINE	BODY	F	G	E
1924		(Steudel)	2 Passenger	1,000	2,200	3,900
1925		(Atas)	4 Passenger	1,000	2,300	4,000

KENWORTHY *(United States, 1920–21)*

YEAR	MODEL	ENGINE	BODY	F	G	E
1920	4-80	4 cyl.	Touring	6,200	12,000	26,000
1920	6-55	6 cyl.	Touring	6,000	13,000	28,000
1920	8-90	8 cyl.	Touring	6,000	14,000	30,000

KEYSTONE *(United States, 1900–15)*

YEAR	MODEL	ENGINE	BODY	F	G	E
1900		1 cyl.	Autocycle	3,800	5,000	12,000
1909	Six-Sixty	6 cyl.	Touring	2,900	8,750	21,000
1910	Light Six	6 cyl.	Roadster	6,000	12,000	24,000
1915	Six-Sixty	6 cyl. (Rutenber)	Touring	4,000	11,000	22,000

KIBLINGER *(United States, 1907–09)*

YEAR	MODEL	ENGINE	BODY	F	G	E
1907	A	2 cyl. (Air-cooled)	Highwheeler	3,000	7,800	15,000
1909	F	2 cyl.	Highwheeler Roadster	3,500	7,000	16,000

KICO *(Germany, 1924)*

YEAR	MODEL	ENGINE	BODY	F	G	E
1924		4 cyl.	Runabout	1,500	2,600	5,750

KIET *(Great Britain, 1950–61)*

YEAR	MODEL	ENGINE	BODY	F	G	E
1950		500cc (Norton)	Sport	800	1,450	3,750
1951		1.5 Litre (MG)	Racing	1,500	2,100	4,750
1951		BSA (650cc)	Sport Runabout	450	1,500	3,250
1953		(Bristol)	Sport	1,750	3,500	7,000
1953		(DeSoto)	Racing	1,900	4,000	7,750
1954			Sport	1,250	2,900	5,750
1954		4 cyl.	Racing	1,250	3,750	7,500

YEAR	MODEL	ENGINE	BODY	F	G	E
KIM-10 *(Soviet Union, 1940–41)*						
1940		4 cyl.	Sedan	1,500	2,100	2,750
1941		1.1 Litre	Sedan	1,200	2,000	2,600
KING *(Great Britain, 1904–70)*						
1904		2 cyl.	Runabout	1,300	3,750	6,500
1957		Ford	Racing	1,550	4,100	8,200
KING *(United States, 1911–24)*						
1911	A	4 cyl.	Coupe	3,500	3,700	16,000
1915	D	V 8 cyl.	Touring	3,900	4,300	17,000
1916	D	V 8 cyl.	Sedan	5,000	8,000	18,000
1917	E	V 8 cyl.	Touring	4,500	9,000	21,000
1918	F	V 8 cyl.	Touring	4,200	9,000	21,000
1919	G	V 8 cyl.	Touring	4,200	8,000	21,000
1920	H	V 8 cyl.	Touring	5,000	10,000	22,000
1924	L	V 8 cyl.	Sedan	4,000	7,500	15,000
KING & BIRD *(Great Britain, 1903)*						
1903		(DeDion)	Dogcart	950	1,900	4,750
KISSEL *(United States, 1907–31)*						
1907	A	4 cyl.	Touring	3,000	7,000	18,000
1909	G9	6 cyl.	Roadster	6,000	12,000	22,000
1910	LD 10	4 cyl.	Touring	4,800	11,000	22,000
1912	30	4 cyl.	Touring	4,000	9,000	19,000
1913	40	4 cyl.	Touring	3,000	5,000	21,000
1917	Double Six	V 12 cyl. (Weidely)	Roadster	5,000	11,000	21,000
1918	Silver Special	6 cyl.	Speedster	6,000	14,000	30,000
1920	Custom Built	6 cyl.	Speedster Runabout	18,000	30,000	40,000
1922	Custom Built	6 cyl.	Sedan	3,000	7,000	15,000
1923	55	6 cyl.	Boattail Speedster	15,000	25,000	40,000
1923	45	6 cyl.	Sedan	3,000	6,000	14,000
1925	75 Deluxe	6 cyl.	4 Passenger Speedster	20,000	30,000	55,000
1926	55 Deluxe	6 cyl.	2 Passenger Speedster	15,000	25,000	50,000
1927	75	6 cyl.	7 Passenger Touring	9,000	20,000	46,000
1928	70	6 cyl.	Cabriolet	9,000	18,000	35,000
1928	8-90	8 cyl.	Sedan	4,000	9,000	20,000
1929		8 cyl.	4 Passenger Speedster	15,000	30,000	55,000
1929	8-95	8 cyl.	Coupe	5,000	12,000	28,000

YEAR	MODEL	ENGINE	BODY	F	G	E
KISSEL *(United States, 1907–31) (continued)*						
1929		8 cyl.	Sedan	4,000	9,000	21,000
KLINE KAR *(United States, 1910–23)*						
1910	6-40	6 cyl.	Runabout	2,400	7,750	14,500
1914	4-40	4 cyl.	Roadster	5,000	10,000	18,000
1920	6-55-J	6 cyl. (Continental)	Touring	4,000	9,000	18,000
1923	6-60-L	6 cyl. (Continental)	Touring	4,000	9,000	18,000
KNAP *(Brazil; France, 1898–1909)*						
1898	3-Wheel	1 cyl.	Voiturette	1,250	2,500	4,500
1899	3-Wheel	2 cyl.	Voiturette	750	1,500	3,000
1900	3-Wheel	4 cyl.	Voiturette	800	1,550	3,500
1900	3-Wheel	6 cyl.	Voiturette	950	1,900	3,750
KNIGHT OF THE ROAD *(Great Britain, 1902–14)*						
1902		1 cyl. (Aster)	2 Passenger	1,950	3,900	6,750
1904	Esculapius	5 hp (Ader)	2 Passenger	1,950	3,900	6,750
1913		4 cyl.	5 Passenger Touring	1,950	4,900	8,750
1913		4 cyl.	2 Passenger	1,900	4,100	7,500

KNOX 1903 MODEL
OPEN

Knox – 1903 "Model C Runabout"

NATIONAL AUTOMOBILE MUSEUM
Reno, Nevada

Featured in this section is a sampling of the holdings in a museum honoring the machines that have touched us all—The William F. Harrah Foundation **NATIONAL AUTOMOBILE MUSEUM.** Through these photographs, the reader can gain a sense of one of our country's newest Automobile Museums. The sensational new facility opened in 1989 with cars representing every era since they were invented.

A visitor will pass through a century of American street scenes and come face to face with the featured attractions—over 200 antique, vintage, classic, and special interest automobiles. Most of them are from the famous collection of gaming pioneer Bill Harrah. And this museum is just like the one he had always imagined—fun for families and fascinating for collectors.

You may wish to start with a theater presentation that traces the history of the automobile with all its humorous twists and turns, stop at the Changing Exhibits Gallery, where a new exhibit opens quarterly, and then check the Masterpiece Circle, themed exhibits of unique cars that are on loan to the museum.

To walk down the four authentic street scenes is like stepping back in time to the turn-of-the-century. Tour history from the blacksmith shop, which was really the first automotive repair shop, on through the 1930s Street and into the 1950s era of suburbia and shopping centers and onward into the future on the Modern Street. On every street, storefronts and creative graphic displays illustrate a century of society's changes brought to us by cars. The museum tells the great story of how the automobile has changed our customs and our society.

On the streets and in the four galleries, the cars are the stars. Some of the special interest cars include:

- The 1892 Philion, one of the oldest existing American-built automobiles which was featured in *Excuse My Dust* with Red Skelton and in *The Magnificent Amberson's* with Orson Wells;
- The 1907 Thomas Flyer, winner of the 1908 New York to Paris Race;
- The 1938 Phantom Corsair, the sleek and sinister star as the Flying Wombat in the 1938 film *The Young in Heart* starring Douglas Fairbanks, Jr.;
- The 1949 Mercury James Dean drove in the film *Rebel Without a Cause;*
- Elvis Presley's 1973 Cadillac Eldorado;
- John F. Kennedy's 1962 Lincoln Continental and;
- John Wayne's 1953 Corvette.

For those of you hooked by the cars you see in this section and lucky enough to visit the museum in Reno, additional treats are the specialty gifts and book shop *"Cruisin' for Gifts,"* and the restaurant on the river for lunch.

The museum is open every day, except Thanksgiving and Christmas Day, from 9:30 A.M. to 5:30 P.M., and is also available for evening receptions and group banquets. Research is available through the world-famous automotive library.

The National Automobile Museum is located at Lake and Mill Street in downtown Reno. For more information, write to them at 10 Lake Street, Reno, Nevada 89501, or call (702) 333-9300.

The National Automobile Museum, Reno, Nevada.

1938 Packard Model 1607 Convertible Coupe. Displayed on the 1930s Street in front of the Palace Theater.

1906 Adams-Farwell Model "A" Convertible Runabout. The only Adams-Farwell known to exist today, this automobile features a unique air-cooled engine and steering system.

1907 Thomas Flyer Model 35. Winner of the 1908 New York to Paris Race. Restored to the condition it was in when it finished its around-the-world odyssey.

1909 White Model "O" Touring. One of the last steamers offered by The White Motor Company of Cleveland, Ohio.

1910 Rolls-Royce Silver Ghost Tourer. One of the earliest Silver Ghosts known to exist in the United States. The Silver Ghost was produced from 1906 to 1925 without substantial change. This model, more than any other produced by Rolls-Royce, established and justified its makers' claim, "The Best Car in the World."

1913 Mercer Series J Type 35 Raceabout. Designed for the amateur sportsmen, the Mercer Raceabouts were often taken at random from the showroom directly to the race track where, with no break-in or special preparation, they set competition records.

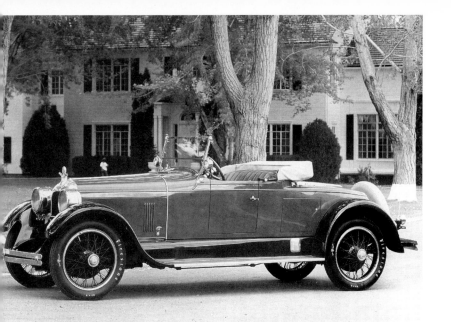

1925 Duesenberg Model A Roadster. Advertised as "The World's Champion Automobile—Built to Outclass, Outrun, and Outlast Any Car on the Road."

1930 Franklin Series 145 Pursuit. "A car of brilliant beauty powered by an airplane-type engine," proclaimed Franklin brochures. Franklins were owned by many famous aviators, such as Charles Lindbergh, Glenn Curtiss, and Amelia Earhart. This Franklin Pursuit is one of only a few remaining today.

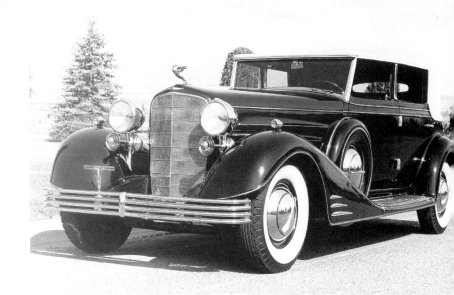

1933 Cadillac All-Weather Phaeton. This All-Weather Phaeton was specially built for Al Jolson, famous singer and movie star of the 1920s and 1930s. It is serial number 56 of only 126 produced in 1933.

1933 Auburn Model 12-161A Custom Speedster. Named for the town of its birth, Auburn, Indiana. Due to the impact of the Depression, only 6,000 cars were built and sold during 1933. Unable to fully recover from the Depression, The Auburn Automobile Company ceased production at the end of the 1936 model year.

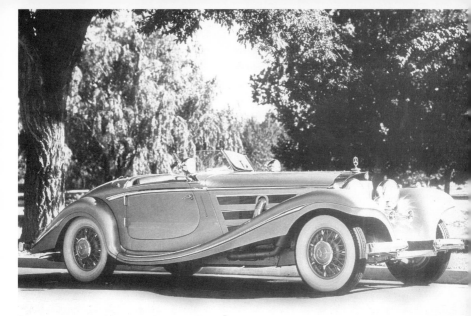

1936 Mercedes-Benz Type 500K Special Roadster. The handsome and luxuriously appointed body is by Sindelfingen. With a supercharged 8 cylinder, 100/160 H.P. engine, this automobile achieved excellent acceleration with a top speed of well over 100 mph.

1937 Cord 812 Supercharged Beverly Sedan. Driven by D. Absalom (Ab) Jenkins, this automobile set records at both the Indianapolis Motor Speedway (June 1937) and the Bonneville Salt Flats (September 1937).

1938 Phantom Corsair Six-Passenger Coupe.
This experimental one-of-a-kind automobile was designed by Rusty Heinz of the "57 Varieties" family. Body by Bohman & Schwartz/ Heinz.

1949 Mercury Series 9CM Six-Passenger Coupe.
Driven by James Dean in the movie *Rebel Without a Cause*. Few automobiles have developed such a "cult" following as this Mercury, one of the most famous movie cars in history.

1962 Lincoln Continental Model 86 Convertible.
Assigned to the late President John F. Kennedy.

YEAR	MODEL	ENGINE	BODY	F	G	E
KNOLLER *(Germany, 1924)*						
1924	Carolette					
	3-Wheel	(Helios)	Cycle	700	1,400	2,750
1924	Carolus	(Helios)	Cycle	750	1,500	3,000
KNOX *(United States, 1900–14)*						
1900	A	1 cyl.	3-Wheel Runabout	4,000	8,000	16,000
1904	Model F-1	1 cyl.	Runabout	5,000	10,000	18,000
1904		2 cyl.	Runabout	4,000	8,000	16,000
1908	H	4 cyl.	Touring	5,000	12,000	25,000
1910	S	6 cyl.	Touring	10,000	20,000	30,000
1912	40	4 cyl.	Raceabout	4,500	9,500	18,000
1914	46	6 cyl.	Touring	6,000	12,000	25,000
KOBOLD *(Germany, 1920)*						
1920		4 cyl.	2 Passenger	750	1,400	3,750
KOCO *(Germany, 1921–26)*						
1921	4/16	2 cyl.	Tonneau	1,400	2,400	5,700
1921	5/25	4 cyl.	Tonneau	1,400	2,400	5,700
1925	6/30	4 cyl.	Tonneau	1,600	3,300	6,000
KOEB-THOMPSON *(United States, 1901–11)*						
1910		4 cyl.	Touring	2,500	7,500	16,000
KOECHLIN *(France, 1910–13)*						
1910		4 cyl.	Racing	1,750	3,500	7,000
1912		4 cyl.	Racing	1,750	3,500	7,000
1913		6 cyl.	Racing	2,150	6,250	13,500
KOEHLER *(United States, 1910–12)*						
1910	Montclair	4 cyl.	Touring	1,900	7,750	16,500
1913		4 cyl.	Touring	2,000	8,000	17,000
KOMNICK *(Germany, 1907–19)*						
1907	K 10	4 cyl. (T-head)	Sedan	1,000	2,500	6,000
1908	K 20	4 cyl. (T-head)	Sedan	1,000	2,550	6,000
1909	K 30	4 cyl. (T-head)	Sedan	1,000	2,600	6,000
1913	C 2	4 cyl.	Sport	1,800	6,750	12,500
1919		4 cyl.	Touring	1,900	6,800	12,500
KORN ET LATIL *(France, 1901–02)*						
1901	Aster	2 cyl.	Voiturette	950	1,900	3,750
1902	Aster	2 cyl.	Voiturette	1,000	2,000	4,000
KORTE *(Great Britain, 1903–05)*						
1903		2 cyl.	Tonneau	750	2,500	6,000
1905		2 cyl.	6 Passenger Tonneau	800	2,650	7,250

YEAR	MODEL	ENGINE	BODY	F	G	E
KORTING *(Germany, 1922–24)*						
1922	6/24	4 cyl. (Selve)	Open	750	2,500	6,000
1924	8/32	4 cyl. (Selve)	Open	800	2,600	6,200
K.R.C. *(Great Britain, 1922–24)*						
1922		V 2 cyl.	Sport	950	2,900	6,750
1923		4 cyl.	Sport	750	2,500	6,000
1924		4 cyl.	Sport	750	2,500	6,000
KRIEGER *(France, 1897–1909)*						
1897		Electric	4 Passenger	4,500	9,000	16,000
1902	Electrolette	Electric	Voiturette	4,800	9,500	17,000
1902		(DeDion)	Voiturette	4,800	9,000	16,000
1903		(Richard-Brasier)	Voiturette	4,500	9,000	16,000
1904		Electric	Brougham	4,300	8,600	15,000
1909		(Brasier)	Brougham	4,000	8,000	14,500
KRIT (K.R.I.T.) *(United States, 1910–15)*						
1910	B	4 cyl.	3 Passenger Roadster	4,000	10,000	20,000
1910	C	4 cyl.	4 Passenger Surrey	3,600	8,000	21,000
1911	A	4 cyl.	Roadster	3,600	8,000	21,000
1913	KR	4 cyl.	Roadster	3,600	8,000	21,000
1915	O	4 cyl.	Touring	3,800	8,800	22,000
KUHLSTEIN *(Germany, 1898–1902)*						
1898		Electric	Avant train	2,100	6,150	13,300
1900		Electric	Vis-a-vis	2,350	6,250	15,500
KURTIS *(United States, 1948–55)*						
1948		V 8 cyl.	Sport	6,000	15,000	25,000
1954	500-F	V 8 cyl. (Mercury)	Racing	8,000	20,000	30,000
1954	500-KK	V 8 cyl. (Mercury)	Racing	8,000	20,000	30,000
1955	500-M	4 cyl. (Supercharged)	Racing	6,000	15,000	25,000

L

YEAR	MODEL	ENGINE	BODY	F	G	E
LABOR *(France, 1907–12)*						
1907		4 cyl.	Landaulet	950	3,900	6,750
1910		4 cyl.	Landaulet	100	4,400	7,900
LA BUIRE *(France, 1904–30)*						
1904		4 cyl.	Sedan	700	1,400	3,750
1906		4 cyl.	Sedan	700	1,400	3,750
1907		4 cyl.	Landaulet	1,000	2,750	5,500
1908	10/14	6 cyl.	Sedan	850	1,650	3,250
1913		4 cyl.	Sport	1,000	2,650	5,300

YEAR	MODEL	ENGINE	BODY	F	G	E
LA BUIRE *(France, 1904–30) (continued)*						
1915		6 cyl.	Landaulet	1,300	2,750	6,500
1920	14/20	6 cyl.	Sedan	850	1,650	3,250
1923	14/46	6 cyl.	Sport	1,000	5,000	11,000
1927	Speed	6 cyl.	Sport	2,000	6,000	12,000
1928	10 AA Long	10 cyl.	Sedan	3,850	7,700	14,400
LACOSTE ET BATTMAN *(France, 1897–1913)*						
1897	L & B	4 hp (Aster)	Voiturette	1,000	2,000	6,000
1897		4 hp (Mutel)	Voiturette	1,000	2,000	6,000
1903		1 cyl.	Runabout	1,050	2,100	5,200
1904		2 cyl.	Runabout	1,150	2,300	6,600
1905		4 cyl. (Mutel)	2 Passenger	1,150	2,250	6,500
1906	Lacoba	4 cyl.	Racing	2,150	5,300	11,600
1907	Proto	1 cyl. (Aster)	Racing	950	2,900	4,800
1907		6 cyl. (Aster)	Racing	3,150	8,250	16,500
LACOUR *(France, 1912–14)*						
1912		V 2 cyl.	Cycle	750	1,500	3,000
LAFAYETTE *(United States, 1921–24)*						
1921	134	V 8 cyl.	Limousine	3,500	8,500	18,000
1923	134	V 8 cyl.	Touring	6,000	12,000	28,000
1924	134	V 8 cyl.	Sedan	4,000	9,500	19,000
LAGONDA *(Great Britain, 1906–63)*						
1906		V 2 cyl.	Sport			
			Touring	2,800	11,300	22,500
1907	20	4 cyl.	Sport			
			Touring	4,000	12,000	26,000
1909	Torpedo	6 cyl.	Sport			
			Touring	8,000	20,000	40,000
1910		4 cyl.	Touring	4,200	13,400	27,000
1911		4 cyl.	Sport			
			Touring	3,200	12,000	25,000
1913		4 cyl.	Sport	3,400	11,800	24,000
1920		2 Litre	Sport			
			Touring	1,650	7,250	16,500
1924	12/24	2 Litre	Sport			
			Touring	1,750	6,500	15,000
1925		1954cc	Sport	1,900	6,750	15,500
1926	14/60	6 cyl.	Semi-Sport			
			Touring	2,150	7,250	16,500
1927	Speed Model	2 Litre	Sport	2,400	5,750	14,500
1928		3 Litre	Sedan	2,000	5,000	10,000
1929		2 Litre	Sedan	1,750	4,500	9,000
1930		2 Litre	Cabriolet	3,150	7,250	16,500

YEAR	MODEL	ENGINE	BODY	F	G	E
LAGONDA (Great Britain, 1906–63) (continued)						
1930		3 Litre	Boattail Speedster	5,400	14,750	37,500
1930		3 Litre	Sport Touring	4,500	10,000	20,000
1931		3 Litre	Sport Touring	4,500	10,000	20,500
1932	Continental	4 cyl.	Sport Touring	4,500	10,000	20,000
1933	16/18	6 cyl.	Sport Touring	5,500	13,000	26,000
1933	M-45	6 cyl. 4.5 Litre	Sport Touring	5,750	13,500	27,000
1934	Selector-Special	6 cyl.	Sport Touring	6,400	14,750	28,750
1935	Rapide	6 cyl. 4.5 Litre	Sedan	2,250	4,500	9,000
1936	LG-45	6 cyl.	Sport Sedan	3,000	5,000	11,000
1937		V 12 cyl.	Convertible Sedan	8,500	23,000	55,000
1938		V 12 cyl.	Sedan	4,250	8,500	16,000
1939		V 12 cyl.	Convertible Victoria	8,650	24,250	56,000
1939		6 cyl.	Convertible Coupe	4,150	12,250	23,500
1939		V 12 cyl.	Drop Head Coupe	6,250	16,500	38,000
1940		V 12 cyl.	Sedan Deville	4,500	9,000	19,000
1948		6 cyl.	Drop Head Coupe	3,250	6,500	13,000
1950		6 cyl.	Sedanca de Ville	3,000	6,000	12,000
1953		6 cyl. 3 Litre	Sedan	2,250	4,500	9,000
1954		6 cyl. 3 Litre	Sedan	2,250	4,500	9,000
1955		6 cyl. 3 Litre	Sedan	2,250	4,500	9,000
1957		6 cyl. 3 Litre	Sedan	2,200	4,400	9,000
1958		6 cyl. 3 Litre	Sedan	2,250	4,250	8,500
1959		4.5 Litre	Sedan	2,300	4,450	9,250
1960	Rapide	3996cc	Sedan	2,300	4,500	9,000
1963	Rapide	DB4	Saloon Sedan	2,300	3,450	8,250
LAMBERT (United States, 1891; 1906–17)						
1891		Gasoline	3 Wheel Buggy		RARE	
1906	A	1 cyl.	Runabout	3,500	8,000	16,000

YEAR	MODEL	ENGINE	BODY	F	G	E
LAMBERT *(United States, 1891; 1906–17) (continued)*						
1906	5	2 cyl.	Touring	3,500	8,000	16,000
1910	36	4 cyl.	Touring	4,250	8,500	20,000
1913	99		Touring	4,750	9,500	25,000
1917	90	4 cyl.	Touring	5,000	10,000	26,000
LAMBERT *(France, 1902–53)*						
1902		1 cyl. (Aster)	Runabout	1,350	2,500	5,250
1903		2 cyl. (DeDion)	Tonneau	1,850	4,700	8,400
1904		2 cyl. (Abeille)	Tonneau	1,900	4,750	8,500
1905		1 cyl.	Touring Side Entrance	1,500	3,900	7,750
1907		2 cyl.	Touring	1,500	3,850	8,650
1926		(Ruby)	Sport	1,100	2,900	7,750
1933		1 cyl.	Cycle	800	1,600	4,200
1945		Electric	2 Passenger	1,000	1,900	5,750
1952	Simplicia	1100cc	Sport	1,050	2,000	5,750
1953		(Lambert-Ruby)	Coupe	1,000	1,900	4,250
LAMBORGHINI *(Italy, 1963 to date)*						
1963		V 12 cyl.	Gran Turismo Coupe	25,000	35,000	50,000
1966	400 GT	V 12 cyl.	Coupe	25,000	40,000	55,000
1967	400	V 12 cyl.	Gran Turismo Coupe 2 + 2	25,000	35,000	42,000
1967	Miura P 400	V 12 cyl.	Gran Turismo Coupe	50,000	75,000	100,000
1967	Marzal	6 cyl.	Coupe	10,000	12,000	18,000
1968	Espada	V 12 cyl.	Coupe	12,000	18,000	28,000

Lamborghini – 1970 "Iselro"

YEAR	MODEL	ENGINE	BODY	F	G	E
LAMBORGHINI *(Italy, 1963 to date) (continued)*						
1970	Jarama	V 12 cyl.	Coupe 2 + 2	20,000	25,000	36,000
1971	Urraco	V 8 cyl.	Coupe	20,000	25,000	36,000
1972	Countach	V 12 cyl.	Coupe	55,000	85,000	125,000
1974	Espada	V 12 cyl.	Coupe			
			Hatchback	27,500	32,500	38,000
LA MINERVE *(France, 1901–06)*						
1901		1 cyl.	Voiturette	950	2,900	6,750
1902		1 cyl.	Voiturette	1,000	3,000	7,000
1902		2 cyl.	Voiturette	1,050	3,100	7,200
1903		2 cyl.	Voiturette	1,100	3,150	7,300
1904		4 cyl.	Voiturette	1,150	3,250	7,500
1905		3 cyl.	Voiturette	1,050	3,100	7,200
1906		4 cyl.	Tonneau	1,150	3,250	7,500
LAMMAS-GRAHAM *(Great Britain, 1936–38)*						
1936		6 cyl. (Graham)	Drop Head			
			Coupe	2,500	5,500	13,000
1937		6 cyl. (Graham)	Sedan	1,200	3,000	6,750
1938		6 cyl. (Graham)	Sport			
			Touring	3,000	8,000	17,000
LANCHESTER *(Great Britain, 1895–1956)*						
1895		2 cyl.	Vis-a-vis	2,150	6,250	12,500
1904		4 cyl.	Landaulet	3,150	9,250	18,500
1906		6 cyl.	Touring	4,150	13,250	26,500
1911	38	6 cyl.	Limousine	3,750	7,500	15,000
1912	25	6 cyl.	Touring	5,500	14,000	28,000
1914	Sporting-Forty	6 cyl.	Sport	5,000	13,000	26,000
1921	Twenty-one	6 cyl.	Sport	4,750	12,500	25,000
1923		6 cyl.	Landaulet	4,150	11,250	22,500
1924		6 cyl.	Limousine	3,650	7,250	15,500
1929	30	8 cyl.	Sedan	2,000	5,000	11,000
1932		6 cyl.	Roadster	4,150	8,250	17,500
1938	Roadrider de		Drop Head			
	Luxe	6 cyl.	Coupe	2,750	5,500	11,000
1939		8 cyl.	Sedan	2,150	4,250	9,500
1952	Fourteen	4 cyl.	Sedan	1,000	2,400	4,750
1954	Dauphin	6 cyl. (Daimler)	Sedan	1,750	3,500	6,000
LANCIA *(Italy, 1906 to date)*						
1906	Alfa	4 cyl.	Touring	4,000	10,000	25,000
1908	Di-Alfa	6 cyl.	Touring	6,000	15,000	30,000
1910	Beta	3.1 Litre	Touring	6,000	15,000	30,000
1911	Eta	4.1 Litre	Limousine	4,000	9,000	20,000
1912	Gamma	4.1 Litre	Touring	4,800	12,500	30,000

YEAR	MODEL	ENGINE	BODY	F	G	E
LANCIA *(Italy, 1906 to date) (continued)*						
1913	Delta	2.6 Litre	Touring	4,000	9,000	20,000
1914	Theta	4.9 Litre	Touring	8,000	20,000	45,000
1919	Kappa	12 cyl.	Coupe	10,000	25,000	50,000
1920	DiKappa	V 8 cyl.	Touring	15,000	35,000	75,000
1920	Torino	6 cyl.	Roadster	15,000	25,000	50,000

Lancia – 1920 "Torino Roadster"

1921	TriKappa	6 cyl.	Saloon Sedan	4,000	10,000	20,000
1922	Lambda	4 cyl.	Sedanca de Ville	3,500	9,000	20,000
1923		2.1 Litre	Torpedo	5,000	12,000	24,000
1924		2.1 Litre	Touring	4,000	8,000	20,000
1926		2.4 Litre	Sedan	3,000	5,000	12,000
1927		2.6 Litre	Sedan	3,000	5,000	12,000
1928		2.1 Litre	Touring	4,000	7,000	14,000
1929	DiLambda	V 8 cyl.	Sedan	3,000	7,000	15,000
1930		2.1 Litre	Sedan	2,000	4,000	10,000
1931	Artena	V 8 cyl.	Sedan	3,000	7,000	13,000
1932	Farina	V 8 cyl.	Sedan	2,000	5,000	12,000
1935	Astura	V 8 cyl.	Coupe	3,000	6,000	12,000
1935	Agusta	4 cyl.	Sedan	1,500	3,000	8,000
1939	Aprilia	1352cc	Sedan	1,500	3,000	8,000
1940	Ardea	V 8 cyl.	Convertible Coupe	8,000	15,000	28,000
1948		1.5 Litre	Sedan	1,500	3,000	6,000
1950		V 6 cyl.	Sedan	2,500	5,000	12,000
1951	Aurelia	2 Litre	Coupe	1,500	3,000	6,000

YEAR	MODEL	ENGINE	BODY	F	G	E
LANCIA *(Italy, 1906 to date) (continued)*						
1953	Ardea	6 cyl.	Touring	3,000	7,000	14,000
1954	B 15	6 cyl.	Sedan	1,500	4,000	6,000
1955	Appia	4 cyl.	Sedan	1,500	4,000	9,000
1956	Flaminia	V 6 cyl.	Coupe	3,000	7,000	15,000
1959		V 8 cyl.	Spyder	4,000	9,000	18,000
LANDAR *(Great Britain, 1965–75)*						
1965	R 3		Racing	1,500	4,000	9,000
1967	R 4		Racing	1,550	4,050	9,100
1967	R 5	(Ford)	Racing	1,600	4,150	9,250
1968	R 6		Racing	1,600	4,150	9,300
1969	R 7		Racing	1,600	4,150	9,300
1972	R 8	(Ford)	Racing	1,650	4,250	9,500
L & E *(United States, 1922–31)*						
1922		6 cyl. (Air-cooled)	Touring	3,950	7,900	17,000
1931		6 cyl. (Air-cooled)	Sedan	2,150	4,250	10,500
LANDGREBE *(Germany, 1921–24)*						
1921	3-Wheel		Cycle	750	1,500	3,000
1924	3-Wheel		Cycle	950	1,900	3,500
LA PERLE *(France, 1913–27)*						
1913		2 cyl.	Cycle	700	1,400	3,000
1914		4 cyl. (Bignan)	Racing	1,200	3,500	6,000
1916		6 cyl.	Racing	2,150	5,250	11,500
LA SALLE *(United States, 1927–40)*						
1927	303	V 8 cyl.	Phaeton	25,000	45,000	80,000
1927	303	V 8 cyl.	Dual Cowl Phaeton	30,000	50,000	86,000
1927	303	V 8 cyl.	Cabriolet	20,000	40,000	74,000
1927	303	V 8 cyl.	Coupe	8,000	18,000	40,000
1927	303	V 8 cyl.	Town	6,600	10,000	32,500
1927	303	V 8 cyl.	Sport Roadster	25,000	40,000	78,000
1928	303	V 8 cyl.	Sedan	9,000	17,000	35,000
1928	303		Convertible	12,000	20,000	39,000
1928	303	V 8 cyl.	Dual Cowl Phaeton	25,000	45,000	84,000
1929	328	V 8 cyl.	Cabriolet	25,000	40,000	74,000
1929	328	V 8 cyl.	Sedan	10,000	20,000	43,000
1929	328	V 8 cyl.	Roadster	20,000	45,000	88,000
1929	328	V 8 cyl.	RS Coupe	11,000	24,000	48,000
1929	328	V 8 cyl.	Sport Phaeton	25,000	50,000	94,000
1929	328	V 8 cyl.	Town Sedan	9,000	20,000	44,000

YEAR	MODEL	ENGINE	BODY	F	G	E
LA SALLE *(United States, 1927–40) (continued)*						
1930	340	V 8 cyl.	7 Passenger			
			Sedan	11,500	28,000	52,000
1930	Fleetway	V 8 cyl.	Cabriolet	30,000	50,000	92,000
1930	Fleetwood	V 8 cyl.	Roadster	35,000	60,000	100,000
1930	340	V 8 cyl.	7 Passenger			
			Sedan	9,000	20,000	45,000
1931	Fleetwood	V 8 cyl.	Cabriolet	35,000	65,000	110,000
1931	345A	V 8 cyl.	Sedan	9,600	15,500	46,500
1932	345B	V 8 cyl.	Convertible	30,000	50,000	98,000
1932	345B	V 8 cyl.	RS Coupe	12,000	26,000	53,000
1932	345B	V 8 cyl.	Town Sedan	9,000	20,000	40,000
1933	345B	V 8 cyl.	Town Coupe	10,000	22,000	48,000
1933	345B	V 8 cyl.	Convertible	30,000	50,000	98,000
1934	350	8 cyl.	Sedan	5,100	8,100	28,200
1935	50	8 cyl.	Convertible	20,000	35,000	60,000
1935	50	8 cyl.	Coupe	5,500	8,800	31,000
1935	50	8 cyl.	Sedan	2,300	5,600	27,000
1936	50	8 cyl.	RS Coupe	2,900	7,800	28,000
1936	50	8 cyl.	Convertible	14,000	25,000	49,000
1936	50	8 cyl.	Sedan	4,000	9,000	19,000
1937	50	V 8 cyl.	4 Passenger			
			Coupe	5,000	12,000	24,000
1937	50	V 8 cyl.	Sedan	4,000	11,000	23,000
1937	50	V 8 cyl.	Convertible			
			Sedan	12,000	25,000	50,000
1937	50	V 8 cyl.	Convertible	18,000	30,000	55,000
1938	50	V 8 cyl.	Sedan	8,000	10,000	23,000
1939	50	V 8 cyl.	Sedan	4,000	8,000	18,000
1939	50	V 8 cyl.	Convertible	15,000	28,000	52,000
1939	50	V 8 cyl.	Coupe	4,500	6,800	30,000
1939	50	V 8 cyl.	Convertible			
			Sedan	18,000	30,000	55,000
1940	50	V 8 cyl.	Sedan	2,000	5,800	18,000
1940	50	V 8 cyl.	Convertible			
			Sedan	18,000	30,000	55,000

YEAR	MODEL	ENGINE	BODY	F	G	E
LA SALLE *(United States, 1927–40) (continued)*						
1940	50	V 8 cyl.	Convertible	15,000	27,000	52,000

La Salle – 1940 "Convertible"

YEAR	MODEL	ENGINE	BODY	F	G	E
1940	52	V 8 cyl.	Convertible Sedan	18,000	30,000	55,000
1940	52	V 8 cyl.	Sedan	16,000	28,000	53,000
1940	52	V 8 cyl.	Coupe	6,000	14,000	29,000
1940	52	V 8 cyl.	Sedan	3,000	8,000	18,000
LA TORPILLE *(France, 1907–23)*						
1907	Tandem	4 cyl. (Ballot)	Cycle	750	1,500	3,500
1909		4 cyl.	Runabout	1,100	2,100	4,600
1911	3-Wheel	1 cyl.	Tandem	700	1,400	2,750
1912	3-Wheel	4 cyl.	Tandem	950	1,700	4,000
LAURIN-KLEMENT *(Austria; Czechoslovakia, 1906–28)*						
1906		2 cyl.	Voiturette	1,150	2,250	4,500
1908		4 cyl.	Voiturette	1,250	3,250	5,500
1909	FF	8 cyl.	Sport	1,400	3,500	6,000
1912		2.6 Litre	Touring	1,350	2,650	5,250
1913	MK	3.3 Litre	Sedan	800	1,600	3,200
1913	RK	4.7 Litre (Knight)	Touring	1,400	3,500	6,000
1924	Type 450	6 cyl.	Sedan	850	1,700	3,400
LA VIOLETTE *(France, 1910–14)*						
1910		1 cyl.	Runabout	1,100	2,300	5,500
1913		2 cyl.	Runabout	1,200	2,900	6,750
1914		4 cyl.	Runabout	1,500	4,000	8,000
LEACH *(United States, 1920–23)*						
1920	20	6 cyl.	7 Passenger Touring	5,000	12,000	27,000
1922	Leach Six	6 cyl.	Roadster	6,000	14,000	29,000

YEAR	MODEL	ENGINE	BODY	F	G	E
LEACH *(United States, 1920–23) (continued)*						
1923	Leach SIx	6 cyl.	6 Passenger Touring	5,000	12,000	27,000
LEADER *(Netherlands, 1904–05)*						
1904		(Aster)	2 Passenger	1,100	2,650	6,250
1905		(DeDion)	2 Passenger	1,200	2,750	6,500
LEADER *(Great Britain, 1905–09)*						
1905	10	4 cyl.		1,300	3,650	7,250
1905	14	4 cyl.	Touring	1,300	3,650	7,300
1906	10/20	4 cyl.	2 Passenger	1,300	3,625	7,250
1906	20/30	4 cyl.	2 Passenger	1,400	3,750	7,500
1907	60	V 8 cyl.	Sport	2,000	6,000	12,000
1909	12/16	4 cyl.	2 Passenger	1,300	3,650	7,250
LEA-FRANCIS *(Great Britain, 1904–60)*						
1904		3 cyl.	Touring	1,500	4,000	8,000
1909		4 cyl.	Coupe	1,500	4,000	8,000
1912		4 cyl.	Roadster	1,600	4,400	8,800
1915		4 cyl.	Roadster	1,500	4,250	8,500
1919		4.5 Litre (Meadows)	Roadster	1,500	4,250	8,500
1922		6 cyl.	Coupe	1,200	2,400	4,750
1925		1.5 Litre	Sport	1,600	4,300	8,500
1926		4 ED (Meadows)	Touring	1,700	4,500	9,000
1927		6 cyl.	Coupe	950	1,900	4,750
1928		6 cyl.	Sport	1,600	4,300	8,000
1929		6 cyl.	Coupe	950	1,900	4,750
1931	Ace of Spades	6 cyl.	Sport	1,500	4,150	8,250
1938	Ace of Spades	2.25 Litre	Sport	1,400	3,250	6,500
1940		6 cyl.	Coupe	950	1,900	4,750
1947		2 Litre (Meadows)	Touring	1,300	3,300	7,500
1951	12	4 cyl.	Sport	1,300	3,250	7,500
1955	14	4 cyl.	Sport	1,400	3,400	7,750
1958	14	4 cyl.	Coupe	950	1,900	4,750
LE BRUN *(France, 1898–1900)*						
1898		V 2 cyl.	Phaeton	1,800	6,000	12,000
1899		V 2 cyl.	Duc	1,100	2,900	7,750
1900		V 2 cyl.	Vis-a-vis	1,400	5,100	11,200
LEDA *(Great Britain, 1969–72)*						
1969	LT 20		Racing	1,650	3,250	7,500
1972	LT 27		Racing	1,850	3,650	7,250
1972	BH 2		Racing	1,850	3,650	7,250

YEAR	MODEL	ENGINE	BODY	F	G	E
LEEDS *(Romania, 1960–64)*						
1960		2 cyl. (Villiers)	Coupe	500	1,200	2,250
1964	L4 MicroCP	2 cyl. (Villiers)	Coupe	500	1,200	2,250
LEESDORFER *(Austria, 1898–1900)*						
1898	Petit Duc	2 cyl.	Duc	1,000	2,000	6,000
1898	Grand Duc	2 cyl.	Duc	1,100	2,150	6,250
LEGROS *(France, 1900–13)*						
1900		1 cyl.	Voiturette	1,200	2,650	6,250
1901	Meynier	Electric	Runabout	2,250	5,250	10,500
1902		(Aster)	Tonneau	1,300	2,900	6,800
1906		(DeDion)	Tonneau	1,300	2,900	6,800
1910		2 cyl.	Tonneau	1,250	2,850	6,650
1913		4 cyl.	Tonneau	1,350	3,900	8,800
LEICHTAUTO *(Germany, 1924)*						
1924		(D.K.W.)	2 Passenger	1,000	2,400	4,800
1924		(Columbus)	2 Passenger	1,200	2,500	5,000
LEIDART *(Great Britain, 1936–38)*						
1936		V 8 cyl. (Ford)	Sport	1,500	4,000	9,000
1937		V 8 cyl. (Ford)	Sport	1,500	4,150	9,250
1938		V 8 cyl. (Ford)	Sedan	1,200	2,450	4,850
L'ELEGANTE *(France, 1903–07)*						
1903		1 cyl. (DeDion)	Voiturette	1,000	3,000	7,000
1904		1 cyl. (DeDion)	Voiturette	1,100	3,150	7,250
1905		2 cyl. (DeDion)	Voiturette	1,300	4,150	9,300
LENARD *(Great Britain, 1904–06)*						
1904		(DeDion)	Voiturette	1,100	2,900	6,750
1906		(Tony Huber)	Roadster	1,400	4,000	8,000
LENHAM *(Great Britain, 1968–75)*						
1968	P 70 GT	(Ford)	Sport	1,000	2,900	5,750
1970	P 80	(Ford)	Spyder	1,000	3,000	6,000
1972		(Repco)	Sport	950	2,900	5,750
1972	T 80	(Ford)	Sport	900	2,800	5,500
LENOX *(United States, 1911–17)*						
1911	A	4 cyl.	Victoria			
			Roadster	3,650	8,250	17,500
1913	4-40	4 cyl.	Touring	3,500	7,000	16,000
1915		4 cyl.	Touring	5,150	10,250	21,500
1917	M	6 cyl.	Touring			
			Speedster	4,500	10,000	24,000
LENTZ *(Italy, 1906–08)*						
1906	14/16	4 cyl.	Roadster	1,100	3,500	7,000
1908	20/24	4 cyl.	Roadster	1,500	4,500	9,000

YEAR	MODEL	ENGINE	BODY	F	G	E
LEON BOLLE; MORRIS-LEON BOLLEE *(France, 1895–1933)*						
1895	Tandem	1 cyl.	Voiturette	1,100	3,150	6,250
1896		1 cyl.	Voiturette	1,100	3,150	6,300
1903	28 hp	4 cyl.	Tonneau	1,150	3,750	7,500
1905	45 hp	4 cyl.	Coach	800	3,600	7,200
1907		6 cyl.	Sedan	800	1,600	3,200
1909	10/14	4 cyl.	Roadster	900	3,800	7,600
1928	18 CV	8 cyl.	Sedan	800	2,600	5,250
1929	15 CV	(LeMans)	Coupe	800	3,600	7,300
1932	12 CV		Sedan	700	1,400	3,750
LEON DUSSEK *(France, 1906–07)*						
1906	16/20	4 cyl.	Runabout	1,100	3,700	7,400
1906	24/30	4 cyl.	Tonneau	1,200	3,750	7,500
1907	35/45	4 cyl.	Tonneau	1,300	3,800	7,500
LEON LAISNE; HARRIS-LEON LAISNE; HARRIS *(France, 1920–37)*						
1920	12 CV	4 cyl. (C.I.M.E.)	Touring	1,100	3,800	7,750
1922		8 cyl. (S.C.A.P.)	Touring	2,500	6,900	12,750
1924		6 cyl. (Hotchkiss)	Touring	1,800	4,000	8,000
1933	Harris Six	6 cyl. (English Standard)	Touring	2,000	3,900	8,750
LESCINA *(United States, 1916)*						
1916	Model V	6 cyl.	7 Passenger Touring	5,000	11,000	24,000
1916	Model X	4 cyl.	5 Passenger Touring	4,000	8,000	18,000
LESPINASSE *(France, 1909)*						
1909		4 cyl.	Runabout	1,200	3,650	6,300
1909		6 cyl.	Touring	1,500	4,100	9,200
LESTER *(Great Britain, 1913–55)*						
1913		(J.A.P.)	Cycle	850	1,650	3,250
1914		(J.A.P.)	Cycle	1,050	2,050	4,100
1949		1.5 Litre	Sport	700	1,400	2,800
1950		(Coventry-Climax)	Coupe	600	1,000	2,500
LE TIGRE *(France, 1920–23)*						
1920		4 cyl. (Fivet)	Torpedo Convertible	2,000	7,900	14,750
1923		4 cyl. (Fivet)	Sedan	700	1,400	3,800
LEWIS *(United States, 1914–16)*						
1914	VI	6 cyl.	Touring	4,000	9,000	19,000
1915	VI	4 cyl.	Touring	2,900	8,000	19,000
1916	VI	6 cyl.	Roadster	6,000	10,000	21,000

YEAR	MODEL	ENGINE	BODY	F	G	E
LEWIS *(Great Britain, 1923–24)*						
1923		V 2 cyl.	2 Passenger	1,800	3,650	6,500
1924		4 cyl.	2 Passenger	2,000	4,400	8,800
LEXINGTON *(United States, 1909–27)*						
1909	D	4 cyl.	5 Passenger Touring	3,250	7,000	17,000
1915	Light Six	6 cyl.	3 Passenger Roadster	4,500	13,500	22,000
1916	6-LA	6 cyl.	Touring	4,200	10,000	20,000
1917	Series 6	6 cyl.	Clubster	3,800	6,000	13,000
1920	Series S	6 cyl.	Touring	3,500	12,000	24,000
1924	Concord	6 cyl.	Sedan	2,500	5,500	13,000
1927	6-50	6 cyl.	Phaeton	4,800	14,500	28,000
LEYAT *(France, 1913–21)*						
1913		2 cyl. (ABC)	Airscrew	850	1,650	4,250
1919	Tandem	3 cyl. (Anzani)	2 Passenger	850	1,650	4,300
1920	Helica	3 cyl. (Anzani)	2 Passenger	900	1,750	4,500
1920		3 cyl. (Anzani)	Saloon	700	1,400	3,800
1921	3-Wheel	3 cyl. (Anzani)	Cycle	600	1,200	3,400
LE ZEBRE *(France, 1909–32)*						
1909		5 hp	Roadster	1,850	4,650	9,250
1911		5 hp	Roadster	2,000	4,400	9,800
1912		4 cyl.	Roadster	1,900	3,800	8,750
1921		4 cyl.	Roadster	1,900	3,800	8,500
LIBERTY *(United States, 1916–23)*						
1916	10A	6 cyl.	Roadster	4,000	8,000	19,000
1917	10B	6 cyl.	Touring	2,500	11,500	22,000
1920	10B	6 cyl.	Touring	2,500	11,500	22,000
1923	10D	6 cyl.	Touring	3,000	12,500	23,500
LIGIER *(France, 1969–75)*						
1969	JS 1	1.8 Litre (Cosworth)	Coupe	900	1,750	3,500
1971	JS 2	V 6 cyl. (Ford)	Gran Turismo Coupe	1,200	2,900	6,000
1972	JS 3	(Cosworth Ford)	Sport	950	1,850	4,700
LILIPUT *(Germany, 1904–07)*						
1904		1 cyl.	2 Passenger	1,200	2,300	5,500
1905		1 cyl.	4 Passenger	1,200	2,300	5,700
1906		2 cyl.	2 Passenger	1,300	3,400	6,550
1907	Libelle	4 cyl.	2 Passenger	1,400	4,450	7,900
LINCOLN *(United States, 1920 to date)*						
1921	Leland	V 8 cyl.	3 Passenger Roadster	9,000	20,000	38,000

YEAR	MODEL	ENGINE	BODY	F	G	E
LINCOLN *(United States, 1920 to date) (continued)*						
1921	Leland	V 8 cyl.	Phaeton	9,000	20,000	38,000
1921	Leland	V 8 cyl.	Touring	9,200	19,900	38,500
1921	Leland	V 8 cyl.	4 Passenger Coupe	6,000	13,600	20,900
1921	Leland	V 8 cyl.	Sedan	8,400	18,000	33,000
1921	Leland	V 8 cyl.	5 Passenger Sedan	8,700	12,000	26,000
1921	Leland	V 8 cyl.	Sub. Touring Sedan	9,200	14,000	27,000
1921	Leland	V 8 cyl.	Town Car Sedan	6,000	15,000	30,000
1922	Leland	V 8 cyl.	Sport Roadster	9,000	20,000	44,000
1922	Leland	V 8 cyl.	Convertible Touring	9,000	20,000	43,000
1922	Leland	V 8 cyl.	7 Passenger Touring	8,200	19,000	40,000
1922	Leland	V 8 cyl.	York Sedan	8,400	17,000	28,000
1922	Leland	V 8 cyl.	Sedan	4,400	7,600	27,000
1923	L	V 8 cyl.	Roadster	8,400	18,000	42,000
1923	L	V 8 cyl.	Phaeton	8,600	19,000	44,000
1923	L	V 8 cyl.	Town Car	8,600	12,500	29,000
1923	L	V 8 cyl.	Coupe	7,600	16,000	30,000
1923	L	V 8 cyl.	7 Passenger Limousine	5,000	10,000	36,000
1923		V 8 cyl.	Touring	10,000	14,500	38,000
1923	L	V 8 cyl.	Sedan	4,200	14,000	29,000
1924	L	V 8 cyl.	Coupe	6,200	17,000	27,000
1924	Judkins-L	V 8 cyl.	Coupe	4,900	14,000	30,000
1924	L	V 8 cyl.	5 Passenger Sedan	4,400	10,000	26,000
1924	L	V 8 cyl.	Touring	9,000	20,000	38,000
1924	L	V 8 cyl.	Roadster	8,700	19,500	42,000
1924	L	V 8 cyl.	Phaeton	9,500	21,000	45,000
1924	L	V 8 cyl.	Limousine	7,700	17,500	31,000
1924	L	V 8 cyl.	Town Car	6,500	10,000	33,000
1925	Brunn-L	V 8 cyl.	Cabriolet	10,000	25,000	48,000
1925	L	V 8 cyl.	4 Passenger Sedan	4,400	12,000	27,000
1925	L	V 8 cyl.	Roadster	8,100	11,500	35,500
1925	L	V 8 cyl.	5 Passenger Sedan	4,400	8,700	26,000
1925	L	V 8 cyl.	Limousine	4,000	14,000	33,000

YEAR	MODEL	ENGINE	BODY	F	G	E
LINCOLN *(United States, 1920 to date) (continued)*						
1925	L	V 8 cyl.	7 Passenger Sedan	4,600	14,000	32,000
1925	L	V 8 cyl.	Dual Cowl Phaeton	9,900	25,000	55,000
1925	L	V 8 cyl.	Coupe	4,200	12,000	32,000
1925	L	V 8 cyl.	Touring Coupe	6,600	15,000	40,000
1925	L	V 8 cyl.	Sport Touring	8,000	19,000	43,000
1926	L	V 8 cyl.	Touring	8,600	20,000	45,000
1926	L	V 8 cyl.	Sport Touring Sedan	9,000	22,000	49,000
1926	L	V 8 cyl.	Dual Cowl Phaeton	10,000	26,000	55,000
1926	L	V 8 cyl.	Roadster	8,500	25,000	50,000
1926	L	V 8 cyl.	Coupe	4,400	11,000	27,000
1926	L	V 8 cyl.	4 Passenger Sedan	3,100	10,000	26,000
1926	L	V 8 cyl.	Berline	8,000	20,000	44,000
1926	Holbrook-L	V 8 cyl.	Cabriolet	8,600	20,000	38,000
1926	Brunn-L	V 8 cyl.	Brougham	6,000	14,000	32,000
1926	L	V 8 cyl.	Limousine	4,000	12,000	29,000
1926	L	V 8 cyl.	7 Passenger Sedan	4,300	10,000	25,000
1926	L	V 8 cyl.	Convertible Phaeton	15,000	27,000	55,000
1927	L	V 8 cyl.	7 Passenger Sedan	4,400	12,000	26,000
1927	L	V 8 cyl.	Coupe	6,000	15,000	32,000
1927	L	V 8 cyl.	Limousine	4,500	15,000	36,000
1927	L	V 8 cyl.	Sport Touring	10,000	22,000	48,000
1927	L	V 8 cyl.	Dual Cowl Phaeton	14,000	28,000	57,000
1927	Holbrook-L	V 8 cyl.	Cabriolet	15,000	25,000	48,000
1927	L	V 8 cyl.	Roadster	17,000	30,000	55,000

YEAR	MODEL	ENGINE	BODY	F	G	E
LINCOLN *(United States, 1920 to date) (continued)*						
1928	Locke	V 8 cyl.	Sport Phaeton	15,000	30,000	64,000

Lincoln – 1928 "7 Passenger Sedan"

				F	G	E
1928		V 8 cyl.	2 Window Sedan	5,400	12,000	29,000
1928	Judkins	8 cyl.	Coupe	7,000	15,000	36,000
1928	Locke	8 cyl.	Roadster	20,000	35,000	60,000
1928		8 cyl.	Sedan	6,000	13,000	29,000
1928	Judkins	8 cyl.	Coupe	9,000	20,000	36,000
1928	L	8 cyl.	Touring	10,000	25,000	53,000
1928	L	8 cyl.	Dual Cowl Phaeton	16,000	33,000	60,000
1929	L	8 cyl.	Brougham Town Cabriolet	12,000	25,000	57,000
1929	L	8 cyl.	Brougham	10,000	20,000	50,000
1929	Locke	V 8 cyl.	Touring	15,000	35,000	75,000
1929	L	V 8 cyl.	5 Passenger Sedan	7,000	17,000	39,000
1929	L	V 8 cyl.	Cabriolet	25,000	40,000	65,000
1929	L	V 8 cyl.	7 Passenger Sedan	8,000	18,000	41,000
1929	L	V 8 cyl.	Club Roadster	25,000	40,000	75,000

YEAR	MODEL	ENGINE	BODY	F	G	E
LINCOLN	*(United States, 1920 to date) (continued)*					
1929	L	V 8 cyl.	Victoria Convertible	15,000	40,000	85,000
1929	L	V 8 cyl.	Sport Phaeton	15,000	38,000	80,000
1929	L	V 8 cyl.	Dual Cowl Phaeton	15,000	40,000	85,000
1930	L	V 8 cyl.	Coupe	8,000	18,000	37,000
1930	L	V 8 cyl.	7 Passenger Sport Phaeton	15,000	40,000	85,000
1930	L	V 8 cyl.	Coupe	6,000	15,000	37,000
1930	L	V 8 cyl.	Cabriolet	10,500	26,000	55,000
1930	L	V 8 cyl.	Town Sedan	5,200	15,000	35,000
1931	L	V 8 cyl.	Roadster Convertible	25,000	45,000	80,000
1931	L	V 8 cyl.	Sport Phaeton	25,000	53,000	85,000
1931	LeBaron	V 8 cyl.	Cabriolet	30,000	50,000	95,000
1931	LeBaron	V 8 cyl.	Sedan	10,000	30,000	75,000
1931	K	V 8 cyl.	Town Sedan	7,000	16,000	36,000
1931		V 8 cyl.	Convertible Coupe	18,000	36,000	78,000
1931			Sport Touring	12,200	21,200	50,000
1932	KA	V 8 cyl.	Roadster	26,000	50,000	90,000
1932	KA	V 8 cyl.	Coupe	8,000	20,000	43,000
1932	KA	V 8 cyl.	Phaeton	25,000	45,000	85,000
1932	KB	V 12 cyl.	Sport Roadster	35,000	60,000	110,000
1932	KB	V 12 cyl.	Sport Phaeton	27,000	50,000	95,000
1932	LeBaron	V 8 cyl.	Convertible Coupe	25,000	45,000	85,000
1932	KA	V 8 cyl.	Sedan	8,000	18,000	42,000
1932	KA	V 8 cyl.	Victoria Sedan	8,000	20,000	42,000
1932	LeBaron	V 8 cyl.	Town Cabriolet	25,000	45,000	85,000
1932	KA	V 8 cyl.	Dual Cowl Phaeton	17,000	42,000	90,000
1932	Custom	V 8 cyl.	Convertible Victoria	19,000	36,000	76,000
1932	KB	V 12 cyl.	Sedan	8,000	20,000	44,000

YEAR	MODEL	ENGINE	BODY	F	G	E
LINCOLN *(United States, 1920 to date) (continued)*						
1932	KB	V 12 cyl.	Limousine	6,000	20,000	45,000
1932	KB	V 12 cyl.	Touring Sedan	8,000	20,000	44,000
1933	KA	V 8 cyl.	Touring	10,000	22,000	46,000
1933	KA	V 8 cyl.	Convertible Roadster	25,000	45,000	85,000
1933	KA	V 8 cyl.	Convertible Sedan	25,000	55,000	110,000
1933	KA	V 8 cyl.	Coupe	8,000	20,000	45,000
1933	Brunn	V 12 cyl. (KA)	Cabriolet	30,000	55,000	100,000
1933		V 12 cyl.	7 Passenger Sedan	8,000	20,000	43,000
1933		V 12 cyl.	Convertible Victoria	17,000	47,000	97,000
1933		V 12 cyl.	Sedan	6,000	16,000	38,000
1933	LeBaron	V 12 cyl.	Coupe	5,400	12,000	46,000
1933	LeBaron	V 12 cyl.	Convertible Sedan	25,000	55,000	110,000
1933	LeBaron	V 12 cyl.	Dual Head Phaeton	40,000	70,000	120,000
1933		V 12 cyl.	Roadster	18,000	47,000	97,000
1934	LeBaron	V 12 cyl.	Roadster	25,000	50,000	90,000

Lincoln – 1934 "Convertible Roadster"

YEAR	MODEL	ENGINE	BODY	F	G	E
LINCOLN (United States, 1920 to date) (continued)						
1934	LeBaron	V 12 cyl.	Convertible Coupe	22,000	45,000	88,000
1934		V 12 cyl.	Sedan	9,000	20,000	44,000
1934		12 cyl.	Convertible Victoria	16,000	44,000	90,000
1934		V 12 cyl.	Coupe	10,000	20,000	46,000
1934		V 12 cyl.	Dual Cowl Phaeton	17,000	42,000	105,000
1934		V 12 cyl.	Limousine	61,000	20,000	47,000
1935		V 12 cyl.	Convertible Victoria	10,000	22,000	47,000
1935		V 12 cyl.	4 Door Convertible Sedan	20,000	45,000	86,000
1935		V 12 cyl.	Touring	15,000	30,000	70,000
1935		V 12 cyl.	Coupe	10,000	23,000	46,000
1935		V 12 cyl.	Convertible Roadster	20,000	40,000	72,000
1936	LeBaron	V 12 cyl.	Convertible	17,000	35,000	70,000
1936		V 12 cyl.	Brougham	8,000	20,000	41,000
1936		V 12 cyl.	7 Passenger Sedan	7,000	17,000	38,000
1936		12 cyl.	Convertible Sedan	12,600	30,000	69,000
1936	LeBaron	V 12 cyl.	Coupe	7,000	16,000	36,000
1936	Zephyr	12 cyl.	Sedan	5,000	12,000	30,000
1936	Zephyr	V 12 cyl.	Phaeton	19,000	38,000	83,000
1936	Zephyr	V 12 cyl.	Cabriolet	17,000	36,000	70,000
1936	Judkins-K	V 12 cyl.	Limousine	8,000	20,000	46,000
1937	Zephyr	V 12 cyl.	Convertible Sedan	15,000	35,000	65,000
1937	K	V 12 cyl.	Phaeton	17,000	38,000	62,000
1937	Zephyr	V 12 cyl.	Coupe	6,000	15,000	32,000
1937	Zephyr	V 12 cyl.	Sedan	9,000	12,000	28,000
1937	K	V 12 cyl.	Sedan	8,000	18,000	39,000
1937	3 Ps K	V 12 cyl.	Coupe	6,000	15,000	34,000
1937	K	V 12 cyl.	Convertible Sedan	14,000	25,000	52,000
1937	K	V 12 cyl.	Roadster	15,000	35,000	65,000
1938	LeBaron-K	V 12 cyl.	Convertible Roadster	15,000	38,000	65,000
1938	Brunn-K	V 12 cyl.	Victoria Convertible	15,000	30,000	60,000

YEAR	MODEL	ENGINE	BODY	F	G	E
LINCOLN *(United States, 1920 to date) (continued)*						
1938	K	V 12 cyl.	Town Sedan	6,000	13,000	29,000
1938	K	V 12 cyl.	Sedan	5,400	12,000	28,000
1938	LeBaron-K	V 12 cyl.	Convertible Sedan	10,000	32,000	68,000
1938	Zephyr	V 12 cyl.	Coupe	7,000	15,000	32,000
1938	Zephyr	V 12 cyl.	Sedan	6,200	10,000	25,000
1938	Zephyr	V 12 cyl.	Convertible Coupe	15,000	25,000	49,000
1938	LeBaron-K	V 12 cyl.	Convertible Sedan	12,000	26,000	50,000
1938	Brunn-K	V 12 cyl.	Town Limousine	8,000	18,000	38,000
1938	Brunn-K	V 12 cyl.	Berline	7,000	17,000	35,000
1939	K	V 12 cyl.	Convertible Sedan	15,000	30,000	58,000

Lincoln – 1939 "Model K Convertible Sedan"

YEAR	MODEL	ENGINE	BODY	F	G	E
1939	K	V 12 cyl.	Town Sedan	6,000	10,000	24,000
1939	Zephyr	V 12 cyl.	Convertible Coupe	12,000	24,000	44,000
1939	Zephyr	V 12 cyl.	3 Window Coupe	7,000	13,000	28,000
1939	Zephyr	V 12 cyl.	Sedan	4,500	11,000	23,000
1939	Zephyr	V 12 cyl.	Town Sedan	9,000	22,000	26,000
1939	K	V 12 cyl.	Phaeton	8,000	14,000	26,000
1940	Continental	V 8 cyl.	Coupe	5,000	15,100	32,000
1940	Zephyr	V 12 cyl.	Limousine	4,000	10,000	27,000
1940	Zephyr	V 12 cyl.	Convertible Coupe	9,700	19,000	40,000
1940	Zephyr	V 12 cyl.	Coupe	6,200	12,000	26,000

YEAR	MODEL	ENGINE	BODY	F	G	E
LINCOLN *(United States, 1920 to date) (continued)*						
1940	Zephyr	V 12 cyl.	Convertible Sedan	14,000	21,000	44,000
1940	Zephyr	V 12 cyl.	Cabriolet	10,000	20,000	44,000
1940	Zephyr	V 12 cyl.	Sedan	4,400	10,000	23,000
1940	Zephyr	V 12 cyl.	Brougham	6,300	12,000	24,000
1940	Zephyr	V 12 cyl. 4.8 Litre	Sedan	6,300	12,000	27,000
1941	Zephyr	V 12 cyl.	3 Window Coupe	5,000	13,000	27,000

Lincoln – 1941 "Zephyr Coupe"

YEAR	MODEL	ENGINE	BODY	F	G	E
1941	Continental	V 12 cyl. 4.8 Litre	Convertible	11,000	23,000	44,000
1941	Continental	V 12 cyl.	Hardtop	8,000	18,000	36,000
1941	Custom	V 12 cyl.	8 Passenger Limousine	5,000	12,000	27,000
1941	Zephyr	V 12 cyl.	Club Coupe	7,000	14,000	28,000
1941	Zephyr	V 12 cyl.	Cabriolet	12,000	20,000	38,000
1941	Zephyr	V 12 cyl.	Sedan	5,000	11,000	23,000
1941	Zephyr	V 12 cyl.	8 Passenger Limousine	4,000	10,000	22,000
1942	Custom	V 12 cyl.	Limousine	4,400	7,400	17,000
1942	Zephyr	V 12 cyl.	Sedan	3,800	6,500	13,000

YEAR	MODEL	ENGINE	BODY	F	G	E
LINCOLN *(United States, 1920 to date) (continued)*						
1942	Custom	V 12 cyl.	Sedan Limousine	4,400	7,400	17,000
1942	72	V 12 cyl.	Coupe	3,800	6,000	13,000
1942	77A	V 12 cyl.	Club Coupe	4,000	8,000	16,000
1942	76	V 12 cyl.	Convertible Coupe	12,000	22,000	40,000
1942	Continental	V 12 cyl.	Cabriolet	14,000	25,000	44,000
1942	Zephyr	V 12 cyl.	Coupe	4,000	8,000	16,000
Postwar Models						
1946	76	V 12 cyl.	Convertible	9,000	20,000	39,000
1946	73	V 12 cyl.	Sedan	2,200	4,200	12,000
1946	Continental	V 12 cyl.	Convertible Cabriole	15,000	27,000	50,000
1946	Continental	V 12 cyl.	Club Coupe	9,000	18,000	36,000
1947	76	V 12 cyl.	Convertible Coupe	12,000	22,000	42,000
1947	77	V 12 cyl.	Club Coupe	2,900	6,000	12,000
1947	73	V 12 cyl.	Sedan	2,700	5,000	12,000

Lincoln – 1947 "Model 73 Sedan"

1947	Continental	V 12 cyl.	Coupe	4,200	7,000	13,000
1948	Continental	V 12 cyl.	Convertible	10,000	20,000	39,000
1948	76	V 12 cyl.	Convertible	12,000	25,000	50,000

YEAR	MODEL	ENGINE	BODY	F	G	E
LINCOLN *(United States, 1920 to date)* *(continued)*						
1948	77	V 12 cyl.	Club Coupe	8,000	18,000	36,000
1949	Cosmopolitn	V 8 cyl.	Fastback Sedan	3,000	5,000	11,000
1949	Cosmopolitn	V 8 cyl.	2 Door Hardtop	4,000	9,000	18,000
1949	Cosmopolitn	V 8 cyl.	Convertible	7,000	15,000	29,000
1949	Cosmopolitn	V 8 cyl.	Club Coupe	3,000	8,000	16,000
1949	Cosmopolitn	V 8 cyl.	Sport Sedan	2,500	5,000	12,000
1950	Cosmopolitn	V 8 cyl.	Convertible	8,000	15,000	29,000
1950	Cosmopolitn	V 8 cyl.	Club Coupe	4,000	8,000	16,000
1950	Cosmopolitn	V 8 cyl.	Sport Sedan	2,500	4,000	9,000
1950	Cosmopolitn	V 8 cyl.	Capri Coupe	4,000	8,000	17,000
1950	Lido	V 8 cyl.	Coupe	4,500	9,000	18,000
1951	Cosmopolitn	V 8 cyl.	Convertible	8,000	15,000	29,000
1951	Lido	V 8 cyl.	Coupe	4,500	9,000	18,000
1951	Cosmopolitn	V 8 cyl.	Sport Sedan	2,500	5,000	10,000
1951	Cosmopolitn	V 8 cyl.	Coupe	4,000	7,000	15,000
1951	Cosmopolitn	V 8 cyl.	Capri Coupe	4,500	8,000	17,000
1952	Capri	V 8 cyl.	2 Door Hardtop	5,000	9,000	18,000
1952	Cosmopolitn	V 8 cyl.	Sedan	2,000	5,000	11,000
1952	Cosmopolitn	V 8 cyl.	Sport Coupe Hardtop	4,000	8,000	17,000
1952	Cosmopolitn	V 8 cyl.	Convertible	7,000	12,000	20,000
1953	Capri	V 8 cyl.	Convertible	9,000	18,000	33,000
1953	Capri	V 8 cyl.	2 Door Hardtop	4,000	8,000	19,000
1953	Capri	V 8 cyl.	Sedan	2,500	5,000	12,000
1953	Cosmopolitn	V 8 cyl.	Sport Coupe Hardtop	4,000	8,000	18,000
1953	Cosmopolitn		Sedan	2,000	5,000	11,000
1954	Capri	V 8 cyl.	2 Door Hardtop	3,500	8,000	19,000
1954	Capri	V 8 cyl.	Sedan	2,500	5,000	12,000
1954	Capri	V 8 cyl.	Convertible	9,000	18,000	35,000
1954	Cosmopolitn	V 8 cyl.	Sedan	2,500	5,000	11,000
1954	Cosmopolitn	V 8 cyl.	Sport Coupe Hardtop	4,500	9,000	18,000
1955	Capri	V 8 cyl.	Sedan	2,000	5,000	12,000
1955	Capri	V 8 cyl.	Coupe Hardtop	5,000	10,000	20,000
1955	Custom	V 8 cyl.	Sedan	2,000	5,000	12,000
1955	Capri	V 8 cyl.	Convertible	8,000	18,000	35,000

YEAR	MODEL	ENGINE	BODY	F	G	E
LINCOLN *(United States, 1920 to date) (continued)*						
1956	Premiere	V 8 cyl.	Sedan	2,500	6,000	13,000
1956	Premiere	V 8 cyl.	Convertible	10,000	22,000	42,000
1956	Capri	V 8 cyl.	Sport Coupe Hardtop	5,000	11,000	23,000
1956	Continental Mark II	V 8 cyl.	2 Door Hardtop	9,000	20,000	45,000
1956	Capri	V 8 cyl.	Sedan	2,000	5,000	12,000
1957	Continental Mark II	V 8 cyl.	2 Door Hardtop	9,000	20,000	40,000
1957	Capri	V 8 cyl.	Sedan	2,000	5,000	9,000
1957	Capri	V 8 cyl.	2 Door Hardtop	5,000	11,000	23,000
1957	Capri	V 8 cyl.	Hardtop Landau	6,000	12,000	24,000
1957	Premiere	V 8 cyl.	2 Door Hardtop Coupe	6,000	12,000	24,000
1957	Premiere	V 8 cyl.	Convertible	12,000	22,000	40,000
1958	Mark III	V 8 cyl.	Sedan	3,000	6,000	12,000
1958	Mark III	V 8 cyl.	Convertible	8,000	17,000	30,000
1958	Mark III	V 8 cyl.	Hardtop Coupe	7,000	17,000	36,000
1958	Capri	V 8 cyl.	Sedan	2,000	4,000	10,000
1958	Capri	V 8 cyl.	2 Door Hardtop	3,500	7,000	15,000
1958	Premiere	V 8 cyl.	4 Door Hardtop	3,000	6,000	13,000
1959	Mark IV	V 8 cyl.	Sedan	3,000	5,000	11,000
1959	Mark IV	V 8 cyl.	Town Car	4,500	9,000	18,000
1959	Mark IV	V 8 cyl.	Executive Limousine	4,000	8,000	16,000
1959	Mark IV	V 8 cyl.	Town Car	3,000	7,000	15,000
1959	Premiere	V 8 cyl.	2 Door Hardtop	4,000	8,000	16,000
1959	Premiere	V 8 cyl.	Sedan	2,000	4,000	9,000
1959	Mark IV	V 8 cyl.	Convertible	9,000	16,000	28,000
1959	Mark IV	V 8 cyl.	Sedan	2,000	5,000	11,000
1960	Continental	V 8 cyl.	2 Door Hardtop	5,000	11,000	22,000
1961	Continental	V 8 cyl.	4 Door Convertible	6,000	12,000	22,000
1962	Continental	V 8 cyl.	4 Door Convertible	5,000	11,000	22,000

YEAR	MODEL	ENGINE	BODY	F	G	E
LINCOLN *(United States, 1920 to date) (continued)*						
1963	Continental	V 8 cyl.	4 Door Sedan	3,000	6,000	12,000
1963	Continental	V 8 cyl.	4 Door Convertible	5,000	10,000	20,000
1964	Continental	V 8 cyl.	4 Door Convertible	5,000	10,000	20,000
1964	Continental	V 8 cyl.	4 Door Sedan	3,000	6,000	12,000
1965	Continental	V 8 cyl.	4 Door Convertible	5,000	10,000	20,000
1965	Continental	V 8 cyl.	4 Door Sedan	3,000	6,000	12,000
1966	Continental	V 8 cyl.	4 Door Convertible	5,000	10,000	20,000
1967	Continental	V 8 cyl.	4 Door Convertible	8,000	14,000	25,000
1968	Continental	V 8 cyl.	2 Door Convertible	4,000	8,000	16,000
1969	Continental Mark III	V 8 cyl.	2 Door Hardtop	3,500	7,000	14,000
1970	Continental Mark III	V 8 cyl.	Coupe	3,000	7,000	15,000
LOTUS *(Great Britain, 1952 to date)*						
1952	Six	4 cyl.	Sport		RARE	
1957	Seven S1	(M.G.) 1.25 Litre	Sport	15,000	20,000	35,000
1958	Elite	1.2 Litre (Coventry-Climax)	Coupe	15,000	20,000	25,000
1958	Seven S2	2.2. Litre	Sport	30,000	35,000	40,000
1959	Elite	1.5 Litre	Coupe	15,000	20,000	25,000
1959	Mark 17	2.2 Litre	Coupe	30,000	35,000	40,000
1960	Elite	1.5 Litre	Coupe	15,000	20,000	25,000
1961	Mark 20	(Cosworth Ford)	Coupe	30,000	40,000	50,000
1961	Super Seven	1.5 Litre	Sport	7,000	10,000	18,000
1962	Elite	1.5 Litre	Coupe	20,000	25,000	30,000
1965	Elan	116 E (Ford)	Convertible	7,000	10,000	18,000
1966	Mark 46 Europa	1.5 Litre	Coupe	5,000	7,000	10,000
1967	Mark 49	(Ford)	Racing	25,000	40,000	60,000
1970	Europa S-2	4 cyl.		6,000	9,000	12,000

YEAR	MODEL	ENGINE	BODY	F	G	E

M

MADISON *(United States, 1915–19)*

YEAR	MODEL	ENGINE	BODY	F	G	E
1916	2 Passenger	6 cyl.	Roadster	5,000	10,000	21,000
1918	4 Passenger	6 cyl.	Roadster	4,000	8,000	12,000

MASERATI *(Italy, 1926 to date)*

YEAR	MODEL	ENGINE	BODY	F	G	E
1926	Tipo 26	1.5 Litre	Sport	100,000	125,000	150,000
1928	28 B	2 Litre	Sport	125,000	150,000	175,000
1929	Tipo 14	2 Litre	Sport	100,000	125,000	150,000
1935	Tipo B	6 cyl.	Touring	225,000	275,000	325,000
1936	V 8 R1	2.6 Litre	Voiturette	250,000	300,000	350,000
1937	6 CM	6 cyl.	Voiturette	135,000	185,000	225,000
1939	4 CL	4 cyl.	Sport	125,000	160,000	200,000
1939	8 CTF	8 cyl.	Sport	250,000	300,000	350,000
1943	A 6	4 cyl.	Grand Prix	150,000	200,000	250,000
1944	A 6	4 cyl.	Grand Prix	125,000	175,000	210,000
1945	A 6	2 Litre	Coupe	60,000	75,000	90,000
1947	4 CLT	4 cyl.	Grand Prix	40,000	60,000	70,000
1948	4 CLT/48	4 cyl.	Grand Prix	40,000	60,000	70,000
1949	4 CLT/48	4 cyl.	Grand Prix	40,000	60,000	70,000
1950	4 CLT/48	4 cyl.	Grand Prix	40,000	60,000	70,000
1953	A 6 SS G	6 cyl.	Grand Prix	50,000	65,000	85,000
1953	A 6 GCS 2000	6 cyl.	Sport	55,000	75,000	95,000
1953	A 6 G 2000	6 cyl.	Touring	55,000	75,000	95,000
1954	250 F	6 cyl.	Grand Prix	50,000	60,000	75,000
1955	300 S	6 cyl.	Sport	60,000	70,000	85,000
1955	150 S	4 cyl.	Sport	30,000	40,000	50,000
1956	200 S	2 Litre	Sport	30,000	40,000	50,000
1957	300 S	6 cyl.	Sport	20,000	25,000	30,000
1957	450 S	V 8 cyl.	Coupe	25,000	30,000	38,000
1958	V-12	V 12 cyl.	Grand Prix	30,000	40,000	55,000
1958	250 F	3.5 Litre	Sport	20,000	25,000	32,000
1958	40 S	V 8 cyl.	Sport	20,000	25,000	30,000
1958	Eldorado	V 8 cyl.	Grand Prix	20,000	25,000	32,000
1959	Tipo 61	4 cyl.	Sport Racing	20,000	25,000	30,000
1960	Tipo 151	V 8 cyl.	Coupe	30,000	38,000	48,000
1965	Iso Grifo	6 cyl.	Grand Prix	30,000	40,000	50,000
1965	3500 GT	6 cyl.	Touring	30,000	35,000	40,000
1966	35000 GTI Sebring	6 cyl.	Touring	6,400	12,000	50,000
1966	Quattro Porte	V 8 cyl.	Touring	25,000	40,000	55,000
1967	Mistral	6 cyl.	Coupe	60,000	75,000	95,000

YEAR	MODEL	ENGINE	BODY	F	G	E
MASERATI	*(Italy, 1926 to date) (continued)*					
1968	Mexico	V 8 cyl.	2 Door Sedan	15,000	20,000	28,000
1969	Ghibli	V 8 cyl.	Coupe	25,000	35,000	40,000
1970	Ghibli SS	V 8 cyl.	Spyder	65,000	85,000	110,000
1971	Indy	V 8 cyl.	Coupe	15,000	20,000	25,000
1972	Indy					
	American	V 8 cyl.	Coupe	10,000	18,000	22,000
1973	Merak	V 6 cyl.	Coupe 2 + 2	15,000	20,000	25,000
1973	Bora	V 8 cyl.	Coupe	25,000	30,000	40,000
1973	Ghibli	V 8 cyl.	Coupe 2 + 2	25,000	30,000	35,000
MASON	*(United States, 1906–14)*					
1907		2 cyl.	5 Passenger Touring	4,000	8,000	25,000
1910		2 cyl.	4 Passenger Touring	4,000	8,000	24,000
1914		4 cyl.	4 Passenger Touring	3,000	6,500	22,000
MATHESON	*(United States, 1903–12)*					
1903	Chain Drive	4 cyl.	7 Passenger Touring	5,000	9,000	19,000
1906	Holyoke	4 cyl.	7 Passenger Touring	5,000	12,000	30,000
1910	M	6 cyl. 65 hp.	5 Passenger Touring	8,000	15,000	31,000
1912	Silent Six	6 cyl.	2 Passenger Speedster	8,000	16,000	37,000
MAXWELL	*(United States, forerunner of the Plymouth, 1905–25)*					
1905	"L"	2 cyl.	2 Passenger Runabout	4,000	8,000	18,000
1910	DA	4 cyl.	5 Passenger Touring	5,000	10,000	22,000
1925	25	4 cyl.	Roadster	6,000	13,000	27,000
MCFARLAN	*(United States, purchased by E. L. Cord, 1910–28)*					
1910		6 cyl.	5 Passenger Touring	3,000	8,000	22,000
1915	T	6 cyl.	2 Passenger Roadster	4,000	9,000	29,000
1920	90	Twin-Valve-6	Cabriolet	9,000	20,000	45,000
1923	"SV"	6 cyl.	4 Passenger Sport	8,000	16,000	32,000
MCINTYRE	*(United States, 1909–15)*					
1912	F-12	4 cyl.	5 Passenger Touring	4,000	9,000	24,000

YEAR	MODEL	ENGINE	BODY	F	G	E
MCINTYRE *(United States, 1909–15) (continued)*						
1915	6-40	6 cyl.	2 Passenger			
			Touring	3,000	6,000	24,000
MERCEDES *(Germany, 1901–1926)*						
1901		4 cyl.	Phaeton	13,000	26,000	52,000
1902		4 cyl.	Tonneau	13,000	26,000	52,000
1902		4 cyl.	Touring	15,000	33,000	70,000
1902		4 cyl.	Phaeton	14,000	29,000	64,000
1903	Simplex	4 cyl.	Tonneau	13,000	26,000	52,000
1903	Simplex	4 cyl.	Touring	15,000	33,000	70,000
1903	Simplex	4 cyl.	Phaeton	14,000	29,000	64,000
1904	Simplex	4 cyl.	Tonneau	19,000	39,000	115,000
1904		4 cyl.	Limousine	13,000	26,000	52,000
1904		4 cyl.	Phaeton	14,000	29,000	64,000
1904		4 cyl.	Touring	14,000	33,000	70,000
1905		4 cyl.	Touring	20,000	41,000	88,000
1905		4 cyl.	Limousine	14,000	29,000	64,000
1905		4 cyl.	Phaeton	13,000	26,000	52,000
1905		4 cyl.	Tonneau	22,000	42,000	88,000
1906	45	4 cyl.	Limousine	13,000	26,000	52,000
1906	18/32	4 cyl.	Landaulet	13,000	26,000	52,000
1906	40/45	4 cyl.	Touring	20,000	42,000	88,000
1907	40/60	6 cyl.	Touring	19,000	39,000	82,000
1907	37/70	6 cyl.	Limousine	9,800	19,000	46,000
1907		6 cyl.	Landaulet	13,000	26,000	49,000
1908		6 cyl.	Landaulet	9,800	19,000	39,000
1909		4.1 Litre	Touring	13,000	26,000	56,000
1909		6 cyl.	Limousine	7,800	14,000	33,000
1909		6 cyl.	Sport	9,600	19,000	39,000
1910	14/30	4 cyl.	Sport	6,700	13,000	26,000
1910	38/80	4 cyl.	Sport	9,600	19,000	39,000
1910	14/30	4 cyl.	Touring	7,900	14,000	33,000
1910	28/60	4 cyl.	Landaulet	9,100	17,000	34,000
1910	28/60	4 cyl.	Phaeton	14,000	33,000	79,000
1911	10/20	4 cyl.	Sport	7,900	15,000	31,000
1911	37/90	4 cyl.	Sport	9,900	19,000	39,000
1911	22/50	4 cyl.	Limousine	7,900	14,000	33,000
1911	16/40	4 cyl.	Touring	7,900	14,000	33,000
1911	16/40	4 cyl.	Phaeton	15,000	32,000	67,000
1912	14/30	4 cyl.	Limousine	7,900	14,000	33,000
1912	38/70	4 cyl.	Sport			
			Phaeton	15,000	33,000	70,000
1912	22/46	4 cyl.	Limousine	7,800	15,000	32,000
1912	29/60	4 cyl.	Limousine	9,200	16,000	33,000

YEAR	MODEL	ENGINE	BODY	F	G	E
MERCEDES *(Germany, 1901–1926) (continued)*						
1912	22/40	4 cyl.	Touring	7,900	14,000	33,000
1913	14/35	4 cyl.	Sport	7,900	14,000	31,000
1913		4 cyl.	Touring	7,900	14,000	33,000
1913		4 cyl.	Limousine	7,900	14,000	33,000
1913	38/70	4 cyl.	Sport			
			Phaeton	11,000	26,000	61,000
1914	28/95	6 cyl.	Touring	9,100	15,000	47,000
1914	28/95	6 cyl.	Sport	7,900	14,000	44,000
1914		4 cyl.	Limousine	7,900	14,000	33,000
1914		4 cyl.	Sport	6,700	13,000	39,000
1915		6 cyl.	Touring	6,700	16,000	42,000
1915		6 cyl.	Sport	7,900	16,000	44,000
1915		6 cyl.	Limousine	9,900	15,000	33,000
1915		4 cyl.	Sport	6,700	16,000	41,000
1916		6 cyl.	Sport	7,900	16,000	44,000
1916		4 cyl.	Sport	6,700	15,000	40,000
1916		6 cyl.	Limousine	8,100	14,000	33,000
1916		6 cyl.	Touring	6,700	16,000	42,000
1917		6 cyl.	Sport	7,900	19,000	44,000
1917		6 cyl.	Touring	7,900	18,000	44,000
1917		6 cyl.	Limousine	7,900	14,000	30,000
1918		6 cyl.	Limousine	7,900	14,000	31,000
1918		6 cyl.	Phaeton	14,000	26,000	70,000
1918		6 cyl.	Touring	10,500	20,000	64,000
1918		6 cyl.	Sport	7,900	16,000	46,000
1919		6 cyl.	Cabriolet	6,700	16,000	46,000
1919		6 cyl.	Touring	7,900	17,000	44,000
1919		4 cyl.	Sport	8,500	17,000	46,000
1920		6 cyl.	Coupe	5,900	11,000	23,000
1920		6 cyl.	Cabriolet	6,700	19,000	44,000
1920		4 cyl.	Sport	6,700	18,000	42,000
1920		4 cyl.	Limousine	7,900	15,000	28,000
1921	28/95	6 cyl.	Sport	9,200	18,000	49,000
1921	6/25/40	4 cyl.	Sport	8,500	16,000	47,000
1921	16/50	6 cyl.	Limousine	7,900	15,000	44,000
1921	6/18	4 cyl.	Sport	7,900	19,000	44,000
1922	10/40/65	4 cyl.	Touring	11,000	23,000	62,000
1922		6 cyl.	Limousine	10,400	15,000	31,000
1923	24/100/140	6 cyl.	Touring	13,000	26,000	71,000
1924	25-40	6 cyl.	Touring	10,400	23,000	64,000
1924	11/40	6 cyl.	Phaeton	9,200	27,000	67,000
1924	24/100/140	6 cyl. (Supercharged)	4 Passenger Touring	16,000	34,000	78,000

YEAR	MODEL	ENGINE	BODY	F	G	E
MERCEDES *(Germany, 1901–1926) (continued)*						
1924		6 cyl.	Roadster	11,000	31,000	65,000
1925	SS	6 cyl.	Touring	19,000	52,000	120,000
1926	K	6 cyl.	Touring	13,000	26,000	78,000
MERCEDES-BENZ *(Germany, 1926 to date)*						
1926	Stuttgart 200	6 cyl.	Cabriolet	10,400	19,000	46,000
1926	Mannheim	6 cyl.	Sedan	5,900	11,000	23,000
1926	SS	6 cyl.	Roadster	28,000	49,000	120,000
1927	S	6 cyl. (Supercharged)	Sport	33,000	97,000	150,000
1927	SSK	6 cyl. (Supercharged)	Sport	44,000	120,000	350,000
1927	K	6 cyl.	Touring	15,000	33,000	99,000
1927	SS	6 cyl.	Touring	26,000	94,000	240,000
1928		8 cyl.	Convertible	19,000	39,000	97,000
1928	SS	6 cyl. (Supercharged)	Sport	26,000	71,000	230,000
1928	15/70/100	6 cyl.	Limousine	10,400	19,000	39,000
1928	Stuttgart 260	6 cyl.	Cabriolet	11,000	33,000	77,000
1928	S	6 cyl.	Speedster	33,000	110,000	180,000
1928		6 cyl.	Touring	19,000	33,000	77,000
1929	230	6 cyl.	Roadster	11,000	27,000	77,000
1929	K	8 cyl.	Limousine	16,000	33,000	52,000
1930	Super Mercedes	8 cyl.	Limousine	13,000	26,000	46,000
1930	'D'	8 cyl.	Coupe	7,900	15,000	28,000
1930		8 cyl.	Cabriolet	11,000	22,000	42,000
1930		8 cyl.	Touring	11,000	19,000	60,000
1931	370S	6 cyl.	Convertible	16,000	46,000	92,000
1932	SSK	8 cyl. (Supercharged)	Roadster	26,000	100,000	340,000
1933	170	6 cyl.	Roadster	8,500	14,000	26,000
1933	170	6 cyl.	Cabriolet	9,200	15,000	26,000
1933	130 H	4 cyl.	Limousine	5,200	9,200	16,000
1933	290	6 cyl.	Convertible	13,000	26,000	50,000
1933	380	8 cyl.	Convertible	20,000	36,000	60,000
1933	380 K	8 cyl.	Sedan	11,000	23,000	36,000

YEAR	MODEL	ENGINE	BODY	F	G	E
MERCEDES-BENZ *(Germany, 1926 to date) (continued)*						
1934	500 K	8 cyl.	Roadster	30,000	100,000	290,000

Mercedes-Benz – 1934 "500 K" Courtesy of White Post Restorations, White Post, Virginia

YEAR	MODEL	ENGINE	BODY	F	G	E
1934	150 H	4 cyl.	Sport	5,200	10,000	20,000
1934	290		Cabriolet	13,000	23,000	44,000
1935	500 K	4 cyl.	Sedan	26,000	55,000	84,000
1935	770 K	8 cyl. (Supercharged)	Limousine P.H.	28,000	110,000	280,000
1935	260 D	4 cyl.	Limousine	10,400	20,000	35,000
1935	170 V	4 cyl.	Limousine	6,300	14,000	27,000
1935	170 V	4 cyl.	Convertible	7,900	16,000	33,000
1936	540 K	8 cyl.	Roadster	46,000	100,000	300,000
1936	540 K	8 cyl. (Supercharged)	Cabriolet	22,000	52,000	130,000
1936	500 K	8 cyl. (Supercharged)	Sport Convertible	50,000	110,000	390,000
1936	500 K	8 cyl. (Supercharged)	Coupe	28,000	64,000	140,000
1936	500 K	8 cyl. (Supercharged)	Touring	34,000	82,000	250,000
1937	320	6 cyl. 78 hp	Limousine	14,000	23,000	39,000
1937	500 K	8 cyl. (Supercharged)	Roadster	50,000	140,000	380,000
1937		4 cyl.	Sport	11,000	23,000	34,000
1937	320	6 cyl.	Cabriolet	14,000	26,000	69,000
1937	500 K	8 cyl.	Convertible Coupe	34,000	67,000	120,000
1938	540 K	8 cyl. (Supercharged)	Coupe	15,000	33,000	80,000
1938	230	6 cyl. 55 hp	Convertible	10,000	20,000	47,000
1938	230	8 cyl. (Supercharged)	Cabriolet	10,000	20,000	47,000
1938	770 K	8 cyl. (Supercharged)	Limousine	34,000	89,000	280,000

YEAR	MODEL	ENGINE	BODY	F	G	E
MERCEDES-BENZ *(Germany, 1926 to date) (continued)*						
1938	540 K	8 cyl. (Supercharged)	Cabriolet	34,000	69,000	140,000

Mercedes-Benz – 1938 "540 K Cabriolet"

YEAR	MODEL	ENGINE	BODY	F	G	E
1938	540 K	8 cyl. (Supercharged)	Roadster	400,000	750,000	1200000
1939	290	8 cyl.	Cabriolet	45,000	65,000	85,000
1939	230	8 cyl.	Roadster	50,000	70,000	90,000
1939	170	4 cyl.	Sport	15,000	25,000	45,000
1939	220	6 cyl.	Sport	20,000	28,000	47,000
1940	770 K	8 cyl. (Supercharged)	Armored Phaeton	300,000	400,000	500,000
Postwar Models						
1947	170 V	4 cyl.	Sedan	7,000	10,000	16,000
1947	170 D	4 cyl.	Coupe	5,000	9,000	15,000
1948	170 D	4 cyl.	Coupe	5,000	9,000	15,000
1948	170 V	4 cyl.	Coupe	5,000	9,000	15,000
1949	170 S	4 cyl.	Limousine	4,000	9,000	20,000
1949	170 D	4 cyl.	Sedan	5,000	8,000	15,000
1949	170 V	4 cyl.	Coupe	8,000	12,000	22,000
1950	170 V	4 cyl.	Sport	10,000	15,000	26,000
1950	170 S	4 cyl.	Convertible Coupe	20,000	45,000	65,000
1950	220	6 cyl.	Sedan	7,000	15,000	25,000
1951	220	6 cyl.	Convertible	25,000	50,000	70,000
1951	300	6 cyl.	Sedan	4,000	7,000	15,000
1951	300	6 cyl.	Coupe	10,000	20,000	35,000
1952	300 S	6 cyl.	Cabriolet	50,000	100,000	150,000
1952	300 S	6 cyl.	Sedan	3,000	15,000	35,000
1952	300 S	6 cyl.	Coupe	25,000	50,000	92,000

YEAR	MODEL	ENGINE	BODY	F	G	E
MERCEDES-BENZ *(Germany, 1926 to date) (continued)*						
1952	170 S	4 cyl.	Cabriolet	15,000	25,000	48,000
1952	170 S	4 cyl.	Limousine	5,000	10,000	21,000
1953	170 SV	4 cyl.	Coupe	7,000	15,000	28,000
1953	300	4 cyl.	Convertible Sedan	40,000	75,000	130,000
1953	300 S	4 cyl.	Convertible Coupe	55,000	100,000	150,000
1953	220	4 cyl.	Cabriolet	15,000	25,000	48,000
1953	300	6 cyl.	Cabriolet	50,000	95,000	132,000
1954	300 B	6 cyl.	Sedan	7,000	15,000	28,000
1954	220	6 cyl.	Limousine	10,000	20,000	32,000
1954	200A	6 cyl.	Coupe	7,900	15,000	33,000

Mercedes-Benz – 1954 "221 A Coupe"

YEAR	MODEL	ENGINE	BODY	F	G	E
1954	300	6 cyl.	Limousine	10,000	20,000	33,000
1954	300S	8 cyl.	Convertible Coupe	50,000	95,000	135,000
1955	190 SL	4 cyl.	Sport Roadster	15,000	25,000	45,000
1955	300 B	6 cyl.	Sedan	10,000	20,000	36,000
1955	300 SC	6 cyl.	Coupe Roadster	40,000	60,000	105,000

YEAR	MODEL	ENGINE	BODY	F	G	E
MERCEDES-BENZ	*(Germany, 1926 to date)*	*(continued)*				
1955	300 SL	8 cyl.	Gullwing Coupe	250,000	350,000	450,000

Mercedes-Benz – 1955 "300 SL Gullwing Coupe"

YEAR	MODEL	ENGINE	BODY	F	G	E
1956	190 SL	4 cyl.	Convertible	15,000	25,000	45,000
1956	200 S	6 cyl.	Sedan	4,000	7,000	12,000
1956	300 C	6 cyl.	Limousine	10,000	20,000	39,000
1956	300 SC	6 cyl.	Sedan	9,000	20,000	50,000
1956	300 C	6 cyl.	Convertible Sedan	75,000	125,000	175,000
1956	300 S	6 cyl.	Cabriolet	100,000	140,000	185,000
1957	180	4 cyl.	Sedan	3,000	5,000	8,000
1957	300 SC	8 cyl.	Roadster	150,000	200,000	250,000
1957	300 SL	8 cyl.	Gullwing Coupe	350,000	475,000	575,000
1957	190 SL	6 cyl.	Roadster	15,000	25,000	45,000
1957	200 S	6 cyl.	Convertible	16,000	35,000	57,000
1958	190 D	4 cyl.	Sedan	2,500	4,000	8,500
1958	220 S	6 cyl.	Coupe	3,300	10,000	20,000
1958	220 S	6 cyl.	Sedan	2,300	5,000	12,000
1958	220 S	6 cyl.	Convertible	15,000	35,000	58,000
1959	180	4 cyl.	Sedan	2,000	4,000	8,000
1959	180 D	4 cyl.	Sedan	1,400	2,800	7,500
1959	220 S	6 cyl.	Coupe	4,000	10,000	22,000

YEAR	MODEL	ENGINE	BODY	F	G	E
MERCEDES-BENZ *(Germany, 1926 to date) (continued)*						
1959	300 D	6 cyl.	Sedan	3,300	6,400	15,000
1959	200 SE	6 cyl.	Sedan	2,800	8,000	16,000
1959	200 SE	6 cyl.	Convertible	15,000	30,000	65,000
1959	190 SL	6 cyl.	Convertible	10,000	20,000	43,000
1959	219	4 cyl.	Sedan	3,000	5,000	11,000

Mercedes-Benz – 1959 "219 Sedan"

YEAR	MODEL	ENGINE	BODY	F	G	E
1962	220 SE	6 cyl.	Coupe	4,400	6,300	14,000
1967	230 SL	6 cyl.	Convertible	6,000	14,000	25,000
1968	280 SL	6 cyl.	Convertible	8,000	17,000	30,000
1970	280 SL	6 cyl.	Convertible	4,900	16,000	35,000
1971	220	6 cyl.	Sedan	2,000	4,000	8,500
1971	220D	6 cyl.	Sedan	1,500	3,000	8,000
1971	280 SE	6 cyl.	Sedan	3,000	7,000	15,000
1971	280 SE	3.5 Litre	Convertible	20,000	45,000	80,000
1971	300 SE	6 cyl.	Convertible	6,600	12,000	24,000
1971	600	8 cyl.	Sedan	5,200	16,000	34,000
1972	250	6 cyl.	Sedan	3,000	6,000	10,000
1972	350 SL	8 cyl.	Convertible	10,000	17,000	35,000
1972	600	8 cyl.	Limousine	5,500	17,000	45,000
1973	220	8 cyl.	Sedan	2,000	4,000	8,500
1973	450 SEL	V 8 cyl.	Convertible	10,000	20,000	27,000
MERCER *(United States, 1910–31)*						
1910	35-R	4 cyl.	Speedster	25,000	60,000	120,000

YEAR	MODEL	ENGINE	BODY	F	G	E
MERCER *(United States, 1910–31) (continued)*						
1917	22-73	4 cyl.	4 Passenger			
			Touring	10,000	30,000	65,000
1922	5	4 cyl.	Coupe	16,000	30,000	52,000
MERCURY *(United States, Ford-built, 1939 to date)*						
1939	99 A	V 8 cyl.	Sport Coupe	1,300	4,200	10,000
1939	99 A	V 8 cyl.	Convertible	6,500	11,000	31,000
1939	99 A	V 8 cyl.	Sedan	1,100	3,700	7,400
1940	09 A	V 8 cyl.	Sport Coupe	1,200	3,100	8,500
1940	09 A	V 8 cyl.	Convertible	6,300	11,000	31,000
1940	09 A	V 8 cyl.	Convertible			
			Sedan	6,000	9,600	28,200
1940	09 A	V 8 cyl.	Tudor	1,100	1,900	9,000
1940	09 A	V 8 cyl.	Fordor	1,100	2,900	8,000
1941	19 A	V 8 cyl.	Convertible	2,800	5,300	27,500
1941	19 A	V 8 cyl.	Business			
			Coupe	800	1,900	8,100
1941	19 A	V 8 cyl.	5 Passenger			
			Coupe	2,000	3,000	8,500
1941	19 A	V 8 cyl.	5 Passenger			
			Coupe	2,200	3,200	9,200
1941	19 A	V 8 cyl.	2 Door Sedan	1,900	2,800	8,000
1941	19 A	V 8 cyl.	Sedan	1,900	2,800	7,500
1941	19 A	V 8 cyl.	Station			
			Wagon	3,700	5,000	16,750
1942	29 A	V 8 cyl.	Convertible	5,000	8,100	18,100
1942	29 A	V 8 cyl.	Business			
			Coupe	2,000	2,900	7,500
1942	29 A	V 8 cyl.	Club Coupe	1,900	2,900	7,500
1942	29 A	V 8 cyl.	2 Door Sedan	1,900	2,800	7,500
1942	29 A	V 8 cyl.	Sedan	1,900	2,800	7,500
1942	29 A	V 8 cyl.	Station			
			Wagon	3,000	5,000	14,750
1946	69 M	V 8 cyl.	2 Door Sedan	1,100	2,300	5,500
1946	69 M	V 8 cyl.	Convertible	6,100	9,600	19,100
1946	69 M	V 8 cyl.	Sportsman			
			Convertible	6,100	12,100	30,500
1946	69 M	V 8 cyl.	Club Coupe	1,100	2,700	6,800
1946	69 M	V 8 cyl.	Sedan	1,100	2,600	5,500
1946	69 M	V 8 cyl.	Station			
			Wagon	2,500	5,100	15,000
1947	79 M	V 8 cyl.	Convertible	6,600	10,100	20,500
1947	79 M	V 8 cyl.	Sportsman			
			Convertible	6,100	12,100	30,500

YEAR	MODEL	ENGINE	BODY	F	G	E
MERCURY *(United States, Ford-built, 1939 to date) (continued)*						
1947	79 M	V 8 cyl.	Club Coupe	1,100	2,700	6,800
1947	79 M	V 8 cyl.	2 Door Sedan	1,100	2,250	5,500
1947	79 M	V 8 cyl.	Station Wagon	2,500	10,000	25,000
1948	89 M	V 8 cyl.	Club Coupe	3,000	5,000	10,000
1948	89 M	V 8 cyl.	Convertible	6,600	14,000	25,000
1948	89 M	V 8 cyl.	Sedan	3,000	4,000	8,000

Mercury – 1948 "Sedan"

YEAR	MODEL	ENGINE	BODY	F	G	E
1948	89 M	V 8 cyl.	Station Wagon	2,800	5,100	15,000
1949	9 CM	V 8 cyl.	Sedan	1,500	2,900	7,100
1949	9 CM	V 8 cyl.	Convertible	6,000	12,000	22,000
1949	89 M	V 8 cyl.	Coupe	2,000	5,000	10,000
1949	9 CM	V 8 cyl.	Station Wagon	2,200	8,000	18,000
1950	0 CM	V 8 cyl.	Convertible	4,200	12,000	21,000
1950	0 CM	V 8 cyl.	Coupe	2,000	5,000	10,000
1950	0 CM	V 8 cyl.	Sedan	3,000	4,000	8,000
1950	0 CM	V 8 cyl.	Station Wagon	3,000	8,000	18,000
1950	Monterey	V 8 cyl.	Coupe	3,000	6,000	13,000
1951		V 8 cyl.	Convertible	7,000	12,000	22,000
1951		V 8 cyl.	Coupe	2,500	5,000	10,000

YEAR	MODEL	ENGINE	BODY	F	G	E
MERCURY *(United States, Ford-built, 1939 to date) (continued)*						
1951	Monterey	V 8 cyl.	Coupe	3,000	5,000	12,000
1951		V 8 cyl.	Sedan	2,000	4,000	9,000
1951		V 8 cyl.	Station Wagon	3,000	8,000	19,000
1952	Monterey	V 8 cyl.	Convertible	6,000	12,000	24,000
1952	Monterey	V 8 cyl.	Hardtop	3,000	8,000	19,000
1952	Monterey	V 8 cyl.	Sedan	2,000	4,000	9,000
1953	Monterey	V 8 cyl.	Hardtop	4,000	8,000	19,000
1953	Monterey	V 8 cyl.	Convertible	7,000	12,000	24,000
1953	Monterey	V 8 cyl.	Station Wagon	2,000	6,000	14,000
1954	Monterey	V 8 cyl.	Hardtop	5,000	11,000	22,000
1954	Sun Valley	V 8 cyl.	Hardtop w/Glass Top	6,000	12,000	26,000
1954	Monterey	V 8 cyl.	Sedan	2,000	3,000	7,000
1955	Monterey	V 8 cyl.	Hardtop	4,000	8,000	18,000
1955	Sun Valley	V 8 cyl.	Hardtop w/Glass Top	6,000	13,000	27,000
1955	Monterey	V 8 cyl.	Sedan	2,000	4,000	8,000
1955	Montclair	V 8 cyl.	Convertible	9,000	18,000	35,000
1956	Custom	V 8 cyl.	Convertible	7,000	15,000	29,000
1956	Montclair	V 8 cyl.	2 Door Hardtop	4,000	8,000	17,000
1956	Montclair	V 8 cyl.	Convertible	8,000	17,000	33,000
1956	Montclair	V 8 cyl.	Sport Sedan	2,000	4,000	9,000
1956	Monterey	V 8 cyl.	4 Door Hardtop	3,000	6,000	12,000
1956	Monterey	V 8 cyl.	Station Wagon	1,700	4,000	9,000
1957	Montclair	V 8 cyl.	Convertible	5,000	12,000	28,000
1957	Turnpike Cruiser	V 8 cyl.	2 Door Hardtop	5,000	10,000	22,000
1957	Turnpike Cruiser	V 8 cyl.	Convertible	8,000	18,000	33,000
1957	Montclair	V 8 cyl.	Sedan	2,000	4,000	7,000
1957	Montclair	V 8 cyl.	2 Door Hardtop	4,000	8,000	16,000
1957	Montclair	V 8 cyl.	Convertible	7,000	15,000	28,000
1958	Montclair	V 8 cyl.	Convertible	6,000	14,000	25,000
1958	Turnpike Cruiser	V 8 cyl.	2 Door Hardtop	4,000	8,000	17,000
1958	Turnpike Cruiser	V 8 cyl.	4 Door Hardtop	3,000	6,000	13,000

YEAR	MODEL	ENGINE	BODY	F	G	E
MERCURY *(United States, Ford-built, 1939 to date) (continued)*						
1959	Parklane	V 8 cyl.	Convertible	6,000	12,000	24,000
1960	Parklane	V 8 cyl.	Convertible	5,000	11,000	22,000
1961	Monterey	V 8 cyl.	Convertible	3,000	5,000	11,000
1962	Custom S-55	V 8 cyl.	Convertible	3,000	7,000	14,000
1962	Custom S-55	V 8 cyl.	2 Door Hardtop	1,500	3,000	8,000
1962	Comet	6 cyl.	Sedan	2,000	3,000	5,000
1962	Comet	6 cyl.	Coupe	2,000	4,000	8,000
1962	Comet	6 cyl.	Station Wagon	900	2,000	5,000
1963	Comet S-22	V 8 cyl.	Convertible	4,000	8,000	14,000
1963	Monterey S-55	V 8 cyl.	Convertible	5,000	9,000	15,000
1963	Marauder S-55	V 8 cyl.	Fastback Coupe	2,000	4,000	8,000
1964	Comet Cyclone 289	V 8 cyl.	2 Door Hardtop	2,500	5,000	10,000
1965	Comet Caliente 289	V 8 cyl.	Convertible	3,000	6,000	12,000
1966	Comet Cyclone GT 390	V 8 cyl.	Convertible	3,000	7,000	15,000
1966	S-55 390	V 8 cyl.	Convertible	3,000	6,000	12,000
1967	Cougar XR7 289	V 8 cyl.	Coupe	2,500	5,000	10,000
1968	Cougar XR7 GTE 428	V 8 cyl.	Coupe	2,000	5,000	11,000
1970	Marauder X100 428	V 8 cyl.	Hardtop	2,000	4,000	8,000
1970	Cyclone GT 428	V 8 cyl.	2 Door Hardtop	1,600	3,300	7,000
1971	Cougar 351	V 8 cyl.	Convertible	3,000	5,000	10,000
METROPOL *(United States, 1913–14)*						
1913		4 cyl.	Speedster	6,000	16,000	36,000
1913		4 cyl.	5 Passenger Touring	5,000	12,000	28,000
1914		4 cyl.	Speedster	6,000	16,000	36,000
1914		4 cyl.	5 Passenger Touring	5,000	12,000	28,000

YEAR	MODEL	ENGINE	BODY	F	G	E
METROPOLITAN *(United States; Great Britain, 1954–62)*						
1954	Nash	4 cyl.	Convertible	3,000	7,000	12,000
1955	Hudson	4 cyl.	Coupe	1,500	4,000	8,000
1956	Nash	4 cyl.	Convertible	4,000	9,000	16,000
1958	AMC	4 cyl.	Coupe	2,000	4,000	9,000
1962	AMC	4 cyl.	Convertible	2,000	4,500	10,000
METZ *(United States, 1909–21)*						
1909		2 cyl.	Roadster	2,000	6,000	14,000
1911		2 cyl.	Roadster	3,000	10,000	20,000
1917	25	4 cyl.	Roadster	3,000	10,000	20,000
1919	Master 6	6 cyl.	Touring	3,500	11,000	24,000
1921	Master 6	6 cyl.	5 Passenger Touring	3,000	10,000	20,000
MEYER *(United States, 1919)*						
1919	2 Passenger	2 cyl.	Runabout	1,500	3,800	9,000
1919	4 Passenger	4 cyl.	Roadster	2,000	4,000	9,000
1919	7 Passenger	6 cyl.	Touring	3,000	10,000	22,000
1919	7 Passenger	12 cyl.	Touring	5,000	12,000	36,000
M.G. *(Great Britain, 1924–80)*						
1924	14/28	1.8. Litre	Sport	4,000	8,000	16,000
1927	14/40		Sport	3,500	7,000	15,000
1927	Morris Six	6 cyl.	Sport	3,000	6,500	11,500
1928	Morris Minor	4 cyl.	Sport	2,000	4,400	7,000
1929	Midget	4 cyl.	Cabriolet	4,000	7,000	15,000
1930	M Type	4 cyl.	Roadster	4,000	8,000	15,000
1930	Midget	4 cyl.	Roadster	2,200	4,800	7,800
1931	J-2	18/80	Roadster	2,500	4,900	8,250
1932	J-2 Midget	4 cyl.	Roadster	2,200	4,700	10,000
1934	LeMans		Roadster	2,600	7,200	15,500
1934	PA	750cc	Roadster	2,300	6,500	14,500
1935	PA	750cc	Roadster	2,300	6,500	14,500
1936	PB	6 cyl.	Touring	1,800	9,000	18,000
1937	TA	4 cyl.	Sport	1,700	8,500	16,750
1938	TA	4 cyl.	Drop Head Coupe	7,000	14,000	27,000
1939	WA	4 cyl.	Convertible Coupe	2,800	8,000	16,500
1947	TC	4 cyl.	Roadster	6,000	12,000	25,000
1948	TC	4 cyl.	Roadster	5,000	11,000	24,000
1949	TC	4 cyl.	Roadster	5,000	11,000	24,000
1950	TD	4 cyl.	Roadster	5,000	10,000	22,000
1951	TD	4 cyl.	Roadster	6,000	12,000	22,000
1952	TD	4 cyl.	Roadster	6,000	12,000	22,000

YEAR	MODEL	ENGINE	BODY	F	G	E
M.G.	*(Great Britain, 1924–80) (continued)*					
1953	TD	4 cyl.	Roadster	6,000	12,000	22,000
1954	TF	4 cyl.	Roadster	5,000	11,000	20,000
1955	TF	4 cyl.	Roadster	4,000	9,000	20,000
1959	MGA	1.6 Litre	Roadster	3,000	8,000	19,000
1960	MGA	1.6 Litre	Roadster	3,000	8,000	19,000
1961	MGA	1.6 Litre	Coupe	3,000	7,000	15,000
1962	MGA	1.6 Litre	Roadster	4,000	9,000	18,000
1962	MGA	4 cyl.	Coupe	1,700	5,500	10,000
1962	MG-Midget	4 cyl.	Roadster	1,500	4,000	7,000
1963	MGB	4 cyl.	Roadster	2,000	5,000	9,000
1963	MG-Midget	4 cyl.	Roadster	1,800	4,500	7,500
1964	MGB	4 cyl.	Roadster	2,000	5,000	9,000
1964	MG-Midget	4 cyl.	Roadster	1,800	4,500	7,500
1965	MGB	4 cyl.	Roadster	2,000	5,000	9,000
1965	MG-Midget	4 cyl.	Roadster	1,500	4,000	6,500
1966	MGB	4 cyl.	Roadster	2,000	4,500	8,000
1966	MG-Midget	4 cyl.	Roadster	1,500	3,500	6,000
1967	MGB	4 cyl.	Roadster	2,000	4,500	8,000
1967	MGB/GT	4 cyl.	Coupe	1,800	4,000	7,000
1967	MG-Midget	4 cyl.	Roadster	1,500	3,500	5,500
1968	MGB	4 cyl.	Roadster	2,000	4,500	8,000
1968	MGB/GT	4 cyl.	Coupe	1,800	4,000	7,000
1968	MGC	6 cyl.	Roadster	2,500	5,500	9,500
1968	MGC/GT	6 cyl.	Coupe	2,000	5,000	8,500
1968	MG-Midget	4 cyl.	Roadster	1,500	3,500	5,500
1969	MGB	4 cyl.	Roadster	2,000	4,500	8,000
1969	MGB/GT	4 cyl.	Coupe	1,800	4,000	7,000
1969	MGC	6 cyl.	Roadster	2,500	5,500	9,500
1969	MGC/GT	6 cyl.	Coupe	2,000	5,000	8,500
1969	MG-Midget	4 cyl.	Roadster	1,000	2,500	4,500
1970	MGB	4 cyl.	Roadster	1,500	3,500	7,000
1970	MGB/GT	4 cyl.	Coupe	1,250	3,000	6,500
1970	MG-Midget	4 cyl.	Roadster	1,000	2,500	4,500
1971	MGB	4 cyl.	Roadster	1,500	3,500	7,000
1971	MGB/GT	4 cyl.	Coupe	1,250	3,000	6,500
1971	MG-Midget	4 cyl.	Roadster	1,000	2,500	4,500
1972	MGB	4 cyl.	Roadster	1,500	3,500	7,000
1972	MGB/GT	4 cyl.	Coupe	1,250	3,000	6,500
1972	MG-Midget	4 cyl.	Roadster	1,000	2,500	4,500
1973	MGB	4 cyl.	Roadster	1,500	3,500	7,000
1973	MGB/GT	4 cyl.	Coupe	1,250	3,000	6,500
1973	MG-Midget	4 cyl.	Roadster	1,000	2,500	4,500
1974	MGB	4 cyl.	Roadster	1,500	3,500	7,000

YEAR	MODEL	ENGINE	BODY	F	G	E
M.G.	*(Great Britain, 1924–80) (continued)*					
1974	MGB/GT	4 cyl.	Coupe	1,250	3,000	6,500
1974	MG-Midget	4 cyl.	Roadster	1,000	2,500	4,500
1975	MGB	4 cyl.	Roadster	1,500	3,500	7,000
1975	MG-Midget	4 cyl.	Roadster	1,000	2,500	4,500
1976	MGB	4 cyl.	Roadster	1,500	3,500	7,000
1976	MG-Midget	4 cyl.	Roadster	1,250	3,000	4,750
1977	MGB	4 cyl.	Roadster	1,500	3,500	7,000
1977	MG-Midget	4 cyl.	Roadster	1,250	3,000	4,750
1978	MGB	4 cyl.	Roadster	1,500	3,500	7,000
1978	MG-Midget	4 cyl.	Roadster	1,500	3,500	5,500
1979	MGB	4 cyl.	Roadster	2,000	4,000	7,500
1979	MG-Midget	4 cyl.	Roadster	1,500	3,500	6,000
1980	MGB	4 cyl.	Roadster	2,500	5,000	8,000
MICHIGAN	*(United States, 1904–13)*					
1904		3½ hp	Buggy	4,000	10,000	21,000
1911	B	4 cyl.	Touring	5,000	10,000	22,000
1912	33	4 cyl.	Roadster	5,000	12,000	26,000
1913	L	4 cyl. 40 hp	5 Passenger Touring	6,000	12,000	28,000
MIDLAND	*(United States, 1908–13)*					
1908	G-9	4 cyl.	Touring		RARE	
1911	L-1	4 cyl.	4 Passenger Roadster	5,000	12,000	24,000
1913	T-6	6 cyl.	2 Passenger Roadster	5,000	16,000	34,000
MILBURN ELECTRIC	*(United States, 1914–23)*					
1914		Electric	Coupe	1,100	3,300	11,000
1922	27L	Electric	Brougham	1,500	3,800	12,000
MITCHELL	*(United States, 1903–23)*					
1903	VI	1 cyl.	Runabout	2,500	6,000	14,000
1910	T	4 cyl.	Touring	3,000	9,000	19,000
1916	16	6 cyl.	5 Passenger Touring	8,000	20,000	42,000
1918	D-5-40	6 cyl.	Touring	7,000	20,000	41,000
1920	E-40	6 cyl.	7 Passenger Touring	6,000	15,000	30,000
1923	F-50	6 cyl.	Phaeton	3,500	7,000	16,000
MOHAWK	*(United States, 1903–05)*					
1903		1 cyl.	Runabout	2,100	4,500	10,000
1904	5 Passenger	2 cyl.	Tonneau	2,800	5,800	13,800

YEAR	MODEL	ENGINE	BODY	F	G	E
MOLINE *(United States, 1904–13)*						
1904		2 cyl.	Runabout	3,000	6,000	12,000
1914	M-40	4 cyl.	Touring	5,000	11,000	22,000
1918	S	4 cyl.	Touring	4,000	9,000	21,000
1919	L	4 cyl.	Sedan	2,100	4,500	10,000
MONARCH *(United States, 1907–19)*						
1907	A	2 cyl.	Runabout	3,000	5,000	11,000
1908		4 cyl.	Touring	1,500	3,200	16,000
1919	J	4 cyl.	Touring	3,000	9,800	22,000
MONITOR *(United States, 1915–22)*						
1915	4-30	4 cyl.	Roadster	2,500	7,000	13,000
1918		4 cyl.	Touring	3,000	7,500	15,800
1922		6 cyl.	Touring	3,800	12,000	26,000
MONROE *(United States, 1914–23)*						
1914	M-2	4 cyl.	Roadster	4,000	8,000	16,000
1916	M-2	4 cyl.	Runabout	3,000	6,000	12,000
1922	S	4 cyl.	5 Passenger Touring	3,500	8,800	19,800
1923	S	4 cyl.	Sedan	3,000	7,000	12,000
MORA *(United States, 1906–10)*						
1906		4 cyl.	Touring	5,000	10,000	21,000
1909	42	6 cyl.	Touring	6,000	12,000	26,000
1910		4 cyl.	Roadster	6,000	12,500	20,000
MORGAN *(Great Britain, 1910 to date)*						
1947	4/4 1	I-4	Roadster	7,500	12,500	20,000
1951	Plus Four 1	I-4	Roadster	6,500	10,000	18,000
1955	Plus Four	I-4	Roadster	5,500	8,000	16,000
1963	Plus Four Plus	I-4	Roadster	6,000	7,000	17,500
1968	Super Sports	I-4	Roadster	10,000	15,000	25,000
1970	Plus 8	V-8	Roadster	10,000	15,000	25,000
MORRISS-LONDON *(United States, 1919–23)*						
1919	Crow	4 cyl.	Roadster	3,500	9,000	20,000
1925	Crow	4 cyl.	Touring	4,000	12,000	28,000
MORSE *(United States, 1910–16)*						
1910	B	4 cyl.	3 Passenger Runabout	7,000	12,000	25,000
1912	D	4 cyl.	5 Passenger Touring	8,000	14,000	27,000
1916	D	4 cyl.	7 Passenger Touring	9,000	14,000	27,000

YEAR	MODEL	ENGINE	BODY	F	G	E
MULTIPLEX *(United States, 1912–13)*						
1912		4 cyl.	Raceabout	6,000	12,000	20,000
1913		4 cyl.	Touring	5,000	10,000	20,000
1913		4 cyl.	Roadster	4,000	9,000	19,000
MURRAY *(United States, 1916–29)*						
1917		V 8 cyl.	Roadster	5,000	11,000	23,000
1918		V 8 cyl.	Touring	5,000	12,000	24,000
1921		6 cyl.	Roadster	6,000	12,000	26,000
1926		6 cyl.	Sedan	4,000	8,000	18,000
1927		6 cyl.	Roadster	6,000	12,000	24,000

NASH *(United States, 1917–57)*						
1918	680	6 cyl.	Coupe	1,000	4,000	9,500
1919	680	6 cyl.	Sedan	1,900	4,500	10,000
1925	Advanced	6 cyl.	Roadster	2,300	7,500	16,750
1928	Standard	6 cyl.	Cabriolet	4,000	9,000	18,000

Nash – 1928 "Cabriolet"

1928	Special	6 cyl.	Sport Touring	3,200	9,300	18,500
1929	Standard	6 cyl.	Sedan	1,900	5,000	9,250
1932	960	6 cyl.	Sedan	1,100	3,250	8,000
1934	Big Six	6 cyl.	2 Door Sedan	1,000	2,500	6,000
1935	Ambassador	8 cyl.	Sedan	1,700	3,200	7,000

YEAR	MODEL	ENGINE	BODY	F	G	E
NASH *(United States, 1917–57) (continued)*						
1936	LaFayette	6 cyl.	Sedan	1,100	2,100	6,000
1939	Ambassador	8 cyl.	Convertible	3,500	8,000	16,000
1940	Ambassador	8 cyl.	Coupe	1,500	3,000	6,500
Postwar Models						
1946	600	6 cyl.	Sedan	800	2,500	5,700
1947	600	6 cyl.	2 Door Brougham	900	1,700	5,950
1948	Ambassador	6 cyl.	Business Coupe	2,500	4,000	7,000
1948	Ambassador	6 cyl.	Sedan	2,000	4,000	8,000
1949	Custom	6 cyl.	Sedan	800	2,500	6,500
1949	Ambassador	6 cyl.	2 Door Brougham	2,000	4,000	8,000
1949	Ambassador	6 cyl.	Sedan	700	2,600	7,000
1950	Statesman	6 cyl.	2 Door Sedan	1,500	3,000	7,000
1950	Ambassador	6 cyl.	Sedan	1,500	3,000	7,000
1950	Ambassador	6 cyl.	2 Door Sedan	2,000	4,000	8,000
1951	Ambassador	6 cyl.	Super Brougham Sedan	2,000	4,000	8,000
1951	Ambassador	6 cyl.	Custom Sedan	2,000	4,000	8,000
1952	Ambassador	6 cyl.	Custom Country Club	2,000	4,500	9,000
1954	Nash-Healey	6 cyl.	Roadster	9,000	20,000	45,000
1955	Ambassador	V 8 cyl.	Sedan	2,000	4,000	8,000
1955	Rambler	6 cyl.	Club Sedan	2,500	4,000	7,000
1956	Ambassador Custom	V 8 cyl.	Sedan	2,000	4,000	8,000
1957	Ambassador Custom	V 8 cyl.	2 Door Hardtop	3,000	6,000	12,000
1957	Ambassador	V 8 cyl.	Sedan	2,000	4,000	8,000
NASH HEALEY *(United States; Great Britain, 1952–54)*						
1951		6 cyl.	Roadster	2,500	8,000	35,000
1953		6 cyl.	Roadster	3,200	9,500	42,000
1954		6 cyl.	Coupe	2,800	5,500	39,000

YEAR	MODEL	ENGINE	BODY	F	G	E

O

OLDSMOBILE *(United States, 1897 to date)*

YEAR	MODEL	ENGINE	BODY	F	G	E
1901	Curved Dash	1 cyl.	Runabout	5,800	10,300	26,000
1902	Curved Dash	1 cyl.	Runabout	5,800	8,600	26,000
1903	Curved Dash	1 cyl.	Runabout	4,600	8,100	24,500
1904	Curved Dash	1 cyl.	Runabout	5,000	8,100	24,500
1905	French Front	1 cyl.	Runabout	6,000	12,000	24,000
1906	Model S	4 cyl.	Touring	7,000	11,200	22,500
1907	F	2 cyl.	Runabout	4,000	8,000	15,000
1908	M-MR	4 cyl.	Roadster	4,500	7,600	20,000
1909	D	4 cyl.	Touring	6,300	10,500	21,500
1909	X	4 cyl.	Runabout	5,000	9,000	15,500
1909	Z	6 cyl.	Touring	5,600	13,000	29,000
1910	Special	4 cyl.	Touring	6,900	14,000	31,000
1911	Special	4 cyl.	Touring	3,100	8,700	21,000
1911	Limited	6 cyl.	Touring	15,000	40,000	78,000
1911	Limited	6 cyl.	Runabout	6,000	19,000	50,000
1911	Autocrat	4 cyl.	Runabout	8,000	14,000	28,000
1912	Limited	6 cyl.	Touring	20,000	30,000	76,000
1912	Autocrat	4 cyl.	Touring	6,300	10,500	21,500
1913	Olds Four	4 cyl.	Touring	3,600	7,900	19,000
1913	Olds Six	6 cyl.	Touring	8,200	16,000	40,000
1914	Baby Olds	4 cyl.	Sedan	3,800	5,800	11,000
1914	54	6 cyl.	Touring	3,800	9,100	21,000
1914	54	6 cyl.	Phaeton	4,400	9,700	23,000
1915	55	6 cyl.	Touring	7,000	9,600	21,500
1915	42	4 cyl.	Touring	3,500	5,400	10,500
1915	42	4 cyl.	Roadster	3,200	5,000	9,750
1916	42	6 cyl.	Sedan	3,400	7,000	13,000
1917	45	V 8 cyl.	Touring	4,600	10,400	30,000
1918	45-A	V 8 cyl.	Touring	5,800	13,000	34,000
1918	37	6 cyl.	Touring	2,400	6,400	12,500
1918	37	6 cyl.	Roadster	2,200	6,000	11,750
1918	37	6 cyl.	Coupe	2,000	5,750	11,250
1919	37-A	6 cyl.	Rumble Seat Roadster	3,300	9,000	20,000
1920	46	V 8 cyl.	Touring	4,800	9,300	26,000
1921	47	V 8 cyl.	Roadster	5,600	9,800	26,000
1922	46	V 8 cyl.	Touring	5,400	9,300	20,000
1923	47	V 8 cyl.	Sport Touring	5,000	6,600	14,500
1924	30-B	6 cyl.	Touring	4,000	8,000	16,000

YEAR	MODEL	ENGINE	BODY	F	G	E
OLDSMOBILE *(United States, 1897 to date) (continued)*						
1924	30-B	6 cyl.	Roadster	3,500	7,500	15,000
1924	30-B	6 cyl.	Sport Touring	3,500	7,500	15,000
1924	30-B	6 cyl.	Sedan	1,600	2,700	7,100
1925	30-C	6 cyl.	Coupe	1,700	3,300	7,100
1926	30-D	6 cyl.	Phaeton	5,800	13,000	32,000
1927	30-E	6 cyl.	Touring	2,900	6,000	12,500
1927	30-E	6 cyl.	Sedan	2,000	4,400	7,750
1927	30-E	6 cyl.	Coupe	3,000	5,500	8,500
1927	30-E	6 cyl.	Landau	2,900	6,000	12,500
1927	30-E	6 cyl.	Sedan	1,900	3,100	7,100
1928	F-28	6 cyl.	Rumble Seat Coupe	2,400	6,400	12,000
1928	F-28	6 cyl.	Touring	2,900	6,000	12,500
1928	F-28	6 cyl.	Roadster	2,500	5,500	12,000
1928	F-28	6 cyl.	Sedan	2,000	4,500	8,000
1928	F-28	6 cyl.	Landau	2,900	6,000	12,500
1929	V-29 Viking	8 cyl.	Cabriolet	6,400	13,000	31,000
1930	V-30 Viking	8 cyl.	Rumble Seat Sport Coupe	2,600	6,600	12,000
1931	F-31	6 cyl.	Sport Coupe	3,200	4,700	10,500
1931	F-31	6 cyl.	Sedan	1,400	3,400	10,500
1931	F-31	6 cyl.	Convertible Roadster	2,750	10,000	22,000
1931	F-31	6 cyl.	Coupe	4,000	5,600	11,500
1932	F-32	6 cyl.	Rumble Seat Coupe	3,200	6,100	11,000
1932	F-32	6 cyl.	Sedan	3,400	5,400	9,000
1932	F-32	6 cyl.	Convertible	5,000	10,000	25,000
1932	L-32	8 cyl.	Coupe	2,400	6,400	12,000
1932	L-32	8 cyl.	Sedan	2,300	5,300	11,000
1933	F-33	6 cyl.	Sedan	3,400	5,000	9,000
1933	F-33	6 cyl.	Coupe	3,200	6,500	11,000
1933	F-33	6 cyl.	Convertible	4,000	8,000	16,000
1933	L-33	8 cyl.	Sedan	2,200	4,800	9,000
1933	L-33	8 cyl.	Coupe	2,500	5,300	9,500
1933	L-33	8 cyl.	Convertible	7,000	11,000	21,500
1934	F-34	8 cyl.	Coupe	2,000	5,500	12,000
1934	F-34	6 cyl.	Sedan	1,750	4,500	7,500
1934	F-34	6 cyl.	Convertible	4,000	8,000	16,000
1934	L-34	8 cyl.	Sedan	3,000	7,000	11,000
1934	L-34	8 cyl.	Coupe	3,400	7,500	12,000

YEAR	MODEL	ENGINE	BODY	F	G	E
OLDSMOBILE *(United States, 1897 to date) (continued)*						
1934	L-34	8 cyl.	Convertible	7,000	11,000	21,500
1935	F-35	8 cyl.	Sedan	2,000	3,300	6,300
1936	F-36	6 cyl.	Coupe	1,400	2,400	10,600
1936	F-36	6 cyl.	Convertible	4,400	9,700	20,000
1936	F-36	8 cyl.	Sedan	1,400	4,600	10,000
1936	L-36	8 cyl.	Convertible	4,700	13,000	34,000
1937	F-37	6 cyl.	Coupe	1,400	3,300	7,700
1937	F-37	6 cyl.	Sedan	1,400	3,300	7,500
1937	F-37	6 cyl.	Convertible	7,000	18,000	30,000
1937	L-37	8 cyl.	Convertible	8,000	16,000	34,000
1937	L-37	8 cyl.	Coupe	1,500	3,200	7,700
1938	F-38	6 cyl.	Convertible	7,000	15,000	30,000
1938	F-38	6 cyl.	Sedan	1,500	3,200	7,500
1938	L-38	8 cyl.	Convertible	8,000	17,000	35,000
1938	L-38	8 cyl.	Coupe	1,400	3,300	7,500
1938	L-38	6 cyl.	Sedan	1,400	3,200	7,500
1939	60	6 cyl.	Coupe	1,400	2,800	7,000
1939	70	6 cyl.	Coupe	1,400	3,000	7,300
1939	70	6 cyl.	Sedan	1,400	2,800	7,000
1939	70	6 cyl.	Convertible	7,000	15,000	29,000
1939	L-39	8 cyl.	Convertible	8,000	17,000	34,000
1940	60	6 cyl.	Convertible	6,000	14,000	27,000
1940	60	6 cyl.	Coupe	1,400	3,100	7,500
1940	60	6 cyl.	Station Wagon	2,300	5,300	11,000
1940	70	6 cyl.	Convertible	7,000	15,000	29,000
1940	70	6 cyl.	Sedan	1,400	3,100	6,000
1940	90	8 cyl.	Convertible	5,200	12,000	30,000
1940	90	8 cyl.	Phaeton	5,800	18,000	39,000
1940	90	8 cyl.	Club Coupe	1,600	4,700	8,700
1940	90	8 cyl.	Sedan	1,500	4,400	7,500
1941	66	6 cyl.	Convertible	6,000	13,000	26,000
1941	66	6 cyl.	Town Sedan	1,400	2,800	6,000
1941	66	6 cyl.	Station Wagon	4,000	8,000	16,000
1941	68	8 cyl.	Station Wagon	4,000	8,000	16,000
1941	76	6 cyl.	Club Sedan	1,400	2,900	7,500
1941	98	8 cyl.	Convertible	8,000	18,000	35,000
1941	98	8 cyl.	Sedan	3,000	5,000	11,000
1941	98	8 cyl.	Club Coupe	1,400	3,000	7,500
1942	66	6 cyl.	Convertible	7,000	14,000	26,000

YEAR	MODEL	ENGINE	BODY	F	G	E
OLDSMOBILE *(United States, 1897 to date) (continued)*						
1942	66	6 cyl.	Station Wagon	5,000	12,000	28,000
1942	78	8 cyl.	Sedan	1,400	2,700	6,500
1942	98	8 cyl.	Convertible	7,000	16,000	32,000
1942	98	8 cyl.	Club Sedan	2,000	4,000	9,000
Postwar Models						
1946	66	6 cyl.	Convertible	7,000	14,000	27,000
1946	66	6 cyl.	Coupe	2,000	4,000	8,000
1946	66	6 cyl.	Station Wagon	5,000	13,000	26,000
1946	78	8 cyl.	Club Sedan	2,000	4,000	9,000
1946	98	8 cyl.	Convertible	8,000	16,000	29,000
1946	98	8 cyl.	Sedan	2,000	5,000	10,000
1947	66	6 cyl.	Club Sedan	1,400	4,000	8,000
1947	66	6 cyl.	Convertible	6,000	14,000	27,000
1947	66	6 cyl.	Station Wagon	5,000	12,000	26,000
1947	78	8 cyl.	Sedan	2,000	4,000	9,000
1947	98	8 cyl.	Convertible	8,000	16,000	30,000
1947	98	8 cyl.	Club Sedan	2,000	4,000	9,000
1948	Dynamic	6 cyl.	Convertible	8,000	15,000	28,000
1948	Dynamic	8 cyl.	Sedan	2,000	4,000	8,000
1948	Dynamic	8 cyl.	Station Wagon	3,000	10,000	25,000
1948	98	8 cyl.	Convertible	7,000	15,000	29,000
1949	Futuramic	V 8 cyl.	Club Coupe	3,000	5,000	10,000
1949	Futuramic	V 8 cyl.	Convertible	8,000	17,000	32,000
1949	Futuramic	V 8 cyl.	Station Wagon	3,000	6,000	14,000
1949	Futuramic	V 8 cyl.	Coupe	3,000	6,000	11,000
1949	98	V 8 cyl.	Convertible	8,000	17,000	33,000
1949	98	V 8 cyl.	Holiday Hardtop	5,000	10,000	20,000
1950	76	6 cyl.	Sedan	2,000	4,000	9,000
1950	76	6 cyl.	Coupe	5,000	8,000	17,000
1950	76	6 cyl.	Station Wagon	3,000	8,000	18,000
1950	88	V 8 cyl.	Convertible	9,000	20,000	38,000
1950	88	V 8 cyl.	Holiday Hardtop	5,000	10,000	22,000
1950	88	V 8 cyl.	2 Door Sedan	2,500	5,000	11,000
1950	98	V 8 cyl.	Convertible	10,000	18,000	34,000

YEAR	MODEL	ENGINE	BODY	F	G	E
OLDSMOBILE	*(United States, 1897 to date) (continued)*					
1950	98	V 8 cyl.	Holiday Hardtop	4,000	8,000	17,000
1950	88	V 8 cyl.	Station Wagon	4,000	10,000	22,000
1950	98	8 cyl.	Sedan	2,000	4,000	10,000
1950	98	8 cyl.	Fastback	2,000	5,000	10,000
1951	S-88	V 8 cyl.	Club Sedan	3,000	5,000	11,000
1951	S-88	V 8 cyl.	Convertible	8,000	15,000	28,000
1951	88 Deluxe	8 cyl.	Sedan	1,500	4,000	10,000
1951	98	V 8 cyl.	Convertible	8,000	15,000	29,000
1951	98	V 8 cyl.	Holiday Hardtop	3,000	7,000	15,000
1951	98	V 8 cyl.	Sedan	2,000	4,000	10,000
1952	S-88	V 8 cyl.	Convertible	8,000	15,000	27,000
1952	S-88	V 8 cyl.	Coupe	2,000	5,000	11,000
1952	98	V 8 cyl.	Convertible	8,000	15,000	29,000
1953	S-88	V 8 cyl.	Convertible	7,000	14,000	27,000
1953	S-88	V 8 cyl.	Holiday Hardtop	4,000	8,000	18,000
1953	S-88	V 8 cyl.	Sedan	2,000	4,000	9,000
1953	88-Super	8 cyl.	Sedan	1,800	4,000	9,000
1953	88-Super	8 cyl.	2 Door Sedan	2,400	4,000	9,000
1953	98	V 8 cyl.	Convertible	9,000	17,000	32,000
1953	98	V 8 cyl.	Holiday Coupe	5,000	10,000	20,000
1953	Fiesta	V 8 cyl.	Convertible	15,000	27,000	50,000
1954	S-88	V 8 cyl.	Convertible	9,000	16,000	30,000
1954	S-88	V 8 cyl.	Holiday Coupe	4,000	9,000	18,000
1954	98 Starfire	V 8 cyl.	Convertible	12,000	22,000	40,000
1954	98	V 8 cyl.	Holiday Coupe	4,000	10,000	22,000
1954	98	V 8 cyl.	Sedan	2,000	5,000	11,000
1955	S-88	V 8 cyl.	Convertible	9,000	17,000	32,000
1955	S-88	V 8 cyl.	Holiday Sedan	4,000	8,000	16,000
1955	88-Super	8 cyl.	Sedan	2,000	5,000	12,000
1955	88-Super	8 cyl.	Convertible	9,000	17,000	32,000
1955	98	V 8 cyl.	Convertible	10,000	18,000	34,000
1955	98	V 8 cyl.	Holiday Coupe	5,000	11,000	24,000
1956	S-88	V 8 cyl.	Convertible	8,000	15,000	29,000

YEAR	MODEL	ENGINE	BODY	F	G	E
OLDSMOBILE	*(United States, 1897 to date) (continued)*					
1956	S-88	V 8 cyl.	Holiday Coupe	3,000	7,000	15,000
1956	S-88	V 8 cyl.	Sedan	2,000	4,000	10,000
1956	98					
	Starfire	V 8 cyl.	Convertible	12,000	22,000	40,000
1956	98	V 8 cyl.	Holiday Coupe	5,000	10,000	21,000
1956	98	8 cyl.	Sedan	2,000	5,000	12,000
1957	S-88	V 8 cyl.	2 Door Sedan	2,000	4,000	10,000
1957	S-88	V 8 cyl.	Holiday Coupe	2,000	6,000	15,000
1957	S-88	V 8 cyl.	Convertible	9,000	16,000	30,000
1957	S-88	V 8 cyl.	Hardtop Wagon	3,000	7,000	14,000
1957	98	V 8 cyl.	Convertible	12,000	22,000	42,000
1957	98	V 8 cyl.	2 Door Hardtop	4,000	10,000	21,000
1957	98	8 cyl.	Sedan	4,000	9,000	20,000
1958	S-88	V 8 cyl.	Convertible	8,000	14,000	24,000
1958	98	V 8 cyl.	Convertible	10,000	18,000	35,000
1958	98	V 8 cyl.	Holiday Sedan	2,500	6,000	14,000
1959	S-88	V 8 cyl.	Holiday Coupe	3,000	8,000	18,000
1959	S-88	V 8 cyl.	Holiday Sedan	3,500	7,000	14,000
1960	S-88	V 8 cyl.	Convertible	8,000	14,000	25,000
1960	98	V 8 cyl.	Convertible	9,000	17,000	32,000
1960	98	V 8 cyl.	Sedan	2,000	4,000	9,000
1960	98	V 8 cyl.	Holiday Coupe	3,000	6,000	14,000
1961	Starfire	V 8 cyl.	Convertible	9,000	16,000	31,000
1961	98	V 8 cyl.	Convertible	6,000	13,000	25,000
1962	Starfire	V 8 cyl.	2 Door Hardtop	4,000	8,000	17,000
1962	98	V 8 cyl.	Convertible	7,000	13,000	24,000
1963	S-88	V 8 cyl.	Convertible	6,000	12,000	20,000
1963	Starfire	V 8 cyl.	2 Door Hardtop	4,000	8,000	16,000
1963	Starfire	V 8 cyl.	Convertible	8,000	14,000	27,000
1963	Jetfire	V 8 cyl.	Coupe	3,000	5,000	10,000
1963	98	V 8 cyl.	Convertible	8,000	14,000	25,000
1964	Starfire	V 8 cyl.	Convertible	7,000	13,000	24,000

YEAR	MODEL	ENGINE	BODY	F	G	E
OLDSMOBILE *(United States, 1897 to date) (continued)*						
1964	Starfire	V 8 cyl.	2 Door Hardtop	4,000	7,000	15,000
1964	98	V 8 cyl.	Convertible	8,000	14,000	25,000
1965	Starfire	V 8 cyl.	Convertible	6,000	10,000	18,000
1965	Starfire	V 8 cyl.	2 Door Hardtop	3,000	5,000	12,000
1965	442	V 8 cyl.	Convertible	5,000	8,000	15,000
1966	Starfire	V 8 cyl.	2 Door Hardtop	2,000	4,000	9,000
1966	Toronado	V 8 cyl.	Custom Hardtop	2,500	5,000	11,000
1967	442	V 8 cyl.	Convertible	6,000	10,000	18,000
1967	Toronado	V 8 cyl.	Custom Hardtop	2,000	4,000	9,000
1969	Hurst/Olds	V 8 cyl.	2 Door Hardtop	4,000	9,000	18,000
1970	Cutlass	V 8 cyl.	Convertible	4,000	8,000	14,000
1971	Cutlass	V 8 cyl.	Convertible	6,000	10,000	18,000
1971	Delta 88	8 cyl.	Sedan	750	1,500	3,250
1971	Delta Royale	8 cyl.	Convertible	2,500	6,000	11,000
1971	Vista Cruiser	8 cyl.	Station Wagon	850	1,750	3,500
1972	Cutlass	V 8 cyl.	Convertible	5,000	10,000	18,000
1973	Cutlass S	V 8 cyl.	Coupe	1,500	3,000	6,000
1973	Cutlass Supreme	V 8 cyl.	Hardtop	2,000	5,000	10,000
1973	Custom Cruiser	V 8 cyl.	Station Wagon	800	2,000	4,000
1973	Delta Royale	V 8 cyl.	2 Door Hardtop	1,500	3,000	6,000
1973	Delta Royale	V 8 cyl.	Convertible	3,000	6,000	10,000
1973	Vista Cruiser	V 8 cyl.	Station Wagon	800	2,000	4,000
1974	Delta Royale	V 8 cyl.	Convertible	3,000	6,000	10,000
1975	Delta Royale	V 8 cyl.	Convertible	4,000	7,000	12,000
OPEL *(Germany, 1898 to date)*						
1898		1 cyl.	Touring	4,000	6,000	12,000
1899		2 cyl.	Touring	3,000	5,000	11,000
1902		2 cyl.	Runabout	3,000	5,000	10,000
1903		4 cyl.	Touring	3,000	4,000	9,000

YEAR	MODEL	ENGINE	BODY	F	G	E
OPEL	*(Germany, 1898 to date) (continued)*					
1905		4 cyl.	Touring	3,000	5,000	9,500
1911		2 cyl.	Roadster	3,000	4,000	9,000
1913		2 cyl.	Touring	2,000	4,000	8,000
1920		4 cyl.	Touring	2,000	4,000	8,000
1924	4/12	4 cyl.	Coupe	2,000	3,500	7,000
1926	Laubfrosch	4 cyl.	Sedan	2,000	3,000	7,000
1928	4/20 hp	4 cyl.	Roadster	6,000	12,000	20,000

Opel – 1928 "4/20 Roadster"

1928		6 cyl.	Sedan	2,000	3,000	6,000
1929	Regent	8 cyl.	Sedan	2,000	4,000	7,000
1930		1 Litre	Coupe	2,000	3,000	6,000
1933		1.2 Litre	Sedan	1,000	2,000	5,000
1935		1.3 Litre	Sedan	1,000	2,000	5,000
1937	Olympia	1.3 Litre	Sedan	1,000	1,900	5,000
1938	Admiral	3.6 Litre	Drophead Coupe	2,000	4,000	7,000
1939	Kapitan	3.6 Litre	Coupe	1,500	3,000	6,000
1947	Olympia	1.3 Litre	Sedan	1,000	2,000	5,000
1948	Kapitan	3.6 Litre	Sedan	1,000	2,000	5,000
1953	Rekord	1488cc	Sedan	1,000	2,000	5,000
1959	Rekord	1897cc	Sedan	1,000	1,600	4,500
1968	Ralley	4 cyl.	Coupe	1,000	1,700	4,000
1970	GT	4 cyl.	Coupe	2,000	4,000	7,000
1973	GT	4 cyl.	Coupe	2,500	5,000	8,000

YEAR	MODEL	ENGINE	BODY	F	G	E

P

PACKARD (United States, 1899–1958)

YEAR	MODEL	ENGINE	BODY	F	G	E
1899	A	1 cyl.	Roadster		RARE	
1900	B	1 cyl.	Roadster		RARE	
1901	C	1 cyl.	Roadster		RARE	
1902	F	1 cyl.	5 Passenger Rear Tonneau	15,000	40,000	75,000
1903	K	4 cyl.	Touring	17,000	35,000	65,000
1904	L	4 cyl.	Touring	11,500	20,000	46,000
1905	N	4 cyl.	Touring	12,500	22,000	49,000
1906	S	4 cyl.	Touring	11,500	20,000	46,000
1907	U	4 cyl.	Touring	10,200	13,700	40,000
1908	UA	4 cyl.	Touring	9,800	17,000	39,000
1909	UB	4 cyl.	Touring	9,900	17,000	40,000
1909	UBS	4 cyl.	Runabout	12,000	19,000	48,000
1909	NA	4 cyl.	Touring	11,000	18,000	41,000
1910	18 UD	4 cyl.	Touring	11,000	19,000	41,000
1910	18 UDS	4 cyl.	Runabout	11,500	21,000	55,000
1910	18 NC	4 cyl.	Touring	10,700	15,700	42,000
1911	UC	4 cyl.	Touring	10,300	19,000	44,000
1911	UCS	4 cyl.	Runabout	9,700	15,000	42,000
1911	NB	4 cyl.	Touring	9,100	14,000	40,000
1912	UEPQ	4 cyl.	Brougham	10,000	16,000	43,000
1912	UESQ	4 cyl.	Coupe	8,900	12,000	30,000
1912	UEFR	4 cyl.	Limousine	9,300	16,000	44,000
1912	UEPJ	4 cyl.	Phaeton	9,900	28,000	50,000
1912	UEST	4 cyl.	Runabout	10,000	21,000	47,000
1912	UEC	4 cyl.	Touring	8,900	15,600	42,000
1912	48	6 cyl.	Touring	10,700	20,000	55,000
1912	PC	6 cyl.	Coupe	10,100	14,700	42,000
1913	TE	6 cyl.	Touring	10,200	15,900	43,000
1913	PB	6 cyl.	Brougham	9,000	14,000	40,000
1913	RC	6 cyl.	Coupe	6,800	11,000	24,000
1913	TG	6 cyl.	Landaulet	11,000	19,000	49,000
1913	TR	6 cyl.	Limousine	8,900	14,900	41,000
1913	PH	6 cyl.	Phaeton	9,200	18,000	49,000
1914	37	6 cyl.	Brougham Saloon Sedan	10,000	18,000	41,000
1914	38	6 cyl.	Coupe	8,900	14,000	30,000
1914	42	6 cyl.	Limousine	9,500	15,900	42,000
1914	51	6 cyl.	Phaeton	10,100	18,000	48,000

YEAR	MODEL	ENGINE	BODY	F	G	E
PACKARD	*(United States, 1899–1958)*	*(continued)*				
1914	46	6 cyl.	Special Touring	10,600	21,000	55,000
1915	79	6 cyl.	Brougham	9,000	15,000	31,000
1915	76	6 cyl.	Laudaulet	9,600	19,000	38,000
1915	72	6 cyl.	Limousine	10,900	16,000	33,000
1915	65	6 cyl.	Phaeton	9,100	16,000	46,000
1915	67	6 cyl.	Runabout	15,000	30,000	60,000
1915	63	6 cyl.	Touring	9,900	17,000	46,000
1915	Twin Six	12 cyl. (Twin 6)	Roadster	16,000	29,000	71,000
1916	111	12 cyl. (Twin 6)	Brougham	11,500	19,000	49,000
1916	102	12 cyl. (Twin 6)	Landaulet	13,900	20,000	51,000
1916	100	12 cyl. (Twin 6)	Limousine	13,000	19,000	49,000
1916	90	12 cyl. (Twin 6)	Touring	13,700	24,000	60,000
1917	151	12 cyl. (Twin 6)	Coupe	10,800	18,000	37,000
1917	161	12 cyl. (Twin 6)	Limousine	11,600	22,000	42,000
1917	156	12 cyl. (Twin 6)	Phaeton	15,000	24,000	62,000
1917	154	12 cyl. (Twin 6)	Touring	14,500	24,000	60,000
1918	172	12 cyl. (Twin 6)	Limousine	13,000	20,000	42,000
1918	168	12 cyl. (Twin 6)	Touring	14,000	23,000	60,000
1918	185	12 cyl. (Twin 6)	Brougham	11,000	20,000	40,000
1918	181	12 cyl. (Twin 6)	Phaeton	12,000	22,000	56,000
1919	177	12 cyl. (Twin 6)	Touring	10,000	18,000	48,000
1919	171	12 cyl. (Twin 6)	Runabout	10,200	22,000	60,000
1919	174	12 cyl. (Twin 6)	Coupe	6,000	14,000	28,000
1920	116	6 cyl.	Runabout	4,100	13,000	28,000
1920	116	6 cyl.	Touring	9,200	14,000	33,000
1920	335	12 cyl. (Twin 6)	Limousine	9,500	13,000	32,000
1921	116	6 cyl.	Touring	10,100	15,000	33,000
1921	335	12 cyl. (Twin 6)	Coupe	8,600	12,000	28,000
1921	335	12 cyl. (Twin 6)	Sedan	7,700	10,200	26,000
1922	126	6 cyl.	Sport Touring	8,300	17,000	36,000
1922	126	6 cyl.	Limousine	7,400	11,000	17,000

YEAR	MODEL	ENGINE	BODY	F	G	E
PACKARD *(United States, 1899–1958) (continued)*						
1923	133	6 cyl.	Touring	7,700	11,700	32,000

Packard – 1923 "Touring Car"

YEAR	MODEL	ENGINE	BODY	F	G	E
1923	136	8 cyl.	Coupe	6,900	10,700	18,000
1924	136	8 cyl.	Limousine	7,700	11,000	22,000
1924	143	8 cyl.	Touring	8,200	14,000	36,000
1925	143	8 cyl.	Sedan	6,100	7,900	18,000
1925	136	8 cyl.	Sport	7,400	17,000	38,000
1926	226	6 cyl.	Touring	7,700	18,000	38,000
1926	236	8 cyl.	Limousine	7,200	10,000	22,000
1926	243	8 cyl.	Touring	8,500	18,000	39,000
1927	336	8 cyl.	Phaeton	8,700	20,000	44,000
1927	343	8 cyl.	Limousine	7,700	11,000	19,000
1927	343	8 cyl.	Touring	7,700	16,000	38,000
1928	426	6 cyl.	Roadster	9,800	16,000	39,000
1928	443	8 cyl.	Convertible Sedan	14,000	26,000	50,000
1928	443	8 cyl.	Roadster	13,000	20,000	50,000
1928	526	6 cyl.	Phaeton	12,000	19,000	38,000
1928	526	6 cyl.	Convertible Coupe	11,000	16,000	38,000
1928	533	8 cyl.	Limousine	6,900	9,100	18,000
1929	626	8 cyl.	Coupe	6,500	15,000	34,000
1929	626	8 cyl.	Convertible Coupe	16,000	30,000	58,000
1929	633	8 cyl.	Roadster	22,000	45,000	82,000
1929	633	8 cyl.	Touring	15,000	30,000	62,000

YEAR	MODEL	ENGINE	BODY	F	G	E
PACKARD *(United States, 1899–1958) (continued)*						
1929	634	8 cyl.	Phaeton	50,000	90,000	180,000

Packard – 1929 "Phaeton"

YEAR	MODEL	ENGINE	BODY	F	G	E
1929	634	8 cyl.	Roadster	65,000	120,000	210,000
1929	640	8 cyl.	Roadster	40,000	75,000	140,000
1929	645	8 cyl.	Roadster	40,000	80,000	145,000
1930	733	8 cyl.	Roadster	35,000	70,000	135,000
1930	733	8 cyl.	Convertible Coupe	20,000	55,000	110,000
1930	734	8 cyl.	Boattail Roadster	60,000	100,000	225,000
1930	734	8 cyl.	Roadster	50,000	100,000	195,000
1930	740	8 cyl.	Roadster	45,000	85,000	175,000
1930	740	8 cyl.	Limousine	10,000	22,000	47,000
1930	740	8 cyl.	Convertible Coupe	25,000	55,000	110,000
1930	745	8 cyl.	Roadster	50,000	110,000	210,000
1931	833	8 cyl.	Convertible Sedan	35,000	70,000	140,000
1931	833	8 cyl.	Phaeton Convertible	35,000	70,000	135,000
1931	840	8 cyl.	Limousine	40,000	90,000	180,000
1931	840	8 cyl.	Roadster	50,000	115,000	225,000
1931	840	8 cyl.	Convertible Sedan	40,000	85,000	175,000
1932	900	8 cyl.	Coupe	7,400	15,000	35,000

YEAR	MODEL	ENGINE	BODY	F	G	E
PACKARD	*(United States, 1899–1958) (continued)*					
1932	900	8 cyl.	Roadster	20,000	35,000	68,000
1932	900	8 cyl.	Sedan	6,900	12,000	30,000

Packard – 1932 "Sedan"

YEAR	MODEL	ENGINE	BODY	F	G	E
1933	1002	8 cyl.	Touring	35,000	60,000	140,000
1933	1004	8 cyl.	Limousine	9,000	20,000	45,000
1933	1004	8 cyl.	Coupe	12,000	25,000	55,000
1933	1005	12 cyl.	Convertible	75,000	140,000	250,000
1933	1005	12 cyl.	Coupe	15,000	25,000	60,000
1934	1100	8 cyl.	Sedan	8,000	20,000	42,000
1934	1101	8 cyl.	Convertible	40,000	75,000	125,000
1934	1101	8 cyl.	Phaeton	40,000	65,000	130,000
1934	1101	8 cyl.	Convertible Sedan	35,000	65,000	135,000
1934	1102	8 cyl.	Limousine	10,000	20,000	45,000
1934	1103	8 cyl.	Sedan	11,000	24,000	49,000
1934	1103	8 cyl.	Victoria Convertible	40,000	75,000	145,000
1935	120A	8 cyl.	Business Coupe	8,000	14,000	24,000
1935	120A	8 cyl.	Sedan	5,000	11,000	23,000
1935	120A	8 cyl.	Touring Sedan	7,000	12,000	24,000

YEAR	MODEL	ENGINE	BODY	F	G	E
PACKARD *(United States, 1899–1958) (continued)*						
1935	120A	8 cyl.	Convertible	15,000	28,000	55,000
1935	120A	8 cyl.	Sport Coupe	8,000	17,000	30,000
1935	1201	8 cyl.	Sedan	7,000	15,000	33,000
1935	1201	8 cyl.	Club Sedan	7,750	16,000	34,000
1935	1201	8 cyl.	Coupe	13,750	25,000	45,000
1935	1201	8 cyl.	Phaeton	14,500	26,500	60,000
1935	1201	8 cyl.	LeBaron Cabriolet	18,000	35,000	68,000
1935	1201	8 cyl.	Victoria Convertible	17,000	30,000	58,000
1935	1202	8 cyl.	LeBaron Town Car	17,500	36,000	78,000
1935	1204	8 cyl.	Roadster	17,500	35,000	68,000

Packard – 1933 "Roadster"

YEAR	MODEL	ENGINE	BODY	F	G	E
1935	1204	8 cyl.	Sedan	7,500	20,000	42,000
1935	1204	8 cyl.	5 Passenger Coupe	9,000	19,000	46,000
1935	1204	8 cyl.	Phaeton	20,000	40,000	70,000
1936	120B	8 cyl.	Touring Coupe	5,900	9,600	19,000
1936	1401	8 cyl.	Victoria Convertible	27,000	50,000	90,000
1936	1401	8 cyl.	Roadster	25,000	45,000	85,000
1936	1401	8 cyl.	Sedan	7,000	15,000	32,000

YEAR	MODEL	ENGINE	BODY	F	G	E
PACKARD *(United States, 1899–1958)* *(continued)*						
1936	1401	8 cyl.	5 Passenger Coupe	7,750	16,000	32,500
1936	1402	8 cyl.	7 Passenger Touring	18,000	40,000	86,000
1936	1405	8 cyl.	Convertible Sedan	30,000	60,000	120,000
1936	1407	V 12 cyl.	Coupe Roadster	45,000	85,000	160,000
1937	115C	6 cyl.	Convertible	12,000	22,000	48,000
1937	115C	6 cyl.	Touring Sedan	4,000	9,000	20,000
1937	120C	6 cyl.	Convertible Sedan	15,000	25,000	55,000
1937	120CD	6 cyl.	Touring Sedan	6,200	12,000	24,000
1937	1501	8 cyl.	Formal Sedan	9,000	14,000	32,000
1937	1501	8 cyl.	Club Sedan	9,000	14,000	35,000
1937	1501	8 cyl.	LeBaron Cabriolet	25,000	50,000	95,000
1937	1501	8 cyl.	Convertible	25,000	45,000	90,000
1937	1502	8 cyl.	Business Limousine	20,000	40,000	75,000
1937	1508	V 12 cyl.	Touring Limousine	8,000	19,000	42,000
1938	1601	6 cyl.	Convertible	12,000	22,000	45,000
1938	1601	8 cyl.	Convertible Sedan	12,000	25,000	50,000
1938	1602	8 cyl.	Touring Sedan	7,000	17,000	35,000
1938	1603	8 cyl.	Touring Sedan	8,000	17,000	38,000
1938	1608	V 12 cyl.	Touring Limousine	15,000	35,000	75,000
1939	1700	6 cyl.	Club Coupe	6,200	7,700	15,000
1939	1701	6 cyl.	Convertible Sedan	12,000	25,000	47,000
1939	1703	8 cyl.	Touring Sedan	5,000	12,000	25,000
1939	1707	V 12 cyl.	Convertible Coupe	50,000	95,000	175,000
1939	1708	V 12 cyl.	Touring Sedan	12,000	30,000	65,000
1940	1800	6 cyl.	Convertible	12,000	22,000	40,000

YEAR	MODEL	ENGINE	BODY	F	G	E
PACKARD	*(United States, 1899–1958) (continued)*					
1940	1801	6 cyl.	Convertible	8,400	17,000	36,000
1940	1803	8 cyl.	Convertible Sedan	25,000	45,000	85,000
1940	1803	8 cyl.	Coupe	8,000	14,000	23,000
1940	1803	8 cyl.	Convertible	20,000	40,000	75,000
1940	1806	8 cyl.	Club Sedan	3,200	10,000	22,000
1940	1807	8 cyl.	Convertible Victoria	22,000	47,000	95,000
1940	1807	8 cyl.	Convertible Sedan	25,000	50,000	98,000
1940	1807-Darrin	8 cyl.	Sport Sedan	15,000	35,000	78,000
1941	1900	6 cyl.	Club Coupe	4,900	7,400	12,000
1941	1901	8 cyl.	Station Wagon	9,000	20,000	45,000
1941	1901	8 cyl.	Sedan	2,000	4,000	10,000
1941	1903	8 cyl.	Convertible Sedan	20,000	40,000	75,000
1941	1903	8 cyl.	Sedan	5,900	7,700	17,000
1941	1905	8 cyl.	Touring Sedan	8,000	14,000	24,000
1941	1907	8 cyl.	LeBaron Sport Brougham	12,000	30,000	65,000
1941	1908	8 cyl.	Town Car	15,000	40,000	85,000
1942	1906	8 cyl.	Convertible Victoria	20,000	40,000	85,000
1942	1907	8 cyl.	Cabriolet	25,000	55,000	100,000
1942	1908	8 cyl.	Town Car	20,000	40,000	85,000
Postwar Models						
1946	2100	6 cyl.	Sedan	4,700	7,100	13,000
1946	2111	8 cyl.	Club Sedan	4,800	7,200	14,000
1947	2126	8 cyl.	Limousine	5,000	14,000	30,000
1948	2201	8 cyl.	Sedan	3,000	6,000	12,000
1949	2301	6 cyl.	Sedan	3,000	7,000	15,000
1949	2302	8 cyl.	Sedan	4,000	8,000	18,000
1950	2301	6 cyl.	Club Sedan	4,000	7,000	15,000
1950	2322	8 cyl.	Limousine	6,000	15,000	30,000
1951	2401	8 cyl.	Coupe	2,500	5,000	10,000
1952	2531	8 cyl.	Convertible	7,000	12,000	20,000
1952	300	8 cyl.	Sedan	3,000	6,000	12,000
1953	2631	8 cyl.	Formal Sedan	4,000	9,000	20,000
1953	2626	8 cyl.	Limousine	3,000	9,000	19,000
1953	2631	8 cyl.	Convertible	8,000	14,000	25,000

YEAR	MODEL	ENGINE	BODY	F	G	E
PACKARD *(United States, 1899–1958) (continued)*						
1954	Clipper	6 cyl.	Club Sedan	3,000	6,000	12,000
1954	5426	8 cyl.	Custom			
			Limousine	3,000	8,000	18,000
1954	Clipper					
	Super	8 cyl.	Sedan	3,000	6,000	12,000
1955	Clipper					
	Custom	8 cyl.	Sedan	2,500	5,000	10,000
1955	Clipper					
	Deluxe	8 cyl.	Sedan	2,000	4,000	9,000
1955	Patrician	V 8 cyl.	Sedan	4,000	7,000	15,000
1955	400	V 8 cyl.	Hardtop	5,000	10,000	20,000
1955	Caribbean	V 8 cyl.	Convertible	9,000	18,000	35,000
1956	"400"	V 8 cyl.	Hardtop	5,000	10,000	20,000
1956	Patrician	V 8 cyl.	Sedan	3,000	7,000	15,000
1956	Caribbean	V 8 cyl.	Hardtop	7,000	14,000	28,000
1956	Caribbean	V 8 cyl.	Convertible	9,000	17,000	35,000
1956	Clipper					
	Custom	V 8 cyl.	Hardtop	3,000	7,000	15,000
1956	Deluxe					
	Clipper	8 cyl.	Sedan	2,000	5,000	10,000
1956	400	8 cyl.	Hardtop	5,100	10,000	20,000
1957	Clipper	V 8 cyl.	Station			
			Wagon	2,000	4,000	8,000
1957	Clipper	V 8 cyl.	Sedan	2,000	4,000	8,000
1958	Hawk	V 8 cyl.	Sport Coupe	7,000	14,000	25,000
1958		V 8 cyl.	Hardtop	3,000	6,000	12,000
1958	L	V 8 cyl.	Station			
			Wagon	1,400	3,500	8,000
PACKET *(United States, 1916–17)*						
1916		4 cyl.	Cycle	1,000	2,900	7,000
PAIGE-DETROIT *(United States, 1909–28)*						
1909	1	3 cyl.	Roadster	6,250	13,500	27,000
1911	C	4 cyl.	Touring	4,900	9,800	18,000
1914	36	4 cyl.	5 Passenger			
			Touring	5,200	13,400	26,000
1915	36	6 cyl.	5 Passenger			
			Touring	4,250	8,500	17,000
1916	6-46	6 cyl.	Roadster	8,000	15,000	30,000
1916	38	6 cyl.	7 Passenger			
			Touring	7,000	15,000	32,000
1918	6-40	6 cyl.	5 Passenger			
			Touring	3,750	10,000	21,000

YEAR	MODEL	ENGINE	BODY	F	G	E
PAIGE-DETROIT	*(United States, 1909–28)*	*(continued)*				
1918	6-55	6 cyl.	Town Car	4,900	13,800	25,500
1919	6-40	6 cyl.	5 Passenger Touring	4,000	10,000	22,000
1919	6-55	6 cyl.	7 Passenger Touring	5,000	12,000	26,000
1921	6-42	6 cyl.	Roadster	7,000	13,000	28,000
1921	6-66	6 cyl.	7 Passenger Touring	7,500	15,500	30,000
1922	6-44	6 cyl.	Touring	5,500	11,000	25,000
1925	6-70	6 cyl.	7 Passenger Phaeton	7,000	15,000	30,000
1927	8-85	8 cyl.	5 Passenger Sedan	4,000	9,000	20,000
PALMER-SINGER	*(United States, 1908–14)*					
1908	Skimabout	4 cyl.	Roadster	8,000	16,000	32,000
1909	6-60	6 cyl.	Runabout	16,000	34,000	68,000
1912	46	6 cyl.	Tonneau	12,000	26,000	55,000
1914	Brighton	6 cyl.	5 Passenger Touring	13,000	27,000	58,000
PAN AMERICAN	*(United States, 1917–22)*					
1917	Chicago	6 cyl.	5 Passenger Touring	7,000	18,000	35,000
1920	American Beauty	6 cyl.	Roadster	8,000	15,000	30,000
1922	6-55	6 cyl.	7 Passenger Touring Sedan	8,000	17,000	34,000
PANHARD	*(France, 1889–1967)*					
1889		V 2 cyl.	Dos-a-dos	4,500	9,500	15,000
1900		2.4 Litre	Voiturette	3,100	7,250	14,500
1905		4 cyl.	Touring	3,100	9,250	22,500
1906		4 cyl. 10.5 Litre	Touring	7,250	18,500	36,000
1910		6 cyl. 6 Litre	Touring	2,250	8,500	20,000
1912		2.6 Litre	Touring	2,100	6,250	12,500
1914		4 cyl. 4.8 Litre	Touring	2,500	7,000	16,000
1919		2.2 Litre	Coupe	950	1,900	4,000
1921		8 cyl.	Sedan	1,300	2,750	6,500
1926		1.5 Litre	Single Passenger	1,250	2,500	5,000
1927		8 cyl.	Sedan	1,300	2,600	6,200
1928	20/60	6 cyl.	Coupe	1,000	2,500	6,000
1929	16/45	1.8 Litre	Coupe	750	1,500	3,000

YEAR	MODEL	ENGINE	BODY	F	G	E
PANHARD *(France, 1889–1967) (continued)*						
1930	18/50	2.3 Litre	Sedan	700	1,400	2,800
1931		6 cyl.	Sedan	1,000	2,500	5,000
1932		8 cyl.	Sedan	1,200	2,600	6,250
1933	6 CS 2	2.5 Litre	Sedan	700	1,400	3,800
1935		8 cyl.	Coupe	1,200	2,750	6,500
1937	Dynamic	2.5 Litre	Coupe	950	1,900	3,800
1938		2.7 Litre	Sedan	800	1,600	3,200
1939		3.8 Litre	Sedan	1,300	2,600	4,250
1945	Dyna	2 cyl.	Sedan	500	1,000	3,000
1946	Dyna	2 cyl. 610cc	Sedan	500	1,000	3,000
1950		750cc	Sedan	500	1,000	3,000
1952	5 CV	850cc	Sedan	550	1,100	3,200
1953	Junior	38 bph	Roadster	1,100	2,300	4,500
1954		62 (Supercharged)	Roadster	1,300	3,100	6,200
1954	Dyna		Sedan	350	750	2,400
1958	Dyna		Sedan	350	750	2,400
1961	Tigre		Sedan	750	2,400	4,600
1964	24 GT	848cc	Coupe	600	1,250	3,400
1967	Dyna		Coupe	700	1,300	3,500
1967	Dyna		Coupe	700	1,300	3,500
PANTHER *(Great Britain, 1971–80)*						
1971	DeVille	4 cyl. (Rolls-Royce)	Sedan	15,000	40,000	98,000
1972	J-72	6 cyl. (Jaguar)	Sport	8,000	20,000	45,000
PARAGON *(United States, 1920–21)*						
1920		4 cyl.	Touring		RARE	
1921		4 cyl.	Roadster		RARE	
PARAMOUNT *(Great Britain, 1950–56)*						
1950		1508cc (Ford Ten)	Touring	1,200	3,200	6,200
1955		(Ford Consul)	Sedan	1,000	2,000	4,000
PARENT *(France, 1913–14)*						
1913		1 cyl.	Runabout	900	3,600	7,000
1914		4 cyl.	Runabout	1,000	4,000	9,000
PARENTI *(United States, 1920–22)*						
1920		8 cyl.	Touring	4,000	13,000	26,000
1921		8 cyl.	Town Car	3,500	8,000	18,000
1922		6 cyl. (Falls)	Roadster	6,000	12,000	22,000
PARISIENNE *(France, 1899–1903)*						
1899		1 cyl. (DeDion)	Victoria	2,200	6,200	12,500
1899		1 cyl. (Aster)	Voiturette	2,000	6,000	12,000
1900		2 cyl. (Aster)	Duc-Spider	1,800	5,500	11,500
1900		2 cyl. (Aster)	Duc-Tonneau	1,900	5,900	11,800

YEAR	MODEL	ENGINE	BODY	F	G	E
PARIS-RHONE *(France, 1947–50)*						
1947	3-Wheel	Electric	Cycle	500	1,900	4,000
1950	3-Wheel	Electric	Coupe	500	1,900	4,000
PARRY; NEW PARRY *(United States, 1910–12)*						
1910	20	4 cyl.	Touring	2,000	8,000	17,000
1912	30	4 cyl.	Touring	2,500	8,800	17,600
PARTIN; PARTIN-PALMER *(United States, 1913–17)*						
1913	38	4 cyl.	6 Passenger Touring	6,000	13,000	27,000
1915	20	4 cyl.	Roadster	6,000	12,000	24,000
1916	8-45	8 cyl.	6 Passenger Touring	4,500	12,000	24,000
1917	32	4 cyl.	Roadster	8,000	14,000	26,000
PASSY-THELLIER *(France, 1903–07)*						
1903		2 cyl. (Aster)	Landaulet	1,500	4,000	9,000
1906		4 cyl. (Aster)	Voiturette	1,600	4,300	9,500
PATERSON *(United States, 1908–23)*						
1908	14	2 cyl. (Air-cooled)	Buggy	2,500	7,800	15,600
1910	30	4 cyl.	5 Passenger Touring	4,000	10,000	21,000
1915	6-48	6 cyl.	5 Passenger Touring	5,000	11,000	24,000
1923	22	6 cyl.	Sport	8,000	15,000	26,000
PATHFINDER *(United States, 1912–17)*						
1912	X11	4 cyl.	Phaeton	3,600	12,000	25,000
1914	XIV-E	6 cyl.	Cruiser	2,600	7,000	15,000
1917	40	V 12 cyl. (Weidely)	Touring	5,500	16,000	36,000
PATIN *(France, 1898–1900)*						
1898	Tandem	Electric	Open	2,600	6,000	14,000
1900	Victoria	Electric	Tonneau	2,800	6,300	14,500
1900	3-Wheel	Electric	Voiturette	2,250	6,300	14,500
PAYNE-MODERN *(United States, 1907–08)*						
1907		4 cyl.	Touring	3,000	9,600	21,500
1908		6 cyl.	Roadster	3,200	10,000	22,000
PAYZE *(Great Britain, 1920–21)*						
1920	10	(Coventry-Simplex)	2 Passenger	1,000	3,000	7,000
1921	Cloverleaf	(Coventry-Simplex)	3 Passenger	1,200	3,250	7,500
PEARSON-COX *(Great Britain, 1909–16)*						
1909		3 cyl.	Runabout	1,000	3,000	7,000
1913		4 cyl.	Touring	1,100	3,250	7,500
1915		2 cyl.	Cycle	900	1,750	3,500

YEAR	MODEL	ENGINE	BODY	F	G	E
PEEL *(Great Britain, 1962–66)*						
1962	3-Wheel	4 cyl.	Cycle	500	1,000	2,500
1964	P 50	49cc (D.K.W.)	Single			
			Passenger			
			Coupe	400	800	2,000
1966	Trident	Electric	Tandem	400	800	2,000
PEER GYNT *(Germany, 1899–1925)*						
1899		1 cyl.	Cycle	1,000	1,800	3,000
1900		1 cyl. (DeDion)	Tonneau	2,200	4,300	8,500
1901		1 cyl. (DeDion)	Touring	2,200	4,300	8,500
1902		1 cyl.	Touring	2,250	4,500	9,000
1903	FC	1 cyl.	Touring	2,500	5,000	10,000
1904		4 cyl.	Racing	5,000	10,000	19,000
1904	Green Dragon	6 cyl.	Racing	6,000	14,500	35,000
1907		6 cyl.	Touring	3,250	6,500	12,500
1915		8 cyl.	Roadster	3,750	12,500	25,000
1917		V 8 cyl.	Opera Coupe	3,000	6,000	12,000
1923	66	6 cyl.	Phaeton	4,500	9,000	18,000
1925	67	8 cyl.	Touring	4,000	8,000	15,000
1926		6 cyl.	Roadster	2,500	5,500	12,000
1927		6 cyl.	Coupe	2,000	4,000	7,800
1927		6 cyl.	Sport Coupe	2,250	4,500	8,000
1928		6 cyl.	Roadster	2,000	6,000	12,000
1929		6 cyl.	Sedan	1,250	2,500	5,000
1929	V-16	V 16 cyl.	Touring	7,500	17,000	35,000
1929			Town Car	2,500	5,000	9,500
1929	Custom 8	8 cyl.	Sedan	2,000	4,000	7,500
1930	Custom 8	8 cyl.	Club Sedan	2,500	5,000	9,750
1930	Custom 8	8 cyl.	Victoria	2,250	4,500	9,000
1931	Custom 8	8 cyl.	Coupe	2,500	5,000	10,000
1932	Deluxe					
	Custom 8	8 cyl.	Sedan	2,500	4,700	9,200
PEGASO *(Spain, 1951–58)*						
1951	Tipo Z 102	V 8 cyl.	Coupe	8,000	15,000	22,000
1953	Tipo 102B	V 8 cyl.	Drop Head			
			Coupe	10,000	18,000	28,000
1954	Tipo 102					
	SS	V 8 cyl.	Sport	18,000	30,000	42,000
PENNINGTON *(United States, 1894–1900)*						
1894	3-Wheel	Electric	Coupe	2,000	6,000	14,000
1896		Electric	Victoria	2,300	6,300	14,000
1897		V 4 cyl. (Kane)	Touring	1,500	5,500	14,000
1898		2 cyl.	Touring	1,500	5,000	12,000

YEAR	MODEL	ENGINE	BODY	F	G	E
PENNINGTON *(United States, 1894–1900) (continued)*						
1900	Type D	4 cyl.	Touring	2,200	6,300	14,500
1900			Tri-car	1,000	4,750	11,500
PENNSYLVANIA *(United States, 1907–11)*						
1907	7	4 cyl.	5 Passenger Touring	3,500	12,500	25,000
1910	H-6	6 cyl.	7 Passenger Touring	12,000	25,000	52,000
PERFECTA *(Italy, 1899–1903)*						
1899		(Gaillardet)		1,100	3,250	7,500
1899		1 cyl. (DeDion)		1,100	3,250	7,500
PERL *(Austria, 1921–27)*						
1921		4 cyl.	Coupe	750	1,400	5,000
1927		4 cyl.	Coupe	850	1,500	5,000
PERRY *(Great Britain, 1913–16)*						
1913		2 cyl.	Sport	1,000	1,750	4,500
1914		4 cyl.	2 Passenger	1,200	3,000	7,000
PETER PAN *(United States, 1914–15)*						
1914	Cyclecar	4 cyl.	4 Passenger Touring	4,000	7,000	14,000
1915	Cyclecar	4 cyl.	Roadster	3,000	6,000	12,000
PETREL *(United States, 1909–12)*						
1909		6 cyl.	Roadster	3,300	7,300	36,000
1912	55	4 cyl.	Touring	3,400	8,400	32,000
PEUGEOT *(France, 1889 to date)*						
1889		Steam	Phaeton	3,250	8,250	17,000
1900		V 2 cyl.	Phaeton	2,250	5,500	11,000
1901		V 2 cyl.	Town Brougham	2,100	4,250	9,500
1902		V 2 cyl.	Town Brougham	2,100	4,250	9,500
1903		V 2 cyl.	Town Brougham	2,100	4,200	9,300
1904		V 2 cyl.	Phaeton	3,200	6,400	12,800
1905		V 2 cyl.	Town Brougham	2,100	4,250	9,500
1906		3.3 Litre	Touring	1,500	3,900	9,000
1907		3.6 Litre	Touring	1,500	3,900	9,000
1908	Type 116	3.6 Litre	Touring	1,500	3,750	8,500
1909		2.2 Litre	Sport	1,000	2,650	6,250
1910		3 Litre	Sport	1,100	2,750	6,500
1911		4.6 Litre	Sport	1,300	2,850	6,750

YEAR	MODEL	ENGINE	BODY	F	G	E
PEUGEOT *(France, 1889 to date) (continued)*						
1912		4.6 Litre	Racing	3,100	7,250	14,500
1913	Bebe	4 cyl.	Runabout	1,000	2,750	6,500
1914		7.6 Litre	Racing	3,750	9,250	26,500
1915		3 Litre	Racing	2,000	5,000	12,000
1916		3 Litre	Touring	1,100	2,250	6,500
1917		3 Litre	Touring	1,100	2,250	6,500
1918		2.5 Litre	Racing	1,500	5,000	10,000
1919		4.5 Litre	Racing	1,700	6,100	13,200
1920		4.5 Litre	Racing	1,700	6,100	13,200
1921	Type 153	3 Litre	Sport Touring	1,200	3,000	7,000
1922		3 Litre	Touring	1,000	2,000	6,000
1923		2.5 Litre	Touring	900	1,750	5,500
1924	Type 174	1.4 Litre	Touring	650	1,250	3,500
1925		6 Litre	Sport	1,500	5,000	10,000
1926		950cc	Sedan	650	1,250	3,500
1927		2 Litre	Coupe	750	1,500	4,000
1928	Type 183	2 Litre	Sedan	700	1,400	3,800
1929	Type 201	1.1 Litre	Coupe	650	1,250	2,500
1930	Type 201	3.8 Litre	Touring	1,800	3,600	7,200
1931		3.8 Litre	Touring	1,800	3,600	7,200
1932		3.8 Litre	Sport Touring	1,900	3,700	8,000
1933	Type 201	1.1 Litre	Coupe	650	1,300	2,600
1934	Type 301	1.5 Litre	Sedan	600	1,200	2,400
1935	Type 601	1.5 Litre	Coupe	650	1,250	2,500
1936		1.5 Litre	Coupe	650	1,250	2,500
1937		1.5 Litre	Touring	750	1,500	3,000
1938	Type 402B	2.1 Litre	Sedan	650	1,250	2,500
1939	Darl Mat	2.1 Litre	Coupe	700	1,400	2,800
1940		3 Litre	Open Sport	1,000	2,250	4,500
1941		2.1 Litre	Cabriolet	750	1,500	3,000
1942		1.5 Litre	Coupe	550	1,100	2,200
1943		2.1 Litre	Cabriolet	750	1,500	3,000
1944		Electric	2 Passenger	850	1,750	3,500
1945	Type 202	1.1 Litre	Sedan	1,000	2,000	5,000
1946	Type 202	1.1 Litre	Sedan	1,000	2,000	5,000
1947	Type 202	1.1 Litre	Sedan	1,000	2,000	5,000
1948	Type 202	1.1 Litre	Sedan	1,000	2,000	5,000
1949	Type 203	1.3 Litre	Sedan	2,000	3,000	6,000
1950	Type 203	1.3 Litre	Sedan	2,000	3,000	6,000
1951		1.3 Litre	Convertible	5,000	8,000	14,000
1952		1.3 Litre	Cabriolet	4,000	7,000	12,000

YEAR	MODEL	ENGINE	BODY	F	G	E
PEUGEOT *(France, 1889 to date) (continued)*						
1953		1.3 Litre	Family			
			Limousine	1,500	3,000	5,500
1954		1.3 Litre	Sedan	2,000	3,000	6,000
1955	Type 403	1.5 Litre	Sedan	2,000	3,000	6,000
1956		1.5 Litre	Convertible			
			Coupe	4,000	7,000	13,000
1957		1.5 Litre	Station			
			Wagon	1,000	2,000	5,000
1958		1.5 Litre	Convertible			
			Coupe	5,000	8,000	14,000
1959		1.5 Litre	Station			
			Wagon	1,000	3,000	7,000
1970	504	1.8 Litre	Sedan	1,000	2,000	4,000
PEUGEOT-CROIZAT *(Italy, 1905–07)*						
1905		1 cyl.	Phaeton	1,200	2,600	6,000
PHANOMEN *(Germany, 1907–27)*						
1907	3-Wheel	V 2 cyl.	Runabout	750	1,500	3,000
1912		4 cyl.	2 Passenger	800	1,600	4,250
1912		4 cyl.	4 Passenger	850	1,750	4,500
1924	412	4 cyl.	Sport	900	1,800	5,500
PHENIX *(France, 1912–14)*						
1912	10	4 cyl.	Racing	2,000	6,000	12,000
1913	12	4 cyl.	Racing	2,100	6,200	12,500
1914	15	4 cyl.	Racing	2,250	6,500	13,000
PHILOS *(France, 1912–23)*						
1912		4 cyl. (Ballot)	2 Passenger	1,000	1,800	4,500
1913		4 cyl. (Altos)	4 Passenger	1,000	1,800	4,500
1914		4 cyl. (Ruby)	2 Passenger	1,000	1,800	4,500
PHIPPS-GRINNELL *(United States, 1911–12)*						
1911	C	Electric		2,400	8,000	16,000
PHOENIX *(Great Britain, 1902–28)*						
1902		2 cyl. (Hudlass)	Voiturette	750	1,500	3,000
1903		3 cyl. (Hudlass)		900	1,700	3,500
1904			Tri-car	800	1,600	3,250
1913	Trimo	1 cyl. (DeDion) 6 hp	Tri-car	960	1,600	3,250
1917		2 cyl.	Voiturette	900	1,500	3,000
1917		3 cyl.	2 Passenger	900	1,500	3,000
1920		4 cyl. 3 Litre				
		(Meadows)	4 Passenger	1,200	3,000	6,000

YEAR	MODEL	ENGINE	BODY	F	G	E
PHOENIX *(ET 1955–56)*						
1955		4 cyl. (Turner)	Super Sport	960	1,300	2,500
1956		2 cyl. (Villiers)	Minicar	600	1,200	2,400
1956	Flamebird	6 cyl. (Fiat)	Sport Coupe	1,200	2,000	4,900
PICCOLO *(Germany, 1904–12)*						
1904		V 2 cyl.	Voiturette	1,200	2,500	6,000
1905		V 2 cyl.	Voiturette	1,200	2,500	6,000
1907		4 cyl.	Voiturette	1,400	3,000	7,000
1909		1 cyl.	Voiturette	900	2,250	4,500
PICK; NEW PICK *(Great Britain, 1898–1925)*						
1898		1 cyl.	Dogcart	1,700	6,300	12,500
1900		1 cyl.	Voiturette	1,250	3,500	7,000
1912		2 cyl.	Racing	2,100	4,250	9,500
1920		4 cyl.	Sport	900	2,800	4,500
1923		4 cyl.	Coupe	750	1,500	3,000
PIC-PIC *(China, 1906–24)*						
1906	20/24	4 cyl.	Touring	1,000	2,000	3,500
1906	35/40	4 cyl.	Limousine	1,000	2,000	3,900
1908	28/32	6 cyl.	Touring	1,600	3,000	5,800
1912	30	6 cyl.	Coupe	1,500	3,000	6,000
1920		V 8 cyl.	Limousine	2,000	3,800	7,500
PIERCE; PIERCE-ARROW *(United States, 1901–38)*						
1901		1 cyl.	Motorette	8,000	15,000	30,000
1902		1 cyl.	Motorette	11,000	20,000	38,000
1903	Motorette	1 cyl.	Runabout	11,900	24,000	40,000
1904	24-28N	4 cyl.	Roadster	15,000	40,000	72,000
1906	Great Arrow	4 cyl.	Victoria Tonneau	16,000	33,000	80,000
1907	Great Arrow	6 cyl.	7 Passenger Touring	16,000	33,000	80,000
1909	24	4 cyl.	Roadster	13,000	26,000	46,000
1910	66	6 cyl.	7 Passenger Touring	15,000	30,800	67,000
1911	48T	6 cyl.	Roadster	16,000	33,000	79,000
1912	66	6 cyl.	Roadster	16,000	33,000	79,000
1913	48-B	6 cyl.	5 Passenger Touring	15,000	31,000	72,000
1914	38-B	6 cyl.	4 Passenger Touring	14,000	28,000	70,000
1915	38-C	6 cyl.	5 Passenger Touring	13,000	27,000	68,000
1916	48-B	6 cyl.	5 Passenger Touring	15,000	40,000	74,000

YEAR	MODEL	ENGINE	BODY	F	G	E
PIERCE; PIERCE-ARROW *(United States, 1901–38) (continued)*						
1917	66	6 cyl.	Roadster	20,000	50,000	85,000
1918	66	6 cyl.	7 Passenger Touring	13,000	28,000	70,000
1919	38	6 cyl.	Brougham Limousine	11,000	23,000	59,000
1920	48	6 cyl.	Brougham	11,000	20,000	55,000
1921	38	6 cyl.	4 Passenger Touring	15,000	35,000	65,000
1922	38	6 cyl.	7 Passenger Touring	18,000	40,000	68,000
1923	38	6 cyl.	7 Passenger Sedan	10,000	25,000	45,000
1924	33	6 cyl.	Limousine	9,200	25,000	55,000
1925	80	6 cyl.	Coupe	10,000	20,000	45,000

Pierce-Arrow – 1925 "Roadster"

YEAR	MODEL	ENGINE	BODY	F	G	E
1926	80	6 cyl.	7 Passenger Sedan	10,000	20,000	45,000
1926	33	6 cyl.	Touring	15,000	30,000	60,000
1926	80	6 cyl.	Roadster	20,000	30,000	55,000
1927	80	6 cyl.	7 Passenger Sedan	8,000	20,000	40,000
1927	36	6 cyl.	Coupe	12,000	25,000	50,000
1927	36	6 cyl.	5 Passenger Sedan	10,000	20,000	40,000
1927	36	6 cyl.	Roadster	20,000	30,000	55,000
1927	36	6 cyl.	Limousine	10,000	25,000	55,000

YEAR	MODEL	ENGINE	BODY	F	G	E
PIERCE; PIERCE-ARROW *(United States, 1901–38) (continued)*						
1928	81	6 cyl.	Brougham	15,000	25,000	55,000
1928	81	6 cyl.	Club Sedan	12,000	25,000	50,000
1929	126	8 cyl.	Convertible Coupe	30,000	50,000	80,000
1929	125	8 cyl.	Twin Sedan	15,000	35,000	65,000
1929	125	8 cyl.	Roadster	20,000	45,000	85,000
1929	143	8 cyl.	Coupe	14,000	24,000	59,000
1929	143	8 cyl.	7 Passenger Sedan	10,000	30,000	60,000
1929	129	8 cyl.	7 Passenger Touring	20,000	40,000	85,000
1930	A	8 cyl.	Convertible Coupe	35,000	60,000	110,000
1930	C	8 cyl.	Sedan	10,000	20,000	40,000
1930	B	8 cyl.	Club Sedan	15,000	35,000	70,000
1930	B	8 cyl.	Dual Cowl Phaeton	19,000	48,000	99,000
1930	A	8 cyl.	Convertible Coupe	35,000	60,000	110,000
1930	B	8 cyl.	Rumble Seat Coupe	15,000	35,000	70,000
1930	B	8 cyl.	Roadster	25,000	55,000	100,000
1931	41	8 cyl.	Touring	25,000	55,000	104,000
1931	42	8 cyl.	Club Sedan	12,000	25,000	50,000
1931	42	8 cyl.	Sport Roadster	40,000	70,000	125,000
1931	42	8 cyl.	Sport Tourer	35,000	60,000	115,000
1931	42	8 cyl.	Rumble Seat Coupe	12,000	25,000	50,000
1931	41	8 cyl.	Sedan	10,400	20,000	63,000
1932	53	V 12 cyl.	Dual Cowl Phaeton	40,000	75,000	140,000
1932	51	V 12 cyl.	Convertible Victoria Coupe	35,000	65,000	120,000
1932	53	V 12 cyl.	Rumble Seat Coupe	15,000	30,000	60,000
1932	52	V 12 cyl.	Club Coupe	15,000	30,000	55,000
1932	53	V 12 cyl.	Convertible Coupe	30,000	55,000	97,000
1932	54	8 cyl.	Convertible Coupe Roadster	30,000	60,000	100,000

YEAR	MODEL	ENGINE	BODY	F	G	E
PIERCE; PIERCE-ARROW *(United States, 1901–38) (continued)*						
1932	54	8 cyl.	Club			
			Brougham	12,000	25,000	50,000
1933	836	8 cyl.	Sedan	10,000	20,000	45,000

Pierce-Arrow – 1933 "Silver Arrow"

1933	1236	V 12 cyl.	Sedan	12,000	25,000	55,000
1933	1236	V 12 cyl.	Club			
			Brougham	14,000	22,000	46,000
1933	1247	V 12 cyl.	4 Passenger			
			Coupe Sedan	15,000	65,000	120,000
1934	1250A	V 12 cyl.	Silver Arrow			
			Sedan	40,000	70,000	125,000
1934	1240A	V 12 cyl.	Sedan	12,000	25,000	55,000
1934	1250A	V 12 cyl.	Limousine	10,000	25,000	65,000
1935	836A	8 cyl.	Sedan	10,000	20,000	45,000
1935	1245	V 12 cyl.	Rumble Seat			
			Coupe	12,000	25,000	55,000
1935	845	8 cyl.	Convertible			
			Roadster	20,000	35,000	65,000
1935	1245	V 12 cyl.	Sedan	10,000	22,000	50,000
1936	Deluxe 8	8 cyl.	Country Club			
			Roadste	20,000	35,000	60,000
1936	Salon	V 12 cyl.	5 Passenger			
			Sedan	5,200	15,000	38,000
1936	Deluxe	8 cyl.	Convertible			
			Sedan	20,000	35,000	65,000
1936	Deluxe	8 cyl.	Rumble Seat			
			Coupe	10,000	20,000	45,000

YEAR	MODEL	ENGINE	BODY	F	G	E
PIERCE; PIERCE-ARROW *(United States, 1901–38) (continued)*						
1937	P-A 8	8 cyl.	Rumble Seat Coupe	10,000	20,000	45,000
1937	P-A12	V 12 cyl.	Sedan	5,900	15,000	38,000
1937	P-A12	V 12 cyl.	Convertible Sedan	20,000	45,000	85,000
1937	P-A 8	8 cyl.	Convertible Roadster	20,000	35,000	65,000
1938	P-A 8	V 12 cyl.	Formal Sedan	9,200	19,000	44,000
1938	P-A12	V 12 cyl.	Rumble Seat Coupe	15,000	30,000	60,000
1938	P-A12	V 12 cyl.	Convertible	25,000	45,000	80,000

Pierce-Arrow – 1934 "Coupe Convertible"

				F	G	E
PILOT *(Great Britain, 1909–14)*						
1909		(White & Poppe)	2 Passenger	1,000	3,750	8,500
1910		(Hillman)	2 Passenger	1,100	3,750	8,500
1911		1 cyl. (Coventry-Simplex)	4 Passenger	1,100	3,250	8,500
1912		4 cyl. (Chapuis-Dornier)	2 Passenger	1,200	3,400	10,000
PILOT *(United States, 1909–24)*						
1909	35	4 cyl.	Roadster	7,000	12,000	20,000
1910	35	4 cyl.	Roadster	7,000	12,000	20,000
1913	60	6 cyl.	Touring	8,000	17,000	35,000
1916	55	6 cyl.	7 Passenger Touring	7,000	15,000	30,000

YEAR	MODEL	ENGINE	BODY	F	G	E
PILOT *(United States, 1909–24) (continued)*						
1916	75	6 cyl.	Roadster	15,000	25,000	45,000
1924	56	6 cyl.	5 Passenger			
			Touring	7,000	15,000	30,000
PIPE *(Brazil, 1898–1922)*						
1898		2 cyl.	Racing	1,250	4,750	9,500
1898	16	4 cyl.	Racing	1,500	5,000	10,000
1905	28/32	6 cyl.	Racing	1,750	5,500	12,000
1918	80	V 8 cyl. 11 Litre	Racing	5,200	13,000	27,000
PIPER *(Great Britain, 1966–73)*						
1966		(Ford)	Sport Racing	2,000	4,000	7,000
1967		(B.M.C.)	Gran Turismo			
			Coupe	700	2,200	5,500
1967		2 Litre (B.R.M.)	Racing	900	2,750	5,500
1971		1600 (Ford GT)	Racing	1,000	3,000	7,000
1973		2 Litre (Ford)	Racing	1,200	2,300	5,500
PIVOT *(France, 1904–07)*						
1904		1 cyl.	Touring	1,200	3,250	8,500
1905		2 cyl.	Town	1,750	4,250	9,500
1906		4 cyl.	Town	2,000	4,750	10,500
1907		4 cyl.	Touring	1,750	5,250	11,500
PLUTON *(France, 1901)*						
1901	Spider	1 cyl.	Runabout	1,300	4,500	9,000
1901		(DeDion)	Tonneau	2,000	5,750	105,000
PLYMOUTH *(United States, 1928 to date)*						
1928	Q	4 cyl.	Roadster	8,000	14,000	26,000
1929	Q	4 cyl.	Touring	6,000	12,000	24,000
1930	U	4 cyl.	Roadster	8,000	15,000	28,000
1931	PA	4 cyl.	Roadster	3,900	13,400	26,000
1932	PA	4 cyl.	Roadster	3,900	13,400	26,000
1933	PC	6 cyl.	Convertible	3,000	12,300	22,500
1934	PE	6 cyl.	Convertible	2,500	12,600	22,000
1935	PJ	6 cyl.	Coupe	2,000	4,000	7,000
1936	P1	6 cyl.	Business			
			Coupe	2,000	4,000	7,000
1937	Roadking	6 cyl.	Coupe	2,000	4,000	7,000
1938	Deluxe	6 cyl.	Sedan	1,200	2,500	6,000
1939	Deluxe	6 cyl.	Convertible			
			Sedan	4,500	13,500	24,000
1941	Special					
	Deluxe	6 cyl.	Convertible	7,000	14,000	26,000
1942	Deluxe	6 cyl.	Sedan	1,200	2,900	5,000

YEAR	MODEL	ENGINE	BODY	F	G	E
PLYMOUTH	*(United States, 1928 to date)* *(continued)*					
1946	P15	6 cyl.	Convertible	6,000	12,000	20,000
1947	P15	6 cyl.	Club Coupe	1,800	3,700	7,900
1948	P15	6 cyl.	Coupe	3,000	5,000	10,000
1949	Special Deluxe	6 cyl.	Convertible	7,000	14,000	22,000
1950	Special Deluxe	6 cyl.	Convertible	6,000	12,000	20,000
1951	P23	6 cyl.	Coupe	2,000	4,000	8,000
1952	Cranbrook	6 cyl.	Hardtop	3,000	6,000	12,000
1953	Cranbrook	6 cyl.	Sedan	2,000	4,000	7,000
1954	Belvedere	6 cyl.	Convertible	6,000	12,000	20,000
1955	Belvedere	V 8 cyl.	2 Door Hardtop	4,000	10,000	18,000
1956	Fury	V 8 cyl.	Hardtop	4,000	10,000	18,000
1957	Plaza	V 8 cyl.	Coupe	2,000	3,000	5,000
1957	Belvedere	V 8 cyl.	Convertible	7,000	14,000	25,000
1958	Belvedere	V 8 cyl.	2 Door Hardtop	4,000	7,000	15,000
1959	Belvedere	V 8 cyl.	4 Door Hardtop	2,000	3,000	6,000
1964	Barracuda	V 8 cyl. 273	Coupe	4,000	7,000	12,000
1967	Barracuda	V 8 cyl. 273	Convertible	6,000	10,000	16,000
1970	Super Bird	V 8 cyl. 440	2 Door Hardtop	10,000	20,000	45,000
POBIEDA; VICTORY	*(Soviet Union, 1946–58)*					
1946		4 cyl.	Sedan	700	1,300	2,500
1950		6 cyl.	Touring	750	1,500	4,000
1952		2.1 Litre	Sedan	450	900	2,000
1955	M-72	6 cyl.	Sedan	500	1,000	2,000
1956	M-20	6 cyl.	Sedan	500	1,000	2,000
1957	Volga 21	6 cyl.	Sedan	500	1,000	2,000
POLYMOBIL	*(Germany, 1904–09)*					
1904	8/10	2 cyl.	Tonneau	1,000	3,000	7,000
1906	16/20	4 cyl.	Runabout	1,300	3,300	7,500
PONTIAC	*(United States, 1926 to date)*					
1926	6-26	6 cyl.	Coupe	3,000	6,000	13,000
1926	6-26	6 cyl.	Sedan	3,000	4,500	12,500
1927	6-27	6 cyl.	Sport Cabriolet	2,200	5,750	12,000
1928	6-28	6 cyl.	Roadster	3,300	12,000	22,000
1929	6-29A	6 cyl.	Roadster	3,400	12,000	23,000

YEAR	MODEL	ENGINE	BODY	F	G	E
PONTIAC *(United States, 1926 to date) (continued)*						
1930	6-30B	6 cyl.	Sport			
			Roadster	3,300	11,000	22,000
1931	401	6 cyl.	Convertible	3,500	12,000	22,000
1932	302	V 8 cyl.	Convertible	8,000	15,000	27,000
1933	601	8 cyl.	2 Door Sedan	1,600	4,900	11,000
1934	603	8 cyl.	Convertible	2,700	12,000	23,000
1935	Deluxe	8 cyl.	Coupe	2,000	5,500	11,000
1936	Deluxe	6 cyl.	Sport Coupe	1,500	4,400	11,000
1937	Deluxe	8 cyl.	Convertible			
			Sedan	7,000	14,000	26,000
1938	Deluxe	8 cyl.	Convertible	6,000	12,000	22,000
1939	Deluxe 8	8 cyl.	Touring			
			Sedan	1,800	4,200	8,000
1940	Model 29	8 cyl.	Sedan	1,800	4,200	8,000
1941	Torpedo	8 cyl.	Convertible			
			Fastback	7,000	12,000	23,000
1942	Streamliner	8 cyl.	Station			
			Wagon	2,600	5,000	12,000
Postwar Models						
1946	Torpedo	8 cyl.	Sport Coupe	1,300	2,800	7,400
1947	Torpedo	8 cyl.	Sedan	1,200	2,500	6,100
1948	Torpedo	8 cyl.	Convertible	7,000	13,000	24,000
1949	Streamline		Station			
	Deluxe	8 cyl.	Wagon			
			(Woodie)	2,200	7,100	14,000
1950	Silver		2 Door			
	Streak	8 cyl.	Hardtop	2,200	7,100	14,000
1951	Chieftain					
	Deluxe	8 cyl.	Coupe Sedan	3,000	6,000	12,000
1952	Chieftain		Hardtop			
	Deluxe	8 cyl.	Super	4,000	9,000	20,000
1953	Catalina	8 cyl.	2 Door			
			Hardtop	3,000	7,000	14,000
1954	Star Chief	V 8 cyl.	2 Door			
			Hardtop	3,000	7,000	15,000
1955	Star Chief	V 8 cyl.	Convertible	8,000	17,000	30,000
1956	Star Chief		Station			
	Safari	V 8 cyl.	Wagon	3,000	7,000	15,000
1957	Star Chief	V 8 cyl.	2 Door			
			Hardtop	4,000	8,000	16,000
1957	Star Chief	V 8 cyl.	Convertible	9,000	16,000	28,000
1957	Bonneville	V 8 cyl. Fl	Convertible	15,000	35,000	60,000

YEAR	MODEL	ENGINE	BODY	F	G	E
PONTIAC *(United States, 1926 to date) (continued)*						
1958	Bonneville	V 8 cyl.	2 Door Hardtop	7,000	16,000	35,000
1959	Bonneville	V 8 cyl.	4 Door Hardtop	2,000	4,000	8,000
1960	Bonneville	V 8 cyl.	Convertible	8,000	15,000	28,000
1961	Ventura	V 8 cyl. 389	2 Door Hardtop	2,000	4,000	9,000
1962	Grand Prix	V 8 cyl. 389	2 Door Hardtop	3,500	7,000	14,000
1963	Grand Prix	V 8 cyl. 389	2 Door Hardtop	3,000	6,000	12,000
1964	GTO	V 8 cyl. 389	Convertible	6,000	12,000	22,000
1966	GTO	V 8 cyl. 389	2 Door Hardtop	3,000	7,000	16,000
1966	Catalina 2 + 2	V 8 cyl. 421	Convertible	6,000	10,000	18,000
1968	Catalina	V 8 cyl.	2 Door Hardtop	1,000	2,400	6,000
1968	Executive	V 8 cyl.	2 Door Hardtop	900	3,000	6,000
1968	Executive	V 8 cyl.	4 Door Hardtop	1,500	4,000	7,000
1968	Executive	V 8 cyl.	Station Wagon	900	2,200	5,000
1968	Tempest	6 cyl.	Hardtop	1,100	2,600	5,500
1968	Tempest	6 cyl.	Sport Coupe	1,000	2,400	5,000
1968	Tempest	6 cyl.	LeMans Convertible	5,000	8,000	14,000
1969	Firebird	V 8 cyl. 389	Convertible	3,000	7,000	12,000
1969	Firebird Trans AM	V 8 cyl. 400	Coupe	3,000	7,000	15,000
1969	Bonneville	V 8 cyl.	2 Door Hardtop	1,500	3,000	6,000
1969	Bonneville	V 8 cyl.	Convertible	3,000	6,000	10,000
1969	Bonneville	V 8 cyl.	Station Wagon	700	1,750	5,000
1969	Catalina	V 8 cyl.	Sedan	700	2,000	4,000
1969	Catalina	V 8 cyl.	2 Door Hardtop	1,000	3,000	5,000
1969	Catalina	V 8 cyl.	Convertible	3,000	5,000	9,000
1969	GTO	V 8 cyl.	Hardtop	4,000	7,000	16,000
1969	GTO	V 8 cyl.	Convertible	6,000	12,000	22,000

YEAR	MODEL	ENGINE	BODY	F	G	E
PONTIAC *(United States, 1926 to date) (continued)*						
1970	Firebird Trans AM	V 8 cyl. 400	Coupe	3,000	7,000	14,000
1970	Bonneville	V 8 cyl.	Sedan	1,000	2,500	5,000
1970	Bonneville	V 8 cyl.	2 Door Hardtop	2,000	4,000	7,000
1970	Bonneville	V 8 cyl.	Convertible	3,000	5,000	10,000
1970	Catalina	V 8 cyl.	Sedan	1,000	2,000	4,000
1970	Catalina	V 8 cyl.	2 Door Hardtop	1,500	3,000	6,000
1970	Catalina	V 8 cyl.	Station Wagon	1,500	3,000	5,000
1970	Executive	V 8 cyl.	Sedan	1,000	2,000	4,500
1970	Executive	V 8 cyl.	2 Door Hardtop	1,500	3,000	6,000
1970	Executive	V 8 cyl.	Station Wagon	1,500	2,500	5,000
1970	Grand Prix	V 8 cyl.	Hardtop "SSJ"	3,000	5,000	10,000
1970	GTO	V 8 cyl.	Convertible	7,000	14,000	24,000
1970	LeMans	6 cyl.	Hardtop	2,000	4,000	8,000
1970	LeMans	6 cyl.	Coupe	2,000	4,000	7,000
1970	Tempest	6 cyl.	Sedan	1,000	2,000	4,000
1970	Tempest	6 cyl.	2 Door Hardtop	1,500	3,000	6,000
1971	Grandville	V 8 cyl.	2 or 4 Door Hardtop	1,000	3,000	5,000
1971	Grandville	V 8 cyl.	Convertible	4,000	7,000	12,000
1971	LeMans GT	V 8 cyl.	2 Door Hardtop	2,000	4,000	9,000
1971	LeMans	V 8 cyl.	2 Door Hardtop	1,250	3,000	6,000
1971	LeMans Sport	V 8 cyl.	Convertible	3,000	6,000	11,000
1971	Ventura	6 cyl.	Sedan	1,000	2,000	4,000
1971	Ventura	6 cyl.	Coupe	1,500	2,500	4,500
1972	Bonneville	V 8 cyl.	2 Door Hardtop Sedan	1,500	3,000	5,000
1972	Bonneville	V 8 cyl.	4 Door Hardtop	800	2,000	4,000
1972	Catalina Brougham	V 8 cyl.	Sedan	700	1,750	3,750

YEAR	MODEL	ENGINE	BODY	F	G	E
PONTIAC *(United States, 1926 to date) (continued)*						
1972	Catalina Brougham	V 8 cyl.	2 Door Hardtop	1,000	3,000	5,000
1972	Safari	V 8 cyl.	Station Wagon	700	1,750	3,750
1973	Grand AM	V 8 cyl.	2 Door Hardtop	1,500	3,250	5,000
1973	LeMans	V 8 cyl.	Sedan	2,000	4,000	7,000
1973	LeMans Luxury	V 8 cyl.	Coupe	700	1,750	3,750
1973	LeMans	V 8 cyl.	Station Wagon	700	1,750	3,750
1973	Ventura	6 cyl.	Coupe	600	1,500	3,500
1974	Grand Prix	V 8 cyl.	Coupe "SJ"	1,000	2,250	5,000
1974	Grand Prix	V 8 cyl.	2 Door Hardtop	1,500	3,000	4,500
1974	Grand AM	V 8 cyl.	2 Door Hardtop	1,300	3,000	7,250
1974	LeMans Sport	V 8 cyl.	Coupe	700	1,750	3,750
POPE-HARTFORD *(United States, 1904–14)*						
1904	A	1 cyl.	Runabout	3,000	7,000	14,000
1905	D	2 cyl.	Tonneau	4,000	8,000	16,000
1907	G	4 cyl.	5 Passenger Touring	4,000	8,000	16,000
1908	M	4 cyl.	Limousine	4,000	7,000	15,000
1910	T	4 cyl.	5 Passenger Touring	5,000	10,000	22,000
1914	35	4 cyl.	Roadster	7,000	14,000	26,000
POPE-TOLEDO *(United States, 1904–09)*						
1904		2 cyl. (Water-cooled)	5 Passenger Touring	4,500	8,500	17,000
1905	VIII	4 cyl.	Tonneau	4,500	9,000	18,000
1907	XV	4 cyl.	Limousine	5,000	10,000	22,000
1909	XXII	4 cyl.	7 Passenger Touring	4,500	12,000	26,000
POPE-TRIBUNE *(United States, 1904–08)*						
1904		1 cyl.	Roadster	6,000	12,000	26,000
1905	IV	2 cyl.	Tonneau	3,750	6,500	15,000
1907	X	4 cyl.	Touring	4,500	9,000	18,000
1908	M	4 cyl.	Runabout	8,000	14,000	25,000

YEAR	MODEL	ENGINE	BODY	F	G	E
PORIER *(France, 1928–58)*						
1928		4 cyl. (Train)	Runabout	900	1,800	4,500
1930	Tandem	4 cyl. (Sach)	Runabout	1,000	1,900	5,000
1937	Monoto XW-5	(Ydral)	Tri-car	800	1,500	4,000
PORSCHE *(Austria; Germany, 1948 to date)*						
1950	356	1100 40 hp	Coupe	10,000	15,000	25,000
1951	356	1100 40 hp	Cabriolet	6,000	12,000	20,000
1954	356	1500 55 hp	Speedster	20,000	30,000	50,000
1955	356 Super	1500 70 hp	Coupe	6,000	12,000	20,000
1956	356A	1600 60 hp	Speedster	20,000	35,000	55,000
1956	356A Super	1600 75 hp	Cabriolet	12,000	20,000	35,000
1956	356A Carrera	1500 100 hp	Speedster	25,000	40,000	60,000
1958	356A	1600 60 hp	Hardtop	8,000	15,000	25,000
1960	356B	1600 60 hp	Coupe	6,000	10,000	20,000
1960	356B Super	1600 75 hp	Roadster	8,000	15,000	25,000
1960	356B Super 90	1600 90 hp	Cabriolet	10,000	16,000	28,000
1961	356B Carrera	2000 130 hp	Cabriolet	15,000	25,000	40,000
1962	356C	1600 95 hp	Coupe SC	8,000	12,000	20,000
1964	356C SC	1600 95 hp	Cabriolet	8,000	12,000	20,000
1966	912	4 cyl. 90 hp	Coupe	5,000	8,000	15,000
1966	911	6 cyl. 130 hp	Coupe	5,000	10,000	18,000
1967	911	6 cyl. 130 hp	Targa	9,000	14,000	20,000
1967	911S	6 cyl. 160 hp	Targa	12,000	18,000	25,000
1968	911L	6 cyl. 130 hp	Targa	9,000	14,000	20,000
1969	912	4 cyl. 90 hp	Coupe	5,000	8,000	15,000
1969	911T	6 cyl. 110 hp	Targa	9,000	14,000	20,000
1969	91E	6 cyl. 140 hp	Coupe	9,000	14,000	20,000
1969	911S	6 cyl. 170 hp	Targa	12,000	18,000	25,000
1970	914	4 cyl. 80 hp	Coupe/Targa	5,000	8,000	12,000
1970	914/6	6 cyl. 110 hp	Coupe/Targa	6,000	10,000	15,000
1970	911T	6 cyl. 125 hp	Targa	5,000	10,000	18,000
1970	911E	6 cyl. 155 hp	Coupe	4,000	9,000	17,000
1970	911S	6 cyl. 180 hp	Targa	12,000	18,000	25,000
1973	914	1800 76 hp	Coupe/Targa	4,000	7,000	12,000
1974	914	1800 76 hp	Coupe/Targa	4,000	7,000	12,000
1974	914/6	2000 95 hp	Coupe/Targa	5,000	9,000	15,000
1974	911	6 cyl. 150 hp	Coupe	5,000	10,000	18,000
1974	911S	6 cyl. 175 hp	Targa	10,000	16,000	22,000
1974	911 Carrera	6 cyl. 175 hp	Targa	16,000	22,000	30,000
1976	930	6 cyl. 245 hp	Coupe	20,000	35,000	45,000
1977	924	4 cyl. 95 hp	Coupe	4,000	7,000	12,000
1977	911 SC	6 cyl. 165 hp	Targa	8,000	12,000	20,000
1977	930	6 cyl. 245 hp	Coupe	20,000	30,000	40,000

YEAR	MODEL	ENGINE	BODY	F	G	E
PORSCHE *(Austria; Germany, 1948 to date) (continued)*						
1978	928	8 cyl.	Coupe	12,000	18,000	25,000
1980	924	4 cyl. Turbo	Coupe	5,000	9,000	15,000
1980	924	4 cyl.	Coupe	4,000	6,000	10,000
1980	911 SC	6 cyl.	Coupe	8,000	12,000	20,000
1980	928	8 cyl.	Coupe	8,000	12,000	20,000
1983	944	4 cyl.	Coupe	4,000	6,000	10,000
1983	911 SC	6 cyl.	Coupe	5,000	10,000	18,000
1983	911 SC	6 cyl.	Targa	8,000	12,000	20,000
1983	911 SC	6 cyl.	Convertible	10,000	16,000	22,000
1983	928	8 cyl.	Coupe	8,000	12,000	20,000
PRAGA *(Austria; Czechoslovakia, 1907–47)*						
1907	Alfa	2 cyl.	Sedan	650	1,300	2,500
1912	Mignon	4 cyl. 2.3 Litre	Sedan	750	1,500	2,900
1921	Grand	3.8 Litre	Sedan	1,000	2,000	4,000
1924	Piccolo	707cc	4 Passenger	750	1,500	3,000
1927	Alf	6 cyl. 1496cc	Cabriolet	900	1,950	4,500
1928	Grand	8 cyl. 3.4 Litre	Sedan	800	1,800	4,200
1932	Grand	4.4 Litre	Cabriolet	1,000	2,000	5,000
1934	Super-Piccolo	6 cyl.	Sedan	750	1,500	2,800
1935	Golden	6 cyl. 3.9 Litre	Sport	900	1,750	3,500
1938	2 S	6 cyl.	Sport	700	1,400	3,000
1939	Piccolo	1.1 Litre	Sedan	600	1,200	2,400
PREMIER *(United States, 1902–26)*						
1903	A	4 cyl. (Weidely)	Runabout	3,750	7,500	17,000
1907	24	4 cyl.	Touring	4,000	9,000	20,000
1911	6-60	6 cyl.	7 Passenger Touring	8,000	17,000	35,000
1913	6-60	6 cyl.	7 Passenger Touring	4,600	10,200	21,000
1914		6 cyl.	Touring	8,000	18,000	36,000
1915	6-50	6 cyl.	7 Passenger Touring	9,000	19,000	37,000
1926		6 cyl.	7 Passenger Touring	8,000	17,000	35,000
PREMIER *(Great Britain, 1906–07; 1912–13)*						
1906	10/12	4 cyl. (Aster)	2 Passenger	1,800	4,250	9,500
1912	Motorette	1 cyl.	Tri-car	1,000	1,800	3,500
1913		2 cyl.	4 Passenger	1,500	4,000	8,000
PREMOCAR *(United States, 1920–23)*						
1921	6-40A	6 cyl. (Falls)	Touring	3,500	9,000	21,500
1923	6-40A	(Rochester-Duesenberg)	Sport Touring	1,000	18,000	35,000

YEAR	MODEL	ENGINE	BODY	F	G	E
PRESTO *(Germany, 1901–27)*						
1901	8/25	2078cc	Runabout	1,000	1,750	6,500
1910	Type D	2350cc	Touring	1,200	2,000	7,000
1914	Type E	6 cyl.	Touring	1,400	2,200	7,000
1926	Type F	6 cyl. 2.6 Litre	Touring	1,500	2,300	7,500
PRIAMUS *(Germany, 1901–23)*						
1901		1 cyl.	Voiturette	1,100	3,300	7,500
1917	15/20	2 cyl.	Tonneau	1,200	3,400	10,000
1920		3 cyl.	Tonneau	1,400	3,500	9,000
PRIMO *(United States, 1910–12)*						
1910	R	4 cyl.	Roadster	2,600	7,500	16,000
1912	FP	4 cyl.	5 Passenger Touring	2,500	6,800	15,500
PUBLIX *(United States; Canada, 1947–48)*						
1947		(Chauffel)	Tri-car Coupe	800	1,900	3,000
PUCH *(Austria, 1906–25)*						
1906		V 2 cyl.	Voiturette	1,500	2,750	6,500
1908		4 cyl. (Daimler-Knight)	Sport	1,600	2,900	7,000
1913	Type III Alpenwagen	3560cc	Touring	2,800	6,500	13,000
PULLMAN *(United States, 1905–17)*						
1905		4 cyl.	Surrey	14,000	19,000	40,000
1910	K	4 cyl.	5 Passenger Touring	5,000	14,000	30,000
1912	6-60	6 cyl.	7 Passenger Touring	6,000	13,000	32,000
1915	Model 6-48	6 cyl.	7 Passenger Touring	7,000	16,000	34,000
1917	424-32	6 cyl.	Roadster	5,000	14,000	25,000
PUNGS-FINCH *(United States, 1904–10)*						
1904		2 cyl.	Runabout	9,000	13,000	22,000
1906	Limited	4 cyl.	Roadster	35,000	45,000	60,000
1910	H	4 cyl.	Runabout	14,000	18,000	28,000
PURITAN *(United States, 1902–14)*						
1902		Steam		3,000	9,500	20,000
1913		(DeLuxe)	Roadster	2,500	7,500	16,000

YEAR	MODEL	ENGINE	BODY	F	G	E

R

RABA *(Hungary, 1912–25)*

1912	Grand	35/45	Touring	1,300	2,500	6,500

RABAG-BUGATTI *(Germany, 1922–26)*

1922	6/25	1453cc	Touring	1,200	4,000	10,000
1926	6/30	1495cc	Sport			
			Touring	2,200	5,000	13,000

R.A.F. *(Austria, 1907–13)*

1907	24/30	4 cyl.	Touring	1,700	4,250	10,500
1910	40/45	4 cyl.	Touring	1,800	5,500	11,000
1912	70	6 cyl.	Touring	2,000	6,000	13,000

RAILTON *(Great Britain, 1933–49)*

1933			Sport	2,600	4,850	9,500
1934		6 cyl. (Hudson)	Sedan	2,200	4,500	8,250
1935		6 cyl. (Hudson)	Sedan	2,300	4,700	8,500
1936	Custom 8	6 cyl. (Standard)	Sedan	1,800	3,500	8,000
1939		6 cyl.	Convertible	5,000	12,500	26,000

RALEIGH *(Great Britain, 1905; 1916; 1933–36)*

1905		4 cyl. (Fafnir)	2 Passenger	1,500	4,000	9,000
1916		2 cyl. (Alpha)	2 Passenger	1,300	3,300	6,600
1936	Safety					
	Seven	V 2 cyl.	Tri-car	750	1,500	3,000

RALLY *(France, 1921–33)*

1921		2 cyl.	Sport			
			Voiturette	1,200	2,500	6,000
1922		4 cyl. (S.C.A.P.)	Sport	1,200	3,750	7,200
1930		4 cyl. (Ruby)	Sport	1,300	3,900	8,000
1933		8 cyl. (C.I.M.E.)	Sport	1,700	5,500	11,000

RAMBLER *(United States, 1897–1913)*

1902		1 cyl.	Runabout	4,000	10,000	21,000
1905		2 cyl.	Touring	2,500	7,000	16,000
1906	14	4 cyl.	Touring	3,000	8,000	18,000
1908	34	4 cyl.	Touring	2,750	7,500	17,000
1910	55	4 cyl.	Touring	5,000	10,000	22,000
1911	63	4 cyl.	Roadster	7,000	14,000	26,000
1913		4 cyl.	Cross Country Touring	8,000	17,000	30,000

YEAR	MODEL	ENGINE	BODY	F	G	E
RANGER (United States, 1907–10)						
1907		2 cyl.	Runabout	1,200	6,300	13,200
1908		2 cyl.	Runabout	1,400	6,700	14,500
1909		2 cyl.	Runabout	1,500	6,900	14,800
1910	D	2 cyl.	Runabout	1,400	6,700	14,500
1910	C	2 cyl.	Runabout	1,500	8,000	16,000
RELIABLE DAYTON (United States, 1906–09)						
1906	C	2 cyl.	Buggy	1,900	6,500	13,500
1909	I	2 cyl.	Surrey	2,000	7,000	14,000
RELIANT (Great Britain, 1952 to date)						
1952	Rebel	747cc	4 Passenger Sport Tri-car	800	1,600	3,200
1957	Sabre	6 cyl.	4 Passenger	850	1,700	3,500
REMINGTON (United States, 1914–16)						
1914	R	4 cyl.	Roadster	7,000	12,000	22,000
1915	R	4 cyl.	Roadster	7,000	14,000	25,000
1915	E	4 cyl.	4 Passenger Touring	6,000	14,000	26,000
1916		4 cyl.	Touring	7,000	14,000	29,000
RENAULT (France, 1898 to date)						
1898		1 cyl.	Voiturette	3,000	6,000	14,000
1899		1 cyl.	Voiturette	3,000	6,000	14,000
1900		500cc	Voiturette	2,500	5,000	12,000
1902		1 cyl.	Runabout	2,500	5,000	12,000
1903		2 cyl.	Touring	2,800	5,600	13,000
1904		4 cyl.	Touring	4,000	9,000	20,000
1905		2 cyl.	Touring	3,000	6,000	17,000
1906		4 cyl. 20 hp	Limousine	3,250	7,000	19,000
1907		2 cyl.	Runabout	3,000	6,000	16,000
1908		4 cyl.	Touring	5,000	13,000	26,000
1909		2 cyl.	Roadster	3,800	7,500	16,000
1910		2 cyl.	Town	4,000	8,000	17,000
1911		4 cyl.	Limousine	6,500	14,000	38,000
1912		4 cyl.	Roadster	5,000	13,000	35,000
1913		4 cyl.	Roadster	5,000	13,000	35,000
1914		4 cyl.	Torpedo Touring	5,500	14,000	37,000
1915		4 cyl.	Town Car	5,500	14,000	37,000
1916		4 cyl.	Roadster	4,500	11,000	32,000
1917		4 cyl.	Roadster	4,500	11,000	32,000
1918		4 cyl.	Limousine	5,000	14,000	35,000
1919	FI	6 cyl.	Touring	8,000	19,000	41,000

YEAR	MODEL	ENGINE	BODY	F	G	E
RENAULT	*(France, 1898 to date) (continued)*					
1920		4 cyl.	Roadster	3,500	9,500	25,000
1921		4 cyl.	Touring	3,000	8,000	22,000
1922		4 cyl.	Touring	3,000	8,000	22,000
1923	KJ	951cc	Touring	1,000	4,000	9,000
1924		4 cyl.	Limousine	7,000	16,500	35,000
1925	45	4 cyl.	Sport Touring	5,000	13,000	30,000
1926	45	4 cyl.	Sport Phaeton	4,000	8,000	26,000
1927	JY	6 cyl.	Touring	4,500	9,000	28,000
1928		3.2 Litre	Sport	4,000	8,000	26,000
1929		6 cyl.	Sport	4,500	9,000	27,500
1930	Reinasetta	8 cyl.	Sport	5,000	10,000	30,000
1931	Monasix	4 cyl.	Sedan	1,200	2,250	5,500
1932	Nerva	8 cyl.	Sedan	1,000	2,900	6,000
1933	Primastella	8 cyl.	Sedan	900	2,400	5,750
1934		6 cyl.	Sport Sedan	1,000	2,000	4,900
1935		6 cyl.	Sedan	1,000	1,900	4,750
1936		4 cyl.	Sport	650	1,250	4,500
1937		8 cyl.	Sedan	1,000	2,000	5,000
1938	Viva Grand Sport	6 cyl.	Sport Sedan	1,250	2,500	6,000
1939		6 cyl.	Sport	900	1,750	5,500
1940		6 cyl.	Sport Sedan	700	1,400	5,000
1941		8 cyl.	Sport Sedan	900	1,750	5,700
1942		6 cyl.	Sedan	650	1,250	4,500
1946		4 cyl.	Sedan	1,000	3,000	6,000
1947		4 cyl.	Sedan	1,000	3,000	6,000
1948	Juraquatre	1 Litre	Coupe	500	2,000	5,000
1949	4 CV	760cc	Coupe	500	2,000	5,000
1950		750cc	Sedan	450	2,000	5,000
1951		2.1 Litre	Sport Sedan	550	2,000	5,000
1952		2 Litre	Sedan	450	1,700	4,000
1953		2 Litre	Sedan	450	1,600	4,000
1954		2.1 Litre	Sedan	450	900	4,000
1955	Fregate	2 Litre	Convertible	2,000	4,000	8,000
1956	Dauphine	845cc	Sedan	1,000	2,000	5,000
1957	Etoile Filante	4 cyl.	Sedan	1,000	2,000	5,000
1958		4 cyl.	Sedan	1,000	2,000	5,000
1959	Floride	845cc	Sport Coupe	1,500	3,000	6,000
1962	Dauphine Deluxe	4 cyl.	Sedan	1,000	2,000	4,000

YEAR	MODEL	ENGINE	BODY	F	G	E
RENAULT *(France, 1898 to date) (continued)*						
1966	R-8 Gordini	4 cyl.	Sedan	1,000	2,000	5,000
REO *(United States, 1905–36)*						
1905		2 cyl.	Tonneau	3,000	6,000	16,000
1905		1 cyl.	Runabout	3,600	6,600	17,000

Reo – 1005 "Runabout"

1906		2 cyl.	Touring	3,500	6,500	16,000
1907		2 cyl.	Touring	3,500	6,500	16,000
1908		2 cyl.	Roadster	3,800	7,000	17,000
1909		1 cyl.	Runabout	3,500	6,500	14,500
1910	R5	4 cyl.	Touring	3,500	7,000	16,500
1912	R5	4 cyl.	Roadster	3,000	6,000	13,500
1912	The 5th	4 cyl.	Touring	4,000	9,500	19,250
1913	The 5th	4 cyl.	Roadster	2,800	5,800	13,000
1915	The 5th	4 cyl.	Touring	3,200	7,500	17,000
1917	M	6 cyl.	Touring	3,500	7,800	17,500
1918	U	6 cyl.	Roadster	3,000	7,000	14,000

YEAR	MODEL	ENGINE	BODY	F	G	E
REO	*(United States, 1905–36)* *(continued)*					
1919	M	6 cyl.	Roadster	4,000	9,000	17,000
1920	T6	6 cyl.	Touring	4,000	9,000	18,000
1923	T6	6 cyl.	Phaeton	4,000	9,000	17,000
1924	T6	6 cyl.	Touring	2,700	8,400	19,500
1924	T6	6 cyl.	Coupe	3,300	11,400	22,000
1924	T6	6 cyl.	Brougham	2,800	6,000	14,000
1925	T6	6 cyl.	Roadster	3,200	9,200	21,500
1925	T6	6 cyl.	Touring	3,500	9,500	22,000
1925	T6	6 cyl.	Sedan	1,900	5,400	10,800
1926	T6	6 cyl.	Coupe	2,000	5,600	11,200
1927	A	6 cyl.	Sport Roadster	3,500	13,700	28,000
1927	Flying Cloud	6 cyl.	Sport Roadster	8,000	14,000	24,000
1928	Flying Cloud	6 cyl.	Coupe	4,000	8,000	17,000
1928	Flying Cloud	6 cyl.	Brougham	4,000	7,000	14,000

Reo – 1928 "Brougham" Courtesy of Reo Club of America, Vermont (Ray M. Wood)

YEAR	MODEL	ENGINE	BODY	F	G	E
1928	Flying Cloud	6 cyl.	Sedan	3,000	6,000	12,000
1928	15	6 cyl.	4 Passenger Coupe	3,000	8,500	18,000
1928	25	6 cyl.	2 Passenger Coupe	4,000	8,000	16,000

YEAR	MODEL	ENGINE	BODY	F	G	E
REO (United States, 1905–36) (continued)						
1930	15	6 cyl.	Sedan	3,000	7,000	15,000
1930	25	6 cyl.	7 Passenger Sedan	4,000	8,000	16,000
1930	Master	6 cyl.	Roadster	8,000	17,000	30,000
1931	15	6 cyl.	5 Passenger Phaeton	7,000	15,000	30,000
1931	20	6 cyl.	Sport Coupe	5,000	10,000	20,000
1931	25	8 cyl.	Victoria	3,000	9,000	18,000
1931	25	8 cyl.	Sport Coupe	3,000	10,000	21,500
1931	25	8 cyl.	Sport Sedan	2,800	7,500	18,000
1931	30	8 cyl.	Coupe	5,000	10,000	22,000
1931	30	8 cyl.	Sedan	4,000	10,000	20,000
1932	S	8 cyl.	Sport Convertible Coupe	9,000	18,000	35,000
1932	S	8 cyl.	Sport Sedan	7,000	14,000	28,000
1933	Royale	8 cyl.	Victoria	6,000	13,000	26,000
1933	Royale	8 cyl.	Cabriolet	15,000	25,000	45,000
1935	Royale	6 cyl.	Convertible Coupe	7,500	15,000	30,000
1935	Flying Cloud	6 cyl.	Sedan	5,000	10,000	20,000
REVERE (United States, 1918–26)						
1917		4 cyl.	Speedster	15,000	20,000	30,000
1920	A	4 cyl.	Roadster	9,000	20,000	40,000
REX; REX-SIMPLEX (Germany, 1901–23)						
1901		1 cyl. (DeDion)	Touring	1,000	4,000	8,000
1914	17/38	2 cyl.	Sport Touring	1,000	4,500	9,000
1923		4 cyl.	Touring	1,750	5,500	11,000
REX (Great Britain, 1901–14)						
1901		1 cyl.	Voiturette	2,000	4,000	8,000
1904	10 hp	2 cyl.	Tonneau	2,100	4,400	8,500
1906	Rexette	V 2 cyl.	2 Passenger	2,100	4,400	9,000
1908	Remo	4 cyl. (T-head)	2 Passenger	2,400	4,800	9,000
1912		V 2 cyl.	Cycle	900	1,750	3,500
REX (United States, 1914)						
1914	Cycle Car	4 cyl.	Roadster	4,000	7,000	15,000
REYROL; PASSE-PARTOUT (France, 1901–30)						
1901		1 cyl. (Aster)	Voiturette	1,100	3,250	8,500
1907		942cc (Buchet)	Racing	2,000	7,750	14,500
1924		(Chapuis-Dornier)	Racing	1,900	7,500	14,000

YEAR	MODEL	ENGINE	BODY	F	G	E
RIKER	*(United States, 1896–1902)*					
1896	3-Wheel	Electric	Open	2,200	7,250	14,500
1899		Electric	Phaeton	3,500	9,000	20,000
1900		Electric	Torpedo			
			Racing	7,000	16,000	35,000
1901		2 cyl.	Runabout	3,500	7,000	14,500
1902		4 cyl.	Dos-a-dos	3,000	6,000	13,000
RILEY	*(Great Britain, 1898–1969)*					
1898		1 cyl.	Voiturette	1,600	3,250	9,000
1899	3-Wheel	1 cyl.		1,100	2,250	6,500
1900		1 cyl.	Voiturette	1,500	3,000	8,000
1901	3-Wheel	1 cyl.		1,000	2,000	6,000
1902		2 cyl.	Touring	1,100	2,250	6,500
1903		2 cyl.	Touring	1,100	2,250	6,500
1904		2 cyl.	Touring	1,100	2,250	6,500
1905	3-Wheel	2 cyl.		1,000	2,000	6,000
1906		2 cyl.	Touring	1,100	2,250	6,500
1907	3-Wheel	V 2 cyl.	Cycle	900	1,750	5,000
1908		V 2 cyl.	Touring	1,000	2,100	6,200
1909	12/18	V 2 cyl.	Torpedo			
			Touring	1,100	3,250	7,500
1910		V 2 cyl.	Touring	1,100	2,100	6,200
1911		V 2 cyl.	Touring	1,000	2,000	6,100
1912		V 2 cyl.	Touring	1,000	2,000	6,000
1913		V 2 cyl.	Touring	1,000	2,000	6,000
1914	2.9	4 cyl.	Touring	1,100	2,250	6,500
1915		4 cyl.	Sport	1,200	2,300	6,500
1916		4 cyl.	Sport	1,200	2,300	6,500
1917		4 cyl.	Touring	1,100	2,200	6,400
1918		4 cyl.	Touring	1,100	2,150	6,500
1919		1.5 Litre	Sport	1,100	3,250	7,500
1920	Eleven	1.5 Litre	Touring	1,000	2,000	6,000
1921		4 cyl.	Touring	1,000	3,000	7,000
1922		4 cyl.	Touring	1,000	3,000	7,000
1923	Redwinger	1.5 Litre	Sport	1,200	2,400	7,000
1924	Twelve	1.5 Litre	Touring	1,100	2,250	6,500
1925		1.5 Litre	Touring	1,100	2,250	6,500
1926	Redwinger	1.5 Litre	Sport	1,250	3,500	7,000
1927		1.5 Litre	Touring	1,100	2,250	6,500
1928	Monaco	1.5 Litre	Fabric Sport			
			Saloon			
			Sedan	1,000	3,500	7,000
1929	Brooklands	1.5 Litre	Sport	1,400	3,750	7,950
1930	Fourteen	6 cyl.	Touring	1,100	4,250	8,500

YEAR	MODEL	ENGINE	BODY	F	G	E
RILEY *(Great Britain, 1898–1969) (continued)*						
1931	Brooklands	6 cyl.	Sport	1,500	5,000	9,000
1932		1.5 Litre	Sport	2,000	3,750	8,500
1933		1.5 Litre	Sport	1,750	3,300	9,000
1934		1.5 Litre	Convertible	2,000	5,000	10,500
1935		1.5 Litre	Sport			
			Roadster	2,250	6,500	14,000
1936	Lynx	1.5 Litre	Sport Sedan	1,000	3,000	6,000
1937		1.5 Litre	Sport			
			Touring	2,000	6,000	12,000
1938		1.5 Litre	Sport	2,000	5,000	10,000
1939		1.5 Litre	Sedan	1,000	2,000	6,000
1940		V 8 cyl.	Sedan	900	1,750	6,500
1941		V 8 cyl.	Sedan	900	1,750	6,500
1942		1.5 Litre	Sedan	750	1,500	5,000
1946		1.5 Litre	Sedan	750	1,500	5,000
1947		1.5 Litre	Sedan	750	1,500	5,000
1948		1.5 Litre	Roadster	2,000	5,250	10,500
1949		1.5 Litre	Roadster	2,000	5,250	10,500
1950		1.5 Litre	Club Sedan	1,200	2,400	6,800
1951		1.5 Litre	Drop Head			
			Coupe	1,600	4,250	8,500
1952		1.5 Litre	Sedan	1,100	2,250	5,500
1953		1.5 Litre	Coupe	1,250	2,500	6,000
1954	Pathfinder	2.5 Litre	Sedan	1,100	2,250	5,500
1955		2.5 Litre	Sedan	1,100	2,250	5,500
1956		2.5 Litre	Coupe	1,200	2,400	6,000
1957		2.5 Litre	Coupe	1,200	2,400	6,000
1958		2.6 Litre	Sedan	900	1,800	4,500
1959		2.6 Litre	Sedan	900	1,800	4,500
1960		2.6 Litre	Sedan	900	1,800	4,500
1961		1.5 Litre	Sedan	750	1,500	4,000
1962		1.5 Litre	Sedan	750	1,500	4,000
1963		1.5 Litre	Sedan	750	1,500	4,000
1964		848cc	Sedan	500	900	3,000
1965		848cc	Sedan	500	900	3,000
1966	Elf Mark	998cc	Sedan	550	1,100	3,250
1967	Elf	998cc	Sedan	650	1,250	3,500
1968	Elf	998cc	Sedan	650	1,250	3,500
1969	Elf	998cc	Sedan	650	1,250	3,500
RIPERT *(France, 1899–1902)*						
1899	6	1 cyl.	Open	1,000	3,000	7,000
1902	12	2 cyl.	Open	1,500	3,200	7,200

YEAR	MODEL	ENGINE	BODY	F	G	E
ROACH *(United States, 1899)*						
1899		2 cyl.	Runabout	2,000	7,750	15,500
ROADER *(United States, 1911–12)*						
1911		4 cyl.	Roadster	6,000	12,000	22,000
ROAMER *(United States, 1916–29)*						
1916		6 cyl. (Continental)	Touring	5,000	12,000	23,000
1919		6 cyl.	Sport	14,000	16,000	35,000
1925	8-88	8 cyl.	5 Passenger Touring	7,000	14,000	29,000
1930	8-88	8 cyl.	Roadster	8,000	16,000	30,000
ROBERTS SIX *(Canada, 1921)*						
1921		6 cyl.	Touring	2,000	5,000	11,000
1921		6 cyl.	Sedan	1,500	3,000	7,000
1921		6 cyl.	Limousine	1,750	3,500	9,000
ROBINSON; POPE-ROBINSON *(United States, 1900–04)*						
1900		2 cyl.	Runabout	2,500	7,000	14,000
1904		4 cyl.	Tonneau	3,500	7,500	16,000
ROBINSON & HOLE *(Great Britain, 1906–07)*						
1906		4 cyl.	Touring	900	2,750	6,250
1907		4 cyl.	Touring	1,500	3,000	7,000
ROB ROY *(Great Britain, 1922–26)*						
1922		2 cyl.	2 Passenger	900	2,800	6,500
1926		4 cyl.	2 Passenger	1,250	3,500	7,000
ROCHDALE *(Great Britain, 1957)*						
1957		1.5 Litre (Riley)	Drop Head Coupe	1,000	1,900	5,000
1957	2/4	(Ford)	Sedan	700	1,400	3,750
ROCHET-SCHNEIDER *(France, 1894–1932)*						
1894		1 cyl.	Tonneau	3,000	5,500	15,000
1905		2 cyl.	Tonneau	2,200	5,000	13,500
1909		4 cyl.	Sedan	2,200	5,000	13,500
1911		6 cyl.	Sedan	2,500	5,500	14,000
1929	20	6 cyl.	Sedan	2,000	4,000	9,500
ROCK *(Hungary, 1905–18)*						
1905	16	4 cyl.	Touring	1,200	2,400	7,000
1913	21/25	6 cyl.	Touring	1,500	2,750	7,500
1918	20/50	6 cyl.	Touring	1,500	2,750	7,500
ROCKNE *(United States, 1932–33)*						
1932	65	6 cyl.	Sedan	1,500	5,200	10,500
1932	75	6 cyl.	Convertible Sedan	9,000	18,000	35,000
1933		6 cyl.	Roadster	6,000	14,000	25,000

YEAR	MODEL	ENGINE	BODY	F	G	E
ROCKNE *(United States, 1932–33) (continued)*						
1933		6 cyl.	Convertible	2,800	11,500	24,000
ROHR *(Germany, 1928–35)*						
1928	Type R	8 cyl.	Sedan	9,000	16,000	30,000
1930	Type RA	8 cyl.	Sedan	9,000	16,000	30,000
1935	Type F	8 cyl.	Sedan	9,000	16,000	30,000
ROLAND-PILAIN *(France, 1906–31)*						
1906	20	4 cyl.	Runabout	1,200	3,250	7,500
1912	18 CV	6 cyl.	Touring	1,350	3,700	8,000
1921	18 CV	8 cyl.	Coupe de Ville	2,200	4,500	9,000
ROLLIN *(United States, 1924–25)*						
1924	G	4 cyl.	Sedan	3,000	7,000	15,000
1925	G	4 cyl.	Coupe Touring Roadster	8,000	1,700	30,000
ROLLO *(Great Britain, 1911–13)*						
1911		1 cyl. (Precision)	Cycle	1,000	1,800	3,500
1913	Tandem	2 cyl. (J.A.P.)	Cycle	1,000	1,800	3,500
ROLLS-ROYCE *(Great Britain, 1904 to date)*						
1904		4 cyl.	Touring	75,000	150,000	350,000
1905		4 cyl.	Touring	75,000	150,000	350,000
1906	Silver Ghost	6 cyl.	Phaeton	8,000	125,000	325,000
1908	Silver Ghost	6 cyl.	Limousine	75,000	175,000	375,000
1909	Silver Ghost	6 cyl.	Roadster	55,000	125,000	325,000
1910	Silver Ghost	6 cyl.	Touring	75,000	150,000	275,000
1911	Silver Ghost	6 cyl.	Town Car	50,000	100,000	225,000
1912	Silver Ghost	6 cyl.	Touring	59,000	150,000	325,000
1913	Silver Ghost	6 cyl.	Roadster	75,000	150,000	300,000
1914	Silver Ghost	6 cyl.	Landaulet	33,000	66,000	150,000
1914	Silver Ghost	6 cyl.	Roadster	75,000	150,000	250,000
1914	Silver Ghost	6 cyl.	Limousine	19,000	39,000	75,000
1915	Silver Ghost	6 cyl.	Touring	26,000	52,000	125,000
1915	Silver Ghost	6 cyl.	Touring Limousine	19,000	39,000	75,000
1916	Silver Ghost	6 cyl.	Roadster	90,000	150,000	275,000
1916	Silver Ghost	6 cyl.	Town Car	26,000	52,000	120,000
1917	Silver Ghost	6 cyl.	Limousine	22,000	46,000	85,000
1918	Silver Ghost	6 cyl.	Touring	26,000	60,000	130,000
1919	Silver Ghost	6 cyl.	Touring	26,000	60,000	130,000
1920	Silver Ghost	6 cyl.	Limousine	10,000	20,000	50,000
1921	Silver Ghost	6 cyl.	Limousine	11,000	22,000	55,000
1921	Silver Ghost	6 cyl.	Town Car	19,000	39,000	79,000

YEAR	MODEL	ENGINE	BODY	F	G	E
ROLLS-ROYCE *(Great Britain, 1904 to date) (continued)*						
1922	20/25	6 cyl.	Estate Wagon	7,000	15,000	35,000
1922	Silver Ghost	6 cyl.	Roadster	37,000	80,000	160,000
1923	Silver Ghost	6 cyl.	Piccadilly Roadster	41,000	99,000	190,000
1923	Silver Ghost	6 cyl.	Pall Mall Phaeton	51,000	99,000	190,000
1923	Silver Ghost	6 cyl.	Sedan	20,000	35,000	75,000
1924	20	6 cyl.	Touring	10,000	20,000	50,000

Rolls-Royce – 1924 "Silver Ghost"

YEAR	MODEL	ENGINE	BODY	F	G	E
1924	20	6 cyl.	Limousine	19,000	20,000	40,000
1925	P I Henley	6 cyl.	Roadster	44,000	110,000	170,000
1925	Silver Ghost	6 cyl.	Roadster	37,000	125,000	225,000
1925	P I	6 cyl.	Sedan Saloon	6,600	16,000	36,000
1925	P I	6 cyl.	Touring	27,000	51,000	140,000
1925	P I Hopper	6 cyl.	Limousine	11,000	33,000	82,000
1926	P I	6 cyl.	Sedanca de Ville	35,000	75,000	125,000
1926	P I Brewster	6 cyl.	Town Car	15,000	35,000	75,000
1926	P I Brewster	6 cyl.	Cabriolet	17,000	40,000	120,000
1926	P I	6 cyl.	Roadster	26,000	79,000	160,000
1926	Silver Ghost	6 cyl.	Limousine	11,000	30,000	79,000
1927	P I	6 cyl.	Ascot Phaeton	50,000	110,000	200,000
1927	Silver Ghost	6 cyl.	Dual Cowl Phaeton	33,000	110,000	220,000
1927	P I	6 cyl.	Saloon Landaulet	11,000	22,000	42,000
1927	P I	6 cyl.	Town Car	9,900	22,000	46,000

YEAR	MODEL	ENGINE	BODY	F	G	E
ROLLS-ROYCE *(Great Britain, 1904 to date) (continued)*						
1927	P I	6 cyl.	7 Passenger Touring	22,000	51,000	120,000
1927	P I	6 cyl.	Limousine	20,000	40,000	75,000
1927	P I	6 cyl.	Dual Cowl Phaeton	31,000	81,000	150,000
1927	P I Brewster	6 cyl.	Cabriolet	40,000	85,000	175,000
1928	P I	6 cyl.	Saloon	8,000	16,000	33,000
1928	P I	6 cyl.	Limousine	17,000	36,000	54,000
1928	P 1 Brewster	6 cyl.	Dual Cowl Phaeton	33,000	79,000	160,000

Rolls-Royce – 1928 "Dual Cowl Phaeton"

YEAR	MODEL	ENGINE	BODY	F	G	E
1928	P I	6 cyl.	Roadster	75,000	150,000	250,000
1928	P I Brewster	6 cyl.	Cabriolet	50,000	90,000	150,000
1928	P I	6 cyl.	4 Door Convertible	36,000	99,000	150,000
1928	P I		Town Car	20,000	40,000	75,000
1929	P I Ward	6 cyl.	Touring	40,000	85,000	175,000
1929	Pall Mall	6 cyl.	Touring	40,000	85,000	175,000
1929	P II	6 cyl.	Convertible Sedan	30,000	65,000	150,000
1929	P II	6 cyl.	Saloon	12,000	23,000	46,000
1929	Brewster	6 cyl.	Town Car	22,000	46,000	75,000
1929	P I	6 cyl.	Limousine	11,000	22,000	46,000
1930	P II	6 cyl.	Boattail Roadster	75,000	125,000	200,000

YEAR	MODEL	ENGINE	BODY	F	G	E
ROLLS-ROYCE	*(Great Britain, 1904 to date)*		*(continued)*			
1930	20/25	6 cyl.	Convertible Sedan	10,400	22,000	81,000
1930	P II	6 cyl.	Sport Phaeton	40,000	90,000	175,000
1930	P II	6 cyl.	Sedanca DeVille	35,000	70,000	125,000
1930	P II	6 cyl.	Limousine	15,000	33,000	77,000
1930	P II	6 cyl.	Saloon	12,000	25,000	55,000
1931	P II	6 cyl.	Limousine	11,000	26,000	58,000

Rolls-Royce – 1931, Courtesy of White Post Restorations, White Post, Virginia

YEAR	MODEL	ENGINE	BODY	F	G	E
1931	P II	6 cyl.	Saloon	12,000	25,000	50,000
1931	P II	6 cyl.	Sport Phaeton	50,000	110,000	200,000
1931	P II	6 cyl.	4 Door Convertible	50,000	95,000	175,000
1931	P II	6 cyl.	Drop Head Coupe	45,000	85,000	150,000
1932	P II	6 cyl.	Convertible Town Car	35,000	75,000	175,000
1932	P II	6 cyl.	Town Car	11,000	29,000	54,000
1932	20-25	6 cyl.	Sport Saloon	7,000	16,000	41,000

YEAR	MODEL	ENGINE	BODY	F	G	E
ROLLS-ROYCE *(Great Britain, 1904 to date) (continued)*						
1932	P II	6 cyl.	Convertible Coupe	40,000	80,000	175,000
1932	Brewster	6 cyl.	Limousine	11,000	23,000	53,000
1932	P II	6 cyl.	Roadster	75,000	150,000	250,000
1933	20-25	6 cyl.	Drop Head Coupe	20,000	40,000	75,000
1933	20-25	6 cyl.	Convertible Sedan	25,000	50,000	90,000
1933	P II	6 cyl.	5 Passenger Saloon	15,000	30,000	65,000
1933	P II	6 cyl.	Limousine	15,000	30,000	60,000

Rolls-Royce – 1933 "Limousine" Courtesy of White Post Restorations, Virginia

1933	Brewster	6 cyl.	Convertible Sedan	25,000	50,000	95,000
1933	Brewster	6 cyl.	Boattail DropHead Phaeton	40,000	85,000	175,000
1934	de Ville	6 cyl.	Coupe	30,000	60,000	125,000
1934	P II	6 cyl.	4 Passenger Coupe	15,000	25,000	50,000
1934	P II	6 cyl.	Victoria Coupe	15,000	35,000	75,000
1934	Brewster	6 cyl.	Roadster	40,000	95,000	175,000
1934	20-25	6 cyl.	Coupe	12,000	25,000	50,000
1934	20-25	6 cyl.	2 Door Convertible	20,000	40,000	75,000

YEAR	MODEL	ENGINE	BODY	F	G	E
ROLLS-ROYCE *(Great Britain, 1904 to date) (continued)*						
1934	P II	6 cyl.	Convertible Sedan	75,000	125,000	225,000
1934	P II	6 cyl.	Continental Boattail	75,000	125,000	225,000
1934	P II	6 cyl.	Convertible Coupe	40,000	85,000	150,000
1935	20-25	6 cyl.	Sport Sedan	7,200	15,000	40,000
1935	P II Hooper	6 cyl.	Limousine	17,000	30,000	65,000
1935	P II	6 cyl.	Convertible Victoria	26,000	80,000	170,000
1935	20-25	6 cyl.	2 Door Coupe	7,900	16,000	38,000
1935	20-25	6 cyl.	7 Passenger Limousine	9,200	17,000	44,000
1935	25-30	6 cyl.	Sport Phaeton	33,000	90,000	160,000
1935	20-25	6 cyl.	2 Door Coupe	11,000	20,000	48,000
1935	20-25	6 cyl.	Convertible Sedan	30,000	50,000	90,000
1936	20-25	6 cyl.	Town Car	18,000	35,000	75,000
1936	20-25	6 cyl.	Saloon	8,000	20,000	40,000
1936	P III	V 12 cyl.	Convertible Sedan	40,000	85,000	150,000
1936	P III	V 12 cyl.	Saloon	15,000	30,000	65,000
1936	P III	V 12 cyl.	7 Passenger Limousine	18,000	35,000	75,000
1936	25-30	6 cyl.	Limousine	9,200	19,000	50,000
1936	25-30	6 cyl.	Opera Coupe	7,900	16,000	34,000
1937	P III	6 cyl.	Touring	30,000	65,000	150,000
1937	25/30	6 cyl.	Limousine	11,000	22,000	41,000
1937	P III	V 12 cyl.	Sedanca de Ville	24,000	60,000	120,000
1937	P II	V 12 cyl.	Victoria Coupe	30,000	65,000	125,000
1937	P III	V 12 cyl.	7 Passenger Saloon	15,000	35,000	75,000
1937	P III	V 12 cyl.	Limousine	20,000	40,000	75,000
1937	P III	V 12 cyl.	Town Car	29,000	80,000	140,000
1937	P III	V 12 cyl.	Convertible Sedan	40,000	85,000	150,000
1937	P III	V 12 cyl.	5 Passenger Saloon	20,000	40,000	75,000
1938	25-30	6 cyl.	Saloon	10,400	18,000	35,000

YEAR	MODEL	ENGINE	BODY	F	G	E
ROLLS-ROYCE *(Great Britain, 1904 to date) (continued)*						
1938	P III	V 12 cyl.	Sedanca de Ville	40,000	85,000	150,000
1938	P III	V 12 cyl.	5 Passenger Saloon	15,000	30,000	60,000
1938	P III	V 12 cyl.	Saloon Limousine	15,000	35,000	70,000
1938	P III	V 12 cyl.	Coupe	20,000	40,000	75,000
1938	P III	V 12 cyl.	Phaeton	75,000	150,000	275,000
1939	Wraith Open Front	6 cyl.	Town Car	20,000	45,000	100,000
1939	Wraith	6 cyl.	Limousine	15,000	25,000	40,000
1939	P III	V 12 cyl.	Convertible Victoria	40,000	95,000	175,000
1939	Wraith	6 cyl.	Sport Sedan Limousine	14,000	22,000	40,000
1940	Wraith	6 cyl.	Saloon	14,000	24,000	52,000
1940	Wraith	6 cyl.	Convertible Sedan	25,000	50,000	95,000
1940	P III	V 12 cyl.	Convertible Coupe	45,000	90,000	175,000
1940	P III	V 12 cyl.	7 Passenger Saloon	20,000	30,000	65,000
Postwar Models						
1947	Silver Wraith	6 cyl.	Sedanca de Ville	11,000	27,000	55,000
1947	Silver Wraith	6 cyl.	Touring Limousine	13,000	20,000	35,000
1947	Silver Wraith	6 cyl.	Saloon	8,400	13,000	36,000
1947	Silver Wraith	6 cyl.	Sport Saloon	12,000	25,000	40,000
1947	Silver Wraith	6 cyl.	Coupe	9,900	21,000	46,000
1947	Silver Wraith	6 cyl.	Drop Head Coupe	20,000	45,000	85,000
1948	Silver Wraith	6 cyl.	Touring Limousine	14,000	22,000	45,000
1948	Silver Wraith	6 cyl.	Saloon	7,900	14,000	35,000
1948	Silver Wraith	6 cyl.	Limousine	11,000	22,000	40,000
1948	Silver Wraith	6 cyl.	Sedanca de Ville	20,000	35,000	65,000

YEAR	MODEL	ENGINE	BODY	F	G	E
ROLLS-ROYCE *(Great Britain, 1904 to date) (continued)*						
1948	Silver Wraith	6 cyl.	Sport Saloon	9,600	20,000	30,000
1948	Silver Wraith	6 cyl.	Drop Head Coupe	25,000	45,000	85,000
1949	Silver Wraith	6 cyl.	Saloon	8,500	18,000	39,000
1949	Silver Dawn	6 cyl.	Saloon	7,900	16,000	39,000
1950	Silver Dawn	6 cyl.	Saloon	9,400	20,000	42,000
1950	P IV P.W.	8 cyl.	Limousine	40,000	75,000	150,000
1950	Silver Wraith	6 cyl.	Saloon	9,200	18,000	35,000
1950	Silver Wraith	6 cyl.	Fixed Head Coupe	9,200	18,000	39,000
1951	Silver Dawn	6 cyl.	Saloon	8,400	18,000	39,000
1951	Silver Wraith	6 cyl.	Sport Saloon	7,900	18,000	40,000
1951	Silver Wraith	6 cyl.	Saloon	9,700	18,000	49,000
1951	Silver Wraith	6 cyl.	Drop Head Coupe	30,000	50,000	95,000
1951	Park Ward	8 cyl.	7 Passenger Limousine	18,000	25,000	40,000
1952	Silver Dawn	6 cyl.	Drop Head Coupe	25,000	40,000	75,000
1952	Silver Dawn	6 cyl.	Saloon	9,000	17,000	35,000
1952	Silver Wraith	6 cyl.	Drop Head Coupe	25,000	40,000	75,000

Rolls-Royce – 1952 "Silver Wraith"

YEAR	MODEL	ENGINE	BODY	F	G	E
1953	Silver Dawn	6 cyl.	Saloon	10,000	23,500	40,000

YEAR	MODEL	ENGINE	BODY	F	G	E
ROLLS-ROYCE *(Great Britain, 1904 to date) (continued)*						
1953	Silver Dawn	6 cyl.	Drop Head Coupe	25,000	40,000	75,000
1953	Silver Wraith	6 cyl.	Saloon	9,900	20,000	46,000
1954	Silver Wraith	6 cyl.	Saloon	10,400	20,000	44,000
1954	Silver Dawn	6 cyl.	Saloon Limousine	8,000	17,000	36,000
1954	Silver Dawn	6 cyl.	Drop Head Coupe	25,000	40,000	75,000
1955	Silver Dawn	6 cyl.	Saloon	7,900	16,000	33,000
1955	Silver Dawn	6 cyl.	Drop Head Coupe	50,000	40,000	75,000
1955	Silver Wraith	6 cyl.	Saloon	7,600	15,000	44,000
1955	Silver Cloud I	V 8 cyl.	Drop Head Coupe	40,000	70,000	125,000
1955	Silver Wraith	6 cyl.	Saloon	9,900	17,000	36,000
1956	Silver Wraith	6 cyl.	Saloon	11,000	20,000	37,000
1956	Silver Cloud I	V 8 cyl.	Saloon	11,000	20,000	30,000
1956	Silver Cloud I	6 cyl.	Drop Head Coupe	40,000	75,000	125,000
1957	Silver Cloud I	6 cyl.	Saloon	8,000	15,000	30,000
1957	Silver Cloud I	6 cyl.	Drop Head Coupe	40,000	75,000	125,000
1957	Silver Wraith	6 cyl.	Saloon	10,600	24,000	40,000
1957	Silver Wraith	6 cyl.	Drop Head Sedan	25,000	45,000	85,000
1957	Silver Wraith	6 cyl. (James Young)	Saloon	11,000	26,000	60,000
1958	Silver Cloud I	6 cyl.	Saloon	9,200	17,000	30,000
1958	Silver Cloud I	6 cyl.	Drop Head Coupe	40,000	75,000	125,000
1958	Silver Wraith	6 cyl.	Drop Head Saloon	15,000	35,000	60,000
1958	Silver Wraith	6 cyl.	Saloon	10,400	20,000	40,000

YEAR	MODEL	ENGINE	BODY	F	G	E
ROLLS-ROYCE *(Great Britain, 1904 to date) (continued)*						
1959	Silver Cloud I	6 cyl.	Saloon	10,400	15,000	30,000

Rolls-Royce – 1959 "Silver Cloud"

YEAR	MODEL	ENGINE	BODY	F	G	E
1959	Silver Cloud I	6 cyl.	Drop Head Coupe	40,000	75,000	125,000
1959	Silver Wraith	6 cyl.	Drop Head Saloon	15,000	35,000	75,000
1959	Silver Wraith	6 cyl.	Saloon	13,000	26,000	40,000
1960	Silver Cloud II	V 8 cyl.	Drop Head Coupe	40,000	85,000	150,000
1960	Silver Cloud II	V 8 cyl.	Saloon	8,000	15,000	30,000
1960	Phantom V	V 8 cyl. (James Young)	Limousine	13,000	35,000	75,000
1960	Phantom V	V 8 cyl.	Limousine	13,000	27,000	60,000
1961	Phantom V	V 8 cyl. (James Young)	Limousine	15,000	40,000	75,000
1961	Phantom V	V 8 cyl. (Park Ward)	Limousine	15,000	30,000	60,000
1961	Silver Cloud II	V 8 cyl.	Drop Head Coupe	28,000	53,000	130,000
1962	Silver Cloud II	V 8 cyl. (James Young)	Limousine	20,000	40,000	75,000
1962	Phantom V	V 8 cyl. (Park Ward)	Limousine	17,000	30,000	60,000

YEAR	MODEL	ENGINE	BODY	F	G	E
ROLLS-ROYCE *(Great Britain, 1904 to date) (continued)*						
1962	Silver Cloud II	V 8 cyl.	Drop Head Coupe	40,000	85,000	150,000
1963	Phantom V	V 8 cyl. (James Young)	Limousine	26,000	40,000	75,000
1963	Silver Cloud III	V 8 cyl.	Saloon	8,000	15,000	30,000
1963	Silver Cloud III	V 8 cyl.	Convertible	35,000	65,000	125,000
1964	Phantom V	V 8 cyl. (James Young)	Limousine	27,000	40,000	75,000
1964	Phantom V	V 8 cyl. (Park Ward)	Limousine	17,000	30,000	60,000
1965	Silver Cloud II	V 8 cyl.	Convertible	27,000	57,000	130,000
1965	Silver Cloud III	V 8 cyl.	Saloon	10,400	18,000	35,000
1966	Phantom V	V 8 cyl. (James Young)	Limousine	27,000	40,000	75,000
1967	Silver Shadow I	V 8 cyl.	Drop Head Coupe	15,000	28,000	40,000
1967	Phantom V	V 8 cyl. (Park Ward)	Limousine	20,000	35,000	60,000
1968	Silver Shadow	V 8 cyl.	Saloon	8,000	15,000	25,000
1968	Phantom V	V 8 cyl. (James Young)	Limousine	26,000	40,000	75,000

Rolls-Royce – 1969 "Silver Shadow"

YEAR	MODEL	ENGINE	BODY	F	G	E
ROLLS-ROYCE (Great Britain, 1904 to date) (continued)						
1969	Silver Shadow I	V 8 cyl.	Saloon	10,000	18,000	30,000
1969	Phantom VI	V 8 cyl.	Limousine	25,000	45,000	85,000
1970	Silver Shadow I	V 8 cyl.	Drop Head Coupe	15,000	25,000	45,000
1971	Corniche	V 8 cyl.	Convertible	17,000	40,000	75,000
1971	Phantom VI	V 8 cyl.	Limousine	29,000	45,000	85,000

Rolls-Royce – 1971 "Limousine"

YEAR	MODEL	ENGINE	BODY	F	G	E
1971	Silver Shadow I	V 8 cyl.	Saloon	15,000	25,000	45,000
1972	Corniche	V 8 cyl.	Convertible	22,900	46,000	75,000
1972	Corniche	V 8 cyl.	Coupe	13,000	26,000	50,000
ROLLS-ROYCE (United States, 1921–35)						
1921	Silver Ghost	6 cyl.	Phaeton	26,000	55,000	120,000
1926	Phantom	6 cyl.	Speedster Phaeton	28,000	57,000	130,000
1931	Phantom	6 cyl.	Speedster Phaeton	29,000	72,000	160,000
ROLUX (France, 1938–52)						
1938		1 cyl.	Minicar	450	1,900	3,000
1952	Doorless	1 cyl.	Minicar	550	1,000	2,000
ROUSSON (France, 1910–14)						
1910	14 CV	4 cyl.	2 Passenger	1,000	3,000	7,000
1914		4 cyl.	4 Passenger	1,100	4,250	8,500

YEAR	MODEL	ENGINE	BODY	F	G	E
ROVER *(Great Britain, 1904 to date)*						
1904	3-Wheel	1 cyl.	Dogcart	1,000	4,000	10,000
1905	3-Wheel	1 cyl.	Dogcart	1,000	4,000	9,750
1906		4 cyl.	Landaulet	1,750	4,750	9,500
1907		4 cyl.	Landaulet	1,750	4,750	9,500
1908		4 cyl.	Landaulet	1,250	4,500	9,000
1909		4 cyl.	Landaulet	1,250	4,500	9,000
1910		4 cyl.	Touring	1,200	4,400	10,000
1911		1.9 Litre	Touring	1,100	3,250	8,500
1912		1.9 Litre	Touring	1,100	3,250	8,500
1913		4 cyl.	Touring	1,250	4,500	9,000
1914		4 cyl.	Roadster	1,400	4,750	9,500
1915		4 cyl.	Roadster	1,400	4,750	9,500
1916		4 cyl.	Roadster	1,400	4,750	9,500
1917		4 cyl.	Touring	1,500	5,000	10,000
1918		4 cyl.	Touring	1,500	5,000	10,000
1919		4 cyl.	Touring	2,500	5,000	10,000
1920		4 cyl.	Roadster	2,800	6,800	13,750
1921		4 cyl.	Roadster	2,500	6,000	13,500
1922		4 cyl.	Roadster	2,250	6,500	13,000
1923		4 cyl.	Roadster	2,250	6,500	13,000
1924	Eight	2.5 Litre	Roadster	2,200	6,400	12,800
1926		2.1 Litre	Sport	2,100	4,250	9,500
1927		2.5 Litre	Sport	2,000	4,100	9,200
1928		2.1 Litre	Roadster	2,000	5,000	11,000
1929		2 Litre	Roadster	2,000	5,000	11,000
1931		6 cyl.	Limousine	3,000	7,000	14,000
1933		2 Litre	Sport	2,000	4,000	8,800
1935		2 Litre	Sport	2,000	4,000	8,000
1936		2 Litre	Limousine	2,000	4,000	8,000
1937		2 Litre	Coupe	2,000	3,000	6,800
1938		2 Litre	Coupe	2,000	3,000	6,800
1939		2 Litre	Sport Sedan	1,900	2,750	6,400
1940		2.6 Litre	Sport	1,900	2,750	6,400
1941		2.6 Litre	Sedan	900	1,750	4,400
1942		2 Litre	Sedan	900	1,750	4,500
1946		2.6 Litre	Sedan	900	1,700	4,400
1947		2.6 Litre	Coupe	1,000	2,000	5,000
1948		2.6 Litre	Sedan	750	1,500	4,250
1949		2 Litre	Sedan	750	1,500	4,000
1950	P 4	2 Litre	Sedan	750	1,500	4,000
1951		2.6 Litre	Sedan	800	1,600	4,250
1952	T 3	2.6 Litre	Coupe	950	1,750	4,500
1953		2.6 Litre	Sedan	750	1,500	4,000

YEAR	MODEL	ENGINE	BODY	F	G	E
ROVER *(Great Britain, 1904 to date) (continued)*						
1954		2.6 Litre	Sedan	700	1,400	5,000
1955		2.6 Litre	Coupe	650	1,250	4,500
1956		2.6 Litre	Coupe	650	1,250	4,500
1957	105 S	2.6 Litre	Sedan	500	1,000	3,000
1958		2.6 Litre	Sedan	500	1,000	3,000
1959		3 Litre	Sedan	550	1,100	3,200
1962		2 Litre	Sedan	650	1,250	3,500
ROYAL & ROYAL PRINCESS *(United States, 1905)*						
1905		Electric	Runabout	2,600	7,000	14,000
1905		2 cyl.	Tonneau	2,500	6,800	13,500
ROYAL STAR *(Brazil, 1904–10)*						
1904		1 cyl.	Open	1,000	3,000	6,000
1908		2 cyl.	Open	1,200	3,250	6,500
1910		4 cyl.	Open	1,500	3,750	7,500
ROYAL TOURIST *(United States, 1904–11)*						
1904	18/20	2 cyl.	Tonneau	4,500	8,500	17,500
1911	48	4 cyl.	Tonneau	5,000	9,500	19,000
RUBY *(France, 1910–22)*						
1910		1 cyl.	Racing	2,250	4,500	9,000
1922		4 cyl.	Racing	3,750	9,250	17,500
RUMPLER *(Germany, 1921–26)*						
1921		6 cyl.	Sedan	1,500	3,600	7,000
1926		4 cyl.	Sport	1,700	3,000	7,000
RUSSELL *(Canada, 1905–16)*						
1905		2 cyl. (DeDion)	Touring	2,500	4,800	9,750
1906		4 cyl.	Touring	3,000	5,900	11,000
1912		6 cyl. (Knight)	Touring	3,500	7,500	17,000
RUSSON *(Great Britain, 1951–52)*						
1951		197cc	3 Passenger	650	1,300	3,500
RUXTON *(United States, 1929–31)*						
1929	Front-Wheel Drive	8 cyl. (Continental)	Roadster	9,000	32,000	72,000
1930		8 cyl.	Roadster	9,000	32,000	72,000
1930		8 cyl.	Sedan	6,000	16,000	35,000
1931		8 cyl.	Sport Phaeton D.W.	17,000	61,000	140,000
1931		8 cyl.	Town Car	12,000	22,000	65,000
R.W.N. *(Germany, 1928–29)*						
1928	3-Wheel	200cc	Cycle	450	1,900	2,800
1929	3-Wheel	500cc	Cycle	500	2,000	3,000

YEAR	MODEL	ENGINE	BODY	F	G	E
RYKNIELD *(Great Britain, 1903–06)*						
1903	10/12	V 2 cyl.	Victoria	2,000	4,000	9,000
1906	20	4 cyl.	Victoria	2,100	5,300	12,500
RYTECRAFT SCOOTACAR *(Great Britain, 1934–40)*						
1934	1 cyl.	(Villiers Midget)	Minicar	450	900	2,000
1940	1 cyl.	(Villiers Midget)	Minicar	500	1,000	2,000

S

YEAR	MODEL	ENGINE	BODY	F	G	E
SAAB *(Sweden, 1950 to date)*						
1966	Sonnett II	V 6 cyl.	Coupe	2,000	3,500	7,000
1968	Sonnett II	V 6 cyl.	Coupe	1,500	3,000	7,500
1970	Sonnett III	V 6 cyl.	Coupe	2,000	4,000	8,000
SABELLA *(Great Britain, 1906–14)*						
1906		1 cyl. (J.A.P.)	Cycle	1,000	1,800	3,500
1910		2 cyl. (J.A.P.)	Cycle	750	1,600	3,200
SANDFORD *(France, 1922–39)*						
1922		4 cyl.	Tri-car	700	1,300	3,500
1927	Tourisme	900cc (Ruby)	Sport	700	1,400	3,800
1930		900cc (Ruby)	Sport	600	1,250	3,500
1936	Super	900cc (Ruby)	Sport	700	1,400	3,800
1939	3-Wheel	900cc (Ruby)	Sport	600	1,200	3,200
S.A.R.A. *(France, 1923–30)*						
1923		4 cyl.	4 Passenger	1,700	3,400	7,800
1925		6 cyl.	4 Passenger	1,800	4,500	9,000
1928		6 cyl.	Drop Head Coupe	1,300	2,800	6,500
SAURER *(China, 1897–1914)*						
1897		1 cyl.	4 Passenger	1,200	2,300	4,500
1910	24/30	4 cyl. (T-head)	Touring	900	2,000	4,000
1914	50/60	6 cyl.	Limousine	1,200	2,500	5,000
S.C.A.R. *(France, 1906–15)*						
1906		4 cyl. (T-head)	2 Passenger	3,750	4,000	6,500
1912		6 cyl.	4 Passenger	4,250	5,000	9,500
1915		6 cyl.	2 Passenger	5,000	5,500	10,000
S.C.A.T. *(Italy, 1906–23)*						
1906	22/32	3.8 Litre	Racing	2,200	7,250	14,500
1910		4.4 Litre	Racing	2,200	7,400	14,800
1914	25/35	4.7 Litre	Racing	3,100	8,250	16,500
1917		2.1 Litre	Racing	2,000	6,800	12,500
1920		4 cyl.	Racing	2,250	7,500	14,000

YEAR	MODEL	ENGINE	BODY	F	G	E
S.C.A.T. *(Italy, 1906–23) (continued)*						
1923		6 cyl.	Racing	4,000	9,000	19,000
SCHACHT *(United States, 1904–13)*						
1904	High-Wheel	2 cyl.	Runabout	2,600	7,000	14,000
1907	B	4 cyl.	Touring	6,000	14,000	25,000

Schacht – 1905 "Runabout"

1913	40 P.P.	4 cyl.	8 Passenger Touring	7,000	16,000	30,000
SCHEELE *(Germany, 1899–1910)*						
1899		Electric	Brougham	2,700	6,300	13,000
1900		Electric	Brougham	2,700	6,300	13,000
1910		Electric	Landaulet	2,800	6,500	13,500
SCHEIBLER *(Germany, 1900–07)*						
1900		2 cyl.	2 Passenger	2,300	4,500	9,000
1904		4 cyl.	4 Passenger	2,500	5,800	10,500
1907		1 cyl.	4 Passenger	1,000	2,900	6,000
SCHULZ *(Germany, 1904–06)*						
1904	18 hp	4 cyl.	2 Passenger	1,000	3,000	6,800
1906	28 hp	6 cyl.	4 Passenger	1,500	4,000	9,000

YEAR	MODEL	ENGINE	BODY	F	G	E
SCHURICHT *(Germany, 1921–25)*						
1921		4 cyl.	2 Passenger	1,000	3,000	6,000
1925		4 cyl.	3 Passenger	700	2,600	5,250
SCOOTACAR *(Great Britain, 1957–64)*						
1957	3-Wheel	324	Coupe	500	1,100	2,250
1957	Tandem	197cc	Minicar	600	1,200	2,300
SCOTSMAN *(Great Britain, 1922–30)*						
1922		4 cyl.	4 Passenger	1,000	2,900	6,800
1925	14/40		2 Passenger	800	2,600	6,500
1929		6 cyl.	2 Passenger	1,800	3,600	8,500
1930	Little Scotsman	(Meadows)	2 Passenger	900	2,750	6,250
SCOUT *(Great Britain, 1904–23)*						
1904	14/17	4 cyl.	Touring	2,000	4,000	8,000
1906	17/20	6 cyl.	Touring	2,200	5,400	12,000
1910		2 cyl.	Racing	1,800	3,500	8,000
1917		6 cyl.	Racing	2,500	8,000	16,000
1920		4 cyl.	Racing	2,200	7,250	14,500
1923		2 cyl.	Coupe	1,200	3,700	6,250
SCRIPPS-BOOTH *(United States, 1912–22)*						
1914	Rocket Tandem	V 2 cyl.	Roadster Cycle	4,000	8,000	16,000
1914	C Staggered	4 cyl. (Sterling)	Roadster	5,000	9,000	18,000
1916	D	8 cyl. (Ferro)	Town Car	4,000	8,000	16,000
1917	G	4 cyl.	Roadster	3,700	8,000	16,000
1917	D	8 cyl.	Roadster	4,000	9,000	17,000
1918	39	6 cyl.	Coupe	4,000	8,000	16,000
1922	F	6 cyl.	Roadster	3,250	11,500	22,500
SEAL *(Great Britain, 1912–24)*						
1912	3-Wheel	V 2 cyl. (J.A.P.)	Cycle	900	1,800	3,500
1914	3-Wheel	980cc (J.A.P.)	Cycle	1,000	1,900	4,000
1920		4 cyl.	2 Passenger	1,200	2,600	6,200
1922		4 cyl.	3 Passenger	1,700	3,800	7,500
1924		4 cyl.	4 Passenger	1,900	4,200	8,500
SEARCHMONT *(United States, 1900–03)*						
1900		1 cyl.	Runabout	2,500	6,500	14,000
1902	III	2 cyl.	Runabout	2,600	6,800	14,800
1903	VI	2 cyl.	Touring	3,200	7,500	18,000
S.E.A.T. *(Spain, 1953–59)*						
1953	1400	4 cyl.	Sedan	850	1,700	4,400
1957	600	6 cyl.	Sedan	900	1,800	4,600
1959	1800	6 cyl.	Sedan	950	1,900	5,000

YEAR	MODEL	ENGINE	BODY	F	G	E
SEATON-PETTER *(Great Britain, 1926–27)*						
1926		V 2 cyl.	Cycle	1,000	2,000	4,000
SECQUEVILLE-HOYAU *(France, 1919–24)*						
1919	10 CV	4 cyl.	Coupe de Ville	1,750	3,500	7,500
SELF *(Sweden, 1916–22)*						
1916		1 cyl.	Cycle	750	1,500	2,750
1919		4 cyl.	Cycle	1,000	2,000	3,800
1922		V 2 cyl.	Cycle	900	1,800	3,500
SELVE *(Germany, 1923–29)*						
1923		4 cyl.	Sedan	1,000	1,800	3,600
1924	8/32	6 cyl.	Sedan	1,500	3,000	7,900
1925	8/40	6 cyl.	Sport	1,200	2,250	6,500
1927	Selecta	6 cyl.	Sedan	1,100	2,000	4,000
SENECHAL *(France, 1921–29)*						
1921		4 cyl. (Ruby)	Racing	1,900	6,800	13,500
1922	Grand Sport	4 cyl.	Sport	1,000	2,900	7,000
1924		6 cyl.	Sport	900	1,800	5,750
1925	SZ	1100cc	Racing	900	6,800	13,500
1927	1500 Special	6 cyl.	Racing	900	6,800	13,500
SERPOLLET *(France, 1900–07)*						
1900		2 cyl.	Landaulet	1,100	3,250	7,500
1904		6 cyl.	Racing	2,200	7,300	14,600
1907		4 cyl.	Tulip Phaeton	1,400	3,800	8,500
S.G.V. *(United States, 1911–15)*						
1911	A	4 cyl.	Landaulet	6,000	12,000	22,000
1915	F	4 cyl.	Tonneau	5,000	1,000	21,000
SHAMROCK *(Ireland, 1959–60)*						
1959		(B.M.C.)	Convertible	1,800	3,800	6,500
SHARP-ARROW *(United States, 1908–10)*						
1908		4 cyl. (Beaver)	Speedabout	8,000	15,000	30,000
1909		4 cyl. (Beaver)	5 Passenger Touring	7,000	14,000	28,000
1910		4 cyl. (Beaver)	Speedabout	9,000	18,000	34,000
SHAW *(United States, 1920–30)*						
1920		4 cyl. (Rochester-Duesenberg)	Phaeton	14,000	19,000	36,000
1923		4 cyl.	Roadster	4,500	9,000	17,000
1925		6 cyl.	Sport Phaeton	7,250	15,000	30,000
1926		V 12 cyl. (Weidely)	Coupe	6,000	17,000	35,000

YEAR	MODEL	ENGINE	BODY	F	G	E
SHAW *(United States, 1920–30) (continued)*						
1928		6 cyl.	Limousine	3,750	9,500	18,000
1930		4 cyl.	Sport			
			Speedster	4,500	8,500	17,000
SHEFFIELD-SIMPLEX *(Great Britain, 1907–22)*						
1907	20	4 cyl.	Touring	2,000	4,000	8,000
1909	45	6 cyl.	Touring	2,100	4,300	11,000
1910	20/30	6 cyl.	Touring	1,900	3,900	8,800
1914	14/20	6 cyl.	Coupe	1,000	2,900	5,900
1917	30	6 cyl.	Coupe	1,000	3,000	6,000
1921	30	6 cyl.	Touring	2,200	5,400	12,000
SHEPPEE *(Great Britain, 1912)*						
1912		2 cyl.	Touring	1,100	3,300	7,500
1912		2 cyl.	Cabriolet	1,000	3,100	7,250
SHOEMAKER *(United States, 1906–08)*						
1907	6	4 cyl.	5 Passenger			
			Touring	5,000	11,000	25,000
1908	C	4 cyl.	5 Passenger			
			Touring	6,000	12,000	26,000
SIATA *(Italy, 1949–70)*						
1949		750cc	Sport	1,000	2,900	7,000
1950	1400	6 cyl.	Touring	2,150	4,350	9,750
1951		6 cyl.	Sport	2,200	4,400	8,800
1952	202	V 8 cyl.	Coupe	1,400	3,750	6,500
1957		V 8 cyl.	Coupe	1,350	3,700	6,400
1959		V 8 cyl.	Coupe	1,250	3,500	6,000
SIDDELEY *(Great Britain, 1902–04)*						
1902		2 cyl. 2.3 Litre	2 Passenger	2,100	4,200	8,400
1903		4 cyl. 3.3 Litre	4 Passenger	3,200	6,400	12,800
1904	6 hp	1 cyl.	2 Passenger	900	2,800	6,650
SIDDELEY-DEASY *(Great Britain, 1912–19)*						
1912		4 cyl. 1.9 Litre	4 Passenger	2,000	4,000	9,000
1913	14/20	4 cyl. 2.6 Litre	2 Passenger	2,100	4,100	9,200
1919	18/24	6 cyl.	Town			
			Carriage	3,150	6,300	12,650
SIMPLEX *(Netherlands, 1899–1914)*						
1899		1 cyl.	Vis-a-vis	1,800	3,600	7,150
1902		1 cyl.	2 Passenger	1,600	3,500	7,000
1907		2 cyl.	4 Passenger	1,900	3,800	7,750
1914		4 cyl.	4 Passenger	2,000	4,000	8,000
SIMPLEX *(United States, 1907–19)*						
1907	50	4 cyl.	Tonneau	14,000	32,000	70,000

YEAR	MODEL	ENGINE	BODY	F	G	E
SIMPLEX *(United States, 1907–19) (continued)*						
1911	38	4 cyl.	7 Passenger Touring	20,000	40,000	85,000
1915	5	6 cyl.	7 Passenger Touring	15,000	35,000	80,000
1916	5	6 cyl.	7 Passenger Touring	20,000	40,000	85,000
SIMPLICITY *(United States, 1906–11)*						
1906		4 cyl.	Touring	3,250	7,500	16,500
1909		4 cyl.	Limousine	2,350	6,750	14,000
1911		4 cyl.	Roadster	3,400	7,800	16,750
SIMSON; SIMSON-SUPRA *(Germany, 1911–32)*						
1911	6/18	2 cyl.	Touring	1,900	3,750	7,500
1919	10/30	4 cyl.	Touring	2,100	4,250	9,500
1924	Type So	4 cyl. 259cc	Touring	2,050	4,100	9,250
1926	Type R	6 cyl. 3538cc	Touring	3,100	6,250	12,500
1928	Type J	4 cyl.	Touring	2,100	4,250	9,500
1930	Type RJ	3358cc	Touring	3,200	6,350	13,640
1932	Type A	8 cyl.	Touring	3,500	7,000	14,000
SINGER *(Great Britain, 1905–70)*						
1905		2 cyl.	Touring	2,000	4,100	9,200
1906		2 cyl.	Touring	2,100	4,500	9,900
1908		4 cyl.	Doctor Coupe	1,850	3,650	6,350
1910		3 cyl.	Coupe	900	2,750	4,500
1911		2 cyl.	Touring	950	2,800	4,950
1913		4 cyl.	Touring	1,900	3,800	7,000
1917	Ten	4 cyl.	Coupe	850	2,500	4,000
1920	20 hp	6 cyl.	Sport	1,900	3,700	7,400
1922		6 cyl.	Sport	1,800	3,600	7,250
1924		6 cyl.	Fabric Sedan	1,700	2,400	4,850
1927	Senior	1.3 Litre	Sedan	1,100	2,200	4,400
1929	Junior	848cc	Coupe	950	1,800	4,000
1932		6 cyl.	Convertible Sedan	2,100	6,250	13,500
1933	Kaye Don	6 cyl.	Coupe	1,700	2,400	5,800
1935	Ten	4 cyl.	Coupe	900	1,800	4,750
1937		6 cyl.	Sedan	850	1,500	3,250
1940		6 cyl.	Sedan	850	1,500	3,250
1940		6 cyl.	Sport	900	1,750	4,500
1948		6 cyl.	Sedan	600	1,200	3,000
1951		6 cyl.	Roadster	1,250	2,600	5,250
1953		6 cyl.	Roadster	1,200	2,500	5,000
1954	Hunter	6 cyl.	Sedan	800	1,600	3,250

YEAR	MODEL	ENGINE	BODY	F	G	E
SINGER (Great Britain, 1905–70) (continued)						
1959		6 cyl.	Sedan	850	1,700	3,400
SINGER (United States, 1914–20)						
1914		6 cyl.	Touring	12,000	25,000	50,000
1917		6 cyl.	7 Passenger			
			Touring	12,000	25,000	50,000
1920		12 cyl.	Roadster	15,000	30,000	65,000
SIRRON (Great Britain, 1909–16)						
1909	10/12	4 cyl.	2 Passenger	2,000	4,000	8,000
1914	12/16	4 cyl.	2 Passenger	2,050	4,100	8,250
1916	16/20	6 cyl.	2 Passenger	2,600	5,250	10,500
SIZAIRE-BERWICK (France; Great Britain, 1913–27)						
1913		4 cyl. 4 Litre	Touring	1,100	3,250	7,500
1917		4 cyl.	Coupe	800	2,000	4,250
1923		6 cyl. 3.2 Litre	Coupe	900	3,750	6,500
1927		6 cyl.	Coupe	900	3,750	6,500
SIZAIRE-FRERES (France; Brazil, 1923–31)						
1923	11 CV	2 Litre	Sport			
			Touring	1,000	1,900	7,000
1927		6 cyl.	Touring	1,000	2,900	8,750
1931		2 Litre	Sedan	750	1,500	3,900
SIZAIRE-NAUDIN (France, 1905–21)						
1905		1 cyl.	Voiturette	1,000	4,000	9,000
1911		4 cyl.	Roadster	2,200	6,300	12,600
1915		4 cyl.	Roadster	3,100	7,250	13,500
1920		4 cyl.	Sedan	1,200	2,400	4,850
1921		4 cyl.	Touring	2,800	6,600	13,250
S.M. SIMPLEX (United States, 1904–07)						
1904		4 cyl.	5 Passenger			
			Touring	4,500	9,000	28,000
1906		4 cyl.	Touring	7,000	15,000	30,000
1907		4 cyl. (T-head)	Racing			
			Runabout	8,000	16,000	29,000
SPITZ (Austria, 1902–07)						
1902		1 cyl.	Racing	1,800	5,750	11,500
1905		2 cyl.	Racing	1,950	6,900	14,000
1907		4 cyl.	Racing	2,000	8,950	16,800
SPOERER (United States, 1908–14)						
1909	DA	4 cyl.	Roadster	6,000	13,000	26,000
1910	30	4 cyl.	5 Passenger			
			Touring	7,000	15,000	30,000
1911	C	4 cyl.	Touring	7,000	15,000	30,000

YEAR	MODEL	ENGINE	BODY	F	G	E
SPOERER *(United States, 1908–14) (continued)*						
1914	40C	4 cyl.	Roadster	8,000	17,000	35,000
SPRINGER *(United States, 1903–05)*						
1903	12	2 cyl.	Runabout	2,300	6,600	14,000
1905	40	4 cyl.	Tonneau	2,800	7,800	15,500
SPRINGFIELD *(United States, 1904–11)*						
1904		1 cyl.	Runabout	2,250	7,500	15,000
1907		4 cyl.	Tonneau	2,300	8,600	16,500
1908		4 cyl.	Torpedo	3,800	11,200	21,000
1911		4 cyl.	Touring	2,400	7,800	15,600
SPYKER; SPIJKER *(Netherlands, 1900–25)*						
1900		2 cyl.	Touring	2,200	6,500	13,000
1902	1.9 Litre	2 cyl.	Touring	2,400	7,800	17,000
1903	12 hp	2 cyl.	Limousine	2,200	7,500	16,000
1904	12/16	4 cyl.	Touring	2,400	8,800	18,600
1905	20/24	4 cyl.	Touring	2,500	9,000	20,000
1906	30/36	4 cyl.	Touring	2,500	9,500	20,500
1910	8.7 Litre	6 cyl.	Racing	5,800	18,800	40,800
1913	1.7 Litre	4 cyl.	Tonneau	2,200	6,600	13,600
1914	1.7 Litre	4 cyl.	Touring	2,000	6,200	13,400
1915	7.2 Litre	4 cyl.	Landaulet	3,000	7,200	15,000
1915	3.4 Litre	6 cyl.	Sport	3,000	8,200	16,600
1916	3.3 Litre	6 cyl.	Sport	4,200	9,800	20,000
1919	16/30	6 cyl.	Sport	4,300	10,600	21,400
1920	13/30	6 cyl.	Sport	3,200	9,200	20,500
1922		6 cyl.	Sport	2,400	8,600	18,500
1925		6 cyl.	Sport	2,800	8,500	19,000
S.S. *(Great Britain, 1900–45)*						
1900		1 cyl.	Runabout	1,100	3,250	7,500
1931		6 cyl.	Coupe	1,300	2,600	7,200
1932	2.5 Litre	6 cyl.	Coupe	1,350	2,750	7,500
1933		6 cyl.	Sport			
			Touring	2,500	6,000	12,000
1934	2.7 Litre	6 cyl.	Sport	1,800	5,100	10,200
1935	Airline	6 cyl.	Sedan	1,750	3,400	7,000
1938		2.7 Litre	Sport Sedan	1,800	3,800	7,250
1940		2.5 Litre	Sedan	1,500	3,000	6,000
S.S. *(United States, 1924–29)*						
1924		6 cyl.	Sedan	7,000	15,000	30,000
1927	Gotham	6 cyl.	Sedan	8,000	16,000	32,000
1929	Lakewood	8 cyl.	8 Passenger			
			Sedan	9,000	17,000	35,000

YEAR	MODEL	ENGINE	BODY	F	G	E
STABILIA *(France, 1908–30)*						
1908	2.2 Litre	4 cyl.	Sport	1,800	3,600	7,250
1912	1.5 Litre	4 cyl.	Sport	1,850	3,700	7,400
1917	1.7 Litre	4 cyl.	Sport	1,900	3,750	7,500
1925	2.7 Litre	4 cyl.	Sport	2,000	3,900	8,000
1927	2.8 Litre	6 cyl.	2 Passenger	2,000	4,000	8,000
1928	1.5 Litre	6 cyl.	2 Passenger	2,000	4,000	8,000
1930	2 Litre	6 cyl.	2 Passenger	2,400	4,750	9,500
STAIGER *(Germany, 1923–24)*						
1923		4 cyl.	2 Passenger	2,900	6,750	12,500
1924		4 cyl.	4 Passenger	3,000	7,800	14,650
STANDARD *(Great Britain, 1903–63)*						
1903	12/15	2 cyl.	Touring	2,100	4,100	9,200
1904		4 cyl.	Coupe	1,000	3,000	6,000
1905	30	4 cyl.	Touring	2,400	5,000	9,900
1907	50	4 cyl.	Touring	2,500	5,800	11,650
1909	3.3 Litre	6 cyl.	Touring	3,000	6,900	13,800
1910		6 cyl.	Touring	3,100	7,000	14,000
1911	4 Litre	4 cyl.	Sport	1,000	3,900	8,800
1912	2.7 Litre	4 cyl.	Sport	1,100	2,800	7,600
1913	RHYL	9.5 hp	Coupe	1,000	2,400	6,800
1919	SLS	1.3 Litre	Sedan	1,000	2,200	4,400
1921	SLO	1.3 Litre	Sedan	1,000	2,000	4,000
1922	SLO 4	1.3 Litre	Sedan	1,000	2,100	4,200
1930	Big Nine	6 cyl.	Sedan	1,000	2,100	4,250
1933		6 cyl.	Sport	2,100	4,300	9,600
1936		6 cyl.	Sport	2,000	4,250	9,500
1939		4 cyl.	Coupe	800	2,000	4,000
1941		V 8 cyl.	Coupe	1,200	2,500	5,000
1947	Twelve	8 cyl.	Sedan	900	1,800	4,600
1953	Fourteen	8 cyl.	Sedan	800	1,700	4,400
1959		8 cyl.	Sport	950	1,900	4,750
STANDARD *(Germany, 1911–35)*						
1911		4 cyl.	Roadster	1,000	3,750	9,500
1933		2 cyl.	Sedan	800	1,600	4,250
STANDARD *(United States, 1914–23)*						
1914		6 cyl.	Touring	6,000	12,000	26,000
1915		8 cyl.	Roadster	4,900	10,800	21,500
1917	E	8 cyl.	Touring	4,750	10,500	21,000
1918	G	8 cyl.	Coupe	4,600	10,250	20,500
1919	G	8 cyl.	Limousine	4,000	10,000	20,000
1920	I	8 cyl.	Sedan	4,800	12,800	23,500
1921	I	8 cyl.	Speedster	10,000	20,000	38,000

YEAR	MODEL	ENGINE	BODY	F	G	E
STANDARD *(United States, 1914–23) (continued)*						
1923	II	8 cyl.	Touring	8,000	17,000	34,000
STANHOPE *(Great Britain, 1915–25)*						
1915	3-Wheel	V 2 cyl.	Cycle	1,000	2,000	3,750
1922		V 2 cyl.	Saloon Sedan	1,000	2,000	3,850
1923		V 2 cyl.	2 Passenger	1,000	2,000	4,200
1925		V 2 cyl.	4 Passenger	1,000	2,700	5,400
STANLEY (STEAM) *(United States, 1897–27)*						
1901	A	2 cyl.	Runabout	7,100	14,250	29,500
1904	C	2 cyl.	Runabout	7,200	14,400	29,800
1906	DX	2 cyl.	Surrey	3,500	8,000	17,500

Stanley – 1905 "Steamer"

1908	M	2 cyl.	Touring	9,500	17,000	35,000
1910	Z	2 cyl.	Wagon	4,750	12,500	25,000
1911	72	2 cyl.	Roadster	5,500	13,000	27,500
1912	63	2 cyl.	Tonneau	5,500	13,000	34,000
1914	607	2 cyl.	Touring	5,750	13,500	28,500
1915	723	2 cyl.	Touring	6,000	14,000	34,000
1917	728	2 cyl.	Touring	6,500	15,000	34,000
1918	735	2 cyl.	Touring	6,500	15,000	34,500
1919	735D	2 cyl.	Sedan	6,500	15,000	34,500
1920	735C	2 cyl.	Coupe	7,500	17,000	36,500
1922	735	2 cyl.	Touring	7,500	17,000	37,500

YEAR	MODEL	ENGINE	BODY	F	G	E
STANLEY (STEAM) *(United States, 1897–27) (continued)*						
1924	740	2 cyl.	Sedan	7,000	15,000	30,000
1927	770	2 cyl.	Touring	7,500	17,000	37,500
STAR; STARLING; STUART *(Great Britain, 1898–1932)*						
1898		1 cyl.	Vis-a-vis	1,100	3,300	8,600
1899		2 cyl.	Touring	2,100	4,350	9,750
1902		2 cyl.	Touring	2,200	4,400	9,800
1908		4 cyl.	Touring	2,200	6,400	12,800
1914		6 cyl.	Touring	3,200	7,450	14,950
1921		6 cyl.	Coupe	3,050	7,100	14,250
1924		2 Litre	Touring	2,050	4,100	9,350
1925		6 cyl.	Coupe	2,000	4,000	8,000
1926		6 cyl. 3 Litre	Coupe	2,000	4,100	8,200
1928		2 Litre	Sedan	1,200	2,600	5,250
1929	18/50	6 cyl.	Sedan	1,500	2,800	6,000
1930	14/40	6 cyl.	Sedan	1,300	2,400	5,800
1931		3.6 Litre	Sedan	1,800	3,600	7,200
1932		2 Litre	Sedan	1,250	2,500	6,000
STAR *(United States, 1922–28)*						
1922		4 cyl.	Runabout	2,250	6,500	14,000
1923		4 cyl.	Coupe	2,300	4,000	8,000
1924		4 cyl.	Sedan	1,500	3,000	6,000
1925	F-25	4 cyl.	Touring	2,000	4,000	9,000
1926		4 cyl.	Touring	3,200	7,500	16,500
1926		6 cyl.	Coupe	1,200	4,100	9,500
1927		4 cyl.	Roadster	3,800	8,300	17,000
1927	M-2	6 cyl.	Touring	4,000	7,000	14,000
1928		4 cyl.	Sport Roadster	5,000	8,000	15,000
STIMULA *(France, 1905–14)*						
1905		1 cyl.	Sport	1,000	4,000	8,000
1910		4 cyl.	Touring	1,100	4,250	9,500
1914		2 cyl.	Touring	1,250	4,500	8,750
STIRLING *(Great Britain, 1897–1903)*						
1897		1 cyl.	Voiturette	1,100	4,250	9,500
1900		1 cyl.	Voiturette	1,150	4,300	9,750
1901		2 cyl.	Doctor Coupe	1,250	3,500	8,000
1902		2 cyl.	Runabout	1,200	4,400	9,000
1903		2 cyl.	Tonneau	1,150	4,800	9,750
STODDARD-DAYTON *(United States, 1904–13)*						
1904		4 cyl.	Touring	5,000	11,000	22,000
1907	F	4 cyl.	Touring	6,000	12,000	26,000
1908	8-G	6 cyl.	Touring	12,000	22,000	45,000

YEAR	MODEL	ENGINE	BODY	F	G	E
STODDARD-DAYTON *(United States, 1904–13) (continued)*						
1913	Knight	6 cyl.	Roadster	13,500	26,000	48,000
STOEWER *(Germany, 1899–1939)*						
1899		2 cyl.	Touring	1,150	4,250	9,500
1900		4 cyl.	Touring	1,300	4,400	10,000
1904	Type T	2 cyl.	Coupe	1,150	4,100	9,200
1910	Type P4	4 cyl.	Touring	1,200	4,250	9,500
1911	Type G4	4 cyl.	Touring	1,150	4,100	9,200
1917	Type P6	6 cyl.	Coupe	1,000	2,900	7,000
1921	Type B1	6 cyl.	Sport	900	3,800	8,600
1938	Type D6	6 cyl.	Sedan	750	2,500	6,000
STONELEIGH *(Great Britain, 1912–24)*						
1912		V 2 cyl.	3 Passenger	900	3,800	8,750
1924		V 2 cyl.	1 Passenger	1,000	3,900	9,000
STORERO *(Italy, 1912–19)*						
1912		4 cyl.	Sport	1,000	2,900	8,750
1915	Type C	6 cyl.	Racing	2,000	7,000	14,000
1919	Type C2	6 cyl.	Racing	2,000	7,100	14,200
STOREY *(Great Britain, 1919–30)*						
1919		4 cyl.	Touring	900	3,750	9,500
1920		4 cyl.	Touring	900	3,800	9,600
1923		4 cyl.	2 Passenger	1,000	2,900	7,750
1925	10/25	4 cyl.	2 Passenger	900	3,800	7,500
1928	14/40	4 cyl.	2 Passenger	650	3,250	7,500
1930		6 cyl.	2 Passenger	1,000	4,300	9,000
STORY *(Netherlands, 1941–44)*						
1941	3-Wheel	Electric	Coupe	800	1,900	5,000
1944	3-Wheel	Electric	Coupe	950	2,100	5,500
STRAKER-SQUIRE *(Great Britain, 1906–26)*						
1906	16/20	4 cyl.	Touring	2,400	4,800	10,000
1908	12/14	4 cyl.	Touring	2,200	4,400	9,000
1910	15	4 cyl.	Sport	2,400	4,800	10,000
1912	15	4 cyl.	Coupe	2,200	4,400	9,000
1919	20/25	6 cyl.	Touring	3,100	6,500	14,000
1921	24/90	6 cyl.	Sport	3,000	6,000	12,500
1924	24/90	6 cyl.	Touring	3,500	7,000	15,000
1926		6 cyl.	Coupe	2,200	4,500	10,000
STRATTON *(United States, 1909–23)*						
1909	High-Wheel	2 cyl.	Buggy	2,600	6,250	13,500
1911	High-Wheel	2 cyl.	Surrey	2,600	6,250	13,500
1923		4 cyl.	2 Passenger	1,800	6,100	12,300

YEAR	MODEL	ENGINE	BODY	F	G	E
STRINGER-WINCO *(Great Britain, 1921–32)*						
1921		4 cyl.	2 Passenger	1,300	3,400	7,750
1922	Type S	4 cyl.	4 Passenger	1,500	3,800	7,600
1929		4 cyl.	2 Passenger	1,400	3,700	7,400
1932		4 cyl.	2 Passenger	1,500	3,800	7,750
STROMMEN; STROMMEN-DODGE *(Norway, 1933–40)*						
1933			Sedan	1,200	2,400	4,850
1937			Sedan	1,250	2,450	4,900
1940			Sedan	1,300	2,500	5,000
STUDEBAKER *(United States; Canada, 1902–66)*						
1904	A	2 cyl.	Touring	4,500	8,000	16,500
1904	B	2 cyl.	Wagon	4,000	7,500	15,500
1904	C	2 cyl.	Touring	4,800	9,600	18,000
1906	E	2 cyl.	Touring	4,800	9,600	18,000
1906	F	2 cyl.	Touring	5,300	10,000	19,500
1906	G	2 cyl.	Touring	6,000	11,000	21,500
1908	H	4 cyl.	Touring	3,000	9,000	22,000
1908	A	4 cyl.	Touring	3,000	9,000	22,000
1908	B	4 cyl.	Touring	4,000	10,000	23,000
1908	B	4 cyl.	Runabout	4,000	10,000	23,000
1909	A	4 cyl.	Touring	3,000	9,000	22,000
1909	B	4 cyl.	Touring	3,750	9,750	22,500
1910	H	4 cyl.	Touring	3,000	9,000	22,000
1910	M	4 cyl.	Touring	3,000	9,000	22,000
1910	M	4 cyl.	Limousine	2,750	8,500	20,500
1911	G-8	4 cyl.	Touring	4,500	11,000	24,500
1911	G-10	4 cyl.	Touring	4,500	11,000	24,500
1913	25	6 cyl.	Touring	5,400	10,400	25,000
1913	35	4 cyl.	Touring	2,200	3,750	12,000
1913	35	4 cyl.	Sedan	2,750	4,500	13,250
1913	35	4 cyl.	Coupe	2,750	4,500	13,250
1914	SC	4 cyl.	Touring	2,500	7,850	18,000
1914	EB	6 cyl.	Touring	2,200	3,750	12,000
1914	EB	6 cyl.	Roadster	2,400	4,500	12,500
1915	EC	6 cyl.	Touring	2,900	8,800	22,000
1915	SD	4 cyl.	Touring	2,600	8,700	16,000
1916	SF	4 cyl.	Touring	2,200	3,750	12,000
1916	SF	4 cyl.	Roadster	2,000	3,500	11,500
1917	ED	6 cyl.	Touring	2,700	9,800	22,000
1917	ED	6 cyl.	Roadster	3,000	10,200	24,000
1918	EG	6 cyl.	Touring	3,700	7,500	15,000
1918	EH	6 cyl.	Roadster	3,700	7,500	15,000
1921	EJ	6 cyl.	Touring	2,700	6,000	12,000

YEAR	MODEL	ENGINE	BODY	F	G	E
STUDEBAKER *(United States; Canada, 1902–66) (continued)*						
1922	Special Six	6 cyl.	Touring	3,300	9,000	23,000
1922	Special Six	6 cyl.	Roadster	3,500	10,500	22,000
1922	Big Six	6 cyl.	Touring	3,000	14,000	24,000
1922	Light Six	6 cyl.	Touring	2,200	3,750	12,000
1922	Light Six	6 cyl.	Roadster	2,000	3,500	11,000
1923	Big Six	6 cyl.	Roadster	3,500	14,000	24,000
1923	Light Six	6 cyl.	Roadster	2,700	10,500	19,000
1923	Special Six	6 cyl.	Sedan	2,000	4,200	10,000
1923	Special Six	6 cyl.	Touring	2,200	3,750	12,000
1923	Special Six	6 cyl.	Roadster	2,600	4,500	13,250
1923	Special Six	6 cyl.	Coupe	1,800	4,200	7,200
1923	Big Six	6 cyl.	Touring	3,200	12,000	24,000
1924	Special Six	6 cyl.	Roadster	2,400	4,500	12,500
1924	Special Six	6 cyl.	Coupe	1,900	4,400	10,000
1924	Big Six	6 cyl.	Touring	3,000	7,500	14,500
1924	Big Six	6 cyl.	Sedan	2,000	4,200	10,500
1924	Big Six	6 cyl.	Coupe	1,700	4,000	9,250
1924	Light Six	6 cyl.	Touring	2,200	3,750	12,000
1924	Light Six	6 cyl.	Sedan	1,700	4,000	9,250
1925	Big Six	6 cyl.	Phaeton	3,700	13,800	26,000
1925	Light Six	6 cyl.	Touring	4,000	10,500	12,000
1926	EP	6 cyl.	Sedan	1,800	4,200	9,500
1926	Big Six	6 cyl.	Roadster	3,600	13,000	26,000
1927	Commander	6 cyl.	Roadster	5,000	10,000	22,000
1927	Commander	6 cyl.	Coupe	2,000	4,200	10,500
1927	Commander	6 cyl.	Phaeton	5,000	10,000	22,000
1927	Dictator	6 cyl.	Touring	4,000	9,000	19,000
1927	Dictator	6 cyl.	Sport Roadster	5,000	10,000	20,000
1927	Dictator	6 cyl.	Coupe	1,500	3,700	8,000
1927	President	6 cyl.	Sedan	1,750	3,900	9,000
1927	President	6 cyl.	Phaeton	3,750	7,500	17,500
1927	Special	6 cyl.	Sport Roadster	4,000	9,000	19,000
1927	Special	6 cyl.	Brougham	1,500	3,700	8,000
1927	Special	6 cyl.	Phaeton	3,750	7,500	17,500

YEAR	MODEL	ENGINE	BODY	F	G	E
STUDEBAKER (United States; Canada, 1902–66) (continued)						
1928	Light Six	6 cyl.	Roadster	6,900	12,000	24,000

Studebaker – 1928 "Roadster"

1928	Dictator	6 cyl.	Sedan	2,200	3,650	12,000
1928	Dictator	6 cyl.	Touring	4,000	9,000	19,000
1928	Dictator	6 cyl.	Coupe	1,750	3,900	9,000
1928	President 8	8 cyl.	Sedan	2,700	7,700	15,000
1928	Commander	8 cyl.	Sedan	3,000	5,900	10,000
1929	President	8 cyl.	Roadster	5,500	16,000	33,000
1929	President	8 cyl.	Cabriolet	5,600	15,000	30,000
1929	Dictator	6 cyl.	Roadster	5,600	15,000	30,000
1929	Commander	8 cyl.	Cabriolet	4,100	13,000	26,000
1930	Dictator-Regal	6 cyl.	Sedan	2,900	6,000	10,000
1930	President	8 cyl.	Sedan	3,300	6,000	12,000
1930	President 8	8 cyl.	Touring	4,100	14,000	26,000
1931	President 8	8 cyl.	Roadster	5,500	20,000	32,000
1931	Commander	8 cyl.	Sedan	3,000	5,900	10,000
1931	Dictator	6 cyl.	Roadster	4,400	18,000	30,000
1931	President	8 cyl.	Sedan	3,800	7,500	14,000
1931	Dictator	6 cyl.	Coupe	3,000	5,000	10,500
1932	President 91	8 cyl.	Sedan	3,600	8,000	20,000
1932	Commander	8 cyl.	Convertible	7,200	18,000	40,000
1932	President	8 cyl.	Roadster	4,800	22,000	36,000
1932	Dictator	6 cyl.	Coupe	2,200	4,200	10,000
1933	President	8 cyl.	Convertible	5,500	16,000	30,000

YEAR	MODEL	ENGINE	BODY	F	G	E
STUDEBAKER *(United States; Canada, 1902–66) (continued)*						
1933	Commander	8 cyl.	Victoria	2,600	7,200	14,000
1934	President	8 cyl.	Convertible Coupe	7,200	19,000	36,000
1934	Dictator	6 cyl.	Sedan	1,200	3,900	9,200
1935	Commander	8 cyl.	Sedan	2,000	4,200	9,750
1938	Commander	8 cyl.	Sedan	1,800	4,000	9,000
1939	Commander	8 cyl.	Sedan	1,800	4,000	9,000
1940	Champion	6 cyl.	Coupe	1,600	4,000	8,400
1940	President	8 cyl.	Sedan	2,000	5,000	9,000
1940	Commander	8 cyl.	2 Door Sedan	1,500	3,000	7,750
1941	President	8 cyl.	Sedan	2,000	4,000	9,300
1941	Champion	6 cyl.	Sedan	1,400	3,000	7,000
1942	President	8 cyl.	Sedan	2,000	4,000	9,750
1948	Commander	6 cyl.	Convertible	7,000	12,000	22,000
1948	Commander	6 cyl.	Club Coupe	2,000	4,000	8,000
1949	Champion	6 cyl.	Convertible	6,000	12,000	20,000
1949	Champion	6 cyl.	Sedan	2,000	4,000	7,000
1949		6 cyl.	Pickup Truck	4,000	6,000	10,000
1950	Champion	6 cyl.	Starlight Coupe	3,000	5,000	9,000
1951	Champion	6 cyl.	3 Window Coupe	2,000	4,000	8,000
1952	Land Cruiser	V 8 cyl.	Sedan	2,000	5,000	10,000
1953	Commander	V 8 cyl.	Hardtop	3,000	7,000	15,000
1954	Commander	V 8 cyl.	Coupe	3,000	6,000	13,000
1955	President	V 8 cyl. 259	Sports Hardtop	5,000	10,000	20,000
1956	Golden Hawk	V 8 cyl.	Hardtop	6,000	12,000	20,000
1956	Power Hawk	V 8 cyl.	Coupe	4,000	7,000	13,000
1957	Golden Hawk	V 8 cyl. (Supercharged)	Sport Hardtop	5,000	10,000	20,000
1958	Golden Hawk	V 8 cyl. 289	Sport Hardtop	4,000	8,000	18,000
1960	Lark Regal	V 8 cyl. 289	Convertible	400	8,000	14,000
1961	Hawk	V 8 cyl.	Sport Coupe	3,000	7,000	15,000
1962	Champ	V 8 cyl.	Pickup Truck	3,000	5,000	8,000
1962	Daytona	V 8 cyl.	Convertible	3,000	7,000	14,000

YEAR	MODEL	ENGINE	BODY	F	G	E

STUDEBAKER *(United States; Canada, 1902–66) (continued)*

YEAR	MODEL	ENGINE	BODY	F	G	E
1962	Gran Turismo	V 8 cyl.	Hardtop	4,000	9,000	17,000

Studebaker – 1962 "Gran Turismo"

YEAR	MODEL	ENGINE	BODY	F	G	E
1963	Lark Regal	V 8 cyl.	Station Wagon	1,500	3,000	7,000
1963	Avanti	V 8 cyl.	Sport Coupe	8,000	14,000	22,000
1964	Daytona	V 8 cyl.	Hardtop	2,000	5,000	10,000
1964	Avanti	V 8 cyl.	Coupe	6,000	12,000	20,000
1965	Cruiser	V 8 cyl.	Sedan	2,000	4,000	7,000

STUTZ *(United States, 1911–35)*

YEAR	MODEL	ENGINE	BODY	F	G	E
1912	A	4 cyl.	Bearcat	50,000	95,000	150,000
1913	B	4 cyl.	Roadster	22,000	40,000	75,000
1914	6E	6 cyl.	Roadster	25,000	45,000	80,000
1915	6F	6 cyl.	Coupe	12,000	20,000	36,000
1916	Bulldog	6 cyl.	Touring	15,000	35,000	65,000
1917	R	4 cyl.	Roadster	14,000	29,000	64,000
1918	Bearcat	4 cyl.	Speedster	29,000	79,000	140,000
1919	Bearcat	4 cyl.	Roadster	45,000	80,000	140,000
1920	H	4 cyl.	Roadster	25,000	40,000	75,000
1921	K	4 cyl.	Coupe	9,600	18,000	38,000
1922	K	6 cyl.	Roadster	25,000	40,000	70,000
1923	Special	6 cyl.	Roadster	20,000	40,000	75,000
1923	Speedway	4 cyl.	Roadster	14,000	28,000	72,000
1924	Special	6 cyl.	Phaeton	16,000	41,000	84,000
1925	394	6 cyl.	Touring	15,000	30,000	65,000
1925	695	6 cyl.	Sportster	25,000	40,000	70,000
1926	AA	8 cyl.	Speedster	40,000	85,000	140,000
1927	AA	8 cyl.	Berline	12,000	25,000	50,000

YEAR	MODEL	ENGINE	BODY	F	G	E
STUTZ *(United States, 1911–35) (continued)*						
1928	BB	8 cyl.	Blackhawk Speedster	45,000	85,000	150,000
1928	BB	8 cyl.	Cabriolet	25,000	55,000	100,000
1929	M	8 cyl.	Speedster	40,000	75,000	140,000

Stutz – 1929 "Dual Cowl Phaeton"

YEAR	MODEL	ENGINE	BODY	F	G	E
1929	M	8 cyl.	Speed Car	40,000	85,000	150,000
1930	MA	8 cyl.	5 Passenger Coupe	12,000	25,000	50,000
1930	MB	8 cyl.	Cabriolet	30,000	50,000	95,000
1931	LA	6 cyl.	Speedster	40,000	75,000	125,000
1931	MA	8 cyl.	Torpedo	25,000	50,000	95,000
1931	MB	8 cyl.	Speedster	45,000	80,000	150,000
1932	LAA	6 cyl.	Sedan	9,000	17,000	40,000
1932	SV-16	8 cyl.	Speedster	40,000	75,000	140,000
1932	SV-16	8 cyl.	Convertible Sedan	40,000	75,000	125,000
1932	DV-32	8 cyl.	Super Bearcat	50,000	110,000	200,000
1933	LAA	6 cyl.	Cabriolet Coupe	20,000	40,000	75,000
1933	SV-16	8 cyl.	Club Sedan	12,000	25,000	50,000
1933	SV-16	8 cyl.	Monte Carlo	20,000	40,000	75,000
1934	SV-16	8 cyl.	Torpedo	40,000	75,000	125,000
1934		8 cyl.	Convertible Coupe	35,000	60,000	100,000
1934	DV-32	8 cyl.	Club Sedan	15,000	30,000	60,000

YEAR	MODEL	ENGINE	BODY	F	G	E
STUTZ (United States, 1911–35) (continued)						
1935	SV-16	8 cyl.	Speedster	25,000	40,000	75,000
1935	DV-32	8 cyl.	Limousine	14,000	30,000	65,000
SUCCESS (United States, 1906–09)						
1906	A	1 cyl.	Runabout			
			Buggy	2,500	6,000	12,500
1907	C	2 cyl.	Runabout			
			Buggy	4,000	9,000	18,000
1909	E	2 cyl.	Runabout			
			Buggy	4,000	9,000	18,000
SUERE (France, 1909–30)						
1909	8 CV	1 cyl.	Touring	1,000	3,900	7,750
1915	8 CV	4 cyl.	Touring	950	4,850	8,750
1922	10 CV	4 cyl.	Saloon Sedan	700	1,400	3,750
1928		V 8 cyl.	Sedan	900	1,800	4,650
1930		6 cyl.	Sedan	750	1,500	4,000
SUMIDA (Japan, 1933–37)						
1933	H		Sedan	700	1,400	3,000
1934	K		Touring	1,250	2,500	6,000
1935	K93		6-Wheel			
			Touring	2,900	4,750	11,500
1937	JC		Touring	1,200	2,400	7,000
SUN (Germany, 1906–24)						
1906	18/22	4 cyl.	2 Passenger	1,500	3,900	9,000
1908	40/50	6 cyl.	2 Passenger	2,200	5,300	11,750
1920		V 2 cyl.	2 Passenger	1,250	2,500	6,000
SUNBEAM (Great Britain, 1899–1974)						
1899		1 cyl.	Voiturette	3,000	6,500	14,000
1901		2 cyl.	Voiturette	2,700	6,000	13,000
1903		2 cyl.	Tonneau	2,500	5,500	12,000
1904		4 cyl.	Coupe	2,500	5,500	10,000
1908	12/16	4 cyl.	Touring	4,500	7,500	15,000
1913	16/20	4 cyl.	Drop Head			
			Coupe	3,500	6,500	12,000
1919	24	6 cyl.	Touring	1,200	3,400	9,000
1920		6 cyl.	Limousine	2,000	6,000	12,000
1922		6 cyl.	Sport	2,100	6,250	12,500
1924		6 cyl.	Sprint	6,000	16,000	32,000
1924		6 cyl.	Sport			
			Touring	6,200	15,400	30,000
1930	16	23.8 hp	Sedan	1,100	2,250	6,500
1933	Speed 20	2.9 Litre	Sport	1,850	3,750	7,500
1934	Dawn	4 cyl.	Sedan	1,500	3,000	4,800

YEAR	MODEL	ENGINE	BODY	F	G	E
SUNBEAM *(Great Britain, 1899–1974) (continued)*						
1935	25	21 hp	Sedan	900	1,750	3,500
1937		6 cyl.	Sport	2,000	4,000	9,000
1938		4 cyl.	Sedan	750	1,500	3,850
1956	Rapier	4 cyl.	Sport Sedan	400	1,400	3,600
1960	Alpine I	4 cyl.	Sport	3,000	4,000	9,000
1961	Alpine II	4 cyl.	Sport	3,500	4,500	9,500
1964	Alpine Tiger I	V 8 cyl.	Sport	5,000	8,000	12,000
1968	Alpine Tiger II	V 8 cyl.	Sport	7,000	12,000	20,000
1970	Alpine	4 cyl.	Hardtop GT	2,000	3,000	5,000
SUNBEAM-TALBOT *(Great Britain, 1938–54)*						
1938		3 Litre	Touring	650	2,250	6,500
1939	Super Snipe	6 cyl.	Touring	700	2,400	6,800
1940		6 cyl.	Touring	750	2,500	6,000
1948	90	2 Litre	Sedan	750	1,500	2,950
1953	Alpine	6 cyl.	Roadster	1,100	3,250	9,500
1954	MK 111	4 cyl.	Sedan	1,200	2,400	2,750
SUPERIOR *(Germany, 1905–06)*						
1905		2 cyl.	Voiturette	1,000	3,000	8,000
1906		4 cyl.	Voiturette	1,200	3,400	10,000

T

YEAR	MODEL	ENGINE	BODY	F	G	E
TALBOT *(Great Britain, 1903–40)*						
1903		1 cyl.	Touring	2,500	4,500	12,000
1904		2 cyl.	Touring	3,000	5,500	14,000
1904		4 cyl.	Coupe	3,000	5,500	14,000
1906		4 cyl.	Touring	3,500	6,500	15,000
1907		4 cyl.	Limousine	3,000	6,000	15,000
1908		4 cyl.	Coupe	2,500	5,500	14,000
1913	15/20	2.6 Litre	Touring	2,500	5,500	14,000
1919	25/50	6 cyl.	Limousine	3,500	8,000	16,000
1923	10/20	6 cyl.	Coupe	1,800	4,000	11,000
1924	23	6 cyl.	Touring	3,400	8,000	16,000
1929	14/45		Sedan	2,000	5,000	12,000
1930		4 Litre	Coupe	2,200	5,700	13,500
1930		6 cyl.	Sport Sedan	3,200	6,400	14,000
1930	75	6 cyl.	Touring	3,500	7,500	18,000
1930	90	6 cyl.	Sport	3,700	7,800	20,000
1931	105	3 Litre	Sport Touring	3,500	7,500	18,000

YEAR	MODEL	ENGINE	BODY	F	G	E
TALBOT *(Great Britain, 1903–40) (continued)*						
1931		3 Litre	Sedan	1,800	3,500	7,000
1931		3 Litre	Sport	2,300	5,000	9,500
1932	65	14/45 hp	Coupe	2,200	4,450	8,900
1933	95	3 Litre	Touring	3,500	6,500	13,000
1935	110	3 Litre	Sport	4,500	8,500	16,000
1938	"Lago"	4 Litre	Coupe	8,500	16,000	32,000
1938		6 cyl.	Sedan	2,500	5,000	9,500
1939	"Lago"	6 cyl.	Cabriolet	6,000	12,000	25,000
1939		6 cyl.	Sport Sedan	2,500	4,500	9,500
T.A.M. *(France, 1908–25)*						
1908	12	4 cyl.	2 Passenger	2,000	4,000	8,000
1913	10/12	4 cyl.	2 Passenger	1,000	1,900	6,750
1925	12/14	4 cyl.	4 Passenger	800	1,600	5,200
TARRANT *(Australia, 1901–07)*						
1901		2 cyl.	Runabout	1,100	3,250	8,500
1902		2 cyl.	Touring	1,150	3,350	8,750
1904		4 cyl.	Touring	2,050	4,100	9,250
1906		4 cyl.	Touring	2,050	4,150	9,350
1907		3 cyl.	Touring	1,100	2,250	6,500
1948			Sport	4,500	9,000	17,500
TASCO *(United States, 1948)*						
1948			Speedster	4,500	18,000	37,500

Tasco – 1948 "Speedster"

YEAR	MODEL	ENGINE	BODY	F	G	E
TATRA *(Czechoslovakia, 1923–75)*						
1923	6.5 Litre	6 cyl.	Touring	1,000	2,000	4,000
1924	Type 11	1066cc	Touring	800	1,600	3,250
1925	Type 12	1066cc	Sport	750	1,500	3,000
1926	Type 30	4 cyl.	Touring	900	1,900	2,750
1927	Type 52	1919cc	Touring	1,700	4,400	9,800
1928	Type 70	6 cyl.	Touring	900	1,750	3,450
1929	Type 80	V 12 cyl.	Sport	2,900	6,800	13,600
1930	Type 49	528cc	Tri-car	550	1,100	3,200
1932	Type 57	1160cc	Sport	600	1,200	3,400
1934	Type 77	V 8 cyl.	Sport	750	1,500	4,000
1935	Type 80	V 12 cyl.	Sedan	1,200	2,400	7,000
1937	Type 87	V 8 cyl.	Sedan	500	1,000	3,000
1939	Type 97	4 cyl.	Sedan	400	800	3,750
1945	Type 57-B	6 cyl.	Sport	450	900	4,000
1957	Type 603	V 8 cyl.	Sedan	500	1,000	4,000
TAU *(Italy, 1924–26)*						
1924	Tipo 95	4 cyl.	Touring	1,000	2,900	7,000
1926	Tipo 90		Sport	900	2,800	6,750
TAURINIA *(Italy, 1902–08)*						
1902		1 cyl.	Voiturette	1,000	3,000	7,850
1906		4 cyl.	Voiturette	2,000	4,000	9,000
1908		3 Litre	Touring	1,100	3,100	8,200
TEMPLAR *(United States, 1917–24)*						
1917		4 cyl.	Roadster	6,000	12,000	25,000
1922		4 cyl.	Touring	6,000	12,000	25,000
1923		4 cyl.	Touring	7,000	12,000	25,000
1923		4 cyl.	Roadster	7,000	14,000	24,000
1924		6 cyl.	5 Passenger Phaeton	8,000	14,000	25,000
TEMPO *(Germany, 1933–56)*						
1933	3-Wheel		Cycle	500	1,000	3,000
1935	V-600	600	Convertible	1,000	2,900	6,850
1950			Convertible	360	700	3,450
1956			Sedan	300	600	2,200
TERRAPLANE *(United States, 1932–38)*						
1933		6 cyl.	Roadster	6,000	11,000	20,000
1933		8 cyl.	Convertible	8,000	14,000	24,000
1933	Deluxe	8 cyl.	Cabriolet	6,000	12,000	22,000
1934	K	8 cyl.	Cabriolet	5,000	11,000	20,000
1935	GU	6 cyl.	Convertible	6,000	12,000	22,000
1936	61	6 cyl.	Convertible	7,000	14,000	24,000
1937	80	6 cyl.	2 Door Sedan	1,000	3,000	5,000

YEAR	MODEL	ENGINE	BODY	F	G	E
TESTE ET MORET *(France, 1898–1903)*						
1898		1 cyl.	Voiturette	1,000	3,000	7,000
1903		2 cyl.	Voiturette	1,000	2,900	7,000
THAMES *(Great Britain, 1906–11)*						
1906		6 cyl.	4 Passenger	2,000	5,900	14,000
1908		4 cyl.	2 Passenger	1,900	3,800	8,500
1910		1 cyl.	2 Passenger	800	2,600	6,200
THOMAS *(Great Britain, 1903)*						
1903		2 cyl.	Touring	1,000	3,900	7,750
1903		1 cyl.	Runabout	1,000	2,000	6,000
1903		2 cyl.	Coupe	1,000	2,000	6,000
THOMAS *(United States, 1903–18)*						
1903	17	1 cyl.	Tonneau	4,500	12,500	25,000
1904	Flyer	3 cyl.	Limousine	7,000	15,000	30,000
1907	Flyer	4 cyl.	Touring	15,000	35,000	75,000
1909	K	6 cyl.	Landaulet	9,000	22,000	56,000
1910	K-6-70	6 cyl.	Flyabout	20,000	45,000	96,000
1912	MC-6-40	6 cyl.	Limousine	12,000	25,000	50,000
1915	MCX	6 cyl.	7 Passenger Touring	20,000	40,000	80,000
1917	MF	6 cyl.	Touring	20,000	40,000	80,000
THOMAS-DETROIT *(United States, 1906–08)*						
1906		4 cyl.	Runabout	7,000	14,000	28,000
1908		4 cyl.	Touring	7,000	15,000	30,000
THOMPSON *(United States, 1901–07)*						
1901		Electric	Runabout	2,500	8,000	16,000
1906		Electric	Wagonette	4,000	8,000	18,000
THOMSON *(France, 1913–28)*						
1913		1.5 Litre	Touring	1,900	3,800	7,650
1913		2 Litre	Touring	1,950	4,900	9,000
1914		4 cyl.	Coupe	1,000	2,800	5,650
1920		4 cyl.	Touring	850	3,750	7,500
1928	40 CV	6 cyl.	Sport	2,000	4,000	8,000
THOR *(Great Britain, 1904–21)*						
1904		2 cyl.	Touring	2,000	4,000	8,000
1910	12/14	2 cyl.	Touring	2,100	4,100	8,200
1914		4 cyl.	Coupe	1,000	2,900	7,000
1918		6 cyl.	Touring	2,150	6,250	13,500
TH. SCHNEIDER *(France, 1910–31)*						
1910		4 cyl.	Touring	1,000	3,800	7,750
1912		6 cyl.	Touring	2,000	6,100	12,200
1914	18/22	6 cyl.	Cabriolet	2,000	5,000	11,000

YEAR	MODEL	ENGINE	BODY	F	G	E
TH. SCHNEIDER *(France, 1910–31) (continued)*						
1916	15	4 cyl.	Touring	1,000	2,900	9,000
1919	14 CV	4 cyl.	Touring	900	2,750	8,500
1921	14 CV	6 cyl.	Coupe	700	1,400	6,000
1927	VL	6 cyl.	Saloon Sedan	650	1,300	5,650
1931		6 cyl.	Coupe	750	1,500	5,000
THULIN *(Sweden, 1920–28)*						
1920		4 cyl.	Sedan	700	1,400	4,000
1924	Type B	4 cyl.	Sedan	700	1,400	3,800
1926	Type B	6 cyl.	Sedan	750	1,500	5,000
1928		6 cyl.	Sedan	750	1,500	5,000
TIDAHOLM *(Sweden, 1906–13)*						
1906		4 cyl.	Shooting Brake	2,200	5,350	11,750
1910		4 cyl.	2 Passenger	1,200	2,400	6,800
1913		4 cyl.	2 Passenger	1,250	2,500	6,950
TINCHER *(United States, 1903–06)*						
1903	20	4 cyl.	Touring	5,000	10,000	20,000
1906	50	4 cyl.	Touring	14,000	28,000	60,000
TINY *(Great Britain, 1913–15)*						
1913		V 2 cyl.	Cycle	1,000	1,900	4,000
1915		4 cyl.	2 Passenger	1,200	2,800	6,650
TOYOTA *(Japan, 1936 to date)*						
1936	AA	6 cyl.	Sedan	800	2,500	6,000
1937	AB	6 cyl.	Sedan	700	2,400	5,700
1938	AC	6 cyl.	Touring	2,200	6,500	13,000
1939	AE	2258cc	Sedan	1,500	3,100	7,200
1943	BA	4 cyl.	Sedan	300	1,600	3,200
1945	B	6 cyl.	Sedan	1,350	2,700	5,400
1949	SA	4 cyl.	Sedan	300	1,600	3,200
1955	Crown	4 cyl.	Sedan	350	1,650	3,250
1958	Corona	1 Litre	Sedan	250	1,500	3,000
1968	2000 GT	6 cyl.	Sport Coupe	2,000	6,000	12,000
TRAVELER *(United States, 1907–15)*						
1907	A	4 cyl.	Touring	6,000	12,000	26,000
1907	B	4 cyl.	Touring	7,000	14,000	28,000
1910	D	4 cyl.	Runabout	5,000	10,000	20,000
1911	D	4 cyl.	Runabout	5,000	10,000	20,000
1914	48	4 cyl.	Roadster	8,000	15,000	28,000
TRIBELHORN *(China, 1902–20)*						
1902		Electric	Victoria	800	2,600	6,250
1910		Electric	Victoria	750	2,500	6,950

YEAR	MODEL	ENGINE	BODY	F	G	E
TRIBELHORN *(China, 1902–20) (continued)*						
1918	3-Wheel	Electric		700	2,400	4,800
1920	3-Wheel	Electric		700	2,400	4,800
TRIBET *(France, 1909–14)*						
1909	8/10	4 cyl.	Sport	1,900	3,800	7,600
1914	4/16	6 cyl.	Racing	2,800	6,650	13,700
TRICOLET *(United States, 1904–06)*						
1904	3-Wheel	2 cyl.	Cycle	3,000	6,000	12,000
1906	4-Wheel	2 cyl.	Cycle	4,000	7,000	14,000
TRIDENT *(France; Great Britain, 1919–20)*						
1919	3-Wheel	2 cyl.	Cycle	700	1,400	4,000
1920	Tandem	2 cyl.	2 Passenger	1,250	2,500	6,000
TRIPPEL *(Germany, 1934–52)*						
1934	Type SG	2.5 Litre	Amphibious	2,100	6,250	13,500
1936		6 cyl.	Amphibious	2,200	6,300	14,000
1937	Type SK	6 cyl.	Amphibious	2,200	6,400	14,000
1948	Type SG-7	V 8 cyl.	Amphibious	2,000	6,900	15,000
1950		498cc	Coupe	850	1,900	4,000
TRIUMPH *(United States, 1907–12)*						
1907	A	4 cyl.	Runabout	7,000	14,000	28,000
1910	A	4 cyl.	Roadster	7,500	15,000	29,000
1912	B	4 cyl.	Touring	8,000	16,000	30,000
TRIUMPH *(Great Britain, 1923–84)*						
1923	TLC	4 cyl.	Touring	1,150	2,250	18,000
1925	TLC	4 cyl.	Touring	1,100	2,250	7,500
1927	TPC	4 cyl.	Sedan	1,000	1,900	4,800
1928	K	832cc (Supercharged)	Sport	2,450	6,300	13,650
1931	S	6 cyl.	Sport	1,800	4,400	12,000
1933	S	6 cyl.	Sedan	1,150	2,300	8,000
1935	G12 Gloria	4 cyl.	4 Passenger Touring	2,250	5,200	11,000
1935	G16 Gloria 6	6 cyl.	4 Passenger Touring	1,500	2,900	6,000
1937	Vitesse/ Dolomite	6 cyl.	Saloon	1,500	2,900	20,000
1938	Dolomite	6 Litre	Sedan	1,650	3,250	15,000
1946	1800	4 cyl.	Roadster	2,250	6,000	14,000
1946	2000	4 cyl.	Roadster	1,250	3,500	14,000

YEAR	MODEL	ENGINE	BODY	F	G	E
TRIUMPH *(Great Britain, 1923–84) (continued)*						
1948	Dolomite	4 Litre	Sedan	1,600	3,200	24,000

Triumph – 1948 "Mayflower"

YEAR	MODEL	ENGINE	BODY	F	G	E
1948	1800	4 cyl.	Roadster	2,200	7,000	12,000
1949	2000	4 cyl.	Roadster	1,250	3,500	14,000
1949	2000 Renown	2.1 Litre	Roadster	2,200	6,575	16,000
1949	Mayflower		Saloon	1,250	3,400	4,000
1953	TR2	4 cyl.	Roadster	2,000	5,000	15,000
1955	TR3	4 cyl.	Roadster	600	2,000	12,000
1957	TR3A	4 cyl.	Roadster	1,100	3,750	15,000
1961	TR4	4 cyl.	Roadster	1,400	2,850	8,000
1962	Spitfire MK I	4 cyl.	Roadster	900	2,750	4,000
1962	TR3B	I-4	Roadster	4,500	7,000	10,500
1963	TR3B	I-4	Roadster	5,000	7,500	11,000
1963	TR4	I-4	Roadster	3,500	5,500	9,000
1963	Spitfire MK II	I-4	Roadster	2,500	3,500	8,000
1964	TR4	I-4	Roadster	3,500	5,500	9,000
1964	TR4	I-4	Coupe	4,000	6,000	9,500
1964	Spitfire II	I-4	Roadster	2,500	3,500	7,500

YEAR	MODEL	ENGINE	BODY	F	G	E
TRIUMPH *(Great Britain, 1923–84) (continued)*						
1965	TR4A	I-4	Roadster	4,500	6,500	10,000
1966	Spitfire II	I-4	Roadster	2,500	3,500	7,500
1967	GT6	I-6	Coupe	2,500	3,500	7,000
1968	TR250	I-6	Roadster	5,000	6,000	11,000
1968	Spitfire III	I-4	Roadster	3,000	3,500	8,000
1969	TR6	I-6	Roadster	5,000	7,500	12,500
1969	GT6+	I-6	Coupe	3,000	3,500	7,500
1969	Spitfire III	I-4	Roadster	3,000	3,500	8,000
1970	TR6	I-6	Roadster	5,000	7,500	12,500
1971	TR6	I-6	Roadster	5,000	7,500	12,500
1971	GT6 III	I-6	Coupe	2,500	3,500	6,500
1971	Spitfire IV	I-4	Roadster	2,500	3,500	7,000
1971	Stag	V-8	Roadster	6,500	8,500	14,000
1972	TR6	I-6	Roadster	5,000	7,500	12,500
1972	GT6 III	I-6	Coupe	2,500	3,500	6,500
1972	Spitfire IV	I-4	Roadster	2,500	3,500	7,000
1972	Stag	V-8	Roadster	6,500	8,500	14,000
1973	TR6	I-6	Roadster	5,000	7,500	12,500
1973	GT6 III	I-6	Coupe	2,500	3,500	6,500
1973	Spitfire IV	I-4	Roadster	2,500	3,500	7,000
1973	Stag	V-8	Roadster	6,500	8,500	14,000
1974	R6	I-6	Roadster	5,000	7,500	12,500
1974	Spitfire 1500	I-4	Roadster	2,500	3,500	7,000
1975	TR6	I-6	Roadster	5,000	7,500	12,500
1975	Spitfire 1500	I-4	Roadster	2,500	3,500	7,000
1975	TR7	I-4	Coupe	2,000	3,500	6,500
1976	TR6	I-6	Roadster	6,000	7,500	14,000
1976	Spitfire 1500	I-4	Roadster	2,500	3,500	7,000
1976	TR7	I-4	Coupe	2,000	3,500	6,500
1977	Spitfire 1500	I-4	Roadster	2,500	3,500	7,000
1977	TR7	I-4	Coupe	2,000	3,500	6,500
1978	Spitfire 1500	I-4	Roadster	2,500	3,500	7,000
1978	TR7	I-4	Coupe	2,000	3,500	6,500
1979	Spitfire 1500	I-4	Roadster	2,500	3,500	7,000
1979	TR7	I-4	Coupe	2,000	3,500	6,500
1979	TR7	I-4	Roadster	3,000	4,500	7,500

YEAR	MODEL	ENGINE	BODY	F	G	E
TRIUMPH *(Great Britain, 1923–84) (continued)*						
1980	Spitfire					
	1500	I-4	Roadster	2,500	3,500	7,000
1980	TR7	I-4	Coupe	2,000	3,500	6,500
1980	TR7	I-4	Roadster	3,000	4,500	7,500
1980	TR8	V-8	Coupe	3,500	5,000	8,500
1980	TR8	V-8	Roadster	4,000	6,500	10,000
TROJAN *(Great Britain, 1922–36)*						
1922		4 cyl.	Sedan	550	1,050	4,100
1924		1.5 Litre	Sedan	550	1,100	4,250
1928	Apollo		Sedan	600	1,200	4,400
1930	RE		Purley Sedan	1,200	2,200	6,400
1935	Mastra	6 cyl.	Sedan	850	1,900	5,000
TRUMBELL *(United States, 1914–15)*						
1914		4 cyl.	Roadster	2,500	6,500	20,000
1915		4 cyl.	Coupe	2,500	6,500	16,000
TSUKUBA *(Japan, 1935–37)*						
1935		V 4 cyl.	2 Passenger	350	750	2,450
1936		V 4 cyl.	Touring	350	700	2,300
1937		V 4 cyl.	Sedan	300	600	2,200
TUAR *(France, 1913–25)*						
1913		4 cyl.	Runabout	1,000	2,900	7,000
1919		6 cyl.	Racing	3,000	7,000	14,000
1925		6 cyl.	Racing	3,100	7,250	14,500
TUCKER *(United States, 1948)*						
1948	R-1	6 cyl.	Sedan	50,000	100,000	175,000
TUDHOPE *(Canada, 1908–13)*						
1908	High-wheel	4 cyl.	Buggy	1,500	4,000	9,000
1910		4 cyl.	Roadster	1,150	3,350	8,750
1913		6 cyl.	Touring	3,250	6,500	12,900
TURBO *(Germany, 1923–24)*						
1923	6/25	1640cc	Sedan	1,200	2,400	7,000
1924	18/32	1980cc	Sedan	1,200	2,500	7,950
TURCAT-MERY *(France, 1898–1928)*						
1898		4 cyl.	Touring	4,000	8,000	16,000
1900		2.6 Litre	Touring	3,000	6,000	11,000
1902		4 cyl.	Touring	3,000	6,000	11,000
1905		6 cyl.	6-Wheel	6,250	12,500	25,000
1907		6 cyl.	Touring	3,000	6,000	11,000
1908		10.2 Litre	Touring	3,100	6,350	11,750
1908	Type FM	6.3 Litre	Racing	3,200	7,400	16,800
1909		2.6 Litre	Touring	1,150	3,350	8,750

YEAR	MODEL	ENGINE	BODY	F	G	E
TURCAT-MERY *(France, 1898–1928) (continued)*						
1911		2.3 Litre	Touring	1,150	3,300	8,600
1912		4 cyl.	Touring	1,100	3,100	8,300
1915		2.6 Litre	Touring	1,100	3,200	8,400
1918		4.1 Litre	Racing	3,000	6,900	14,850
1920		6.1 Litre	Racing	3,700	8,100	19,250
1924	Type UG	2.4 Litre	Sport	1,000	3,000	8,000
1926	7 CV	1.2 Litre	Sport	850	1,700	5,400
1928	Type VF	1.6 Litre	Sport	900	1,750	5,500
1928		8 cyl.	Racing	6,000	12,000	24,000
TURGAN-FOY *(France, 1899–1906)*						
1899		1 cyl.	Tonneau	1,500	3,000	7,000
1900		1 cyl.	Tonneau	1,500	3,100	7,250
1901		2 cyl.	Tonneau	2,050	4,100	8,250
1903		4 cyl.	Touring	2,300	4,900	9,800
1905		4 cyl.	Touring	2,500	5,000	9,950
1906		4 cyl.	Touring	2,000	4,000	9,000
TURNER *(United States, 1901–03)*						
1901	Lilliputian	1 cyl.	Tri-car	2,200	4,500	8,000
1901	Gadabout	1 cyl.	Voiturette	2,000	5,000	10,000
TURNER *(Great Britain, 1906–66)*						
1906	20/25	4 cyl.	Touring	1,000	1,900	4,800
1909		V 2 cyl.	Cycle	800	1,600	3,200
1912		4 cyl.	Touring	1,000	2,100	7,250
1913	Fifteen	2.1 Litre	Touring	1,100	2,250	6,500
1914	Ten	4 cyl.	Drop Head Coupe	1,000	2,000	5,000
1915	Ten	4 cyl.	Drop Head Coupe	1,000	2,000	5,000
1916	12/20	4 cyl.	Touring	1,900	3,750	7,500
1918		1.8 Litre	Coupe	900	1,800	4,750
1920		2.3 Litre	Touring	1,000	2,500	6,000
1922	All Weather	4 cyl.	Touring	1,250	2,800	7,750
1924	Colonial	2.1 Litre	Touring	900	2,600	6,500
1926	Twelve	4 cyl.	Coupe	850	1,850	5,250
1930		1.4 Litre	Sedan	750	1,500	4,000
1951		4 cyl. 500cc	Sport	1,100	2,200	6,400
1955		4 cyl.	Single Passenger	650	1,850	4,500
TURNER-MIESSE *(Great Britain, 1902–13)*						
1902		3 cyl.	Landaulet	1,200	2,400	7,000
1903		3 cyl.	Landaulet	1,150	2,350	6,750
1904		2 cyl.	Runabout	1,150	2,300	6,000

YEAR	MODEL	ENGINE	BODY	F	G	E
TURNER-MIESSE *(Great Britain, 1902–13) (continued)*						
1905		4 cyl.	Landaulet	1,100	2,200	6,400
1906		4 cyl.	Landaulet	1,100	2,200	6,400
1908		4 cyl.	2 Passenger	1,100	2,250	6,500
1913		4 cyl.	4 Passenger	1,200	3,400	8,000
1919		4 cyl.	2 Passenger	1,150	3,300	7,750
T.V.R. *(Great Britain, 1954 to date)*						
1954	Mark 1	1.2 Litre	Coupe	900	1,200	3,200
1957	Mark 1	1.2 Litre	Coupe	950	1,800	3,300
1959	Mark 1	1.2 Litre	Coupe	950	1,800	3,400
TWOMBLY *(United States, 1913–15)*						
1913	Cycle Car	2 cyl.	Tandem Touring Roadster	2,000	6,900	14,000
1914	Cycle Car	4 cyl.	Tandem Roadster	2,900	5,800	11,750
1915	Light Car	4 cyl.	4 Passenger Touring	3,000	6,000	13,000
TWYFORD *(United States, 1904–07)*						
1904		2 cyl.	Stanhope	2,500	6,600	13,500
1905	B	2 cyl.	Tonneau	2,400	6,500	13,200
1907	C	2 cyl.	Roadster	2,000	6,000	12,000
TYNE *(Great Britain, 1904)*						
1904		1 cyl.	Runabout	1,750	3,500	7,000
1904		2 cyl.	Tonneau	2,000	4,100	8,200

U

YEAR	MODEL	ENGINE	BODY	F	G	E
ULTIMA *(France, 1912–14)*						
1912	10	1 cyl.	Open	1,250	3,800	8,750
1914	10/12	4 cyl.	Open	1,600	4,000	9,000
UNDERBERG *(France, 1899–1909)*						
1899		1 cyl.	Voiturette	1,000	4,000	9,000
1906		2 cyl.	Voiturette	1,100	5,200	10,500
1909		4 cyl.	Tonneau	1,150	6,300	11,750
UNIC *(France, 1904–39)*						
1904		1 cyl.	Touring	2,500	4,500	8,500
1904	10/12	2 cyl.	Coupe	2,500	4,500	8,500
1907	12/14	4 cyl.	Touring	2,700	4,700	8,700
1909		6 cyl.	Touring	3,500	6,500	14,500
1914		6 cyl.	Coupe	1,500	3,500	6,700
1920	Type L	1847cc	Sport	2,750	4,500	9,000

YEAR	MODEL	ENGINE	BODY	F	G	E
UNIC *(France, 1904–39) (continued)*						
1923		1.8 Litre	Sport	700	1,400	3,750
1925	Type L313	2 Litre	Sport	800	1,600	4,200
1926		6 cyl.	Touring	1,950	5,900	12,800
1928		8 cyl.	Sport	1,600	5,000	11,000
1931	15 CV	8 cyl.	Coupe	1,200	3,700	7,400
1932		2 Litre	Touring	1,400	3,900	9,000
1934	U-4	4 cyl.	Sedan	1,200	2,400	5,000
1937	U-6	6 cyl.	Sedan	1,300	2,600	5,400
1939	U-4D	2150cc	Sedan	1,300	2,600	5,200
UNION *(United States, 1902–14)*						
1902		4 cyl.	Roadster	2,400	7,800	15,500
1903		2 cyl.	Runabout	2,200	6,200	12,400
1904		2 cyl.	Tonneau	2,200	6,200	12,400
1911		4 cyl.	Touring	2,350	7,600	14,500
UNIT *(Great Britain, 1920–23)*						
1920		2 cyl.	2 Passenger	700	2,400	7,000
1923		4 cyl.	2 Passenger	800	2,600	7,250
UPTON *(United States, 1900–07)*						
1900		1 cyl.	Runabout	2,250	6,500	13,000
1901		4 cyl.	Touring	3,000	7,600	16,200
1905		4 cyl.	Tonneau	2,600	6,900	14,500
U.S. LONG DISTANCE *(United States, 1901–03)*						
1901		1 cyl.	Runabout	2,200	6,500	13,000
1903		2 cyl.	Tonneau	2,400	6,700	14,400
UTILIS *(France, 1923–25)*						
1923		1 cyl.	Cycle	950	1,850	3,750
1925		2 cyl.	Cycle	950	1,850	3,750
UTILITY *(United States, 1921–22)*						
1921		4 cyl.	Roadster	2,850	6,800	13,000
1922		4 cyl.	Touring	2,900	6,900	13,500
1922		4 cyl.	Station Wagon	2,000	4,000	8,500

YEAR	MODEL	ENGINE	BODY	F	G	E

V

VABIS *(Sweden, 1897–1915)*

YEAR	MODEL	ENGINE	BODY	F	G	E
1897		2 cyl.	Touring	950	2,900	7,850
1900		4 cyl.	Touring	1,000	4,000	9,000
1903	Type G4	2 Litre	Touring	950	3,850	8,750
1910		4 cyl.	Touring	900	3,800	9,600
1915		4 cyl.	Touring	850	3,700	8,400

VALE *(Great Britain, 1932–36)*

YEAR	MODEL	ENGINE	BODY	F	G	E
1932		832cc	Sport	1,800	3,600	8,250
1933		4 cyl.	Roadster	2,000	4,000	9,000
1933	Tourette	4 cyl.	Touring	1,875	3,750	8,500
1935		4 cyl.	Sport	1,900	3,800	8,750
1936		6 cyl.	Racing	4,950	11,900	23,800

VALLEE *(France, 1895–1901)*

YEAR	MODEL	ENGINE	BODY	F	G	E
1895		2 cyl.	Touring	1,950	3,850	8,750
1900		2 cyl.	Touring	1,975	3,950	8,900
1901		2 cyl.	Racing	2,050	6,100	13,250
1901		4 cyl.	Brake	2,050	3,100	8,250

VALVELESS; LUCAS VALVELESS *(Great Britain; 1901–14)*

YEAR	MODEL	ENGINE	BODY	F	G	E
1901		2 cyl.	Touring	1,950	4,950	8,850
1905	25	2 cyl.	Landaulet	2,000	5,000	9,000
1908	20	2 cyl.	Landaulet	1,600	3,900	8,000
1910	15	4 cyl.	Touring	1,875	4,750	8,500
1914		4 cyl.	Touring	1,900	4,800	8,750

VARLEY-WOODS *(Great Britain, 1918–21)*

YEAR	MODEL	ENGINE	BODY	F	G	E
1918		4 cyl.	Torpedo	2,200	6,400	13,750
1920		4 cyl.	Touring	1,100	3,250	8,500
1921		4 cyl.	Sedan	800	1,600	4,200

VAUXHALL *(Great Britain, 1903 to date)*

YEAR	MODEL	ENGINE	BODY	F	G	E
1903		1 cyl.	Runabout	2,500	3,700	8,500
1905	7/9	3 cyl.	Runabout	2,800	4,000	9,000
1907		4 cyl.	Sport	3,000	4,800	11,000
1910		4 Litre	Sport	2,800	4,500	10,500
1912	30/98	6 cyl.	Touring	3,500	6,800	14,500
1914	Type D	4 Litre	Touring	2,500	4,500	11,000
1916	Type B	6 cyl.	Touring	3,500	6,500	14,000
1917		3 Litre	Racing	4,200	10,000	20,000
1919	Type E	6 cyl.	Sport	2,700	4,400	11,500
1922	Type M	6 cyl.	Touring	3,500	6,500	14,000
1925	Princeton	6 cyl.	Touring	3,500	6,500	14,000
1928	20/60	6 cyl.	Coupe	2,200	4,000	10,000

YEAR	MODEL	ENGINE	BODY	F	G	E
VAUXHALL *(Great Britain, 1903 to date) (continued)*						
1930		6 cyl.	Roadster	3,500	7,500	15,000
1930	Cadat	3 Litre	Sedan Saloon	2,800	3,600	9,000

Vauxhall – 1930 "Cadat Saloon Sedan"

1932	T-80	3.3 Litre	Sport	2,600	3,800	9,000
1933	Cadat	2.4 Litre	Sedan	1,400	2,800	7,000
1935		6 cyl.	Speedster	6,500	17,000	34,000
1935	Big Six	6 cyl.	Landaulet	2,900	4,800	9,000
1940	Ten	4 cyl.	Saloon	1,500	2,500	5,000
1940	Twelve	4 cyl.	Saloon	1,500	3,000	6,000
1948	Velox	6 cyl.	Saloon	1,200	2,500	7,200
1953	Wyvern	1.4 Litre	Saloon	2,000	4,000	7,000
1955	Fourteen	6 cyl.	Saloon	1,100	2,100	6,900
1957	Victor	1.5 Litre	Station Wagon	1,500	3,000	6,000
1962	Victor FB Super	4 cyl.	4 Door Sedan	1,000	2,000	5,000
VEDRINE *(France, 1904–10)*						
1904		Electric	Brougham	1,950	5,900	12,000
1907		Electric	Landaulet	2,000	6,000	12,000
1910		Electric	Landaulet	2,000	6,050	12,100
VEHAL *(France, 1899–1901)*						
1899		1 cyl.	Tonneau	1,200	2,700	6,400
1901		2 cyl.	Tonneau	1,400	2,800	7,250

YEAR	MODEL	ENGINE	BODY	F	G	E
VELIE *(United States, 1909–29)*						
1909	A	4 cyl.	5 Passenger Touring	2,500	6,000	24,000
1914	10	6 cyl.	5 Passenger Touring	2,800	6,300	28,000
1915	Big Four	4 cyl.	5 Passenger Touring	3,200	7,000	28,000
1916	22	6 cyl.	Roadster	3,300	7,200	22,000
1917	28	6 cyl.	Touring Coupe	3,500	7,300	18,000
1918	38	6 cyl.	Cabriolet	3,500	7,000	25,000
1923	58	6 cyl.	Sedan	3,800	7,500	15,000
1925	60	6 cyl.	Phaeton	4,000	8,500	36,000
1929	77	6 cyl.	Royal Sedan	1,900	4,200	18,000
1929	88	8 cyl.	Special Sedan	2,500	5,500	25,000
VELOMOBILE *(Germany, 1905–07)*						
1905	3-Wheel		Cycle	800	1,600	3,250
1907	3-Wheel		Cycle	850	1,700	3,500
VELOX *(Austria, 1906–10)*						
1906		1 cyl.	Coupe	850	1,700	4,400
1910		1 cyl.	Coupe	900	1,800	4,750
VIPEN *(Great Britain, 1898–1904)*						
1898		2 cyl.	Tonneau	1,000	3,000	7,000
1904		2 cyl.	Tonneau	1,100	3,250	7,500
VIRINUS *(Brazil, 1899–1912)*						
1899		1 cyl.	Voiturette	1,700	3,500	7,000
1900		2 cyl.	Voiturette	1,800	3,600	7,250
1909		2 cyl.	Voiturette	1,850	3,650	7,300
1910	15/18	4 cyl.	Touring	1,900	3,800	9,750
1912	16/20	6 cyl.	Limousine	2,000	3,900	9,750
VOGTLAND *(Germany, 1910–12)*						
1910	6/12	4 cyl.	2 Passenger	1,200	2,800	7,600
1912	10/20	4 cyl.	6 Passenger	2,000	4,000	9,000
VOISIN *(France, 1919–39)*						
1919	Type C-1	4 cyl.	Coupe	4,290	13,000	18,000
1921	Type C-4	1.25 Litre	Coupe	3,900	10,000	14,000
1923			Coupe de Ville	3,000	8,000	12,000
1927		6 cyl.	Sedan	1,500	3,800	6,800
1930	Type C-18	4.8 Litre	Sedan	1,500	3,800	6,800
1931		6 cyl.	Coupe	2,250	4,500	9,000

YEAR	MODEL	ENGINE	BODY	F	G	E
VOISIN *(France, 1919–39) (continued)*						
1933	Sirocco	V 12 cyl.	Coupe	8,000	16,000	30,000
1934	Chamant	6 cyl.	Sedan	3,000	6,000	12,000
1936		12 cyl.	Sport	10,000	32,000	50,000
1938		6 cyl.	Drop Head			
			Coupe	4,250	8,500	15,000
VOLKSWAGEN *(Germany, 1936 to date)*						
1936	VW3		Touring		RARE	
1937	VW 30	704cc	Touring		RARE	
1938	VW 38	784cc	Touring		RARE	
1945	Standard	1131cc	Sedan	3,000	5,000	10,000
1949	Deluxe	1131cc	Convertible	2,400	6,200	13,000
1953	Micro Bus	4 cyl.	Station			
			Wagon	2,000	4,000	8,000
1954	Deluxe	1192cc	Sedan	1,000	3,700	6,000
1956	Karmann Ghia	1192cc	Coupe	3,000	7,000	12,000
1959	Standard	1192cc	Convertible	4,000	6,000	10,000
1960	Karmann Ghia	4 cyl.	Convertible	800	3,500	9,750
1966	1600		Fastback	500	1,500	3,000
1967	Karmann Ghia	1500cc	Convertible	1,200	5,200	11,200
1971	Type 3		Fastback	500	1,500	3,000
1974	Karmann Ghia		Convertible			
			Coupe	2,000	7,000	12,000
1974	Thing			1,000	4,000	6,000
1979	Super Bug		Convertible	4,000	6,000	10,000
VOLVO *(Sweden, 1927 to date)*						
1927	P4	1 cyl.	Sedan	4,000	6,000	8,000
1929	PV 651	6 cyl.	Sedan	5,000	6,500	8,500
1936	PV 36	3.7 Litre	Sedan	2,000	4,000	7,000
1939	60	3.6 Litre	Sedan	2,000	4,000	7,000
1944	PV 444	1.4 Litre	2 Door Sedan	4,000	6,000	8,000
1957	PV 444	4 cyl.	2 Door Sedan	4,000	6,000	8,000
1965	PV 544	4 cyl.	2 Door Sedan	2,000	4,000	7,000
1970	1800E	4 cyl.	Coupe	4,000	6,000	10,000

YEAR	MODEL	ENGINE	BODY	F	G	E

VOLVO *(Sweden, 1927 to date) (continued)*

| 1971 | 1800E | 4 cyl. | Coupe | 4,500 | 5,500 | 9,500 |

Volvo – 1971

YEAR	MODEL	ENGINE	BODY	F	G	E
1973	1800ES	4 cyl.	Sport Wagon	5,000	8,000	12,000

VORAN *(Germany, 1926–28)*

| 1926 | 4/20 | 4 cyl. | 2 Passenger | 950 | 1,900 | 5,000 |

VOUSEMOI *(France, 1904)*

| 1904 | 10 | 2 cyl. | 2 Passenger | 950 | 2,900 | 7,000 |
| 1904 | 16/20 | 4 cyl. | 2 Passenger | 1,000 | 4,000 | 9,000 |

VULCAN *(Great Britain, 1902–28)*

1902		1 cyl.	Voiturette	950	2,900	6,750
1904		4 cyl.	Touring	2,000	5,000	11,000
1905		4 cyl.	Touring	2,050	5,100	11,200
1906		5.2 Litre	Sport	2,150	5,250	11,500
1908		6 cyl.	Sport	2,200	5,400	12,500
1910		2.4 Litre	Sport			
			Touring	950	2,900	7,800
1912		6 cyl.	Touring	2,400	5,800	11,650
1918	3.5 Litre	V 8 cyl.	Touring	3,000	7,000	14,000
1920	3.6 Litre	4 cyl.	Sport			
			Touring	1,800	3,600	8,250
1925	3.3 Litre	4 cyl.	Sedan	750	2,500	5,050
1927	Gainsborough	4 cyl.	Sedan	800	2,600	5,200

VULCAN *(United States, 1913–15)*

1913	27	4 cyl.	Roadster	4,000	8,000	16,000
1915	27	4 cyl.	5 Passenger			
			Touring	4,000	8,000	16,000

VULPES *(France, 1905–10)*

| 1905 | | 1 cyl. | Voiturette | 1,000 | 3,000 | 7,000 |
| 1906 | 30/40 | 4 cyl. | Touring | 950 | 3,900 | 9,000 |

YEAR	MODEL	ENGINE	BODY	F	G	E
VULPES *(France, 1905–10) (continued)*						
1908		4 cyl.	Touring	900	3,800	8,650
1910		4 cyl.	Touring	950	3,900	8,750

W

WADDINGTON *(Great Britain, 1903–04)*						
1903		1 cyl.	Runabout	1,500	3,900	7,850
1904		2 cyl.	Tonneau	1,700	4,000	9,000
W.A.F. *(Austria, 1910–26)*						
1910	25	4 cyl.	Touring	1,000	2,000	96,000
1917	35	4 cyl.	Touring	1,050	2,100	6,200
1922	45	4 cyl.	Touring	1,100	2,150	6,350
1926	70	6 cyl.	Touring	2,200	5,400	12,000
WAGENHALS *(United States, 1910–15)*						
1913	25	4 cyl.	Tri-car	1,500	3,000	8,000
WALTER *(United States, 1902–09)*						
1902	40	2 cyl.	Touring	2,400	6,900	14,000
1903	50	4 cyl.	Touring	4,000	8,000	16,000
WALTER *(Austria; Czechoslovakia, 1908–36)*						
1908		V 2 cyl.	Tri-car	800	1,600	5,200
1913		4 cyl.	2 Passenger	900	1,750	5,500
1920		4 cyl.	4 Passenger	900	1,800	5,750
1929	Six B Super	3.3 Litre	Sedan	700	1,450	5,850
1931		V 12 cyl.	Sedan	1,950	4,900	14,000
1934	Regent	3.2 Litre	Cabriolet	900	1,800	5,750
WALTHAM *(United States, 1905–22)*						
1905	Orient	1 cyl.	Buckboard	5,000	10,000	15,000
1908	E	2 cyl.	Tonneau	4,000	9,000	18,000
1922		6 cyl.	5 Passenger Touring	8,000	15,000	28,000
WANDERER *(Germany, 1911–39)*						
1911		2 cyl.		950	2,900	6,850
1915	Tandem	4 cyl.	2 Passenger	1,150	2,250	6,500
1920	1.5 Litre	4 cyl.	3 Passenger	1,200	2,400	6,850
1923		4 cyl.	4 Passenger	1,600	3,250	7,500
1927		6 cyl.	Touring	2,000	4,000	8,000
1931	10/50	6 cyl.	Cabriolet	2,250	4,500	9,000
1936	W 25 K	2 Litre	Sport	1,200	2,400	4,850
1937		6 cyl.	Sedan	1,250	2,400	5,000

YEAR	MODEL	ENGINE	BODY	F	G	E
WARD (United States, 1914–16)						
1914		Electric	4 Passenger Coupe	2,400	6,750	15,500
1916		Electric	4 Passenger Coupe	4,000	8,000	16,000
WARREN; WARREN-DETROIT (United States, 1910–13)						
1910	10	4 cyl.	Runabout	6,000	12,000	24,000
1911	11	4 cyl.	Torpedo	4,800	10,600	21,500
1913	Resolute	6 cyl.	7 Passenger Touring	9,000	18,000	35,000
WARREN-LAMBERT (Great Britain, 1912–22)						
1912		2 cyl.	Cycle	800	1,600	4,250
1919		4 cyl.	Sport	1,875	3,750	8,500
1922		1.5 Litre	Sport	1,300	2,800	7,650
WARTBURG (Germany, 1898–1904)						
1898		2 cyl.	Tonneau	1,100	2,200	7,500
1901		2 cyl.	Tonneau	1,060	2,100	7,250
1902		4 cyl.	Touring	1,950	3,900	9,850
1903	45	4 cyl.	Touring	2,000	4,000	10,000
1904		3 cyl.	Sedan	850	1,750	3,200
WASHINGTON (United States, 1909–24)						
1909	A-1	4 cyl.	5 Passenger Touring	6,000	12,000	24,000
1910	A-2	4.6 Litre	Tonneau	7,000	15,000	30,000
1912	E-40	4 cyl.	4 Passenger Roadster	8,000	16,000	32,000
1921	B	6 cyl.	Touring	9,000	18,000	36,000
1924	C	6 cyl.	5 Passenger Sedan	4,000	8,000	16,000
WEYHER ET RICHEMOND (France, 1905–10)						
1905	15	4 cyl.	Runabout	1,900	4,850	9,650
1906	20	4 cyl.	Tonneau	1,950	4,900	9,750
1908	28	6 cyl.	Touring	2,500	6,950	13,850
1910	30	6 cyl.	Touring	2,500	7,000	14,000
W.F.S. (United States, 1911–13)						
1911		4 cyl.	Coupe	1,800	4,000	8,500
1911		4 cyl.	Runabout	2,100	6,000	13,500
1912		6 cyl.	Touring	2,400	6,800	13,750
1913		4 cyl.	Limousine	2,000	5,800	11,900
WHITE (United States, 1900–18)						
1900	A	Steam	Stanhope	12,000	24,000	45,000
1905	E	Steam	Touring	11,000	22,000	45,000

YEAR	MODEL	ENGINE	BODY	F	G	E
WHITE *(United States, 1900–18) (continued)*						
1908	L	Steam	Touring	10,000	20,000	40,000
1909	M	Steam	7 Passenger			
			Touring	10,000	22,000	45,000
1910	GA	4 cyl.	Touring	7,000	15,000	30,000
1910	MM	Steam	Touring	9,000	20,500	40,000
1914	Sixty	6 cyl.	Limousine	7,000	16,000	28,000

White – 1911 "Roadster"

				F	G	E
1918		1.5 Litre	Cabriolet	7,000	14,000	25,000
WHITING *(United States, 1910–12)*						
1910	20	4 cyl.	Roadster	2,300	6,600	14,500
1912	40	4 cyl.	Touring	2,500	6,800	14,000
WHITLOCK *(Great Britain, 1903–32)*						
1903		1 cyl.	Touring	1,000	3,000	7,000
1907		1 cyl.	Touring	1,000	3,000	7,000
1910		2 cyl.	Touring	1,050	2,100	6,000

YEAR	MODEL	ENGINE	BODY	F	G	E
WHITLOCK *(Great Britain, 1903–32) (continued)*						
1917		2 cyl.	Coupe	850	1,700	3,400
1920	20/30	4 cyl.	Coupe	750	1,500	4,000
1924		6 cyl.	Touring	1,850	3,700	9,400
1928	20/70	6 cyl.	Drop Head Coupe	2,700	5,450	10,750
1933		6 cyl.	Coupe	1,950	3,900	8,750
WHITNEY *(United States, 1897–1905)*						
1897		1 cyl.	Runabout	3,400	6,500	14,700
1900		2 cyl.	Runabout	3,200	7,300	16,750
1905		2 cyl.	Surrey	2,200	6,300	13,000
WICHITA *(United States, 1914)*						
1914		2 cyl.	Cycle	1,600	2,500	5,800
1914	Tandem	2 cyl.	Cycle	1,600	2,500	5,800
WIKOV *(Czechoslovakia, 1929–36)*						
1929		4 cyl.	Sedan	800	1,600	4,200
1933		1.5 Litre	Sport	850	1,700	4,400
1936		2 Litre	Sedan	770	1,550	4,050
WILLS SAINTE CLAIRE *(United States, 1921–27)*						
1922	A-68	V 8 cyl.	Sedan	3,000	7,000	16,000
1923	A-68	V 8 cyl.	Roadster	9,000	19,000	36,000
1923	A-68	V 8 cyl.	Brougham	4,000	8,000	16,000
1925	B-68	V 8 cyl.	Roadster	7,000	16,000	34,000
1927	W-6	6 cyl.	Roadster	12,000	22,000	45,000
WILLYS *(United States, 1914–63)*						
1915	K-19	4 cyl.	Touring	3,000	6,500	14,500
1917	88-4	4 cyl.	Touring	2,800	6,000	14,000
1918	88-8	8 cyl.	Touring	8,000	14,000	25,000
1921	20	4 cyl.	Roadster	4,000	8,000	14,000
1923	67	4 cyl.	Touring Coupe	2,500	4,000	7,000
1924	64	4 cyl.	Touring	2,500	5,800	13,500
1925	66	6 cyl.	Sedan	1,400	3,200	8,200
1926	66	6 cyl.	Roadster	5,000	11,000	20,000
1926	70	6 cyl.	Coupe	1,200	2,800	6,500
1927	66A	6 cyl.	Sedan	2,000	4,000	8,000
1927	70A	6 cyl.	Roadster	2,600	7,300	16,600
1927	70A	6 cyl.	Cabriolet	2,500	6,100	14,400
1928	70A	6 cyl.	Sedan	1,600	3,800	8,000
1929	56	6 cyl.	Roadster	6,000	12,500	20,000
1929	66A	6 cyl.	Roadster	4,000	13,000	26,000
1929	70B	6 cyl.	Sedan	1,600	3,800	8,000
1930	98B	6 cyl.	Touring	4,000	13,000	26,000

YEAR	MODEL	ENGINE	BODY	F	G	E
WILLYS	*(United States, 1914–63) (continued)*					
1930	6-87	6 cyl.	Roadster	5,000	10,000	18,000
1930	70B	6 cyl.	Roadster	6,000	13,000	22,000
1931	6-87	6 cyl.	Sedan	1,200	3,500	8,200
1931	66D	6 cyl.	Victoria	1,800	3,900	9,000
1931	98D	6 cyl.	Sedan	2,000	4,000	8,000
1931	6-97	6 cyl.	Roadster	4,000	8,000	16,000

Willys – 1931 "Roadster"

YEAR	MODEL	ENGINE	BODY	F	G	E
1932	90	6 cyl.	Victoria Coupe	3,000	6,000	10,000
1932	8-88	8 cyl.	Roadster	6,000	12,000	20,000
1932	8-88	8 cyl.	Coupe	2,500	5,000	10,000
1932	6-66D	6 cyl.	Victoria	4,000	7,000	12,000
1933	77	6 cyl.	Coupe	2,000	4,000	8,000
1933	4-77	2.2 Litre	Custom Coupe	2,000	4,500	9,000
1934	4-77	2.2 Litre	Coupe	2,000	4,000	8,000
1935	4-77	2.2 Litre	Custom Sedan	2,500	4,800	8,000
1936	4-77	4 cyl.	Sedan	1,300	2,600	7,200
1939	48	4 cyl.	Coupe	1,400	2,500	7,000
1941	Americar	4 cyl.	Sedan	1,200	3,200	6,000
1942	Americar	2.2 Litre	Coupe	1,400	3,000	7,000
1947	Jeepster	4 cyl.	Convertible	3,000	6,000	11,000
1949	Jeepster	6 cyl.	Convertible	4,000	7,000	12,000

YEAR	MODEL	ENGINE	BODY	F	G	E
WILLYS *(United States, 1914–63) (continued)*						
1952	Ace	6 cyl.	Sedan	1,500	3,000	6,000
1954	Eagle	6 cyl.	2 Door Hardtop	2,000	3,000	6,000
1955	Bermuda	6 cyl.	Hardtop	2,000	6,000	12,000
WILSON *(Great Britain, 1922–36)*						
1922		4 cyl.	Coupe	1,100	2,600	6,200
1935		Electric	Coupe	1,850	3,700	9,400
WILSON-PILCHER *(Great Britain, 1901–07)*						
1901		Electric	Coupe	1,950	5,950	13,850
1905		4 cyl.	Touring	1,200	3,800	9,600
1907		6 cyl.	Touring	2,100	6,900	14,000
WILTON *(Great Britain, 1912–24)*						
1912		V 2 cyl.	Coupe	1,000	2,600	6,250
1924		4 cyl.	Coupe	1,100	2,750	6,500
WINDHOFF *(Germany, 1908–14)*						
1908		4 cyl.	Touring	1,100	3,900	9,000
1914		6 cyl.	Sport	1,300	5,000	12,000
WINDSOR *(United States, 1929–30)*						
1929	8-82	8 cyl.	Cabriolet	8,000	15,000	30,000
1929	8-92	8 cyl.	Roadster	10,000	22,000	40,000
1930	6-69	6 cyl.	Roadster	10,000	20,000	36,000
WINTON *(United States, 1896–1924)*						
1901		1 cyl.	Runabout	7,000	14,000	25,000
1905	B	4 cyl.	Touring	7,000	15,750	30,000
1911	17-B	6 cyl.	Roadster	9,000	18,000	35,000
1917	48	6 cyl.	Runabout	10,000	22,000	45,000
1918	33	6 cyl.	Coupelet	8,000	16,000	30,000
1919	48	6 cyl.	Coupe	6,500	17,000	35,000
1922	25	6 cyl.	Touring	12,000	25,000	50,000
1924	40	6 cyl.	Phaeton	14,000	27,000	55,000
WISCO *(United States, 1910)*						
1910		4 cyl.	Tonneau	5,000	10,000	20,000
1910		4 cyl.	Touring	6,000	12,000	24,000
WITHERS *(Great Britain, 1906–15)*						
1906	12/14	4 cyl.	Open	1,100	3,750	8,500
1910	20/24	4 cyl.	Runabout	1,200	3,800	9,750
1915	24/30	4 cyl.	Touring	1,300	4,900	12,750
WITTEKIND *(Germany, 1922–25)*						
1922		4 cyl.	2 Passenger	1,100	3,750	7,500
1925		4 cyl.	3 Passenger	1,500	4,800	8,750

YEAR	MODEL	ENGINE	BODY	F	G	E
W.M.	*(Poland, 1927–28)*					
1927	Open	2 cyl.	Touring	500	1,000	3,000
1928		2 cyl.	Saloon Sedan	450	900	1,800
WOLSELEY; WOLSELEY-SIDDELEY			*(Great Britain, 1899–1975)*			
1899		2 cyl.	Tri-Car	1,100	3,150	6,250
1900		1 cyl.	Touring	1,500	4,000	9,000
1902		2 cyl.	Racing	2,400	7,800	15,600
1905		2 cyl.	Racing	2,600	8,350	16,500
1907		4 cyl.	Racing	2,750	8,500	17,000
1908		6 cyl.	Touring	1,900	6,750	13,500
1909		6 cyl.	Racing	5,100	13,250	28,500
1910		2 cyl.	Touring	1,875	3,750	9,500
1912		4 cyl.	Touring	2,000	6,000	12,000
1914		6 cyl.	Touring	2,700	8,900	19,750
1917		V 8 cyl.	Racing	6,500	14,000	30,000
1920	All Weather	30/40 hp	Touring	2,250	8,500	19,000
1921		4 cyl.	Coupe de Ville	2,000	4,000	8,000
1925		11/22 hp	Touring	1,900	4,800	9,600
1927	Silent Six	2 Litre	Touring	1,950	4,900	9,800
1929		8 cyl.	Touring	3,000	9,000	18,000
1930	Viper	16 hp	Sedan	1,250	3,500	8,000
1932		6 cyl.	Touring	1,900	3,750	12,500
1934	Hornet	6 cyl.	Sport	2,100	4,250	9,500
1935	Wasp	6 cyl.	Coupe	1,200	2,400	5,850
1940	Ten	4 cyl.	Drop Head Coupe	1,450	2,900	6,750
1945		4 cyl.	Sedan	1,000	2,000	4,000
1949		6 cyl.	Coupe	900	1,800	3,600
1953	4/44	4 cyl.	Sedan	700	1,400	2,800
1959		4 cyl.	Sedan	1,000	2,200	4,400
WOLVERINE; WOLVERINE SPECIAL			*(United States, 1904–28)*			
1904		2 cyl.	Runabout	2,500	6,000	14,000
1906		2 cyl.	Tonneau	2,400	5,800	13,600
1917		4 cyl.	Speedster	2,400	8,000	16,000
1927		6 cyl.	Sedan	1,200	2,800	8,200
1927		6 cyl.	Coupe	1,200	2,800	8,300
1928		6 cyl.	Sedan	1,200	2,800	8,300
1928		6 cyl.	Rumble Seat Coupe	1,200	2,800	8,300
1928		6 cyl.	Cabriolet	2,300	4,500	9,000

YEAR	MODEL	ENGINE	BODY	F	G	E
WOODILL	(United States, 1952–58)					
1952		V 8 cyl.	Sport Roadster	1,800	8,000	17,000
WOODS ELECTRIC	(United States, 1899–1919)					
1899		Electric	Tonneau	4,000	14,500	31,000
1903	2	Electric	Buggy	3,000	6,500	14,000
1907	214A	Electric	Brougham	7,000	13,500	24,000
1912	1318	Electric	Limousine	5,000	10,000	20,000
1914		Electric	Brougham	3,800	8,500	17,800
1918	Dual Power	Electric	Coupe	6,000	12,000	25,000
WOODS MOBILETTE	(United States, 1913–16)					
1914	10/12	4 cyl.	Cycle	4,000	8,000	16,000
1916	Tandem	4 cyl.	Cycle	3,500	7,000	15,000
WORTHINGTON BOLLEE	(United States, 1904)					
1904	24/32	4 cyl.	Tonneau	3,400	7,800	15,500
WUNDERLICH	(Germany, 1902)					
1902		2 cyl.	Voiturette	1,100	2,250	6,500

Y

YEAR	MODEL	ENGINE	BODY	F	G	E
YALE	(United States, 1902–18)					
1903	A	2 cyl.	Tonneau	5,000	10,000	20,000
1904	C	2 cyl.	Touring	5,000	10,000	20,000
1905	F	2 cyl.	Touring Roadster	3,600	8,000	18,000
1918		V 8 cyl.	Touring Speedster	8,000	14,000	28,000
YANKEE	(United States, 1910)					
1910	MB	2 cyl.	Buggy	2,500	6,000	13,500
1910	RR	2 cyl.	Roadster	2,400	5,800	13,300
YAXA	(China, 1912–14)					
1912		4 cyl.	Torpedo Touring	1,200	3,850	8,750
1914		4 cyl.	Touring	950	2,900	7,000
YORK	(Germany, 1922)					
1922		V 2 cyl.	Cycle	950	1,950	3,750

YEAR	MODEL	ENGINE	BODY	F	G	E

Z

Z *(Czechoslovakia, 1924–39)*

YEAR	MODEL	ENGINE	BODY	F	G	E
1924	Z-1	1 cyl.	Touring	900	3,000	5,900
1929	Z-2	6 cyl.	Touring	1,800	4,100	10,750
1930	Z-9	2 cyl.	Touring	1,600	2,300	8,200
1931	Z-13	8 cyl.	Sport	1,700	3,400	10,700
1935	Z-5	4 cyl.	Touring	1,600	2,300	5,200
1936	Z-6	2 cyl.	Sedan	7,100	2,100	3,000
1938	Z-9	2 cyl.	Sedan	1,600	2,100	3,000

ZEDEL *(France; China, 1906–23)*

YEAR	ENGINE	BODY	F	G	E
1906	4 cyl.	Roadster	1,200	2,400	4,000
1907	4 cyl.	Roadster	1,200	2,400	4,000
1908	15 hp	Roadster	1,200	2,400	4,000
1909	4 cyl.	Roadster	1,000	1,900	3,000
1912	4 cyl.	Touring	2,250	4,500	8,200
1920	4 cyl.	Touring	2,000	4,000	8,000
1923	4 cyl.	Touring	2,000	4,000	8,000

ZEILLER ET FOURNIER *(France, 1920–24)*

YEAR	ENGINE	BODY	F	G	E
1920	4 cyl.	2 Passenger	1,300	2,600	6,750
1924	4 cyl.	2 Passenger	1,400	2,600	6,750

ZENA *(Italy, 1906–08)*

YEAR	ENGINE	BODY	F	G	E
1906	1 cyl.	Runabout	990	2,900	7,100
1906	1 cyl.	Touring	1,400	3,100	7,200
1907	4 cyl.	Touring	1,200	4,000	8,200
1908	4 cyl.	Touring	1,300	4,100	8,300

ZENITH *(France, 1910)*

YEAR	ENGINE	BODY	F	G	E
1910	1 cyl.	Voiturette	1,100	2,200	6,750

ZEPHYR *(Great Britain, 1919–20)*

YEAR	MODEL	ENGINE	BODY	F	G	E
1919	11.9 hp	4 cyl.	2 Passenger	990	2,900	7,500
1920		4 cyl.	4 Passenger	990	3,200	7,250

ZEVACO *(France, 1923–25)*

YEAR	ENGINE	BODY	F	G	E
1924	2 cyl.	Cycle	1,300	2,500	3,250
1925	4 cyl.	Cycle	1,600	2,200	3,000

YEAR	MODEL	ENGINE	BODY	F	G	E

ZIM *(Soviet Union, 1950–57)*

| 1950 | | 6 cyl. | Sedan | 1,900 | 3,500 | 6,000 |

Zim – 1950 "Sedan"

| 1957 | | 3.5 Litre | Sedan | 2,200 | 3,900 | 7,000 |

ZIMMERMAN *(United States, 1908–15)*

1908	G	2 cyl.	Runabout	2,200	8,800	16,500
1910	I	2 cyl.	Surrey Touring	3,100	9,500	18,500
1915	Z-6	6 cyl.	Touring	5,800	15,000	30,500

ZIS *(Soviet Union, 1936–56)*

1936	101	8 cyl.	Limousine	2,700	9,500	12,500
1939		5.5 Litre	Sedan	3,000	6,000	9,500
1940	102	8 cyl.	Open Touring	3,800	8,300	17,000
1945	110	8 cyl.	Limousine	3,000	5,500	9,500
1950	110	5.4 Litre	Convertible	3,300	6,000	11,500
1956		5 cyl.	Limousine	2,200	2,800	3,900

ZUNDAPP *(Germany, 1956–58)*

| 1956 | Janus | 7.4 Litre | Sedan | 380 | 750 | 2,000 |

INTRODUCTION TO TRUCKS

The U.S. trucking industry dates to the early twentieth century when trucks were tested in New York for capacity, speed and economy. They proved worthy of replacing the horse and wagon. Five years later more than 4,000 trucks were in use, and within a decade there were more than 100,000 trucks. One million trucks were on the road in 1920, and by 1978 close to four million trucks were sold and more than thirty million trucks were registered.

Two of the oldest trucking companies in America are the Morris Wheeler Steel Company, based in Philadelphia and founded in 1828; and B. vonParis and Sons, founded in 1892 and based in Timonium, Maryland. Between the years 1900 and 1970, metropolitan Chicago was the home for more than 140 truck manufacturers and competition was stiff. The first National Truck Show opened in Madison Square Garden in 1911.

During these early years winter played an important role in the evolution of the truck. Horses were better in the snow, so trucks weren't used during bad weather. In fact, trucks weren't expected to be used in the winter, and some manuals suggested removing the fan belt. Later advice cited alcohol as the best anti-freeze.

Trucks had to be designed for winter, with more protection for the driver. The cab evolved and included a windshield, top, side curtains, doors, heater, and fan defrosters. The wheel and tire tread designs developed; radiators were fitted with covers to heat faster; and trucks were fitted with snow plows.

1890–1900

In 1890, W. H. Christie began his company in Kane, Pennsylvania hauling goods by horse and wagon across the Allegheny Mountains. William Walter arrived from Switzerland in 1898 and developed the Walter Car. He didn't like using a lever or crank, so he made a fifth wheel for steering.

1900–1909

Mack introduced a 20-passenger, gasoline-powered bus in 1900. Eight years later it was converted to a truck. The White brothers introduced a steam-powered light delivery truck in 1900. In 1901, they produced a five-ton steam truck.

In 1900 two brothers, Max and Morris Grabowsky, designed a truck with a horizontal gas engine. Selling their first truck in 1902, they began the Rapid Motor Vehicle Company of Detroit. The Rapid operation along with The Reliance Motor Company were soon acquired by General Motors.

In 1904, Walter introduced the first American car with select instead of progressive gears. The Detroit Auto Company developed a gasoline-powered delivery wagon in 1900 while in 1901 Heil began developing vehicle bodies in Milwaukee.

International Harvester organized in 1902 through a merger of McCormick Company, Deering, Plano, Milwaukee, and Warder, Bushnell and Glessner. The high model truck was introduced in 1905 and in 1907 the plant moved to Akron, Ohio where the first automotive vehicle was built.

The Diamond T Motor Car Company of Chicago was formed in 1905 by C. A. Tilt. Other motor trucks were introduced in 1906 by the Knox Motor Truck Company. C. G. Strang, of Brooklyn, established a household moving van service in 1907 and the Sternberg Manufacturing Company was formed in West Allis, Wisconsin.

The FWD truck, made in 1908, became the first four-wheel drive vehicle. And 1908 also produced a front-drive motor truck by the International Motor Car Company. The Hackett Motor Car Company, based in New York, began in 1907 with one truck. By 1910 the company had ten trucks—all Mack-Manhattans.

1910–1919

The Rapid company and Reliance company changed to GMC in 1911, and manufacturing operations moved to Pontiac, Michigan in 1913. The General Motors Truck Company was then organized as the manufacturing and sales subsidiary of GM.

Warwick Saunders and his sons established the Ford Livery in 1916. Known today as the Saunders System, this was the first company to rent and lease cars and trucks. They rented Model-T Fords and some trucks.

In 1911 Richard Corbitt found the competition too stiff for automobiles and turned to trucks. By 1916 he had developed an extensive line of trucks that were used by the U.S. Army as well as in many foreign countries. Magnus Hendrickson and his two sons founded the Hendrickson Motor Truck Company in 1913. Very early they established a reputation for specially equipped trucks.

The Walter Motor Truck Company, best known for snow removal equipment, was formed in 1911. The same year International Motors was formed by consolidating Mack, Sauer, and Hewitt. Marmon introduced a 1,500 pound delivery truck in 1912.

The Mack AC "Bulldog" model was introduced in 1914. Gerlinger Manufacturing Company formed in 1915 in Portland, Oregon, and in 1917 the name changed to Gersix.

In 1918, Nash was the largest producer of trucks with an army contract for more than 11,000 vehicles.

1920–1929

The Ford Livery Company became the Saunders Drive It Yourself System in 1923. By 1926 Saunders had 86 branches in 56 cities. Other rental agencies followed their lead, including Hertz and GM.

In 1925 General Motors Truck Company merged with the Yellow Cab Manufacturing Company to become the Yellow Truck and Coach Manufacturing Company.

By 1920, standard features on the Mack trucks included high-door cabs to protect drivers during cold weather. In 1922 Mack Trucks, Inc. was founded and took over International Motor Company.

Based on the patents of William Besserdich, The Wisconsin Auto Company was formed to produce a four-wheel drive truck. Later the company became the Osh-Kosh Truck Corporation. The Gersix Truck company became Kenworth.

Chrysler Corporation emerged in 1925, developing from Maxwell-Chalmers. Dodge purchased the majority interest in Graham Brothers in 1925, and in 1928 Chrysler bought Dodge.

1930–1939

Typical of western trucks in the 1930s was the Fageol with side-mounted spare tires, cable from radiator to cab, and shutters to moderate cooling the engine.

In 1932, E. Ward King saw the possibility of a two-way haul between Kingsport,

Tennessee and New York City, and he began a company with three rigs. In 1933 his company officially became Mason and Dixon Lines, Inc., and by 1935 Mason and Dixon was allowed to operate as a regulated carrier between Atlanta and New York City.

Saunders did well until the stock market crash and the death of the president Warwick Saunders. Then the company was forced into bankruptcy. The Saunders brothers bought some of the branches and the Saunders System continued on a small scale as they tried to rebuild the company.

1940–1949

This decade saw Powel Crosley, Jr. introducing small, economical trucks to go with his small, economical cars. He presented a station wagon and a Parkway Delivery truck in 1940.

In 1943, GM acquired the Yellow Truck and Coach Company and GMC Truck and Coach Division was established. Corbett trucks were doing well—the '30s and '40s were the best years for the Corbetts. The up-to-date, well-equipped, high speed models all had the same look. For many years they also built school buses, trailers and farm tractors.

With World War II, the Hendrickson company became involved in high-tech components such as split shaft power take-offs and axle power dividers. Kenworth also produced for the military. They made vehicles, wreckers and bomber nose assemblies.

Since then Kenworth has been noted for meeting the trucking industry's needs through engineering, testing and quality control.

1950–1959

By 1953 The Saunders System had been rebuilt. In 1954 the company moved to Birmingham, Alabama where it is successful today.

Corbett trucks did well until 1952 and the death of Mr. Corbett. The company was left with an unprepared management and a low inventory.

The '50s saw major changes for Mason and Dixon. A Civil War mansion in Virginia became a relay station for north/south runs. Mason and Dixon Tank Lines, Inc. emerged in 1957—the result of buying Robinson Transfer Motor Lines.

1960–1969

The 1963 purchase of Silver Fleet Motor Express added more than 5,000 miles and service between Chicago and Birmingham for Mason and Dixon.

W. H. Christie & Sons was carried on by the sons and moved to Kane, Pennsylvania.

1970–PRESENT

Scot Trucks formed in Eastern Canada in 1972 as a specialty truck to carry fuel oil. High costs and the devaluation of the Canadian dollar caused the end of Scot in 1980.

In 1981, GM established the worldwide Truck and Bus Group in a regrouping of the corporation's truck and bus operations. In 1982 GMC Truck and Coach merged with several GM Assembly Divisions and Chevrolet motor divisions to become the GM Truck and Bus Manufacturing Division.

PRICING. Condition plays the most important role in antique truck pricing. The prices in the following listing are the average condition price for the stated year. For a truck in mint condition add as much as one hundred percent to the listed price. For a truck in good condition add forty to fifty percent. For a vehicle that is missing several parts and needs considerable restoration subtract forty to fifty percent off the listed price.

Collectors must study manufacturers, prices and types of trucks, before visualizing the finished restoration. Obviously, there are numerous truck collector makers.

YEAR	MODEL	ENGINE	BODY	F	G	E
CHEVROLET						
1926	Superior V	4 cyl.	1 Ton, 8 ft. Bed	2000	3500	7000
1928	Pickup	4 cyl.	1 Ton	2100	3500	7000
1929	Pickup	6 cyl.	1/2 Ton	2700	4000	8000
1931	Flatbed	6 cyl.	2 Ton	3250	5000	10000
1931	Pickup	6 cyl.	1 1/2 Ton	2500	4000	8000
1933	Stake	6 cyl.	1 1/2 Ton, Red Oak Bed	2880	4500	9000
1935	Pickup	6 cyl.	1 1/2 Ton, 12 Bed	2600	4500	9000
1936	Pickup	6 cyl.	Express	2000	3500	7000
1937	Pickup	6 cyl., 4-Speed	1/2 Ton	2200	3500	7000
1938	Pickup	6 cyl.	Stepside	1750	4000	8000
1939	Pickup	6 cyl.	1 Ton	2180	3500	7000
1939	Pickup	6 cyl.	1 Ton	2350	3500	7000
1940	Carryall	6 cyl.	Closed Back	2500	4000	8000
1940	Pickup	6 cyl., 3-Speed		2300	4000	8000
1941	Panel		3/4 Ton	2500	4000	8000
1941	Pickup	6 cyl.	1 Ton	2200	4000	8000
1941	Pickup	6 cyl., 4-Speed		2150	3500	7000
1941	Pickup	4-Speed		1800	3500	7000
1941	Pickup	4-Speed	3/4 Ton	1800	3500	7000
1941	Pickup	216, 4-Speed	1/2 Ton	2500	4000	8000
1942	Dump	Diesel, 2-Speed		1750	3000	6000
1942	Pickup	6 cyl.	1/2 Ton	1800	5000	9000
1942	Pickup	6 cyl.	1/2 Ton	1950	3000	6000
1945	Stake	6 cyl.	Highside	2500	4000	8000
1946	Pickup		1/2 Ton, Oak Bed	2000	4000	8000
1946	Pickup		1/2 Ton	2100	3500	7000
1946	Pickup		1/2 Ton	2000	3500	7000
1946	Pickup	6 cyl.	1/2 Ton	2000	3500	7000
1946	Pickup	6 cyl.	3/4 Ton	1500	3000	6000
1946	Pickup	6 cyl., 3-Speed	3/4 Ton	1500	3000	6000
1946	Pickup	6 cyl., 235		2000	3500	7000
1946	Pickup	4 cyl.	1/2 Ton	1700	3500	7000
1947	Thriftmaster	6 cyl.	Closed Box	2500	4000	8000
1948	Loadmaster		1 1/2 Ton, Flatbed	2400	3500	7000
1948	Pickup	6 cyl.	1/2 Ton, Deluxe Package	2750	4500	9000
1948	Wrecker		1 1/2 Ton	2300	3500	7000
1950	Panel	6 cyl.	1 Ton	2100	3500	7000
1950	Pickup		3/4 Ton	1500	3000	6000
1950	Pickup		3/4 Ton	1500	3000	6000
1950	Pickup	6 cyl., 3-Speed	1/2 Ton, Maplewood Bed	2200	3500	7000

YEAR	MODEL	ENGINE	BODY	F	G	E
1950	Suburban Carryall	6 cyl.	½ Ton	1900	3500	7000
1951	Pickup	6 cyl.	¾ Ton	1650	3000	6000
1951	Pickup	6 cyl.	½ Ton	1600	3000	6000
1951	Suburban Carryall	6 cyl.	Closed Body	2000	4000	6000
1952	Panel	6 cyl.	1 Ton	2200	4000	6000
1952	Pickup		6 ft. Steel Bed	2400	5000	7000
1953	Pickup	6 cyl.	¾ Ton	1950	4000	6000
1953	Pickup	6 cyl., 4-Speed	½ Ton	1900	4000	6000
1953	Pickup	235, 6 cyl., 4-Speed	½ Ton	2000	4000	6000
1954	Pickup	4-Speed	½ Ton	2000	4000	6000
1954	Pickup	6 cyl., 4-Speed		2100	4000	6000
1954	Pickup	6 cyl., 4-Speed	½ Ton	2000	4000	6000
1954	Pickup	235, 6 cyl., 4-Speed	½ Ton	2050	4000	6000
1954	Pickup	6 cyl., 4-Speed	½ Ton	1950	4000	6000
1955	3100 Pickup	6 cyl., 3-Speed 13-Speed, Overdrive	Short Bed	2600	5000	8000
1955	Pickup	6 cyl., 3-Speed		2450	4000	7000
1955	Pickup	6 cyl., 3-Speed	½ Ton	2350	5000	8000
1955	Pickup	6 cyl., 4-Speed	½ Ton	2400	4000	7000
1956	Pickup	6 cyl.	½ Ton	2700	5000	8000
1956	Pickup	6 cyl., 3-Speed		2700	5000	8000
1956	Pickup	(V) 8 cyl.	Short Bed, Deluxe Package	2800	5000	8000
1956	Pickup	(V) 8 cyl., 4-Speed	½ Ton	2750	5000	8000
1956	Stake	(V) 8 cyl.	1½ Ton, Oakwood Sides	2850	4000	8000
1957	Pickup		1½ Ton	2500	4000	8000
1957	Pickup	6 cyl.	Stepside	2350	3500	7000
1957	Pickup	6 cyl., 4-Speed		2400	3500	7000
1957	Pickup	6 cyl., 4-Speed	½ Ton	2300	3500	7000
1957	Pickup	6 cyl., 4-Speed	¾ Ton	2450	4000	8000
1957	Pickup	6 cyl., 4-Speed	¾ Ton, 4 x 4	2450	4000	8000
1957	Pickup	6 cyl.	½ Ton, Short Bed	2300	3500	7000
1957	Pickup	(V) 8 cyl., 4-Speed		2700	5000	8000
1957	Stepside	(V) 8 cyl.	Deluxe Package	2750	4000	8000
1957	Pickup	(V) 8 cyl. 265, 4-Speed	Cameo	2750	4000	8000
1957	Pickup	(V) 8 cyl., 283		2650	4000	8000
1957	Pickup	(V) 8 cyl., 4-Speed		2650	4000	8000
1957	Pickup	(V) 8 cyl., 4-Speed	½ Ton, Deluxe Package	2750	4000	8000

YEAR	MODEL	ENGINE	BODY	F	G	E
1958	Pickup	6 cyl.	Fleetside, Big Window	2850	4500	9000
1958	Pickup		½ Ton, Stepside	2500	4000	8000
1958	Pickup	6 cyl., Standard Transmission	Fleetside Deluxe Cab	2850	4500	9000
1958	Pickup	6 cyl., 3-Speed	½ Ton	2000	4000	8000
1959	Apache 31	6 cyl., 4-Speed		2000	3500	7000
1959	Pickup	6 cyl.	½ Ton	2350	4000	8000
1959	Pickup	(V) 8 cyl.	½ Ton	2450	4000	8000
1959	Pickup	(V) 8 cyl.	Short Stepside, Deluxe Package	2650	4000	8000
1961	Corvair	6 cyl.	Rampside	2100	3500	7000
1961	Pickup	6 cyl., 3-Speed	½ Ton, Stepside	2250	3500	7000
1962	Pickup	6 cyl.	½ Ton	2100	3500	7000
1964	Pickup	6 cyl., 4-Speed	½ Ton, 4 x 4, Stepside	2500	2750	3100
1965	Pickup	(V) 8 cyl., 3-Speed	Custom Wide Short Bed	2000	3500	5400
1965	Pickup	(V) 8 cyl., Automatic		2500	4000	8000
1966	Pickup	(V) 8 cyl. 238	Fleetside, Long Bed	2750	4000	8000
1966	Pickup	(V) 8 cyl. 327	½ Ton, 8 ft. Bed	2800	3100	3400
1967	Pickup	6 cyl., Automatic		2400	2600	2900
1968	Pickup	327 Automatic	½ Ton	2000	2350	2700
1968	Pickup	6 cyl., 3-Speed	½ Ton	2100	2400	3000
1969	K10	(V) 8 cyl. 350	4 x 4, Stepside	3000	3480	3700
1969	Pickup	(V) 8 cyl. 396, 3-Speed	Deluxe Package	3100	3500	4000
1969	Garwood Series 50	350, 5-Speed	Diamond Plate Rollback Platform	2000	4000	4750
1970	Ultra Van	(V) 8 cyl.	Windowed	2000	3000	6000
1971	Cheyenne Pickup		Short Bed	2500	4000	5500
1982	Silverado Pickup	454 Automatic		3000	4000	6000

DODGE

Formed by John and Horace Dodge in November 1914, Dodge's first full production vehicle—the 4-cylinder touring car—became America's third best selling model. Chrysler Corporation of Detroit, Michigan bought the company in 1928. By 1930, Dodge produced America's fourth best selling truck. By 1941, truck buyers had a wide selection to choose from including six engines, seventeen axle ratios, twenty-three frames, four clutches, six types of brakes and eight rear axles. In 1975, Dodge discontinued its entire heavy truck line opting instead to produce lightweight trucks with new features: servo front disc brakes, 4-litre, 6-cylinder diesel, and fancy color and trim packages.

YEAR	MODEL	ENGINE	BODY	F	G	E
1930	Stake Truck	6 cyl.	¾ Ton	1000	2000	4000
1936	Panel		1 Ton	2000	2300	4200
1936	Panel	6 cyl.	Deluxe Package	3500	4000	4500
1937	Pickup	6 cyl.	¾ Ton	1950	3000	6000
1939	Panel	6 cyl.	½ Ton	2000	4000	9000
1947	WC Pickup	6 cyl.	½ Ton	2000	4000	7000
1948	Tow Platform	6 cyl.		1000	2000	4500
1950	Pickup	6 cyl.	1 Ton	1000	2750	5000
1950	Pickup	6 cyl.	½ Ton	1000	3000	6000
1953	Pickup	6 cyl.	½ Ton, Short Bed	1500	3000	6000
1953	Pickup	6 cyl.	½ Ton	1500	3200	6500
1953	Power Wagon	6 cyl.	½ Ton	2000	5000	10000
1953	Pickup	6 cyl.	¾ Ton	1000	2350	6000
1953	Van	6 cyl. (Flathead)		3000	3500	3900
1954	Pickup	6 cyl.	½ Ton	1000	3000	7000
1956	Pickup	6 cyl.	½ Ton, Oak Bed & Running Boards	1500	3000	6000
1956	Pickup	(V) 8 cyl.	1 Ton	2550	4000	7000
1959	Sweptside	(V) 8 cyl.	½ Ton	1000	3000	6500
1960	Power Wagon	6 cyl.	Stepside	2350	4000	8000
1962	Power Wagon	6 cyl., 4-Speed 2 Speed Transfer	1 Ton	2600	4500	9000
1962	Utiline	6 cyl.	½ Ton	950	2700	5500
1962	Sweptline	6 cyl.	½ Ton	1100	2700	5500
1963	Crew Cab	6 cyl.	¾ Ton	900	2500	5000
1963	Sweptline	6 cyl.	½ Ton	950	2700	5500
1964	Panel	6 cyl.	½ Ton	900	3000	6000
1964	Sweptline	6 cyl.	½ Ton	1000	2700	5500
1965	Compact	6 cyl.	½ Ton	1500	3200	5500
1965	Sweptline	6 cyl.	½ Ton	1500	3000	6000
1966	Wagon	6 cyl.	½ Ton	1200	3000	6000
1966	Sweptline	6 cyl.	½ Ton	875	3200	6500
1967	Van	6 cyl.	½ Ton	850	2500	5000
1967	Sweptline	6 cyl.	½ Ton	900	3000	6000
1968	Platform	6 cyl.	½ Ton	900	2500	5500
1968	Sweptline	6 cyl.	½ Ton	1200	2500	5000
1969	Crew Cab	6 cyl.	½ Ton	1200	2500	5500
1969	Crew Cab	(V) 8 cyl.	½ Ton	1500	3000	6000
1969	Sweptline	6 cyl.	½ Ton	1800	3000	6000
1969	Sweptline	(V) 8 cyl.	½ Ton	1500	3200	6500
1970	Power Wagon	6 cyl.	½ Ton	1000	2200	5000
1970	Power Wagon	(V) 8 cyl.	½ Ton	1100	2500	5500
1970	Sweptline	6 cyl.	½ Ton	900	2500	5500
1970	Sweptline	(V) 8 cyl.	½ Ton	1000	3000	6000
1971	Van	6 cyl.	½ Ton	900	1500	4000
1971	Van	(V) 8 cyl.	½ Ton	1000	2000	4500

YEAR	MODEL	ENGINE	BODY	F	G	E
1972	Utiline	6 cyl.	½ Ton	900	2000	5000
1972	Utiline	(V) 8 cyl.	½ Ton	1000	2500	5500
1972	Sweptline	6 cyl.	½ Ton	900	2200	5200

FORD

The company was begun in 1905 in Detroit, Michigan, by Henry Ford. Three years later, Ford produced the Model T, a 4-cylinder, L-head engine, with 2-speed-and-reverse transmission truck. In 1917, Ford built the first 1-ton truck named the Model TT. More than a million of this model were sold in ten years. Because of it popularity, Ford pulled in 51 percent of the U.S. truck market by 1926, contrasting Chevrolet's 1-ton truck which held only two percent of the market. Production ceased on the Model T in 1927. Its replacement was the Model A. In 1936, the three millionth Ford truck was produced and two years later Ford added two more lines. By 1948 Ford had a major restyling—the first step in the process of range-widening which characterized all U.S. volume producers. Ten years later more than 300 models were available with an automobile-inspired pickup design styling, new grills, dual headlights, customized interiors and two-tone color combinations. By 1978, Ford had sold almost 22 million trucks. There is no doubt, Ford's pioneering achievements played an important role in the U.S. trucking industry.

YEAR	MODEL	ENGINE	BODY	F	G	E
1920	Model T	4 cyl.	Delivery	4500	7000	12000
1923	Model T	4 cyl.	Roadster	6000	12000	14000
1925	Model TT	4 cyl.	C-Cab Panel	3500	6000	12000
1925	Model TT	4 cyl.	1 Ton	2000	4000	8000
1928	Model A	4 cyl.	Short Bed	4000	8000	16000
1930	Model A	4 cyl.	Panel	3000	6000	12000
1931	Model A	4 cyl.	Deluxe Pickup	3000	5000	10000
1931	Model AA	4 cyl.	Sedan Delivery	3800	9000	16000
1931	Model AA	4 cyl.	Short Box	2000	4200	9000
1932	B-18	(V) 8 cyl.	Open Cab Pickup	4000	8000	15000
1932	Model B	4 cyl.	Closed Cab Pickup	2650	4500	9000
1932	B-18	(V) 8 cyl.	Standard Panel	2100	4000	8000
1933	46	(V) 8 cyl.	Pickup	2000	4000	9000
1933	Model 46	4 cyl.	Panel	2750	5000	9000
1934	46	(V) 8 cyl.	Pickup	2800	4500	9000
1935	50	(V) 8 cyl.	Panel	3000	4500	9000
1935	48	(V) 8 cyl.	Sedan Delivery	2300	4000	8000
1936	67	(V) 8 cyl.	Deluxe Panel	2200	5000	8000
1937	73	(V) 8 cyl.	Flatbed	1750	3500	7000
1937	77	4-Speed	¾ Ton Pickup	2050	4000	8000
1937	Stake 73	(V) 8 cyl.	½ Ton Pickup	2000	3500	7000
1938	82C	6 cyl.	Pickup	1700	4000	8000
1938	82C	(V) 8 cyl.	Platform	2150	3500	7000

YEAR	MODEL	ENGINE	BODY	F	G	E
1938	Pickup	(V) 8 cyl.	1½ Ton	2000	3500	7000
1938	Pickup	(V) 8 cyl.		1950	3500	7000
1938	Pickup	(V) 8 cyl.	Wood Bed	2100	4000	8000
1938	Wrecker	(V) 8 cyl.	4-Speed	2500	4000	8000
1939	Pickup	(V) 8 cyl.	¾ Ton	1500	3500	7000
1939	Stake	(V) 8 cyl.	1½ Ton, Oak body	2300	4000	8000
1940	Pickup	6 cyl.	½ Ton	1950	5000	10000
1940	Pickup	(V) 8 cyl.	½ Ton	2000	4000	8000
1940		(V) 8 cyl.	2 Ton	800	3500	7000
1941	Pickup	(V) 8 cyl.	½ Ton	2000	4000	8000
1941	Pickup	(V) 8 cyl.	1½ Ton, Winch	2200	4000	8000
1941	Pickup	(V) 8 cyl., 3-Speed		2100	4000	8000
1941	Pickup	4 cyl.	½ Ton	2100	3500	7000
1941	F-1 Stake	(V) 8 cyl.	8-Foot Bed	2500	5000	9000
1942	Pickup	6 cyl.	¾ Ton	2000	3500	7000
1942	Pickup	(V) 8 cyl., 3-Speed	½ Ton	1550	3000	6000
1942	Pickup	(V) 8 cyl.	¾ Ton	2000	3500	7000
1946	Panel	(V) 8 cyl.	1 Ton	3000	5000	9000
1946	Panel	(V) 8 cyl., 3-Speed	½ Ton	2000	3500	7000
1946	Pickup		½ Ton	2450	3500	7000
1946	Pickup	6 cyl.	Flatbed Rear	1850	3000	6000
1946	Pickup	6 cyl.	½ Ton	1900	3000	6000
1946	Pickup	(V) 8 cyl.	Low Body	2200	3000	6000
1946	Pickup	(V) 8 cyl., 2-Speed Rear Axle	1½ Ton	1900	3500	7000
1946	Pickup	(V) 8 cyl., 4-Speed	½ Ton	2250	4000	8000
1946	Stake	(V) 8 cyl., 4-Speed		2100	4000	8000
1947	Flatbed	(V) 8 cyl., 3-Speed	½ Ton	1450	3500	7000
1947	Flatbed	(V) 8 cyl., 4-Speed	½ Ton	1400	3500	7000
1947	Panel	6 cyl., 3-Speed	½ Ton	995	3000	6000
1947	Pickup	6 cyl., 4-Speed	1 Ton	900	3000	6000
1947	Pickup		½ Ton	1500	3500	7000
1947	Pickup	(V) 8 cyl.	1½ Ton	1500	3500	7000
1947	Pickup	(V) 8 cyl., 3-Speed	½ Ton	1500	3500	7000
1948	Pickup	6 cyl.	½ Ton	1500	3500	7000
1948	F-1 Pickup	6 cyl., 3-Speed		2000	4000	8000
1948	Pickup	(V) 8 cyl., 239		1500	3500	7000
1948	Pickup	(V) 8 cyl., Flathead	Short Bed	1600	3500	7000
1948	Stake	(V) 8 cyl., 4-Speed	1 Ton, Flatbed	1600	3500	7000
1949	F-1			1350	3500	7000
1949	F-1	(V) 8 cyl.		1550	3500	7000
1949	F-1	(V) 8 cyl. Flathead 4-Speed		2000	4000	7000
1949	Panel	(V) 8 cyl.	½ Ton	1500	3000	7000
1949	Pickup	6 cyl., 3-Speed	½ Ton	1200	3000	6000
1949	Pickup	(V) 8 cyl.	½ Ton	1300	3000	6000

YEAR	MODEL	ENGINE	BODY	F	G	E
1949	Pickup	4-Speed	1 Ton, 8-Foot Box	2250	4500	8000
1950	F-1	(V) 8 cyl., 4-Speed		2000	4000	7000
1950	F-1	(V) 8 cyl. Flathead		2000	4000	7000
1950	Model F4 Delivery	(V) 8 cyl.	1 Ton	2000	4000	7000
1950	Model F4 Delivery	(V) 8 cyl. Flathead	1 Ton	2000	4000	7000
1950	Pickup	(V) 8 cyl.	½ Ton	1150	3000	6000
1950	Pickup	(V) 8 cyl. Flathead, 3-Speed	½ Ton	2000	4000	7000
1950	Pickup	(V) 8 cyl. Flathead, 4-Speed	½ Ton	1275	3000	6000
1951	F-1	(V) 8 cyl. Flathead, 3-Speed		1800	4000	7000
1951	Flatbed	(V) 8 cyl., 4-Speed	1½ Ton	1700	4000	7000
1951	Pickup	6 cyl.		1400	3000	6000
1951	Pickup	6 cyl.	½ Ton	1500	3000	7000
1951	Pickup	(V) 8 cyl.	½ Ton	1600	3000	7000
1951	Pickup	(V) 8 cyl.	Stepside	2000	4000	8000
1951	Pickup	(V) 8 cyl., 3-Speed		1850	4000	7000
1951	Pickup	(V) 8 cyl. Flathead, 3-Speed	½ Ton	1650	3000	6000
1951	Pickup	(V) 8 cyl.	¾ Ton	2000	4000	8000
1952	F-1	6 cyl.	½ Ton	1950	3000	7000
1952	F-1	(V) 8 cyl.	Stepside	2300	4000	7000
1952	F-100			1750	4000	7000
1952	F-250	(V) 8 cyl. Flathead, 3-Speed	Stepside	2250	4000	8000
1952	Pickup	(V) 8 cyl.	½ Ton	2000	3000	7000
1952	Pickup	(V) 8 cyl. Flathead	½ Ton	1950	3000	7000
1952	Pickup	(V) 8 cyl. Flathead	½ Ton, Oak Bed	2500	4000	8000
1952	Pickup	(V) 8 cyl. Flathead	Stepside	2150	3500	7000
1953	F-100	(V) 8 cyl., 4-Speed		1550	3000	6000
1953	F-100	6 cyl.	Deluxe Package	3250	4500	9000
1953	F-100	6 cyl., 3-Speed		1550	3000	6000
1953	Pickup	6 cyl., 4-Speed	¾ Ton	1495	3000	6000
1953	Pickup	6 cyl., 3-Speed		1450	2500	5000
1953	Pickup	6 cyl.	1½ Ton	1500	3000	6000
1953	Pickup	6 cyl., 3-Speed	½ Ton	1500	3000	6000
1953	Pickup	(V) 8 cyl.	½ Ton	1750	3000	6000
1954	F-100	6 cyl.	Rack Side	1600	3000	6000
1954	Pickup	(V) 8 cyl.	Standard Shift	1650	3000	6000
1954	Pickup	6 cyl.		1500	2500	5000
1954	Pickup	6 cyl., 3-Speed	½ Ton, Stepside	1550	2500	5000
1954	Pickup	6 cyl., 4-Speed	Cedar Flatbed	1750	3000	6000

YEAR	MODEL	ENGINE	BODY	F	G	E
1955	F-100	6 cyl., 4-Speed		2000	3500	7000
1955	F-100	(V) 8cyl., 3-Speed	Deluxe Package	2500	5000	10000
1955	F-100	4-Speed	Deluxe Package	3900	6000	11000
1955	F-100	(V) 8 cyl.	1½ Ton, Stake Bed	1500	3500	7000
1955	Pickup	(V) 8 cyl., 4-Speed	½ Ton	1500	3000	6000
1956	F-100		Custom Cab	2500	4000	8000
1956	F-100	(V) 8 cyl.	Custom Cab	2000	4000	8000
1956	F-100	(V) 8 cyl., 4-Speed		2250	3500	7000
1956	F-100	6 cyl., 3-Speed		2000	3500	7000
1956	F-100	292		2250	3500	7000
1956	F-100		Deluxe Package	3500	6000	12000
1956	F-250	(V) 8 cyl.	Long Bed	2000	3500	7000
1956	Flatbed		1 Ton	2000	3500	7000
1956	Pickup	6 cyl.	½ Ton	1500	3000	6000
1956	Pickup	6 cyl., 3-Speed	Stepside	2000	3500	7000
1956	Pickup	(V) 8 cyl.	½ Ton	1500	3500	7000
1956	Pickup	(V) 8 cyl.	½ Ton, Custom Cab	2600	4000	8000
1956	Pickup	(V) 8 cyl.	½ Ton, Long Bed	2200	3500	7000
1956	Pickup	(V) 8 cyl., 3-Speed		2100	3500	7000
1956	Pickup	(V) 8 cyl., 3-Speed		2200	4000	8000
1956	Pickup	(V) 8 cyl.	½ Ton	2100	3500	7000
1956	Pickup	(V) 8 cyl.	½ Ton, Deluxe Package	3000	6000	12000
1957	F-100	6 cyl.	Stepside	2000	3500	7000
1957	F-100	(V) 8 cyl. 272, 4-Speed		2450	4000	8000
1957	Pickup	(V) 8 cyl.	Short Bed	2400	3500	7000
1959	F-100	(V) 8 cyl. 292		2400	3500	7000
1959	Pickup	6 cyl., 3-Speed		2300	3500	7000
1959	Pickup	(V) 8 cyl.	Deluxe Package	2700	4000	8000
1959	F-100	(V) 8 cyl.	½ Ton	2375	3500	7000
1959	F-100	(V) 8 cyl., 3-Speed	6 Foot Bed	2500	4000	8000
1960	F-100	Fleetside Bed		2400	4000	8000
1961	Pickup	6 cyl., 3-Speed		2300	4000	8000
1961	F-100					
	Pickup	(V) 8 cyl. 292 3-Speed	Custom Cab	2000	4000	8000
1962	Pickup	(V) 8 cyl. 292 4-Speed	4 X 4	2450	4000	8000
1962	Van	(V) 8 cyl., 4-Speed	1 Ton	2100	3500	7000
1963	F-100	6 cyl.	6 Foot Bed	2450	3500	7000

YEAR	MODEL	ENGINE	BODY	F	G	E
1963	Tow	(V) 8 cyl., 4-Speed		2850	5000	9000
1964	Pickup	6 cyl., 3-Speed	½ Ton	2300	3500	7000
1965	Van	6 cyl. Automatic	Deluxe Package	4000	6000	12000
1966	Pickup	6 cyl., 3-Speed		2450	3500	7000
1966	Pickup	(V) 8 cyl. 352, 4-Speed		2400	4000	8000
1966	Pickup	(V) 8 cyl. 352	¾ Ton	2200	4000	8000
1966	Pickup	(V) 8 cyl. 352	High Side	2000	3500	7000
1966	Pickup	(V) 8 cyl. 352	Short Bed	2000	4000	8000
1966	Pickup	(V) 8 cyl. 352	Short Bed, Custom Cab	2600	4000	8000
1966	Pickup	(V) 8 cyl. 352	Short Bed, Deluxe Package	2500	4000	8000
1967	Pickup	(V) 8 cyl., 4-Speed	Flatbed	2000	3500	7000
1970	Pickup	6 cyl.	½ Ton	2000	3500	7000
1971	Flareside	6 cyl.		2000	4000	8000
1971	Flareside	(V) 8 cyl.		2000	4000	8000
1971	Styleside	6 cyl.		2000	4500	9000
1971	Styleside	(V) 8 cyl.		2000	4500	9000
1971	Ranchero	6 cyl.		2000	4500	9000
1971	Ranchero	(V) 8 cyl.		3000	5000	10000
1972	Flareside	6 cyl.		2000	4000	8000
1972	Styleside	(V) 8 cyl.		2500	4500	9000
1972	Styleside	6 cyl.		2500	4500	9000
1972	Ranchero	6 cyl.		2500	4500	9000
1972	Ranchero	(V) 8 cyl.		2500	4500	9000

GENERAL MOTORS CORPORATION

General Motors began production in 1911 by merging Rapid and Reliance Truck Companies. In 1918, GMC began a new division called Chevrolet. The first Chevy was a Series T, 1-ton, 4-cylinder, 3-speed truck. Enclosed cabs were featured with the 1926 R-series and the ½-ton range extended to include a roadster pickup which became a favorite style of the company. In 1930, Chevrolet sold 118,253 trucks but could not catch Ford until 1933 only to lose the truck market wars again in 1935 and 1937. As with other truck companies, Chevrolet had its share of innovations including a new heavy duty engine option covering fifteen basic models in the one-half-to two-ton range offered in 1942. Early 1950s improvements included a power-glide, automatic option on light models, full-pressure lubrication and a bigger six-cylinder engine. Today, Chevrolet is very competitive in the light and heavy truck market.

YEAR	MODEL	ENGINE	BODY	F	G	E
1942	Stake	6 cyl.	1½ Ton	1500	3000	5000
1943	Military		1½ Ton, 4 X 4	1500	3000	5000
1949	Pickup	6 cyl., 4-Speed	¾ Ton	1850	3000	5000
1950	Pickup	6 cyl.	Canopy Top	2200	4000	6000
1950	Refrigerator Truck	6 cyl., 4-Speed	1½ Ton	2000	4000	6000

YEAR	MODEL	ENGINE	BODY	F	G	E
1954	Tow		1½ Ton	2000	3500	5000
1954	Van	6 cyl.	1½ Ton	2000	3500	5000
1955	Pickup	6 cyl.	½ Ton	2000	3500	5000
1955	Pickup	6 cyl. (Hydramatic)	¾ Ton	1500	3000	5000
1956	Panel	6 cyl., 3-Speed	Deluxe Package	2500	4000	8000
1956	Pickup	(V) 8 cyl.	½ Ton	1500	3500	5000
1956	Pickup	(V) 8 cyl. (Automatic)		1850	4000	6000
1956	Pickup	(V) 8 cyl., 3-Speed		1800	4000	6000

INTERNATIONAL HARVESTER

Although the company officially began in 1907 in Chicago, Illinois, its predecessor companies have roots dating back to 1840 when Cyrus McCormick sold two grain reapers. In the early days, IHC's main goal was to manufacture agricultural vehicles, but they also produced motor vehicles for farms. In 1907, the company manufactured 100 IHC "auto buggies." In 1914, the name "International" first appeared replacing the "IHC" logo. By 1915, the company had new mechanical and styling changes including four-cylinder engines, three-speed transmissions and shaft-drives to internal gear axles. Internationals were good sellers in the early teens capturing four percent of the truck market. In 1924, the company made another dramatic style change on the one- to five-ton models. The radiator was placed in front and the engine covered with a butterfly hood. By 1940, the company had become the third ranking truck producer in the U.S. and it was believed that it sold more trucks of two tons and over than any three companies combined. The current International logo—red **I** over black **H**—first appeared in 1945. Since 1961, International offers 12 truck lines, is the fifth ranking U.S. truck dealer and its lifetime production is one of the largest attained in the world.

YEAR	MODEL	ENGINE	BODY	F	G	E
1917	G			3500	5500	9000
1925	S	4 cyl., 2-Speed Rear		2700	5000	8000
1927	Pickup	4 cyl., 3-Speed	1 Ton, Grain Bed	3500	5500	9000
1928	A	4 cyl.	1½ Ton	2800	5000	8000
1928	Pickup	4 cyl.	1½ Ton	2600	5000	8000
1935	C-1, Pickup	6 cyl.	Straight Side	2600	5000	8000
1935	C-1, Pickup		½ Ton	2500	5000	8000
1936	Pickup	6 cyl.	½ Ton	2550	5000	8000
1941	Pickup	4-Speed		2000	3500	7000
1955	Pickup	6 cyl., 3-Speed	½ Ton	2000	3500	7000
1966	Pickup	6 cyl., 4-Speed		2000	3500	7000
1967	Pickup	6 cyl.	½ Ton	2000	3500	7000

STUDEBAKER

1945	Pickup	6 cyl.	1 Ton	1500	3000	6000
1947	Pickup	6 cyl.	½ Ton	1400	3000	6000
1949	Pickup	6 cyl.	½ Ton	1450	3000	6000
1950	Pickup			1300	3000	6000
1950	Pickup		½ Ton	1350	3000	6000
1951	Pickup		Sidestep	1450	3000	6000
1952	Pickup	6 cyl.	¾ Ton	1600	3000	6000

YEAR	MODEL	ENGINE	BODY	F	G	E
1953	Pichup	6 cyl., 4-Speed	1½ Ton	1850	3000	6000
1960	Champ	(V) 8 cyl.	Short Bed	1600	3000	6000
1961	Pickup	(V) 8 cyl., 3-Speed	¾ Ton	1500	3000	6000
1962	Pickup			1800	3000	6000
1963	Pickup	(V) 8 cyl.	½ Ton	1500	3000	6000
1964		6 cyl.	½ Ton	3000	5000	8000
1964		(V) 8 cyl.	½ Ton	3000	5000	8000

INTRODUCTION TO MOTORCYCLES

Gottlieb Daimler is considered the father of the motor engine and is credited with great engineering feats and inventions. In 1885, an accommodating bicycle was the first display of his air-cooled four cycle engine, and although the invention of the motor was an instant success, the mode of transportation fell by the wayside. Nevertheless, this great mechanic patented his motorized bike and it became the first production of a booming industry.

The mechanical revolution at the turn of the century was responsible for many of the technological advances that modernized this country. Although it always had been at the fringes of the phenomenal boom in vehicle manufacture, the motorcycle had its share of ingenious inventors. Four-wheel production was the focus of most engineering interest and the first motorcycles were nothing more than adapted bicycles. They were volatile, bumpy and required a great deal of effort. But when the Werner Brothers improved the design with an inframe engine and replaced the pedals with a transmission, they created the sport of motorcycling. The hobby has a huge following for collectibles and antiques, as well as for restored and running tourers.

YEAR	MODEL/ENGINE	G	E	YEAR	MODEL/ENGINE	G	E
AJS				1947	Red Hunter		
1916	V Twin	7000	10000		500 Twin	3000	4000
1925	V Twin	3000	5000	1948	RH 500cc	2500	3000
1949	7R	10000	14000	1950	Square Four 1000	5000	8000
1955	500 Single	3000	4000	1951	Square Four	4000	8000
1959	Model 16 MA	800	1200	1955	Square Four	5000	12000
ARIEL				1956	Hunter 500cc		
1930	Ariel	6000	12000		Single	2500	3000
1946	21 c.i.	2000	3000	1957	Square Four	5000	12000
				1957	Square Four II	5000	12000
				1958	Square Four	5000	12000

BMW

The Bavarian Motor Works have been manufacturing high quality, advanced technology motorcycles since the 1920s. They developed and perfected the twin cylinder, horizontally opposed engine in the early days, later innovating their quiet, powerful transverse flat engine.

YEAR	MODEL/ENGINE	G	E	YEAR	MODEL/ENGINE	G	E
1942	R75M	10000	15000	1957	R50,		
1951	R67	3000	4000		500cc	2000	3500
1955	R67 Three			1961	R26	1500	2500
	with sidecar	10000	15000	1961	R50	5000	8000

YEAR	MODEL/ENGINE	G	E
1961	TR500 with Steib sidecar	4000	8000
1962	R60 with Steib sidecar	15000	20000
1962	R69S	3000	4000
1963	R69S	2000	3000
1964	R27, 2500cc single	2000	3000
1964	R69S	3000	4000
1965	R69S	6000	8000
1965	R80/7	3000	4000
1966	R27	3500	5000
1966	Thumper R27	3500	5000
1967	Combi R60, 600cc	7000	10000
1967	Combi R60 with sidecar	9000	14000
1967	R27	5000	7000
1967	R60 with Steib sidecar	12000	16000
1967	Thumper R27, 250cc single	6000	8000
1968	R60 Twin	6000	8000
1968	R69S with Watsonian sidecar	10000	15000
1968	R69US	7000	10000
1969	R27	4000	6000
1969	R27LS	6000	8000
1969	R60US, 600cc	6000	8000
1969	R69S	4000	6000
1969	R60S European	8000	12000
1969	R69US	7000	10000
1969	R69US with Spirit of America sidecar	3000	4000
1970	R60US, 600cc	6000	8000
1970	R69S	2000	3000
1979	R100RT	9000	14000

BROUGH

YEAR	MODEL/ENGINE	G	E
1931	Superior	8000	12000
1933	Superior SS100	10000	15000
1938	Superior V-Twin	6000	8000

B.S.A.

YEAR	MODEL/ENGINE	G	E
1939	M20	3000	4000
1947	Twin, 500cc	8000	12000
1955	A10, 650cc	1200	1800
1955	B33, 500cc	2000	2500
1955	Goldstar, 500cc, single	4000	6000
1956	Goldstar DBD	1500	2000
1956	Goldstar 350	4000	6000
1958	Road Rocket	1500	2000
1958	Goldstar, DBD-34	3000	4000
1960	Goldstar 500cc	5000	7000
1960	Goldstar Clubman	6000	8000
1961	Goldstar Clubman	11000	16000
1965	Victor 441cc Street	1000	1500
1966	Bantam	1500	2000
1966	Lightning	3000	4000
1966	Super Bantam	1200	1700
1967	Lightning 650	2000	3000
1967	Shooting Star 441	1500	2000
1968	250cc	1200	1800
1968	Firebird Scrambler	2000	3000
1968	Hornet 650	1500	2000
1968	Lightning 650cc	3500	4500
1968	Victor 441	1000	1600
1969	Rocket Three	3000	4000
1969	Thunderbolt, 650cc	2000	3000
1969	Victor 441cc	1500	2500
1970	Rocket-3	3000	4000
1970	Starfire, 250cc	1000	1500
1970	Victor 441	1500	2000
1970	Victor 441 Special	2000	3000
1971	750cc	1000	1500
1972	B50ss Goldstar	1500	2000
1972	Goldstar	1200	1800
1972	Lightning 650	2000	3000

HARLEY DAVIDSON

Harley Davidson is now and has always been a top name in motorcycle manufacturing. The ponderous, patrician V twin engine has sustained thousands of heavy touring models with power, comfort, and smoothness. They started in 1903 with a 2 h.p. single cylinder engine, and built an empire that no economic downturn has been able to stifle. They bought out their arch rival, Indian, in the early seventies, ceasing one of the most avid and interesting industrial competitions in the 20th century.

YEAR	MODEL/ENGINE	G	E	YEAR	MODEL/ENGINE	G	E
1912	Single	6000	9000	1941	VL80 with sidecar, 4 cyl.	10000	15000
1916	Twin	7000	10000	1942	Flathead 75 with sidecar	12000	18000
1918	Cleveland Single	15000	20000	1942	Fulldress 74 c.i. with sidecar	8000	13000
1918	Twin Magneto with sidecar	17000	22000	1942	Model XA	5000	7000
1924	JD with sidecar	4000	6500	1942	VL, 74 c.i.	10000	15000
1925	JD with sidecar	12000	16000	1942	XA opposed cylinder	4000	6000
1929	Single	12000	16000	1945	Flathead 74 c.i. with sidecar	11000	16000
1930	VL	4000	6000	1945	Solo Civilian	6000	8000
1931	VL	4000	6000	1946	Flathead 74 with sidecar, 4 cyl., 3-speed	14000	20000
1932	VL	3000	5000	1946	"45" Solo	6000	8000
1933	VL	6000	8000	1946	Knucklehead 61 c.i.	7500	10000
1933	45	6000	8000	1946	Three-wheeler, 45 c.i.	4000	7000
1934	VL	7500	11000	1946	WL-45	4000	7000
1935	74VLD	11000	14000	1947	Knucklehead 1200cc	13000	19000
1936	VL-TT with Snoop sidecar	10000	15000	1947	Servicar	4000	6000
1937	74VL, Flathead	6000	8000	1947	Three-wheeler	9000	14000
1937	Deluxe 74	9000	14000	1947	VL74	8000	11000
1938	EL	6000	8000	1947	WL45	7000	10000
1939	Flathead 45	10000	15000	1948	Dresser 610HV	7000	10000
1939	Flathead 74	8000	12000	1948	FL	8000	12000
1940	Knucklehead 61 EL	14000	19000	1948	Hummer, 125cc	1500	2000
1940	45	4000	6000	1948	Knucklehead	12000	18000
1940	61"	15000	20000	1948	Panhead, 61 c.i.	8000	13000
1941	Dresser with sidecar 74 c.i.	10000	15000	1948	Panhead with sidecar	11000	16000
1941	Fl with sidecar	13000	18000				
1941	Knucklehead 74 with sidecar	18000	24000				
1941	45	4000	6000				

YEAR	MODEL/ENGINE	G	E
1948	Three-wheeler	8000	13000
1948	WL45	6000	10000
1949	Hummer, 125cc	1500	2000
1949	Knucklehead	11000	16000
1949	Panhead	8000	12000
1949	Servicycle	6000	9000
1949	Three-wheeler 74	3000	5000
1950	Saviour Chopper	10000	15000
1950	WL45 Solo	6000	8000
1951	45 c.i.	11000	16000
1951	61 c.i.	12000	18000
1952	Hummer	2000	3000
1952	Model K	3000	4000
1954	Hummer, 125cc	800	1200
1954	Norton Special	6000	8000
1954	Three-wheeler police bike	5000	7000
1955	FL	4000	6000
1956	Hydraglide	2000	3000
1956	K Model	4000	6000
1956	Panhead with sidecar	9000	14000
1957	FLH Dresser	8000	12000
1957	VL74	7000	10000
1958	Duoglide	7000	10000
1958	Electraglide Flathead	8000	11000
1958	Flathead	7000	10000
1959	Panther with sidecar	7000	10000
1959	Superglide, panhead	4000	6000
1960	Duoglide Dresser with Chrome	8000	12000
1960	Dresser	8500	13000
1960	Flathead	8500	13000
1960	RR250	3000	5000
1960	Sportster	7000	10000
1961	Duoglide	8000	12000
1961	FLH Wideglide 1200cc	8000	12000
1961	Servicar	7000	10000
1962	Duoglide	5000	8000
1962	Harley Topper	1500	2000
1962	Sportster XLH	3000	5000
1963	H Model	6000	9000
1963	Sprint H, 250cc	850	1300
1964	Duoglide	8000	12000
1964	Duoglide Chopper	5000	8000
1964	FLH 1200 Dresser	15000	20000
1964	FLH Panhead	5000	8000
1964	Servicar police special, 3 wheel	4000	8000
1964	Sprint	2000	3000
1965	Sidecar with fittings	3000	5000
1965	Three-wheeler police special	4000	8000
1966	Electraglide	10000	15000
1967	Police Special	3000	6000
1968	Electraglide dresser	2000	3000
1968	Three-wheeler police special	4000	8000
1969	Electraglide	15000	20000
1969	Three-wheeler, 750cc	3000	5000
1970	Dresser	12000	18000
1970	Wideglide	13000	19000
1972	Sportster	8000	12000
1973	Harley Servicar	4000	8000
1978	Flathead 4100	10000	15000
1979	Dresser	17000	22000
1979	XLCH	12000	18000
1981	Milwaukee Sportster	10000	15000

HENDERSON

YEAR	MODEL/ENGINE	G	E
1924	Deluxe with sidecar	15000	20000
1928	KJ	11000	17000
1929	KJ Streamline	4000	6000
1931	Four	7000	10000

INDIAN

Indian motorcycles were created by Oscar Hedstrom and George Hendee. In 1901, the Hendee Manufacturing Company produced its first single cylinder 1¾ h.p. motorcycle. The horsepower doubled within five years, setting the fast pace for technological advances that Indian maintained for decades. Their bikes were an instant success, and the company ran neck and neck with Harley Davidson from those first days.

YEAR	MODEL/ENGINE	G	E	YEAR	MODEL/ENGINE	G	E
1911	Single belt	8000	12000	1939	Four	15000	20000
1913	Excelsior	7000	10000	1939	Knuckles	7000	10000
1913	Single	9000	14000	1939	Scout	9000	14000
1915	Motorbike	3000	4000	1940	Four	11000	17000
1917	Twin	9000	14000	1940	Knuckle	7000	10000
1918	Cleveland			1940	Scout	3000	5000
	single	8000	13000	1941	Chief	2000	3500
1923	Chief, 74 c.i.	4000	6000	1941	Four	18000	24000
1923	Scout	4500	7000	1941	Military	15000	20000
1923	Scout "45"	7000	10000	1941	Scout 101, 4 cyl.	12000	16000
1924	Chief	7500	12000	1941	Scoutsport	4000	6000
1925	Henderson			1941	Touring	30000	38000
	Deluxe	9000	14000	1941	V Twin	8000	12000
1926	Chief			1941	Woodsman,		
	1200ccs with				4 cyl.	20000	30000
	Princess			1941	Chief with		
	sidecar	7500	12000		sidecar,		
1926	With Princess				1200cc	15000	20000
	sidecar	10000	15000	1942	Chief	3000	5000
1927	Chief with			1942	Four	16000	22000
	sidecar	8000	13000	1942	Scout	4000	6500
1927	Four with			1942	WLA	3000	4000
	sidecar	6500	11000	1942	WLD	8500	13000
1928	Four 401	9000	14000	1942	Woodsman,		
1930	4 cyl.	8000	13000		4 cyl.	12000	16000
1931	Scout 101	12000	18000	1945	74	4000	6000
1932	Pony Scout	12000	16000	1946	Chief	9000	14000
1933	Pony Scout	8000	12000	1946	U	4000	6000
1934	UL 4 cyl.	7000	10000	1946	UL	4000	6000
1935	Chief	6000	8000	1947	Bonneville 74	5000	8000
1936	Chief	12000	16000	1947	Chief, 4 cyl.	8000	12000
1936	Four	9000	14000	1947	Chief, Starkelite		
1937	Chief, 1200cc	9000	14000		eng.	7500	11000
1937	Junior Scout	8000	12000	1947	CZ	2000	3000
1937	Sport Scout	4500	6500	1947	WLD	1500	2500
1937	UL4	18000	23000	1948	Chief	15000	20000
1938	Chief, 4 cyl.	12000	16000	1948	Flathead	7000	10000
1938	Four	15000	20000	1949	Scout, 426cc	4000	6000
1938	Scout	7000	10000	1949	Scout twin		
1939	Dispatch	2000	3000		sport	4000	6000

YEAR	MODEL/ENGINE	G	E	YEAR	MODEL/ENGINE	G	E
1949	Springfield Scout	7000	10000	1955	Endfield Woodsman	1000	2000
1949	Warrior	2000	3000	1955	Woodsman, 500cc	1200	1600
1950	HD Three-Wheeler	8000	12000	1959	Endfield Chief	3000	4000
1951	Chief 80	7500	11000	1960	Chief	3000	4000
1951	Dispatch	18000	25000	1960	Scout Special	3500	5000
1951	Warrior II	4000	7000	1960	Shoveltop	7500	11000
1952	Brave, 4 cyl.	4000	7000	1961	Flathead	8500	13000
1952	Enfield	6000	8000	1964	45 c.i. H.D. Chopper	3000	5000
1953	Chief, 80 c.i.	7000	10000	1967	FLH	6000	8000
1953	Woodsman 80	8500	9500	1970	Vello	6500	8500

TRIUMPH

Triumph is one of the earliest and most successful English racing motorcycle manufacturers. They have built a reputation on year after year of technical inventions aimed at increasing power.

YEAR	MODEL/ENGINE	G	E	YEAR	MODEL/ENGINE	G	E
1907	Triumph	10000	15000	1969	Richman Trident 4 Speed	4500	7000
1920	Model H	6000	8000	1969	Trident 750cc	3000	4000
1921	Baby	2000	3500	1969	Trophy 250	1500	2000
1955	Triumph T110	3000	4500	1970	Bonneville, 650cc	5000	7000
1956	T110	3200	5000	1973	Hurricane TRX, 750cc	7000	10000
1959	T110, 650cc	15000	20000	1974	Trident, 750cc	2000	3000
1963	5TA twin	4000	6000	1978	Bonneville 750	4500	7000
1966	GT Thunderbird	1500	2500	1979	Bonneville 750	5000	7500
1966	Tr6SR	2500	3500				
1967	Bonneville 650	4000	6000		**VELOCETTE**		
1967	Mountain Cub, 800cc	1500	2000	1952	Velocette, 350cc	4000	6000
1968	Richman Trident	4000	6000	1956	350	2000	3000
1968	Tr6, 650cc	3000	4000	1963	Endurance	4000	6000
1968	X-75 Hurricane	6000	8000	1967	Thruxton	7000	10000
1969	Hurricane	7000	10000	1969	Thruxton Scrambler	9500	14000
				1970	Thruxton	8000	12000

VINCENT

The Vincent Motorcycle Manufacturing Company was known from its first days as the makers of a well-engineered, fast and expensive product. Some of the Black Shadow series command the top collector dollar in this lucrative market.

YEAR	MODEL/ENGINE	G	E	YEAR	MODEL/ENGINE	G	E
1942	Comet, Series C	11000	17000	1949	HRD Radide, 1000cc	8000	12000
1948	Black Lightning	32000	40000	1950	Black Shadow, Series A	12000	18000
1948	Black Shadow, Series A	6000	9000	1950	Black Shadow, Series B	12000	18000
1948	Black Shadow, Series B	14000	20000	1951	Black Shadow	15000	20000
1948	Model B Rapide	12000	18000	1951	Comet	12000	18000
1949	Black Shadow	11000	17000	1956	Black Shadow	8000	12000

COLLECTOR CAR CLUBS

Penn-Ohio **A Ford** Club, Inc.
139 E. Main St.
Shelby, OH 44875

The **Abarth** Register
1298 Birch St.
Uniondale, NY 11553

AC Owners Club
11955 S.W. Faircrest St.
Portland, OR 97225

Airflow Club of America
1000 Tallmadge Ave.
Akron, OH 44310

Airflow Club of America
2029 Minoru Dr.
Altadena, CA 91001

Alfa Romeo Owners Club
2468 Gum Tree Lane
Fallbrook, CA 92028

Allante Appreciation Group
2558 Ingram Rd.
Duluth, GA 30136

Alvis Owners Club—N. America
P.O. Box 46—146 Race St.
Bainbridge, PA 17502

AMC Rambler Club
2645 Aston Rd.
Cleveland, OH 44118

AMC Pacer Club
2628 Queenstown Rd.
Cleveland Heights, OH 44118

AMC Rambler Club
2645 Ashton Rd.
Cleveland Heights, OH 44118

AMC World Clubs, Inc.
7963 Depew St.
Arvada, CO 80003

American Austin/Bantam Club
Rt. 1, Box 137—351 Wilson Rd.
Willshire, OH 45898

American Motors Owners Assoc.
2836 Hundred Oaks Ave.
Baton Rouge, LA 70808

American Motors Owners Assoc.
6756 Cornell St.
Portage, MI 49002

Amercian Truck Historical Society
201 Office Park Dr.
Birmingham, AL 35223

Amphibious Auto Club of America
3281 Elk Ct.
Yorktown Heights, NY 10598

National **Amphicar** Club
13 Bluebird Lane
Gloversville, NY 12078

AMX Club
1135 Bloomfield Rd.
San Pedro, CA 90732

AMX Club, Classic International
501 Indian Terrace
Rockford, IL 61103

Southern California Classic **AMX** Club
1135 Bloomwood Rd.
San Pedro, CA 90732

Classic **AMX** Club International
7963 Depew St.
Arvada, CO 80003

Classic **AMX** Registry
21 Creek Rd.
Dauphin, PA 17018

Anglia Obsolete
1311 York Dr.
Vista, CA 92084

Antique Automobile Club of
    America (AACA)
501 W. Governor Rd.
P.O. Box 417
Hershey, PA 17033

Antique Motor Club of Greater
    Baltimore, Inc.
208 Brightside Ave.
Pikesville, MD 21208

Antique Motorcycle Club
Lake Ave.
Harrisonville, NJ 08039

Antique Riders
Rt. 1, 202 Tenth St.
Locksport, LA 70374

Arkansas Traveler Antique Auto Club
7521 Gable Dr.
Little Rock, AR 72205

Armstrong Siddeley Club of America
1906 W. Spruce St.
Orange, CA 92668

Aston Martin Owners Club
USA Centre
Atlanta, GA 30327

Atlantic Coast Old Timers
4 Elm Dr.
Newton, CT 06470

Auburn Cord Duesenberg
18 Poplar Rd.
Ringoes, NJ 08551

Auburn Cord Duesenburg
963 W. Hathaway Rd.
Harbor Springs, MI 49740

Quattro Club (**Audi**)
7700 Quattro Dr.
Chanhassen, MN 55317

Austin/Bantam Car Club
1104 Beechwood Dr.
Hagerstown, MD 21740

Austin Healey Club of America, Inc.
603 E. Euclid Ave.
Arlington Heights, IL 60004

Austin Healey Club Pacific Centre, Inc.
P.O. Box 6267
San Jose, CA 95150

Austin Healey Sports & Touring Club
P.O. Box 3539
York, PA 17402

Austin Works East
359 N. Union St.
Kennet Square, PA 19348

Automobilists of the Upper Hudson
    Valley, Inc.
Drawer G
Clarksville, NY 12041

Avanti Owners Assoc.
7840 Michelle Dr.
La Mesa, CA 92041

Avanti Owners Assoc.
P.O. Box 28788
Dallas, TX 75228

Avanti Owners Assoc. International
P.O. Box 322
Uxbridge, MA 01569

Total Performance **Avanti** Club
1511 19th Ave.
Bradenton, FL 34205

Pacific **Bantam Austin** Club
12304 Lambert Ave.
El Monte, CA 91732

Barracuda Owners Club
167 Clarence St.
Torrington, CT 06790

Bentley Drivers Club—Western
Region USA
2139 Torrey Pines Rd.
La Jolla, CA 92007

Berkeley Register
P.O. Box 162282
Austin, TX 78716

BMW 507 Club USA
Hilltown Pike
Hilltown, PA 18927

BMW Automobile Club of America
Box 401
Hollywood, CA 90028

BMW Car Club of America
2130 Massachusetts Ave.
Cambridge, MA 02140

BMW Car Club of America
345 Harvard St.
Cambridge, MA 02138

BMW Vintage Club of America, Inc.
P.O. Box S
San Rafael, CA 94903

BMW Vintage Club of America, Inc.
148 Linden St.
Wellesley, MA 02181

Borgward Owners Club
77 New Hampshire Ave.
Bay Shore, NY 11706

Bricklin International
4815 Garden Brook Lane
Orlando, FL 32809

Bricklin International Owners Club
P.O. Box 310
Cedar Ridge, CA 95924

Bricklin International Owners Club
20 Bradford St.
New Providence, NJ 07974

Organization of **Bricklin** Owners
P.O. Box 24775
Rochester, NY 14624

Bristol Owners Club
P.O. Box 60
Brooklandville, MD 21022

The American **British Cab Society**
4470 Cerritos Ave.
Long Beach, CA 90807

Brough Superior Club
Box 393
Cos Cob, CT 06807

Brougham Owners Assoc.
P.O. Box 254
Berea, OH 44017

Brougham Owners Assoc.
829 W. Wesley Rd.
Atlanta, GA 30327

Brush Owners Assoc.
67 Rockland Ave.
Larchmont, NY 10538

American **Bugatti** Club
4484 Howe Hill Rd.
Camden, ME 04843

1932 **Buick** Registry
3000 Warren Rd.
Indiana, PA 15701

1937–38 **Buick** Club
1005 Rilma Lane
Los Altos, CA 94022

1950 **Buick** Registry
54 Madison St.
Pequannock, NJ 07440

1966–67 **Buick** Riviera Directory
Box 825
Dearborn, MI 48121

Buick Club of America
P.O. Box 401927
Hesperia, CA 92340

Buick Club of America
P.O. Box 898
Garden Grove, CA 92642

New **Buick GN/T**-Type Assoc.
14305 S.E. Johnson Rd.
Milwaukie, OR 97267

Buick GS Club of America
1213 Gornto Rd.
Valdosta, GA 31602

1953–54 **Buick Skylark** Club
P.O. Box 57
Eagle Bay, NY 13331

International **Bus** Collectors
18 Lambert Ave.
Lynn, MA 01902

Motor **Bus** Society
P.O. Box 251
Paramus, NJ 07653

1958 Cadillac Owners Assoc.
P.O. Box 850029
Braintree, MA 02185

Cadillac Convertible Owners of
America
P.O. Box 269
Ossining, NY 10562

Cadillac Drivers Club
5825 Vista Ave.
Sacramento, CA 95824

Cadillac LaSalle Club, Inc.
3340 Poplar Dr.
Warren, MI 48091

Cadillac-LaSalle Club, Inc.
223 S. Fairfield Rd.
Devon, PA 19333

Cadillac Single Cylinder Registry
18714 N.E. Halsey
Portland, OR 97230

Association of **California Car** Clubs
13272 Rainbow St.
Garden Grove, CA 92643

Camaro Owners of America
701 N. Keyser Ave.
Scranton, PA 18508

International **Camaro** Club, Inc.
2001 Pittson Ave.
Scranton, PA 18505

U.S. **Camaro** Club
P.O. Box 608167
Orlando, FL 32860

Capri Car Club Ltd.
P.O. Box 111221
Aurora, CO 80042

Capri Club
422 Bradrick Dr.
San Leandro, CA 94578

J.I. **Case** Collectors' Assoc., Inc.
Rt. 2, Box 242
Vinton, OH 45686

Chalmers Automobile Registry
110 Sourwood Dr.
Hatboro, PA 19040

Checker Car Club of America
15536 Sky Hawk Dr.
Sun City West, AZ 85375

National **Chevelle** Owners Assoc.
7343-j W. Friendly Ave.
Greensboro, NC 27410

1965–66 Full Size **Chevrolet** Club
15615 State Rd. 23
Granger, IN 46530

National Assoc. of **Chevrolet** Owners
P.O. Box 9879
Bowling Green, KY 42102

Vintage **Chevrolet** Club of America
P.O. Box 5387
Orange, CA 92613

Bow Tie **Chevy** Assoc.
P.O. Box 608108
Orlando, FL 32860

Chevy Club
19493 Meekland Ave.
Hayward, CA 94541

Chevy Club National Classic
P.O. Box 17188
Orlando, FL 32860

Chevy Owners Assoc.
157 Coram-Mt. Sinai Rd.
Coram, NY 11727

Late Great **Chevys** Club
P.O Box 607824
Orlando, FL 32860

The National **Chevy** Assoc.
947 Arcade St.
St. Paul, MN 55106

Tri-**Chevy** Assoc.
24862 Ridge Rd.
Elwood, IL 60421

Chrysler 300 Club, Inc.
P.O. Box 6613
Texarkana, TX 75501

Chrysler 300 Club International
4900 Jonesville Rd.
Jonesville, MI 49250

Chrysler 300 Club International, Inc.
19 Donegal Ct.
Ann Arbor, MI 48105

Chrysler Product Club
3768 De Garmo
Sylmar, CA 91342

Chrysler Maserati TC Registry
P.O. Box 66813
Chicago, IL 60666

Chrysler Product Owners Club, Inc.
1506 Wheaton Lane
Silver Spring, MD 20902

Chrysler Town & Country Owners
    Register
4500 E. Speedway, Suite 22
Tucson, AZ 85712

National **Chrysler** Products Club
14 Princeton Dr.
New Providence, NJ 07974

Walter P. **Chrysler** Club
Box 4706
N. Hollywood, CA 91607

Citroen Car Club
P.O. Box 743
Hollywood, CA 90078

Citroen Concours of America
8180 Miramar Rd.
San Diego, CA 92126

Citroen Quarterly
P.O. Box 30, Hanover Station
Boston, MA 02113

Classic Car Club of America
1645 Des Plaines River Rd., Suite 7
Des Plaines, IL 60018

Club Elite
6238 Ralston Ave.
Richmond, CA 94805

Club Elite of N. America
17053 Paulette Place
Granada Hills, CA 91344

Cobra Jet Registry
6890 Plainfield Rd.
Dearborn, MI 48127

Cole Motor Car Club of America
4716 Northeastern Ave.
Indianapolis, IN 46239

Connecticut Council of Car Clubs
1195 Dunbar Hill Rd.
Hamden, CT 06514

Connecticut Historical Automobile
    Society
149 Jennifer Rd.
Hamden, CT 06514

Contemporary Historical Vehicle
    Assoc., Inc.
P.O. Box 98
Tecumseh, KS 66542

Contemporary Autos of South Oregon
450 W. Pine
Central Point, OR 95701

Contemporary Historical Vehicle
    Assoc., Inc.
P.O. Box 40, Dept. VAA
Antioch, TN 37013

Continental MK II Owners Assoc.
17230 Oldenberg Rd.
Apple Valley, CA 92307

Colorado Linc-Cont **Convertible** Club
14180 Foothill Circle
Golden, CO 80401

Hoosier **Convertible** Club, Inc.
6419 S. Woodwind Dr.
Indianapolis, IN 46217

Pacific N.W. **Convertible** Club
40400 N.E. Larch Mountain Rd.
Corbett, OR 97019

Southern California **Convertible** Club
P.O. Box 784
Vista, CA 92083

Convertibles of Houston
107 E. John Alber
Houston, TX 77037

Cooper Car Club
14 Biscayne Dr.
Ramsey, NJ 07446

Central Pa. **Corvair** Club
1751 Chesley Rd.
York, PA 17403

Corvair Society of America
P.O. Box 2488
Pensacola, FL 32503

Corvair Society of America
P.O. Box 607
Lemont, IL 60439

Lakewood-Monza Group (**Corvair**)
1306 Friar Rd.
Newark, DE 19713

Milwaukee **Corvair** Club
2523 E. Armour Ave.
Milwaukee, WI 53207

State **Corvair** Club
415 E. Bryan St.
Bryan, OH 43506

Cascade **Corvette** Club
P.O. Box 363
Eugene, OR 97440

Corvette Club-N.C.O.A.
P.O. Box 111
Falls Church, VA 22046

Corvette Club of America
P.O. Box 3355
Gaithersburg, MD 20885

LT-1 **Corvette** Registy
25 Lido Blvd.
Lido Beach, NY 11561

Miami **Corvette** Association
249 Lafayette Dr.
Miami Springs, FL 33166

National **Corvette** Owners Association
404 S. Maple Ave.
Falls Church, VA 22046

National **Corvette** Restorers Society
6291 Day Rd.
Cincinnati, OH 45247

National Council of **Corvette** Clubs
P.O. Box 5032
Lafayette, IN 47903

National Council of **Corvette** Clubs
P.O. Box 325
Troy, OH 45373

Six-Cylinder **Corvette** Club
1512 Bellmore Ave.
Bellmore, NY 11710

Straight-Axle **Corvette** Enthusiasts
P.O. Box 2288
N. Highlands, CA 95660

Vintage **Corvette** Club of America
P.O. Box 325, Box T
Troy, OH 45373

Corvette ZR-1 Registry
29 Lucille Dr.
Sayville, NY 11782

Cougar Club of America
0-4211 N. 120th Ave.
Holland, MI 49424

Cougar Owners Club
1526 Ericson Place
Bronx, NY 10461

Crosley Automobile Club
4825 Ridge Rd. E.
Williamson, NY 14289

Crosley Automobile Club
217 N. Gilbert
Iowa City, IA 52245

Crown Victoria Assoc.
P.O. Box 226
Bryan, OH 43506

DAF Club USA
293 Hudson St.
Hackensack, NJ 07601

Datsun Owners Assoc.
12966 Crowley St.
Arleta, CA 91331

Datsun Roadster Owners Club
P.O. Box 60997
Pasadena, CA 91116

United 510 Owners (**Datsun**)
3780 Starr King
Palo Alto, CA 94306

Windy City Z Club (**Datsun**)
1419 Adams St.
Lake in the Hills, IL 60102

Daytona Superbird Assoc.
120 Bradshaw Ave.
Hendersonville, NC 28739

Daytona Superbird Auto Club
13717 W. Green Meadow
New Berlin, WI 53151

De Vaux Registry
240 Greenridge N.W.
Grand Rapids, MI 49504

DeLorean Club International
P.O. Box 23040
Seattle, WA 98102

DeLorean Owners Assoc.
879 Randolph Rd.
Santa Barbara, CA 93111

DeSoto Club of America
105 E. 96th St.
Kansas City, MO 64114

National **DeSoto** Club, Inc.
1521 Van Cleave Rd. N.W.
Albuquerque, NM 87107

Diamond T Register
P.O. Box 1657
St. Cloud, MN 56302

DKW Club of America
260 Santa Margarita Ave.
Menlo Park, CA 94025

Dodge Brothers Club, Inc.
P.O. Box 151
N. Salem, NY 10560

Matko Early **Dodge** Club
Rt. 1, Box 88
Nardin, OK 74646

T/A-ARR Special Interest Auto Club
  (**Dodge**)
P.O. Box 30022
Columbus, OH 43230

Duluth Special Interest Car Club
1411 Ecklund Ave.
Duluth, MN 55811

Durango Old Car Club
215 Riverview Dr.
Durango, CO 81301

Eastern Upper Peninsula Antique
  Auto Club
905 McCandless St.
Sault Ste. Marie, MI 49783

Arizona **Edsel** Club
8324 E. Via Dorado
Scottsdale, AZ 85258

Edsel Owners Club, Inc.
West Liberty, IL 62475

Edsel Owners Club, Inc.
4713 Queal Dr.
Shawnee, KS 66203

International **Edsel** Club
P.O. Box 371
Sully, IA 50251

International **Edsel** Club
P.O. Box 86
Polo, IL 61064

Elva Owners of America
318 Adrian
Berea, OH 44017

The **Erkine** Register
441 E. St. Clair
Almont, MI 48003

Tri-State **F-100's**
2510 Minton Rd.
Hamilton, OH 45013

Fairlane Club of America
2116 Manville Rd.
Muncie, IN 47302

Fairlane Club of America
721 Drexel Ave.
Drexel Hill, PA 19026

Falcon Club of America
P.O. Box 113
Jacksonville, AR 72078

Ferrari Club of America
P.O. Box 720597
Atlanta, GA 30358

Ferrari Owners Club
20850 Leapwood Street, Suite L
Carson, CA 90746

Ferrari Owners Club
15910 Ventura Blvd.#1201
Encino, CA 91436

Ferrari Owners Club
7364 El Cajon Blvd.#103A
San Diego, CA 92115

Fiat 600/600D Exchange Club
5220 Brittany Dr. S, Apt. 1406
St. Petersburgh, FL 33715

Fiat Club of America, Inc.
Union Square, P.O. Box 192
Somerville, MA 02143

Rear Engine **Fiat** Club
P.O. Box 682
Sun Valley, CA 91353

Topolino Register of N. America (**Fiat**)
3301 Shetland Rd.
Beavercreek, OH 45385

Fiat-Lancia Unlimited
P.O. Box 193
Shillington, PA 19607

Fiero Owners Club of America
2165 Dupont Circle, Unit 1
Anaheim, CA 92860

Fifty's Automobile Club of America
1114 Furman Dr.
Linwood, NJ 08221

National **Firebird** Club
Box 11238
Chicago, IL 60611

Flint Hills Antique Car Club
713 Commercial St.
Emporial, KA 66801

FoMoCo Owners Club
P.O. Box 19665
Denver, CO 80219

'49–'50 **Ford** Owners Assoc.
12204 43rd Ave.
S. Tukwila, WA 98178

'54 **Ford** Club of America
1517 N. Wilmot #144
Tucson, AZ 85712

'58 **Ford** Fairland Club
2911 Seton Dr.
Mattews, NC 28105

1930–31 **Ford** A Deluxe Phaeton Club
P.O. Box 20847
Castro Valley, CA 94646

Associated **Fords** of the '50s
P.O. Box 66161
Portland, OR 97266

Early V-8 **Ford** Club of America
P.O. Box 2122
San Leandro, CA 94577

Fabulous Fifties **Ford** Club of America
P.O. Box 286
Riverside, CA 92502

Ford Falcon Club
500 Ruxton Ave.
Spring Valley, CA 92077

Ford Falcon Club of America
629 N. Hospital Dr.
Jacksonville, AR 72076

Ford Falcon Club of San Diego
P.O. Box 33306
San Diego, CA 92103

Great Lakes Roadster Club (**Ford**)
P.O. Box 302
Bath, OH 44210

International **Ford** Retractable Club
P.O. Box 92
Jerseyville, IL 62052

International **Ford** Retractable Club
Box 389
Marlboro, MA 01752

Mid-Century **Ford** Club
6312 Marywood Rd.
Bethesda, MD 20034

Model A **Ford** Club of America
250 S. Cypress St.
La Habra, CA 90631

Model T **Ford** Club of America
P.O. Box 743936
Dallas, TX 75374

Nifty Fifties **Fords** of N. Ohio
P.O. Box 111
Macedonia, OH 44056

Performance **Ford** Club of America
P.O. Box 32
Ashville, OH 43101

Ford Galaxie Club of America
P.O. Box 2206
Bremerton, WA 98310

'49-'50-'51 **Ford/Mercury** Owners
P.O. Box 30647
Midwest City, OK 73140

Ford-Mercury Club of America
P.O. Box 3551
Hayward, CA 94540

Ford-Mercury Restorers Club
P.O. Box 2133
Dearborn, MI 48123

Special Interest **Fords** of the '50s
246 Silvercreek
Ducanville, TX 75137

Long Island **Ford/Mercury** Club
P.O. Box 336
Ronkonkoma, NY 11779

48 and Under Club
708 Water St.
Sauk City, WI 53583

Franklin Syndicate Auto Club
115 Lincoln Center
Stockton, CA 95207

H.H. **Franklin** Club
Cazenovia College
Cazenovia, NY 13035

Gadsden Antique Automobile Club
113 Buckingham Place
Gadsden, AL 35901

Gardner Automobile Register
341 Fitch Hill Rd.
Uncasville, CT 06382

Dual **Ghia** Owners Assoc.
29 Forgedale Rd.
Fleetwood, PA 19522

Graham Owners Club
P.O. Box 105
Burlington, MA 01803

Graham Owners Club International
5262 N.W. Westgate Rd.
Silverdale, WA 98383

Graham Vintage Auto Club
907 Brazos
Graham, TX 76046

Pontiac **Grand Prix** Chapter
357 Marvin Place
Wheeling, IL 60090

Great Autos of Yesteryear
P.O. Box 4
Yorba Linda, CA 92686

GT Torino
2911 Seton Dr.
Matthews, NC 28105

GTO Assoc. of America
5829 Stroebel Rd.
Saginaw, MI 48609

GTO Club of Wisconsin, Inc.
P.O. Box 18348
Milwaukee, WI 53218

Orginal **GTO** Club
P.O. Box 18438
Milwaukee, WI 53218

N. American **Heinkel & Trojan** Register
164 E. Crescent Pkwy.
S. Plainfield, NJ 07080

Heinkel-Messerschmitt-Isetta Club
P.O. Box 90
Topango, CA 90290

Early **Hemi** Assoc.
233 Rogue River Hwy., Suite 354
Grants Pass, OR 97527

National **Hemi** Owners Assoc.
1693 S. Reese Rd.
Reese, MI 48757

. National **Hemi** Owners Assoc.
7010 Darby Ave.
Reseda, CA 91335

Hispano Suiza Society
P.O. Box 688
Hayward, CA 94543

Hispano-Suiza Society
175 St. Germain Ave.
San Francisco, CA 94114

Historical Automobile Assoc., Inc.
P.O. Box 10313
Fort Wayne, IN 46851

Honda International
P.O. Box 242
Deptford, NJ 08096

Hondacar International
Box 242
Deptford, NJ 08096

Horseless Carriage Club of America
9031 E. Florence Ave.
Downey, CA 90240q

Horseless Carriage Club of America
128 S. Cypress St.
Orange, CA 92666

Hudson Essex Terraplane Club, Inc.
100 E. Cross
Ypsilanti, MI 48197

Hudson Essex Terraplane Club, Inc.
P.O. Box 715
Milford, IN 46542

Humpmobile Club, Inc.
Box AA
Rosemead, CA 91770

Hupmobile Club, Inc.
158 Pond Rd.
N. Franklin, CT 06254

Hurst 300 Registry
5844 W. Eddy St.
Chicago, IL 60634

IH Collectors
648 Northwest Hwy, Box 250
Park Ridge, IL 60068

National **Impala** Assoc.
P.O. Box 968
Spearfish, SD 57783

National **Impala** Assoc.
1752 South Blvd.
Idaho Falls, ID 83401

Classic Years **Imperial** Register
20 Creekline Dr.
Roswell, GA 30076

Imperial Owners Club International
P.O. Box 991-OC
Scranton, PA 18503

International Society for Vehicle
  Preservation
P.O. Box 50046
Tucson, AZ 85703

Iron Clad Cruising Club
665 Fairview Ave.
Piscataway, NJ 08854

Iso & Bizzarini Owners Club
2025 Drake Dr.
Oakland, CA 94611

Historic Registry of **Isotta Fraschini**
1001 Park Ave.
New York, NY 10028

Itasca Vintage Car Club, Inc.
P.O. Box 131
Grand Rapids, MI 55744

Classic **Jaguar** Assoc., Inc.
P.O. Box 61
Costa Messa, CA 92627

Jaguar Clubs of N. America
600 Willow Tree Rd.
Leonia, NJ 07605

Jaguar Owners Club, Inc.
1724 Dalton Rd.
Palos Verdes Estates, CA 90274

Sacramento **Jaguar** Club
1375 Exposition Blvd.
Sacramento, CA 95815

The **Jeep** Registry
172 Long Hill Rd.
Oakland, NJ 07436

Midstates **Jeepster** Assoc.
12700 W. Cortez Dr.
New Berlin, WI 53151

Assoc. of **Jensen** Owners
Rt. 7, Box 605
Morgantown, NC 28655

Jensen Interceptor Owners Club
5771 Trophy
Huntington Beach, CA 92649

Jensen-Healey Preservation Society
2950 Airway Ave., A-9
Costa Mesa, CA 92626

Jewette Owners Club
24005 Clawiter Rd.
Hayward, CA 94545

Jordan Register
5231 Stratford Ave.
Westminster, CA 92683

Judge Convertible Registry
1250 Brair St.
Wayzata, MN 55391

Judge GTO International
114 Prince George Dr.
Hampton, VA 23669

Kaiser-Darrin Owner's Roster
R.D. Box 36, Antram Rd.
Somerset, PA 15501

Kaiser-Frazer Owners Club, Inc.
P.O. Box 1251
Wellsville, NY 14895

King Midget International Car Club
385 Cavan Dr.
Pittsburgh, PA 15236

Kissel Kar Club
147 N. Rual St.
Hartford, WI 53027

The **Kurtis-Kraft** Register
Drawer 220
Oneonta, NY 13820

Lagonda Car Club U.S. Section
Ten Crestwood Trail
Sparta, NJ 07871

Lamborghini Owners Club
P.O. Box 7214
St. Petersburgh, FL 33734

American **Lancia** Club
723 Plainfield Ave.
Berkley Heights, NJ 07922

North Land **Late Eight** Chapter
6989 Ashwood Rd. 102
Woodbury, MN 55125

Les Amis De Panhard and Deutsch
    Bonnet
P.O. Box 1172
Mineda, FL 34755

Automobile **License Plate** Collectors
    Assoc., Inc.
P.O. Box 712
Weston, WV 26452

Light Commercial Vehicle Assoc.
Box 5211
Salem, OR 97304

Lincoln Owners Club
P.O. Box 1434
Minocqua, WI 54548

Lincoln Owners Club
P.O. Box 189
Algonquin, IL 60102

Lincoln Registry
Box 10075
Elmwood, CT 06110

Road Race **Lincoln** Register
91 Knollwood Rd.
Farmington, CT 06032

Lincoln Continental Owners Club
P.O. Box 549
Nogales, AZ 85621

Lincoln & Continental Owners Club
P.O. Box 157
Boring, OR 97009

Lincoln-Mercury Enthusiast
925 West St.
Tonganoxie, KS 66086

Lincoln Zephyr Owners Club
P.O. Box 16-5835
Miami, FL 33116

Lincoln Zephyr Owners Club
2107 Steinruck Rd.
Elizabethtown, PA 17022

Locomobile Society of America
3165 California St.
San Francisco, CA 94115

Club Elite (**Lotus**)
23999 Box Canyon Rd.
Canoga Park, CA 91304

Lotus LTD
P.O. Box L
College Park, MD 20741

Maine Obsolete Auto League
RFD 2, Box 307
Cumberland Center, ME 04021

Malone Auto Club
9 Finney Blvd.
Malone, NY 12953

Marlin Owners Club
Rd. 5, Box 187
Coatesville, PA 19320

Marmon Club
629 Orangewood Dr.
Dunedin, FL 33528

Marmon Club
3044 Gainsborough Dr.
Pasadena, CA 91107

Maserati Club of America
945 Middle Country Rd.
Selden, NY 11784

Maserati Information Exchange
P.O. Box 772
Mercer Island, WA 98040

Maserati Owners Club of N. America
Box 6554
Orange, CA 92667

Maxwell Registry
RD 4, Box 8
Ligonier, PA 15658

Maxwell Briscoe Registry
55 E. Golden Lake Rd.
Circle Pines, MN 55014

Mazda Club
P.O. Box 11238
Chicago, IL 60611

Mazda RX-7 Club
1774 S. Alvira St.
Los Angeles, CA 90035

McClean County Antique Auto Club
1340 E. Empire St.
Bloomington, IL 61701

Mercedes Benz 190SL Group
3 Westpark Court
Ferndale, MD 21061

Mercedes Benz Club of America
P.O. Box 9985
Colorado Springs, CO 80912

Mercedes Benz Club of America
954 Grand Maral
Grosse Point, MI 48230

Mercedes Gull Wing Group
2229 Via Cerritos
Palos Verdes, CA 90274

Mercer Associates
414 Lincoln Ave.
Havertown, PA 19083

70/71 **Mercury** Montego/Cyclone
   Registry
19 Glyn Dr.
Newark, DE 19713

Big M **Mercury** Club
5 Robinson Rd.
W. Woburn, MA 01801

International **Mercury** Owners Assoc.
6445 W. Grand Ave.
Chicago, IL 60635

Mercury Club of America
P.O. Box 3551
Hayward, CA 94540

Mid-Century **Mercury** Car Club
1816 E. Elmwood Dr.
Lindenhurst, IL 60046

Mid-Century **Mercury** Car Club
5707 35th Ave.
Kenosha, WI 53142

Messerschmitt Owners Club
39 Sylvan Way
W. Caldwell, NJ 07006

Metropolitan Owners Club
49 Carleton
Westbury, NY 11590

Metropolitan Owners Club of
   N. America
839 W. Race St.
Somerset, PA 15501

Metropolitan Owners Club of
   N. America
5009 Barton Rd.
Madison, WI 53711

Metz Chain Gang
63 Commercial St.
Honesdale, PA 18431

Classic **MG** Club
1307 Ridgecrest Rd.
Orlando, FL 32806

MG Car Club of N. America
P.O. Box 1446
Kellar, TX 76244

MG Vintage Racers
35 Laurel
Clifton, NJ 07012

Milwaukee & G.L. **MG** Motorcar Group
5235 N. Diversey Blvd.
Whitefish Bay, WI 53217

N. American **MG** Register
412 Whitree Lane
Chesterfield, MO 63017

New England **MG** T Register Ltd.
Drawer 220
Oneonta, NY 13820

Midwest **MGA** Club
11731 W. 101st St.
Overland Park, KS 66214

American **MGB** Assoc.
P.O. Box 11401
Chicago, IL 60611

N. American **MGB** Register
P.O. Box MGB
Akin, IL 62805

American **MGC** Register
12 Charles St.
Islip Terrace, NY 11752

Michigan License Plate Collectors
   Assoc.
601 Duchess Rd.
Milford, MI 48042

Microcar and Minicar Club
P.O. Box 43137
Upper Montclair, NJ 07043

Mid-American Old Time Auto Assoc.
Morriton, AR 72110

Mid-Mo Old Car Club
P.O. Box 1594
Jefferson City, MO 65102

Milestone Car Society
P.O. Box 50850
Indianapolis, IN 46250

Military Vehicle Collectors Club
P.O. Box 33697
Thornton, CA 80233

Military Vehicle Preservation Assoc.
P.O. Box 520378-T
Independence, MO 64052

Mini-Owners
100 Prince St.
Fairfield, CT 06430

Mitchell Roster
717 N. Main St.
Port Byron, IL 61275

Model A Ford Cabriolet Club
P.O. Box 515
Porter, TX 77365

Model A Ford Club of America
250 S. Cypress
La Habra, CA 90631

Model A Restorers Club
24800 Michigan Ave.
Dearborn, MI 48124

Model T Ford Club of America
P.O. Box 7400
Burbank, CA 91510

Model T Ford Club International
P.O. Box 915
Elgin, IL 60120

Model T Ford Club International, Inc.
P.O. Box 438315
Chicago, IL 60643

Model T Ford Owners of America
Box 1711
Oceanside, CA 92054

National **Monte Carlo** Owners Assoc.
P.O. Box 187
Independence, KY 41051

Moon Owners Registry
1600 N. Woodlawn
St. Louis, MO 63124

Mopar Muscle Club
4910 Leigh
Amarillo, TX 79110

Mopar Rapid Transit Club
10705 Old Beatly Ford
Rockwell, NC 28138

Morgan Car Club
616 Gist Ave.
Silver Spring, MD 20910

Morgan Three-Wheeler Club
1432 Yale St. #6
Santa Monica, CA 90404

Morgan Three-Wheeler Club
1490 Francisco
San Francisco, CA 94123

Morris Minor Registry
P.O. Box 6848
Stanford, CT 94305

Morris Minor Registry of N. America
318 Hampton Park
Westerville, OH 43081

1982–'93 **Mustang** GT Registry
6582 N.W. 56th St.
Johnston, IA 50131

1984 GT 350 **Mustang** National Owners
Assoc.
P.O. Box 318
Mt. Airy, GA 30563

1985 **Mustang** GT Convertible Registry
4311 John Goff Rd.
Watervliet, MI 49098

Late Model **Mustang** Owners Assoc.
P.O. Box 2526
Dearborn, MI 48123

Mustang & Classic Ford Club of New
England
P.O. Box 963
North Attleboro, MA 02761

Mustang Club of America
P.O. Box 447
Lithonia, GA 30058

Mustang Club of Southern California
15168 Ashwood Lane
Chino, CA 91710

Mustang Collector Club
850 Pershing
Jonesboro, LA 71251

Mustang Owners of California
P.O. Box 7321
Van Nuys, CA 91409

Mustang Owners Club International
2720 Tennessee N.E.
Albuquerque, NM 87110

National Capital Region **Mustang** Club
7602 Mineral Spring
Springfield, VA 22153

1935–'36 **Nash** Register
2412 Lincoln Ave.
Alameda, CA 94551

C.W. **Nash** Assoc.
2412 Lincoln Ave.
Alameda, CA 94501

Nash Car Club of America
P.O. Box 80279
Indianapolis, IN 46280

Nash Car Club of America
111 McCormick
Bel Air, MD 21014

Nash Club of America
Rt. 1, Box 253
Clinton, IA 52732

Nash Metropolitan Club
2244 Cross St.
La Canada, CA 91011

Nash-Healey Car Club International
530 Edgewood Ave.
Trafford, PA 15085

National Classic Half Ton Club
1141 S. Lewis Ave.
Tulsa, OK 74104

National **409** Club
2510 E. 14th St.
Long Beach, CA 90804

National Nomad Club
P.O. Box 606
Arvada, CO 80002

National Panel Delivery Club
4002 1/2 Hermitage
Richmond, VA 23227

Chevrolet **Nomad** Assoc.
8653 W. Hwy. 2
Cairo, NE 68824

National Nostalgic **Nova**
P.O. Box 2344
York, PA 17405

NSU Club of America
717 N. 68th St.
Seattle, WA 98103

NSU Enthusiasts USA
2909 Utah Place
Alton, IL 62002

Henry **Nyberg** Society
17822 Chicago Ave.
Lansing, IL 60438

All American **Oakland** Chapter
22 Washington St.
Millinocket, ME 04462

Oakland/Pontiac Enthusiasts
    Organization, Inc.
P.O. Box 0371
Drayton Plains, MI 48330

Olde Tyme Auto Club
P.O. Box 302
Evansville, IN 47701

Curved Dash **Olds** Owners Club
72 Northwood Ave.
Demarest, NJ 07627

Hurst/**Olds** Club of America
455 131st Ave.
Wayland, MI 49348

1960 **Oldsmobile** Chapter
10895 E. Hibma Rd.
Tustin, MI 49688

Curved Dash **Oldsmobile** Club
3455 Florida Ave.
N. Minneapolis, MN 55427

National Antique **Oldsmobile** Club
11730 Moffit Lane
Manassas, VA 22111

National Antique **Oldsmobile** Club
P.O. Box 483
Elmont, NY 11003

Oldsmobile Club of America
P.O. Box 16216
Lansing, MI 48901

N. American **Opel** GT Club
15 Valewood Rd.
W. Chicago, IL 60185

Opel Motorsport Club
4608 Cathann St.
Toffance, CA 90503

Opel U.S.A.
64 Eaton Rd.
Tolland, CT 06084

1937 **Packard** Six International Roster
3174 Whitetail Lane
Adel, IA 50003

Eastern **Packard** Club, Inc.
P.O. Box 153
Fairfield, CT 06430

Old Dominion **Packard** Club
901 Dirk Dr.
Richmond, VA 23227

Packard Automobile Classics, Inc.
420 S. Ludlow St.
Dayton, OH 45402

Packard Caribbean Register
P.O. Box 765
Huntington Beach, CA 92648

Packard Club
P.O. Box 2808
Oakland, CA 94618

Packard International Motor Car Club
302 French St.
Santa Ana, CA 92701

Packard Truck Organization
1196 Mountain Dr.
York Springs, PA 17372

Packards International
302 French St.
Santa Ana, CA 92701

Paige Registry
P.O. Box 66
Shady, NY 12409

Pantera International
5540 Farralone Ave.
Woodland Hills, CA 91367

Pantera Owners Club of America
1048 Camino Del Cerritos
San Dimas, CA 91773

Peerless Motor Car Club
1749 Baldwin Dr.
Millersville, MD 21108

Pierce-Arrow Society, Inc.
135 Edgerton St.
Rochester, NY 14607

Pioneer Antique Auto Club of the
    Mid-Ohio Valley
Rt. 2, Box 10
Washington, WV 26181

Pioneer Antique Auto Club of
    Northwest Ohio
403 E. Findlay St.
Carey, OH 43316

Pioneer Automobile Assoc. of St.
    Joseph Valley, Inc.
922 E. Jefferson
Mishawaka, IN 46544

Pioneer Automobile Touring Club
374 Harvard Ave.
Palmerton, PA 18071

Plumas Antique Auto Club
Box 315
Quincy, CA 59571

Plymouth 4- & 6-Cylinder Owners
    Club, Inc.
203 Main St. E.
Cavalier, ND 58220

Plymouth Owners Club, Inc.
P.O. Box 416
Cavalier, ND 58220

Police Car Owners of America
Rt. 6, Box 112
Eureka Springs, AR 72632

Pontiac-Oakland Club International
P.O. Box 5108
Salem, OR 97304

Pontiac-Oakland Club International, Inc.
P.O. Box 9569
Brandenton, FL 34206

356 Registry (**Porsche**)
27244 Ryan Rd.
Warren, MI 48092

Porsche 914 Owners Assoc. & 914-6
    Club USA
100 S. Sunrise Hwy., Suite 116H
Palm Springs, CA 92262

Porsche Club of America
P.O. Box 30100
Alexandria, VA 22310

Porsche Club of America
5616 Claremont Dr.
Alexandria, VA 22310

Porsche Owners Club
P.O. Box 54910
Los Angeles, CA 90054

Professional Car Society
12505 Bennett Rd.
Herndon, VA 22071

Ford **Ranchero** Club
1339 Beverly Rd.
Portvue, PA 15133

Ranchero-Torino Club
8307 E. Calexico St.
Tucson, AZ 85730

Renault Owners Club of America
1380 156th Ave. N.E., Suite 204
Bellevue, WA 98007

United **Renault** Club of America
P.O. Box 2277
Cypress, CA 90630

Reo Club of America
Rt. 2, Box 190
Forest, OH 45843

Reo Club of America
29 Congress St.
St. Albans, VT 05478

Reo Club of America, Inc.
P.O. Box 336
Sea Bright, NJ 07760

Reo One & Two-Cylinder Registry
3506 Nord Rd.
Bakersfield, CA 93312

Rickenbacker Car Club of America
HCR-1, Box 92B
Saranac Lake, NY 12983

Riley Motor Club USA, Inc.
P.O. Box 4162
Anaheim, CA 92803

Riviera Club
2603 N. 36 St. E.
Phoenix, AZ 85008

Riviera Owners Assoc.
P.O. Box 26344
Lakewood, CO 80226

Roaring 20s Antique and Classic Car
    Club, Inc.
Box 1187
Waterbury, CT 06721

Rolls-Royce Owners Club
P.O. Box 2001
Mechanicsburg, PA 17055

Rolls-Royce Owners Club
191 Hempt Rd.
Mechanicsburg, PA 17055

Silver Ghost Assoc. (**Rolls-Royce**)
Box 737
Salina, KS 67402

Rover Owners Club of N. America
P.O. Box 43005
Tucson, AZ 85719

Saab Club of N. America
2416 London Rd. #900-H
Duluth, MN 55812

Sabra Connection
7040 N. Navajo Ave.
Milwaukee, WI 53217

Saxon Registry
5230 N.W. Highland Dr.
Corvallis, OR 97330

Scorpion Registry
4 Trieste Way
Chico, CA 95926

Scout & IH Truck Assoc.
4026 Senour Rd.
Indianapolis, IN 46239

Shelby Owners of America
P.O. Drawer 1429
Great Bend, KS 67530

Shelby-American Auto Club
4150 Dorchester Ave.
Reading, PA 19609

Shelby American Automobile Club
P.O. Box 788
Sharon, CT 06069

Shelby Dodge Automobile Club
P.O. Box 4631
Lutherville, MD 21094

Simplex Motorbike Register
839 W. Race St.
Somerset, PA 15501

N. American **Singer** Owners Club
P.O. Box 501
Lawrence, MA 01842

N. American **Singer** Owners Club
19365 Aramario Rd.
Soulsbyville, CA 95372

N. American **Singer** Owners Club
2113 Avenida Planeta
Tucson, AZ 85710

Single-Cylinder Cadillac Registry
311 Nature Trail Dr.
Greer, SC 29651

Slant 6 Club of America
P.O. Box 4414
Salem, OR 97302

Society of Automotive Historians, Inc.
5201 Woodward Ave.
Detroit, MI 48202

Society of Automotive Historians (SAH)
P.O. Box 339
Matamoras, PA 18336

Society for the Perpetuation of Three-
Wheeled Vehicles
P.O. Box 3212
Bristol, TN 37625

New England **Sonnet** Club
P.O. Box 4362
Manchester, NH 03108

Sports Car Collectors Society of
America
201 San Pablo Rd.
Jacksonville, FL 32225

Squire SS-100 Registry
11826 S. 51st St.
Phoenix, AZ 85044

Station Wagon Owners Assoc.
6110 Bethesda Way
Indianapolis, IN 46254

Steam Automobile Club of America
Box 529
Pleasant Garden, NC 27313

Steam Automobile Club of America, Inc.
1227 W. Voorhees St.
Danville, IL 61832

Stephens Registry
1034 Henderson
Freeport, IL 61032

Stevens-Duryea Associates
3565 Newhaven Rd.
Pasadena, CA 91107

'56 **Studebaker** Golden Hawk Owners
Register
1025 Nodding Pines Way
Casselbary, FL 32707

Antique **Studebaker** Club
P.O. Box 28845
Dallas, TX 75228

Studebaker Drivers Club
P.O. Box 28788
Dallas, TX 75228

Studebaker Lark Club
2333 Feather Sound Dr., Suite B206
Clearwater, FL 34622

Stutz Club, Inc.
7400 Lantern Rd.
Indianapolis, IN 46256

Subaru 360 Drivers Club
1421 N. Grady Ave.
Tucson, AZ 85715

California Assoc. of Tiger Owners
   (Sunbeam)
18321 Vista Del Lago
Yorba Linda, CA 92686

N. American **Super Sports**
109 Mound St.
Tiltonsville, OH 43963

Suburban Driver Club
P.O. Box 292
Orchard Park, NY 14127

Tatra Enthusiasts
14200 New Hampshire Ave.
Silver Spring, MD 20904

TC America, Inc.
7200 Montgomery N.E. #400
Albuquerque, NM 87109

Classic **Thunderbird** Club, Inc.
P.O. Box 4148
Santa Fe Springs, CA 90670

Heartland Vintage **Thunderbird** Club
5002 Gardner
Kansas City, MO 64120

Heartland Vintage **Thunderbird** Club of
   America
P.O. Box 18113
Kansas City, MO 64133

International **Thunderbird** Club
8 Stag Trail
Fairfield, NJ 07004

Thunderbirds of America
P.O. Box 2766
Cedar Rapids, IA 52406

Vintage **Thunderbird** Club, Int.
P.O. Box 2250
Dearborn, MI 48123

Toyota 2000 GT Owners Club
P.O. Box 617
Saco, ME 04072

TR8 Car Club of America
266 Linden St.
Rochester, NY 14620

American Union of **Trabant** Owners
P.O. Box 2004
Bellaire, TX 77402

Bandit **Trans Am** Club
P.O. Box 322
Cleveland, WI 53015

Trans Am Club
P.O. Box 917
Champaign, IL 61820

Trans Am Club of America
P.O. Box 07084
Milwaukee, WI 53207

Trans Am Club of America
P.O. Box 33085
North Royalton, OH 44133

6-Pack **Triumph** TR6 Owners Club
1012 W. Ninth Ave.
Oshkosh, WI 54901

Triumph Register of America
1641 N. Memorial Dr., Suite TR3
Lancaster, OH 43130

Vintage **Triumph** Register
15218 W. Warren Ave.
Dearborn, MI 48126

American **Truck** Historical Society (ATHS)
P.O. Box 531168
Birmingham, AL 35253

Antique **Truck** Club of America
89 115th St.
College Point, NY 11356

Antique **Truck** Club of
America (ATCA)
P.O. Box 291
Hershey, PA 17033

Antique **Truck** Club of New England
280 W. First St.
S. Boston, MA 02127

Ford F-100 **Truck** Club
1315 Hollos Terrace
Bremerton, WA 98310

Tucker Automobile Club
of America, Inc.
311 W. 18th St.
Tifton, GA 31794

TVR Car Club—N. America
4450 S. Park Ave, #1609
Chevy Chase, MD 20815

Vanden Plas Princess Owners Club
14200 New Hampshire Ave.
Silver Spring, MD 20904

Cosworth **Vega** Owners Assoc.
147 Hiram St.
Pittsburgh, PA 15209

Cosworth **Vega** Owners Assoc.
P.O. Box 910
El Toro, CA 92630

Vehicle Preservation Society
P.O. Box 9800
San Diego, CA 92169

Velie Owners Registry
1811 E. Stella Lane
Phoenix, AZ 85016

Veteran Motor Car Club (VMCCA)
P.O. Box 360788
Strongville, OH 44136

Vintage **Volkswagen** Club of America
5705 Gordon Dr.
Harrisburg, PA 17112

Volkswagen Club of America
P.O. Box 154
North Aurora, IL 60542

Volkswagen The Thing/Type 181
Registry
P.O. Box 56056
Riverside, CA 92506

Volvo Club of America
P.O. Box 16
Afton, NY 13730

Volvo Enthusiasts Club
1902 Barber Dr.
Stoughton, WI 53589

Volvo Sports America 1800
1203 Cheltenham Ave.
Melrose Park, 19027

Vintage **White** Truck Assoc.
719 Ohms Way
Costa Mesa, CA 92627

White Steam Registry
923 Minnesota Ave.
Chickasha, OK 73018

Willis St. Claire Registry
721 Jenkinson St.
Port Huron, MI 48060

Willy's Aero Survival Count
952 Ashbury Heights Ct.
Decatur, GA 30030

Willy's Areo Survival Count
3248 Washington Place
La Crescenta, CA 91214

Willys Club
137 Plymouth Ave.
Oreland, PA 19075

Willys-Overland-Knight Registry
1440 Woodacre Dr.
Mclean, VA 22101

National **Woodie** Club
P.O. Box 6134
Lincoln, NE 68506

National **Woodie** Club
5522 W. 140th St.
Hawthorne, CA 90250

COLLECTOR CAR MUSEUMS

ALABAMA
The Vintage Motor Museum
850 Government
Mobile, AL 36602

ALASKA
Alaska Historical & Transportation
  Museum
Box 902
Palmer, AK 99645

Museum of Automobiles
Rt. 3
Morrilton, AK 72110

ARIZONA
Grand Old Cars
8722 E. Joshua Tree Lane
Scottsdale, AZ 85253

Hall of Fame Museum
6101 E. Van Buren
Phoenix, AZ 85008

ARKANSAS
Museum of Automobiles
State Rd. 154 at Petit Jean—Mountain
  State Park
Morrilton, AR 72110

Reed's Museum of Automobiles
714 Central Ave.
Hot Springs, AR 71901

CALIFORNIA
Blackhawk Auto Collection
1975 San Romon Valley Blvd.
San Ramon, CA 94583

Boses Collection
1028 N. Labrea Ave.
W. Hollywood, CA 90038

Briggs Cunningham Automotive
  Museum
250 Baker St.
Costa Mesa, CA 92626

Concours Moter Cars
619 E. Fourth St.
Santa Ana, CA 92703

Deer Park Auto Museum
29013 Champagne Blvd.
Escondido, CA 92026

Los Angeles County Museum of Natural
  History
900 Exposition Blvd.
Los Angeles, CA 90007

Merle Norman Classic Beauty Collection
San Sylmar, CA 91342

Metropolitan Historical Collection
5330 Laurel Canyon Blvd.
N. Hollywood, CA 91607

Miller's Horse & Buggy Ranch
9425 Yosemite Blvd.
Modesto, CA 95351

Movieworld Cars of the Stars
6920 Orangethorpe Ave.
Buena Park, CA 90620

Museums at Blackhawk: The Behring
  Auto Museum
3700 Blackhawk Plaza Circle
Danville, CA 94506

Nethercut Collection
4734G LaVilla Marine
Marina del Rey, CA 90291

Petersen Automotive Museum
Los Angeles Museum of Natural History
6060 Wilshire Blvd.
Los Angeles, CA 90036

Route 66 Territory Museum
8916-C Foothill Blvd.
Ranch Cucamonga, CA 91730

San Diego Aerospace Museum
Pan American Plaza in Balboa Park
San Diego, CA 92112

Towe Ford Museum
2200 Front St.
Sacramento, CA 95818

Wagons to Wings Museum
15060 Foothill Rd.
Morgan Hill, CA 95037

COLORADO
Buckskin Joe Museum
1193 Fremont County Rd. 3A
Canon City, CO 81212

Dougherty Museum Collection
US 287 (one mile south of Longmont)
Longmont, CO 80501

Forney Transportation Museum
1416 Platte St.
Denver, CO 80202

Front Wheel Drive Auto Museum
250 N. Main St.
Brighton, CO 80601

Pikes Peak Auto Hill Climb Museum
135 Manitou Ave.
Colorado Springs, CO 80829

Ray Dougherty Collection
Rt. 2, Box 253-A
Longmont, CO 80501

Robert Esboreon Classic Cars
14959 W. 69th St.
Denver, CO 80401

Veteran Car Museum
2030 S. Cherokee
Denver, CO 80223

CONNECTICUT
Antique Auto Museum
P.O. Box 430
Manchester, CT 06040

Bradley Air Museum
Bradley International Airport
Windsor Locks, CT 06096

Hartford Automobile Club
815 Farmington Ave.
W. Hartford, CT 06119

Museum of Connecticut History
231 Capitol Ave.
Hartford, CT 06115

DELAWARE
Delaware Agricultural Museum
866 N. Dupoint Hwy.
Dover, DE 19901

Majic Age of Steam
P.O. Box 127, Rt. 82
Yorkyln, DE 19726

Memours Mansion & Gardens
P.O. Box 109 Rockland Rd.
Wilmington, DE 19899

Wrangle Hill Classic & Antique Car
    Museum
2780 Pulaski Hwy. (US 40)
Glasgow, DE 19702

DISTRICT OF COLUMBIA
National Museum of American History
Constitution Ave.
Washington, DC 20560

FLORIDA
Bellm's Cars and Music of Yesterday
5500 N. Tamiami Trail
Sarasota, FL 33580

Birthplace of Speed Museum
160 E. Granada Blvd.
Ormans Beach, FL 32176

Don Garlit's Museum of Drag Racing
13700 S.W. 16th Ave.
Ocala, FL 32676

Early American Museum
P.O. Box 188
Silver Springs, FL 32688

Eilliott Museum
Hutchinson Island
Stuart, FL 33494

Horseless Carriage Shop
P.O. Box 898, 1881 Main St.
Dunedin, FL 33528

Silver Springs Antique Car Collection
State Rd. 40
Ocala, FL 32670

Tragedy in U.S. History Museum
7 Williams St.
St. Augustine, FL 32084

GEORGIA
Antique Auto & Music Museum
Georgia's Stone Mountain Park
Stone Mountain, GA 30086

Museo Abarth Museum
1111 Via Bayless
Marietta, GA 30066

HAWAII
Automotive Museum of the Pacific
197 Sand Island Rd.
Honolulu, HA 96819

IDAHO
Grant's Antique Cars and Museum
5606 Franklin Rd.
Boise, ID 83705

Museum of Transportation—Old Idaho
   Penitentiary
Main St. at 2445 Penitentiary Rd.
Boise, ID 83712

Vintage Wheel Museum
218 Cedar St.
Sandpoint, ID 83864

ILLINOIS
Bortz Auto Collection
Gurnee Mills Mall
Gurnee, IL 60035

Excalibur Motorcars Ltd.
3610 Skokie Valley Rd.
Highland Park, IL 60035

Fagan's Antique & Classic Automobile
   Museum
162nd St. and Clairmont Ave.
Markham, IL 60426

Gasoline Alley
c/o Hitchin-Post Inn
1765 N. Milwaukee
Libertyville, IL 60048

Grant Hills Antique Auto Museum
US Hwy. 20
Galena, IL 61036

Gray's Ride through History Museum
1608 E. Main St.
West Frankfort, IL 62896

Hartung's Automotive Museum
3623 W. Lake St.
Glenview, IL 60025

Lazarus Motor Museum
Box 368, 211 Walnut
Forrenston, IL 61030

Martin's Antique Automobile Museum
RR 1, Rt. 16
Metamora, IL 61548

Max Nordeen's Wheels Museum
(2 miles north of downtown Woodhull)
Woodhull, IL 61490

McDonald's Des Plaines Museum
400 N. Lee St.
Des Plaines, IL 60016

Mississippi Valley Historic Auto Club
   Museum
Front and Cedar Sts.
Quincy, IL 62301

Museum of Science and Industry
57th St. and Lake Shore Dr.
Chicago, IL 60637

Quinsippi Island Antique Auto Museum
2215 Spruce
Quincy, IL 62301

Time Was Village Museum
1325 Burlington St.
Mendota, IL 61342

Volo Antique Museum and Village
27582 W. Hwy. 120
Volo, IL 60073

Wheels O'Time Museum
11923 N. Knoxville Ave.
Dunlap, IL 61525

Wheels through Time Museum
12th and Waltonville Rd.
Mount Vernon, IL 62864

INDIANA

Antique Classic Car Museum
S. Ray Miller Foundation, Inc.
2130 Middlebury St.
Elkhart, IN 46516

Auburn-Cord-Duesenberg Museum
1600 S. Wayne St.
Auburn, IN 46706

Bill Goodwin Museum
757 S. Harrison St.
Frankford, IN 46041

Cars of Yesterday
5226 Nob Lane
Indianapolis, IN 46226

Early Wheels Museum
817 Wabash Ave.
Terre Haute, IN 47801

Elwood Haynes Museum
1915 S. Webster St.
Kokomo, IN 46902

Historical Military Armour Museum
2330 Crystal St.
Anderson, IN

Indiana Museum of Transportation
    Communication, Inc.
Forest Park, P.O. Box 83
Noblesville, IN 46060

Indianapolis Motor Speedway & Hall of
    Fame Museum
4790 W. 16th St.
Speedway, IN 46224

Maclyn Museum—Antique Motor Cars
    and Mechanical Apparatus
US Hwy. 52
Metamora, IN 47030

National Automotive and Truck Museum
    of the United States
1000 Gordon Buehrig Place
Auburn, IN 46706

Northern Indiana Historical Society
    Museum
112 S. Lafayette Blvd.
South Bend, IN 46601

Plew's Indy 500 Museum
9648 W. Morris St.
Indianapolis, IN 46231

Recreational Vehicle/Motor Home Hall
    of Fame Museum
801 Benham Ave.
Elkhart, IN 45616

Studebaker National Museum
120 South St., Joseph St.
South Bend, IN 46600

IOWA

Don Jensen Museum
411 4th Ave.
N. Humbolt, IA 50548

Iowa State Historical Museum
East 12th and Grand Ave.
Des Moines, IA 50319

Kinney Pioneer Museum
US Hwy. 18 W. at Mason City Airport
Mason City, IA 50401

Olson Linn Museum
Village Square
Villisca, IA 50864

Scheid International Museum
805 W. Bremer Ave.
Waverly, IA 50677

Van Horn's Truck Museum
Hwy. 65 N.
Mason City, IA 50401

KANSAS

Eisenhower Center
SR 14 at SE 4th St.
Abilene, KS 67410

Kansas State Historical Society Museum
120 W. Tenth St.
Topeka, KS 66612

Reo Antique Auto Museum
100 N. Harrison
Lindsborg, KS 67456

KENTUCKY
National Corvette Museum
(off I-65 south of GM Corvette
   Assembly Plant)
Bowling Green, KY 42101

LOUISIANA
Cars of Yesteryear Museum
12137 Airline Hwy.
Baton Rouge, LA 70801

MAINE
Boothbay Auto Museum
Box 123, Rt. 27
Boothbay, ME 04537

Cole Land Transportation Museum
405 Perry Rd.
Bangor, ME 04401

Owls Head Transportation Museum
Knox County Airport
Owls Head, ME 04854

Wells Auto Museum
Rt. 1
Wells, ME 04090

MASSACHUSETTS
Heritage Plantation Auto Museum
Grove and Pine Sts. (off SR 130)
Sandwich, MA 02563

Indian Motorcycle Museum
33 Hendee St.
Springfield, MA 01139

Museum of Transportation
15 Newton St.—Larz Anderson Park
Brookline, MA 02146

MICHIGAN
Alfred P. Sloan Museum
1221 E. Kearsley St.
Flint, MI 48500

Automotive Hall of Fame, Inc.
Northwood Institute, P.O. Box 1742
Midland, MI 48649

Gilmore Classic Car Museum
6865 Hickory Rd.
Hickory Corners, MI 49060

Henry Ford Museum & Greenfield
   Village
20900 Oakwood Blvd.
Dearborn, MI 48120

National Automotive History Collection
Detroit Public Library
5201 Woodward Ave.
Detroit, MI 48202

Poll Museum of Transportation
353 E. Sixth St.
Holland, MI 49423

Pontiac Museum
One Pontiac Plaza
Pontiac, MI 48053

R.E. Olds Museum
240 Museum Dr.
Lansing, MI 48933

MINNESOTA
Roaring 20s Auto Museum
Hwy. 55
Brooten, MN 56316

MISSISSIPPI
Frank's Museum and Antiques
Hwy. 45 S.
Booneville, MS 38829

MISSOURI
Kelsey's Antique Cars
US 54 E.
Camdenton, MO 65020

Memoryville, U.S.A.—Autos of
   Yesteryear
Rt. 63 N.
Rolla, MO 65401

National Museum of Transportation
3015 Barrett Station Rd.
St. Louis, MO 63122

Ozark Auto Show & Museum
West Hwy. 76
Branson, MO 65616

Patee House Museum
Box 1022, 12th and Penn Sts.
St. Joseph, MO 64503

Turpen Enterprises—Classic & Antique
    Cars
1206 West Hwy. 76
Branson, MO 65616

MONTANA
Oscar's Dreamland
Rt. 9
Billings, MT 59102

Towe Antique Ford Collection
1106 Main St.
Deer Lodge, MT 56701

NEBRASKA
Chevyland U.S.A.
Rt. 2
Elm Creek, NE 68836

Hastings Museum
1330 N. Burlington
Hastings, NE 68901

NEVADA
Imperial Palace Auto Collection
3535 Las Vegas Blvd.
Las Vegas, NV 89109

National Automobile Museum
10 Lake St. S.
Reno, NV 89501

NEW HAMPSHIRE
Crossroads of America
Rt. 302 and Trudeau Rd.
Bethleham, NH 03579

Grand Manor
Rts. 16 and 302
Glen, NH 03838

Westminster MG Car Museum
South St.
Walpole, NH 03608

NEW JERSEY
Roaring 20s Autos
RD 1, Box 178-G, Hwy. 34
Wall, NJ 07719

NEW MEXICO
Antique Auto Barn
National Parks Hwy. 16-180
Carlsbad, NM 88220

Callahan's Auto Museum
410 Cedar St.
Truth or Consequences, NM 87901

NEW YORK
Ausable Chasm Antiques Auto Museum
Rt. 9
Ausable Chasm, NY 12911

Auto Memories
County Rd. 38
Arkville, NY 12406

Automobile Museum of Rome and
    Restoration Shoppe
6 Pilimore Dr. Rt. 49 W.
Rome, NY 13440

Bridgewater Auto Museum
US Rt. 20
Bridgewater, NY 13313

Cavalcade of Cars—Gaslight
    Village, Inc.
Box 511, Rt. 9
Lake George, NY 12845

Collector Cars, Inc.
56 W. Merrick Rd.
Freeport, NY 11520

Corvette Americana Hall of Fame
SR 38 S.
Cooperstown, NY 13326

Golden Age Auto Museum
W. Grand St.
Palarine Bridge, NY 13428

Hall of Fame and Classic Car Museum—
    D.I.R.T. Motorsports
1 Speedway Dr.
Weedsport, NY 13166

Harry Resnick Motor Museum
46 Canal St.
Ellenville, NY 12428

Himes Museum of Motor Racing
    Nostalgia
15 O'Neil Ave.
Bay Shore, NY 11706

Long Island Automotive Museum
Meadow Spring
Glen Cove, NY 11542

Long Island Automotive Museum
Rt. 27
Southampton, NY 11968

Upstate Auto Museum
Box 152, Main St.
Bridgewater, NY 13313

Watkins Glen Racing Museum
110 N. Franklin St.
Watkins Glen, NY 14891

NORTH CAROLINA
Estes-Winn-Blomberg Antique Car
    Museum
Grovewood Rd.
Asheville, NC 28806

North Carolina Transportation Museum
Spencer Shops Historic Site
Spencer, NC 28159

Rearview Mirror Museum
300 E. Baltic Ave.
Nags Head, NC 28159

NORTH DAKOTA
Bonanzaville USA
I-94 and US 10, P.O. Box 719
West Fargo, ND 58078

OHIO
Allen County Museum
620 W. Market St.
Lima, OH 45801

Canton Classic Car Museum
555 Market Ave. S.
Canton, OH 44702

Carillion Park
Patterson and Carillion Blvd.
Dayton, OH 45409

Charlie Sens Antique Auto Museum
Pole Lane Rd.
Marion, OH 43302

Frederick C. Crawford Auto-Aviation
    Museum
10825 East Blvd.
Cleveland, OH 44106

Goodyear World of Rubber
1144 E. Market St.
Akron, OH 44316

Motorcycle Heritage Museum
33 Collegeview Rd.
Westerville, OH 43081

Welsh Jaguar Classic Car Museum
5th and Washington Sts.
Steubenville, OH 43952

OKLAHOMA
Antiques, Inc.
P.O. Box 1887, 2115 W. Shawnee
Muskogee, OK 74401

Bob Townsend Classic Auto Museum
SR 18 N.
Shawnee, OK 74801

Museum of Special Interest
    Automobiles
13700 US 177 S.
Shawnee, OK 74801

PENNSYLVANIA
Alan Dent Antique Auto Museum
Box 254
Lightstreet, PA 17839

Boyertown Museum of Historical
    Vehicles
Warwick St. and Reading Ave.
Boyretown, PA 19512

Colonial Flying Corps Museum
Box 17, Newark Rd.
Toughkenamon, PA 19374

Gast Classic Motorcars
Rt. 986, RD 2, Box 1G
Strasburg, PA 17579

Jem Classic Car Museum
SR 443
San Andreas, PA 18211

Kelly Auto Museum
Lehigh Rd. and SR 507
Gouldsboro, PA 18424

Mack Trucks Historical Museum
Main St.
Macungie, PA 18062

Magee Transportation
Box 150
Bloomsburg, PA 17815

Pollock Auto Showcase 1
70 S. Franklin St.
Pottstown, PA 19464

Reilly Classic Motors
175 Market St.
Kingston, PA 18704

Station Square Transportation Museum
450 The Landmarks Bldg.,
One Station Square
Pittsburgh, PA 15219

SOUTH CAROLINA
Joe Weatherly Stock Car Museum
Hwy. 34 W., Box 500
Darlington, SC 29532

Wings and Wheels
P.O. Box 93
Santee, SC 29142

SOUTH DAKOTA
Autos of Yesteryear Museum
Alcester, SD 57701

Horseless Carriage Museum
Keystone Rt. Box 255
Rapid City, SD 57701

Ledbetter's Auto Museum
US 16 W.
Custer, SD 57730

Mitchell Car Museum
1130 S. Burr St.
Mitchell, SD 57301

National Motorcycle Museum & Hall of
Fame
2348 Junction Ave.
Sturgis, SD 57785

Pioneer Auto Museum
Box 76
Murdo, SD 57559

TENNESSEE
Car Collector Hall of Fame
1534 Demon Breun St.
Nashville, TN 37203

Cox's Car Museum
P.O. Box 253
Gatlinburg, TN 37738

Dixie Gun Works Old Car Museum
US Hwy. 51 S.
Union City, TN 38261

Marty Robbins Memorial Showcase
2613A McGavock Pike
Nashville, TN 37214

Old Car Museum
Hwy 51 S.
Union City, TN 38261

Reed's 1950 Antique Car Museum
Rt. 2, Lost Sea Pike
Sweetwater, TN 37874

Smoky Mountain Car Museum
US 441 Hwy.
Pigeon Forge, TN 37863

World Famous Car Collectors Hall of Fame
1534 Demonbreun St.
Nashville, TN 37203

TEXAS
Alamo Classic Car Museum
I-35 and Ingel Rd.
New Braunfels, TX 78130

Central Texas Museum of Automotive
History
Hwy. 304
Rosanky, TX 78953

Chapman Auto Museum
Rt. 3, Box 120A
Rickweel, TX 75087

Classic Showcase
Star Rt. 543
Kerrville, TX 78028

David Taylor Classic Car Museum
1918 Mechanic St.
Galveston. TX 77750

Galveston Automobile Museum
1309 Tremont St.
Galveston, TX 77550

Jerry J. Moore's Classic Auto Museum
505 N. Loop W.
Houston, TX 77008

McAllen Hudson Museum
3100 Colbath Rd.
McAllen, TX 78501

Museum of Time and Travel
Rt. 1, Box 90, 1101 Pool Rd.
Odessa, TX 79763

Panhandle-Plains Historical Museum
W.T. Station—US 87 on 4th Ave.
Canyon, TX 79016

Pate Museum of Transportation
P.O. Box 711, Hwy. 377 S.
Fort Worth, TX 76101

San Antonio Museum of
    Transportation
Hemis Fair Plaza
San Antonio, TX 78205

Vidas Vintage Vehicles
I-45 N.
Spring, TX 77380

UTAH

Bonneville Speedway Museum
P.O. Box 39
Wendover, UT 84083

Classic Cars International Auto Museum
355 W. 700 South St.
Salt Lake City, UT 84101

Kimball-Browning Car Museum
25th St. and Wall Ave.
Ogden, UT 84401

VERMONT

The Westminster MG Car Museum
Westminster, VT 05158

VIRGINIA

Automobile Museum of Hampton
    Roads
3535 Airline Blvd.
Portsmouth, VA 23701

Historic Car & Carriage Caravan
Box 748—Luray Caverns
Luray, VA 28835

Lowery's Car Collection
528 Church Lane
Tappahannock, VA 22560

Pettit's Museum of Motoring
P.O. Box 445
Louisa, VA 23093

Roanoke Transportation Museum
802 Wiley Drive S.W.
Roanoke, VA 24015

Roaring Twenties Antique Car
    Museum
Rt. 1, Box 198
Hood, VA 22723

Virginia Museum of Transportation
303 Norfolk Ave.
Roanoke, VA 24016

WISCONSIN

Brooks Stevens Automotive
    Museum
10325 N. Port Washington Rd.
Mequon, WI 53092

Dells Auto Museum
591 Wisconsin Dells Pkwy.
Wisconsin Dells, WI 53965

Hartford Heritage Auto Museum
147 N. Rural St.
Hartford, WI 53027

Midway Auto Museum
Rt. 2, Hwy. 52
Birnamwood, WI 54414

SUGGESTED READINGS

The author would like to thank Steve Fields of Import Car Parts Marketing, 7944 Clover Hill Lane, Fair Oaks, CA 95628, for the compilation of the following data. Mr. Fields issues an extensive list of out-of-print automotive books offered for sale, and may be reached at the address above or by phone at 916-863-5513; fax 916-863-5519.

ALFA ROMEO
  Alfa Romeo Tradition, Borgeson (1990)
  Alfa Romeo Story, Wherry (1967)
  Alfa Romeo Catalogue Raisonne, Fusi and Lurani (1978)

AMERICAN MOTORS
  American Motors: The Last Independent, Marquez
  Standard Catalog of American Motors, Gunnell

ASTON MARTIN
  Aston Martin and Lagonda, Frostick (1977)
  Aston Martin Postwar Road Cars, Rasmussen (1988)
  Aston Martin DB4/5/6: The Complete Story, Wood

AUBURN/CORD/DUESENBERG
  Rolling Sculpture, Buehrig (1975)
  Classic Cord, Post (1952)
  Auburn, Cord, Duesenberg, Butler

AUSTIN HEALEY
  Story of the Big Healeys, Healey (1977)
  Austin Healey: The Handsome Brut, Harvey (1978)
  Healeys and Austin Healeys, Browning (1970)

BMW
  BMW: A History, Schrader (1979)
  BMW: A Celebration, Dymock
  The BMW Story: A Company in Its Time, Monnich

BUGATTI
  Bugatti Story, Boddy (1960)
  Bugatti Book, Eaglesfield (1954)
  Bugatti, Conway

BUICK
The Buick: A Complete History, Gustin and Dunham
Buick Postwar Years, Norbye (1978)

CADILLAC
Cadillac: The American Standard, Bonsall
Standard Catalog of Cadillac 1903–1990, Sieber and Buttolph
Cadillac Standard of Excellence, Langworth (1980)

CHEVROLET
Chevrolet: A History From 1911, Kimes
Chevrolet Spotters Guide 1920–1992, Burness
Chevrolet USA-1: An Illustrated History of Chevrolet's Passenger Cars 1946–1959, Miller
75 Years of Chevrolet, Dammann
Camaro! Chevy's Classy Chassis, Miller
Camaro: From Challenger to Champion, Witzenburg
Corvette: America's Star Spangled Sports Car, Ludvigson
Corvette: A Piece of the Action, Mitchell and Girdler

CHRYSLER (Dodge, Plymouth)
Complete History of the Chrysler Corporation 1924–1985, Langworth and Norbye
The Dodge Story, McPherson
Mighty Mopars, Young
Chrysler and Imperial 1946–1975: The Classic Postwar Years, Langworth

DE LOREAN
Stainless Steel Illusion, Lamm (1983)
Dream Maker: The Rise and Fall of John De Lorean, Fallon and Srodes (1983)

FERRARI
The Complete Ferrari, Eaton (1986)
Ferrari, Tanner (1959)
Ferrari Sports and GT Cars, Fitzgerald, Merritt, and Thompson (1968)
Ferrari: Forty Years on the Road, Nowack (1988)
Inside Ferrari, Dregni

FIAT
All the Fiats, Domus
Automobili Fiat, Anselmi
Fiat Sports Cars From 1945 to X1/9, Robson (1984)

FORD
Ford Pickup Color History, Brownell and Mueller
Ford Trucks Since 1905, Wagner
Fords Forever, Sorensen
Illustrated History of Ford, Dammann
The Model T-Ford: From Here to Obscurity, Miller and McCally
Henry's Lady: Illustrated History of the Model A, Miller
Mustang Does It, Miller
Mustang: The Complete History of America's Ponycar, Witzenburg
Shelby Mustang, Cororan
Thunderbird: An Illustrated History of the Ford T-Bird 1955–1966, Miller

The Ford Road: 75th Anniversary of Ford, Sorensen (1978)
Ford: Decline and Rebirth 1933–1962, Nevins and Hill (1962)
Ford: Expansion and Challenge 1915–1933, Nevins and Hill (1957)
Ford: The Times, The Man, The Company, Nevins and Hill (1954)

HONDA
Honda/Acura Driver/Owner Guide: Maximize the Potential of Your Honda and Acura 1962–1990, Krause

HUDSON
Hudson 1946–1957: The Classic Postwar Years, Langworth
The History of Hudson, Butler

JAGUAR
The Jaguar Tradition, Frostick (1973)
Jaguar Companion, Ullyet (1959)
Jaguar Sports Cars, Skilleter (1975)
Jaguar: The Definitive History of a Great British Sports Car, Whyte
Jaguar in America, Dugdale
Jaguar: An Illustrated History, Mennem

JEEP
The Jeep Bible, King
Jeep Owner's Bible, Ludel

KAISER FRAZER
Kaiser Frazer: The Last Onslaught on Detroit, Langworth

LAMBORGHINI
History of Lamborghini, Crump and de la Box (1974)
Lamborghini Cars From Sant' Agata, Crump and de la Box (1981)
Lamborghini Catalogue Raisonne 1963–88, Automobilia

LANCIA
La Lancia, Oude Weernink
Lancia Catalogue Raisonne, Automobilia
Lancia: The Shield and the Flag, Trow (1980)

LINCOLN
The Cars of Lincoln-Mercury, Dammann and Wagner
The Lincoln Motorcar, Bonsall
Lincoln Motorcar: 60 Years of Excellence, Bonsall (1981)

LOTUS
Lotus Esprit: The Complete Story, Walton
Legend of Lotus Seven, Ortenburger (1981)
Lotus: All the Cars, Pritchard (1990)
Story of Lotus 1947–1960, Smith (1970)
Story of Lotus 1961–1971, Nye (1972)

MASERATI
Maserati Catalog Raisonne 1926–1990, Automobilia
Maserati: Sports, Racing, and GT Cars from 1926, Crump and de la Box

Maserati: A History, Pritchard (1976)
Maserati Postwar Sportsracing Cars, Finn (1977)

MERCEDES
Mercedes-Benz Catalogue Raisonne 1886–1990, Automobilia
Mercedes-Benz Production Models 1946–1990, Nitske
Mercedes-Benz: The First Hundred Years, Langworth (1984)
Mercedes-Benz SL and SLC Autohistory, Setright (1979)
Three-Pointed Star, Scott-Moncrieff (1955)
Mercedes-Benz: The Star and the Laurel, Kimes (1986)

MERCURY
Fifty Years of Lincoln-Mercury, Dammann (1971)
55 Years of Mercury, Gunnell
The Cars of Lincoln-Mercury, Dammann and Wagner

MG
MG by McComb, McComb
MG Log: A Celebration of the World's Favorite Sports Car, Haining
MGB: The Illustrated History, Wood
MG A, B, and C, Harvey (1980)
MG Story, Wherry (1967)
T Series MG, Knudson (1973)

MINI
The Big Mini Book, Hubner
Mighty Minis, Harvey
Mini-Cooper and S Autohistory, Walton (1982)

MORGAN
Morgan, Harvey
Morgan: First and Last of the Real Sports Cars, Bowden
Morgan in the Colonies, Sheally (1978)

OLDSMOBILE
The Cars of Oldsmobile, Casteele
Oldsmobile 1946–1980: The Classic Postwar Years, Norbye and Dunne
Oldsmobile Muscle Cars, Holder and Kunz
Oldsmobile: The First Seventy-Five Years, Kimes and Langworth, (1972)

PACKARD
The Coachbuilt Packard, Pfau
Packard: A History of the Motor Car and the Company, Kimes
Packard Guide, Marvin (1987)

PANTERA
DeTomaso: The Man and the Machines, Wyss
DeTomaso Pantera Autohistory, Norbye (1980)

PIERCE-ARROW
Pierce-Arrow: The Golden Age, Ralston (1984)
Pierce-Arrow, Ralston

PONTIAC
Firebird: America's Premier Performance Car, Witzenburg
GTO Resource Guide: 30th Anniversary Edition, Bonsall
Pontiac! They Build Excitement, Bonsall
Pontiac 1946–1978: The Classic Postwar Years, Norbye and Dunne
Fabulous Firebird, Lamm (1979)
Pontiac: The Complete History 1926–1986, Bonsall (1985)
Seventy-Five Years of Pontiac-Oakland, Gunnell (1982)

PORSCHE
Excellence Was Expected, Ludvigson
Porsche Catalogue Raisonne 1947–1993, Automobilia
Porsche: The Fine Art of the Sports Car, Lewis
Porsche 911: The Complete Story, Vivian
Porsche 911, Harvey (1980)
Project Porsche 928, Whiteman and Steinemann (1978)
Porsche Panorama: The First 25 Years, Barrett/PCA (1982)
Porsche: Portrait of a Legend, Seiff (1985)
We at Porsche, Bentley (1976)

RENAULT
Renault 1898–1965, Richard (1965)

ROLLS-ROYCE (+ Bentley)
Rolls-Royce Excellence Continues, Dalton (1971)
Those Elegant Rolls-Royce, Dalton (1967)
Engines Were Rolls-Royce, Harker (1979)
The Magic of a Name, Nockolds (1945)
Rolls-Royce Motor Car, Bird and Hallows (1964)
Rolls-Royce and Bentley: A History of the Cars 1904 On, Robfeldt
Rolls-Royce: The Best Car in the World, Oliver
A Pride of Bentleys, Adams (1978)
Bentley: 50 Years of the Marque, Green (1969)
Bentley: The Cars From Crewe, Steel

ROVER
The Land Rover Experience, Sheppard
Rover: The First Ninety Years, One of Britain's Fine Cars 1904–1994, Dymock
Range Rover / Land-Rover, Robson (1979)

SAAB
Saab 9000 Turbo, Automobilia
Saab: The Innovator, Chatterton (1980)
Saab Turbo Autohistory, Robson (1983)

STUDEBAKER
Avanti, Bonsall
Studebaker 1946–1966: The Classic Postwar Years, Langworth
Studebaker: The Complete Story, Cannon and Fox (1981)
A Century on Wheels, Longstreet (1952)

SUNBEAM
The Rootes Brothers: Story of a Motoring Empire, Bullock
Tiger: The Making of a Sports Car, Taylor

TRIUMPH

TR for Triumph, Harvey
Triumph TR's: The Complete Story, Robson
Story of Triumph Sports Cars, Robson (1973)

TUCKER

Design and Destiny: The Making of the Tucker Automobile, Egan
Indomitable Tin Goose, Pearson (1960)

TVR

TVR: The Complete Story, Tipler
TVR: Success Against the Odds, Filby (1976)

VOLVO

Volvo Cars From the 20's to the 90's, Lindh
Volvo, Nichol (1975)

VW

The Origin and Evolution of the VW Beetle, Shuler
Original VW Beetle, Meredith
Volkswagen Bug! The Peoples Car, Miller
Volkswagen: Nine Lives Later, Post
VW Beetle and Karmann Ghia: A Collector's Guide, Wood
Small Wonder, Nelson (1965+)
Beyond Expectation: The VW Story, Hopfinger (1954)
VW Beetle, Fry (1980)

REFERENCE PERIODICALS

Automobile Quarterly
P.O. Box 348
Kutztown, PA 19530

British Car Magazine
P.O. Box 9099
Canoga Park, CA 91309

The Car Collector and Car Classic
  Magazine
1241 Canton St.
Roswell, GA 30075

Cars and Parts Magazine
P.O. Box 482
Sidney, OH 45365

CSK Publishing Co., Inc.
299 Market St.
Saddle Brook, NJ 07662

du Pont Registry
P.O. Box 25237
Tampa, FL 33622
800-233-1731

Hemmings Motor News
P.O. Box 100
Bennington, VT 05201

J.C. Whitney Accessories Catalog
P.O. Box 8410
Chicago, IL 60680

Old Cars Weekly
700 E. State St.
Iola, WI 54990

Skinned Knuckles
175 May Ave.
Monrovia, CA 91016

Special Interest Autos
P.O. Box 196
Bennington, VT 05201

Sports Car International
42 Digital Dr. #5
Novato, CA 94949

This Old Truck Magazine
P.O. Box 562
Yellow Springs, OH 45387

GLOSSARY

AIR-COOLED. A process whereby an engine is cooled directly by a flow of air rather than a water radiator system.

AIR INTAKE. An opening located at the front or side of the car; permits air in for the cooling of water, oil, or brakes.

ANTIQUE. An antique car is one manufactured before 1935. An antique car may be ugly, rundown, or poorly made.

ATMOSPHERIC ENGINE. An early form of the steam engine.

AUTOMATIC TRANSMISSION. A transmission that shifts according to speed and the road.

BATTERY. A storage device for electrical energy. In automobiles, it is used to start the engine and to operate all electrical devices when the engine is shut off.

BLOWN ENGINE. An engine that is supercharged.

BODY. The part of the vehicle that carries the cargo, driver, and/or passengers.

BONNET. Hood of car in British English.

BRASS ERA. The earliest age of commercial auto manufacturing includes cars made before World War I. Components were made of solid brass in these cars. Later, brass was abandoned because of rising costs and the belief that it was outdated.

CABRIOLET. An auto with a collapsible top. Sometimes called a drop-head coupe and, most often, a convertible.

CATALYTIC CONVERTER. An antipollution device in the auto's exhaust system.

CHASSIS. The auto frame; includes the engine, suspension, wheels, brakes, and drive train.

CHOKE. Restriction in the carburetor that results in a reduction of air flow that helps in starting the car.

CLUTCH. A device that uses friction to connect the engine to the drive train.

COMPACT CAR. A passenger car that has a wheelbase measure of 100–111″.

CONVERTIBLE. Any car with a collapsible roof; also called drophead coupé.

COUPE. Smaller than a sedan, has a capacity of two to five passengers.

CUSTOM CAR. A restyled automobile.

CYCLE CAR. A small car made mostly from motorcycle parts. Usually had a one- or two-cylinder engine. Made prior to 1922.

DISC (DISK) BRAKE. Two friction pads attached to a steel disc to form a brake.

DOS-A-DOS. A four-passenger car in which the seats face each other or are back-to-back.

DROPHEAD COUPÉ. *See* Convertible.

FASTBACK. A car designed so the rear window slopes at less than a 45-degree angle and has an unbroken curved line from the top of the roof roughly to the rear bumper.

FOUR-WHEEL DRIVE. A drive system on four wheels instead of the usual two.

G.T. Grand Touring (from the Italian Gran Turismo) car combines characteristics of both sedans and sports cars.

HAND CRANK. A device used to start gas-powered engines. Not used anymore due to modern ignition systems.

HATCHBACK. Follows the design of the fastback but the rear seats fold out for trunk space and the rear window opens out.

HORSEPOWER. A unit used to measure the power output of a given engine. The term is believed to have been originated by Captain Thomas Savery, the British military engineer who developed an atmospheric steam engine that enjoyed widespread success in 18th-century England.

HOT ROD. A vehicle that has undergone modifications in speed capabilities.

LANDAU. A cabriolet limousine.

LIMOUSINE. An automobile in which the driver is separated from the passengers by glass.

MANUAL TRANSMISSION. The driver is responsible for the lever and the clutch in order to change from gear to gear.

MONOCAR. Single-seat cycle cars, circa 1915.

PHAETON. An open two-, three-, or four-seat motorcar with spoked wheels.

PONY CAR. A car which is capable of better performance and handling than the average automobile, but is not a sports car (i.e. Z-28 or Mustang).

ROADSTER. A sporty, two-seat passenger car, circa 1920–40.

RUNABOUT. An open, sporty, and lightweight vehicle with two seats, circa 1900s.

SALOON. The British term for a sedan.

SEDAN. A closed car with the capacity of four or more passengers.

SPORTS CAR. Easily managed, tightly sprung vehicles.

SPYDER. Two-seater car, circa early 1900s.

SUPERCHARGER. An air compressor fitted to an engine to further increase the power of the engine.

TACHOMETER. A device that gauges the number of revolutions per minute that the engine is turning. Commonly referred to as a "tach."

TORPEDO. A long sports car, circa 1910–20.

TURBOCHARGER. A supercharging device.

VICTORIA. An open vehicle with a large, collapsible hood, two seats, circa 1900.

ABOUT THE AUTHOR

Robert H. Balderson is a free-lance writer and editor. He holds a BA in economics, with a minor in history, and an MBA. Both degrees are with honors and he holds the Wall Street Journal Student Achievement Award. He has taught classes at California State University encompassing economics, investments, marketing, and appraisal. His other works include *The Official Price Guide to Antique and Modern Firearms*, and he is currently working on two more books. He has edited works on a broad range of topics that include cooking, skiing, marketing, real estate, and personal law.

For twenty years Robert Balderson has been involved in the area of antiques and collectibles as a collector, dealer, appraiser, writer, and bookseller. His comprehension of varying prices, based on regional preferences, is derived from traveling nationally as a full-time dealer for ten years, and having resided and maintained business operations on both coasts. Numerous widely known collections have been appraised, purchased, and cataloged by Mr. Balderson. He is frequently called upon to act in an advisory capacity and as agent for both buyers and sellers, he aids in searches for rare and hard-to-find pieces, and he oversees the settlement of estates.

Rarely has any young man amassed such an extraordinary combination of advanced academic credentials, wide-ranging successful professional experience, and distinguished personal accomplishments. Driven by a passion to learn and a sincere interest in his topics, Mr. Balderson has attained an immense level of knowledge, remarkably blending economics, humanities, history, industrial and decorative arts, and business; thus, his unique insight into collectors and the antiques and collectibles market is unsurpassed.

Originally from Baltimore, Robert served in the U.S. Air Force as a flight engineer and is a Vietnam veteran. His professional career has been diverse and reflects a record of steadily increasing challenge and recognition. He has successfully managed businesses ranging from small to multinational international corporations. Like most of his generation, he was a car enthusiast before he was old enough to drive. Today, Robert Balderson resides in Sacramento, California, is a business consultant, and continues to sell collectibles and related books while writing and editing.

Respected sources, including the Smithsonian Institution and *Maloney's Antiques and Collectibles Resource Directory*, list Mr. Balderson as an authority in several areas of the antiques and collectibles field. His library contains over 500 volumes on related subjects, and his individual research is a storehouse of information. Robert H. Balderson may be contacted as a consultant or appraiser at P.O. Box 254886, Sacramento, CA 95865. For appraisals, he requests that as much information (description, photographs, etc.) as possible be included with the first correspondence.